Constraint Processing

AUTHOR BIOGRAPHY

Rina Dechter is a professor of Computer Science at the University of California, Irvine. She received her Ph.D. in Computer Science at UCLA in 1985, an M.S. degree in Applied Mathematics from the Weizman Institute and a B.S. in Mathematics and Statistics from the Hebrew University, Jerusalem. Her research centers on computational aspects of automated reasoning and knowledge representation including search, constraint processing, and probabilistic reasoning. Professor Dechter has authored over 50 research papers, and has served on the editorial boards of: Artificial Intelligence, the Constraint Journal, Journal of Artificial Intelligence Research and the Encyclopedia of AI. She was awarded the Presidential Young Investigator award in 1991 and is a fellow of the American Association of Artificial Intelligence.

Chapter 11 Authors

David Cohen
Department of Computer Science
Royal Holloway, University of London
Egham, Surrey TW20 0EX, England

David Cohen is a Senior Lecturer in Computer Science at Royal Holloway College, University of London, England. He obtained his Ph.D. in Mathematics from the University of Oxford in 1986. His main research interest is the theory of tractability as it applies to constraint satisfaction problems. In this area, with Peter Jeavons, he has proved some important results both on structural tractability, and on constraint languages.

Peter Jeavons
Oxford University Computing Laboratory
Wolfson Building
Parks Road
Oxford OX1 3QD

Peter Jeavons is a Reader in Computer Science at the University of Oxford, UK. He obtained his Ph.D. in Computer Science from the University of London in 1992. His main research interest is the study of algorithms and complexity, especially in the analysis of constraint satisfaction problems. Dr. Jeavons is currently investigating the use of constraint satisfaction and other algorithmic techniques in computational molecular biology.

Chapter 15 Author

Francesca Rossi
Department of Pure and Applied Mathematics
University of Padova
Via G. B. Belzoni 7
35131 Padova, Italy

Francesca Rossi is a professor of Computer Science at the University of Padova, Italy. She obtained her Ph.D. in Computer Science from the University of Pisa in 1993. Her main research interest is constraint programming and solving, with an emphasis on soft constraints. Dr. Rossi has served on a number of organizing committees of international conferences on logic programming, constraint programming, and general AI, including serving as the conference chair of CP 1998, and as the program chair of CP 2003. She is also on the editorial boards of the Constraint Journal and the Journal of AI Research.

Constraint Processing

Rina Dechter

University of California, Irvine

With contributions by

David Cohen, Royal Holloway, University of London
Peter Jeavons, Oxford University Computing Laboratory
Francesca Rossi, University of Padova, Italy

MORGAN KAUFMANN PUBLISHERS

AN IMPRINT OF ELSEVIER SCIENCE

SAN FRANCISCO   SAN DIEGO   NEW YORK   BOSTON
LONDON   SYDNEY   TOKYO

Publishing Director	Diane Cerra
Senior Editor	Denise Penrose
Publishing Services Manager	Simon Crump
Editorial Coordinator	Emilia Thiuri
Project Management	Matrix Productions, Inc.
Project Manager	George Morrison
Cover Design Manager	Cate Rickard Barr
Text Design	Rebecca Evans
Composition	Cepha Imaging Pvt. Ltd.
Technical Illustration	Dartmouth Publishing, Inc.
Copyeditor	Ken Dellapenta
Proofreader	Jennifer McClain
Indexer	Ty Koontz
Interior printer	Maple—Vail Book Manufacturing Group
Cover printer	Phoenix Color Corp.

Designations used by companies to distinguish their products are often claimed as trademarks or registered trademarks. In all instances in which Morgan Kaufmann Publishers is aware of a claim, the product names appear in initial capital or all capital letters. Readers, however, should contact the appropriate companies for more complete information regarding trademarks and registration.

Permissions may be sought directly from Elsevier's Science and Technology Rights Department in Oxford, UK. Phone: (44) 1865 843830, Fax: (44) 1865 853333, e-mail: permissions@elsevier.co.uk. You may also complete your request on-line via the Elsevier homepage: http://www.elsevier.com by selecting "Customer Support" and then "Obtaining Permissions".

Morgan Kaufmann Publishers
An Imprint of Elsevier Science
340 Pine Street, Sixth Floor
San Francisco, CA 94104-3205
www.mkp.com

Printed and bound in the United Kingdom

Transferred to Digital Printing, 2011

Library of Congress Cataloging-in Publication Data

Dechter, Rina, 1950-
   Constraint processing/Rina Dechter.
      p. cm.
   Includes bibliographical references and index.
   ISBN-13: 978-1-55860-890-0   ISBN-10: 1-55860-890-7
   1. Constraint Programming (Computer Science) I. Title.

QA76.612.D43 2003
005.1'1—dc21

2003044562

This book is printed on acid-free paper.

Foreword

Constraint Processing by Rina Dechter

Constraint satisfaction is a simple but powerful idea. If we can pose our world knowledge as a set of local constraints on the values assigned to variables in global solutions to a problem, then when we satisfy those constraints we solve the problem. Over the last three to four decades, that idea has motivated a community of researchers to pursue the goal of realizing the constraint satisfaction paradigm. This book captures that spirit, documents that pursuit, and provides a valuable systematic map of the territory discovered.

Constraint satisfaction has a unitary theoretical model with myriad practical applications. The research community has advanced the theoretical base by noting significant experimental results, developing explanations, proving theorems, generalizing the results, and importing and exporting ideas from and to neighboring disciplines, occasionally, unfortunately, rediscovering them and renaming them. The applications themselves have often been the source of new theoretical hypotheses. The constraint processing story is an archetypal case of scientific and engineering development. Parenthetically, that story would make a perfect doctoral thesis topic in the history of science.

Scientists are explorers. The game of science, like geographical exploration, is characterized by an intriguing mix of collaboration and competition. Rina Dechter, as a seasoned explorer with several discoveries to her credit, is well positioned to write this synthesis. Indeed, by bringing together so many disparate research results in this coherent treatment, she has made another substantial contribution to the evolution of the field.

For an optimist, a constraint specifies the possible; for a pessimist, equivalently, the impossible. A constraint may be, for example, in the form of a database relation, a prepositional logic clause, an equation or an inequality. These restricted, modular knowledge representations are natural to humans, yet, because they are so restricted, uniform constraint processing algorithms can efficiently explicate some or all of the consequences of a set of constraints. Spreadsheets and databases, for example, can be seen as simple constraint satisfaction systems. Because those representations fit their applications so naturally, they became two of the 'killer apps' that drove the personal computer revolution. The lesson is that constraint-based systems are tools that let us make computation more transparent, efficient and reliable—in short, more useful.

Dechter clearly develops the major theme in constraint processing, namely, constraint propagation: the process of taking the given explicit local constraints, discovering new implicit constraints, and making them explicit, once and for all. Then, of course, the new and original constraints can give rise to more implicit constraints, which can be made explicit and so forth. The parallel with logical inference is, not surprisingly, exact. Given a logical theory in the form of a set of sentences as axioms, we can use rules of inference to deduce new sentences as logical consequences of those axioms.

The power of making the implicit constraints explicit is that they can, in turn, control the search for global solutions, quickly terminating impossible partial solutions or sub-problems and avoiding thrashing search behavior. This can make the search vastly more efficient, sometimes even making apparently intractable problems tractable. The level of constraint explicitness to be achieved is controlled through the degree of consistency, which is, essentially, the size of the scope of the constraint, that is the number of variables participating in it. These local consistency-enforcing algorithms are, precise, specialized logical inference methods that reformulate a constraint satisfaction problem as an equivalent problem with more explicit constraints that may well be easier to solve and, incidentally, easier for humans to understand. One reason these algorithms are so practical is that we can easily tradeoff the degree of consistency, and thus the level of explicitness, with the work required to compute it.

Dechter provides a reader-friendly organization: covering self-contained basic topics in the first half and following with advanced treatments right up to the contemporary research frontier. She introduces the two basic approaches to constraint processing, inferential consistency algorithms and search algorithms, separately, and then presents methods for their integration. The links to topics in tractable sublanguages, temporal reasoning, probabilistic networks, constraint logic programming, and constraint optimization are clearly and concisely explored. Embedding constraint solving techniques in constraint programming languages makes them more widely available. That embedding also allows us to see that logic programming, as embodied in Prolog, is just a special case of constraint logic programming with unification as the constraint solver.

This book is accessible to novice researchers, software developers, and readers who are simply intellectually curious. But it will also appeal to mature researchers and practitioners in constraint processing and related areas such as database, logic and constraint programming, satisfiability, formal verification, operations research, and the theory of algorithms and complexity.

Think of this book as a well-equipped base camp for exploration, complete with a new map of the terrain. It will serve us well, both for short day hikes, and for major expeditions into uncharted territory.

Alan K. Mackworth
Professor, Department of Computer Science,
University of British Columbia,
Director of the UBC Laboratory for Computational Intelligence

To my parents, Chaim (1918–2002)
and Shoshana Kahana.

Contents

Preface

A constraint is a restriction on a space of possibilities; it is a piece of knowledge that narrows the scope of this space. Because constraints arise naturally in most areas of human endeavor, they are the most general means for formulating regularities that govern our computational, physical, biological, and social worlds. Some examples: the angles of a triangle must sum to 180 degrees; the four nucleotides that make up DNA strands can only combine in particular sequences; the sum of the currents flowing into a node must equal zero; Susan cannot be married to both John and Bill at the same time. Although observable in diverse disciplines, they all share one feature in common: they identify the impossible, narrow down the realm of possibilities, and thus permit us to focus more effectively on the possible.

Formulating problems in terms of constraints has proven useful for modeling fundamental cognitive activities such as vision, language comprehension, default reasoning, diagnosis, scheduling, and temporal and spatial reasoning, as well as having application for engineering tasks, biological modeling, and electronic commerce. Formulating problems in terms of constraints enables a natural, declarative formulation of *what* must be satisfied, without having to say *how* it should be satisfied.

This book provides comprehensive, in-depth coverage of the theory that underlies constraint processing algorithms as they have emerged in the last three decades, primarily in the area of artificial intelligence. The intended audience is readers in diverse areas of computer science, including artificial intelligence, databases, programming languages, and systems, as well as practitioners of related fields such as operations research, management science, and applied mathematics.

This book focuses on the fundamental tools and principles that underlie reasoning with constraints, with special emphasis on the representation and analysis of constraint satisfaction algorithms that operate over discrete and finite domains. We first describe the basic principles underlying relational representation and then present processing algorithms across two main categories: search based and inference based. Search algorithms are characterized by backtracking search and its various enhancements, while inference algorithms are presented through a variety of constraint propagation methods (also known as consistency-enforcing methods).

In order to enhance the understanding and analysis of the various methods, we emphasize a graph-based view of both types of algorithms throughout the book. This graphical preference also allows us to tie in constraint networks and constraint processing with the emerging framework of graphical models that cuts across deterministic and probabilistic knowledge bases.

We seek to take the reader on a step-by-step journey through the world of constraints, offering definitions, examples, theory, algorithms, and complexity analysis. The text is intended primarily for graduate students, senior undergraduates, researchers, and practitioners, and it could be used in a quarter/semester course dedicated to this topic, or as a reference book in a general class on artificial intelligence and operations research. To accommodate different levels of reading, some chapters can be skipped without disturbing the flow. Each chapter starts with the basic and practical aspects of its topic, and proceeds to more advanced issues, including those under current research.

This book is divided into two parts. Chapters 2 through 7 provide the basic material, while Chapters 8 through 15 provide more advanced elaboration. Two chapters are contributed by outside authors, experts in their respective areas: Chapter 11, which focuses on tractable languages, and Chapter 15, which provides a bridging introduction into the whole area of constraint programming languages. Chapters 12, 13, and 14 extend constraint processing to temporal reasoning, optimization tasks, and probabilistic reasoning, respectively.

The chapter flow tree in Figure P.1 provides a precedence order for reading the chapters. A detailed overview of the chapters is provided in Chapter 1.

Acknowledgments

It is a pleasure for me to thank the many colleagues whose work influenced the content of this book. First and foremost, I would like to acknowledge the pioneering work of Ugo Montanari, Alan Mackworth, and Eugene Freuder, whose seminal papers triggered and influenced much of my work, as well as that of the entire constraint processing field. Second, I would like to thank collaborators and students in my group whose work forms the basis for large portions of this book: Itay Meiri, Rachel Ben-Eliyahoo-Zohari, Dan Frost, Eddie Schwalb, Irina Rish, Kalev Kask, Javier Larrosa, Lluis Vila, and Yousri El-Fattah.

Special thanks for many influential interactions to the members of the UCLA cognitive science lab: Hector Geffner, Dan Geiger, and Adnan Darwiche, and most of all, to Judea Pearl, who has inspired me throughout my academic life, and whose encouragement and support is invaluable.

Special thanks also to Peter van Beek, with whom the book idea was born, and whose collaboration and advice throughout the years have always been beneficial, and to Krzystoff Apt for forcefully encouraging me to get this project through.

I am grateful to every one of my colleagues who has contributed comments on the many versions of this manuscript: Pedro Meseguer, Francesca Rossi,

Toby Walsh, Barbara Smith, Carla Gomes, Bart Selman, Henry Kautz, Roberto Bayardo, Manolis Koubarakis, Jean-Charles Regin, Faheim Bacchus, and Weixiong Zhang. Pedro and Carla in particular provided thorough and in-depth comments. Thanks also go to anonymous reviewers of the final draft.

I am indebted to all the students who have perused many versions of this book in the past six years and have provided careful criticism, and in particular to my recent group: Robert Mateescu, Radu Marinescu, David Larkin, and Bozhena Bidyuk.

The National Science Foundation deserves acknowledgment for sponsoring research that allowed the creation of this book, with special thanks to Larry Reaker. Other sponsors include the Office of Naval Research, with special thanks to Wendy Martinez, and the Air Force Office of Scientific Research, with special thanks to Abraham Waksman.

Thanks to Nira Brand for her dedicated editing of the first six chapters of this book, and to Mario Espinoza for assisting in drawing many of the figures and incorporating revisions.

Finally, I owe a great debt to my family for their encouragement throughout the years: to Gadi, for harnessing his wonderful language skills as a developmental editor for the book; to Dani, for his inspiring songs that influenced the final months of this work; and to Eyal, for his thought-provoking questions that forced me to deal with basic issues. Finally, thanks to Avi, my husband of more than 30 years, whose daily support and companionship have made this book, and many more things, possible.

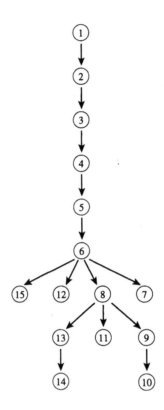

Figure P.1 Chapter flow diagram.

chapter 1

Introduction

The work under our labour grows luxurious by restraint.
  John Milton, Paradise Lost

We regularly encounter constraint in our day-to-day lives—for instance, a finite amount of memory in our PCs, seats in the car, hours in the day, money in the bank. And we regularly engage in solving constraint satisfaction problems: how to live well but within our means, how to eat healthy but still enjoy food. Most of the time, we don't require sophisticated computer-processed algorithms to figure out whether to splurge on a ski vacation or eat the triple-layer chocolate cake. But consider the complexity encountered when the number of constraints to be satisfied, and variables involved, begins to grow. For example, we find it takes a surprisingly long time to determine the optimal seating arrangement for a dinner party, or choose one movie rental for a large group of friends.

Now imagine the difficulty in scheduling classrooms for a semester of university instruction. We need to allocate a classroom for every course while simultaneously satisfying the constraints that no two classes may be held in the same classroom at the same time, no professor can teach in two different classrooms at the same time, no class may be scheduled in the middle of the night, all classes must be offered in appropriately sized rooms or lecture halls, certain classes must not be scheduled at the same time, and so on.

As the complexity of the problem grows, we turn to computers to help us find an acceptable solution. Computer scientists have devised language to model *constraint satisfaction problems* and have developed methods for solving them. The language of constraints is used to model simple cognitive tasks such as vision, language comprehension, default reasoning and abduction, as well as tasks that require high levels of human expertise such as scheduling, design, diagnosis, and temporal and spatial reasoning.

In general, the tasks posed in the language of constraints are computationally intractable (NP-hard), which means that you cannot expect to design algorithms that scale efficiently with the problem size, in all cases. However, it is possible and desirable to identify special properties of a problem class that can accommodate efficient solutions and to develop general algorithms that are efficient for as many problems as possible.

Indeed, over the last two to three decades, a great deal of theoretical and experimental research has focused on developing and improving the performance of general algorithms for solving constraint satisfaction problems, on identifying restricted subclasses that can be solved efficiently, called tractable classes, and on developing approximation algorithms. This book describes the theory and practice underlying such constraint processing methods.

The remainder of this chapter is divided into three parts. First is an informal overview of constraint networks, starting with common examples of problems that can be modeled as constraint satisfaction problems. Second is an overview of the book by chapter. Third is a review of mathematical concepts and some preliminaries relevant to our discussion throughout the book.

1.1 Basic Concepts and Examples

In general, constraint satisfaction problems include two important components of variables with associated domains and constraints. Let's define each component and then take a look at several examples that formally model constraint satisfaction problems. First, every constraint problem must include *variables*: objects or items that can take on a variety of values. The set of possible values for a given variable is called its *domain*. For example, in trying to find an acceptable seating arrangement for a dinner party, we may choose to see the chairs as our variables, each with the same domain, which is the list of all guests.

The second component to every constraint problem is the set of constraints themselves. *Constraints* are rules that impose a limitation on the values that a variable, or a combination of variables, may be assigned. If the host and hostess must sit at the two ends of the table, then their choices of seats are constrained. If two feuding guests must not be placed next to or directly opposite one another, then we must include this constraint in our overall problem statement.

Note that there is often more than one way to model a problem. In the previous example, we could just as logically have decided to call the guests our variables and their domains the set of chairs at the table. In this case, assuming a one-to-one correspondence between chairs and guests, the choice makes little difference, but in other cases, one formulation of a problem may lend itself more readily to solution techniques than another.

A model that includes variables, their domains, and constraints is called a *constraint network*, also called a *constraint problem*. Use of the term "network" can be traced to the early days of constraint satisfaction work when the research focus was restricted to sets of constraints whose dependencies were naturally captured by simple graphs. We prefer this term because it emphasizes the importance of a constraint dependency structure in reasoning algorithms.

A *solution* is an assignment of a single value from its domain to each variable such that no constraint is violated. A problem may have one, many, or no solutions. A problem that has one or more solutions is *satisfiable* or *consistent*. If there is no possible assignment of values to variables that satisfies all the constraints, then the network is *unsatisfiable* or *inconsistent*.

Typical tasks over constraint networks are determining whether a solution exists, finding one or all solutions, finding whether a partial instantiation can be extended to a full solution, and finding an optimal solution relative to a given cost function. Such tasks are referred to as *constraint satisfaction problems* (CSPs).

Let's look at some common examples of problems that can be intuitively modeled as constraint satisfaction problems, including both simple puzzle problems that help illustrate the principles involved, as well as more complex real-world problems. At this point the specification of the constraints will be made informally. We will revisit some of these examples in greater detail in the following chapter and throughout the book.

The n-Queens Problem

The classic example used to illustrate a constraint satisfaction problem is the n-queens problem. The task is to place n queens on an $n \times n$ chessboard such that the placement of no queen constitutes an attack on any other. One possible constraint network formulation of the problem is the following: there is a variable for each column of the chessboard $x_1, \ldots, x_n$, the domains of the variables are the possible row positions $D_i = \{1, \ldots, n\}$, and the constraint on each pair of columns is that the two queens must not share a row or diagonal. An interesting property of this problem is that the number of variables is always the same as the number of values in each domain.

Crossword Puzzles

Crossword puzzles have also been used in evaluating constraint satisfaction algorithms. The task is to assign words from the dictionary (or from a given set of words) into vertical or horizontal slots according to certain constraints. If we allow each word to be placed in any space of correct length, a possible constraint network formulation of the crossword puzzle in Figure 1.1 is the following: each white square is a variable, the domain of each variable is the alphabet, and the constraints are dictated by the input of possible words:

{HOSES, LASER, SHEET, SNAIL, STEER, ALSO, EARN, HIKE, IRON,

SAME, EAT, LET, RUN, SUN, TEN, YES, BE, IT, NO, US}

Figure 1.1 A crossword puzzle.

So, for example, there is a constraint over the variables x_8, x_9, x_{10}, x_{11} that allows assigning only the four-letter words from the list to these four variables. This constraint can be described by the relation $C = \{(A, L, S, O), (E, A, R, N),$ $(H, I, K, E), (I, R, O, N), (S, A, M, E)\}$. This means that x_8, x_9, x_{10}, x_{11} can be assigned, respectively, either $\{A, L, S, O\}$ or $\{E, A, R, N\}$, and so on. A solution to the constraint problem will generate an assignment of letters to the squares so that only these four-letter words are entered.

Map Coloring and k-Colorability

The map-coloring problem is a well-known problem that asks whether it is possible to color a map with only four colors when no two adjacent countries may share the same color. The problem was open for many years until it was solved in 1976 by a combination of mathematics and computer simulation (Appel and Haken 1976). Many resource allocation and communication problems can be abstracted to this problem, known in the field of classical graph theory as *k-colorability*. Examples of this type of problem are *radio link frequency assignment problems*—communication problems where the goal is to assign frequencies to a set of radio links in such a way that all the links may operate together without noticeable interference.

   In graph coloring, the map can be abstracted to a graph with a node for each country and an edge joining any two neighboring countries. Given a graph of arbitrary size, the problem is to decide whether or not the nodes can be colored with only k colors such that any two adjacent nodes in the graph must be of different colors. If the answer is yes, then a possible k-coloring of the graph's nodes should be given.

   The graph k-colorability problem is formulated as a constraint satisfaction problem where each node in the graph is a variable, the domains of the variables are the possible colors (when $k = 3$ for every variable x_i, its domain is $D_i = \{red, blue, green\}$

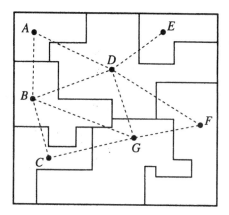

Figure 1.2   A map-coloring problem.

or $D_i = \{1, 2, 3\}$), and the constraints are that every two adjacent nodes must be assigned different values (if x_i is connected to x_j, then $x_i \neq x_j$). A specific example is given in Figure 1.2, where the variables are the countries denoted A, B, C, D, E, F, and G. A solution to this constraint satisfaction problem is a legal 3-coloring of the graph. A property of k-colorability problems is that their *not-equal* constraints appear in many problems and are among the "loosest" constraints, namely, they forbid only k out of the k^2 possible value combinations between any two constrained variables. A solution to the graph-coloring problem in Figure 1.2, using three colors, is ($A = green, D = red, E = blue, B = blue, F = blue, C = red, G = green$).

Configuration and Design

Configuration and allocation problems are a particularly interesting class for which constraint satisfaction formalism is useful. These problems arise in applications as diverse as automobile transmission design, microcomputer system configuration, and floor plan layout. Let us consider a simple example from the domain of architectural site location. Consider the map in Figure 1.3, showing eight lots available for development.[1] Five developments are to be located on these lots: a recreation area, an apartment complex, a cluster of 50 single-family houses, a large cemetery, and a dump site. Assume the following information and conditions:

- The recreation area must be near the lake.
- Steep slopes must be avoided for all but the recreation area.

---

1. This example was popularized by Nadel (1989).

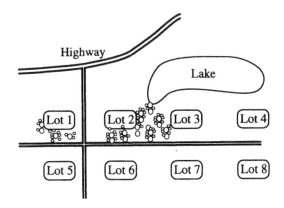

Figure 1.3 Development map.

- Poor soil must be avoided for developments that involve construction, namely, the apartments and the houses.
- Because it is noisy, the highway must not be near the apartments, the houses, or the recreation area.
- The dump site must not be visible from the apartments, the houses, or the lake.
- Lots 3 and 4 have poor soil.
- Lots 3, 4, 7, and 8 are on steep slopes.
- Lots 2, 3, and 4 are near the lake.
- Lots 1 and 2 are near the highway.

The problem of siting the five developments on the eight available lots while satisfying the given conditions can be naturally formulated as a constraint satisfaction problem. A variable can be associated with each development:

- *Recreation, Apartments, Houses, Cemetery,* and *Dump*

The eight development sites constitute our variables' common domain:

- *Domain* = {1, 2, 3, 4, 5, 6, 7, 8}

The information and conditions above suggest the constraints on the variables. For instance, the statement of the solution incorporates the implicit constraints that no two developments may occur on the same lot. This can be formulated using the "not-equal" constraints as we see in graph coloring.

Fork:

Arrow:

Ell:

Tee:

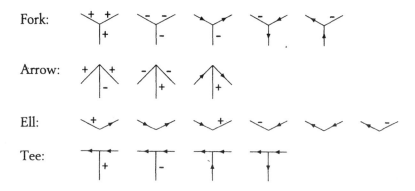

Figure 1.4 Huffman-Clowes junction labelings.

Huffman-Clowes Scene Labeling

One of the earliest constraint satisfaction problems was introduced in the early 1970s. This problem concerns the three-dimensional interpretation of a two-dimensional drawing. Huffman and Clowes (1975) developed a basic labeling scheme of the arcs in a block world picture graph, where + stands for a convex edge, − for a concave edge, and → for occluding boundaries. They demonstrated that the possible combination of legal labelings associated with different junctions in such scenes can be enumerated as in Figure 1.4. The interpretation problem is to label the junction of a given drawing such that every junction type is labeled according to one of its legal labeling combinations and that edges common to two junctions receive the same label. One formulation of the cube instance as a constraint satisfaction problem assigns variables for the lines in the figure with their domains being the possible labelings $\{+, -, \rightarrow, \leftarrow\}$. The labeling of adjacent lines in a junction are constrained according to the junction type. The possible consistent labelings of a cube are presented in Figure 1.5.

Scheduling Problems

Scheduling problems naturally lend themselves to constraint satisfaction formulation. These problems typically involve scheduling activities or jobs, while satisfying given resource and temporal precedence constraints. A well-known problem class is job shop scheduling, where a typical resource is the availability of a machine for processing certain tasks. Another class is time-tabling problems, which involve scheduling rooms and teachers to classes and time slots while satisfying natural constraints. In such problems it is common to associate the *tasks* with variables, their domain with the *starting time* of the task, and the constraints restrict the relevant variables. A simple example will be given in Chapter 2.

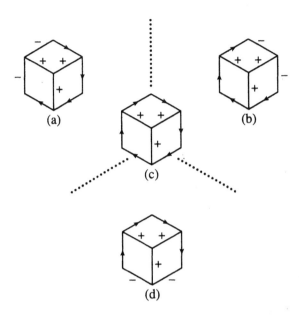

Figure 1.5 Solutions: (a) stuck on left wall, (b) stuck on right wall, (c) suspended in midair, and (d) resting on floor.

We have looked at several examples of problems, and described them—informally—as constraint problems. A formal treatment will be given in Chapter 2. We conclude this chapter with an overview of the remaining chapters, and with a discussion of the mathematical concepts and background used throughout the book.

1.2 **Overview by Chapter**

The remainder of this book is divided into two parts. The first (Chapters 2 through 7) contains the basic core information for constraint processing. The second (Chapters 8 through 15) includes more advanced areas and related material. Techniques for processing constraints can be classified into two main categories: (1) inference and (2) search, and these techniques may also be combined. Both inference and search techniques offer methods that are systematic and complete, as well as stochastic and incomplete. We call an algorithm complete if it is guaranteed to solve the problem, or it can prove that the problem is unsolvable. Incomplete (or approximation) algorithms sometimes solve hard problems quickly, but they are not guaranteed to solve the problem even with unbounded time and space.

1.2.1 Inference

Chapters 3 and 4 in the first part of the book and Chapters 8 and 9 in the second part focus on inference algorithms. Inference algorithms create equivalent problems through problem reformulation. They usually create simpler problems that are subsequently easy to solve by a search algorithm. Occasionally, inference methods can deliver a solution or prove the inconsistency of the network without requiring further search.

Chapter 3 focuses on the main concepts associated with inference methods applied to constraint networks called *local consistency* algorithms. These algorithms take a telescopic view of subparts of the constraint network and demand that they contain no obviously extraneous or contradictory parts. For example, if a network consists of several variables $x_1, \dots, x_n$, all with domains $D = \{1, \dots, 10\}$, and if x_1 is constrained such that its value must be strictly greater than the value of every other variable, then we can infer that there is no need for the value 1 in x_1's domain.

In the language of constraint networks, the value 1 is *inconsistent* and should be removed from x_1's domain because there is no solution to the problem that assigns $x_1 = 1$. (We could similarly reason that the value 10 should be removed from the domain of x_2 and x_3 and so on.)

In general, local consistency algorithms (also known as *constraint propagation*) are polynomial algorithms that transform a given constraint network into an equivalent, yet more explicit, network by deducing new constraints, which are then added to the problem. For example, the most basic consistency algorithm we will present, called *arc-consistency*, ensures that any legal value in the domain of a single variable has a legal match in the domain of any other selected variable. This is the sort of consistency enforcing that we saw in the above example. *Path-consistency* ensures that any consistent solution to any two variables is extensible to any third variable, and, in general, *i-consistency* algorithms guarantee that any locally consistent instantiation of $i - 1$ variables is extensible to any ith variables. We can transform a given network to an *i*-consistent one by inferring some constraints. However, enforcing *i*-consistency is computationally expensive; it can be accomplished in time and space exponential in i. While these methods are not guaranteed to find a solution, sometimes they eliminate domain values to the point of completely emptying one or more domains, allowing us to declare the network *inconsistent*.

Chapters 4 and 8 continue our discussion of advanced inference methods, some of which are guaranteed to find a solution to the problem by making the problem *globally consistent*. We will present less expensive directional consistency algorithms that enforce *global consistency* only relative to a certain variable ordering, such as ADAPTIVE-CONSISTENCY, an inference algorithm typical of a class of variable elimination algorithms. A unifying description of such algorithms is the focus of Chapter 8. Chapters 4 and 8 will expose you to structure-based analysis and parameters, such as *induced width*, that accompany many of the subsequent chapters. Some tractable classes, exploiting the notions of tight domains and tight constraints, and row-convex constraints, are also introduced in Chapter 8. The chapter also includes the specialized language and consistency methods of propositional theories and the constraints expressed by linear inequalities.

1.2.2 Search

Chapters 5 and 6 focus on complete search algorithms. The most common algorithm for performing systematic search is *backtracking* that traverses the space of partial solutions in a depth-first manner. Each step in the search represents the assignment of a value to one additional variable, thus extending a *candidate* partial solution. When a variable is encountered such that none of its possible values are consistent with the current candidate solution, a situation referred to as a *dead-end*, backtracking takes place. Namely, the algorithm returns to an earlier variable and attempts to assign it a new value such that the dead-end can be avoided. The best scenario for a backtracking algorithm occurs when the algorithm is able to successfully assign a value to every variable without encountering any dead-ends. In such problem instances, backtracking is very efficient. Worst-case performance, encountering many dead-ends, however, still requires exponential time.

Improvements to backtracking have focused on the two phases of the algorithm: moving-forward activity (look-ahead schemes), described in Chapter 5, and backtracking activity (look-back schemes), the focus of Chapter 6. When moving forward to extend a partial solution, look-ahead schemes perform some computation to decide which variable and even which of that variable's values to assign next in order to enhance the efficiency of the search. For example, variables that participate in many constraints maximally constrain the rest of the search space and are thus preferred. In choosing a value from the domain of the selected variable, however, the least constraining value is preferred, in order to maximize options for future instantiations.

Look-back schemes are described in Chapter 6. They are invoked when the algorithm encounters a dead-end and perform two functions: First, they decide how far to backtrack by analyzing the reasons for the dead-end, a process often referred to as *backjumping*. Second, they record the reasons for the dead-end in the form of new constraints, so that the same conflict does not arise again, a process known as *constraint learning* or *no-good recording*.

Chapter 7 describes *stochastic local search* (SLS) strategies, which approximate search. These methods move in a hill-climbing manner, traversing the space of complete instantiations of all the variables. The algorithm improves its current instantiation by iteratively changing (or "flipping") the value of the variable to maximize the number of constraints satisfied. Such search algorithms are incomplete, may get stuck in a local optimum of their guiding cost function, and cannot prove inconsistency. Nevertheless, when equipped with some heuristics for randomizing the search or for revising the guiding criterion function (constraint reweighting), they have been demonstrated successful in solving large and hard problems that are frequently too difficult for backtracking-style search. The chapter also shows how these local search algorithms can be combined with inference using a method known as the *cycle-cutset scheme*. This method is also elaborated on in Chapter 10.

Local search algorithms flourished initially for solving *satisfiability*, namely, finding a truth assignment to a set of propositional variables that satisfies a set of Boolean clauses. Satisfiability is a central constraint satisfaction problem that received targeted attention in a variety of communities. In this book we treat satisfiability as a special case of constraint solving in each of the relevant chapters.

The second part of the book, Chapters 8 through 15, focuses on advanced structure-based inference, search, and their hybrids, and discusses tractable classes that are derived from the constraint types. It also includes topics such as temporal constraints, constraint optimization, probabilistic networks, and constraint programming. Each of the latter constitutes an area of its own significance and deserves its own book. Here we only seek to open a window into these topics, as they emerge naturally from within the constraint processing framework.

Chapter 8 was discussed earlier. Chapter 9 continues with advanced inference algorithms, concentrating on a structure-based compilation method called *tree-clustering*. This method belongs to *structure-driven algorithms* that depict constraint networks as graphs where nodes represent variables and edges represent constraints. These techniques emerged from an attempt to characterize easy-to-solve constraint problems by their graph characteristics. The basic network structure that supports tractability is a tree. This has been observed repeatedly in areas of constraint networks, complexity theory, and database theory. Tree-clustering compiles a constraint problem into an equivalent tree of subproblems whose respective solutions can be efficiently combined into a solution to the whole problem. The ADAPTIVE-CONSISTENCY algorithm, described in Chapters 4 and 8, is quite related to tree-clustering, and both are time and space exponentially bounded in a parameter of the constraint graph called *induced width*.

Chapter 10 focuses on hybrids of search and inference. When a problem is computationally hard for inference, it can be solved by bounding the amount of constraint propagation and augmenting the algorithm with a search component. We start by presenting the *cycle-cutset scheme*, a search and inference hybrid, which is exponentially bounded by the graph's *cycle-cutset*. We then extend this approach to a general parameterized hybrid scheme whose parameter b bounds the level of inference allowed. Such combined methods also allow trade-offs between time and space.

Chapter 11 extends the theory of tractable constraint problems by restricting the language by which the constraints themselves can be expressed. It presents a theory of both the expressiveness and the complexity of constraint languages and characterizes both for constraints over finite domains. The tractable cases discussed include *implicational* and *max-ordered constraints* and linear constraints.

In Chapter 12, we introduce special classes of constraints associated with temporal reasoning that have received much attention in the last decade. These tractable classes include subsets of the *qualitative interval algebra*, expressing relationships such as "time interval A overlaps or precedes time interval B," as well as quantitative binary linear inequalities over real numbers of the form $X - Y \le a$.

Chapter 13 extends the constraint processing task to combinatorial optimization. It is often the case that the problem at hand requires specifying preferences among solutions. Such problems can be expressed by augmenting the constraint problem with a cost function. The chapter extends search and inference approaches to optimization. It summarizes the two best-known approaches for optimization developed in operations research: branch-and-bound and dynamic programming.

Chapter 14 takes you one step beyond deterministic constraints to networks involving probabilistic relationships such as Bayesian networks. It shows that the principles for computing answers to relevant queries over Bayesian networks can be addressed in a way similar to that of processing constraints and optimization problems, namely, by using inference and search. In particular, the inference-type bucket elimination algorithms for finding posterior probabilities and for computing most likely tuples are given.

The practice of designing models for given problems is only casually addressed in this book, via sporadic examples and exercises. Although important, this aspect of constraint networks is something of an art and not well-understood. Our final chapter, Chapter 15, provides a window into a language approach for addressing the modeling issue. It also provides an introduction to a class of languages that exploit constraint processing algorithms known as "constraint programming."

Some chapters throughout the book include empirical testing of relevant algorithms. Our examples aim at giving the flavor of empirical testing, but they are by no means inclusive. For a comprehensive treatment of empirical testing, see Frost (1997).

1.3 **Mathematical Background**

The formalization of constraint networks relies upon concepts drawn from the related areas of discrete mathematics, logic, the theory of relational databases, and graph theory. This section is a summary of the mathematical knowledge needed for understanding the formalization of constraint networks and the analyses presented in subsequent chapters. Here we present the basic notations and definitions for sets, relations, operations on relations, and graphs. If you are already familiar with these topics, a skim of this material will suffice to ensure your understanding of the notation used in this book.

1.3.1 **Sets, Domains, and Tuples**

A *set* is a collection of distinguishable objects, and an object in the collection is called a *member* or an *element* of the set. A set cannot contain the same object more than once, and its elements are not ordered. If an object x is a member of set A, we write $x \in A$; if an object x is not a member of set A, we write $x \notin A$. A set can be defined explicitly, by listing the members of the set, or implicitly, by stating a property satisfied by elements of the set. For example, $A = \{1, 2, 3\}$ and $A = \{x \mid x$ an integer and $1 \leq x \leq 3\}$ both represent the same set with three members, 1, 2 and 3. If each element of a set A is also an element of set B, then we write $A \subseteq B$ and say that A is a *subset* of B. Set A is a *proper subset* of B, written $A \subset B$, if $A \subseteq B$ but $A \neq B$.

Given two sets A and B, we can also define new sets by applying set operations: the *intersection* of two sets A and B is the set $A \cap B = \{x \mid x \in A$ and $x \in B\}$, the *union* of two sets A and B is the set $A \cup B = \{x \mid x \in A$ or $x \in B\}$, and the *difference* of two sets A and B is the set $A - B = \{x \mid x \in A$ and $x \notin B\}$. A set containing no members is called an *empty set* and is denoted $\emptyset$. The number of elements in a set S is called the *size* (or *cardinality*) of the set and is denoted $|S|$. Two sets A and B are *disjoint* if they have no elements in common; that is, if $A \cap B = \emptyset$.

A variable is a collection of values, called a *domain*. That is, the domain of a variable is simply a set that lists all of the possible objects that a variable can denote or all of the possible values that a variable can be assigned. A *k-tuple* (or simply a *tuple*) is a sequence of k not necessarily distinct objects denoted by $(a_1, \ldots, a_k)$, and an object in the sequence is called a *component*. The *Cartesian product* (or simply the *product*) of a list of domains $D_1, \ldots, D_k$, written $D_1 \times \cdots \times D_k$, is the set of all k-tuples $(a_1, \ldots, a_k)$ such that a_1 is in D_1, a_2 is in D_2, and so on.

EXAMPLE 1.1   Let $D_1 = \{$black, green$\}$ and $D_2 = \{$apple juice, coffee, tea$\}$. The Cartesian product $D_1 \times D_2$ is the set of tuples $\{$(black, apple juice), (black, coffee), (black, tea), (green, apple juice), (green, coffee), (green, tea)$\}$.   ●

1.3.2 **Relations**

Given a set of variables $X = \{x_1, \ldots, x_k\}$, each associated with a domain $D_1, \ldots, D_k$, respectively, a *relation* R on the set of variables is any subset of the Cartesian product of their domains. The set of variables on which a relation is defined is called the *scope* of the relation, denoted $scope(R)$. Each relation that is a subset of some product $D_1 \times \cdots \times D_k$ of k domains is said to have *arity* k. If $k = 1, 2,$ or 3, then the relation is called a *unary*, *binary*, or *ternary* relation, respectively. If $R = D_1 \times \cdots \times D_k$, then R is called a *universal* relation. We will frequently denote a relation defined on a scope S by R_S.

EXAMPLE
1.2

Let $D_1 = \{black, green\}$ be the domain of variable x_1 and let $D_2 = \{apple$ juice, coffee, tea$\}$ be the domain of variable x_2. The set of tuples $\{(black, coffee), (black, tea), (green, tea)\}$ is a relation on $\{x_1, x_2\}$, since the tuples are a subset of the product of D_1 and D_2. The scope of this relation is $\{x_1, x_2\}$.   ●

The empty set is another example of a relation.

Representing Relations

Relations are sets of tuples defined over the same scope, and, as discussed above for sets, they may be either explicitly or implicitly defined. For example, let R be a relation on the set of variables $\{x_1, x_2\}$, where $D_1 = \{black, green\}$ and $D_2 = \{apple juice, coffee, tea\}$. Then the relation R_1 on the scope $\{x_1, x_2\}$ given by $R_1 = \{(black, coffee), (black, tea), (green, tea)\}$ and $R_2 = \{(x_1, x_2) \mid x_1 \in D_1, x_2 \in D_2,$ and x_1 is before x_2 in dictionary ordering$\}$ both represent the same relation. Using arithmetic expressions, we can also write more succinctly $x_1 \leq x_2$, where $\leq$ is a lexicographic ordering.

Two additional ways to explicitly express a relation make use of tables and (0, 1)-matrices. In a table representation each row is a tuple and each column corresponds to one component of the tuple. Each column is identified by the variable associated with that component (in the database community, the names of columns are called *attributes*). The ordering of the columns is inconsequential; two relations that differ only in the ordering of their columns are considered the same.

A binary relation between two variables x_i and x_j can be represented as a (0, 1)-matrix with $|D_i|$ rows and $|D_j|$ columns by imposing an ordering on the domains of the variables. A 0 entry at row a column b means that the pair consisting of the ath element of D_i and the bth element of D_j is not in the relation, while a 1 entry means that the pair is in the relation. The (0, 1)-matrix representation can be generalized to nonbinary relations by increasing the number of dimensions of the matrix.

Figure 1.6 shows two graphical representations of the binary relation R on the scope $\{x_1, x_2\}$, where $D_1 = \{black, green\}$ and $D_2 = \{apple juice, coffee, tea\}$.

Operations on Relations

Having introduced the mathematical notion of a relation, let's now consider operations on relations. First we discuss how general set operations apply to relations, and then we focus on three operations specific to relations: selection, projection, and join.

Intersection, Union, and Difference. Given two relations, R and R', on the same scope, the intersection of R and R', denoted $R \cap R'$, is the relation containing all tuples that are in both R and R'. The union $R \cup R'$ is the relation containing all the tuples that are in either R or R' or both. The difference $R - R'$ is the relation

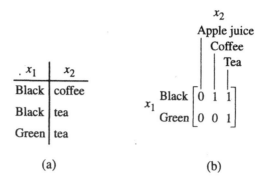

x_1	x_2
Black	coffee
Black	tea
Green	tea

(a)

(b)

Figure 1.6 Two graphical views of relation $R = \{$(black, coffee), (black, tea), (green, tea)$\}$: (a) table and (b) (0, 1)-matrix.

x_1	x_2	x_3
a	b	c
b	b	c
c	b	c
c	b	s

x_1	x_2	x_3
b	b	c
c	b	c
c	n	n

x_2	x_3	x_4
a	a	1
b	c	2
b	c	3

(a)   (b)   (c)

Figure 1.7 Three relations: (a) relation R, (b) relation R', and (c) relation R''.

containing those tuples that are in R but not in R'. The scope of the resulting relations is the same as the scope of the relations R and R'.

EXAMPLE 1.3   Let the relations R, R', and R'' be as shown in Figure 1.7. The relations R and R' have the same scopes $\{x_1, x_2, x_3\}$, so the set operations intersection, union, and difference are well-defined for these sets. Since the scope of R'' is not the same, none of these three operations is well-defined for R'' in conjunction with either of the other two relations. Figure 1.8 shows the relations $R \cap R'$, $R \cup R'$, and $R - R'$.   ●

Let us now consider operations specific to relations.

Selection. A selection takes a relation R and yields a new relation: the subset of tuples of R with specified values on specified variables. In a table representation of a relation, selection chooses a subset of the rows. Let R be a relation, let $x_1, \ldots, x_k$ be variables in the scope of R, and let a_i be an element of D_i, the domain of x_i. We use

x_1	x_2	x_3
a	b	c
b	b	c
c	b	c
c	b	s
c	n	n

x_1	x_2	x_3
b	b	c
c	b	c

x_1	x_2	x_3
a	b	c
c	b	s

(a)   (b)   (c)

Figure 1.8 Examples of (a) intersection $(R \cap R')$, (b) union $(R \cup R')$, and (c) difference $(R - R')$ operations applied to relations.

the notation $\sigma_{x_1=a_1,\dots,x_k=a_k}(R)$ to denote the selection of those tuples in R that have the value a_1 for variable x_1, the value a_2 for variable x_2, and so on. An alternative and more succinct notation is $\sigma_{Y=t}(R)$ if $Y = \{x_1,\dots,x_k\}$ and $t = (a_1,\dots,a_k)$. The scope of the resulting relation is the same as the scope of R.

Projection. Projection takes a relation R and yields a new relation that consists of the tuples of R with certain components removed. In a table representation of a relation, projection chooses a subset of the columns. Let R be a relation, and let $Y = \{x_1,\dots,x_k\}$ be a subset of the variables in the scope of R. We use the notation $\pi_Y(R)$ to denote the projection of R onto Y, that is, the set of tuples obtained by taking in turn each tuple in R and forming from it a smaller tuple, keeping only those components associated with variables in Y. Projection specifies a subset of the variables of a relation, and so the scope of the resulting relation is that subset of variables.

Join. The join operator takes two relations R_S and R_T, and yields a new relation that consists of the tuples of R_S and R_T combined on all their common variables in S and T. For illustration, let R_S be a relation with scope S, and R_T a relation with scope T. A tuple r is in the join of R_S and R_T, denoted $R_S \bowtie R_T$, if it can be constructed according to the following steps: (1) take a tuple s from R_S, (2) select a tuple t from R_T such that the components of s and t agree on the variables that R_S and R_T have in common (that is, on the variables in $S \cap T$), and (3) form a new tuple r by combining the components of s and t, keeping only one copy of those components corresponding to variables in $S \cap T$. The scope of the resulting relation is the union of the scopes of R and S, that is, $S \cup T$. We can see now that a join of two relations with the same scopes is equivalent to the intersection of the two relations.

EXAMPLE 1.4 Let the relations R, R', and R'' be as shown in Figure 1.7. Figure 1.9 shows examples of the selection, projection, and join operations applied to these relations. The relation $\sigma_{x_3=c}(R')$ consists of those tuples in R' that have

x_1	x_2	x_3
b	b	c
c	b	c

(a)

x_2	x_3
b	c
n	n

(b)

x_1	x_2	x_3	x_4
b	b	c	2
b	b	c	3
c	b	c	2
c	b	c	3

(c)

Figure 1.9 Example of (a) selection $(\sigma_{x_3=c}(R'))$, (b) projection $(\pi_{\{x_2,x_3\}}(R'))$, and (c) join $(R' \bowtie R'')$ operations on relations.

the value c for variable x_3. The relation $\pi_{\{x_2,x_3\}}(R')$ consists of the tuples in R', each with the component that corresponds to the variable x_1 removed; only the components that correspond to variables x_2 and x_3 are kept. Duplicate entries are removed, since a relation is a set and sets do not contain duplicate objects. The relation $R' \bowtie R''$ consists of tuples that are combinations of pairs of tuples from R' and R'' that share common variables $\{x_2, x_3\}$. To construct $R' \bowtie R''$, we consider each tuple in R', match it up with all possible tuples in R'' that agree with it on the common variables, and delete duplicate components associated with these variables. For example, the tuple (b, b, c) in R' agrees with the tuples (b, c, 2) and (b, c, 3) in R'', resulting in the tuples (b, b, c, 2) and (b, b, c, 3). Similarly, the tuple (c, b, c) in R' results in the tuples (c, b, c, 2) and (c, b, c, 3). The tuple (c, n, n) in R' does not agree with any tuple in R'' on variables x_2 and x_3, so no additional tuples are added to $R' \bowtie R''$.   ●

1.3.3 Graphs: General Concepts

A *graph* $G = (V, E)$ is a structure that consists of a finite set of *vertices* or *nodes*, $V = \{v_1, \ldots, v_n\}$, and a set of *edges* or *arcs*, $E = \{e_1, e_2, \ldots, e_l\}$. Each edge e is incident to an unordered pair of vertices $\{u, v\}$ that are not necessarily distinct (as in the case of a loop). Although the vertices are unordered, they will often be written as an ordered pair (u, v). If $e = (u, v) \in E$, we say that e connects u and v and that u and v are *adjacent* or *neighbors*. The degree $d(u)$ of a vertex u in a graph is the number of its adjacent vertices.

A *path* is a sequence of edges $e_1, e_2, \ldots, e_k$ such that e_i and e_{i+1} share an endpoint. Namely, if $e_i = (u_1, v_1)$ and $e_{i+1} = (u_2, v_2)$, then v_1 and u_2 are the same. It is also convenient to describe a path using its vertices $v_0, v_1, \ldots, v_k$, where $e_i = (v_{i-1}, v_i)$. In this case node v_o is called the *start vertex* of the path, v_k is called the *end vertex*, and the length of the path is k. A *cycle* is a path whose start and end vertices are the same. A path is *simple* if no vertex appears on it more than once.

A cycle is *simple* if no vertex other than the start-end vertex appears more than once and the start-end vertex does not appear elsewhere in the cycle. If for every two vertices u and v in the graph there exists a path from u to v, then the graph is said to be *connected*. An undirected graph with no cycles is called a *tree*. Given a subset of the nodes S in the graph G, a *subgraph* relative to S, denoted G_S, is the graph whose nodes are in S and whose edges, all in G, are incident only to nodes in S. A graph is *complete* if every two nodes are adjacent. A *clique* in a graph is a complete subgraph.

A *directed graph (digraph)* is defined similarly to an undirected graph except that the pair of endpoints of an edge is now ordered; the first endpoint is the *start vertex* of the edge and the second is the *end vertex*. The edge $e = (u, v)$, also denoted $u \to v$, is said to be directed from u to v. The *outdegree* of a vertex v is the number of edges that have v as their start vertex; the *indegree* of v is the number of edges that have v as their end vertex. The set of nodes that point to node u is its *parents* and is denoted $pa(u)$. Similarly, the set of vertices to which u points is called the set of *child nodes* of u and is denoted $ch(u)$. A *directed path* is a sequence of edges $e_1, e_2, \ldots, e_k$ such that the end vertex of e_{i-1} is the start vertex of e_i. A directed path is a *directed cycle* if the start vertex of the path is the same as the end vertex. A directed graph is *strongly connected* if for every vertex u and every vertex v there is a directed path from u to v. A directed graph is *acyclic* if it has no directed cycles. The following example illustrates these definitions.

EXAMPLE 1.5

The graph G_1 in Figure 1.10(a) is an undirected graph over vertices $\{A, B, C, D, E, F\}$. The edge $e = (A, B)$ is in the graph, while (B, C) is not. The sequence (A, B, D, F) is a path whose start vertex is A and whose end vertex is F. The path (A, B, D, C, A) is a simple cycle. The degree of vertex D is 3. The subgraph $\{A, B, E\}$ is a clique. The subgraph $\{A, B, E, D\}$ contains

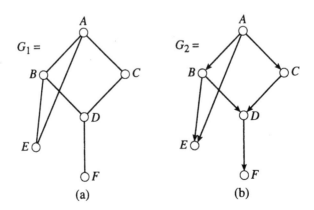

Figure 1.10   Two graphs: (a) undirected and (b) directed.

four edges: $\{(A, B), (B, E), (A, E), (B, D)\}$. The graph G_2 in Figure 1.10(b) is an acyclic directed graph. The indegree of D is 2, and its outdegree is 1; D in G_2 has two parents and one child node.   •

1.3.4   Background in Complexity

Throughout the book we will analyze the complexity of algorithms by determining their asymptotic efficiency. That is, we are concerned with how the running time of an algorithm increases with the size of the input, as the size of the input increases without bound. Usually, an algorithm that is asymptotically more efficient will be the best choice for all but very small inputs to the algorithm. An excellent comprehensive introduction into the asymptotic analysis of algorithms is given in Leiserson, Cormen, and Rivest (1990, Chapters 1 and 2). We briefly summarize from Chapter 2 several relevant concepts used throughout this book:

In general, an algorithm's complexity is its worst-case running time $T(n)$ over all its inputs of a fixed size n. The asymptotic analysis of algorithms uses special notation for characterizing the running time. We will use the O-notation. Intuitively, if we say that an algorithm's complexity is $O(f(n))$, we mean that for large enough inputs the number of basic steps of the algorithm as a function of its input size n is bounded below by $c \cdot f(n)$ for some constant c. Formally, the O-notation describes the asymptotic upper bound. For a given function $g(n)$, $O(g(n))$ denotes the set of functions

$$O(g(n)) = \{f(n): \text{there exist positive constants } c \text{ and } n_0 \text{ such that}$$
$$0 \le f(n) \le cg(n) \text{ for all } n \ge n_0\}$$

For all values n greater than n_0, the value of $f(n)$ is on or below $g(n)$. To indicate that a function $f(n)$ is a member of $O(g(n))$, we write $f(n) = O(g(n))$.

The asymptotic upper bound provided by O-notation is meant to be tight. The bound $2n^2 = O(n^2)$ is asymptotically tight, but the bound $2n = O(n^2)$ is not. o-notation (small "o") is used to denote an upper bound that is *not* asymptotically tight. Formally:

$$o(g(n)) = \{f(n): \text{for any positive constant } c \text{ and } n_0$$
$$0 \le f(n) \le c \cdot g(n) \text{ for all } n \ge n_0\}$$

The main difference between O-notation and o-notation is that in $f(n) = O(g(n))$, the bound $0 \le f(n) \le c \cdot g(n)$ holds for some constant $c > 0$, whereas in $f(n) = o(g(n))$, the bound $0 \le f(n) \le c \cdot g(n)$ holds for every constant $c > 0$. Intuitively, in the o-notation, the function $f(n)$ becomes insignificant relative to $g(n)$ as n approaches infinity.

Additional notations commonly used for performance evaluation are Ω-notation, which is analogous to O-notation but denotes asymptotic lower bounds that are tight, and ω-notation, where ω to Ω is like o to O. Finally, θ-notation is used to denote an asymptotic tight function that is both a lower and an upper bound. In the book we use O-notation primarily, even when the claims can be strengthened using θ-notation.

Two additional central concepts we use when discussing complexity are *polynomial complexity* are *exponential complexity*. A *polynomial of degree d* is a function $p(n)$ of the form

$$p(n) = \sum_{i=1}^{d} a_i n^i$$

where the a_i are constants. A polynomial is asymptotically positive iff $a_d > 0$. We say that a function $f(n)$ is polynomially bounded if $f(n) = O(n^k)$ for some constant k.

For a constant a the function $f(n) = a^n$ is an exponential function. The rate of growth of exponential functions and polynomials can be related by the fact that for all a and b, such that $a > 1$

$$\lim_{n \to \infty} \frac{n^b}{a^n} = 0$$

An algorithm is *tractable* if it has polynomial complexity. A class of problems is tractable if there exists a polynomial algorithm to solve it and intractable if it is known that there does not exist a polynomial algorithm for its solution.

NP-complete problems are a class of problems that are believed to be worst-case exponential. Namely, it is believed that for any algorithm that solves a problem in this class, there are some instances for which the algorithm will take an exponential number of steps in the problem size. Up to polynomial differences, the NP-complete problems all have the same complexity. That is, if there is a polynomial time algorithm for any NP-complete problem, then this would yield a polynomial time algorithm for every NP-complete problem. NP-complete problems have the property that a potential solution to the problem can be verified in polynomial time. The class of *NP-hard problems* is at least as difficult as NP-complete problems. For the NP-hard class, there is no known way to verify a solution in polynomial time.

Constraint satisfaction problems, the focus of this book, are known to be NP-complete, and therefore, general-purpose polynomial algorithms are clearly unavailable. The thrust of all constraint processing is to develop algorithms that work well in a wide range of problem classes.

1.4 **Bibliographical Notes**

Work in constraints in artificial intelligence began with Waltz's attempts to formally identify three-dimensional interpretation from two-dimensional drawing (Waltz 1975). It was followed by the seminal work of Montanari (1974), who formally introduced the concept of constraint networks, establishing many of the concepts that later became the building blocks of this area, such as path-consistency. Mackworth (1977a) further extended and popularized this work, defining notions of node-, arc-, and path-consistency, and discussing the implication of these methods to search technique. Existing surveys on various aspects of constraint-based reasoning include Mackworth (1987), Dechter (1992a), and Kumar (1992). More recent surveys can be found in Dechter (1999b). There is also an alternative full-length book treatment of the subject by Tsang (1993) and a new book on constraint programming (Marriott and Stuckey 1998). For surveys on constraint programming see Jaffar and Lassez (1994).

For mathematical foundation see Cormen, Leiserson, and Rivest (1990). This is a useful reference for some of the elements of discrete mathematics discussed in this chapter and for material on asymptotic notation and algorithm analyses, which are used but not presented in this book. There is a close relationship between constraint networks and the relational data model in database systems, as both use relations as the primary notation for representing data or knowledge. Maier (1983) and Ullman (1998) are useful references for relational databases and for the mathematical language employed in expressing queries to the database, called the *relational algebra*, from which our operations on relations are drawn.

A significant parallel development is constraint programming. This field develops programming languages that address modeling issues, focusing on the expression of constraints. Such languages have enabled the practical solution of many constraint satisfaction problems (Marriott and Stuckey 1998).

1.5 **Exercises**

1. Let $R_1 = \{(a, b), (c, d), (d, e)\}$ and $R_2 = \{(b, c), (e, a), (b, d)\}$.

   (a) Compute $R_1 \cup R_2$.

   (b) Compute $R_1 - R_2$.

   (c) Assume the scope of R_1 is $\{x, y\}$ and the scope of R_2 is $\{y, z\}$. Compute

       i. $R_{xy} \bowtie R_{yz}$

       ii. $\pi_x R_{xy}$

       iii. $\sigma_{x=c}(R_{xy} \bowtie R_{yz})$

2. Provide a description of the 3-colorability problem for the map problem in Figure 1.2.

3. Provide the constraints for the development problem in Figure 1.3.

4. Provide an elaborated description as a constraint problem for the cube recognition problem.

part one

Basics of Constraint Processing

chapter 2

Constraint Networks

Nature, like liberty, is but restrain'd by the same laws
which first herself ordain'd.

Alexander Pope, An Essay on Criticism

In this chapter we begin formally modeling constraint satisfaction problems as constraint networks. The initial formal work on constraint networks introduced by Montanari (1974) was restricted to binary constraints, defined on pairs of variables only. Much of the early research, experiments in particular, was limited to the binary case. Indeed, it is possible to show that any set of constraints can be mapped to the binary case. Nevertheless, we will always assume the general case, where constraints are defined on sets of variables of arbitrary size, and will explicitly refer to the special case of binary constraints when appropriate.

2.1 Constraint Networks and Constraint Satisfaction

We start with formal definition of the central concepts.

2.1.1 The Basics of the Framework

A *constraint network* $\mathcal{R}$ consists of a finite set of *variables* $X = \{x_1, \ldots, x_n\}$, with respective *domains* $D = \{D_1, \ldots, D_n\}$ which list the possible values for each variable $D_i = \{v_1, \ldots, v_k\}$, and a set of *constraints* $C = \{C_1, \ldots, C_t\}$. Thus, a constraint network can be viewed as a triple (X, D, C).

A constraint C_i is a relation R_i defined on a subset of variables S_i, $S_i \subseteq X$. The relation denotes the variables' simultaneous legal value assignments. S_i is called the *scope* of R_i. If $S_i = \{x_{i_1}, \ldots, x_{i_r}\}$, then R_i is a subset of the Cartesian product $D_{i_1} \times \cdots \times D_{i_r}$. Thus, a constraint can also be viewed as a pair $C_i = \langle S_i, R_i \rangle$. When the scope's identity is clear, we will often identify the constraint C_i with its relation

R_i. Alternatively, for clarity, a constraint relation may be denoted R_{S_i}. A scope will be denoted explicitly as $\{x, y, z\}$, or, if there is no possibility of confusion, as xyz. For example, we can denote as R_{xyz} (or $\langle xyz, R \rangle$) the constraint defined over the variables x, y, and z whose relation is R. The set of scopes $S = \{S_1, \ldots, S_i, \ldots, S_t\}$ is called the network *scheme*. Without loss of generality, we assume for relational constraints that only a single constraint is defined over a subset S_i in S. Namely, if $i \neq j$, then $S_i \neq S_j$. This assumption may be removed when discussing algebraic or Boolean constraints.

The *arity* of a constraint refers to the cardinality, or size, of its scope. A *unary constraint* is defined on a single variable; a *binary constraint*, on two variables. A *binary constraint network* has only unary and binary constraints.

Formulating the n-Queens Problem

Let's return to the n-queens problem and explore a possible constraint network formulation. We can think of the columns of the chessboard as the variables, $x_1, \ldots, x_n$, and the possible row positions, $D_i = \{1, \ldots, n\}$, as domains of the variables. Assigning a value $j \in D_i$ to a variable x_i means to place a queen in row j on column x_i of the board. The constraints, binary in this case, are that no two queens should attack one another, namely, that no two queens should be placed on the same row or diagonal. Figure 2.1(a) shows the chessboard for the 4-queens problem, and Figure 2.1(b) shows all of the constraints in relational form. For example, the tuple $(1, 3)$ is in the relation R_{12} defined over $\{x_1, x_2\}$, which means that simultaneously assigning the value 1 to variable x_1 and the value 3 to variable x_2 (a queen on row 1 of column 1 and on row 3 of column 2) is allowed by the constraint. The complete definition of the 4-queens problem is $\mathcal{R} = (X, D, C)$, where $X = \{x_1, x_2, x_3, x_4\}$, and for every i, $D_i = \{1, 2, 3, 4\}$. There are six constraints: $C_1 = R_{12}$, $C_2 = R_{13}$, $C_3 = R_{14}$, $C_4 = R_{23}$, $C_5 = R_{24}$, and $C_6 = R_{34}$.

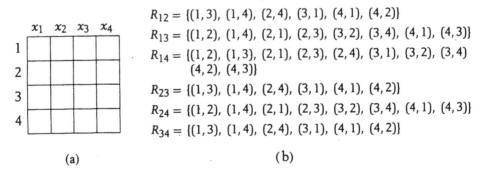

$$R_{12} = \{(1,3), (1,4), (2,4), (3,1), (4,1), (4,2)\}$$
$$R_{13} = \{(1,2), (1,4), (2,1), (2,3), (3,2), (3,4), (4,1), (4,3)\}$$
$$R_{14} = \{(1,2), (1,3), (2,1), (2,3), (2,4), (3,1), (3,2), (3,4)$$
$$(4,2), (4,3)\}$$
$$R_{23} = \{(1,3), (1,4), (2,4), (3,1), (4,1), (4,2)\}$$
$$R_{24} = \{(1,2), (1,4), (2,1), (2,3), (3,2), (3,4), (4,1), (4,3)\}$$
$$R_{34} = \{(1,3), (1,4), (2,4), (3,1), (4,1), (4,2)\}$$

(a)   (b)

Figure 2.1 The 4-queens constraint network. The network has four variables, all with domains $D_i = \{1, 2, 3, 4\}$. (a) The labeled chessboard. (b) The constraints between variables.

2.1.2 **Solutions of a Constraint Network**

When a variable is assigned a value from its domain, we say that the variable has been *instantiated*.

Instantiation

An *instantiation* of a subset of variables is an assignment from its domain to each variable in the subset. Formally, an instantiation of a set of variables $\{x_{i_1}, \ldots, x_{i_k}\}$ is a tuple of ordered pairs $(\langle x_{i_1}, a_{i_1} \rangle, \ldots, \langle x_{i_k}, a_{i_k} \rangle)$, where each pair $\langle x, a \rangle$ represents an assignment of the value a to the variable x, and where a is in the domain of x. We also use the notation $(x_1 = a_1, \ldots, x_i = a_i)$. For simplicity we often abbreviate $(\langle x_1, a_1 \rangle, \ldots, \langle x_i, a_i \rangle)$ to $\bar{a} = (a_1, \ldots, a_i)$, and understand an instantiation or tuple as a relation over some scope having a single tuple.

Satisfying a Constraint

An instantiation or tuple $\bar{a}$ satisfies a constraint $\langle S, R \rangle$ iff it is defined over all the variables in S and the components of the tuple $\bar{a}$ associated with S are present in the relation R. For example, let $R_{xyz} = \{(1, 1, 1), (1, 0, 1), (0, 0, 0)\}$. Then the instantiation $\bar{a}$, whose scope is $\{x, y, z, t\}$, given by $\bar{a} = (\langle x, 1 \rangle, \langle y, 1 \rangle, \langle z, 1 \rangle, \langle t, 0 \rangle)$, satisfies R_{xyz} because its projection on $\{x, y, z\}$ is $(1, 1, 1)$, which is an element of R_{xyz}. However, the instantiation $(\langle x, 1 \rangle, \langle y, 0 \rangle, \langle z, 0 \rangle, \langle t, 0 \rangle)$ violates R_{xyz} because $(1, 0, 0)$ is not a member of R_{xyz}. Or we could put it more formally as the following.

A Consistent Partial Instantiation

A partial instantiation is *consistent* if it satisfies all of the constraints whose scopes have no uninstantiated variables. A *projection* of a tuple $\bar{a}$ on a subset of its scope S is denoted also by $\bar{a}[S_i]$ (as well as $\pi_{S_i}(\bar{a})$). Using this notation, $\bar{a}$ over S is consistent relative to network $\mathcal{R}$ iff for all S_i in the scheme of $\mathcal{R}$, such that $S_i \subseteq S$, $\bar{a}[S_i] \in R_{S_i}$.

Solution

A *solution* of a constraint network $\mathcal{R} = (X, D, C)$, where $X = \{x_1, \ldots, x_n\}$, is an instantiation of all its variables that satisfies all the constraints. The solution relation $sol(\mathcal{R})$, also denoted ρ_X, is hence defined by

$$sol(\mathcal{R}) = \{\bar{a} = (a_1, \ldots, a_n) | a_i \in D_i, \forall S_i \in \text{scheme of } \mathcal{R}, \ \bar{a}[S_i] \in R_i\}$$

A network of constraints is said to *express* or *represent* the relation of all its solutions. If we have a constraint network $\mathcal{R}$ over X and a subset of variables $A \subseteq X$, $sol(A)$ or ρ_A is the set of all consistent instantiations over A.

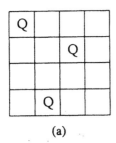 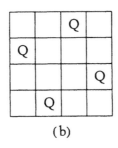 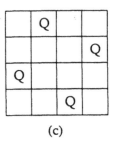

(a)   (b)   (c)

Figure 2.2 Not all consistent instantiations are part of a solution: (a) A consistent instantiation that is not part of a solution. (b) The placement of the queens corresponding to the solution (2, 4, 1, 3). (c) The placement of the queens corresponding to the solution (3, 1, 4, 2).

Consider again the constraint network for the 4-queens problem. As there is a constraint between every pair of variables, the scheme of the network is given by $\{\{x_1, x_2\}, \{x_1, x_3\}, \ldots, \{x_3, x_4\}\}$. Consider the set of variables $Y = \{x_1, x_2, x_3\}$. The instantiation $\bar{a} = (\langle x_1, 1 \rangle, \langle x_2, 4 \rangle, \langle x_3, 2 \rangle)$ shown in Figure 2.2(a) is consistent, since

$$\bar{a}[\{x_1, x_2\}] = (1, 4) \quad \text{and} \quad (1, 4) \in R_{12}$$

$$\bar{a}[\{x_1, x_3\}] = (1, 2) \quad \text{and} \quad (1, 2) \in R_{13}$$

$$\bar{a}[\{x_2, x_3\}] = (4, 2) \quad \text{and} \quad (4, 2) \in R_{23}$$

although $\bar{a}$ is not part of any full solution. There are only two full solutions to the 4-queens problem, as shown in Figure 2.2(b) and (c). The 4-queens problem represents the relation $\rho_{1234} = \{(2, 4, 1, 3)(3, 1, 4, 2)\}$.

The crossword puzzle

We return now to our crossword puzzle example from Chapter 1 (Figure 1.1 on page 4). A formal constraint network specification is the following: there is a variable for each square that can hold a character, $x_1, \ldots, x_{13}$, the domains of the variables are the alphabet letters, and the constraints are the possible words. For this example, the constraints are given by

$$R_{\{1,2,3,4,5\}} = \{(H, O, S, E, S), (L, A, S, E, R), (S, H, E, E, T), (S, N, A, I, L),$$
$$(S, T, E, E, R)\}$$

$$R_{\{3,6,9,12\}} = \{(A, L, S, O), (E, A, R, N), (H, I, K, E), (I, R, O, N), (S, A, M, E)\}$$

$$R_{\{5,7,11\}} = \{(E, A, T), (L, E, T), (R, U, N), (S, U, N), (T, E, N), (Y, E, S)\}$$

$$R_{\{8,9,10,11\}} = R_{\{3,6,9,12\}}$$

$$R_{\{10,13\}} = \{(B, E), (I, T), (N, O), (U, S)\}$$

$$R_{\{12,13\}} = R_{\{10,13\}}$$

Verify for yourself that the consistent partial assignments over the set of variables $\{x_1, x_2, x_3, x_4, x_5, x_6, x_9, x_{12}\}$ are

$$\begin{aligned}
\rho_{\{1,2,3,4,5,6,9,12\}} = \{&(H, O, S, E, S, A, M, E), (L, A, S, E, R, A, M, E), \\
&(S, H, E, E, T, A, R, N), (S, N, A, I, L, L, S, O), \\
&(S, T, E, E, R, A, R, N)\}
\end{aligned}$$

An alternative constraint formulation of the crossword puzzle associates each digit that can start a word with a variable and its possible word assignments as domain values. In this case, the variables are x_1 (1, horizontal), x_2 (3, vertical), x_3 (5, vertical), x_4 (8, horizontal), x_5 (12, horizontal), and x_6 (10, vertical). The scheme of this problem is $\{\{x_1, x_2\}, \{x_1, x_3\}, \{x_4, x_2\}, \{x_4, x_3\}, \{x_5, x_2\}, \{x_6, x_4\}, \{x_6, x_5\}\}$ because there is a constraint between x_1 (1, horizontal) and x_2 (3, vertical), and so on. The domains are $D_1 = \{hoses, laser, sheet, snail, steer\}$, $D_2 = D_4 = \{also, earn, hike, iron, same\}$, $D_3 = \{eat, let, run, sun, ten, yes\}$, and $D_5 = D_6 = \{be, it, no, us\}$. The constraint between x_1 and x_2 is given by

$$R_{12} = \{(hoses, same)(laser, same), (sheet, earn)(snail, also), (steer, earn)\}$$

A partial consistent tuple in this case is $(x_1 = sheet, x_2 = earn, x_3 = ten, x_4 = iron, x_5 = no)$. Note that this formulation of the problem is binary, namely, involving constraints on pairs of variables only. Note also that the network has no solutions.

2.1.3 Constraint Graphs

Graph concepts play a central role in capturing the structure of a constraint problem and in its solution process.

Primal Constraint Graphs

A constraint network can be represented by a graph called a *primal constraint graph* or just a *constraint graph*, where each node represents a variable and the arcs connect all nodes whose variables are included in a constraint scope of the problem. The absence of an arc between two nodes indicates that there is no direct constraint—one that is specified in the input—between the corresponding variables. For binary constraints a missing arc means that there is implicitly a *universal binary relation* allowing every pair of values. Figure 2.3(a) shows the constraint graph associated with our second formulation of the crossword puzzle, and Figure 2.3(b) shows the constraint graph of the 4-queens problem, which is complete.

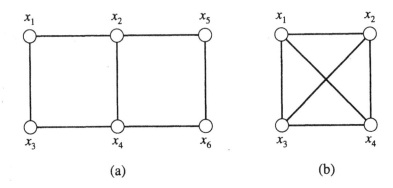

Figure 2.3 Constraint graphs of (a) the crossword puzzle and (b) the 4-queens problem.

A Scheduling Example

The constraint framework is useful for expressing and solving scheduling problems. Consider the problem of scheduling five tasks, $T1, T2, T3, T4, T5$, each of which takes one hour to complete. The tasks may start at 1:00, 2:00, or 3:00. Tasks can be executed simultaneously, subject to the restrictions that $T1$ must start after $T3$, $T3$ must start before $T4$ and after $T5$, $T2$ cannot execute at the same time as $T1$ or $T4$, and $T4$ cannot start at 2:00.

Given our five tasks and three time slots, we can model the scheduling problem by creating five variables, one for each task, and giving each variable the domain {1:00, 2:00, 3:00}. Another possible approach is to create three variables, one for each starting time, and to assign each of these variables a domain that is the powerset of $\{T1, T2, T3, T4, T5\}$ denoting tasks that start at that time point. This second approach is somewhat awkward and is left as an exercise at the end of the chapter. The problem's constraint graph for the first formulation is shown in Figure 2.4, along with the constraint relations.

Dual Constraint Graphs and Hypergraphs

The primal constraint graph is well-defined for both binary and nonbinary constraints. However, a hypergraph representation more accurately maintains the association between arcs and constraints in the nonbinary case.

DEFINITION   **(hypergraph)**
2.1
A hypergraph is a structure $\mathcal{H} = (V, S)$ that consists of vertices $V = \{v_1, \ldots, v_n\}$ and a set of subsets of these vertices $S = \{S_1, \ldots, S_l\}$, $S_i \subseteq V$, called hyperedges. The hyperedges differ from regular edges in that they may "connect" (or are defined over) more than one or two variables.   •

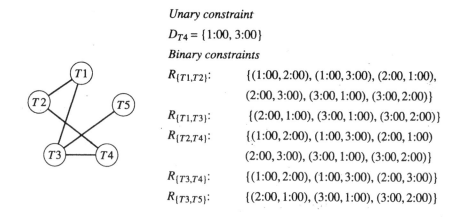

Unary constraint

$D_{T4} = \{1:00, 3:00\}$

Binary constraints

$R_{\{T1,T2\}}$: $\{(1:00, 2:00), (1:00, 3:00), (2:00, 1:00),$
$(2:00, 3:00), (3:00, 1:00), (3:00, 2:00)\}$

$R_{\{T1,T3\}}$: $\{(2:00, 1:00), (3:00, 1:00), (3:00, 2:00)\}$

$R_{\{T2,T4\}}$: $\{(1:00, 2:00), (1:00, 3:00), (2:00, 1:00)$
$(2:00, 3:00), (3:00, 1:00), (3:00, 2:00)\}$

$R_{\{T3,T4\}}$: $\{(1:00, 2:00), (1:00, 3:00), (2:00, 3:00)\}$

$R_{\{T3,T5\}}$: $\{(2:00, 1:00), (3:00, 1:00), (3:00, 2:00)\}$

Figure 2.4 The constraint graph and constraint relations of the scheduling problem example.

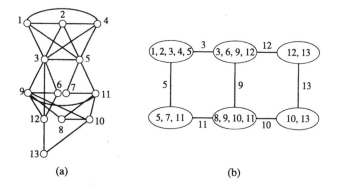

(a)   (b)

Figure 2.5 Constraint graphs of the crossword problem: (a) primal and (b) dual.

In the *constraint hypergraph* representation of a constraint problem, nodes represent the variables, and *hyperarcs* (drawn as regions) are the scopes of constraints. The hyperarcs group those variables that belong to the same scope. A related representation is the *dual constraint graph*. A dual constraint graph represents each constraint scope by a node and associates a labeled arc with any two nodes whose constraint scopes share variables. The arcs are labeled by the shared variables. Figure 2.5 depicts the primal and the dual graphs of our first formulation of the crossword puzzle.

Notice that the structure of the dual graph of the first formulation in Figure 2.5(b) is identical to the structure of the primal constraint graph of the second formulation in Figure 2.3(a). Indeed, the dual constraint graph suggests a transformation of a nonbinary network into a special type of binary network called the *dual problem*, where the constraints themselves (of the primary problem) are the variables, denoted *c-variables*. The domain of each c-variable ranges over all possible value combinations permitted by the corresponding constraint. There exists a constraint between any two adjacent c-variables enforcing the restriction that their shared (original) variables must be assigned the same values (i.e., the c-variables are bound by equality constraints). In this way, any set of constraints can be transformed into a binary constraint network and solved by binary network techniques. For the crossword puzzle, both the dual and the primal representations are intuitive; people will frequently come up with either of these formulations as their first representation of the problem.

The Radio Link Frequency Assignment Problem

Radio link frequency assignment problems are communication problems where the goal is to assign frequencies to a set of radio links in such a way that all the links may operate together without noticeable interference. The French Centre d'Electronique de l'Armement (CELAR) has made available a set of radio link frequency assignment benchmark problems (RLFAP) built from a real network with simplified data.[1] The constraints are all binary nonlinear, and the variables have finite domains. These are real-world size problems, the larger instances having around 1000 variables and more than 5000 constraints. All these instances have been built from a unique real instance of 916 links and 5744 constraints in 11 connected components. Each radio link is represented by a variable whose domain is the set of all frequencies available for that link. The essential constraints involve two variables F_1 and F_2: $|F1-F2| > k_{12}$. The two variables represent two radio links, and the constant k_{12} depends on the position of the two links and also on the physical environment. For each pair of sites, two frequencies must be assigned, one for the communications from A to B, and the other for the communications from B to A.

Figure 2.6 shows three constraint graphs of instances of the radio link frequency assignment problems from the CELAR benchmark, showing the diversity in structure for some problems.

The Huffman-Clowes Labeling

The Huffman-Clowes junction labeling is another example of intuitive dual-primal formulation. In one formulation of the problem as a constraint network, the various junctions in the problem instance are variables, their domains are the possible label combinations on junction types, and the constraints can be expressed using (0, 1)-matrices as in Figure 2.7. For example, x_i denotes junction i in the cube. Since 1 is a fork junction, the values of x_1 are the label combinations that can be assigned such a junction. The label assignments are constrained by the requirement that if an edge connects two junctions, it must get the same label

---

1. See *www.inra.fr/hia/schiex/DOC/CELARE.html* and also Schiex (1999).

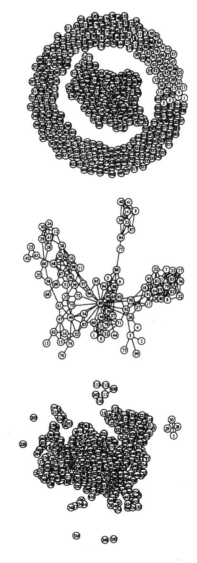

Figure 2.6 Constraint graphs of three instances of the radio frequency assignment problem in CELAR's benchmark.

from each junction. The $(0, 1)$-matrix constraints representation R_{ij} assumes that the domains of each junction variable (in Figure 1.4 on page 7) are ordered from left to right. The columns are indexed by X_i's domains and the rows by X_j's domain. In this formulation, all the constraints are binary, and the constraint graph is identical to the input problem graph as shown in Figure 2.7. The set of solutions to this problem is given in Figure 1.5 (page 8).

$$R_{21} = \begin{bmatrix} 0\,1\,1\,0\,0 \\ 1\,0\,0\,0\,0 \\ 1\,0\,0\,0\,0 \end{bmatrix} \quad R_{31} = \begin{bmatrix} 0\,1\,0\,1\,0 \\ 1\,0\,0\,0\,0 \\ 1\,0\,0\,0\,0 \end{bmatrix} \quad R_{51} = \begin{bmatrix} 0\,1\,0\,0\,1 \\ 1\,0\,0\,0\,0 \\ 1\,0\,0\,0\,0 \end{bmatrix}$$

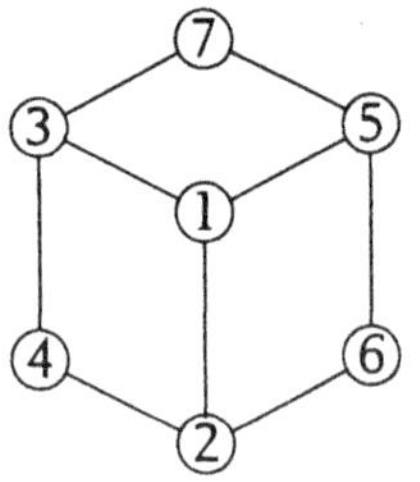

$$R_{24} = R_{37} = R_{56} = \begin{bmatrix} 0\,0\,1\,0\,0\,0 \\ 0\,0\,0\,0\,0\,1 \\ 0\,0\,0\,1\,1\,0 \end{bmatrix}$$

$$R_{26} = R_{34} = R_{57} = \begin{bmatrix} 1\,0\,0\,0\,0\,0 \\ 0\,0\,0\,1\,0\,0 \\ 0\,0\,0\,0\,1\,1 \end{bmatrix}$$

Figure 2.7   Scene-labeling constraint network.

The above formulation may also be perceived as the dual graph of a second non-binary formulation that views the edges as the variables, each having the domains of $\{+, -, \rightarrow, \leftarrow\}$, and the constraints as binary or ternary depending on the junction types. For example, the edges $(1, 3)$, $(1, 5)$, $(1, 2)$ are three variables in a scope of a single constraint in the second formulation. In the primal constraint graph of this second formulation, two nodes (representing edges) will be connected if they participate in the same junction (see Exercise 4).

2.2 Numeric and Boolean Constraints

By explicitly specifying the allowed tuples via the syntax of relations, we do a good job of describing the underlying meaning of a constraint. However, as we saw in Section 2.1.2, this method of specification is sometimes tedious and unwieldy. In many instances, mathematical conventions can describe the relationships between objects more concisely or conveniently than relational descriptions. Arithmetic constraints and Boolean constraints are examples of alternative languages for describing constraints. The first allows for more concise expression, while the second, in addition to being restricted to bivalued domains, expresses the forbidden tuples rather than the legal ones.

2.2.1 Numeric Constraints

Numeric constraints express constraints by arithmetic expressions. Consider expressing our 4-queens problem with numeric constraints. Instead of describing the constraints by enumerating the allowed elements of each relation, we can quite succinctly state that every two variables x_i and x_j should satisfy $\forall i, j, x_i \neq x_j$, and $|x_i - x_j| \neq |i - j|$, defining the relation

$$R_{ij} = \{(x_i, x_j) \mid x_i \in D_i, x_j \in D_j, x_i \neq x_j, \text{ and } |x_i - x_j| \neq |i - j|\}$$

In another example, let the domains of the variables be finite subsets of the integers, and let a binary constraint between two variables be a conjunction of linear inequalities of the form $ax_i - bx_j = c$, $ax_i - bx_j < c$, or $ax_i - bx_j \leq c$, where a, b, and c are integer constants. For example, the conjunction

$$(3x_i + 2x_j \leq 3) \wedge (-4x_i + 5x_j < 1)$$

is a legitimate constraint between variables x_i and x_j. A network with constraints of this form can be formulated as an "integer linear program" where each constraint is defined over two variables, and the domains of the variables are restricted to being finite subsets of the integers. Linear constraints are a special subclass of numeric constraints widely applicable in the areas of scheduling and temporal and spatial reasoning.

Crypto-arithmetic Puzzles

One class of toy problems that can be easily formulated with linear constraints are the *crypto-arithmetic puzzles*, such as SEND + MORE = MONEY. Here we are asked to replace each letter by a different digit so that the above equation is correct. The constraint formulation of these puzzles will associate each letter with a variable whose domains are the digits $\{0..9\}$. The exact formulation of this problem is left to you as an exercise (see Exercise 6).

2.2.2 Boolean Constraints and Propositional CNF

When the variables of a constraint problem range over two values, we frequently use a Boolean propositional language to describe the various relationships. Assume that you would like to invite your friends Alex, Bill, and Chris to a party. Let A, B, and C denote the propositions "Alex comes," "Bill comes," and "Chris comes," respectively. You know that if Alex comes to the party, Bill will come as well, and if Chris comes, then Alex will too. This can be expressed in propositional calculus as $(A \rightarrow B) \wedge (C \rightarrow A)$, or equivalently as $(\neg A \vee B) \wedge (\neg C \vee A)$. Assume now that Chris came to the party; should you expect to see Bill? Or, in propositional logic, does the propositional theory $\varphi = C \wedge (A \rightarrow B) \wedge (C \rightarrow A)$ entail B? A common way to answer this query is to assume that Bill will not come and check whether this is a plausible situation (i.e., decide if $\varphi\prime = \varphi \wedge \neg B$ is satisfiable). If $\varphi\prime$ is unsatisfiable, we can conclude that φ entails B. We next provide the formal definitions.

Propositional variables take only two values: $\{true, false\}$ or "1" and "0." We denote propositional *variables* by uppercase letters $P, Q, R, \ldots$; propositional literals (i.e., P, $\neg P$) stand for $P =$ "*true*" or $P =$ "*false*"; and disjunctions of literals, or *clauses* are denoted by $\alpha, \beta, \ldots$. For instance, $\alpha = (P \vee Q \vee R)$ is a clause. We will sometimes denote by $\{P, Q, R\}$ the clause $(P \vee Q \vee R)$. A *unit clause* is a clause of size 1. The notation $(\alpha \vee T)$, when $\alpha = (P \vee Q \vee R)$, is shorthand for the disjunction $(P \vee Q \vee R \vee T)$. $\alpha \vee \beta$ denotes the clause whose literal appears in either α or β. The *resolution* operation over two clauses $(\alpha \vee Q)$ and $(\beta \vee \neg Q)$ results in a clause $(\alpha \vee \beta)$, thus eliminating Q. A formula φ in *conjunctive normal form* (CNF), referred to as a *theory*, is a set of clauses $\varphi = \{\alpha_1, \ldots, \alpha_t\}$ that denotes their conjunction. The set of *models* or *solutions* of a theory φ is the set of all truth assignments to all variables that do not violate any clause.

In general, a CNF theory can be viewed as a constraint network whose variables are the propositions, and whose domains have two values {*true, false*} or {0, 1}. Each clause is a constraint on the corresponding propositional variables. For instance, the CNF theory $\varphi = (A \vee B) \wedge (C \vee \neg B)$ has three variables and two constraints. The constraint $A \vee B$ expresses the relation $R_{AB} = \{(0, 1), (1, 0), (1, 1)\}$. Note that we may have more than one clause defined on the same set of propositional variables.

The propositional satisfiability problem (SAT) is to decide whether a given CNF theory has a *model* (that is, a truth assignment that does not violate any clause), or alternatively, whether the associated constraint problem is consistent. The structure of a propositional theory can be described by an *interaction graph* that corresponds to the (primal) constraint graph. The interaction graph of a propositional theory φ, denoted $G(\varphi)$, is an undirected graph that contains a node for each propositional variable and an edge for each pair of nodes that correspond to variables appearing in the same clause. For example, the interaction graph of theory $\varphi_1 = \{(\neg C), (A \vee B \vee C), (\neg A \vee B \vee E), (\neg B \vee C \vee D)\}$ is shown in Figure 2.8.

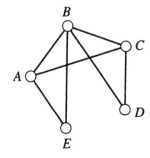

Figure 2.8 The interaction graph of theory $\varphi_1 = \{(\neg C), (A \vee B \vee C), (\neg A \vee B \vee E), (\neg B \vee C \vee D)\}$.

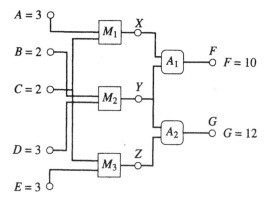

Figure 2.9 A combinatorial circuit: *M* is a multiplier; *A* is an adder.

2.2.3 Combinatorial Circuits Diagnosis

Boolean propositional languages are often used to express combinatorial circuits built out of AND, OR, and XOR gates (see Figure 2.9). The diagnosis task over such circuits can be formulated as a constraint satisfaction problem. In *circuit diagnosis* we are given a description of the circuit, composed of combined inputs through Boolean gates to their respective outputs. If the expected output is different from the observed output, our task is to identify a subset of the gates that, if assumed to be faulty, explains the observed output.

One method of formulating the diagnosis task within a constraint network is to associate each gate, as well as its inputs and outputs, with a variable and then to describe by Boolean constraints the relationship between the input and output of each gate under the assumption that the gate is either proper or faulty. Once we observe an output fault, the task of explaining the circuit behavior is completed by identifying a set of faulty gates. (Often the minimal such set is required.) Such an explanation amounts to finding a consistent solution for the formulated network.

In the example in Figure 2.9 there are three multipliers and two adders. The constraint formulation will have a variable for each input $\{A, B, C, D, E\}$, output $\{F, G\}$, and intermediate output $\{X, Y, Z\}$, and for each component M_1, M_2, M_3, A_1, A_2. The domains of the input and output variables are any number (integer or Boolean if we so choose to restrict the problem). The domain of the components are $\{0, 1\}$, where 1 indicates a faulty behavior of the component and 0 a correct behavior. A constraint is associated with each component variable, its input variables and output variables, yielding five constraints, each defined over four variables.

If the inputs and outputs are Boolean variables, the constraints can be expressed by a Boolean expression. For example, if M_1 is an AND gate, its associated constraint can be $M_1 \rightarrow (A \wedge C \rightarrow X)$. You will be asked to formulate a detailed description of the constraints in the exercises.

2.3 Properties of Binary Constraint Networks

Many constraint processing concepts were initially introduced for binary networks. It is helpful to discuss binary networks separately in this section because many important concepts are more easily digested in this restricted case. Understanding concepts such as minimal networks and decomposability will allow deep understanding of issues that underlie the general theory of constraints.

2.3.1 Equivalence and Deduction with Constraints

A central concept of constraint processing is constraint deduction or *constraint inference*. New constraints can be inferred from an initial set of constraints. These newly inferred constraints might take the form of constraints between variables that were not initially constrained or might be tightenings of existing constraints. For instance, from the algebraic constraints $x \geq y$ and $y \geq z$ we can infer that $x \geq z$. Note that adding the inferred constraint $x \geq z$ yields an equivalent constraint network. The next example demonstrates constraint inference using relational representation.

EXAMPLE 2.1   Consider the graph-coloring problem in Figure 2.10(a). The problem can be described by a constraint network with three variables, x_1, x_2, and x_3, one for each node, all defined on the same domain values {*red, blue*}, and the not-equal constraints $R_{21} = R_{32} = \{(blue, red), (red, blue)\}$. The lack of an arc between x_1 and x_3 represents the universal relation $R_{13} = \{(red, blue), (blue, red), (red, red), (blue, blue)\}$. The problem has two solutions: $\rho_{123} = \{(red, blue, red)(blue, red, blue)\}$. Assume now that we tighten the constraint between x_1 and x_3, disallowing the pair $(\langle x_1, red \rangle, \langle x_3, blue \rangle)$. Since this pair does not participate in any of the original problem's solutions, this restriction does not alter the set of solutions. In fact, if we add the constraint $R'_{13} = \{(red, red)(blue, blue)\}$, we get a new constraint network $\mathcal{R}'$ having the same set of solutions, as in Figure 2.10(b). Indeed, the constraint R'_{13}, which enforces $x_1 = x_3$, can be *inferred* from the original network $\mathcal{R}$. The two networks $\mathcal{R}$ and $\mathcal{R}'$ are said to be *equivalent*. •

An inferred constraint can also be viewed as *redundant* relative to a constraint network since its deletion from the network will not change the set of all solutions.

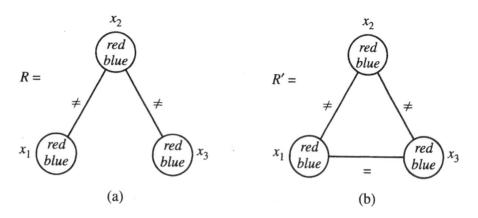

Figure 2.10   (a) A graph $\mathcal{R}$ to be colored by two colors and (b) an equivalent representation $\mathcal{R}'$ having a newly inferred constraint between x_1 and x_3.

In $\mathcal{R}'$, for instance, the not-equal constraint between x_1 and x_2 is redundant since its deletion does not change the set of solutions. The same redundancy exists for each of the other two constraints. However, once R'_{12} is removed from $\mathcal{R}'$, the other constraints are no longer redundant. In summary, two constraint networks are equivalent if they are defined on the *same set of variables* and express the same set of solutions. A constraint R_{ij} is redundant relative to $\mathcal{R}'$ iff $\mathcal{R}'$ is equivalent to $\mathcal{R}$ when R_{ij} is removed.

Constraint deduction can be accomplished through the *composition* operation.

DEFINITION 2.2   **(composition)**

Given two binary or unary constraints R_{xy} and R_{yz}, the composition $R_{xy} \cdot R_{yz}$ generates the binary relation R_{xz} defined by

$$R_{xz} = \{(a,b)|a \in D_x,\ b \in D_z ,\ \exists c \in D_y \text{ such that } (a,c) \in R_{xy} \text{ and } (c,b) \in R_{yz}\}$$

•

An alternative, operational definition of composition is formulated in terms of the join and projection operators:

$$R_{xz} = R_{xy} \cdot R_{yz} = \pi_{\{x,z\}}(R_{xy} \bowtie R_{yz})$$

In Figure 2.10(a), we deduced that $R'_{13} = \pi_{\{x_1,x_3\}}(R_{12} \bowtie R_{23}) = \{(red, red), (blue, blue)\}$, thus yielding the equivalent network in Figure 2.10(b). The composition operation can also be described via Boolean matrix multiplication when binary relations are expressed using $(0, 1)$-matrices.

EXAMPLE
2.2

Continuing with our simple graph-coloring example, the two inequality constraints can be expressed as 2×2 matrices having zeros along the main diagonal:

$$R_{12} = \left(\begin{array}{c|cc} & red & blue \\ \hline red & 0 & 1 \\ blue & 1 & 0 \end{array}\right) \qquad R_{23} = \left(\begin{array}{c|cc} & red & blue \\ \hline red & 0 & 1 \\ blue & 1 & 0 \end{array}\right)$$

Multiplying two such matrices yields the following two-dimensional identity matrix:

$$R_{12} \cdot R_{23} = R_{13} = \left(\begin{array}{cc} 0 & 1 \\ 1 & 0 \end{array}\right) \times \left(\begin{array}{cc} 0 & 1 \\ 1 & 0 \end{array}\right) = \left(\begin{array}{cc} 1 & 0 \\ 0 & 1 \end{array}\right) = \left(\begin{array}{c|cc} & red & blue \\ \hline red & 1 & 0 \\ blue & 0 & 1 \end{array}\right)$$

•

Note that composition is not generally distributive with respect to intersection, namely, $R_{12} \cdot (R_{23} \cap R'_{23}) \neq (R_{12} \cdot R_{23}) \cap (R_{12} \cdot R'_{23})$.

2.3.2   **The Minimal and the Projection Networks**

In his seminal paper, Montanari (1974) considers the expressive power of binary networks. The question of interest is whether an arbitrary relation can be a set of solutions to some underlying binary constraint network having the same set of variables. In other words, can any relation be represented as a binary constraint network?

In fact, most relations cannot be represented by a collection of binary constraints, since there are many more different relations possible on n variables than there are networks of binary constraints on n variables. Given n variables each having a domain of size k, cardinality arguments dictate that the number of different relations on n variables is 2^{k^n}, which is far greater than the number of different binary constraint networks, $2^{k^2 \frac{n(n-1)}{2}}$. The proof of this argument is left to you as an exercise. Accordingly, those special cases where a relation is expressible by a binary constraint network are highly desirable, since they may require less space to specify.

A relation that cannot be expressed by a binary network may still be approximated by one. Let's consider the approximation of a relation by its binary *projection network*.

DEFINITION
2.3

(projection network)

The projection network of a relation ρ is obtained by projecting ρ onto each pair of its variables. Formally, if ρ is a relation over $X = \{x_1, \ldots, x_n\}$, its projection network, $P(\rho)$, is defined by the network $\mathcal{P} = (X, D, P)$ where $D = \{D_i\}$, $D_i = \pi_i(\rho)$, $P = \{P_{ij}\}$, and $P_{ij} = \pi_{x_i, x_j}(\rho)$.   •

**EXAMPLE
2.3**

Let $\rho_{123} = \{(1, 1, 2)(1, 2, 2)(1, 2, 1)\}$. The projection network $P(\rho)$ includes the constraints $P_{12} = \{(1, 1)(1, 2)\}$, $P_{13} = \{(1, 2)(1, 1)\}$, and $P_{23} = \{(1, 2)(2, 2)(2, 1)\}$. Generating all solutions of $P(\rho)$ yields $sol(P(\rho)) = \{(1, 1, 2)(1, 2, 2)(1, 2, 1)\}$. •

What is the relationship between the original relation and its approximation, between ρ and $P(\rho)$? Generating all solutions of $P(\rho)$, in Example 2.3, yields back the relation ρ. But this cannot be characteristic of the general case, or else we would have proven that every relation has a binary network representation by its projection network, and we know this to be false due to the cardinality argument presented earlier. What does hold in general is that the projection network is the best *upper bound network approximation* of a relation. That is, for every relation ρ, the solution set of $P(\rho)$ contains ρ. Moreover, as we will show, any other upper bound network will express a solution set that includes the projection network's solutions. The following example illustrates this useful feature of the projection network.

**EXAMPLE
2.4**

Consider a slightly different relation ρ:

x_1	x_2	x_3
1	1	2
1	2	2
2	1	3
2	2	2

The projection network $P(\rho)$ has the following constraints: $P_{12} = \{(1, 1)(1, 2)(2, 1)(2, 2)\}$, $P_{23} = \{(1, 2)(2, 2)(1, 3)\}$, and $P_{13} = \{(1, 2)(2, 3)(2, 2)\}$. The set of solutions to $P(\rho)$, $sol(P(\rho))$, is

x_1	x_2	x_3
1	1	2
1	2	2
2	1	2
2	1	3
2	2	2

•

We see that all the tuples of ρ appear in the solution set of $P(\rho)$, while some additional solutions to $P(\rho)$ are not in ρ. In general:

**THEOREM
2.1**   For every relation ρ, $\rho \subseteq sol(P(\rho))$.

Proof   Let $t \in \rho$. We have to show only that $t \in sol(P(\rho))$, namely, that it satisfies every binary constraint in $P(\rho)$. This is clearly true, since, by its definition, every pair of values of t was included, by projection, in the corresponding constraint of $P(\rho)$.   ●

Is there another binary network of constraints $\mathcal{R}'$ whose solution set contains ρ but is smaller than $P(\rho)$? Might we discover such a network by tightening the constraints of $P = P(\rho)$? Let's try to eliminate the superfluous tuple $(2, 1, 2)$ from $sol(P)$ in Example 2.4 by deleting the pair $(2, 1)$ from the projection constraint P_{12}. Unfortunately, when we do this, we also exclude the tuple $(2, 1, 3)$, which is in ρ. Similarly, when we try to exclude $(2, 1, 2)$ by deleting the pair $(1, 2)$ from P_{23}, we eliminate $(1, 1, 2)$, which is also in ρ. And, if we exclude $(2, 2)$ from P_{13}, we eliminate $(2, 2, 2)$. Indeed, $P(\rho)$ cannot be tightened any further if its solutions are to include all the tuples in ρ. In fact,

**THEOREM
2.2**   The projection network $P(\rho)$ is the tightest upper bound binary network representation of ρ; there is no binary network $\mathcal{R}'$, such that $\rho \subseteq sol(R') \subset sol(P(\rho))$.   ●

Consequently, if a relation is not expressible by its projection network, it cannot be expressed by any binary network of constraints.

Theorem 2.2 shows that the projection network is the most accurate binary network upper bound for a relation. But is it also the tightest explicit description of relation $sol(P(\rho))$? This question leads us to the notion of a partial order of tightness among binary constraint networks. As we have seen in Figure 2.10(a) and (b), the networks $\mathcal{R}$ and $\mathcal{R}'$ are semantically equivalent since they represent the same set of solutions, yet $\mathcal{R}'$ is tighter than $\mathcal{R}$ using a pair-wise comparison of their binary relations.

**DEFINITION
2.4**   **("tighter than" network relationship)**

Given two binary networks, $\mathcal{R}'$ and $\mathcal{R}$, on the same set of variables $x_1, \ldots, x_n$, $\mathcal{R}'$ is at least as tight as $\mathcal{R}$ iff for every i and j, $R'_{ij} \subseteq R_{ij}$.   ●

Obviously, if $\mathcal{R}'$ is tighter than $\mathcal{R}$, then the solution set of $\mathcal{R}'$ is contained in the solution set of $\mathcal{R}$. Often, however, the tighter network still expresses the same set of solutions. Moreover, if we take the intersection of two equivalent networks (by intersecting constraints pair-wise), we get yet another equivalent network that is tighter than either.

DEFINITION **(intersection on networks)**
2.5
The intersection of two networks $\mathcal{R}$ and $\mathcal{R}'$, denoted $\mathcal{R} \cap \mathcal{R}'$, is the binary network obtained by pair-wise intersection of the corresponding constraints in the two networks.   •

Clearly,

PROPOSITION If $\mathcal{R}$ and $\mathcal{R}'$ are two equivalent networks, then $\mathcal{R} \cap \mathcal{R}'$ is equivalent to and
2.1 is at least as tight as both.   •

The proof is left as an exercise.

EXAMPLE Consider the network in Figure 2.10(a) and the network in Figure 2.10(b)
2.5 without R_{23}. Intersecting the two networks yields the equivalent network in Figure 2.10(b) that is tighter than either.   •

There exists, therefore, a partial order of tightness among all equivalent networks. If we intersect all these networks, we get one unique network that is both equivalent to all the networks and at least as tight as all networks. This network is called the *minimal network*. The minimal network $M(\mathcal{R})$ of a binary network $\mathcal{R}$ is the tightest network equivalent to $\mathcal{R}$. $M(\mathcal{R})$ is also denoted $M(\rho)$ when ρ is the set of solutions to $\mathcal{R}$.

DEFINITION **(minimal network)**
2.6
Let $\{\mathcal{R}_1, \ldots, \mathcal{R}_l\}$ be the set of all networks equivalent to $\mathcal{R}_0$ and let $\rho = sol(\mathcal{R}_0)$. Then the minimal network M of $\mathcal{R}_0$ or of ρ is defined by $M(\mathcal{R}_0) = M(\rho) = \cap_{i=1}^{l} \mathcal{R}_i$.   •

Finally, it is possible to show that the minimal network is identical to the projection network of the minimal network's set of solutions.

THEOREM For every binary network $\mathcal{R}$ such that $\rho = sol(\mathcal{R})$, $M(\rho) = P(\rho)$.   •
2.3
The proof is left as an exercise.

Figure 2.11 shows the constraint graph and the binary minimal constraints of the 4-queens problem. We denote the binary constraints in the minimal network by M_{ij}. The unary constraints are the reduced domains. (Compare this network to the equivalent one in Figure 2.1.) The minimal network is perfectly explicit for unary and binary constraints. That is to say, if a pair of values is permitted by the minimal constraints, then it is guaranteed to appear in at least one solution. Indeed, the next proposition immediately follows from Theorem 2.3.

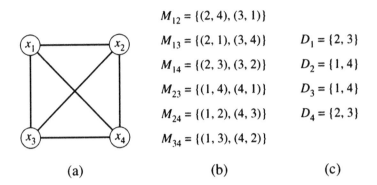

$$M_{12} = \{(2, 4), (3, 1)\}$$

$$M_{13} = \{(2, 1), (3, 4)\} \qquad D_1 = \{2, 3\}$$

$$M_{14} = \{(2, 3), (3, 2)\} \qquad D_2 = \{1, 4\}$$

$$M_{23} = \{(1, 4), (4, 1)\} \qquad D_3 = \{1, 4\}$$

$$M_{24} = \{(1, 2), (4, 3)\} \qquad D_4 = \{2, 3\}$$

$$M_{34} = \{(1, 3), (4, 2)\}$$

(a)   (b)   (c)

Figure 2.11   The 4-queens constraint network: (a) the constraint graph, (b) the minimal binary constraints, and (c) the minimal unary constraints (the domains).

PROPOSITION   If $(a, b) \in M_{ij}$ then $\exists\, t \in sol(M)$ such that $t[i] = a$ and $t[j] = b$.   •
   2.2

We should note here that finding a single solution of a minimal network of constraints is not guaranteed to be easy. In fact, deciding whether ρ can be representable by its projection network is NP-hard (Ullman, 1991). It is still not clear, however, whether or not generating a single solution of a minimal network is hard, even though empirical experience shows that it is normally easy. Nevertheless, we do speculate that generating a single solution from the minimal network is hard, and we leave this as an exercise.

2.3.3   Binary-Decomposable Networks

While we can always easily find a partial solution of size 2 that is part of a full solution when given a minimal network, we cannot guarantee that we can extend a two-variable solution to a third variable such that the obtained triplet is part of a full solution unless the minimal network is also *binary-decomposable*.

We know by now that a relation has a binary network representation iff it is equivalent to its projection network. We also know that the projection network is the relation's most explicit form. It turns out, however, that a relation may be representable by a binary network even if many of its projections are not.

EXAMPLE   Consider the relations
   2.6

$$
\rho = \begin{pmatrix}
x & y & z & t \\
a & a & a & a \\
a & b & b & b \\
b & b & a & c
\end{pmatrix}
\qquad
\pi_{xyz}\rho = \begin{pmatrix}
x & y & z \\
a & a & a \\
a & b & b \\
b & b & a
\end{pmatrix}
$$

You can easily verify that ρ is representable by a binary constraint network. However, the projected relation $\pi_{xyz}\rho$ is not expressible by binary networks, that is,

$$\pi_{xyz}\rho \subset sol(P(\pi_{xyz}\rho)) \qquad \bullet$$

**DEFINITION
2.7**

(binary-decomposable)

A relation is *binary-decomposable* if it is expressible by a network of binary constraints and iff each of its projected relations is also expressible by a binary network of constraints. $\qquad \bullet$

If a relation is binary-decomposable, then the projection network expresses the relation and all its projections. In other words, if ρ is a binary decomposable relation and S is a subset of the variables, then $\pi_S\rho$ is expressible by the subnetwork of $P(\rho)$ whose variables are restricted to the variables in S (see exercises).

2.4 Summary

In this chapter we provided a formal presentation of constraint networks, their solutions, and their graph representations and have demonstrated these concepts through examples. We ended it by focusing on some formal properties of binary constraint networks. We defined concepts such as inferred constraint, redundant constraint, partial order of tightness between constraints, the projection network, and the minimal network. We showed that those two latter notions coincide. Finally, we defined the concept of binary-decomposable networks.

2.5 Bibliographical Notes

Graphical properties of constraint networks were initially investigated through the class of binary constraint networks. Montanari (1974) was the first to formally define these networks. Montanari also introduced most of the concepts mentioned in the second part of this chapter, including minimal network, projection network, and binary-decomposable network. He also discussed important notions of constraint propagations, which are the focus of the next chapter.

2.6 Exercises

1. Nadel (1989) proposes a variant of the *n*-queens problem called *confused n-queens*. The problem is to find all ways to place n queens on an $n \times n$

chessboard, one queen per column, so that all pairs of queens *do* attack each other. Propose a formulation of the problem as a constraint network. Identify variables, domains, and constraints.

2. A Latin square of order n is defined to be an $n \times n$ array made out of n distinct symbols (usually the integers $1, 2, \ldots, n$) with the defining characteristic that each of the n symbols occurs exactly once in each row of the array and exactly once in each column. For example,

$$\begin{bmatrix} 3 & 2 & 1 \\ 1 & 3 & 2 \\ 2 & 1 & 3 \end{bmatrix}$$

Orthogonal Latin squares: Let **A** and **B** be Latin squares of order n and let the entry in the ith row and the jth column of **A** and **B** be denoted as a_{ij} and b_{ij}, respectively, with $i, j = 1, 2, \ldots, n$. **A** and **B** are *orthogonal* if the n^2 order pairs (a_{ij}, b_{ij}) are all distinct. For example, the following juxtaposed Latin squares are orthogonal:

$$\begin{bmatrix} (3,2) & (2,3) & (1,1) \\ (2,1) & (1,2) & (3,3) \\ (1,3) & (3,1) & (2,2) \end{bmatrix}$$

Propose a formulation of the problem as a constraint network. Identify variables, domains, and constraints.

3. Using the starting times as variables, formulate the scheduling example as a constraint network problem.

4. Formulate the Huffman-Clowes labeling problem as a constraint network where each arc in the drawing is a variable. Draw the primal constraint graph and the dual constraint graph of such formulation of the cube three-dimensional interpretation.

5. The zebra problem: There are five houses in a row, each of a different color, inhabited by women of different nationalities. The owner of each house owns a different pet, serves different drinks, and smokes different cigarettes from the other owners. The following facts are also known:

The Englishwoman lives in the red house.

The Spaniard owns a dog.

Coffee is drunk in the green house.

The Ukrainian drinks tea.

The green house is immediately to the right of the ivory house.

The Oldgold smoker owns the snail.

Kools are smoked in the yellow house.

Milk is drunk in the middle house.

The Norwegian lives in the first house on the left.

The Chesterfield smoker lives next to the fox owner.

The yellow house is next to the horse owner.

The Lucky Strike smoker drinks orange juice.

The Japanese smokes Parliament.

The Norwegian lives next to the blue house.

The question: Who drinks water and who owns the zebra?

Formulate the zebra problem as a constraint network. Provide the variables, domains, and constraints. Draw its primal constraint graph.

6. Provide two formulations for each of the crypto-arithmetic problems below as a constraint network. Provide the variables, domains, and constraints. Draw the primal and the dual constraint graphs. Discuss which formulation is superior in your opinion.

          SEND
(a) + MORE
       ―――――――
       MONEY

(b) HOCUS + POCUS = PRESTO

(c) GERALD + DONALD = ROBERT

7. Provide a detailed formulation of the circuit diagnosis problem in Figure 2.9.

8. Provide a detailed formulation of the design problem presented in Figure 1.3.

9. Provide a formal definition for the radio link frequency assignment problem. The goal is to assign frequencies to a set of radio links in such a way that all the links can work together with no interference.

10. A magic square of order n is an $n \times n$ array of the integers $1, 2, \ldots, n^2$ arranged so that the sum of every row, column, and the two main diagonals is the same. Since

$$\sum_{i=1}^{n^2} = \frac{1}{2}n^2(n^2 + 1)$$

the sum must be $\frac{1}{2}n(n^2 + 1)$. For example,

$$\begin{bmatrix} 1 & 15 & 24 & 8 & 17 \\ 23 & 7 & 16 & 5 & 14 \\ 20 & 4 & 13 & 22 & 6 \\ 12 & 21 & 10 & 19 & 3 \\ 9 & 18 & 2 & 11 & 25 \end{bmatrix}$$

is a magic square of order 5; each row, column, and main diagonal add up to $\frac{1}{2}5(5^2 + 1) = 65$.

Formulate the 3×3 magic square as a constraint problem. Draw its primal and dual graphs.

11. Find the minimal network of the crossword puzzle (Figure 1.1) when the problem is formulated as a set of binary constraints.

12. Consider the following relation ρ on variables x, y, z, t:

$$\rho_{xyzt} = \{(a, a, a, a)(a, b, b, b)(b, b, a, c)\}$$

(a) Find the projection network $P(\rho)$. Is ρ representable by a network of binary constraints? Justify your answer.

(b) Is the projection $\pi_{xyz}(\rho)$ representable by a network of binary constraints? Is ρ binary decomposable?

(c) A search space is backtrack-free along an order of its variables, d, if any partial solution along this order can be extended to a full solution. Can you find an ordering such that $P(\rho)$ is backtrack-free?

(d) Is there a binary network representation of ρ that is backtrack-free in the order x, y, z, t? Is there a binary network representing ρ that is binary decomposable?

13. Prove that if $\mathcal{R}$ and $\mathcal{R}'$ are two equivalent networks, then $\mathcal{R} \cap \mathcal{R}'$ is equivalent to, and is at least as tight as, both.

14. Let $\mathcal{R}_1$ and $\mathcal{R}_2$ be two binary networks on the same n variables and the same domains. Prove that if $\mathcal{R}_1$ is tighter than $\mathcal{R}_2$, then $sol(\mathcal{R}_1) \subseteq sol(\mathcal{R}_2)$.

15. Prove: for every binary network $\mathcal{R}$ whose set of solutions is ρ, $M(\rho) = P(\rho)$.

16. (a) Is the set of solutions of the 4-queens problem binary-decomposable?

(b) Prove that if ρ is a binary-decomposable relation and S is a subset of its variables, then $\pi_S(\rho)$ is expressible by the subnetwork restricted to variables in S of the projection network $P(\rho)$.

(c) Is the minimal network always binary-decomposable? Prove or show a counterexample.

17. Prove that the number of relations over n variables with domain size k is 2^{k^n}, while the number of binary constraint networks is $2^{k^2 n^2}$.

18. Prove that composition is not generally distributive with respect to intersection. Namely, $R_{12} \cdot (R_{23} \cap R'_{23}) \neq (R_{12} \cdot R_{23}) \cap (R_{12} \cdot R'_{23})$.

19. Show or dispute the following claim: generating a single solution given a binary minimal network is NP-complete.

20. Prove Theorem 2.2.

chapter 3

Consistency-Enforcing and Constraint Propagation

> Knowledge of what is possible is the beginning of happiness.
>
> *George Santayana, Little Essays*

Perhaps the most exciting and fundamental concept that drives the constraint processing area is *constraint propagation*. These are inference methods used by us in everyday life that can be imitated by computers to exhibit intelligent inference.

Assume again our party example in Chapter 2 where we would like to invite Alex, Bill, and Chris to a party. Let A, B, and C denote the propositions "Alex comes," "Bill comes," and "Chris comes," respectively. If Alex comes to the party, Bill will come as well, and if Chris comes, then Alex will too. This is expressed using Boolean constraints as $(A \rightarrow B)$ and $(C \rightarrow A)$. Assume now that Chris will definitely come to the party, namely, C is a fact (a unary constraint, or a domain constraint). Using the constraint $(C \rightarrow A)$ and C, we can immediately infer A, that Alex will be at the party. Now, using the new deduced fact A and the single constraint $(A \rightarrow B)$, you can immediately conclude B, that Bill will be at the party. We can similarly reason in the reverse order. Suppose you know the two rules above and also that Bill did not go to the party after all. That is, you know $\neg B$. From $\neg B$ and $(A \rightarrow B)$ you can deduce $\neg A$. From $\neg A$ and $(C \rightarrow A)$ you can infer $\neg C$. Both chains of reasoning demonstrate (Boolean) constraint propagation, the simplest form of inference. Each deduction step involves just a single variable and a single constraint. The deduction is performed by *propagating* the local reasoning steps. Propagation is efficient, requiring minimal new memory, and yields valuable conclusions. Constraint propagation is at the heart of all the more complex inference methods, which are the essence of constraint techniques.

3.1 Why Propagate Constraints?

This chapter deals with the processing and solving of constraint systems by inference, a concept we encountered in Section 2.3.1 in the context of binary networks.

In general, inference, as it is applied to constraints, narrows the search space of possible partial solutions by creating equivalent, yet more explicit, networks. We demonstrate the relevant concepts employing example constraints such as $x \neq y$ or $x = y$ that are easy to specify and manipulate. Consider the constraint network having three variables x, y, z, all with domains $D = \{red, blue\}$, and three constraints: (1) $x = y$, (2) $y = z$, and (3) $x \neq z$. From the first two constraints, we can infer that $x = z$. Since this inferred constraint conflicts with the constraint $x \neq z$, we can conclude that the set of three constraints is inconsistent.

Consider now the set of just two constraints $\mathcal{R} = \{x = y, \ y = z\}$. From $\mathcal{R}$ we can infer $x = z$, which we can add to the set of constraints, resulting in the new network $\mathcal{R}' = \{x = y, \ y = z, \ x = z\}$. The two networks $\mathcal{R}$ and $\mathcal{R}'$ are equivalent (as discussed in Section 2.3.1), meaning that they have the same set of solutions, but $\mathcal{R}'$ is more explicit than $\mathcal{R}$; it includes a relationship not made explicit in $\mathcal{R}$.

Suppose now that we want to generate a solution for these networks by assigning values to the variables along the ordering x, z, y. Using $\mathcal{R}$, we can generate the partial solution ($x = red, z = blue$) and will only then realize that there is not a consistent extension to y. In other words, the two values in the domain of the remaining variable, y, are both inconsistent with at least one value assignment in the partial solution. Therefore, we have to backtrack and try another assignment for z. This time, only $z = red$ remains, which yields a full solution.

Let's now assign values along the same ordering while consulting network $\mathcal{R}'$. Since the constraint $x = z$ is explicit in $\mathcal{R}'$, it will not allow us to assign a value to z that differs from the value assigned to x. Therefore, the partial assignment above is not a partial solution of $\mathcal{R}'$, and we will avoid the dead-end we encountered with $\mathcal{R}$.

In general, the more explicit and tight (but equivalent) constraint networks are, the more restricted the search space of all possible partial solutions will be, and consequently, any search becomes more efficient. In fact the problem may become explicit enough (by inferring additional constraints or by tightening existing ones) that the search will be directed to a solution without encountering a dead-end.

Indeed, constraint inference can be used to find a complete solution. It can deduce constraints from the given initial set either until an inconsistency is encountered, or until an equivalent constraint network is created from which every solution can be derived by a depth-first search that encounters no dead-ends.

Unfortunately, solving a complete problem by inference is frequently too hard, requiring the addition of an exponential number of new constraints. A more conservative approach is to infer only a restricted set of new constraints, yielding a reduced search space. The resulting new network may encounter some dead-ends, but it may allow finding a solution, or concluding inconsistency, relatively quickly. Algorithms that perform a bounded amount of constraint inference are called *local consistency-enforcing*, *bounded consistency inference*, or *constraint propagation* algorithms.

Since consistency-enforcing algorithms are introduced to assist search, they are defined in terms of extending a solution of a fixed length $i - 1$ by one more variable. Intuitively, a consistency-enforcing algorithm makes any partial solution of a small subnetwork extendible to some surrounding network. The primary characteristic of consistency inference algorithms is the *size* of the subnetwork involved in the inference. Size can be defined by the number of variables or by the number of constraints involved. Algorithms that infer constraints based on pairs of variables are called *arc-consistency algorithms*. Arc-consistency ensures that any legal value in the domain of a single variable has a legal match in the domain of any other selected variable. Algorithms that infer constraints based on subnetworks of size 3 are called *path-consistency algorithms*. Path-consistency ensures that any consistent solution to a two-variable subnetwork is extendible to any third variable. More generally, algorithms that infer constraints based on subnetworks having i variables are called *i-consistency algorithms*. These algorithms guarantee that any consistent instantiation of $i - 1$ variables is extendible to any ith variable. If a network is i-consistent for all i, we call it *globally consistent*.

How much consistency should be enforced on the network before commencing search? Although any search algorithm will benefit from representations that have a high level of consistency, the time and space cost of enforcing i-consistency is exponential in i. Thus, there is a trade-off between the effort spent on preprocessing by i-consistency and that spent on subsequent search. Experimental analysis of local consistency enforcement, both before and during search, focuses on this trade-off.

The remainder of this chapter covers the basics of local consistency methods. We present consistency-enforcing methods whose level is determined by the number of variables involved. Most of the chapter focuses on arc- and path-consistency, which are inherently binary network concepts. Higher levels of local consistency, as well as extensions of arc-consistency to the nonbinary case, are introduced toward the end. Chapter 4 extends this concept to directional inference. In Chapter 8 we will return to local consistency. We will focus on definitions and methods based on the number of constraints involved and apply the entire exposition to general constraints.

Before we move on, let's review the definition of the central concept of *consistency of a partial solution*.

DEFINITION 3.1   (partial solution)

Given a constraint network $\mathcal{R}$, we say that an assignment of values to a subset of the variables $S = \{x_1, \ldots, x_j\}$ given by $\bar{a} = (\langle x_1, a_1 \rangle, \langle x_2, a_2 \rangle, \ldots, \langle x_j, a_j \rangle)$ is consistent relative to $\mathcal{R}$ iff it satisfies every constraint R_{S_i} such that $S_i \subseteq S$. The assignment $\bar{a}$ is also called a partial solution of $\mathcal{R}$. The set of all partial solutions of a subset of variables S is denoted by ρ_S or $\rho(S)$.   ●

3.2 **Arc-Consistency**

Note that the minimal network has the following local consistency property: any value in the domain of a single variable can be extended consistently by any other variable (this follows immediately from Proposition 2.2). This property is termed *arc-consistency*, and it can be satisfied by nonminimal networks as well. Arc-consistency can be enforced on any network by an efficient computation that, because of its local and distributed character, is often called *propagation*.

The following example more clearly demonstrates the notion of arc-consistency. We speak both of a constraint being arc-consistent (or not) relative to a given variable and of a variable being arc-consistent (or not) relative to other variables. In both cases, the underlying meaning is the same.

EXAMPLE 3.1

Consider the variables x and y, whose domains are $D_x = D_y = \{1, 2, 3\}$, and the single constraint R_{xy} expressing the relation $x < y$. The constraint R_{xy} is depicted in a *matching diagram*[1] in Figure 3.1(a), where the domain of each variable is an enclosed set of points, and arcs connect points that correspond to consistent pairs of values. (Note: This type of diagram should not be confused with the constraint graph of the network.) Because the value $3 \in D_x$ has no consistent matching value in D_y, we say that the constraint R_{xy} is not arc-consistent relative to x. Similarly, R_{xy} is not arc-consistent relative to y, since $y = 1$ has no consistent match in x. In matching diagrams, a constraint is not arc-consistent if any of its variables have *lonely* values.

Now, if we shrink the domains of both x and y such that $D_x = \{1, 2\}$ and $D_y = \{2, 3\}$, then x is arc-consistent relative to y, and y is arc-consistent relative to x. The matching diagram of the arc-consistent constraint network is depicted in Figure 3.1(b). If we shrink the domains even further to $D_x = \{1\}$ and $D_y = \{2\}$, we will still have an arc-consistent constraint. However, the latter is no longer equivalent to the original constraint since we may have deleted solutions from the whole set of solutions.   •

DEFINITION 3.2

(arc-consistency)

Given a constraint network $\mathcal{R} = (X, D, C)$, with $R_{ij} \in C$, a variable x_i is *arc-consistent* relative to x_j if and only if for every value $a_i \in D_i$ there exists a value $a_j \in D_j$ such that $(a_i, a_j) \in R_{ij}$. The subnetwork (alternatively, the arc) defined by $\{x_i, x_j\}$ is arc-consistent if and only if x_i is arc-consistent relative to x_j and x_j is arc-consistent relative to x_i. A network of constraints is called *arc-consistent* iff all of its arcs (e.g., subnetworks of size 2) are arc-consistent.   •

---

1. Also called a *microstructure* (Jégou 1993).

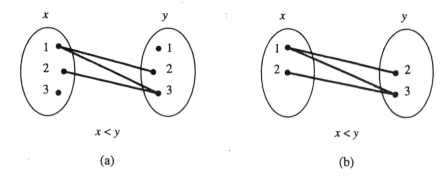

Figure 3.1 A matching diagram describing the arc-consistency of two variables x and y: (a) The variables are not arc-consistent. (b) The domains have been reduced, and the variables are now arc-consistent.

REVISE((x_i), x_j)

Input: A subnetwork defined by two variables $X = \{x_i, x_j\}$, a distinguished variable x_i, domains D_i and D_j, and constraint R_{ij}.

Output: D_i, such that x_i is arc-consistent relative to x_j.

1. **for** each $a_i \in D_i$
2.   **if** there is no $a_j \in D_j$ such that $(a_i, a_j) \in R_{ij}$
3.   **then** delete a_i from D_i
4.   **endif**
5. **endfor**

Figure 3.2 The REVISE procedure.

As we saw in the earlier example, we can make a binary constraint arc-consistent by shrinking the domains of the variables in its scope. If a value does not participate in a solution of a two-variable subnetwork, it will clearly not be part of a complete solution. But how do we ensure that we only eliminate values that will not affect the set of the network's solutions? The simple procedure REVISE($(x_i), x_j)$, shown in Figure 3.2, if applied to two variables, x_i and x_j, returns the largest domain D_i of x_i for which x_i is arc-consistent relative to x_j. It simply tests each value of x_i and eliminates those values having no match in x_j.

Since each value in D_i is compared, in the worst case, with each value in D_j, REVISE has the following complexity:

PROPOSITION 3.1 The complexity of REVISE is $O(k^2)$, where k bounds the domain size. •

REVISE can also be described using composition; namely, lines 1, 2, and 3 can be replaced by

$$D_i \leftarrow D_i \cap \pi_i(R_{ij} \bowtie D_j) \qquad (3.1a)$$

In this case, D_i stands for the one-column relation over x_i. (Consult Section 1.3 for the definitions of the join and project operators.) Remember that the subscript i is shorthand for variable x_i.

Arc-consistency may be imposed on some pairs of variables, on all pairs from some subset of variables, or over an entire network. Arc-consistency of a whole network is accomplished by applying the REVISE procedure to all pairs of variables, although applying the procedure just once to each pair of variables is sometimes not enough to ensure the arc-consistency of a network, as we see in the following example.

EXAMPLE 3.2   Consider now the matching diagram of the three-variable constraint network depicted in Figure 3.3(a). Without knowing the nature of the constraint between y and x, we can see that the two are arc-consistent relative to one another because each value in the domains of the two variables can be matched to an element from the other. However, their arc-consistency is violated in the process of making the adjacent constraints arc-consistent. Specifically, to make $\{x, z\}$ arc-consistent, we must delete a value from the domain of x, which will leave y no longer arc-consistent relative to x. Consequently, REVISE may need to be applied more than once to each constraint until there is no change in the domain of any variable in the network.   •

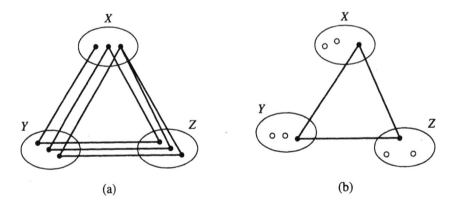

(a)   (b)

Figure 3.3   (a) Matching diagram describing a network of constraints that is not arc-consistent. (b) An arc-consistent equivalent network.

AC-1($\mathcal{R}$)

Input: A network of constraints $\mathcal{R} = (X, D, C)$.

Output: $\mathcal{R}'$, which is the largest arc-consistent network equivalent to $\mathcal{R}$.

1. **repeat**
2.   **for** every pair $\{x_i, x_j\}$ that participates in a constraint
3.   REVISE($(x_i), x_j$) (or $D_i \leftarrow D_i \cap \pi_i (R_{ij} \bowtie D_j)$)
4.   REVISE($(x_j), x_i$) (or $D_j \leftarrow D_j \cap \pi_j (R_{ij} \bowtie D_i)$)
5.   **endfor**
6. **until** no domain is changed

Figure 3.4 ARC-CONSISTENCY-1 (AC-1).

Algorithm ARC-CONSISTENCY-1 (AC-1), a brute-force algorithm that enforces arc-consistency over the network, is given in Figure 3.4. The algorithm applies the REVISE rule to all pairs of variables that participate in a constraint until a full cycle ensures that no domain has been altered. The arc-consistent equivalent of the network in the matching diagram of Figure 3.3(a) is given in Figure 3.3(b).

Occasionally, arc-consistency enforcing may discover inconsistency.

EXAMPLE 3.3 Consider a binary network over three variables $\{x, y, z\}$, where the domains of all the variables are $\{1, 2, 3\}$ and the constraints are $x < y$, $y < z$, $z < x$. Applying arc-consistency to the variables that participate in constraints in the sequence R_{xy}, R_{yz}, R_{zx}, we get first (when revising R_{xy} in both directions) that D_x is reduced to $\{1, 2\}$ and D_y to $\{2, 3\}$. Then, processing constraint R_{yz}, the domain of y is further reduced to $\{2\}$ and the domain of z to $\{3\}$. When R_{zx} is processed, the domain of z becomes empty. Subsequent processing will empty the domains of y and z, and we conclude that the network is inconsistent. •

As we have seen, algorithm AC-1 generates an equivalent arc-consistent network, and when an empty domain is encountered, we conclude that the network has no solution. AC-1 has the following complexity:

PROPOSITION 3.2 Given a constraint network $\mathcal{R}$ having n variables, with domain sizes bounded by k, and e binary constraints, the complexity of AC-1 is $O(enk^3)$.

Proof In AC-1, one cycle through all the binary constraints (steps 2–5) takes $O(ek^2)$. Since, in the worst case, one cycle may cause the deletion of just one value from one domain, and since, overall, there are nk values, the maximum number of such cycles is nk, resulting in the overall bound of $O(n \cdot ek^3)$. •

AC-3($\mathcal{R}$)

Input: A network of constraints $\mathcal{R} = (X, D, C)$.

Output: $\mathcal{R}'$, which is the largest arc-consistent network equivalent to $\mathcal{R}$.

1. **for** every pair $\{x_i, x_j\}$ that participates in a constraint $R_{ij} \in \mathcal{R}$

2. $queue \leftarrow queue \cup \{(x_i, x_j), (x_j, x_i)\}$

3. **endfor**

4. **while** $queue \neq \{\}$

5.   select and delete (x_i, x_j) from $queue$

6.   REVISE$((x_i), x_j)$

7.   **if** REVISE$((x_i), x_j)$ causes a change in D_i

8.   **then** $queue \leftarrow queue \cup \{(x_k, x_i), k \neq i, k \neq j, R_{ki} \in \mathcal{R}\}$

9.   **endif**

10. **endwhile**

Figure 3.5   ARC-CONSISTENCY-3 (AC-3).

Algorithm AC-1 can be improved. There is no need to process all the constraints if only a few domains were reduced in the previous round. The improved version of arc-consistency establishes and maintains a queue of constraints to be processed. Initially, each pair of variables that participates in a constraint is placed in the queue twice (once for each ordering of the pair of variables). Once an ordered pair of variables is processed, it is removed from the queue and is placed back in the queue only if the domain of its second variable is modified as a result of the processing of adjacent constraints. We name this algorithm ARC-CONSISTENCY-3 (AC-3) to conform to the usage already established in the community. A previous improvement called AC-2 provides only a minor advancement step in between these two versions. Algorithm AC-3, which uses a queue data structure, is presented in Figure 3.5.

EXAMPLE 3.4   Consider a three-variable network: z, x, y with $D_z = \{2, 5\}$, $D_x = \{2, 5\}$, $D_y = \{2, 4\}$. There are two constraints: R_{zx}, specifying that z evenly divides x, and R_{zy}, specifying that z evenly divides y. The constraint graph of this problem is depicted in Figure 3.6(a). Assume that we apply AC-3 to the network. We put $(z, x), (x, z), (z, y)$, and (y, z) onto the queue. Processing the pairs (z, x) and (x, z) does not change the problem, since the domains of z and x are already arc-consistent relative to R_{zx}. When we process (z, y), we delete 5 from D_z, and consequently place (x, z) back on the queue. Processing (y, z) causes no further change, but when (x, z) is revised,

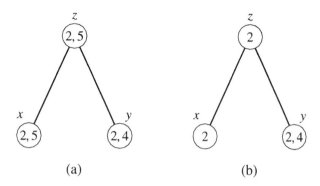

Figure 3.6 A three-variable network, with two constraints: z divides x, and z divides y (a) before and (b) after AC-3 is applied.

5 will be deleted from D_x. At this point, no further constraints will be inserted into the queue (remember, no constraint already in the queue needs to be inserted), and the algorithm terminates with the domains $D_x = \{2\}$, $D_z = \{2\}$, and $D_y = \{2, 4\}$.　　　　　　●

Algorithm AC-3 processes each constraint at most $2k$ times, where k bounds the domain size, since each time it is reintroduced into the queue, the domain of a variable in its scope has just been reduced by at least one value, and there are at most $2k$ such values. Since there are e binary constraints, and processing each one takes $O(k^2)$, we can conclude the following:

PROPOSITION 3.3　　The time complexity of AC-3 is $O(ek^3)$.　　　　　　●

Is AC-3's performance optimal? It seems that no algorithm can have time complexity below ek^2, since the worst case of merely verifying the arc-consistency of a network requires ek^2 operations. Indeed, algorithm ARC-CONSISTENCY-4 (AC-4) achieves this optimal performance. AC-4 does not use REVISE or the composition operator as an atomic operation. Instead, it exploits the underlying microstructure of the constraint relation and tunes its operation to that level.

AC-4 associates each value a_i in the domain of x_i with the amount of *support from variable x_j*, that is, the number of values in the domain of x_j that are consistent with value a_i. A value a_i is then removed from the domain D_i if it has no support from some neighboring variable. The algorithm maintains a *List* of currently unsupported variable-value pairs, a counter array *counter*(x_i, a_i, x_j) of supports for a_i from x_j, and an array $S_{(x_j, a_j)}$ that points to all values in other variables supported by $\langle x_j, a_j \rangle$. In each step, the algorithm picks up an unsupported value from *List*, adds it to the *removed* list M, and updates all the supports of potentially affected values. Those

AC-4($\mathcal{R}$)

Input: A network of constraints $\mathcal{R}$.

Output: An arc-consistent network equivalent to $\mathcal{R}$.

1. Initialization: $M \leftarrow \emptyset$

2.   initialize $S_{(x_i,c_i)}$, *counter*(i, a_i, j) for all R_{ij}

3.   **for** all counters

4.   **if** *counter*$(x_i, a_i, x_j) = 0$ (if $\langle x_i, a_i \rangle$ is unsupported by x_j)

5.   **then** add $\langle x_i, a_i \rangle$ to *List*

6.   **endif**

7.   **endfor**

8. **while** *List* is not empty

9.   choose $\langle x_i, a_i \rangle$ from *List*, remove it, and add it to M

10.   **for** each $\langle x_j, a_j \rangle$ in $S_{(x_i, a_i)}$

11.   decrement *counter*(x_j, a_j, x_i)

12.   **if** *counter*$(x_j, a_j, x_i) = 0$

13.   **then** add $\langle x_j, a_j \rangle$ to *List*

14.   **endif**

15.   **endfor**

16. **endwhile**

Figure 3.7   ARC-CONSISTENCY-4 (AC-4).

values that became unsupported as a result are placed in *List*. If a_j is unsupported, the counters of values that it supports will be reduced. Algorithm AC-4 is given in Figure 3.7.

EXAMPLE 3.5   Consider the problem in Figure 3.6. Initializing the $S_{(x,a)}$ arrays (indicating all the variable-value pairs that each $\langle x, a \rangle$ supports), we have

$$S_{(z,2)} = \{\langle x, 2\rangle, \langle y, 2\rangle, \langle y, 4\rangle\}, S_{(z,5)} = \{\langle x, 5\rangle\}, S_{(x,2)} = \{\langle z, 2\rangle\},$$

$$S_{(x,5)} = \{\langle z, 5\rangle\}, S_{(y,2)} = \{\langle z, 2\rangle\}, S_{(y,4)} = \{\langle z, 2\rangle\}.$$

For counters we have *counter*$(x, 2, z) = 1$, *counter*$(x, 5, z) = 1$, *counter*$(z, 2, x) = 1$, *counter*$(z, 5, x) = 1$, *counter*$(z, 2, y) = 2$, *counter*$(z, 5, y) = 0$, *counter*$(y, 2, z) = 1$, *counter*$(y, 4, z) = 1$. (Note that we do not need to add counters between variables that are not directly constrained, such as x and y.) Finally, *List* $= \{\langle z, 5\rangle\}$, $M = \emptyset$. Once $\langle z, 5\rangle$ is removed from *List* and placed in *M*, the counter of $\langle x, 5 \rangle$ is updated to *counter*$(x, 5, z) = 0$, and $\langle x, 5 \rangle$ is placed in *List*. Then, $\langle x, 5 \rangle$ is removed from *List* and placed in *M*. Since the only value it supports is $\langle z, 5 \rangle$ and since $\langle z, 5 \rangle$ is already in *M*, *List* remains empty and the process stops.   •

The initialization step that creates the counter of supports and the pointers requires, at most, $O(ek^2)$ steps. The number of elements in $S_{(x_j, a_j)}$ is on the order of ek^2. We can show:

PROPOSITION   The time and space complexity of AC-4 is $O(ek^2)$.
3.4

  Proof   See Exercise 4.   •

Since worst-case complexity often overestimates, and since average-case analysis is hard to achieve, it is sometimes useful to introduce more refined parameters into the analysis. Instead of using $O(k^2)$—which is the size of the universal relation (remember that arc-consistency is relevant only to the binary constraints)—as a bound for each relation size, we can use a *tightness* parameter t that stands for the maximum number of tuples in each binary relation. Frequently the constraints can be quite tight, as in the case of functional constraints where $t = O(k)$.

Revisiting our worst-case analysis, the REVISE procedure can be modified to have a complexity of $O(t)$. Consequently, the complexity of AC-1 is modified to $O(n \cdot k \cdot e \cdot t)$, that of AC-3 to $O(e \cdot k \cdot t)$, and that of AC-4 to $O(e \cdot t)$.

Analyzing the best-case performance of these algorithms may also provide insight. The best case of AC-1 and AC-3 is $e \cdot k$ steps because the problem may already be arc-consistent. The best case of AC-4 remains at ek^2, which is the time necessary to create the special data structures in its initialization phase. Consequently, when the constraints are loose (i.e., when t is closest to k^2), AC-1 and AC-3 may frequently outperform AC-4, even though AC-4 is optimal in the worst case.

3.3 **Path-Consistency**

As we saw in Example 3.3, arc-consistency can sometimes decide inconsistency by discovering an empty domain. However, arc-consistency is not complete for deciding consistency because it makes inferences based on a single (binary) constraint and single domain constraints.

EXAMPLE   Consider the example we mentioned at the outset having three vari-
3.6   ables x, y, z with respective domains {*red, blue*} and constrained by $x \neq y$, $y \neq z$, $z \neq x$. This constraint network is arc-consistent without reducing any domains, and therefore AC enforcement will not reveal the network's inconsistency. Although the constraint R_{xy}, which is $x \neq y$, allows the assignment

$(\langle x, red \rangle, \langle y, blue \rangle)$, no color for z will be consistent with both $\langle x, red \rangle$ and $\langle y, blue \rangle$. Indeed, we can infer something about this network: since our domain size is 2, $x \neq y$ and $y \neq z$ imply $x = z$, but $x = z$ is not explicit in this network. Not only that, it contradicts another explicit constraint.   •

The consistency level violated here is called *path-consistency*, requiring consistency relative to paths of length 3 (the path from x to y that goes through z). It is interesting to note that in the minimal network path-consistency is maintained; any consistent pair of values can be consistently extended by any third variable (see Exercise 6).

In general, the notion of path-consistency involves inferences using subnetworks having three variables. However, since the original definition of path-consistency involves only binary constraints, it is relevant only to the binary constraints of the network. An extension of the definition to nonbinary constraints is presented later; it constitutes only a minor change that is relevant when the network also has ternary constraints.

DEFINITION 3.3

(path-consistency)

Given a constraint network $\mathcal{R} = (X, D, C)$, a two-variable set $\{x_i, x_j\}$ is path-consistent relative to variable x_k if and only if for every consistent assignment $(\langle x_i, a_i \rangle, \langle x_j, a_j \rangle)$ there is a value $a_k \in D_k$ such that the assignment $(\langle x_i, a_i \rangle, \langle x_k, a_k \rangle)$ is consistent and $(\langle x_k, a_k \rangle, \langle x_j, a_j \rangle)$ is consistent. Alternatively, a binary constraint R_{ij} is path-consistent relative to x_k iff for every pair $(a_i, a_j) \in R_{ij}$, where a_i and a_j are from their respective domains, there is a value $a_k \in D_k$ such that $(a_i, a_k) \in R_{ik}$ and $(a_k, a_j) \in R_{kj}$. A subnetwork over three variables $\{x_i, x_j, x_k\}$ is path-consistent iff for any permutation of (i, j, k), R_{ij} is path-consistent relative to x_k. A network is path-consistent iff for every R_{ij} (including universal binary relations) and for every $k \neq i, j$ R_{ij} is path-consistent relative to x_k.   •

Pictorially, a connected pair of points in the matching diagram (denoting a legal pair of values in R_{xy}) satisfies path-consistency iff the connected pair can be extended to a triangle with a third value as is shown in Figure 3.8(b). When a three-variable subnetwork is not path-consistent, we can enforce path-consistency by making the necessary inferences. So, if in the input specification there is no constraint between x and y (meaning that everything is allowed), we can deduce a new constraint by the length-3 path from x to y through z. In this case, the necessary inferences are adding binary constraints or tightening binary constraints (deleting tuples from the relation). In the coloring example (see the matching diagram in Figure 3.8(a)), if we attempt to make R_{xy} path-consistent relative to z, this implies emptying the constraint R_{xy} and declaring inconsistency.

Alternatively, consider again the network of three variables $\{x, y, z\}$ where all variables have the same domain and the equality constraints $R_{xz} : x = z$ and

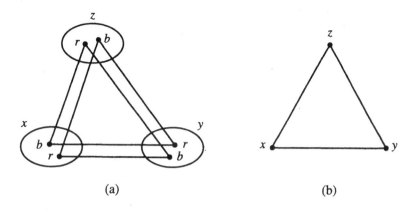

Figure 3.8 (a) The matching diagram of a two-value graph-coloring problem. (b) Graphical picture of path-consistency using the matching diagram.

REVISE-3$((x, y), z)$

Input: A three-variable subnetwork over (x, y, z), R_{xy}, R_{yz}, R_{xz}.

Output: Revised R_{xy} path-consistent with z.

1. **for** each pair $(a, b) \in R_{xy}$

2.   **if** no value $c \in D_z$ exists such that $(a, c) \in R_{xz}$ and $(b, c) \in R_{yz}$

3.   **then** delete (a, b) from R_{xy}.

4.   **endif**

5. **endfor**

Figure 3.9 REVISE-3.

$R_{yz} : y = z$. To make this network path-consistent, we should infer and add to the network the constraint $R_{xy} : x = y$.

To use an analog of REVISE for arc-consistency, we define a procedure REVISE-3$((x,y), z)$ (Figure 3.9). This procedure takes a pair of variables (x, y) and their constraint that we wish to modify, R_{xy} (and which can also be the universal constraint), and a third variable, z, and returns the loosest constraint R'_{xy} that satisfies path-consistency. REVISE-3 tests if each pair of consistent values in R_{xy} can be extended consistently to a value of z, and if not, it deletes the violating pair.

REVISE-3$((x, y), z)$ can be expressed succinctly as the composition

$$R_{xy} \leftarrow R_{xy} \cap \pi_{xy}(R_{xz} \bowtie D_z \bowtie R_{zy}) \tag{3.1b}$$

PC-1 ($\mathcal{R}$)

Input: A network $\mathcal{R} = (X, D, C)$.

Output: A path-consistent network equivalent to $\mathcal{R}$.

1. **repeat**
2.   **for** $k \leftarrow 1$ to n
3.   **for** $i, j \leftarrow 1$ to n
4. $R_{ij} \leftarrow R_{ij} \cap \pi_{ij} (R_{ik} \bowtie D_k \bowtie R_{kj})$/* (REVISE-3$((i, j), k)$)
5.   **endfor**
6.   **endfor**
7. **until** no constraint is changed.

Figure 3.10   PATH-CONSISTENCY-1 (PC-1).

As you can see, REVISE-3 makes the minimal necessary changes to make R_{xy} path-consistent relative to z. You can verify that its performance is characterized by the following:

PROPOSITION 3.5   The complexity of REVISE-3 is $O(k^3)$ and $O(t \cdot k)$ where k bounds the domain size and t bounds the constraint tightness.   ●

The claim of the proposition assumes that testing the consistency $(a, b) \in R_{xy}$ can be done in constant time using hash tables. Otherwise a $\log k$ factor should be introduced. When using the tightness parameter t, the best performance of REVISE-3 may take just t steps.

Path-consistency can be applied to a subnetwork, or it can be fully enforced with respect to all subnetworks of size 3, yielding a completely path-consistent network. The following two algorithms, PATH-CONSISTENCY-1 (PC-1) and PATH-CONSISTENCY-2 (PC-2), enforce path-consistency on a network in a manner analogous to AC-1 and AC-3, respectively. PC-1 applies REVISE-3 in a brute-force manner to every triplet of variables until there is one full cycle with no change, as shown in Figure 3.10. Its complexity analysis is similar to AC-1's.

PROPOSITION 3.6   Given a network $\mathcal{R}$, when k bounds the domain sizes and t bounds the tightness of the constraints, PC-1 generates an equivalent path-consistent network, with complexity $O(n^5 k^5)$ or $O(n^5 \cdot t^2 \cdot k)$.

Proof   Since in each cycle (steps 3, 4, and 5) we may eliminate only one pair of values from one constraint, the number of cycles is $O(n^2 k^2)$ (respectively, $O(n^2 \cdot t)$). Since we have $O(n^3)$ triplets of variables, and since processing

PC-2($\mathcal{R}$)

Input: A network $\mathcal{R} = (X, D, C)$.

Output: $\mathcal{R}'$ a path-consistent network equivalent to $\mathcal{R}$.

1. $Q \leftarrow \{(i, k, j) \mid 1 \le i < j \le n,\ 1 \le k \le n,\ k \ne i,\ k \ne j\}$

2. **while** Q is not empty

3.   select and delete a 3-tuple (i, k, j) from Q

4. $R_{ij} \leftarrow R_{ij} \cap \pi_{ij} (R_{ik} \bowtie D_k \bowtie R_{kj})$ /* (REVISE-3$((i, j), k)$)

5.   **if** R_{ij} changed **then**

6. $Q \leftarrow Q \cup \{(l, i, j)\ (l, j, i) \mid 1 \le l \le n,\ l \ne i,\ l \ne j\}$

7. **endwhile**

Figure 3.11 PATH-CONSISTENCY-2 (PC-2).

each triplet by REVISE-3 is $O(k^3)$ (respectively, $O(t \cdot k)$), each cycle costs $O(n^3 k^3)$ (respectively, $O(n^3 \cdot t \cdot k)$), yielding the above bound.   •

Algorithm PC-2 (Figure 3.11) improves on PC-1 by maintaining a queue of ordered triplets to be processed (or reprocessed). Once a constraint R_{ij} is modified, thus deleting a pair of its values, all the triplets involving x_i and x_j, and any third variable x_k, are reprocessed.

Note that in order to make the network fully path-consistent, all ordered triplets should be included in the initial queue, even those containing pairs of variables that have no direct binary constraint.

PROPOSITION 3.7   Given a network $\mathcal{R}$, algorithm PC-2 generates an equivalent path-consistent network, and its complexity is $O(n^3 k^5)$ ($O(n^3 \cdot t^2 \cdot k)$, respectively), where k and t represent the tightness of domains and constraints, respectively.

Proof See Exercise 13.   •

EXAMPLE 3.7   Consider the graph-coloring problem on a four-variable network where the domains contain only two possible colors $D_1 = D_2 = D_3 = D_4 = \{red, blue\}$, and the constraints are $x_1 \ne x_2$, $x_2 \ne x_3$, $x_3 \ne x_4$, $x_4 \ne x_1$. The constraint graph of this problem is depicted in Figure 3.12(a). The network is currently arc-consistent, but not path-consistent. For example, the universal constraint between x_3 and x_1 allows the assignment $x_1 = red$ and $x_3 = blue$, yet there is no assignment to x_4 satisfying the unequal constraints with this instantiation. Enforcing path-consistency requires adding the constraint $x_1 = x_3$. Path-consistency will similarly add the

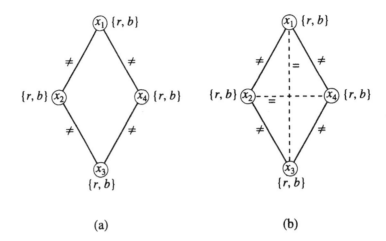

Figure 3.12 A graph-coloring graph (a) before path-consistency and (b) after path-consistency.

constraint $x_2 = x_4$. The path-consistent constraint network version of this example is depicted in Figure 3.12(b). If we generate a path-consistent network by applying PC-1 to the original network, the algorithm's first cycle applies REVISE-3 to four triplets, generating the two equality constraints. A full cycle will then be executed to verify that nothing changes. This verification requires a second processing of each triplet. On the other hand, if we enforce path-consistency by PC-2, we may be able to process each triplet only once, assuming the right ordering is picked. If we apply REVISE-3 first to (x_1, x_3, x_2), that is, to the universal constraint between x_1 and x_3, and then to (x_2, x_4, x_1), each triplet would be processed just once.   •

Like its arc-consistent counterpart (AC-3), PC-2 is not optimal, although we can devise an optimal algorithm, akin to AC-4. It would require operating on the relation level and maintaining *supports* for pairs of values. An algorithm exploiting such low-level consistency maintenance, which we will call PC-4, is available (Mohr and Henderson 1986),and its complexity bound is $O(n^3 k^3)$ or $O(n^3 tk)$. It is an optimal algorithm, since even verifying path-consistency has that lower bound; namely, it is $\Omega(n^3 k^3)$.

Regarding best-case performance, we observe that PC-1, PC-2, and PC-4 have properties that parallel those of arc-consistency. Algorithms PC-1 and PC-2 can be as good as $O(n^3 \cdot t)$ and $O(n^3 \cdot k^2)$, respectively, while algorithm PC-4 (which was not presented explicitly) requires an order of $O(n^3 k^3)$ (or $O(n^3 \cdot t \cdot k)$) even in the best case because of its initialization (see Exercise 14).

Let's conclude our introduction to path-consistency by giving an alternative definition that may explain the origin of the term.

DEFINITION
3.4

(path-consistent constraint)

A constraint R_{ij} is path-consistent, relative to the path of length m through the nodes $(i = i_0, i_1, \ldots, i_m = j)$, if for any pair $(a_i, a_j) \in R_{ij}$ there is a sequence of values $a_{i_l} \in D_{i_l}$ such that $(a_i = a_{i_0}, a_{i_1}) \in R_{i_0 i_1}$, $(a_{i_0}, a_{i_1}) \in R_{i_0 i_1}, \ldots$, and $(a_{i_{m-1}}, a_{i_m} = a_j) \in R_{i_{m-1} i_m}$. ●

For a constraint graph that is complete, the two definitions can be shown to be the same. However, if we require path-consistency in Definition 3.4 to hold relative to only real paths in the constraint graph, then the two above-referenced definitions are not the same (see Exercise 15).

3.4 Higher Levels of *i*-Consistency

Arc- and path-consistency algorithms process subnetworks of size 2 and 3, respectively. We're now ready to generalize the concept of local consistency to subnetworks of size i. In this case nonbinary constraints also come into play.

DEFINITION
3.5

(*i*-consistency, global consistency)

Given a general network of constraints $\mathcal{R} = (X, D, C)$, a relation $R_S \in C$ where $|S| = i - 1$ is i-consistent relative to a variable y not in S iff for every $t \in R_S$, there exists a value $a \in D_y$, such that (t, a) is consistent. A network is i-*consistent* iff given any consistent instantiation of any $i - 1$ distinct variables, there exists an instantiation of any ith variable such that the i values taken together satisfy all of the constraints among the i variables. A network is *strongly i-consistent* iff it is j-consistent for all $j \le i$. A strongly n-consistent network, where n is the number of variables in the network, is called *globally consistent*. ●

Globally consistent networks are characterized by the property that any consistent instantiation of a subset of the variables can be extended to a consistent instantiation of all of the variables without encountering any dead-ends.

EXAMPLE
3.8

Consider the constraint network for the 4-queens problem. We see that the network is 2-consistent since, given that we have placed a single queen on the board, we can always place a second queen on any remaining column such that the two queens do not attack each other. This network is not 3-consistent, however; given the consistent placement of two queens shown in Figure 3.13(a), there is no way to place a queen in the third column that is consistent with the previously placed queens. Similarly, the network is not 4-consistent (Figure 3.13(b)). ●

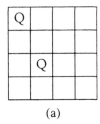   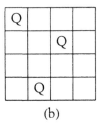

    (a)   (b)

Figure 3.13   (a) Not 3-consistent; (b) not 4-consistent.

REVISE-i $(\langle x_1, x_2,\ldots, x_{i-1}\rangle, x_i)$

Input: A network $\mathcal{R} = (X, D, C)$, a constraint R_S, (which may be universal).

Output: A constraint R_S ($S = \{x_1,\ldots, x_{i-1}\}$), which is i-consistent relative to x_i.

1. **for** each instantiation $\bar{a}_{i-1} = (\langle x_1, a_1\rangle, \langle x_2, a_2\rangle,\ldots, \langle x_{i-1}, a_{i-1}\rangle) \in R_S$ **do**,

2. **if** no value of $a_i \in D_i$ exists such that $(\bar{a}_{i-1}, a_i)$ is consistent

    then delete $\bar{a}_{i-1}$ from R_S

    (Alternatively, let $\mathcal{S}$ be the set of all subsets of $\{x_1,\ldots, x_i\}$ that contain

    x_i and appear as scopes of constraints of $\mathcal{R}$, then

    $R_S \leftarrow R_S \cap \pi_S(\bowtie_{S' \subseteq \mathcal{S}} R_{S'}))$

3. **endfor**

Figure 3.14   REVISE-i.

Enforcing higher levels of consistency requires recording constraints on more than two variables. Consider first the i-level REVISE rule. If a consistent instantiation of $i - 1$ variables cannot be consistently extended to an ith variable, we need to *rule out* that instantiation, labeling it as a *no-good*. This means that we should record an explicit constraint over the scope of these $i - 1$ variables that excludes that particular no-good assignment. As a consequence of this exclusion, even if the input network is binary, enforcing i-consistency may result in a nonbinary network having constraints of arity $i - 1$. For example, to make the 4-queens example 4-consistent, we need to add, among other constraints, the ternary constraint over x_1, x_2, x_3 that forbids the tuple $(\langle x_1, 1\rangle\langle x_2, 4\rangle\langle x_3, 2\rangle)$. The REVISE-$i$ operation carries out this task, which is defined in Figure 3.14.

The complexity of brute-force REVISE-i is $O(k^i)$ if we assume that the input specification includes binary constraints only. However, when arbitrary constraints are involved, REVISE-i by itself can be as complex as $O((2k)^i)$ because there may be $O(2^i)$ constraints that need to be tested for each tuple. If e bounds the number of constraints, the complexity is $o(ek^i)$.

---

i-CONSISTENCY($\mathcal{R}$)

Input: A network $\mathcal{R}$.

Output: An *i*-consistent network equivalent to $\mathcal{R}$.

1. **repeat**

2.   **for** every subset $S \subseteq X$ of size $i - 1$, and for every x_i, do

3.   let $\mathcal{S}$ be the set of all subsets of $\{x_1, \dots, x_i\}$ in *scheme*($\mathcal{R}$) that contain x_i

4. $R_S \leftarrow R_S \cap \pi_S(\bowtie_{S' \in \mathcal{S}} R_{S'})$ (this is REVISE-*i*(S, x_i))

5.   **endfor**

6. **until** no constraint is changed.

Figure 3.15 *i*-CONSISTENCY.

Several algorithms for enforcing *i*-consistency have been developed. When REVISE-*i* is incorporated into a brute-force algorithm enforcing *i*-consistency over a given network $\mathcal{R}$, as in algorithm *i*-CONSISTENCY in Figure 3.15, all subsets of size $i - 1$ need to be modified, requiring $O(n^i(2k)^i) = O((2nk)^i)$ steps. These steps should be repeated until a complete cycle produces no change. The number of such cycles equals $O(n^i k^{i-1})$, yielding overall time complexity of $O((nk)^{2i} 2^i)$ and space complexity of $O(n^i k^i)$. On the other hand, a lower bound for enforcing *i*-consistency is $\Omega((nk)^i)$ (for more details see Dechter 1990). Indeed there exists an optimal algorithm that achieves this bound (using complex data structures) that is analogous to AC-4 and PC-4 (Cooper 1990). In summary, we have the following:

THEOREM 3.1   **(complexity of *i*-consistency)**

The time and space complexity of brute-force *i*-consistency is $O(2^i(nk)^{2i})$ and $O(n^i k^i)$, respectively. A lower bound for enforcing *i*-consistency is $\Omega(n^i k^i)$.   •

3.4.1 A Note on 3-Consistency and Path-Consistency

For binary constraint networks, 3-consistency is identical to path-consistency. When the network also has ternary constraints, the definition of 3-consistency requires also testing ternary constraints.

EXAMPLE 3.9   Suppose a constraint network involves three variables x, y, z having domains $\{0, 1\}$ and a single ternary constraint $R_{xyz} = \{(0, 0, 0)\}$. Application of the path-consistency algorithm will produce nothing since there are no binary constraints to test; the network is already path-consistent. However, the network is *not* 3-consistent. While we can assign the values $(\langle x, 1 \rangle, \langle y, 1 \rangle)$ (since there is no constraint), we cannot extend this assignment to z in a way that satisfies the given ternary constraint. Indeed, if we apply 3-consistency to this network, we will add at least the constraint $R_{xy} = \{(\langle x, 0 \rangle \langle y, 0 \rangle)\}$ in addition to the constraint $R_x = \{(\langle x, 0 \rangle)\}$.   •

You can see here that the REVISE-3 operation, as depicted in Figure 3.14, will indeed test consistency relative to ternary constraints as well as binary ones.

3.5 Arc-Consistency for Nonbinary Constraints

Many variants of local consistency algorithms exist in the literature. We will revisit this topic when we introduce relational consistency in Chapter 8. There we characterize consistency level by the number of constraints involved rather than by the number of variables. We conclude with a simple extension of arc-consistency to nonbinary constraints. This extension is a special case of relational consistency elaborated on Chapter 8.

3.5.1 Generalized Arc-Consistency

So far, the notion of constraint propagation, as reflected by arc-consistency, is restricted to pairs of variables only. In applications, constraints are most often nonbinary, so an extension of this simplest form of constraint propagation to the nonbinary case is called for. There are many simple local inferences that can be made between a single nonbinary constraint and a single variable. For example, a constraint such as $x + y + z \leq 15$, together with a domain constraint $z \geq 13$, can immediately lead us to restrict y to $y \leq 2$ and x to $x \leq 2$. As another example, we can have a nonbinary party constraint saying that if Alex (A) and Bill (B) go to the party, then Gill goes to the party (G), that is, $A \wedge B \to G$. If we learn that Gill did not go to the party (that is, $\neg G$) we can conclude $\neg A \vee \neg B$. In both cases inference is local, relying on a single constraint and a single variable. In one case, local propagation reduces only the domain. In the others, we can infer constraints on more than a single variable.

Hence an extension of arc-consistency to nonbinary constraints can be done in two complementary ways. Both definitions take a constraint and a single variable. The first extension is called *generalized arc-consistency* and leads to concepts such as domain reduction or domain propagation.

DEFINITION
3.6

(generalized arc-consistency)

Given a constraint network $\mathcal{R} = (X, D, C)$, with $R_S \in C$, a variable x is *arc-consistent* relative to R_S if and only if for every value $a \in D_x$ there exists a tuple, in the domain of variables in S, $t \in R_S$ such that $t[x] = a$. t can be called a *support* for a. The constraint R_S is called arc-consistent iff it is arc-consistent relative to each of the variables in its scope. A constraint network is arc-consistent if all its constraints are arc-consistent. Remember that a domain of a subset of variables is the Cartesian product of the respective domains.   •

We can enforce generalized arc-consistency on a constraint by shrinking the domains of its variables. A simple extension of the REVISE procedure can be obtained using Equation (3.1), applied to a nonbinary relation, namely, by

$$D_x \leftarrow D_x \cap \pi_x(R_S \bowtie D_{S-\{x\}}) \tag{3.2}$$

Since each value in D_x is compared, in the worst case, with each tuple of R_S, we get the following:

PROPOSITION
3.8

The complexity of the rule in Equation (3.2) is $O(t \cdot k)$ where k bounds the domain size and t is the constraint tightness. Note that $t \leq k^r$ when r is the constraint scope size.   •

The second extension of arc-consistency is complementary in the sense that it records the inferred constraint on the entire scope of the constraint except for the single variable involved in the inference. This inference is called *relational arc-consistency*, and it can be enforced for every constraint R_S and a variable $x \in S$ by

$$R_{S-\{x\}} \leftarrow \pi_{S-\{x\}}(R_S \bowtie D_x) \tag{3.3}$$

3.5.2 Global Constraints

So far we have discussed constraint propagation relative to specified input constraints that are assumed to be available in relational form. However, the task of modeling real applications as constraint problems requires developing specialized propagation algorithms for frequently used constraints, either because a relational description is unrealistic, or because standard propagation rules are inefficient, not effective, or both.

The most well-known example is the *alldifferent* constraint, *alldifferent* $(x_1, x_2, \ldots, x_l)$, which requires that the values assigned to each variable among the set will be mutually different. This constraint appears in almost every assignment and resource allocation problem, and it can be expressed by a collection of binary not-equal constraints. Applying arc-consistency over such a binary network yields little or no effect because such networks are often already arc-consistent (unless there are single-valued domains). Consequently, specialized filtering algorithms were developed.

Many such constraints that appear often in modeling, and for which specialized domain reduction propagation algorithms have been developed, are called *global constraints*. Typically, a global constraint is well defined over any size scope (e.g., alldifferent). The level of consistency enforced on such constraints can be described as (generalized) arc-consistency relative to their underlying implicit relation. Since it takes advantage of the structure of the global constraint, the method for achieving the targeted level of consistency is specialized and domain-dependent.

Consider the problem of scheduling speakers in a conference. Each talk is a one-hour slot, and the speakers are available only at certain time slots. Assume we have the following speakers: Alfred (A) who can talk in slots $\{3, 4, 5, 6\}$, Bob (B) in $\{3, 4\}$, Cindy (C) in $\{2, 3, 4, 5\}$, Debby (D) in $\{2, 3, 4\}$, Eldridge (E) in $\{3, 4\}$, and Fred (F) in $\{1, 2, 3, 4, 5, 6\}$. There can be many additional constraints, such as that Cindy and Debby should teach one following the other, and so on. Modeling the problem can be done by a set of binary not-equal constraints between every pair of distinct variables: $A \neq B$, $B \neq C$, and so on, for every pair of variables. A quick look reveals that all these constraints are arc-consistent, and therefore no domain pruning will occur by enforcing arc-consistency. Suppose now that we view the set of not-equal binary constraints as a single global alldifferent constraint $R(A, B, C, D, E, F)$ on all the variables. Namely, it denotes the implicit constraint, representing all solutions to the unary (domain constraints) and binary (not-equal) constraints.

If we apply generalized arc-consistency to this global constraint we will see that the domain of the variables will be reduced considerably. For example, $D_A = \{6\}$, $D_F = \{1\}$, and so on (see Exercise 19). Clearly, a brute-force algorithm for achieving this level of consistency amounts to solving a subproblem and projecting its set of solutions on each single domain using the rule in Equation (3.2). This process is quite costly, however, and in general it makes little practical sense. However, some specialized constraints may allow efficient processing for achieving that level of consistency.

In particular, it can be shown that generalized arc-consistency over the global alldifferent constraint can be accomplished by a bipartite matching algorithm between variables and values leading an algorithm whose complexity is $O(k \cdot n^{1.5})$. Additional specialized global constraints (e.g., global cardinality constraints) are also shown to possess efficient arc-consistency methods.

The list of global constraints is long. Among the most popular are the following: (1) The alldifferent constraints were discussed earlier. (2) A constraint of sum makes one variable equal to the sum of k other variables. (3) Global cardinality constraints generalize the alldifferent constraint. (4) The cumulative constraint enforces, at each point in time, that the cumulative resource consumption of a set of tasks that overlaps does not exceed the specified capacity. Each task has a start, a duration, and a resource consumption, which are all domain variables.

In summary, a global constraint $C = \{C(i)\}$ is a family of scope-parameterized constraints (normally $i \geq 2$), where $C(i)$ is a constraint whose relation is often defined implicitly either by a natural language statement or as a set of solutions to a subproblem defined by lower-arity explicit constraints (e.g., alldifferent). It is associated with one or more specialized propagation algorithms trying to achieve generalized arc-consistency relative to $C(i)$ (or an approximation of it) in a way that is more efficient than a brute-force approach.

3.5.3 Bounds-Consistency

In some cases the application of arc-consistency is too costly. This is the case when the domains of the variables are large sets of integers and occurs often (but not only) when developing arc-consistency algorithms for the kinds of global constraints discussed above. In such cases a weaker notion of consistency called *bounds-consistency* appears to be highly cost-effective. It is less costly than applying full arc-consistency on either input or global constraints. The idea is to bound the domain of each variable by an interval and make sure that only the end-points of the intervals obey the arc-consistency requirement. If not, the upper and lower bounds of the intervals can be tightened until bounds-consistency is achieved.

DEFINITION 3.7 **(bounds-consistency)**

Given a constraint C over a scope S and domain constraints, a variable $x \in S$ (when D_x is a well-defined ordered set), is bounds-consistent relative to C if the value $\min\{D_x\}$ (respectively, $\max\{D_x\}$) can be extended to a full tuple t of C, when t's values are from the respective domains. We say that t supports $\min\{D_x\}$ (respectively, $\max\{D_x\}$). A constraint C is bounds-consistent if each of its variables is bounds-consistent. •

A constraint problem can be made bounds-consistent by repeatedly removing unsupported lower and upper values from the domains of its variables. This level of consistency can be far more efficient to achieve for large domains and for global constraints than (generalized) arc-consistency.

EXAMPLE 3.10

Consider the constraint problem with variables $x_1, \ldots, x_6$, each with domains $1, \ldots, 6$, and constraints

$$C_1 : x_4 \geq x_1 + 3$$

$$C_2 : x_4 \geq x_2 + 3$$

$$C_3 : x_5 \geq x_3 + 3$$

$$C_4 : x_5 \geq x_4 + 1$$

$$C_5 : alldifferent\{x_1, x_2, x_3, x_4, x_5\}$$

The constraints are not bounds-consistent. For example, the minimum value 1 in the domain of x_4 does not have support in constraint C_1 as there is no corresponding value for x_1 that satisfies the constraint. Enforcing bounds-consistency using constraints C_1 through C_4 reduces the domains of the variables as follows: $D_1 = \{1, 2\}$, $D_2 = \{1, 2\}$, $D_3 = \{1, 2, 3\}$, $D_4 = \{4, 5\}$, and $D_5 = \{5, 6\}$. Subsequently, enforcing bounds-consistency using constraint C_5 further reduces the domain of x_3 to $D_3 = \{3\}$. Now constraint C_3 is no longer bounds-consistent. Reestablishing bounds-consistency causes the domain of x_5 to be reduced to $\{6\}$. Is the resulting problem already arc-consistent?   •

For the alldifferent constraints bounds-consistency can be enforced in $O(n \log n)$. The concepts of global constraints and bounds-consistency were developed in the context of constraint programming languages and will be discussed again in Chapter 15.

3.6   Constraint Propagation for Numeric and Boolean Constraints

When we process constraint systems that have a special syntactic form, such as numeric constraints expressed algebraically or Boolean constraints expressed by Boolean expressions, the composition operation can be applied directly to the syntactic form of those expressions. We will demonstrate the implication of arc- and path-consistency, generalized arc-consistency, and relational arc-consistency on these specialized languages.

3.6.1   Algebraic Constraints

Consider the following unary and binary numeric constraints restricted to the integers and defined over closed intervals:

$$D_x : x \in [1, 10], \quad D_y : y \in [5, 15], \quad R_{xy} : x + y = 10$$

Clearly, x is not arc-consistent relative to y, nor is y arc-consistent relative to x. For example, $x = 10$ is in D_x but there is no value of y in D_y satisfying $x + y = 10$. Enforcing arc-consistency would restrict the domain of x to $x \in [1, 5]$ and the domain of y to $[5, 9]$. In this case, the composition operator in Equation (3.1a) can be expressed as linear elimination; from $x + y = 10$ and $-y \leq -5$ we infer $x \leq 5$ by *summing* the first two expressions.

Now assume that we also have variable z with domain $D_z : z \in [-10, 10]$ and a constraint $R_{yz} : y + z \leq 3$. Clearly, x and z are not path-consistent relative to y since, for example, the pair $x = 1, z = -3$ cannot be consistently extended to a value of y. We can make x, z path-consistent relative to y by adding the constraint $x - z \geq 7$, which is obtained by *summing* $x + y = 10$ and $-y - z \geq -3$ (see also Exercise 17). Again, the composition in Equation (3.1b) can be accomplished by summation that eliminates one variable. This operator is called "linear elimination."

Finally, as we already saw, if we also have nonbinary numeric constraints such as $x + y + z \leq 10$ over nonnegative integer domains, applying generalized arc-consistency yields $x \leq 10, y \leq 10$, and $z \leq 10$. Enforcing relational arc-consistency requires additional constraints such as $x + y \leq 10$ that can be generated by linear elimination, which will be further discussed in Section 8.6.

3.6.2 **Boolean Constraint Propagation**

Consider two clauses:

$$(A \vee \neg B) \text{ and } (B)$$

(A) is equivalent to the proposition that "A is true," and $(\neg B)$ is equivalent to the proposition that "B is false." In this case, B is arc-consistent relative to A, but A is not arc-consistent relative to B. This is because, if A is false, B has to be false, but it is restricted to being true. Arc-consistency is achieved if we add the unary constraint (A), restricting A's domain to be true. In this Boolean domain, the composition operation in Equation (3.1a) takes the form of *resolution*: from $(A \vee \neg B)$ and (B), we can infer (A). If we have, in addition, the clause $B \vee C$, then enforcing path-consistency relative to B requires the additional clause $A \vee C$. This clause can be obtained by resolution over B of the two clauses $(A \vee \neg B)$ and $(B \vee C)$.

Notice that applying generalized arc-consistency to nonbinary clauses will not yield any domain reduction (a unit clause). Relational arc-consistency, however, will require additional clauses to be deduced. Observe that since a domain constraint in CNF theories appears as a unit literal, the relational arc-consistency rule of Equation (3.3) translates to unit resolution, that is, a resolution between a unit clause and an arbitrary clause. Indeed, UNIT-PROPAGATION is an algorithm equivalent to applying the rule in Equation (3.3) until no new clauses can be deduced, at which point the set of clauses will satisfy relational arc-consistency. This yields a cost-effective inference algorithm for CNF theories that runs in linear time. Algorithm UNIT-PROPAGATION is given in Figure 3.16.

THEOREM   Algorithm UNIT-PROPAGATION has a linear time complexity.
3.2

> **Proof** Each unit resolution or unit subsumption operation causes either the elimination of a clause or the shortening of a clause by one. The number of unit resolutions is at most the length of the CNF formula. Therefore, if we have

---

procedure UNIT-PROPAGATION

Input: A CNF theory φ, $d = Q_1, \ldots, Q_n$.

Output: An equivalent theory such that no unit clause
  appears in any nonunit clause.

1. queue = all unit clauses.

2. **while** queue is not empty, do:

3. $T \leftarrow$ next unit clause from Queue.

4.   **for** every clause β containing T or $\neg T$

5.   **if** β contains T delete β (subsumption elimination)

6.   **else**, $\gamma \leftarrow resolve(\beta, T)$,

               if γ, the resolvent, is empty, the theory is unsatisfiable.

7.   **else**, add the resolvent γ to the theory and delete β.

               if γ is a unit clause, add γ to Queue.

8.   **endfor**.

9. **endwhile**.

Figure 3.16 UNIT-PROPAGATION algorithm.

an efficient indexing to access all clauses containing a literal, the argument
follows.   •

3.7 Trees, Bivalued Networks, and Horn Theories

As we have seen, both arc- and path-consistency can sometimes decide inconsistency. For some restricted classes of constraint problems, they are even guaranteed to solve the problem. Such *tractable* classes will be discussed at length in later chapters. At this stage, we will only mention three such cases.

Consider a binary constraint network whose graph is a tree, without cycles. If arc-consistency is enforced on such a tree network, and if no domain becomes empty as a result, then the problem can be shown to be consistent (see Exercise 12).

Next, consider the case of an arbitrary binary constraint network whose domain sizes are bounded to 2 (i.e., $k = 2$). If we apply path-consistency to such a bivalued binary constraint network and no constraint becomes empty, then the network is guaranteed to have a solution. Moreover, a path-consistent bivalued binary network is guaranteed to be minimal (see Exercise 7). An immediate implication of this observation for CNF theories is that if a CNF theory has clauses of length 1 or 2 only, then if we apply resolution (until nothing new can be generated) without deriving the empty clause, the theory is consistent.

Finally, assume a Horn CNF theory, that is, each clause has at most one single positive literal. If we apply unit propagation to such a Horn theory without generating the empty clause, then the theory is satisfiable. We summarize all these three cases in the next theorem.

**THEOREM
3.3**

1. The consistency of binary constraint networks having no cycles can be decided by arc-consistency.

2. The consistency of binary constraint networks with bivalued domains can be decided by path-consistency.

3. The consistency of Horn CNF theories can be decided by unit propagation. •

The above theorem illustrates two types of tractable classes. The first is characterized by the topological properties of the constraint graph (e.g., trees), while the second by restriction on the constraints themselves (bivalued, Horn). These examples will be generalized in Chapters 8, 9 and 11.

3.8 **Summary**

In this chapter we introduced the basic inference algorithms for constraint processing: arc-, path-, and i-consistency. Figure 3.17 demonstrates schematically how arc-, path-, and i-consistency are applied to one, two, or $i - 1$ variables. Arc-consistency applies to subnetworks of size 2, path-consistency to subnetworks of size 3, and i-consistency to subnetworks of size i.

i-bounded consistency algorithms are polynomial (exponential in i) and are not guaranteed to solve the problem. As i increases, the ability of these algorithms to determine consistency also increases. Because consistency-enforcing algorithms infer new constraints, they change the structure of the network. Arc-consistency restricts the domains of variables, path-consistency restricts and add constraints on pairs of variables, and i-consistency enforces constraints of arity $i - 1$. These changes can be reflected in the problem's constraint graph, as depicted in Figure 3.18. We further demonstrated the form of these consistency-enforcing methods for Boolean and numeric constraints. We also extended the basic constraint propagation algorithms to nonbinary constraints via concepts such as generalized arc-consistency, relational arc-consistency, global constraints, and bounds-consistency. In Chapter 8 we will present another class of consistency algorithms that are defined by the constraints themselves.

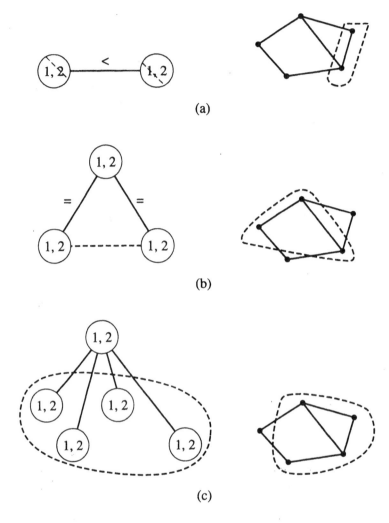

Figure 3.17 The scope of consistency enforcing: (a) arc-consistency, (b) path-consistency, and (c) i-consistency.

3.9 **Bibliographical Notes**

Work on constraint propagation and consistency algorithms was initiated by Waltz (1975), who introduced a constraint propagation algorithm, later called arc-consistency, for three-dimensional cubic drawing interpretations. He demonstrated empirically that for some polyhedral figures, basic propagation algorithms are sufficient to solve these problems. This work was formalized and extended by Montanari

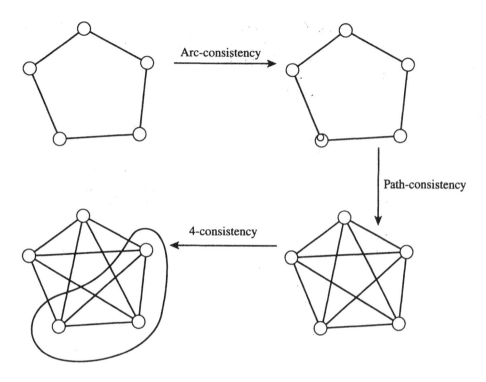

Figure 3.18 Changes in the network graph as a result of arc-consistency, path-consistency, and 4-consistency.

(1974), who also introduced the term "constraint networks." Montanari defined the notion of path-consistency and presented algorithms and analysis. Building upon these two works, Mackworth (1977a) distinguished three properties that characterize local consistency of binary networks (node-, arc-, and path-consistency) and also introduced several algorithms. He introduced AC-1, AC-2, and AC-3 for imposing arc-consistency, and PC-1 and PC-2 for imposing path-consistency. The complexity of these algorithms was subsequently analyzed by Mackworth and Freuder (1985), where they also observed that arc-consistency can solve treelike problems. Mackworth also introduced generalized arc-consistency (also sometimes called hyperarc consistency) for nonbinary constraints (1977b). Freuder (1978) then generalized these notions to k-consistency. Mohr and Henderson (1986) presented optimal algorithms for arc- and path-consistency, called AC-4 and PC-4, both of which were based on Lauriere's earlier work on a language for solving combinatorial problems (Lauriere 1978). Mohr and Henderson's optimal algorithms were generalized for i-consistency in Cooper (1990). It was still observed that in practice the average performance of AC-3 is better than AC-4 (Wallace 1993). Several authors have developed more efficient and refined arc-consistency algorithms for special classes of constraints, such as monotonic and functional constraints (Deville and Van Hentenryck 1991; Deville, Van Hentenryck, and Teng 1992). Subsequent algorithms continue the numbering tradition (AC-5, AC-6, AC-7, PC-5, PC-6, and PC-7). Particularly noteworthy is AC-6 (Bessière and Cordier 1993), which is able to achieve optimal worst-case complexity while avoiding some of the bad average cases of AC-4, making it a serious competitor to both AC-4 and AC-3. Subsequent fine-tuning of AC-3- type algorithms toward being both worst-case optimal and average-case competitive were presented by Bessière and Régin (2001) and Zhang and Yap (2001).

Boolean constraint propagation was described by McAllester (1980, 1990) within the work of truth maintenance systems. Finally, in the context of constraint programming languages (see Chapter 15) the specialized types of constraint propagation algorithms for global constraints were developed for a variety of constraints. Most noteworthy are alldifferent constraints (Régin 1994; van Hoeve 2001), global cardinality constraints (gcc) that generalize the alldifferent constraint (Régin 1996), the cumulative constraint (Aggoun and Beldiceanu 1992; Caseau and Laburthe 1996), and the cycle constraint (Beldiceanu and Contejean 1994). Bounds-consistency was introduced in Puget (1998) and improved for the alldifferent constraint in Mehlhorn and Thiel (2000).

3.10 Exercises

1. Consider a network having eight variables named $1, 2, \ldots, 8$, each having domains $\{1, 2, 3, 4\}$, whose constraints and graph are in Figure 3.19. Find an equivalent arc- and path-consistent network. Is the path-consistent network minimal? Is it globally consistent?

2. Consider the CSP formulation of the zebra problem, where you have 25 variables, divided into clusters where the domains are house numbers (see Exercise 5 in Chapter 2). The constraint graph of a possible formulation is given in Figure 3.20. Is your CSP formulation of the zebra problem arc-consistent? If not, describe an equivalent arc-consistent network. Is it path-consistent?

3. Prove that algorithm AC-1 generates an equivalent arc-consistent network. Prove also that when an empty domain is encountered, the network has no solution.

4. Prove that the time and space complexity of AC-4 is $O(ek^2)$, where e is the number of constraints and k bounds the domain size.

5. Consider a binary network formulation of the crossword puzzle in Figure 1.1, and suppose that we are to fill it with the words from the following list, using each word not more than once:

   • HOSES, LASER, SAILS, SHEET, STEER

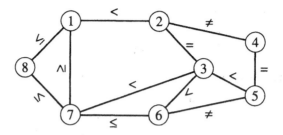

Figure 3.19 A constraint graph.

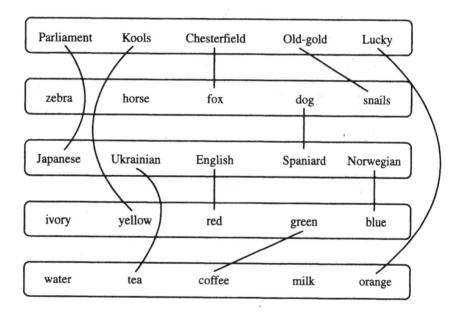

Figure 3.20 Constraint graph of the zebra problem.

- HEEL, HIKE, KEEL, KNOT, LINE
- AFT, ALE, EEL, LEE, TIE

Is the problem arc-consistent? If not, find an equivalent arc-consistent network. Is the network path-consistent? If not, enforce path-consistency.

6. Prove that a minimal network is always path-consistent: any consistent pair of values can be consistently extended by any third variable.

7. Prove that a bivalued, nonempty, path-consistent binary network is consistent. Prove that it is also a minimal network.

8. Is a binary-decomposable network globally consistent? Prove your claim.

9. Implement algorithms AC-3 and AC-4.

   (a) Apply the algorithms to a set of randomly generated binary problems created using the four parameters N, K, C, T, where N is the number of variables, K is the number of values in each domain, T is the tightness of each constraint (the number of allowed pairs divided by the total number of pairs), and C is the number of constraints. For each N, K, we select C pairs of variables uniformly at random, and for each T, we select pairs of values for each constraint randomly as allowed pairs. Which algorithm is better? AC-3 or AC-4?

   (b) Apply AC-3 and AC-4 to the n-queens problem.

10. Consider a graph-coloring problem with three colors having four nodes x_1, x_2, x_3, x_4 where every two nodes are connected. Is the problem arc-consistent? Path-consistent? 4-consistent? If not, enforce strong 4-consistency. Can you make the problem 4-consistent by adding only binary constraints?

11. Let $\mathcal{R}$ be an arbitrary graph 3-coloring problem.

    (a) Discuss what would be the effect of enforcing 2- and 3-consistency on $\mathcal{R}$.
    (b) What would be the effect of enforcing 2-, 3-, 4-, ..., $(k-1)$-, k-, $(k+1)$-consistency on a k-coloring problem?

12. Prove that an arc-consistent binary network that has no cycle is consistent.

13. Derive a worst-case complexity analysis for algorithm PC-2.

14. Read algorithm PC-4 in Mohr and Henderson (1986) and show that the best-case performance of PC-4 is $O(n^3 k^3)$ or $O(n^3 tk)$, where n is the number of variables, k bounds the domain sizes, and t bounds the number of pairs in a binary relation.

15. Show that the two definitions of path-consistency (Definitions 3.3 and 3.4) are equivalent only when the constraint graph is complete.

16. A graph is *transitively closed* iff any two nodes connected by a path are directly connected. Prove that the constraint graph of a path-consistent network is transitively closed.

17. Generate an arc- and path-consistent network equivalent to the network given by

$$D_x : x \in [1, 10], \quad D_y : y \in [5, 15], \quad R_{xy} : x + y = 10$$
$$D_z : z \in [-10, 10], \quad R_{yz} : y + z \le 3$$

18. (Due to J.-C. Régin) Consider the global alldifferent constraints over $\{x_1, \ldots, x_{n/2}\}$ with domains $[0 .. n]$ where the variables of $x_{n/2+1}, x_{n/2+2}$ are $[1 .. 2]$, $x_{n/2+3}, x_{n/2+4}$ have domains $[4 .. 5]$, $x_{n/2+5}, x_{n/2+6}$ have domains $[7 .. 8]$. Make the global constraint bounds-consistent and analyze the complexity of your algorithm.

19. Derive the constraint alldifferent for the speaker problem presented in Section 3.5.2 and make this global constraint arc-consistent.

20. Analyze the complexity of deciding the consistency of binary tree networks, of bivalued binary networks, and of Horn theories.

chapter 4

Directional Consistency

Law is order, and good law is good order.

Aristotle, Politics

How do we explain how people perform so well on tasks that are theoretically intractable? One explanation is to assume that intelligent behavior is actually grounded in approximation methods that are based on idealized, easy-to-solve models. In other words, we assume people intuitively transform hard tasks into a series of more manageable, simple tasks, which, taken together, approximate the original task. Some real-life problems may naturally fall into such easy classes and can thus be solved efficiently. Likewise, some difficult problems may be transformed into simplified versions that are not too distant from the original problems. Following this line of reasoning, one approach in artificial intelligence is to imitate the assumed human reasoning process and find ways to idealize (i.e., simplify) the task environment. These simplifications can then be used to provide either approximate solutions or heuristic advice to guide the search toward an exact solution of the original problem. We will indeed see that although the general constraint satisfaction problem is hard, there are many subclasses of constraint networks that are easy to process (some of which we already saw in Chapter 3.)

In general, a problem class is considered *easy* when it allows a solution in polynomial time. Because of the popularity of backtracking search as the primary problem-solving method for constraint satisfaction problems, a CSP is considered easy if it is backtrack-free, that is, if backtracking search (the focus of Chapters 5 and 6) can solve the problem without encountering any dead-ends. In such a case, a solution is produced in time linear in the size of the problem, as defined by the number of variables and the overall size of the constraints.

As mentioned in Chapter 3, the primary means by which a constraint problem can avoid dead-ends is by making its representation more explicit via *inference*. If a bounded, polynomial-time inference method generates a backtrack-free representation, the whole problem can be solved efficiently. This concept has prompted a theoretical investigation into the level of local consistency that suffices for ensuring a backtrack-free search, leading to topological and constraint properties for which a restricted level of consistency enforcing is sufficient for transforming such networks into backtrack-free representations.

Let's first define the notion of backtrack-free search:

DEFINITION   **(backtrack-free search)**
4.1

A constraint network is backtrack-free relative to a given ordering $d = (x_1, \ldots, x_n)$ if for every $i \leq n$, every partial solution of $(x_1, \ldots, x_i)$ can be consistently extended to include x_{i+1}.   •

The various successful approaches for identifying tractable classes of constraint satisfaction problems can be divided into two main groups. The first is *tractability by restricted structure*, which is based solely on the structure of the constraint graph of the problem, independently of the actual constraint relations. This class will be the focus of the current chapter, as well as Chapters 8 and 9. The second group, *tractability by restricted constraint relations*, or constraint languages that identify classes that are tractable thanks to special properties of the constraint relations, is the focus of Chapter 11.

Tractability due to restricted structure can be reasoned from the topological properties of the constraint graph and its hypergraph. We will start by reviewing relevant graph concepts.

4.1 Graph Concepts: Induced Width

Topological characterization is centered on the graphical parameter known as *induced width*. Given an undirected graph $G = (V, E)$, an *ordered graph* is a pair (G, d), where $V = \{v_1, \ldots, v_n\}$ is the set of nodes, E is a set of arcs over V, and $d = (v_1, \ldots, v_n)$ is an ordering of the nodes. The nodes adjacent to v that precede it in the ordering are called its *parents*. The *width of a node* in an ordered graph is its number of parents. The *width of an ordering d*, denoted $w(d)$, is the maximum width over all nodes. The *width of a graph* is the minimum width over all the orderings of the graph.

EXAMPLE   Figure 4.1 presents a constraint graph G over six nodes, along with three
4.1   orderings of the graph: $d_1 = (F, E, D, C, B, A)$, its reversed ordering $d_2 = (A, B, C, D, E, F)$, and $d_3 = (F, D, C, B, A, E)$. Note that we depict the orderings from bottom to top, so that the first node is at the bottom of the figure and the last node is at the top. The arcs of the graph are depicted by the solid lines. The parents of A along d_1 are $\{B, C, E\}$. The width of A along d_1 is 3, the width of C along d_1 is 1, and the width of A along d_3 is 2. The width of these three orderings are $w(d_1) = 3$, $w(d_2) = 2$, and $w(d_3) = 2$. The width of graph G is 2.   •

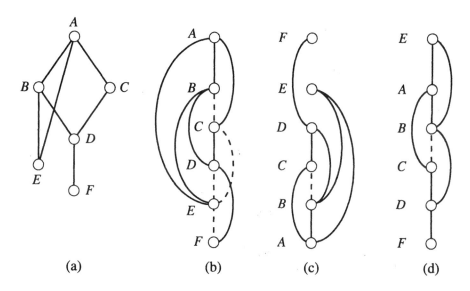

Figure 4.1 (a) Graph G, and three orderings of the graph: (b) $d_1 = (F, E, D, C, B, A)$, (c) $d_2 = (A, B, C, D, E, F)$, and (d) $d_3 = (F, D, C, B, A, E)$. Broken lines indicate edges added in the induced graph of each ordering.

The *induced graph* of an ordered graph (G, d) is an ordered graph (G^*, d) where G^* is obtained from G as follows: The nodes of G are processed from last to first (top to bottom) along d. When a node v is processed, all of its parents are connected. The *induced width of an ordered graph*, (G, d), denoted $w^*(d)$, is the width of the induced ordered graph (G^*, d). The *induced width of a graph*, w^*, is the minimal induced width over all its orderings.

EXAMPLE 4.2   Consider again Figure 4.1. For each ordering d, (G, d) is the graph depicted without the broken edges, while (G^*, d) is the corresponding induced graph that includes the broken edges. We see that the induced width of B along d_1 is 3, and that the overall induced width of this ordered graph is 3. The induced widths of the graph along orderings d_2 and d_3 both remain 2, and, therefore, the induced width of the graph G is 2. •

A rather important observation is that a graph is a tree (has no cycles) if and only if it has a width-1 ordering. The reason a width-1 graph cannot have a cycle is that, for any ordering, at least one node on the cycle would have two parents, thus contradicting the width-1 assumption. And vice versa: if a graph has no cycles, it can always be converted into a rooted directed tree by directing all edges away from a designated root node. In such a directed tree, every node has exactly one node pointing to it—its parent. Therefore, any ordering in which every parent node precedes its child nodes in the rooted tree has a width of 1. Furthermore, given

---

MIN-WIDTH (MW)

Input: A graph $G = (V, E)$, $V = \{v_1, \ldots, v_n\}$.

Output: A min-width ordering of the nodes $d = (v_1, \ldots, v_n)$.

1. **for** $j = n$ to 1 by -1 do
2. $r \leftarrow$ a node in G with smallest degree.
3.   Put r in position j and $G \leftarrow G - r$.
       (Delete from V node r and from E all its adjacent edges)
4. **endfor**

Figure 4.2   The MIN-WIDTH (MW) ordering procedure.

an ordering having a width of 1, its induced ordered graph has no additional arcs, yielding an induced width of 1, as well. In summary, we have the following:

PROPOSITION 4.1   A graph is a tree iff it has induced width of 1.   •

4.1.1   Greedy Algorithms for Finding Induced Widths

Finding a minimum-width ordering of a graph can be accomplished by the greedy algorithm MIN-WIDTH (see Figure 4.2). The algorithm orders variables from last to first as follows: In the first step, a variable with a minimum number of neighbors is selected and put last in the ordering. The variable and all its adjacent edges are then eliminated from the original graph, and selection of the next variable continues recursively with the remaining graph. Ordering d_2 of G in Figure 4.1(c) could have been generated by a min-width ordering.

PROPOSITION 4.2   Algorithm MIN-WIDTH (MW) finds a minimum-width ordering of a graph.

> **Proof**   See Exercise 2.   •

Though finding the min-width ordering of a graph is easy, finding the minimum *induced width* of a graph is hard (NP-complete). Nevertheless, deciding whether there exists an ordering whose induced width is less than a constant k takes $O(n^k)$ time.

A decent greedy algorithm, obtained by a small modification to the MIN-WIDTH algorithm, is the MIN-INDUCED-WIDTH (MIW) algorithm (Figure 4.3). It orders the variables from last to first according to the following procedure: The algorithm selects a variable with minimum degree and places it last in the ordering. The algorithm next connects the node's neighbors in the graph to each other, and only

---

MIN-INDUCED-WIDTH (MIW)

Input: A graph $G = (V, E)$, $V = \{v_1, \ldots, v_n\}$.

Output: An ordering of the nodes $d = (v_1, \ldots, v_n)$.

1. **for** $j = n$ to 1 by -1 do
2. $r \leftarrow$ a node in V with smallest degree.
3.   Put r in position j.
4.   Connect r's neighbors: $E \leftarrow E \cup \{(v_i, v_j) | (v_i, r) \in E, (v_j, r) \in E\}$.
5.   Remove r from the resulting graph: $V \leftarrow V - \{r\}$.

Figure 4.3 The MIN-INDUCED-WIDTH (MIW) procedure.

MIN-FILL (MF)

Input: A graph $G = (V, E)$, $V = \{v_1, \ldots, v_n\}$.

Output: An ordering of the nodes $d = (v_1, \ldots, v_n)$.

1. **for** $j = n$ to 1 by -1 do
2. $r \leftarrow$ a node in V with smallest fill edges for his parents.
3.   Put r in position j.
4.   Connect r's neighbors: $E \leftarrow E \cup \{(v_i, v_j) | (v_i, r) \in E, (v_j, r) \in E\}$.
5.   Remove r from the resulting graph: $V \leftarrow V - \{r\}$.

Figure 4.4 The MIN-FILL (MF) procedure.

then removes the selected node and its adjacent edges from the graph, continuing recursively with the resulting graph. The ordered graph in Figure 4.1(c) could have also been generated by a min-induced-width ordering of G. In this case, it so happens that the algorithm achieves the overall minimum induced width of the graph, w^*. Another variation yields a greedy algorithm known as MIN-FILL. Rather than order the nodes in order of their min-degree, it uses the *min-fill set*, that is, the number of edges needed to be filled so that its parent set is fully connected, as an ordering criterion. This min-fill heuristic, described in Figure 4.4, was demonstrated empirically to be somewhat superior to the MIN-INDUCED-WIDTH algorithm. The ordered graph in Figure 4.1(c) could have been generated by a min-fill ordering of G, while the ordering d_1 or d_3 in parts (a) and (d) could not.

The notions of width and induced width, and their relationships with various graph parameters, have been studied extensively in the past two decades. Here we will focus only on those aspects that are relevant to constraint processing.

4.1.2   **Chordal Graphs**

Computing the induced width for chordal graphs is easy. A graph is *chordal* if every cycle of length at least 4 has a chord, that is, an edge connecting two non-adjacent vertices. For example, G in Figure 4.1(a) is not chordal since the cycle (A, B, D, C, A) does not have a chord. The graph can be made chordal if we add the edge (B, C) or the edge (A, D).

Many difficult graph problems become easy on chordal graphs. For example, finding all the maximal (largest) *cliques* (completely connected subgraphs) in a graph—an NP-complete task on general graphs—is easy for chordal graphs. This task (finding maximal cliques in chordal graphs) is facilitated by using yet another ordering procedure called the *max-cardinality ordering* (Tarjan and Yannakakis 1984). A max-cardinality ordering of a graph orders the vertices from *first to last* according to the following rule: The first node is chosen arbitrarily. From this point on, a node that is connected to a maximal number of already ordered vertices is selected, and so on. (See Figure 4.5.)

A max-cardinality ordering can be used to identify chordal graphs. Namely, a graph is chordal iff in a max-cardinality ordering each vertex and all its parents form a clique. You can thereby enumerate all maximal cliques associated with each vertex (by listing the sets of each vertex and its parents, and then identifying the maximal size of a clique). Notice that there are at most n cliques: each vertex and its parents are one such clique. Consequently, when using a max-cardinality ordering of a chordal graph, the ordered graph is identical to its induced graph, and therefore its width is identical to its induced width. Also:

PROPOSITION 4.3   If G^* is the induced graph of a graph G, along some ordering, then G^* is chordal.

Proof   See Exercise 3.   •

MAX-CARDINALITY (MC)

Input: A graph $G = (V, E)$, $V = \{v_1, \ldots, v_n\}$.

Output: An ordering of the nodes $d = (v_1, \ldots, v_n)$.

1. Place an arbitrary node in position 0.

2. **for** $j = 1$ to n **do**

3. $r \leftarrow$ a node in G that is connected to a largest subset of nodes in positions 1 to $j - 1$, breaking ties arbitrarily.

4. **endfor**

Figure 4.5   The MAX-CARDINALITY (MC) ordering procedure.

EXAMPLE
4.3
We see again that G in Figure 4.1(a) is not chordal since the parents of A are not connected in the max-cardinality ordering in Figure 4.1(d). If we connect B and C, the resulting induced graph is chordal.   •

4.1.3 *k*-Trees

A subclass of chordal graphs is *k-trees*. A *k*-tree is a chordal graph whose maximal cliques are of size $k + 1$, and it can be defined recursively as follows: (1) A complete graph with k vertices is a *k*-tree. (2) A *k*-tree with r vertices can be extended to $r + 1$ vertices by connecting the new vertex to all the vertices in any clique of size k.

k-trees were investigated extensively in the graph-theoretical literature. It was shown, for example, that a graph can be *embedded* in a *k*-tree if and only if it has an induced width $w^* \leq k$ (Arnborg 1985).

4.2 **Directional Local Consistency**

We now return to the primary target of this chapter: determining the amount of inference that can guarantee a backtrack-free solution.

The level of inference applied to a given constraint network can be restricted in a variety of ways. A general approach discussed in Chapter 3 is bounding the number of variables that participate in an inference to yield propagation methods such as arc-consistency or path-consistency. Another orthogonal approach is to restrict inference relative to a given ordering of the variables, in anticipation of subsequent processing by search.

Indeed, securing full arc-consistency, full path-consistency, and full *i*-consistency is sometimes unnecessary if a solution is going to be generated by search along a fixed variable ordering. Consider, for example, the task of applying search on a problem whose ordered constraint graph is given in Figure 4.6. To ensure that the search algorithm encounters no dead-ends when assigning values using ordering $d = (x_1, x_2, x_3, x_4)$, we need only make sure that any assignment to x_1 will have at

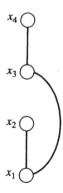

Figure 4.6 An ordered constraint graph.

least one consistent corresponding value in x_2 and x_3, and that, subsequently, any assignment to x_3 will have at least one consistent corresponding value in x_4. This can be achieved by making x_1 arc-consistent relative to x_2 and x_3, and x_3 arc-consistent relative to x_4. We don't need to ensure that x_2 and x_3 are arc-consistent relative to x_1, or that x_4 is arc-consistent relative to x_3. In other words, arc-consistency is required only in the direction to be exploited by the search algorithm.

In this section we develop the idea of *directional consistency*—restricting inference to a given variable ordering. We present algorithms for enforcing varying levels of directional consistency. We will see how graphical properties of the constraint graph can shed light on the design and analysis of such algorithms. We will further show that directional inference leads to a general and complete variable elimination algorithm called ADAPTIVE-CONSISTENCY. In Chapter 8 these ideas are extended to relational consistency.

Since we start with directional arc- and path-consistency that in their simplest form are relevant only to binary constraints, we will initially assume that the networks in question are binary, and then generalize to arbitrary constraints, to include the notions of generalized arc-consistency and relational consistency (in Chapter 8).

4.2.1 Directional Arc-Consistency

DEFINITION 4.2

(directional arc-consistency)

A network is *directional arc-consistent* relative to order $d = (x_1, \ldots, x_n)$ iff every variable x_i is arc-consistent relative to every variable x_j such that $i \leq j$. •

An algorithm DAC for achieving directional arc-consistency along ordering $d = (x_1, \ldots, x_n)$ is given in Figure 4.7. It processes the variables in reverse order of d. When processing x_i, all the binary constraints incident to x_i, R_{ki} such that $k \leq i$, are considered and the corresponding domains D_k of x_k are tightened.

DAC($\mathcal{R}$)

Input: A network $\mathcal{R} = (X, D, C)$, its constraint graph G, and an ordering $d = (x_1, \ldots, x_n)$.

Output: A directional arc-consistent network.

1. **for** $i = n$ to 1 by -1 **do**
2.   **for each** $j < i$ such that $R_{ji} \in \mathcal{R}$, do
3. $D_j \leftarrow D_j \cap \pi_j (R_{ji} \bowtie D_i)$, (this is REVISE($(x_j)$, x_i)).
4. **endfor**

Figure 4.7 Directional arc-consistency (DAC).

**EXAMPLE
4.4**

Assume that the constraints and the domains of the problem in Figure 4.6 are specified below.

$$D_1 = \{red, white, black\}$$
$$D_2 = \{green, white, black\}$$
$$D_3 = \{red, white, blue\}$$
$$D_4 = \{white, blue, black\}$$
$$R_{12} : \ x_1 = x_2$$
$$R_{13} : \ x_1 = x_3$$
$$R_{34} : \ x_3 = x_4$$

Using the ordering $d = (x_1, x_2, x_3, x_4)$, the algorithm processes the variables in the reverse order along the ordered graph in Figure 4.6. Starting with x_4, DAC first revises x_3 relative to x_4, deleting *red* from D_3 (since *red* of x_3 has no match in D_4), yielding $D_3 = \{white, blue\}$. Since x_4 has only this one constraint, processing proceeds with x_3, and the constraint R_{13} is tested to ensure that x_1 is arc-consistent relative to x_3. As a result, *red* and *black* are eliminated from D_1 since they have no equals in the updated domain of D_3. When x_2 is next processed, nothing changes because x_1, with its current domain $D_1 = \{white\}$, is already arc-consistent relative to x_2. The final resulting domains are $D_1 = \{white\}$, $D_2 = \{green, white, black\}$, $D_3 = \{white, blue\}$, $D_4 = \{white, blue, black\}$, yielding a directional arc-consistent network relative to the given ordering.

Is the resulting network also full arc-consistent? Checking the constraint R_{31}, we see a violation of arc-consistency: variable x_3 is not arc-consistent relative to x_1; *blue* in D_3 has no match in D_1. Nevertheless, if we now try to assign values in the forward direction of ordering $d = (x_1, x_2, x_3, x_4)$, we will assign $x_1 = white$ (the only value in x_1's domain), then $x_2 = white$ (the only way to satisfy the equality constraint between x_1 and x_2), and similarly, $x_3 = white$ and $x_4 = white$. We see that despite lack of full arc-consistency a consistent assignment was made to every variable, and that no dead-end was encountered. •

There is a distinct computational advantage to enforcing directional arc-consistency rather than full arc-consistency: each constraint is processed exactly once. Indeed, we have the following:

**PROPOSITION
4.4**

Given a network $\mathcal{R}$, and an ordering of its variables d, algorithm DAC generates a directional arc-consistent network relative to d, with time complexity of $O(ek^2)$, where e is the number of binary constraints (i.e., number of arcs) and k bounds the domain size.

Proof   Because of the processing order, once the arc-consistency of x_i relative to a later x_j is enforced, the domain of x_j will not be revised again. In addition, even if the domain of x_i is subsequently revised (in order to enforce arc-consistency with another, intermediate variable), it can only shrink in size; no new members will be added to the domain of x_i, and therefore the enforced arc-consistency of x_i relative to x_j will be maintained. Since there are e binary constraints, each processed just once, and since the complexity of REVISE is $O(k^2)$, the complexity of DAC is bounded by $O(ek^2)$.   •

Algorithm DAC seems optimal for achieving directional arc-consistency. To merely *verify* directional arc-consistency, each constraint needs to be inspected at least once, requiring $O(ek^2)$ consistency tests.

EXAMPLE 4.5   Let's now examine another constraint network. This time the constraints are between every pair of variables and are all not-equal constraints (R_{ij} : $x_i \neq x_j, i \neq j$), and the domains will all be {*red, blue*}. This network is already full arc-consistent, and so, by definition, it is also directional arc-consistent for any ordering. Therefore, applying DAC in any order will not change the domains of the variables. Does the network's directional arc-consistent standing guarantee a backtrack-free search for a consistent solution? Well, we see that it is possible to make the consistent partial assignment ($\langle x_1, red \rangle, \langle x_2, blue \rangle$). However, there is no assignment to x_3 that satisfies both $R_{23} : x_2 \neq x_3$ and $R_{13} : x_1 \neq x_3$, and therefore a dead-end is encountered. We see that like full arc-consistency, DAC is insufficient to guarantee that every problem will be backtrack-free; higher levels of consistency may be necessary.   •

4.2.2   Directional Path-Consistency

The same principle of restricting inference to a specific ordering can also be applied to path-consistency and to *i*-consistency in general. These consistency properties can be achieved more efficiently relative to one specific ordering than can the corresponding full consistency.

DEFINITION 4.3   **(directional path-consistency)**

A network $\mathcal{R}$ is *directional path-consistent* relative to order $d = (x_1, \dots, x_n)$ iff for every $k \geq i, j$, the pair {x_i, x_j} is path-consistent relative to x_k.   •

EXAMPLE 4.6   Consider again the graph-coloring problem whose ordered constraint graph along $d = (x_1, x_2, x_3, x_4)$, having the domains {*red, blue*}, is depicted in Figure 4.8(a). As we saw in Chapter 3, this network is arc-consistent, but not path-consistent. For example, the (universal) constraint between

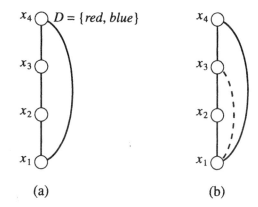

Figure 4.8 (a) An ordered constraint graph and (b) its induced graph.

x_3 and x_1 allows the assignment $x_1 = red$ and $x_3 = blue$, while there is no assignment to x_4 that both satisfies the relevant constraints and agrees with this instantiation. Enforcing full path-consistency on this network requires adding the constraints $R_{13} : x_1 = x_3$ and $R_{24} : x_2 = x_4$. However, for directional path-consistency relative to d only, we only need to add the constraint $x_1 = x_3$. This allows a solution to be assembled along order d without encountering dead-ends.

As implied by the previous example, when the network is not directional path-consistent, directional path-consistency can be enforced. Algorithm DPC (Figure 4.9) achieves strong directional path-consistency (namely, both directional arc-consistency and directional path-consistency). The DPC algorithm processes the variables in reverse order of d. When processing variable x_k, it makes all the constraints R_{ij}, $i, j < k$, path-consistent relative to x_k, and it also enforces arc-consistency on all the variables x_i, $i < k$, relative to x_k. Step 3 of the algorithm is equivalent to REVISE$((x_i), x_k)$, and performs directional arc-consistency. Step 5 is equivalent to REVISE-3$((x_i, x_j), x_k)$: recording or updating the binary constraints inferred by a later third variable.

A new feature of this algorithm is its explicit reference to the underlying constraint graph; the algorithm manages not only the changes made to the constraints but also the changes made to the constraint graph, namely, adding new arcs that correspond to the added new constraints.

THEOREM 4.1   Given a binary network $\mathcal{R}$ and an ordering d, algorithm DPC generates a largest equivalent, strong, directional path-consistent network relative to d. The time and space complexity of DPC is $O(n^3 k^3)$, where n is the number of variables and k bounds the domain sizes.

DPC($\mathcal{R}$)

Input: A binary network $\mathcal{R} = (X, D, C)$ and its constraint graph $G = (V, E)$,
   $d = (x_1, \ldots, x_n)$.

Output: A strong directional path-consistent network and its graph $G' = (V, E')$.

Initialize: $E' \leftarrow E$.

1.   **for** $k = n$ to 1 by -1 **do**
2.   (a) $\forall\ i \leq k$ such that x_i is connected to x_k in the graph, **do**
3. $D_i \leftarrow D_i \cap \pi_i (R_{ik} \bowtie D_k)$ (REVISE $((x_i), x_k)$)
4.   (b) $\forall\ i,j \leq k$ such that $(x_i, x_k), (x_j, x_k) \in E'$ **do**
5. $R_{ij} \leftarrow R_{ij} \cap \pi_{ij} (R_{ik} \bowtie D_k \bowtie R_{kj})$ (REVISE-3$((x_i, x_j), x_k)$)
6. $E' \leftarrow E' \cup (x_i, x_j)$
7.   **endfor**
8.   **return** the revised constraint network $\mathcal{R}$ and $G' = (V, E')$.

Figure 4.9   Directional path-consistency (DPC).

Proof   To prove the above theorem, all we need to show is that when DPC terminates every pair (x_i, x_j) is path-consistent relative to x_k, assuming $i \leq j \leq k$ in d. We know that when x_k was processed (step 5), the pair (x_i, x_j) was made path-consistent relative to x_k. We also know that this condition may be violated only if the domain of x_k is later reduced, or if the two binary constraints R_{ik} and R_{jk} are changed. However, by the time x_k is processed, these two constraints already have their final form determined because they can be affected only when processing variables appearing later than x_k, and those were all processed before x_k. Regarding complexity, the number of times the inner loop (steps 4, 5, and 6) is executed for variable x_i is at most $O(n^2)$ (the number of different pairs of earlier neighbors of variable x_i), and each step is at most $O(k^3)$, yielding an overall complexity of $O(n^3 k^3)$. Since the computation of steps 2 and 3 is completely dominated by the computation of steps 4, 5, and 6, we find that the overall complexity is $O(n^3 k^3)$.   •

4.2.3   **Directional *i*-Consistency**

In the previous two subsections we restricted our attention to binary networks because the constraints recorded were binary or unary only. Generalizing to directional *i*-consistency must account for constraints with larger scopes. We can lift the restriction of binary constraints and apply DAC or DPC to a general network, but we must restrict operation of these two algorithms to their binary subnetworks only.

With this approach, algorithm DAC still yields a directional arc-consistent network, and DPC yields a directional path-consistent network.

DEFINITION **(directional *i*-consistency)**
4.4

A network is *directional i-consistent* relative to order $d = (x_1, \dots, x_n)$ iff every $i - 1$ variables are i-consistent relative to every variable that succeeds them in the ordering. A network is *strong directional i-consistent* if it is directional j-consistent for every $j \leq i$. ●

When extending directional consistency to i-consistency, we consider subnetworks defined on i variables. Given a general constraint network, algorithms for enforcing directional i-consistency can be obtained by generalizing DPC, replacing the composition operator in DPC (step 5) by the REVISE-i operator. A description of the generalized algorithm is given in Figure 4.10. Note that in this algorithm we use a generic REVISE procedure that operates on any size set as its first parameter. If the parent set of a variable has no more than $i - 1$ variables, the procedure records a single constraint over the parent set (steps 2–4). Otherwise, we record a constraint over every subset of size $i - 1$ of the parent set (step 6). Algorithm DIC$_i$ enforces

---

Directional *i*-consistency (DIC$_i$ ($\mathcal{R}$))

Input: A network $\mathcal{R} = (X, D, C)$, its constraint graph $G = (V, E)$, $d = (x_1, \dots, x_n)$.

Output: A strong directional *i*-consistent network along d and its graph $G' = (V, E')$.

Initialize: $E' \leftarrow E$, $C' \leftarrow C$.

1. **for** $j = n$ to 1 by -1 **do**
2.   **let** $P = parents(x_j)$.
3.   **if** $|P| \leq i - 1$ then
4.   Revise (P, x_j)
5.   **else, for** each subset of $i - 1$ variables S, $S \subseteq P$, **do**
6.   Revise (S, x_j)
7.   **endfor**
8. $C' \leftarrow C' \cup$ all generated constraints.
9. $E' \leftarrow E' \cup \{(x_k, x_m) | x_k, x_m \in P\}$ (connect all parents of x_j)
10. **endfor**
11. **return** C' and E'.

Figure 4.10 Algorithm directional *i*-consistency (DIC$_j$).

strong directional i-consistency (see Exercise 9). Its complexity will be addressed later using induced width.

EXAMPLE 4.7   Applying DIC3 to the network $\mathcal{R} = \{R_{xyz}\}$ in Example 3.9, along ordering $d = (x, y, z)$, will add the constraint $R_{xy} = \{(\langle x, 0 \rangle \langle y, 0 \rangle)\}$ in addition to the constraint $R_x = \{(\langle x, 0 \rangle)\}$.   •

Note that DIC3 and DPC are identical if the input network is binary, but they handle ternary constraints differently.

4.2.4   Graph Aspects of Directional Consistency

Neither directional arc-consistency nor full arc-consistency can change the constraint graph. Higher levels of directional consistency do change the constraint graph, although to a lesser extent than their nondirectional counterparts. For example, applying DPC to the network whose ordered graph is given in Figure 4.8(a) results in a network having the graph in Figure 4.8(b), where arc (x_1, x_3) is added. If we apply DPC to the problem in Figure 4.6, no constraint will be added, since the changes are only those caused by arc-consistency. Full path-consistency, on the other hand, will make the constraint graph of Figure 4.6 complete. Before continuing with this section, you should refresh your memory of the graph concepts defined in Section 4.1, if necessary.

During processing by DPC, a variable x_k only affects the constraint between a pair of earlier variables when it is constrained via binary constraints[1] and is thus connected to both earlier variables in the graph. In this case, a new constraint and a corresponding new arc may be added to the graph. Algorithm DPC recursively connects the parents of every two nodes in the ordered constraint graph, thus generating the *induced ordered graph*. Indeed, the graph in Figure 4.8(b) is the induced graph of the ordered graph in Figure 4.8(a).

PROPOSITION 4.5   Let (G, d) be the ordered constraint graph of a binary network $\mathcal{R}$. If *DPC* is applied to $\mathcal{R}$ relative to order d, then the graph of the resulting constraint network is subsumed by the induced graph (G^*, d).

Proof   Let G be the original constraint graph of $\mathcal{R}$, and let G_1 be the constraint graph of the problem generated by applying DPC to $\mathcal{R}$ along d. We prove the above claim by induction on the variables along the reverse ordering of $d = (x_1, \ldots, x_n)$. The induction hypothesis is that all the arcs incident to $x_n, \ldots, x_i$ in G_1 appear also in (G^*, d). The claim is true for x_n (the induction base step), since its connectivity is equivalent in both graphs.

---

1. Remember that, as defined, DPC manipulates only the binary constraints.

Assume that the claim is true for $x_n, \ldots, x_i$, and we will show that it holds also for $i - 1$ (i.e., for $x_n, \ldots, x_{i-1}$). Namely, we will show that if (x_{i-1}, x_j), $j < i - 1$, is an arc in G_1, then it is also in (G^*, d). There are two cases: either x_{i-1} and x_j are connected in G_1 (i.e., they have a binary constraint in $\mathcal{R}$, and therefore they will stay connected in (G^*, d)), or a binary constraint over $\{x_{i-1}, x_j\}$ was added by DPC. In the second case, this new binary constraint was obtained while processing some later variable x_t, $t > i - 1$. Since a constraint over x_{i-1} and x_j is generated by DPC, both x_j and x_{i-1} must be connected to x_t in G_1 and, following the induction hypothesis, each will also be connected to x_t in (G^*, d). Therefore, x_{i-1} and x_j will become connected when generating the induced graph (G^*, d) (i.e., when connecting the parents of x_t). ●

The induced graph and its induced width can be used to refine the worst-case complexity of DPC along d. Since DPC processes only pairs of variables selected from the set of *current* parents in the ordered constraint graph, the number of such pairs can be bounded by the parent set size of each variable, namely, by $w^*(d)$. We conclude the following:

THEOREM 4.2 Given a binary network $\mathcal{R}$ and an ordering d, the complexity of DPC along d is $O((w^*(d))^2 \cdot n \cdot k^3)$, where $w^*(d)$ is the induced width of the ordered constraint graph along d.

Proof Proposition 4.5 asserts that when a variable x is being processed by DPC it is connected to at most $w^*(d)$ parents. Therefore the number of triplets that a variable can share with its parents is $O(w^*(d)^2)$. Since processing each triplet is $O(k^3)$, and since there are n variables altogether, we get the complexity bound claimed above. ●

Consequently, orderings with a small induced width allow DPC to be more efficient. Rather than being governed by cubic complexity, DPC is linear in the number of variables for networks whose constraint graph has bounded induced width.

The complexity of general DIC_i can be bounded using the induced width as well. Given a general network whose constraint scopes are bounded by i, applying DIC_i in any ordering connects the parents of every node in the ordered *primal* constraint graph (restricted to constraints of arity i or less), yielding again its induced graph. We can now extend Proposition 4.5 and Theorem 4.2 to the general i-consistency case.

PROPOSITION 4.6 Given a network $\mathcal{R}$ whose constraint arity is bounded by i, if DIC_i is applied to $\mathcal{R}$ relative to order d, then the primal graph of the resulting constraint network is subsumed by the induced graph (G^*, d).

Proof See Exercise 8. ●

The complexity of the algorithm is determined by the REVISE procedure. If the algorithm records a constraint on a set of size j, its complexity is $O((2k)^j)$. Since the size of the parent set is bounded by $w^*(d)$, and the number of its subsets of size i is bounded by $O((w^*(d))^i)$, we conclude the following:

THEOREM
4.3

Given a general constraint network $\mathcal{R}$ whose constraints' arity is bounded by i, and an ordering d, the complexity of DIC$_i$ along d is $O(n(w^*(d))^i \cdot (2k)^i)$.   •

4.3   Width versus Local Consistency

In Example 4.6, we saw that DPC changed the network so that a solution could be found in a backtrack-free manner. However, it is easy to come up with examples where DPC (or even full path-consistency) would not suffice for making the network backtrack-free. Clearly, it would be highly desirable to have a criterion that could identify, *in advance*, the level of consistency sufficient for generating a backtrack-free representation for a given constraint network. Such a criterion can be provided, based on the induced width of the network's graph. Let's start with the special case of width 1.

4.3.1   Solving Trees: Case of Width 1

In the example graph of Figure 4.6, we saw that directional arc-consistency generated a backtrack-free network. However, it will not generate a backtrack-free network when we add a not-equal constraint between x_2 and x_4 augmenting Example 4.4. Notice also that the graph of Figure 4.6 did not have cycles, although it did once we added the constraint. Indeed these examples illustrate the general characteristics that any arc-consistent tree-structured binary network is backtrack-free for a variety of orderings. Moreover, if a tree network is not arc-consistent, arc-consistency can be enforced. We will use the concept of width to express this relationship between graphs and local consistency. Remember (from Section 4.1) that a graph is a tree iff it has a width-1 ordering.

However, as we observed before, attaining full arc-consistency is not necessary for achieving backtrack-free solutions on trees. For example, if the constraint network in Figure 4.11 is assigned values (by backtrack search) along ordering $d_1 = (x_1, x_2, x_3, x_4, x_5, x_6, x_7)$, we need only make sure that any value assigned to variable x_1 will have at least one consistent value in x_2. Notice that the tree in Figure 4.11, along $d_1 = (x_1, x_2, x_3, x_4, x_5, x_6, x_7)$, has a width of 1, while along the ordering $d_2 = (x_4, x_5, x_6, x_7, x_2, x_3, x_1)$, the width is 2. We can conclude the following.

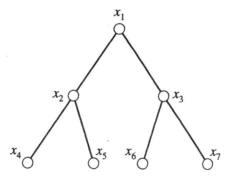

Figure 4.11 A tree network.

TREE-SOLVING

Input: A tree network $T = (X, D, C)$.

Output: A backtrack-free network along an ordering d.

   1.   Generate a width-1 ordering, $d = x_1, \ldots, x_n$ along a rooted tree.

   2.   **let** $x_{p(i)}$ denote the parent of x_i in the rooted ordered tree.

   3.   **for** $i = n$ to 1 **do**

   4.   REVISE $((x_{p(i)}), x_i)$;

   5.   **if** the domain of $x_{p(i)}$ is empty, exit (no solution exists).

   6.   **endfor**

Figure 4.12 TREE-SOLVING algorithm.

THEOREM **(width 1 and directional arc-consistency)**
4.4

Let d be a width-1 ordering of a constraint tree T. If T is directional arc-consistent relative to d, then the network is backtrack-free along d.

Proof Consider a width-1 ordering $d = (x_1, \ldots, x_n)$. Let's assume that a subset of variables $x_1, \ldots, x_i$ was instantiated consistently and that we now need to instantiate x_{i+1}. Since d is a width-1 ordering, there is only one parent variable x_j ($j < i$) that may constrain x_{i+1}. Since x_j is arc-consistent relative to x_{i+1}, it must have a legal value consistent with the current assignment to x_j, and this value provides a consistent extension to the partial solution. •

So, if we have a width-1 ordering of a binary constraint network, we can apply algorithm DAC along that ordering, thus enforcing directional arc-consistency, and then find a backtrack-free solution. The tree-solving algorithm in Figure 4.12 presents these steps explicitly. Step 1 generates a *rooted-directed* tree that corresponds to various width-1 orderings. Steps 3–5 apply directional arc-consistency. Clearly (from Theorem 4.4) the tree-solving algorithm is complete for trees, and its complexity is $O(nk^2)$, the complexity of DAC.

Interestingly enough, if we apply DAC relative to a width-1 order d and *then* apply DAC relative to the reverse order of d, we will achieve full arc-consistency for binary trees in $O(nk^2)$ steps. In contrast, if algorithm AC-3 had been applied to a tree, its worst-case performance is $O(nk^3)$. If algorithm AC-4 is applied to trees, it also has a complexity of $O(nk^2)$, but at the cost of a much more involved implementation.

4.3.2 Solving Width-2 Problems

Can we also make a width-2 network backtrack-free? To some extent, the answer is yes. Let's extend the relationship observed in Theorem 4.4:

THEOREM 4.5   **(width 2 and directional path-consistency)**

If $\mathcal{R}$ is directional arc- and path-consistent along d, and if it also has width 2 along d, then it is backtrack-free along d.

Proof   To ensure that a width-2 ordered constraint network is backtrack-free, it is required that each variable selected for instantiation will have some values in its domain that are consistent with all previously chosen values. Suppose that $x_1, x_2, \ldots, x_k$ were already instantiated. Having a width-2 ordering implies that variable x_{k+1} is constrained with at most two previous variables, x_i and x_j, $i, j \leq k$. Since the problem is directional path-consistent, for any assignment of values to x_i and x_j, there exists a consistent assignment for x_{k+1}. If x_{k+1} is constrained by only one previous variable, directional arc-consistency ensures the existence of a consistent extension to x_{k+1} as well.   ●

If a problem has a width-2 ordering but is *not* directional path-consistent, then we may consider enforcing directional path-consistency by DPC. However, as we saw in Section 4.2.2, applying DPC may add arcs to the problem's graph and increase its width, now its induced width $w^*(d)$, above 2. Therefore, applying DPC to width-2 problems does *not* guarantee a backtrack-free solution, unless $w^*(d) = 2$. A ring is a good example of a problem whose width and induced width is 2. Figure 4.13 shows an ordered ring and its induced graph. Both graphs have a width of 2.

THEOREM 4.6   A binary constraint network $\mathcal{R}$ having an induced width of 2 can be solved in linear time in the number of variables namely in $O(nk^3)$.

Proof   Let d be an ordering of a binary constraint network $\mathcal{R}$ for which $w(d) = w^*(d) = 2$. Such a problem can be solved by first applying DPC

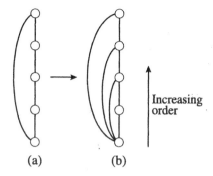

Figure 4.13   An induced width-2 graph. (a) Width-2. (b) Its induced width-2 graph.

relative to d, followed by a backtrack-free value assignment. For problems having an induced width of 2, DPC is bounded by $O(nk^3)$ steps.   •

How easy is it to determine if a graph has an ordering with an induced width of 2? Clearly, enumerating all orderings may be hard. Fortunately there is a linear time algorithm for recognizing such graphs: the MIN-INDUCED-WIDTH (MIW) algorithm described in Section 4.1. Remember, MIW orders the nodes in decreasing order. It selects a node with smallest degree, places it last in the ordering, connects its neighbors, removes it from the graph, and continues recursively. If at anytime a selected node's degree is larger than 2, the graph must have an induced width higher than 2 (see Exercise 14).

4.3.3   Solving Width-*i* Problems

The relationship between graph width and the tractability of the problem can be extended to general nonbinary networks. A problem is *backtrack-free* along d if the *level* of its directional strong consistency along this order is greater than the *width* of the ordered constraint graph.

The intuition behind this claim rests on the fact that when backtracking works along a given ordering, it only tests the consistency of the relevant constraints among past and current variables. If these past constraints already ensure that a *locally consistent* partial solution will remain consistent relative to future variables, a dead-end will not occur. When a future variable is constrained with many past variables (i.e., when it has a high *width*) the required level of local consistency on past variables is higher. Generalizing previous theorems yields the following:

THEOREM   **(Width *i* − 1 and directional *i*-consistency)**
4.7

Given a general network $\mathcal{R}$, if its ordered constraint graph along d has a width of $i - 1$, and if it is also strong directional i-consistent, then $\mathcal{R}$ is *backtrack-free* along d.

Proof Assume a network with width $i - 1$ along d that is strong i-consistent. Then, given any partial solution $\bar{a} = (\langle x_1, a_1 \rangle, \ldots, \langle x_{i-1}, a_{l-1} \rangle)$ and given the next variable x_l, because the width is $i - 1$, x_l is connected to a subset of variables S_i, $S_i \subseteq \{x_1, \ldots, x_l\}$, of at most $i - 1$ variables. Because of strong i-consistency, the partial assignment $\bar{a}$ restricted to S_i, $\bar{a}[S_i]$, which is of length $i - 1$ or less, is consistent with some value of x_l. Therefore, there exists a consistent extension of $\bar{a}$ to x_l.   •

Because most problem instances do not satisfy the desired relationship between width and local consistency, we may want to increase the level of strong directional consistency until it matches the width of the problem. Specifically, if a width-$(i-1)$ problem is not i-consistent, algorithms enforcing directional i-consistency should be applied.

However, as in the case of width 2, algorithm DIC$_i$ augments the network with additional constraints (either binary or nonbinary), yielding a denser constraint graph. The resulting graph is identical to (or subsumed by) the induced ordered graph along the processed ordering. In other words, enforcing directional i-consistency guarantees a backtrack-free solution if the network's *induced* width along the processed order is $i - 1$. This leads us to a simple procedure. Given a problem, select an ordering having a small width $w(d)$, compute its induced width $w^*(d)$, and then apply strong directional $(w^*(d) + 1)$-consistency. The resulting network must satisfy the desired relationship—and is therefore backtrack-free.

4.4 Adaptive Consistency and Bucket Elimination

Algorithm ADAPTIVE-CONSISTENCY (ADC1) in Figure 4.14 implements the adaptive procedure suggested at the end of the previous section. Given an ordering d, ADC1 establishes directional i-consistency recursively, changing levels from node to node to *adapt* to the changing width of nodes at the time of processing. The algorithm is just DIC$_i$, when i is adaptive. This approach works because by the time a node is processed, its final induced width is determined, and the matching level of consistency can be achieved. The procedure may impose new constraints over certain subsets of variables, as well as tighten existing constraints.

Another way to look at adaptive consistency is as a variable elimination algorithm. That is, at each step, one variable and all its related constraints are solved, and a constraint is inferred on all the rest of the participating variables. We next provide an alternative description of adaptive consistency that employs a data structure, called *buckets*, which provides a convenient way for describing variable elimination algorithms, avoiding an explicit reference to the constraint graph. This description highlights important properties of the algorithm and unifies variable elimination algorithms for a variety of tasks. The idea is to associate a bucket with each variable

---

ADAPTIVE-CONSISTENCY (ADC1)

Input: A constraint network $\mathcal{R} = (X, D, C)$, its constraint graph $G = (V, E)$, $d = (x_1, \ldots, x_n)$.

output: A backtrack-free network along d.

Initialize: $C' \leftarrow C, E' \leftarrow E$

1. **for** $j = n$ to 1 **do**

2.   Let $S \leftarrow parents(x_j)$.

3. $R_S \leftarrow$ REVISE (S, x_j) (generate all partial solutions over S that can be extended to x_j).

4. $C' \leftarrow C' \cup R_S$

5. $E' \leftarrow E' \cup \{(x_k, x_r) | x_k, x_r \in parents(x_j)\}$ (connect all parents of x_j)

6. **endfor**

Figure 4.14 Algorithm ADAPTIVE-CONSISTENCY—version 1.

and, given an ordering, to place each constraint into the bucket of the variable that appears latest in its scope. By doing so, we will have collected in the various buckets all the constraints that share the same latest variable in their scope. Subsequently, buckets are processed in reverse order. Processing a bucket means solving a subproblem and recording its solutions as a new constraint. This operation is equivalent to the REVISE procedure. The newly generated constraint is placed in the bucket of *its* latest variable. The *bucket elimination* algorithm adaptive consistency ADC in Figure 4.15 does precisely this. You can verify that the two descriptions of adaptive consistency coincide. From our earlier discussion, we obtain the following:

PROPOSITION 4.7   Let $\mathcal{R}$ be a constraint network and d an ordering for which $w^*(d) = i$. Then (1) applying adaptive consistency is identical to applying strong directional $(i + 1)$-consistency along d, and (2) the constraint graph of the resulting network has width bounded by i.   •

THEOREM 4.8   Given a network $\mathcal{R}$, adaptive consistency (either version ADC1 or ADC) determines the consistency of $\mathcal{R}$, and if the network is consistent, it also generates an equivalent representation $E_d(\mathcal{R})$ that is backtrack-free along d.

Proof   From Proposition 4.7 it follows that ADC generates a width-i problem that is $(i + 1)$-consistent, for some i, and thus, from Proposition 4.7, it follows that the resulting network $E_d(\mathcal{R})$ is backtrack-free along the order of processing.   •

ADAPTIVE-CONSISTENCY (ADC)

Input: A constraint network $\mathcal{R}$, an ordering $d = (x_1,...,x_n)$.

Output: A backtrack-free network, denoted $E_d(\mathcal{R})$, along d, if the empty constraint was not generated. Else, the problem is inconsistent.

1.   Partition constraints into $bucket_1,...,bucket_n$ as follows:

      for $i \leftarrow n$ **downto** 1, put in $bucket_i$ all unplaced constraints mentioning x_i.

2.   **for** $p \leftarrow n$ **downto** 1 **do**

3.   **for** all the constraints $R_{S_1},...,R_{S_j}$ in $bucket_p$ **do**

4. $A \leftarrow \bigcup_{i=1}^{j} S_i - \{x_p\}$

5. $R_A \leftarrow \pi_A(\bowtie_{i=1}^{j} R_{S_i})$

6.   **if** R_A is not the empty relation **then** add R_A to the bucket of the latest variable in scope A,

7.   **else**   exit and return the empty network

8.   **return** $E_d(\mathcal{R}) = (X, D, bucket_1 \cup bucket_2 \cup \cdots \cup bucket_n)$

Figure 4.15 ADAPTIVE-CONSISTENCY as a bucket elimination algorithm.

EXAMPLE 4.8

Consider the graph-coloring problem depicted in Figure 4.16 (domains are numbers). The figure shows a schematic execution of adaptive consistency using the bucket data structure for the two orderings $d_1 = (E, B, C, D, A)$ and $d_2 = (A, B, C, D, E)$. The initial constraints, partitioned into buckets for both orderings, are displayed in the figure to the left of the double bars, while the constraints generated by the algorithm are displayed to the right of the double bars, in their respective buckets. Focusing on ordering d_2, adaptive consistency proceeds from E to A and imposes constraints on the parents of each processed variable, which are those variables appearing in its bucket. Processing the bucket of E, the problem, composed of three constraints in the buckets, is solved and the solution is projected over D, C, B, recording the ternary constraint R_{DCB}, which is placed in the bucket of D. Next, the algorithm processes D's bucket, which contains $D \neq A$ and the new constraint R_{DCB}. Joining these two constraints and projecting out D yields a constraint R_{ACB}, which is placed in the bucket of C, and so on. Processing the buckets along ordering d_1 causes the generation of a different set of constraints. Observe that while only binary constraints are created along order d_1, it is possible that ternary constraints are generated along ordering d_2. Notice also that along ordering d_1 two

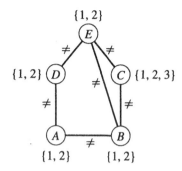

Ordering d_1

Bucket(A): $A \neq D, A \neq B$

Bucket(D): $D \neq E \parallel R_{DB}$

Bucket(C): $C \neq B, C \neq E$

Bucket(B): $B \neq E \parallel R^1_{BE}, R^2_{BE}$

Bucket(E): $\parallel R_E$

Ordering d_2

Bucket(E): $E \neq D, E \neq C, E \neq B$

Bucket(D): $D \neq A \parallel R_{DCB}$

Bucket(C): $C \neq B \parallel R_{ACB}$

Bucket(B): $B \neq E \parallel R_{AB}$

Bucket(A): $\parallel R_A$

Figure 4.16 Execution of ADC along two orderings.

constraints on scope B and E are generated, in the bucket of C and in the bucket of D, denoted R^1_{BE} and R^2_{BE}, respectively, in the figure.

Furthermore, the constraint R^1_{BE} means $B \neq E$ and is displayed—for illustration only—in the bucket of B, since there is already an identical original constraint. Also, the constraint R^2_{BE} is the universal constraint and should therefore not be recorded at all; we chose to display it only to illustrate the general case. When processing along ordering d_2, we only indicated the scheme of the constraints (i.e., their scope), leaving out their explicit description. ●

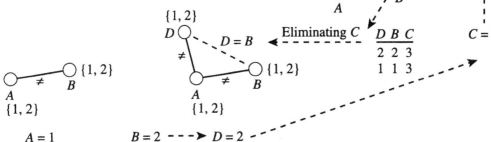

Figure 4.17   A schematic variable elimination and solution generation process is backtrack-free.

An alternative graphical illustration of the algorithm's performance along d_2 is given in Figure 4.17. The figure shows, through the changing graph, how constraints are generated in one ordering, and how a solution is created in the reverse order.

Generating the induced graph along the orderings $d_1 = E, B, C, D, A$ and $d_2 = A, B, C, D, E$ leads to the two graphs in Figure 4.18. The broken arcs are the newly added arcs. The induced width along d_1 and d_2 are 3 and 2, respectively, suggesting different complexity bounds for adaptive consistency. Algorithm ADC is linear in the number of buckets n and in the time to process each bucket. However, since processing each bucket amounts to generating all the solutions of a subproblem, its complexity is exponential in the number of variables appearing in the bucket. The important observation is that the number of variables in a bucket is bounded by

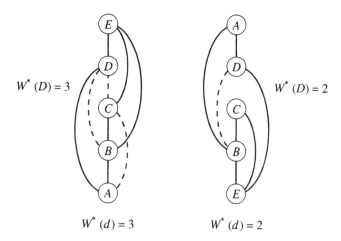

$W^*(D) = 3$ $W^*(D) = 2$

$W^*(d) = 3$ $W^*(d) = 2$

Figure 4.18 The induced width along the orderings: $d_2 = A, B, C, D, E$ and $d_1 = E, B, C, D, A$.

the number of parents of the corresponding variable in the induced ordered graph, namely, by the induced width.

THEOREM 4.9 The time and space complexity of ADAPTIVE-CONSISTENCY is $O(n \cdot (2k)^{w*+1})$ and $O(n \cdot k^{w*})$, respectively, where n is the number of variables, k bounds the domain size, and $w*$ is the induced width along the order of processing. When r bounds the number of constraints, the complexity can be bounded by $O(rk^{w^*+1})$.

Proof The number of constraints (relations) in each bucket will increase to at most 2^{w^*+1} relations because there are at most $w^* + 1$ variables in a bucket. Therefore testing that many constraints over all $O((k)^{w^*+1})$ tuples yields the overall complexity of $O(n \cdot (2k)^{w^*+1})$. Alternatively, since the total number of function input and those generated is bounded by $2r$, and since the computation in a bucket is $O(r_i k^{w^*+1})$, where r_i is the number of functions in a bucket, the total over-all buckets is $O(rk^{w^*+1})$. •

The analysis in this chapter yields a class of tractable problems based on the induced width of the constraint graph. Problems having bounded induced width $(w^* \leq b)$ for some constant b can be solved in polynomial time. In particular, when applied to trees, ADC coincides with DAC (directional arc-consistency), as demonstrated in Figure 4.19. Since the graph is cycle-free, when ordered along $d = (A, B, C, D, E, F, G)$, its width and induced width are 1. Indeed, as demonstrated by the schematic execution along d in Figure 4.19, ADC generates only unary relationships.

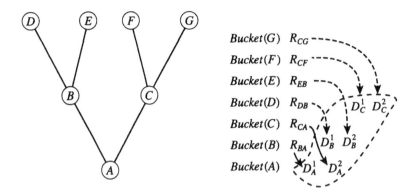

Figure 4.19 Schematic execution of ADAPTIVE-CONSISTENCY on a tree network. D_X denotes unary constraints over X.

Although finding the induced width of a graph is hard, deciding if the width is less than a constant b can be done in polynomial time. Consequently, w^* yields a characterization of a subclass of constraint networks that is tractable. In summary, we have the following:

THEOREM   **(w*-based tractability)**
4.10

The class of constraint problems whose induced width is bounded by a constant b is solvable in polynomial time and space.   •

ADAPTIVE-CONSISTENCY should be evaluated not merely as a procedure for deciding consistency, but also as a compilation algorithm since it transforms the constraint problem into an equivalent network from which *every* solution can be assembled in linear time. Therefore, when the output network can be substantially compacted, ADC may be cost-effective for compilation, even if it takes substantial time to generate the compiled network. However, when the worst-case space complexity reflects the actual output network, the value of adaptive consistency—both as a one-time solution process and as a compilation algorithm—is governed by the same induced-width parameter.

4.5 Summary

This chapter introduced the notion of bounded directional consistency algorithms such as directional arc-, path-, and i-consistency. These are incomplete inference algorithms that can sometimes decide inconsistency and that are designed as preprocessing algorithms to be used before backtracking search. As we'll see in the next chapter, such algorithms can also be interleaved with search. We also presented a relationship between induced width and consistency levels that guarantees a backtrack-free solution: if the problem has width i and it is $(i + 1)$-consistent, then it is backtrack-free. This condition yields the identification of tractable problem classes based on the induced width: if a problem has induced width b, then it can be made backtrack-free by $\text{DIC}_{(b+1)}$, which coincides with adaptive consistency.

While finding the induced width of a problem is NP-complete, determining if the induced width of a graph is less than a constant b can be done in polynomial time, exponential in b (Arnborg 1985), and therefore the induced width indeed identifies tractability classes for constraint satisfaction problems. In particular, trees and problems having induced width 2 can be solved linearly. Finally, the inference algorithm ADAPTIVE-CONSISTENCY (ADC) was shown to make any problem backtrack-free relative to a given variable ordering. It is described as a variable elimination algorithm using the bucket data structure.

The chapter also provides a background section to graph concepts such as width and induced width. Related graph concepts (e.g., tree width) will be presented in Chapter 9. Chapter 8 extends algorithms appearing in this chapter to the more general consistency notion of relational consistency.

4.6 Bibliographical Notes

The fundamental relationship between width and consistency level that guarantees a backtrack-free solution was introduced by Freuder (1982). This relationship was extended by Dechter and Pearl (1987b) to the more restricted concept of directional consistency. It also led to algorithm ADAPTIVE-CONSISTENCY and to the identification of the induced width as the principal graph parameter that controls the algorithms's complexity. A similar elimination algorithm was introduced earlier by Seidel (1981). It was observed that these algorithms belong to the class of dynamic programming algorithms as presented in Bertele and Brioschi (1972). In Dechter and Pearl (1989), the connection between ADAPTIVE-CONSISTENCY and tree-clustering algorithms was made explicit, as will be shown in Chapter 9.

The analysis of the role of graph-based parameters in the complexity of various variable elimination algorithms, and the connection between tree width, induced width, hypertrees, and join-trees was observed independently in the areas of relational databases (Maier 1983), dynamic programming (Bertele and Brioschi 1972), and graph theory (Arnborg 1985; Corneil, Arnborg, and Proskourowski 1987; Arnborg and Proskourowski 1989).

In their book on nonserial dynamic programming, Bertele and Brioschi (1972) show the dependence of variable elimination algorithms for solving optimization tasks on a graph parameter (which they called "dimension" and what we call "induced width"). They suggest several greedy heuristics, including the MIN-INDUCED-WIDTH (not under this name) ordering, and show that it is complete for graphs having an induced width of 2. Montanari (1974) also observes that series-parallel binary constraint networks are tractable, a class that is identical to networks having an induced width of 2. In the field of relational databases the concept of join-tree was defined and observed as a desired representation. The connection between join-trees and chordal graphs was identified (Beeri et al. 1983), and the max-cardinality order was shown to be an identifier of chordal graphs by Tarjan and Yannakakis (1984). The practical value of the min-fill heuristic has been experimentally shown to produce elimination orders with small induced width by Kjaerulff, (1990, 1992).

Finally an extensive analysis of related concepts defined over hypertrees and the notion of tree width, and their connection with a variety of graph properties, were comprehensively analyzed in several papers by Arnborg and his colleagues (Arnborg 1985; Corneil, Arnborg, and Proskourowski 1987; Arnbourg and Proskourowski 1989). In particular, Arnborg proved that finding the tree width of an arbitrary graph is NP-complete. Nevertheless, deciding whether there exists an ordering whose induced width is less than a constant b takes $O(n^b)$ time. A more recent analysis is given by Bodlaender (1997). Approximation algorithms with some good guarantees have been and continue to be developed (Bar-Yehuda, Becker, and Geiger 1999; Shoiket and Geiger 1997).

4.7 **Exercises**

1. (*) Show that it takes $O(n^b)$ time to decide whether a graph G has an ordering whose induced width is less than a constant b.[2]

2. Prove that algorithm MIN-WIDTH achieves min-width ordering of a graph.

3. Let (G^*, d) be an ordered induced graph. Prove that G^* is chordal.

4. Prove that if you apply arc-consistency on a tree, from leaves to root and back, you get an arc-consistent network.

5. Prove that the tree-solving algorithm in Figure 4.12 is optimal.

6. Generate a directional path-consistent 4-queens problem along the columns ordered from left to right.

7. Consider the graph in Figure 4.20.

   (a) What is the induced width of the graph? Provide an ordering having minimum induced width.

   (b) Assume that the graph expresses a binary constraint network with some arbitrary constraints (e.g., not-equal). Provide a complexity bound using

---

2. An asterisk (*) indicates a relatively difficult problem.

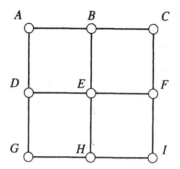

Figure 4.20 Grid with nine nodes.

the induced width for applying algorithm DPC along the optimal induced-width ordering of this problem.

(c) Can algorithm DPC always determine consistency of every constraint problem having an $n \times n$ grid constraint graph?

8. Prove Proposition 4.6.

9. Prove that algorithm DIC$_i$ generates a strong directional i-consistent network.

10. Consider 2-CNF formulas (conjunction of clauses of length 2).

(a) Describe a DAC-type algorithm for enforcing directional arc-consistency of 2-CNF formulas using resolution.

(b) Describe a DPC-type algorithm for enforcing directional path-consistency on 2-CNFs using resolution.

11. Consider the graph-coloring problem given in Figure 4.21. The constraints are not-equal constraints and the domains are indicated inside the nodes in the graph.

(a) Generate a directional strong path-consistent network for this problem.

(b) Generate a backtrack-free problem using adaptive consistency.

(c) Find a solution to the problem.

12. Consider the crossword puzzle in Figure 4.22.

(a) Model the problem as a binary CSP with the words as variables. Draw its constraint graph.

(b) Generate a min-induced-width and max-cardinality ordering of the constraint graph. Generate the induced graph along these orderings. What is the w^* of this problem?

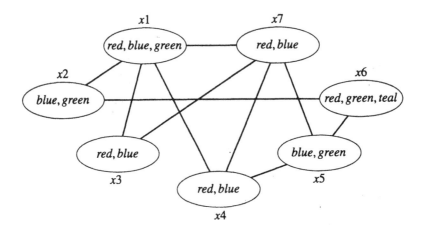

Figure 4.21 A coloring problem.

1		2		3

|4| |5|

|6| |7|

|8|

Word list

aft	laser
ale	lee
eel	line
heel	sails
hike	sheet
hoses	steer
keel	tie
knot	

Figure 4.22 A crossword puzzle.

(c) What level of directional i-consistency is guaranteed to generate a backtrack-free representation for the ordered graphs that you picked, assuming you know nothing about the constraints themselves?

(d) Using the min-induced-width ordering, show the constraints that will be recorded for this problem when applying

   i. directional arc-consistency

   ii. directional path-consistency

iii. adaptive consistency (in this case, show the constraint subsets generated for all buckets, and also the actual constraints generated when processing the first three buckets)

13. Consider the crypto-arithmetic problem TA + DB = GBA when using the formulation of the problem with carries.

    (a) Draw the primal constraint graph of the problem.
    (b) Find an ordering of the variables using the MIN-INDUCED-WIDTH and MIN-FILL algorithms. What is the width of the orderings you generated? Compute the induced graph and the induced width of the orderings generated.
    (c) Hand-simulate algorithm ADAPTIVE-CONSISTENCY on the ordering you created in (b). First describe the schemes of the initial partitioning into buckets, then show how new relations are created. Describe only the scopes of the relations.
    (d) Bound the complexity of the algorithm on the ordering of your choice.
    (e) Code algorithm ADAPTIVE-CONSISTENCY and apply it to this problem.

14. Prove that the MIW algorithm (Figure 4.3) can decide if a graph has an induced width of 2.

chapter 5

General Search Strategies: Look-Ahead

> Who is wise? One who foresees what is coming.
>
> *Talmud: Tamid* 32a

No matter how much we *reason* about a problem, after some consideration we are left with choices, and the only way to proceed is *trial and error* or *guessing and testing* (if the guess is consistent with previous choices and how it affects future choices). That is, we must search the space of possible choices. So, if we have 12 guests for dinner, we may have already determined the seats of the host and hostess, and that Jill, who will help with serving, must sit next to the hostess. And we know that Jill's ex-husband must not sit next to her nor face her. So who will sit next to Jill? We have 8 possible guests. Let's choose one arbitrarily and see how it plays out with the rest of the constraints.

Indeed, most CSP algorithms employ either search or deduction principles; more sophisticated algorithms often combine both. The term *search* characterizes a large category of algorithms that solve problems by guessing the next operation to perform, sometimes with the aid of a heuristic. A good guess results in a new state that is nearer to the goal. If the operation does not result in progress toward the goal (this may not be apparent until later in the search), then the step can be retracted and another operation can be tried.

For CSPs, search is epitomized by the backtracking algorithm. Backtracking search for CSPs extends a current partial solution by assigning values to variables. Starting with the first variable, the algorithm assigns a provisional value to each variable in turn, making sure that each assigned value is consistent with values assigned thus far before proceeding to the next variable. When the algorithm encounters a variable for which no domain value is consistent with previous assignments, a *dead-end* occurs. At this point, *backtracking* takes place; that is, the value assigned to the variable immediately preceding the dead-end variable is changed—if possible—and the search continues. The algorithm halts either when the required number of solutions has been found or when it can be concluded that no solution, or no more solutions, exist. Backtracking requires only linear space, but in the worst case it requires time exponential in the number of variables.

Much of the work in constraint satisfaction during the last decade has been devoted to improving the performance of backtracking search. The performance of backtracking can be improved by reducing the size of its *explored* search space, which is determined both by the size of the *underlying* search space and by the algorithm's control strategy. The size of the underlying search space depends on the level of local consistency possessed by the problem, and on the order of variable instantiation. Using these factors, two types of improvement procedures have emerged: those that bound the size of the underlying search space and are employed *before* performing the search, and those used dynamically *during* the search that decide which parts of the search space will not be visited. Commonly used preprocessing techniques are arc- and path-consistency algorithms, as well as heuristic approaches that determine the variable ordering.

For the remainder of this chapter, we will take a closer look at search spaces for CSPs, at backtracking in general, and at look-ahead schemes that improve basic backtracking. Look-back improvement schemes will be covered in Chapter 6.

5.1 The State Space Search

A *state space* is generally defined by four elements: a set S of states, a set O of operators that map states to states, an initial state $s_0 \in S$, and a set $S_g \subseteq S$ of goal states. The fundamental task is to find a solution—a sequence of operators that transforms the initial state into a goal state. The state space can be effectively represented by a directed *search graph*, where each node represents a state and where a directed arc from s_i to s_j means that there is an operator transforming s_i into s_j. Terminal or leaf nodes are nodes lacking outwardly directed arcs. Goal nodes represent solutions, and nongoal terminal nodes represent dead-ends. Any search algorithm for finding a solution can thus be understood as a traversal algorithm looking for a solution path in a search graph. For details about state spaces and general search algorithms, see Nillson (1980) and Pearl (1984).

Search algorithms for CSPs can be viewed as traversing a state space graph whose nodes (the states) are consistent partial instantiations and whose arcs represent operators that take a partial solution $(\langle x_1, a_1 \rangle, \ldots, \langle x_j, a_j \rangle)$, $1 \leq j \leq n$, and augment it with an instantiation of an additional variable that does not conflict with prior assignments, yielding $(\langle x_1, a_1 \rangle, \ldots, \langle x_j, a_j \rangle, \langle x_{j+1}, a_{j+1} \rangle)$. The *initial state* is the empty instantiation, and *goal states* are full solutions. Variables are processed in some order, which may be either specified prior to search or determined dynamically during search. To demonstrate concepts of search space we use a simple and small problem example so that the visual depiction of the search space stays feasible.

**EXAMPLE
5.1**

Consider a constraint network $\mathcal{R}$ having four variables x, y, l, z with domains $D_x = \{2, 3, 4\}$, $D_y = \{2, 3, 4\}$, $D_l = \{2, 5, 6\}$, and $D_z = \{2, 3, 5\}$. There is a constraint between z and each of the other variables. These constraints require that the value assigned to z evenly divides the values assigned to x, y, and l. The constraint graph of this problem is depicted in Figure 5.1(a). State space graphs for the problem along the orderings $d_1 = (z, x, y, l)$ and $d_2 = (x, y, l, z)$ are given in Figure 5.1(b) and (c). Filled nodes in Figure 5.1(b) and (c) denote legal states. Light-colored ovals denote goal states, black ovals denote intermediary states, and black boxes denote dead-ends. The hollow boxes connected by broken lines represent illegal states that correspond to failed instantiation attempts. These illegal states are sometimes depicted in the search graph because they express problem-solving activity. (In fact, some search space definitions include these leaf nodes as legal states in the search space.) •

Next, we look at two factors that contribute to the size of a search space: variable ordering and consistency level.

5.1.1 Variable Ordering

As illustrated in Figure 5.1(b) and (c), a constraint network may have different search spaces, depending on the variable ordering. The search graph for ordering d_1 includes 20 legal states, whereas the search graph for ordering d_2 includes 48 legal states. Since the search space includes all solutions, one way to assess whether its size is excessive is by counting the number of dead-end leaves. Ordering d_1, for instance, renders a search graph with only one dead-end leaf (a black box), while the search graph for ordering d_2 has 18 dead-end leaves.

When variable ordering is unrestricted, the ordering of the variables is left to the search algorithm rather than fixed in advance, and the underlying search space includes all possible orderings of variables. Because of its large size, the unordered search space may seem undesirable and appear unable to effectively bound the search. Nevertheless, as we shall see, its flexibility frequently leads to a comparatively small *explored* graph.

5.1.2 Consistency Level

The second factor affecting the search space of a CSP is the level of local consistency, which shrinks the search space as we change the representation of a problem to an equivalent but tighter set of constraints.

**EXAMPLE
5.2**

Consider again the constraint network in Example 5.1. As given, the network is not arc-consistent. The value 5 of z, for instance, does not

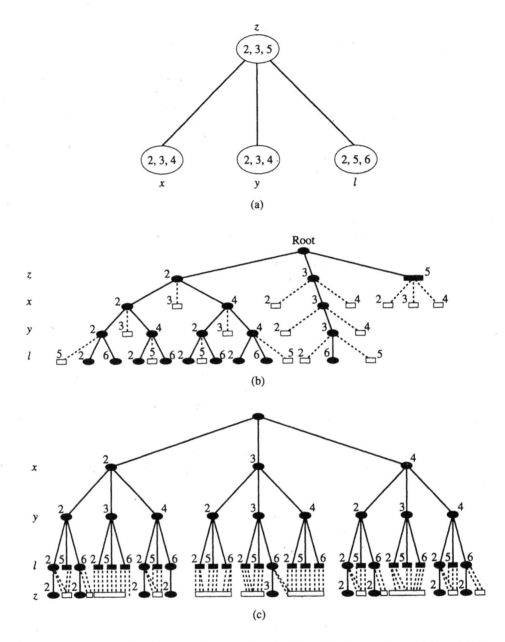

Figure 5.1 (a) A constraint graph, (b) its search space along ordering $d_1 = (z, x, y, l)$, and (c) its search space along ordering $d_2 = (x, y, l, z)$. Hollow nodes and bars in the search space graphs represent illegal states that may be considered, but will be rejected. Numbers next to the nodes represent value assignments.

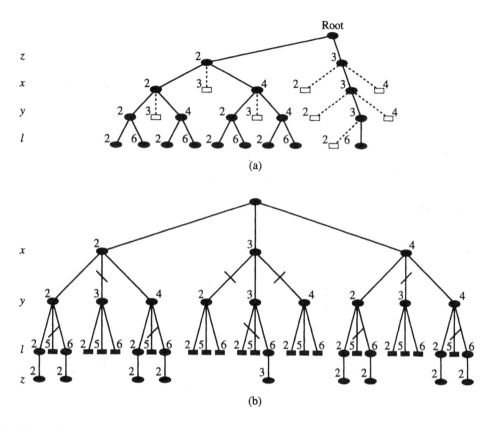

Figure 5.2 (a) Search space for Example 5.1 with ordering d_1 after arc-consistency. (b) Search space for ordering d_2 with reduction effects from enforcing path-consistency marked with slashes.

evenly divide any of x's values. Applying arc-consistency to the network would result in the deletion of the value 5 from the domains of z and l. Consequently, in the resulting arc-consistent network the search space along ordering d_1 will no longer include the dead-end at node $z = 5$, which emanates from the root in Figure 5.1(b). The new search space is shown in Figure 5.2(a). Similarly, enforcing arc-consistency would eliminate nine dead-end leaves (all corresponding to removing $\langle l, 5 \rangle$) from the search space along ordering d_2. The network, as given, is also not path-consistent. For instance, the assignment $(\langle x, 2 \rangle, \langle y, 3 \rangle)$ is consistent, but cannot be extended to any value of z. To enforce path-consistency, we introduce a collection of binary constraints and we get a path-consistent network $\mathcal{R}'$, which includes the following set of constraints:

$$R'_{zx} = \{(2,2), (2,4), (3,3)\}$$
$$R'_{zy} = \{(2,2), (2,4), (3,3)\}$$

$$R'_{zl} = \{(2,2),(2,6),(3,6)\}$$
$$R'_{xy} = \{(2,2),(2,4),(4,2),(4,4),(3,3)\}$$
$$R'_{xl} = \{(2,2),(2,6),(4,2),(4,6),(3,6)\}$$
$$R'_{yl} = \{(2,2),(2,6),(4,2),(4,6),(3,6)\}$$

The search graphs of $\mathcal{R}'$ and $\mathcal{R}$ along ordering d_2 are compared in Figure 5.2(b). Note the amount of pruning of the search space (indicated by slash marks across the pruned branches) that results from tightening the representation.   •

THEOREM 5.1   Let $\mathcal{R}'$ be a tighter network than $\mathcal{R}$, where both represent the same set of solutions. For any ordering d, any path appearing in the search graph derived from $\mathcal{R}'$ also appears in the search graph derived from $\mathcal{R}$.   •

The above discussion suggests that you should make the representation of a problem as explicit as possible by inference before searching for a solution. However, too much thought process in the form of local consistency algorithm is costly, and its cost may not always be offset by the smaller search space. Tighter representations normally include many more explicit constraints than looser ones and may require many additional constraint checks (each testing if a given assignment satisfies a single constraint). If the constraints are binary, we will never have more than $O(n)$ consistency checks per state generation. However, in the general case, the number of constraints may be very large, as high as $O(n^{r-1})$ when r bounds the constraints' arity.

EXAMPLE 5.3   To observe the trade-off associated with preprocessing by path-consistency, let's continue Example 5.2. When generating the search space for $\mathcal{R}$ along ordering d_1, exactly one constraint is tested for each new node generated. In contrast, when using $\mathcal{R}'$, which has an explicit constraint for every pair of variables, each node generated at level 1 of the search tree requires one constraint check; at level 2 each node requires two constraint checks; and three checks are required for each node generated at level 3. Overall, using ordering d_1, fewer constraint tests, around 20, are performed when generating the whole search tree for R, while many more constraint checks, around 40, are required for $\mathcal{R}'$. When generating the search graph for $\mathcal{R}$ along ordering d_2 (Figure 5.2(b)), on the other hand, the first three levels of the tree require no constraint checks (there are no explicit constraints between variables x, y, l), but generating the fourth level in the search tree may require as many as three constraint checks per node, yielding between 45 and 81 constraint tests depending on the order of constraint testing. When using $\mathcal{R}'$ along ordering d_2, constraint checks are performed in each of the first three levels in the tree (one per node in the first level, two per node in the second, three per node in the third). This search graph has only nine nodes at level 4, each requiring three tests. Thus, for ordering d_2, enforcing path-consistency pays off: the maximum number of required tests is higher, around 80, before enforcing path-consistency, whereas afterwards, it is reduced considerably, to about 50. •

Finally, observe that after the application of arc-consistency, the search space along ordering d_1 in Figure 5.2(a) contains solution paths only. This is an extremely desirable state of affairs since any depth-first search of such a space is now guaranteed to find a solution in linear time (provided that the cost of state generation is bounded). Next, we redefine this *backtrack-free* search space.

DEFINITION **(backtrack-free network)**
5.1
A network R is said to be *backtrack-free* along ordering d if every leaf node in the corresponding search graph is a solution. •

Let's refresh our memory on relevant notation. We denote by $\vec{a}_i$ the subtuple of consecutive values $(a_1, \ldots, a_i)$ for a given ordering of the variables $x_1, \ldots, x_i$.

5.2 **Backtracking**

The BACKTRACKING algorithm traverses the state space of partial instantiations in a depth-first manner. Backtracking has two phases. The first is a forward phase during which the variables are selected in sequence, and a current partial solution is extended by assigning a consistent value, if one exists, for the next variable. The second phase is a backward one in which, when no consistent solution exists for the current variable, the algorithm returns to the previous variable assigned. Figure 5.3 describes a basic backtracking algorithm. The BACKTRACKING procedure employs a series of mutable value domains D_i', where D_i' holds the subset of D_i that has not yet been examined under the current partial instantiation of earlier variables.

EXAMPLE Consider the graph-coloring problem in Figure 5.4. Assume a backtrack-
5.4 ing search for a solution using two possible orderings: $d_1 = x_1, x_2, x_3, x_4,$ x_5, x_6, x_7 and $d_2 = x_1, x_7, x_4, x_5, x_6, x_3, x_2$. The search graphs along orderings d_1 and d_2, as well as those portions explicated by backtracking from left to right, are depicted in Figure 5.5(a) and (b), respectively. Only legal states, namely, partial solutions, are depicted in the figure. •

In its description, BACKTRACKING repeatedly calls the SELECT-VALUE subprocedure to find a value for the current variable, x_i, that is consistent with the current partial instantiation, $\vec{a}_{i-1}$. This subprocedure describes the work associated with generating the next node in the search space. SELECT-VALUE, in turn, relies on the CONSISTENT

---

procedure BACKTRACKING

Input: A constraint network $\mathcal{R} = (X, D, C)$.

Output: Either a solution, or notification that the network is inconsistent.

   $i \leftarrow 1$ (initialize variable counter)

   $D'_i \leftarrow D_i$ (copy domain)

   while $1 \leq i \leq n$

      instantiate $x_i \leftarrow$ SELECT-VALUE

      if x_i is null   (no value was returned)

         $i \leftarrow i - 1$ (backtrack)

      else

         $i \leftarrow i + 1$ (step forward)

         $D'_i \leftarrow D_i$

   end while

   if $i = 0$

      return "inconsistent"

   else

      return instantiated values of $\{x_1, \ldots, x_n\}$

end procedure

subprocedure SELECT-VALUE   (return a value in D'_i consistent with $\vec{a}_{i-1}$)

   while D'_i is not empty

      select an arbitrary element $a \in D'_i$, and remove a from D'_i

      if CONSISTENT $(\vec{a}_{i-1}, x_i = a)$

         return a

   end while

   return null   (no consistent value)

end procedure

Figure 5.3 The BACKTRACKING algorithm.

subprocedure, which returns *true* only if the current partial solution is consistent with the candidate assignment to the next variable. If SELECT-VALUE succeeds in finding a value, BACKTRACKING proceeds to the next variable, x_{i+1}. If SELECT-VALUE cannot find a consistent value for x_i, a *dead-end* occurs and BACKTRACKING looks for a new value for the previous variable, x_{i-1}. The algorithm terminates when all

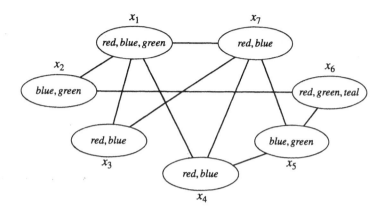

Figure 5.4 A coloring problem with variables $(x_1, x_2, \ldots, x_7)$. The domain of each variable is written inside the corresponding node. Each arc represents the constraint that the two variables it connects must be assigned different colors.

variables have consistent assignments, or when it has proven that all values of x_1 cannot lead to a solution, and thus that the problem is unsolvable. Our presentation of BACKTRACKING stops after a single solution has been found, but it could be easily modified to return all or a desired number of solutions.

The SELECT-VALUE and CONSISTENT subprocedures are separated from the main BACKTRACKING routine for clarity. (Both have access to the local variables and parameters of the main procedure.) For simplicity's sake, our examples involve binary constraints, but the description is completely general. The CONSISTENT subprocedure handles general binary and nonbinary constraints; its implementation, which is not specified, depends on how constraints are represented by the computer program. Next, we analyze its complexity.

5.2.1 Complexity of Extending a Partial Solution

We can determine the complexities of CONSISTENT and SELECT-VALUE by conceptualizing the constraints as stored in tables. Let e be the number of constraints in the problem, and let t be the maximum number of tuples in a constraint. Let k be the maximum size of any domain in D. If the maximum constraint arity is r, then $t \leq k^r$. The constraints can be organized to permit finding a tuple of a given constraint in worst-case logarithmic time: $\log t \leq r \log k \leq n \log k$. Since a variable may participate in up to e constraints, the worst-case time complexity of CONSISTENT is $O(e \log t)$, which is also bounded by $O(e r \log k)$. SELECT-VALUE may invoke CONSISTENT up to k times so the worst-case time complexity of SELECT-VALUE is $O(e k r \log k)$, or $O(e k \log t)$.

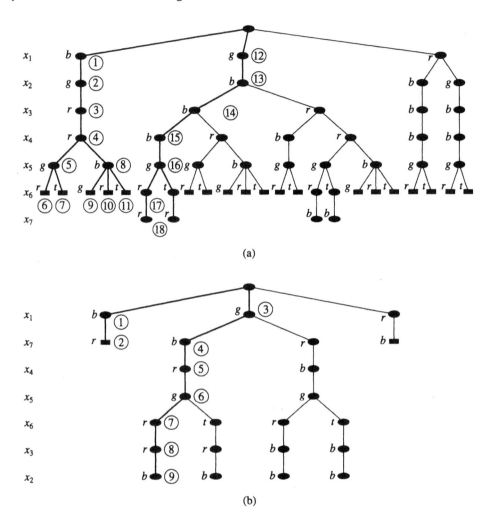

Figure 5.5   Backtracking search for the orderings (a) $d_1 = x_1, x_2, x_3, x_4, x_5, x_6, x_7$ and (b) $d_2 = x_1, x_7,$ x_4, x_5, x_6, x_3, x_2 on the example instance in Figure 5.4. Intermediate states are indicated by filled ovals, dead-ends by filled rectangles, and solutions by gray ovals. The colors are considered in order (*blue, green, red, teal*),[1] and are denoted by first letters. Bold lines represent the portion of the search space explored by backtracking when stopping after the first solution. Circled numbers indicate the order in which nodes are expanded.

In general we will assume that when given a partial solution $\vec{a}_i$, CONSISTENT tests the consistency of a specific assignment to x_{i+1} by looking at the relevant constraints in an arbitrary ordering. Let e_i be the number of constraints that are defined over x_i. Clearly, the ordering of contraint testing can have an impact on performance, and

---

1. Except for x_5 where "g" is before "b".

rejecting an inconsistent extension can cost between 1 to e_{i+1} constraint checks. Therefore, the best-case performance of SELECT-VALUE is $O(k \log t)$.

For the special case of a binary CSP, the tentative instantiation $\langle x_i, a \rangle$ must then be checked with at most n earlier variables, effectively yielding $O(n)$ complexity for CONSISTENT and $O(n k)$ complexity for SELECT-VALUE. Of course, if CONSISTENT performs computations other than table lookups, its complexity is dependent on the nature of these computations. In summary, we have the following:

PROPOSITION For general CSPs having n variables, e constraints, a constraint arity boun-
5.1 ded by r, number of tuples in a constraint bounded by t, and at most k domain values, the time complexity of CONSISTENT is $O(e \log t)$ or $O(e r \log k)$, and the time complexity of SELECT-VALUE is $O(e k r \log k)$ or $O(e k \log t)$. For binary CSPs, the complexity of SELECT-VALUE is $O(n k)$. •

5.2.2 Improvements to Backtracking

Backtracking frequently suffers from *thrashing*—repeatedly rediscovering the same inconsistencies and partial successes during search. An efficient cure for thrashing in all cases is unlikely, since the problem is NP-complete. Still, backtracking performance can be improved by employing preprocessing algorithms that reduce the size of the *underlying* search space, and by dynamically improving the algorithm's control strategy during search. The procedures for dynamically improving the pruning power of backtracking during search are split into *look-ahead schemes* and *look-back schemes*, as they relate to backtracking's two main phases: going forward to assemble a solution and going back in case of a dead-end.

Look-ahead schemes can be invoked whenever the algorithm is preparing to assign a value to the next variable. These schemes attempt to discover, from a restricted amount of inference, that is, constraint propagation, how current decisions about variable and value selection will restrict future search. Once a certain amount of forward constraint propagation is complete, the algorithm can use the information to do the following:

1. Decide which variable to instantiate next, if the order is not predetermined. It is generally advantageous to first instantiate those variables that maximally constrain the rest of the search space. Therefore, the most highly constrained variable having the least number of viable values is usually selected.

2. Decide which value to assign to the next variable. When searching for a single solution, an attempt is made to assign the value that maximizes the number of options available for future assignments.

Look-back schemes are invoked when the algorithm prepares to backtrack after encountering a dead-end. These schemes perform two functions:

1. Decide how deep to backtrack. By analyzing the reasons for the dead-end, irrelevant backtrack points can often be avoided so that the algorithm goes

directly back to the source of failure. This procedure is often referred to as *backjumping*.

2. Record the reasons for the dead-end in the form of new constraints, so that the same conflicts do not arise again later in the search. The terms used to describe this function are *constraint recording* and *learning*.

We return to look-back schemes in Chapter 6. The remainder of this chapter focuses on look-ahead algorithms. But before we proceed, let us conclude this section by looking at one of the earliest procedures for improving the state generation cost, *backmarking*, which does not quite fit as either a look-ahead or look-back scheme.

Backmarking

By keeping track of where past consistency tests failed, BACKMARKING can eliminate the need to repeat previously performed checks.

Recall that a backtracking algorithm moves either forward or backward in the search space. Suppose that the current variable is x_i and that x_p is the earliest variable in the ordering whose value has changed since the last visit to x_i. Clearly, any testing of constraints whose scope includes x_i and only those variables preceding x_p will produce the same results as in the earlier visit to x_i. If it failed against earlier instantiations, it will fail again; if it succeeded earlier, it will succeed again. By maintaining the right information from earlier parts of the search, therefore, either values in the domain of x_i can be immediately recognized as inconsistent, or else the only constraints to be tested are those involving instantiations starting from x_p.

Backmarking acts on this insight by maintaining two new tables. First, for each variable x_i and for each of its values a_v, backmarking remembers the earliest prior variable x_p such that the current partial instantiation $\vec{a}_p$ conflicted with $x_i = a_v$. This information is maintained in a table with elements $M_{i,v}$. (Note: This approach assumes that constraints involving earlier variables are tested before those involving later variables.) If $x_i = a_v$ is consistent with all earlier partial instantiations $\vec{a}_j$, $j < i$, then $M_{i,v} = i$. The second table, containing elements low_i, records the earliest variable that changed value since the last time x_i was instantiated. This information is put to use at every step of node generation. If $M_{i,v}$ is less than low_i, then the algorithm knows that the variable pointed to by $M_{i,v}$ did not change and that $x_i = a_v$ will fail again when checked against $\vec{a}_{M_{i,v}}$, so no further consistency checking is needed for rejecting $x_i = a_v$. If $M_{i,v}$ is greater than or equal to low_i, then $x_i = a_v$ is consistent with $\vec{a}_{low_i}$, and the relevant consistency checks can be skipped. The BACKMARKING algorithm is presented in Figure 5.6.

EXAMPLE 5.5   Consider again the example in Figure 5.4, and assume that backmarking uses ordering $d_1 = (x_1, x_2, x_3, x_4, x_5, x_6, x_7)$. Once the algorithm encounters the first dead-end at variable x_7 with the assignment $\langle x_1, blue \rangle$,

procedure BACKMARKING
Input: A constraint network $\mathcal{R} = (X, D, C)$.
Output: A solution or conclusion that the network is inconsistent.

    $M_{i,v} \leftarrow 0,\ low_i \leftarrow 0$ for all i and v (initialize tables)
    $i \leftarrow 1$ (initialize variable counter)
    $D'_i \leftarrow D_i$ (copy domain)
    while $1 \le i \le n$
        instantiate $x_i \leftarrow$ SELECT-VALUE-BACKMARKING
        if x_i is null   (no value was returned)
            $low_i \leftarrow i - 1$
            $i \leftarrow i - 1$ (backtrack)
        else
            $i \leftarrow i + 1$ (step forward)
            $D'_i \leftarrow D_i$
    end while
    if $i = 0$
        return "inconsistent"
    else
        return instantiated values of $\{x_1, \ldots, x_n\}$
end procedure

procedure SELECT-VALUE-BACKMARKING
    remove from D'_i all a_v for which $M_{i,v} < low_i$
    while D'_i is not empty
        select an arbitrary element $a_v \in D'_i$, and remove a_v from D'_i
        consistent $\leftarrow$ *true*
        $k \leftarrow low_i$
        while $k < i$ and *consistent*
        if not CONSISTENT $(\vec{a}_k, x_i = a_v)$
            $M_{i,v} \leftarrow k$
            consistent $\leftarrow$ *false*
        else
            $k \leftarrow k + 1$
        end while
        if *consistent*
            $M_{i,v} \leftarrow i$
            for all $j,\ i < j \le n,$ (update *low* of future variables)
                if $i < low_j$
                    $low_j \leftarrow i$
            return a_v
    end while
    return null   (no consistent value)
end procedure

Figure 5.6 The BACKMARKING algorithm.

$\langle x_2, green\rangle, \langle x_3, red\rangle, \langle x_4, red\rangle, \langle x_5, green\rangle, \langle x_6, red\rangle)$ (see the search graph in Figure 5.5(a)), table M has the following values: $M(1, blue) = 1$, $M(2, green) = 2$, $M(3, blue) = 1$, $M(3, red) = 3$, $M(4, blue) = 1$, $M(4, red) = 4$, $M(5, blue) = 5$, $M(6, green) = 2$, $M(6, red) = 6$, $M(7, red) = 3$, $M(7, blue) = 1$. Upon backtracking from x_7 to x_6, $low(7) = 6$ and $x_6 = teal$ is assigned. Then, when trying to instantiate a new value for x_7, the algorithm notices that the M values are smaller than $low(7)$ for both values of x_7 (*red, blue*) and, consequently, both values are determined inconsistent without performing any other consistency checks.   •

Although backmarking does no pruning of the search space, it does replace a number of consistency checks with table lookups and table updating. The cost of updating a table for each node generation is constant. The overall extra space required is $O(n \cdot k)$, where n is the number of variables and k the number of values. For each new node generated, one table lookup can replace as many as $O(e)$ consistency tests.

5.3 Look-Ahead Strategies

Look-ahead schemes are invoked whenever the algorithm is preparing to select the next variable or the next value. These schemes seek to discover, from a restricted amount of consistency enforcing, how current decisions about variable and value selection will affect future search. Specifically, the decision to accept or reject a value of the current variable is based on the impact that assignment has when constraint propagation is applied to the uninstantiated "future" variables. Once a certain amount of reasoning via constraint propagation is completed, the algorithm can use the results to decide which *variable* to instantiate next, if the order is not predetermined, and which *value* to assign to the next variable.

EXAMPLE 5.6   Consider again the coloring problem in Figure 5.4. Assume that variable x_1 is first in the ordering and that it is assigned the value *red*. A look-ahead procedure notes that the value *red* in the domains of x_3, x_4, and x_7 is incompatible with the current partial instantiation $\langle x_1, red\rangle$ and thus provisionally removes those values. A more extensive look-ahead procedure may then note that x_3 and x_7 are connected and are thereby left with incompatible values; each variable has the domain {*blue*} and the problem with $x_1 = red$ is therefore not arc-consistent. The scheme concludes that assigning *red* to x_1 will inevitably lead to a dead-end, cannot be part of a solution, and should be rejected. The same is true for $x_1 = blue$. So, for this level of constraint propagation, both partial solutions $\langle x_1 = red\rangle$ or $\langle x_1 = blue\rangle$ will be determined as dead-ends and the corresponding branches below them will be pruned.   •

Look-ahead strategies incur an extra cost for each instantiation request, but they can provide important benefits. For example, if *all* values of an uninstantiated variable are removed by looking ahead, then the current instantiation cannot be part of a solution and the algorithm knows to backtrack. Consequently, dead-ends occur earlier in the search, and much smaller portions of the search space need be explored. In general, the stronger the level of constraint propagation used for look-ahead, the smaller the search space explored and the higher the computational overhead.

Finally, by removing from the domains of each future variable all values inconsistent with the current partial instantiation via constraint propagation, we eliminate the need to test the consistency of values of the current variable with previous variables.

Look-ahead strategies rarely yield better worst-case performance guarantees over naive backtracking. The key challenge is to strike a practical cost-effective balance between look-ahead's effectiveness and its overhead.

Algorithm GENERALIZED-LOOK-AHEAD in Figure 5.7 presents a framework for look-ahead algorithms that can be specialized based on the level of constraint propagation, as expressed in the specific SELECT-VALUE subprocedure employed.[2] GENERALIZED-LOOK-AHEAD initially sets all the tentative domains (the D' sets) to equal the original domains (the D sets), and the SELECT-VALUE subprocedure propagates the current instantiation to remove values from the D' sets. At this stage, the algorithm may also record inferred constraints on future variables, although to bound the overhead of constraint propagation, most look-ahead methods modify future domains only. Upon backtracking, GENERALIZED-LOOK-AHEAD resets D' sets in order to rescind modifications that were contingent on partial instantiations no longer applicable. As we see in our upcoming implementation discussion, n copies of each D' set—one for each level in the search tree—are usually maintained in order to permit the reset action to be performed efficiently.

5.3.1 Look-Ahead Algorithms for Value Selection

In this section, we will define four levels of look-ahead that are based on arc-consistency. We will focus first on their use for value selection strategies.

Forward-Checking

The first of our four look-ahead algorithms, *forward-checking*, produces the most limited form of constraint propagation during search. It propagates the effect of a tentative value selection to each future variable, *separately*. If the domain of one of these future variables becomes empty, the value under consideration is not selected

---

2. Note the subtle difference between BACKTRACKING and GENERALIZED-LOOK-AHEAD.

---

procedure GENERALIZED-LOOK-AHEAD

Input: A constraint network $\mathcal{R} = (X, D, C)$.

Output: Either a solution, or notification that the network is inconsistent.

    $D_i' \leftarrow D_i$ for $1 \leq i \leq n$ (copy all domains)

    $i \leftarrow 1$ (initialize variable counter)

    while $1 \leq i \leq n$

        instantiate $x_i \leftarrow$ SELECT-VALUE-XXX

        if x_i is null   (no value was returned)

            $i \leftarrow i - 1$ (backtrack)

            reset each D_k', $k > i$, to its value before x_i was last instantiated

        else

            $i \leftarrow i + 1$ (step forward)

    end while

    if $i = 0$

        return "inconsistent"

    else

        return instantiated values of $\{x_1, \ldots, x_n\}$

end procedure

Figure 5.7 A common framework for several look-ahead-based search algorithms. By replacing SELECT-VALUE-XXX with SELECT-VALUE-FORWARD-CHECKING, the forward-checking algorithm is obtained. Similarly, using SELECT-VALUE-ARC-CONSISTENCY yields an algorithm that interweaves arc-consistency and search.

and the next candidate value is tried. Forward-checking uses the SELECT-VALUE-FORWARD-CHECKING subprocedure, presented in Figure 5.8. Specifically, if variables x_1 through x_{i-1} have been instantiated, and if x_i is the current variable to be assigned, then for the tentative partial solution $\vec{a}_i = (\vec{a}_{i-1}, x_i = a_i)$, $n - i$ subproblems can be created by combining $\vec{a}_i$ with one uninstantiated variable x_u. The only constraints of interest in each subproblem are those whose scope includes x_i, x_u, and a subset of $\{x_1, \ldots, x_{i-1}\}$. Enforcing consistency on a subproblem is achieved by removing from x_u's domain any value that conflicts with $\vec{a}_i$ for some relevant constraint. Forward-checking treats these $n - i$ subproblems independently of each other, removing values from the domains of future variables—from the D' sets—as necessary. If the domain of one of the future variables x_u becomes empty, then the partial instantiation $\vec{a}_i$ cannot be extended consistently to x_u, and therefore $\langle x_i, a_i \rangle$

```
procedure SELECT-VALUE-FORWARD-CHECKING
    while Dᵢ' is not empty
        select an arbitrary element a ∈ Dᵢ'. and remove a from Dᵢ'
        for all k, i < k ≤ n
            for all values b in Dₖ'
                if not CONSISTENT(āᵢ₋₁, xᵢ = a, xₖ = b)
                    remove b from Dₖ'
            end for
            if Dₖ' is empty              (xᵢ = a leads to a dead-end don't select a)
            reset each Dₖ', i < k ≤ n to value before a was selected
            else
            return a
        end while
        return null                      (no consistent value)
end procedure
```

Figure 5.8 The SELECT-VALUE subprocedure for the forward-checking algorithm.

is rejected and another value for x_i is considered. Notice that forward-checking is by no means restricted to binary constraints. Given a partial solution, all constraints having at most two variables that are not assigned (one of which is the current variable) can affect this look-ahead.

Complexity of SELECT-VALUE-FORWARD-CHECKING

If the complexity of a constraint check is $O(1)$, then SELECT-VALUE-FORWARD-CHECKING's complexity is $O(ek^2)$, where k is the cardinality of the largest domain and e is the number of constraints. How do we arrive at this figure? For a given tentative value of x_i the procedure tests the consistency of $\vec{a}_i$ against each of the k values of each future variable x_u, each involving e_u constraints, yielding $O(e_u k)$ tests. Summing over all future variables yields $O(ek)$ tests because $e = \sum_u e_u$. Finally, the procedure cycles through all the values of x_i, resulting in $O(ek^2)$ constraint checks.

EXAMPLE 5.7 Consider again the coloring problem in Figure 5.4. In this problem, instantiating $x_1 = red$ reduces the domains of x_3, x_4, and x_7. Instantiating $x_2 = blue$ does not affect any future variable. The domain of x_3 includes only *blue*, and selecting that value causes the domain of x_7 to be empty,

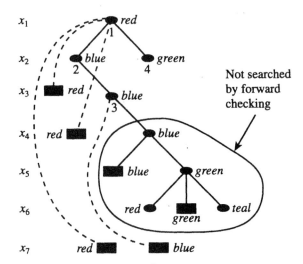

Figure 5.9 Part of the search space explored by forward-checking in the example in Figure 5.4. Only the search space below $x_1 = red$ and $x_2 = blue$ is drawn. Dotted lines connect values with future values that are filtered out.

so $x_3 = blue$ is rejected and x_3 is determined to be a dead-end. See Figure 5.9.   •

Arc-Consistency Look-Ahead

Arc-consistency look-ahead algorithms enforce full arc-consistency on all uninstantiated variables following each tentative value assignment to the current variable. Clearly, this look-ahead method does more work at each instantiation than does forward-checking. If a variable's domain becomes empty during the process of enforcing arc-consistency, then the current candidate value is rejected. SELECT-VALUE-ARC-CONSISTENCY in Figure 5.10 implements this approach. The **repeat** ... **until** loop in the subprocedure is essentially the arc-consistency algorithm AC-1 when some of the variables are instantiated. More efficient arc-consistency procedures can also be used within a SELECT-VALUE subprocedure.

Complexity of SELECT-VALUE-ARC-CONSISTENCY

The general optimal time complexity for any arc-consistency procedure is $O(ek^2)$, where e is the number of constraints in the subproblem, and k is the cardinality of the largest domain. Since arc-consistency may need to be applied for each value of the current variable, SELECT-VALUE-ARC-CONSISTENCY yields a worst-case bound of $O(ek^3)$ checks, if an optimal arc-consistency algorithm is used. As presented, however, SELECT-VALUE-ARC-CONSISTENCY has worse complexity bounds since it uses the AC-1 algorithm. Its analysis is left as an exercise (Exercise 5).

---

subprocedure SELECT-VALUE-ARC-CONSISTENCY

    while D_i^j is not empty

        select an arbitrary element $a \in D_i^j$, and remove a from D_i^j

        repeat

        removed-value $\leftarrow$ *false*

            for all $j, i < j \le n$

                for all $k, k \ne j, i < k \le n$

                    for each value b in D_j^i

                        if there is no value $c \in D_k^i$ such that

                            CONSISTENT$(\vec{a}_{i-1}, x_i = a, x_j = b, x_k = c)$

                        remove b from D_j^i

                        removed-value $\leftarrow$ *true*

                  end for

              end for

            end for

        until *removed-value* = *false*

        if any future domain is empty   (don't select a)

            reset each $D_j^i, i < j \le n$, to value before a was selected

        else

            return a

    end while

    return null   (no consistent value)

end procedure

Figure 5.10 The SELECT-VALUE subprocedure for arc-consistency, based on the AC-1 algorithm.

Algorithm arc-consistency look-ahead is sometimes called *real full look-ahead* to be contrasted with the full and partial look-ahead methods presented later. A popular variant of full arc-consistency is MAINTAINING-ARC-CONSISTENCY (MAC), which performs full arc-consistency after each domain value is rejected. In other words, assume that we select a value for the current variable x that has four values $\{1, 2, 3, 4\}$. First, tentatively assign $x = 1$ and apply full arc-consistency. If this choice causes an empty domain, $x = 1$ is rejected, and the domain of x reduces to $\{2, 3, 4\}$. Now apply full arc-consistency again with this reduced domain. If it causes an empty domain, conclude that the problem has no solutions. Otherwise (following the propagation by arc-consistency) resume value selection with the next variable (any other variable can be selected at this point). We can view MAC as if it searches a virtual binary tree, where at any value selection point, the choice is between a single value $x = a$ to the current variable, and assigning any other value to this variable ($x = \neg a$). This distinction when associated with full arc-consistency at each such choice $\{a, \neg a\}$ sometimes yields more effective pruning. It also allows richer variable ordering strategies (see Exercise 7).

Full and Partial Look-Ahead

Two algorithms that do more work than forward-checking and less work than enforcing full arc-consistency at each state are *full looking ahead* and *partial looking ahead*. The full looking ahead algorithm makes a single pass through the future variables; in effect the **repeat** and **until** lines in SELECT-VALUE-ARC-CONSISTENCY are removed.

Partial looking ahead (PLA) does less work than full looking ahead. It applies directional arc-consistency to the future variables. In addition to removing the **repeat** loop from SELECT-VALUE-ARC-CONSISTENCY, partial looking ahead replaces "**for** all $k, i < k \leq n$" with "**for** all $k, j < k \leq n$." That is, future variables are only compared with those variables following them.

EXAMPLE 5.8   Consider the problem in Figure 5.4 using the same ordering of variables and values as in Figure 5.9. Partial look-ahead starts by considering $x_1 = red$. Applying directional arc-consistency from x_1 toward x_7 will first shrink the domains of x_3, x_4, and x_7 (when processing x_1), as was the case for forward-checking. Later, when directional arc-consistency processes x_4 (with its only value, *blue*) against x_7 (with its only value, *blue*), the domain of x_4 will become empty, and the value *red* for x_1 will be rejected. Likewise, the value $x_1 = blue$ will be rejected. Therefore, the whole tree in Figure 5.9 will not be visited if either partial look-ahead or the more extensive look-ahead schemes are used. With this level of look-ahead only the subtree below $x_1 = green$ will be expanded.   •

Complexity of Partial Look-Ahead

SELECT-VALUE-PARTIAL-LOOK-AHEAD applies directional arc-consistency to k subproblems, each requiring in the worst case $O(ek^2)$ complexity. The total complexity is therefore bounded by $O(ek^3)$. As this bound is identical to that of optimal arc-consistency look-ahead, it is clear that it does not reflect the actual complexity well. Notice, however, that SELECT-VALUE-PARTIAL-LOOK-AHEAD will not require a complex implementation of arc-consistency.

Dynamic Look-Ahead Value Orderings

We can also use the information gathered from constraint propagation to rank-order the promise of nonrejected values by estimating their likelihood to lead to a solution. Such a *look-ahead value ordering* (LVO) algorithm can be based on forward-checking or any higher level of constraint propagation. Rather than just accepting the current variable's first value not shown to lead to a dead-end, LVO tentatively instantiates each value of the current variable and examines the effects of a forward-checking or arc-consistency-style look-ahead on the domains of future variables. (Each instantiation and its effects are retracted before the next instantiation is made.) LVO's strategies can vary by the amount of look-ahead performed and also by the heuristic measure they use to transform the propagated information into a ranking of the values. We list several popular LVO heuristics next.

One, called min-conflicts (MC), chooses the value that removes the smallest number of values from the domains of future variables. Namely, it considers each value in the domain of the current variable and associates with it the total number of values in the domains of future variables with which it conflicts but that are consistent with the current partial assignment. The current variable's values are then selected in increasing order of this count.

A second heuristic is inspired by the intuition that a subproblem that includes variables having small domains (e.g., single-valued domains) is more likely to be inconsistent. Note that each of the search trees rooted at an instantiation of x_i is a different subproblem. The max-domain-size (MD) heuristic prefers the value in the current variable that creates the largest *minimum* domain size in the future variables. For example, if after instantiating x_i with value a the $min_{j \in \{i+1,...,n\}} |D'_j|$ is 2 and with $x_i = b$ the minimum is 1, then a will be preferred.

A third heuristic attempts to estimate the number of solutions in each potential subproblem. The ES (estimate solutions) computes an upper bound on the number of solutions by multiplying together the domain sizes of each future variable, after values incompatible with the candidate value of the current variable have been removed. The value that leads to the highest upper bound on the number of solutions is selected first.

Finally, another useful value ordering heuristic is to prefer the most recent value assigned to x_i (when it was last assigned, and since retracted) in order to capitalize on previously assembled partial solutions.

Experimental results indicate that the cost of performing the additional look-ahead, while not justified on smaller and easier problems, can certainly be valuable on consistent large and hard problems. In particular the MC heuristic emerged as best among the above measures on a variety of randomly generated instances.

5.3.2 Look-Ahead for Variable Ordering

The ordering of variables has a tremendous impact on the size of the search space. Empirical and theoretical studies have shown that certain fixed orderings are generally effective at producing smaller search spaces. In particular, the min-width ordering and max-cardinality ordering introduced in Chapter 4, both of which use information from the constraint graph, are quite effective.

Dynamic Variable Orderings

When dynamically determining variable ordering during search, one common heuristic, known as "fail-first," is to select as the next variable the one likely to constrain the remainder of the search space the most. All other factors being equal, the variable with the smallest number of viable values in its (current) domain will have the fewest subtrees rooted at those values, and therefore the smallest search space below it. Given a current partial solution $\vec{a}_i$, we wish to determine the domain values for each future variable that are consistent with $\vec{a}_i$. We may estimate the domain sizes of future variables using the various levels of look-ahead propagation discussed above. Such methods are called *dynamic variable ordering* (DVO) strategies. A possible formulation is given in the SELECT-VARIABLE subprocedure in Figure 5.11. GENERALIZED-LOOK-AHEAD can be modified to employ dynamic variable ordering by calling SELECT-VARIABLE after the initialization step "$i \leftarrow 1$" and after the forward step "$i \leftarrow i + 1$."

For clarity we explicitly specify DVO with forward-checking. Forward-checking, which performs the least amount of look-ahead, has proven cost-effective in many empirical studies.[3] We call this weak form of DVO *dynamic variable forward-checking* (DVFC). In DVFC, given a state $\vec{a}_i = (a_1, \ldots, a_i)$, the algorithm updates the domain of each future variable to include only values consistent with $\vec{a}_i$. Then, a variable with a domain of minimal size is selected. If any future variable has an empty domain, it is placed next in the ordering, and a dead-end will occur when this next variable becomes the current variable. This algorithm is described in Figure 5.12.

---

subprocedure SELECT-VARIABLE

$m \leftarrow min_{i \leq j \leq n}|D'_j|$ (find size of smallest future domain)

Select an arbitrary uninstantiated variable x_k such that $|D'_k| = m$

Rearrange future variables so that x_k is the ith variable

end subprocedure

Figure 5.11   The subprocedure SELECT-VARIABLE, which employs a heuristic based on the D' sets to choose the next variable to be instantiated.

---

3. As far as we know, no empirical testing has been carried out for full look-ahead or partial look-ahead based variable orderings.

procedure DVFC

Input: A constraint network $\mathcal{R} = (X, D, C)$.

Output: Either a solution, or notification that the network is inconsistent.

    $D_i' \leftarrow D_i$ for $1 \leq i \leq n$ (copy all domains)

    $i \leftarrow 1$ (initialize variable counter)

            $s = min_{i < j \leq n} |D_j'|$ (find future variable with smallest domain)

            $x_i \leftarrow x_s$ (rearrange variables so that x_s is the first variable)

while $1 \leq i \leq n$

    instantiate $x_i \leftarrow$ SELECT-VALUE-FORWARD-CHECKING

    if x_i is null   (no value was returned)

        reset each D' set to its value before x_i was last instantiated

        $i \leftarrow i - 1$ (backtrack)

    else

        if $i < n$

            $s = argmin_j |D_j|$ (find future variable with smallest domain)

            $x_{i+1} \leftarrow x_s$ (rearrange variables so that x_s follows x_i)

            $i \leftarrow i + 1$ (step forward to x_s)

end while

if $i = 0$

    return "inconsistent"

else

    return instantiated values of $\{x_1, \dots, x_n\}$

end procedure

Figure 5.12 The DVFC algorithm. It uses the SELECT-VALUE-FORWARD-CHECKING subprocedure given in Figure 5.8.

EXAMPLE 5.9   Consider again the example in Figure 5.4. Initially, all variables have domain size of 2 or more. DVFC picks x_7, whose domain size is 2, and the value $\langle x_7, blue \rangle$. Forward-checking propagation of this choice to each future variable restricts the domains of x_3, x_4, and x_5 to single values, and reduces the size of x_1's domain by one. DVFC selects x_3 and assigns it its only possible value, *red*. Subsequently, forward-checking causes variable

x_1 to also have a singleton domain. The algorithm chooses x_1 and its only consistent value, *green*. After propagating this choice, we see that x_4 has one value, *red*; it is selected and assigned the value. Then x_2 can be selected and assigned its only consistent value, *blue*. Propagating this assignment does not further shrink any future domain. Next, x_5 can be selected and assigned *green*. The solution is then completed, without dead-ends, by assigning *red* or *teal* to x_6.   •

It is important to note that DVFC also accomplishes the same value pruning associated with forward-checking.

Randomized Backtracking

Since value and variable orderings can have a dramatic effect on the performance of the backtracking algorithm with huge variances even on a single instance due to varying tie-breaking rules, and since finding a heuristic that will work well in all cases is unlikely, an alternative strategy explores randomness in values and variable selection. For example, when the algorithm needs to select a variable, it can use a variable selection heuristic such as min-domain, but breaks ties randomly. Similarly, a value may be selected randomly, or a random tie-breaking rule can be employed on top of a popular value selection heuristic. In order to capitalize on the huge performance variance exhibited by randomized backtracking algorithms, it is common to restart the randomized algorithm after being aborted due to a self-imposed time cutoff. When running a sequence of such randomized backtracking algorithms with increasing cutoff times, the resulting scheme is guaranteed to find a solution if one exists or to report that the problem is inconsistent. Such randomized strategies have proven highly effective on various domains in recent years.

5.3.3 The Cycle-Cutset Effect

We next present a relationship between the structure of the constraint graph and some forms of look-ahead. We will see more such properties in other chapters as well.

DEFINITION   **(cycle-cutset)**
5.2
Given an undirected graph, a subset of nodes in the graph is a *cycle-cutset* if its removal results in a graph having no cycles.   •

Once a variable is instantiated, the flow of interaction through this variable is terminated. This can be graphically expressed by deleting the corresponding variable from the constraint graph. Therefore, once the set of variables that forms a cycle-cutset is instantiated, the remaining problem can be perceived as a tree. As noted in Chapter 4, a tree can be solved by directional arc-consistency, and therefore partial looking ahead performing directional arc-consistency at each node is guaranteed to solve the problem once the cycle-cutset variables initiate the search ordering. Search will not be deeper than the cycle-cutset (See also Chapter 10).

PROPOSITION 5.2 A constraint problem whose graph has a cycle-cutset of size c can be solved by the partial looking ahead algorithm in a time of $O((n - c) \cdot k^{c+2})$.

Proof Since there are k^c possible instantiations of the cutset variables, and since each remaining tree created by each instantiation is solved in $(n - c)k^2$ consistency checks, the above-proposed complexity follows. ●

5.3.4 An Implementation Issue

The cost of node expansion when implementing a look-ahead strategy can be controlled if certain information is cached and maintained. One possibility is to maintain for each variable a table containing viable domain values relative to the partial solution currently being assembled. When testing a new value of the current variable, or after committing to a value for the current variable, the tables will tentatively be updated following the application of constraint propagation. This strategy requires an additional $O(n \cdot k)$ space. However, whenever a dead-end occurs, the algorithm has to recompute the tables associated with the state to which the algorithm retracted. This may require n times the node generation cost depending on the level of look-ahead used.

Another approach is to maintain a table of pruned domains for each variable and for each level in the search tree, which results in additional space of $O(n^2 \cdot k)$. Upon reaching a dead-end, the algorithm retracts to the previous level and uses the tables maintained at that level. Consequently, the only cost of node generation is the usual partial solution extension and that of updating the tables.

5.3.5 Extensions to Stronger Look-Aheads

The collection of look-ahead techniques we've described is not meant to be exhaustive. For example, a search algorithm could enforce a degree of consistency higher than arc-consistency following each instantiation. Doing so entails not only deleting values from domains, but also adding new constraints. More recent work has shown that as larger and more difficult problems are considered, higher levels of look-ahead become more useful. Therefore, it is likely that as experiments are conducted with larger and harder problems, look-ahead based on path-consistency becomes cost-effective.

Look-ahead algorithms can also be extended to handle some generalized definitions of consistency, such as relational consistency, described in Chapter 8. Those definitions focus on constraints rather than on variables and are particularly well-suited for the nonbinary case. The "generalized arc-consistency" condition defined in Chapter 3 is particularly appropriate since it reduces domains only. You can try to extend SELECT-VALUE-ARC-CONSISTENCY and forward-checking to the generalized arc-consistency definition (see Exercise 2).

5.4 Satisfiability: Look-Ahead in Backtracking

The backtracking algorithm and its advances are applicable to the special case of propositional satisfiability. The most well-known, and still one of the best, variation of backtracking for this representation is known as the *Davis-Putnam, Logemann, and Loveland procedure* (DPLL) (Davis, Logemann, and Loveland 1962). This is a backtracking algorithm applied to a CNF theory (a set of clauses) augmented with unit propagation as the look-ahead method (see Figure 3.16 in Chapter 3). This level of look-ahead is akin to applying a type of full arc-consistency (i.e., relational arc-consistency) at each node.

Figure 5.13 presents DPLL. Unlike our general exposition of search algorithms, we define this one recursively. The algorithm systematically searches the space of

---

DPLL(φ)

Input: A CNF theory φ.

Output: A decision of whether φ is satisfiable.

1. Unit_propagate(φ);

2. **If** the empty clause is generated, return(*false*);

3. **Else**, if all variables are assigned, return(*true*);

4. **Else**

5. Q = some unassigned variable;

6.   **return**(DPLL($\varphi \wedge Q$) $\vee$

        DPLL($\varphi \wedge \neg Q$)) and if consistent, a truth assignment.

Figure 5.13 The DPLL procedure.

partial truth assignments of propositional variables. Step 1 applies unit propagation (line 1), accomplishing some level of dynamic variable and value selection automatically within unit propagation. Additional value and variable selection can be done at step 5 of Figure 5.13.

EXAMPLE 5.10

Consider the party problem with the following rules: If Alex attends the party, then Bill will as well. If Chris attends, then Alex will, and if both Alex and Bill do not attend, then David will. Assume we also know that Chris did attend the party. The CNF theory for this story is $\varphi = \{(\neg A \vee B), (\neg C \vee A), (A \vee B \vee D), (C)\}$. The search tree of our party example along ordering A, B, D, C is shown in Figure 5.14. We see that there are two consistent scenarios. Suppose we now apply the DPLL algorithm. Applying unit propagation will resolve unit clause C, yielding unit clause A, which in turn is resolved, yielding the unit clause B. Unit propagation terminates and we have three variable assignments $((A = 1, B = 1, C = 1)$. In step 5 the algorithm will select the only variable D. Since both of its truth assignments are consistent, we have two solutions. In this case the algorithm encountered no dead-ends. The portion of the search space explored is enclosed in Figure 5.14.   •

Higher levels of look-ahead using stronger resolution-based inference, which enforce higher levels of local consistency, can naturally be considered here. Different levels of bounded resolution, restricted by the size of the generated resolvents or by the size of the participating clauses, can be considered for propagation at each node in the search tree. The level of such propagation that is cost-effective is not clear, leading to the common trade-off between more inference at each node versus exploration of fewer nodes in the search tree. Clearly, when

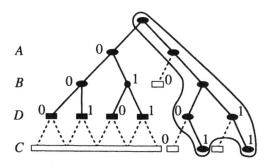

Figure 5.14 A state search tree along the variables A, B, D, C for a CNF theory $\varphi = \{(\neg A \vee B), (\neg C \vee A), (A \vee B \vee D), C\}$. Hollow nodes and bars in the search tree represent illegal states; gray ovals represent solutions. The enclosed area corresponds to DPLL with unit propagation when D is before C.

problems are larger and harder, more intensive look-ahead is likely to become cost-effective, as already observed for general constraints. One possible extension of unit propagation is to apply path-consistency at each node. In the context of CNF theories, path-consistency is equivalent to applying resolution between clauses of length 2 at the most. Indeed, adding such *binary clause reasoning* has recently produced very effective versions of look-ahead on top of DPLL.

Finally, look-ahead methods can also be used for variable ordering, as we saw in the general case. A useful heuristic for variable ordering that has been reported for these DPLL-based algorithms is the *2-literal clause heuristic*. This heuristic suggests preferring a variable that would cause the largest number of unit propagations, where the number of possible unit propagations is approximated by the number of 2-literal clauses in which the variable appears. The augmented algorithm was demonstrated to significantly outperform a DPLL that doesn't employ this heuristic.

5.5 **Summary**

This chapter introduced backtracking search for solving constraint satisfaction problems and focused on enhancements that use look-ahead algorithms. The primary variants of look-ahead—forward-checking, full look-ahead, partial look-ahead, and arc-consistency look-ahead—were introduced, and their use for variable and value selection was discussed. The complexity overheads of these methods were analyzed, and the worst-case complexity bound as a function of the problem's cycle-cutset was presented. Finally the chapter presented the DPLL-based backtracking search with look-ahead for satisfiability.

5.6 **Bibliographical Notes**

Most current work on improving backtracking algorithms for solving constraint satisfaction problems uses Bitner and Reingold's (1975) formulation of the algorithm. One of the early and still one of the influential ideas for improving backtracking's performance on constraint satisfaction problems was introduced by Waltz (1975). Waltz demonstrated that when constraint propagation in the form of arc-consistency is applied to a two-dimensional line drawing interpretation, the problem can often be solved without encountering any dead-ends. Golomb and Baumert (1965) may have been the first to informally describe this idea. Consistency techniques for look-ahead are used in Lauriere's Alice system (Lauriere 1978). Explicit algorithms employing this idea have been given by Gaschnig (1979), who described a backtracking algorithm that incorporates arc-consistency; McGregor (1979), who described backtracking combined with forward-checking; Haralick and Elliott (1980), who added the various look-ahead methods described in this chapter (forward-checking, full look-ahead, and partial look-ahead); and Nadel (1989), who discussed backtracking combined with many partial and full arc-consistency variations. Gaschnig (1979) has compared Waltz-style look-ahead backtracking (which corresponds to arc-consistency look-ahead) with look-back improvements that he introduced, such as backjumping and backmarking. Haralick and Elliot (1980) did a relatively comprehensive study of look-ahead and look-back methods at the time, in which they compared the performance of the various methods on the *n*-queens problem and on randomly generated instances. Based on their empirical evaluation, they concluded that forward-checking, the algorithm that uses the weakest form of constraint propagation, is superior. This conclusion was maintained for two decades until larger and more difficult problem classes were tested by Sabin and Freuder (1994) and by Frost and Dechter (1995,1996). In these later studies, forward-checking lost its superiority in many problem instances to arc-consistency looking ahead, MAC and full looking ahead, and other stronger looking ahead variants. Various value ordering heuristics (MC, MD, ES) were tested empirically by Frost and Dechter (1995). Learning schemes for value ordering heuristics were also investigated (Wallace et al. 2002). Empirical evaluation of backtracking with dynamic variable ordering on the *n*-queens problem was reported by Stone and Stone (1986). More sophisticated DVO schemes have been investigated by Prosser et al. (1995,1996) and Smith and Grant (1998), focusing on computational trade-off of various such heuristics. Recent work has demonstrated the effectiveness of stronger propagation methods on hard problems (Debruyne 1998). Following the introduction of graph-based methods (Freuder 1982; Dechter and Pearl 1987b), Dechter and Pearl introduced *advice generation*, a look-ahead value selection method that prefers a value if it leads to a larger number of solutions based on a tree approximation of the problem at each node. Dechter (1990) introduced the cycle-cutset scheme and its complexity bound as a function of the cycle-cutset size. The balance between overhead and pruning is a topic of frequent study (Frost and Dechter 1995; Sabin and Freuder 1994; Baker 1995; Frost 1997).

Since 1997, many solution methods combine different algorithms, or exploit nondeterminism in the randomized version of backtracking search using either random restarts or randomizing backtrack points (Gomes, Selman, and Kautz 1998; Prestwich 2000). These ideas were described initially by Sinclair, Luby, and Zuckerman (1993) and followed up by extensive empirical investigations (Gomes, Selman, Crato, and Kautz 2000; Gomes and Selman 2001).

In the context of solving propositional satisfiability, the most notable development was the Davis, Logemann, and Loveland (1962) backtracking search algorithm (called DPLL) that uses look-ahead in the form of *unit propagation*, which is similar to arc-consistency. Interestingly, the algorithm was preceded by a complete resolution algorithm, called the Davis-Putnam algorithm (Davis and Putnam 1960), which was confused for a long time with the search-based algorithm presented in 1962. Such confusions are still occurring today.

The *2-literal clause heuristic* was proposed by Crawford and Auton (1993). For at least one decade this algorithm was perceived as one of the most successful DPLL versions for satisfiability. It provided the key idea for many subsequent heuristics for variable selection, namely, estimating the variable whose assignment will lead to the greatest amount of forward propagation. Another popular DPLL-based algorithm named SATO (Zhang 1997) incorporated a sophisticated data structure called a *watch list* that allows a quick recognition of clauses that became unit clauses.

Methods for incorporating stronger resolutions for constraint propagation were also tried and often failed to be cost-effective. One such approach that is focused on the binary clauses resolution was recently demonstrated by Bacchus (2002) to be effective if augmented with additional heuristics.

In the past 10 years, the basic DPLL procedure was improved dramatically using both look-ahead methods described in this chapter and look-back methods, to be described in the next chapter. Sophisticated data structures and engineering ideas contributed to the effectiveness of these schemes considerably. We elaborate more in Chapter 6.

Analytical average-case analysis for some backtracking algorithms has also been pursued for satisfiability (Purdom 1983) and for constraint satisfaction (Haralick and Elliot 1980; Nadel 1983; Nadel 1990).

5.7 **Exercises**

1. The two primary search algorithms for exploring any search graph are depth-first search (DFS) and best-first search (BFS). These algorithms have complementary properties. For instance, when BFS terminates, it finds an optimal solution although it may require exponential space to do so. DFS requires only linear space, but may not terminate on infinite search spaces.

   Why are DFS-based algorithms the algorithms of choice for exploring constraint satisfaction state spaces?

2. Extend the forward-checking and arc-consistency look-ahead algorithm to exploit the generalized arc-consistency definition.

3. Let G be a constraint graph of a problem having five variables x_1, x_2, x_3, x_4, x_5 with arcs (x_1, x_2), (x_2, x_3) (x_3, x_4) (x_4, x_1) (x_4, x_5) (x_5, x_2). (See Figure 5.15.) Assume the domains of all variables are $\{1, 2, 3\}$. Assume not-equal constraints. For a problem having the constraint graph G and using ordering $d_1 = x_1, x_2, x_3, x_4, x_5$, answer the following—and justify your answer:

   (a) Will backmarking help when searching this problem?

   (b) Apply forward-checking.

   (c) Apply arc-consistency look-ahead.

   (d) Apply partial look-ahead.

4. Consider the crossword puzzle in Figure 1.1 and in Chapter 2 (page 28) formulated using the dual-graph representation. Using the ordering

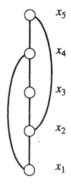

Figure 5.15 A constraint graph.

$x_1, x_2, x_5, x_6, x_4, x_3$, show a trace, whose length is limited by a 1-page description, for each of the following algorithms:

(a) BACKTRACKING

(b) BACKMARKING

(c) FORWARD-CHECKING

(d) DVFC

(e) PARTIAL LOOK-AHEAD Bound the complexity of partial look-ahead as a function of the constraint graph

5. Analyze the complexity of SELECT-VALUE-ARC-CONSISTENCY when using

(a) AC-3

(b) AC-4

for arc-consistency.

6. Analyze the overhead of each of the following algorithms:

(a) BACKTRACKING

(b) BACKMARKING

(c) FORWARD-CHECKING

(d) PARTIAL LOOK-AHEAD

(e) ARC-CONSISTENCY LOOK-AHEAD

Assume that you are maintaining a table of current domains at each level of the search tree. Analyze the complexity of node generation and the complexity of generating a path along the search tree.

7. Apply the following algorithms to the 5-queens problem. Show only the search graph generated for finding all solutions.

(a) Forward-checking

(b) Dynamic variable ordering (DVFC)

(c) Arc-consistency look-ahead

(d) Maintaining arc-consistency (MAC)

8. Implement DVO algorithms for three levels of look-ahead: forward-checking, arc-consistency, and partial look-ahead. Run these algorithms on various random and real benchmarks, and compute three performance measures: the size of the search graph (or number of dead-ends), the number of consistency checks, and CPU time. Present a comparison of your experiments.

9. We say that a problem is backtrack-free at level k of the search if a backtracking algorithm, once it reaches this level, is guaranteed to be backtrack-free. Assume that we apply DPC as a look-ahead propagation at each level of the search.

   (a) Assuming a fixed variable ordering, can you identify a level for which DPC is backtrack-free?

   (b) Can you bound the complexity of DPC as a function of a width-2 cutset (a cutset is of width 2 if its removal from the graph yields a graph having induced width of 2)?

10. Describe algorithm DPLL augmented with a look-ahead scheme that does bounded resolution such that any two clauses creating a clause whose size is bounded by 2 are carried out at each step.

11. A set of literals that reduces a CNF theory to a Horn theory via unit propagation is called a literal Horn cutset. A set of propositions such that any of its truth assignments is a literal Horn cutset is called a Horn cutset.

    (a) Assume that a CNF theory has a Horn cutset of size h. Can you bound the complexity of DPLL as a function of h?

    (b) Suggest an algorithm for finding a small-size Horn cutset.

12. The Golomb ruler problem asks to place a set of n markers $x_1 > \cdots > x_n$ on the integer line (assigning a positive integer to each marker) such that the distances between any two markers are all different, and such that the *length of the ruler*, namely, the assignment to $x_n - x_1$, is the smallest possible.

    (a) Provide two ways of formulating the Golomb ruler as a constraint satisfaction problem. Assume that you know the optimal length l and you have to provide values for the markers. Demonstrate your formulation on a problem of small size (five variables).

    (b) Discuss the solution of the problem by look-ahead methods such as DVFC, forward-checking, full arc-consistency look-ahead, and partial look-ahead.

    (c) Propose two algorithms to apply and test for the problem.

13. The combinatorial auction problem: There is a set of items $S = \{a_1, \ldots, a_n\}$ and a set of m bids $B = \{b_1, \ldots, b_m\}$. Each bid is $b_i = (S_i, r_i)$ where $S_i \subseteq S$ and

$r_i = r(b_i)$ is the cost to be paid for bid b_i. The task is to find a subset of bids $B' \subseteq B$ such that any two bids in B' do not share an item and to maximize, $R(B') : R(B_i) = \sum_{b \in B_i} r(b)$. Assume knowledge of the value of the optimal solution, $R(B')$.

Answer items (a), (b), and (c) of the previous exercise.

14. The rain problem: Given a communication network modeled as a graph $G = (N, E)$, where the set of nodes are processing nodes and the links are bidirectional communication links, each link e is associated with *bandwidth capacity* $c(e)$. A *demand* is a communication need between a pair of nodes $d_u = (x_u, y_u, \beta_u)$, where x_u is the source, y_u is the destination, and β_u is the required bandwidth. Given a set of demands $\{d_1, \ldots, d_m\}$, the task is to assign a route (a simple path) from source to destination for each demand such that the total capacity used over each link is below the available bandwidth. Assume again knowledge of the value of an optimal solution.

Answer items (a), (b), and (c) of Exercise 12.

chapter 6

General Search Strategies: Look-Back

Yet knowing how way leads on to way, I doubted if I
should ever come back.

Robert Frost, "The Road Not Taken"

We have now looked at the basic backtracking algorithm as it applies to CSPs,
and at some schemes developed to foresee and avoid some future traps during
the algorithm's *forward* phase (Chapter 5). This chapter introduces another class
of improvement schemes that attempt to counteract backtracking's propensity for
thrashing, or repeatedly rediscovering the same inconsistencies and partial successes
during search. These schemes are invoked when the algorithm gets stuck in a dead-
end and prepares to backtrack. Collectively, these are called *look-back* schemes, and
they can be divided into two main categories. The aim of the first type is to improve
upon the standard policy of retreating just one step backwards when encountering
a dead-end. By analyzing the reasons for the dead-end, irrelevant backtrack points
can often be avoided so that the algorithm jumps back directly to the source of
failure, instead of just to the immediately preceding variable in the ordering. The
aim of the second type of look-back scheme, called *constraint recording* or *no-good
learning*, is to record the reasons for the dead-end in the form of new constraints,
so that the same conflicts will not arise again later in the search. In this chapter, we
will take a deep look at several algorithms that exemplify some of the many ways
in which these two categories of improvement schemes can be implemented.

6.1 Conflict Sets

Backjumping schemes are one of the primary tools for reducing backtracking's
unfortunate tendency to repeatedly rediscover the same dead-ends. A dead-end
occurs if x_i has no consistent values left relative to the current partial solution, in
which case the backtracking algorithm will go back to x_{i-1}. Suppose that a new

value for x_{i-1} exists and that there is no constraint whose scope includes x_i and x_{i-1}. In this case, x_{i-1} cannot be a cause for the dead-end at x_i, and a dead-end will again be reached at x_i, for each value of x_{i-1}, until all values of x_{i-1} have been exhausted. For instance, returning to our coloring problem (Figure 5.4 on page 125), if we apply backtracking along the ordering $d_1 = (x_1, x_2, x_3, x_4, x_5, x_6, x_7)$, we will encounter a dead-end at x_7, given the assignment ($\langle x_1, red \rangle$, $\langle x_2, blue \rangle$, $\langle x_3, blue \rangle$, $\langle x_4, blue \rangle$, $\langle x_5, green \rangle$, $\langle x_6, red \rangle$). Backtracking will then return to x_6 and instantiate it as $x_6 = teal$, but the same dead-end will be encountered at x_7 because the value assigned at x_6 was not relevant to the cause of the dead-end at x_7.

We can ameliorate this situation by identifying a *culprit variable* responsible for the dead-end, and then immediately jump back and reinstantiate the culprit variable, instead of repeatedly instantiating the chronologically previous variable. Identification of culprit variables in backtracking is based on the notion of *conflict sets*. For ease of exposition, in the following discussion we assume a fixed ordering of the variables $d = (x_1, \dots, x_n)$. This restriction can be lifted without affecting correctness, thus allowing dynamic variable orderings in all the algorithms.

DEFINITION   (dead-end)
6.1

A dead-end state at level i indicates that a current partial instantiation $\vec{a}_i = (a_1, \dots, a_i)$ conflicts with every possible value of x_{i+1}. $(a_1, \dots, a_i)$ is called a *dead-end state*, and x_{i+1} is called a *dead-end variable*. That is, backtracking generated the consistent tuple $\vec{a}_i = (a_1, \dots, a_i)$ and tried to extend it to the next variable, x_{i+1}, but failed; no value of x_{i+1} was consistent with all the values in $\vec{a}_i$.   ●

The subtuple $\vec{a}_{i-1} = (a_1, \dots, a_{i-1})$ may also be in conflict with x_{i+1}, and therefore going back to x_i only and changing its value will not always resolve the dead-end at variable x_{i+1}. In general, a tuple $\vec{a}_i$ that is a dead-end state may contain many subtuples that are in conflict with x_{i+1}. Any such partial instantiation will not be part of any solution. Backtracking's normal control strategy often retreats to a subtuple $\vec{a}_j$ (alternately, to variable x_j) without resolving all or even any of these conflict sets. Therefore, rather than going to the previous variable, the algorithm should jump back from the dead-end state at $\vec{a}_i = (a_1, \dots, a_i)$ to the most recent variable x_b such that $\vec{a}_{b-1} = (a_1, \dots, a_{b-1})$ contains no conflict sets of the dead-end variable x_{i+1}. As it turns out, identifying this culprit variable is fairly easy. We next give a few definitions to capture the necessary concepts.

DEFINITION   (conflict set)
6.2

Let $\vec{a} = (a_{i_1}, \dots, a_{i_k})$ be a consistent instantiation of an arbitrary subset of variables, and let x be a variable not yet instantiated. If there is no value b in the domain of x such that $(\vec{a}, x = b)$ is consistent, we say that $\vec{a}$ is a *conflict set* of x, or that $\vec{a}$ conflicts with variable x. If, in addition, $\vec{a}$ does not contain a subtuple that is in conflict with x, $\vec{a}$ is called a *minimal* conflict set of x.   ●

DEFINITION 6.3

(leaf dead-end)

Let $\vec{a}_i = (a_1, \ldots, a_i)$ be a consistent tuple. If $\vec{a}_i$ is in conflict with x_{i+1}, it is called a *leaf dead-end* and x_{i+1} is a leaf dead-end variable. •

DEFINITION 6.4

(no-good)

Given a network $\mathcal{R} = (X, D, C)$, any partial instantiation $\bar{a}$ that does not appear in any solution of $\mathcal{R}$ is called a *no-good*. *Minimal* no-goods have no no-good subtuples. •

A conflict set is clearly a no-good, but there also exist no-goods that are not conflict sets of any single variable. That is, they may conflict with two or more variables simultaneously.

EXAMPLE 6.1

For the problem in Figure 5.4, the tuple $(\langle x_1, red \rangle, \langle x_2, blue \rangle, \langle x_3, blue \rangle, \langle x_4, blue \rangle, \langle x_5, green \rangle, \langle x_6, red \rangle)$ is a conflict set relative to x_7 because it cannot be consistently extended to any value of x_7. It is also a leaf dead-end. Notice that the assignment $(\langle x_1, blue \rangle, \langle x_2, green \rangle, \langle x_3, red \rangle)$ is a no-good that is not a conflict set relative to any single variable. •

Whenever backjumping discovers a dead-end, it seeks to jump back as far as possible without skipping potential solutions. While the issue of *safety* in jumping can be made algorithm independent, the *maximality* in the magnitude of a jump needs to be defined relative to the information recorded by the algorithm. What is maximal for one style of backjumping may not be maximal for another, especially if they are engaged in different levels of information gathering.

DEFINITION 6.5

(safe jump)

Let $\vec{a}_i = (a_1, \ldots, a_i)$ be a leaf dead-end state. We say that x_j, where $j \le i$, is *safe* (relative to $\vec{a}_i$) if the partial instantiation $\vec{a}_j = (a_1, \ldots, a_j)$ is a no-good, namely, it cannot be extended to a solution. •

In other words, we know that if x_j's value is changed from a_j to another value, we will never explore again any solution that starts with $\vec{a}_j = (a_1, \ldots, a_j)$. But since $\vec{a}_j$ is a no-good, no solution will be missed.

6.2 Backjumping Styles

Next we present three styles of backjumping. *Gaschnig's backjumping* jumps back to the culprit variable only at leaf dead-ends. *Graph-based backjumping* extracts information about irrelevant backtrack points exclusively from the constraint graph and jumps back at nonleaf (internal) dead-ends as well. *Conflict-directed backjumping* combines maximal backjumps at both leaf and internal dead-ends, but is not restricted to graph information alone.

6.2.1   Gaschnig's Backjumping

We first define the notion of culprit that is used in Gaschnig's backjumping.

DEFINITION   **(culprit variable)**
6.6

Let $\vec{a}_i = (a_1, \ldots, a_i)$ be a leaf dead-end. The *culprit index* relative to $\vec{a}_i$ is defined by $b = min\{j \leq i| \ \vec{a}_j$ conflicts with $x_{i+1}\}$. We define the *culprit variable* of $\vec{a}_i$ to be x_b.   •

We use the notions of culprit tuple $\vec{a}_b$ and culprit variable x_b interchangeably. By definition, $\vec{a}_b$ is a conflict set that is minimal relative to prefix tuples, namely, tuples associated with a prefix subset of the ordered variables. We claim that x_b is both safe and maximal. That is, we make the following claim:

PROPOSITION   If $\vec{a}_i$ is a leaf dead-end and x_b is its culprit variable, then $\vec{a}_b$ is a safe backjump
6.1   destination and $\vec{a}_j$, $j < b$, is not.

Proof   By definition of a culprit, $\vec{a}_b$ is a conflict set of x_{i+1} and is therefore a no-good. Consequently, jumping to x_b and changing the value a_b of x_b to another consistent value of x_b (if one exists) will not result in skipping a potential solution. On the other hand, it is easy to construct a case where backing up further than x_b skips solutions (left as Exercise 2).   •

Computing the culprit variable of $\vec{a}_i$ is relatively simple since at most i subtuples need to be tested for consistency with x_{i+1}. Moreover, it can be computed during search by gathering some basic information while assembling $\vec{a}_i$. An alternative description is that the culprit variable of a dead-end state $\vec{a}_i = (a_1, \ldots, a_i)$ is the most recent variable in $\{x_1, \ldots, x_i\}$, whose assigned value in $\vec{a}_i$ renders inconsistent the last remaining values in the domain of x_{i+1} not ruled out by prior variable value assignments.

Rather than waiting for a dead-end $\vec{a}_i$ to occur, Gaschnig's backjumping uses information recorded while generating $\vec{a}_i$ to determine the dead-end's culprit variable x_b. The algorithm uses a marking technique whereby each variable x_j maintains a pointer *latest*$_j$ to the *most recently instantiated* predecessor found incompatible with any of the variable's values. The pointer identifies the most recent variable tested for consistency with x_j and found to have a value in conflict with a new value in D'_j. For example, if no compatible values exist for x_j and if $latest_j = 3$, the pointer indicates that $\vec{a}_3$ is a conflict set of x_j. If x_j does have a consistent value, then $latest_j$ is assigned the value $j - 1$ (which allows backtracking chronologically in nonleaf dead-ends). The algorithm jumps from a dead-end variable x_{i+1} (or a leaf dead-end $\vec{a}_i$) back to $x_{latest_{i+1}}$, its culprit. Gaschnig's backjumping algorithm is presented in Figure 6.1.

EXAMPLE 6.2
Consider the problem in Figure 5.4 and the order d_1. At the dead-end for x_7 that results from the partial instantiation $(\langle x_1, red \rangle, \langle x_2, blue \rangle, \langle x_3, blue \rangle, \langle x_4, blue \rangle, \langle x_5, green \rangle, \langle x_6, red \rangle)$, $latest_7 = 3$, because $x_7 = red$ was ruled out by $\langle x_1, red \rangle$, $x_7 = blue$ was ruled out by $\langle x_3, blue \rangle$, and no later variable had to be examined. On returning to x_3, the algorithm finds no further values to try ($D'_3 = \emptyset$). Since $latest_3 = 2$, the next variable examined will be x_2. Thus we see the algorithm's ability to backjump at leaf dead-ends. On subsequent dead-ends, as in x_3, it goes back to its preceding variable only. An example of the algorithm's practice of pruning the search space is given in Figure 6.2. •

PROPOSITION 6.2
Gaschnig's backjumping implements only safe and maximal backjumps in leaf dead-ends.

Proof Whenever there is a leaf dead-end x_i, the algorithm has a partial instantiation of $\vec{a}_{i-1} = (a_1, \ldots, a_{i-1})$. We only need to show that $latest_i$ is the culprit of x_i. Let $j = latest_i$. $\vec{a}_j$ is clearly in conflict with x_i, so we only have to show that $\vec{a}_j$ is minimal relative to prefix tuples. Since $j = latest_i$ when the domain of x_i is exhausted, and since a dead-end did not previously happen, any earlier $\vec{a}_k$ for $k < j$ is not a conflict set of x_i, and therefore x_j is the culprit variable as defined by Definition 6.6. From Proposition 6.1, it follows that this algorithm is safe and maximal. •

6.2.2 Graph-Based Backjumping

If a backtracking algorithm jumps back to a previous variable x_j from a leaf dead-end, and if x_j has no more candidate values to instantiate, then x_j is termed an *internal dead-end variable*, and $\vec{a}_{j-1}$ is an *internal dead-end state*.

EXAMPLE 6.3
In Figure 6.3, all of the backjumps illustrated lead to internal dead-ends, except for the jump back to $(\langle x_1, green \rangle, \langle x_2, blue \rangle, \langle x_3, red \rangle, \langle x_4, blue \rangle)$, because this is the only case where another value exists in the domain of the culprit variable. •

In Gaschnig's backjumping, a jump of more than one level happens only at leaf dead-ends. At internal dead-ends, the algorithm takes the most conservative step of jumping back only one level. Algorithm *graph-based backjumping*

procedure GASCHNIG'S-BACKJUMPING

Input: A constraint network $\mathcal{R} = (X, D, C)$.

Output: Either a solution, or a decision that the network is inconsistent.

$i \leftarrow 1$ (initialize variable counter)
$D_i' \leftarrow D_i$ (copy domain)
$latest_i \leftarrow 0$ (initialize pointer to culprit)
while $1 \leq i \leq n$
    instantiate $x_i \leftarrow$ SELECT-VALUE-GBJ
    if x_i is null   (no value was returned)
      $i \leftarrow latest_i$ (backjump)
    else
      $i \leftarrow i + 1$
      $D_i' \leftarrow D_i$
      $latest_i \leftarrow 0$
end while
if $i = 0$
    return "inconsistent"
else
    return instantiated values of $\{x_1, \dots, x_n\}$
end procedure

procedure SELECT-VALUE-GBJ

    while D_i' is not empty
      select an arbitrary element $a \in D_i'$, and remove a from D_i'
      $consistent \leftarrow true$
      $k \leftarrow 1$
      while $k < i$ and $consistent$
        if $k > latest_i$
          $latest_i \leftarrow k$
        if not CONSISTENT$(\vec{a}_k, x_i = a)$
          $consistent \leftarrow false$
        else
          $k \leftarrow k + 1$
      end while
      if $consistent$
        return a
    end while
    return null   (no consistent value)
end procedure

Figure 6.1   Gaschnig's backjumping algorithm.

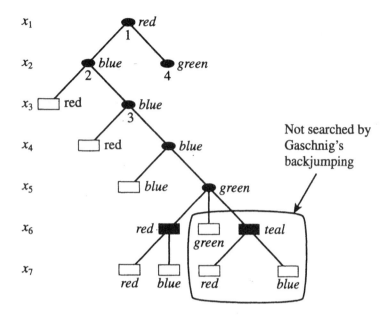

Figure 6.2 Portion of the search space explored by Gaschnig's backjumping, on the example network in Figure 5.4 under $x_1 = red$. The nodes circled are explored by backtracking but not by Gaschnig's backjumping. Notice that unlike previous examples we explicitly display leaf dead-end nodes although they are not legal states in the search space.

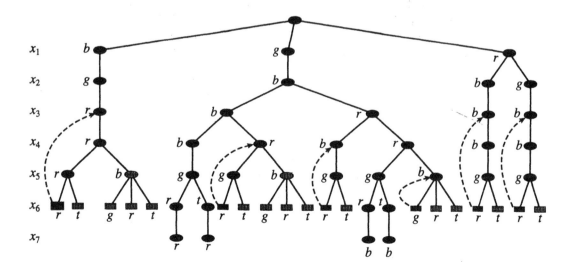

Figure 6.3 The search space for the graph-coloring problem from Figure 5.4. Dashed arrows show the jumps performed at leaf dead-ends by Gaschnig's backjumping. Cross-hatched nodes are those avoided by this technique.

implements jumps of more than one level at both internal dead-ends and leaf dead-ends.

Graph-based backjumping extracts knowledge about possible conflict sets from the structure of the constraint graph exclusively (that is, it recognizes variables, and the presence or absence of constraints between variables, but it does not use information about the domains of the variables or the nature of the constraints). Whenever a dead-end occurs and a solution cannot be extended to the next variable x, the algorithm jumps back to the most recent variable y that is *connected* to x in the constraint graph; if y has no more values, the algorithm jumps back again, this time to the most recent variable z connected to x *or* y; and so on. The second and any further jumps are jumps at *internal dead-ends*. By using the precompiled information encoded in the graph, the algorithm avoids computing *latest$_i$* during each consistency test.

Graph-based backjumping uses the subset of earlier variables adjacent to x_{i+1} as an approximation of a minimal conflict set of x_{i+1}. It is an approximation because even when a constraint exists between two variables x_u and x_{i+1}, the particular value currently being assigned to x_u may not conflict with any potential value of x_{i+1}. For instance, assigning *blue* to x_2 in our graph-coloring problem of Figure 5.4 has no effect on x_6 because *blue* is not in x_6's domain. Since graph-based backjumping does not maintain domain value information, it fills in this gap by assuming the worst: that the subset of variables connected to x_{i+1} is a minimal conflict set of x_{i+1}. Under this assumption, the latest variable in the ordering that precedes x_{i+1} and is connected to x_{i+1} is the culprit variable.

Studying graph-based backjumping is important because algorithms with performance tied to the constraint graph allow us to determine graph-theoretic complexity bounds, and thus to develop graph-based heuristics aimed at reducing these bounds. Such bounds are also applicable to algorithms that use refined run-time information such as Gaschnig's backjumping and conflict-directed backjumping (described in Section 6.4).

We now introduce some graph terminology that will be used in the following pages:

DEFINITION 6.7   **(ancestors, parent)**

Given a constraint graph and an ordering of the nodes d, the *ancestor set* of variable x, denoted $anc(x)$, is the subset of the variables that precede and are connected to x. The *parent* of x, denoted $p(x)$, is the most recent (or latest) variable in $anc(x)$. If $\vec{a}_i = (a_1, \ldots, a_i)$ is a dead-end, we equate $anc(\vec{a}_i)$ with $anc(x_{i+1})$, and $p(\vec{a}_i)$ with $p(x_{i+1})$.   •

EXAMPLE 6.4   The graph of Figure 5.4 is given in Figure 6.4(a) ordered along $d_1 = (x_1, \ldots, x_7)$. In this example, $anc(x_7) = \{x_1, x_3, x_4, x_5\}$ and $p(x_7) = x_5$. The parent of the leaf dead-end $\vec{a}_6 = (\textit{blue, green, red, red, blue, red})$ is x_5, which is the parent of x_7.   •

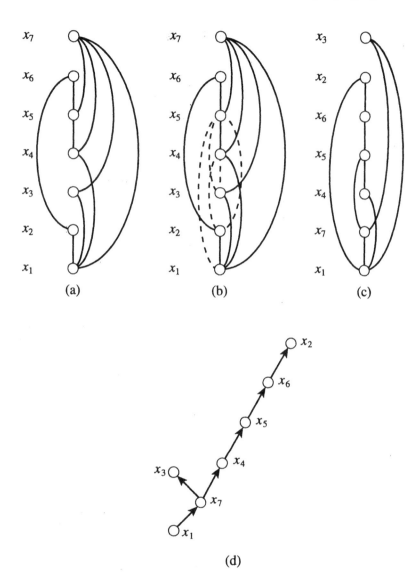

Figure 6.4 Several ordered constraint graphs of the problem in Figure 5.4: (a) along ordering $d_1 = (x_1, x_2, x_3, x_4, x_5, x_6, x_7)$, (b) the induced graph along d_1, (c) along ordering $d_2 = (x_1, x_7, x_4, x_5, x_6, x_2, x_3)$, and (d) a DFS spanning tree along ordering d_2.

It is easy to show that if $\vec{a}_i$ is a leaf dead-end, $p(\vec{a}_i)$ is safe. Moreover, if only graph-based information is utilized and if culprit variables are not compiled as in Gaschnig's backjumping, it is unsafe to jump back any further. When facing an internal dead-end at x_i, however, it may not be safe to jump to its parent $p(x_i)$, as we see in the next example.

EXAMPLE
6.5

In the constraint network in Figure 5.4 with ordering $d_1 = x_1, \ldots, x_7$. x_1 is the parent of x_4. Assume that a dead-end occurs at node x_5 and that the algorithm returns to x_4. If x_4 has no more values to try, it will be perfectly safe to jump back to its parent x_1. Now let us consider a different scenario. The algorithm encounters a leaf dead-end at x_7, so it jumps back to x_5. If x_5 is an internal dead-end, control is returned to x_4. If x_4 is also an internal dead-end, then jumping to x_1 is now unsafe, since changing the value of x_3 could theoretically undo the dead-end at x_7 that started this latest retreat. If, however, the dead-end variable that initiated this latest retreat was x_6, it *would* be safe to jump as far back as x_2, if we encounter an internal dead-end at x_4.   ●

Clearly, when encountering an internal dead-end, it matters which node initiated the retreat. The following few definitions identify the graph-based culprit variable via the *induced ancestor set* in the current *session*.

DEFINITION
6.8

(invisit, session)

We say that backtracking *invisits* x_i if it processes x_i coming from a variable earlier in the ordering. The session of x_i starts upon the invisiting of x_i and ends when retracting to a variable that precedes x_i. At a given state of the search where variable x_i is already instantiated, the *current session* of x_i is the set of variables processed by the algorithm since the most recent *invisit* to x_i. The current session of x_i includes x_i, and therefore the session of a leaf dead-end variable has a single variable.   ●

DEFINITION
6.9

(relevant dead-ends)

The relevant dead-ends of x_i's session, denoted $r(x_i)$, are defined recursively as follows. The relevant dead-ends in the session of a leaf dead-end x_i are just x_i. If x_i is a variable to which the algorithm retracted due to a dead-end at x_j, then the relevant dead-ends of $x_i's$ session are the union of its current relevant dead-ends and the ones inherited from x_j, namely, $r(x_i) = r(x_i) \cup r(x_j)$.   ●

The above definition of relevant dead-ends seems involved. However, this complication is necessary if we want to allow the biggest graph-based backjumping possible.

DEFINITION
6.10

(induced ancestors, graph-based culprit)

Let x_i be a dead-end variable. Let Y be the set of all the relevant dead-ends in x_i's current session. The *induced ancestor set* of x_i relative to Y, $I_i(Y)$, is the union of all Y's ancestors, restricted to variables that precede x_i. Formally, $I_i(Y) = \cup_{y \in Y} anc(y) \cap \{x_1, \ldots, x_{i-1}\}$. The induced parent of x_i

relative to Y, $P_i(Y)$, is the latest variable in $I_i(Y)$. We call $P_i(Y)$ the graph-based culprit of x_i.   •

THEOREM 6.1

Let $\vec{a}_{i-1}$ be a dead-end (leaf or internal) and let Y be the set of relevant dead-end variables in the current session of x_i. If only graph information is used, the graph-based culprit, $x_j = P_i(Y)$, is the earliest variable to which it is safe to jump for graph-based backjumping.

Proof *Sketch:* By definition of x_j, all the variables between x_j and the dead-end variable do not participate in any constraint with any of the relevant dead-end variables Y in x_i's current session. Consequently, any change of value to any of these variables will not perturb any of the no-goods that caused the dead-end in $\vec{a}_i$, and so jumping to x_j is safe.

Next we argue that if the algorithm had jumped to a variable *earlier* than x_j, some solutions might have been skipped. Let y_i be the first (relative to the ordering) relevant dead-end variable in Y that is connected to x_j encountered by backtracking. We argue that there is no way, based on graph information only, to rule out the possibility that there exists an alternative value of x_j for which y_i may not lead to a dead-end. If y_i is a leaf dead-end, and since x_j is an ancestor of y_i, there exists a constraint R whose scope S contains x_j and y_i, such that the current assignment $\vec{a}_i$ restricted to S cannot be extended to a legal tuple of R. Clearly, had the value of x_j been changed, the current assignment may have been extendible to a legal tuple of R and the dead-end at y_i may not have occurred. If y_i is an internal dead-end, there were no values of y_i that both were consistent with $\vec{a}_j$ and could be extended to a solution. It is not ruled out (when using the graph only) that different values of x_j, if attempted, could permit new values of y_i for which a solution might exist. Exercise 4 asks you to construct a counterexample to make the above intuitive argument exact.   •

EXAMPLE 6.6

Consider again the ordered graph in Figure 6.4(a), and let x_4 be a dead-end variable. If x_4 is a leaf dead-end, then $Y = \{x_4\}$, and x_1 is the sole member in its induced ancestor set $I_4(Y)$. The algorithm may jump safely to x_1. If x_4 is an internal dead-end with $Y = \{x_4, x_5, x_6\}$, the induced ancestor set of x_4 is $I_4(\{x_4, x_5, x_6\}) = \{x_1, x_2\}$, and the algorithm can safely jump to x_2. However, if $Y = \{x_4, x_5, x_7\}$, the corresponding induced parent set $I_4(\{x_4, x_5, x_7\}) = \{x_1, x_3\}$, and upon encountering a dead-end at x_4, the algorithm should retract to x_3. If x_3 is also an internal dead-end, the algorithm retracts to x_1 since $I_3(\{x_3, x_4, x_5, x_7\}) = \{x_1\}$. If, however, $Y = \{x_4, x_5, x_6, x_7\}$, when a dead-end at x_4 is encountered (we could have a dead-end at x_7, jump back to x_5, go forward and jump back again at x_6, and yet again at x_5), then $I_4(\{x_4, x_5, x_6, x_7\}) = \{x_1, x_2, x_3\}$. The algorithm then retracts to x_3, and if it is a dead-end, it will retract further to x_2, since $I_3(\{x_3, x_4, x_5, x_6, x_7\}) = \{x_1, x_2\}$.   •

Algorithm GRAPH-BASED-BACKJUMPING is given in Figure 6.5. It can be shown that it jumps back at leaf and internal dead-ends as far as graph-based information allows. That is, for each variable x_i, the algorithm maintains x_i's induced ancestor set I_i relative to the relevant dead-ends in x_i's current session.

6.2.3   Conflict-Directed Backjumping

The two backjumping ideas we have discussed; jumping back to a variable that, *as instantiated*, the current state is in conflict with the current variable, and jumping back at internal dead-ends, can be integrated into a single algorithm: the *conflict-directed backjumping* algorithm. This algorithm uses the scheme we have already outlined for graph-based backjumping, but, rather than relying on graph information, exploits information gathered during search. For each variable, the algorithm maintains an induced *jumpback set*. Given a dead-end tuple $\vec{a}_i$, we define next the jumpback set of $\vec{a}_i$ as the variables participating in $\vec{a}_i$'s *earliest minimal conflict set* of all relevant dead-ends in its session. We first define an ordering between constraints. Let $scope(R)$ denote the scope of constraint R.

DEFINITION 6.11   **(earlier constraint)**

Given an ordering of the variables in a constraint network, we say that constraint R is *earlier* than constraint Q if the latest variable in $scope(R) - scope(Q)$ precedes the latest variable in $scope(Q) - scope(R)$.   •

For instance, under the variable ordering $(x_1, x_2, \ldots)$, if the scope of constraint R_1 is (x_3, x_5, x_8, x_9) and the scope of constraint R_2 is (x_2, x_6, x_8, x_9), then R_1 is earlier than R_2 because x_5 precedes x_6. Given an ordering of all the variables in X, the *earlier* relation defines a total ordering on the constraints in C.

DEFINITION 6.12   **(earliest minimal conflict set)**

For a network $\mathcal{R} = (X, D, C)$ with an ordering of the variables d, let $\vec{a}_i$ be a tuple whose potential dead-end variable is x_{i+1}. The *earliest minimal conflict set* of $\vec{a}_i$, (or of x_{i+1}) denoted $emc(\vec{a}_i)$, can be generated as follows. Consider the constraints in $C = \{R_1, \ldots, R_c\}$ with scopes $\{S_1, \ldots, S_c\}$, in order as defined in Definition 6.11. For $j = 1$ to c, if there exists $b \in D_{i+1}$ such that R_j is violated by $(\vec{a}_i, x_{i+1} = b)$, but no constraint earlier than R_j is violated by $(\vec{a}_i, x_{i+1} = b)$, then $var\text{-}emc(\vec{a}_i) \leftarrow var\text{-}emc(\vec{a}_i) \cup S_j$. $emc(\vec{a}_i)$ is the subtuple of $\vec{a}_i$ projected over $var\text{-}emc(\vec{a}_i)$. Namely, $emc(\vec{a}_i) = \vec{a}_i[var\text{-}emc(\vec{a}_i)]$.   •

DEFINITION 6.13   **(jumpback set)**

The *jumpback set* J_{i+1} of a leaf dead-end x_{i+1} is its $var\text{-}emc(\vec{a}_i)$. The jump-back set of an internal state $\vec{a}_i$ (or of variable x_{i+1}) includes all the

procedure GRAPH-BASED-BACKJUMPING

Input: A constraint network $\mathcal{R} = (X, D, C)$.

Output: Either a solution, or a decision that the network is inconsistent.

    compute $anc(x_i)$ for each x_i (see Definition 6.7 in text)

    $i \leftarrow 1$ (initialize variable counter)

    $D_i' \leftarrow D_i$ (copy domain)

    $I_i \leftarrow anc(x_i)$ (copy of anc( ) that can change)

    while $1 \leq i \leq n$

        instantiate $x_i \leftarrow$ SELECT-VALUE

        if x_i is null   (no value was returned)

            $iprev \leftarrow i$

            $i \leftarrow$ latest index in I_i (backjump)

            $I_i \leftarrow I_i \cup I_{iprev} - \{x_i\}$

        else

            $i \leftarrow i + 1$

            $D_i' \leftarrow D_i$

            $I_i \leftarrow anc(x_i)$

    end while

    if $i = 0$

        return "inconsistent"

    else

        return instantiated values of $\{x_1, \ldots, x_n\}$

end procedure

procedure SELECT-VALUE   (same as BACKTRACKING's)

    while D_i' is not empty

        select an arbitrary element $a \in D_i'$, and remove a from D_i'

        if CONSISTENT($\vec{a}_{i-1}, x_i = a$)

            return a

    end while

    return null   (no consistent value)

end procedure

Figure 6.5 The GRAPH-BASED-BACKJUMPING algorithm.

var-emc($\vec{a}_j$) of all the relevant dead-ends $\vec{a}_j$, $j \geq i$, that occurred in the current session of x_i. Formally, $J_i = \bigcup \{var\text{-}emc(\vec{a}_j) \mid \vec{a}_j$ is a relevant dead-end in x_i's session$\}$. •

The definition of relevant dead-ends is exactly the same as in the graph-based case, when replacing *anc*($\vec{a}_i$) by *var-emc*($\vec{a}_i$). In other words, *var-emc*($\vec{a}_i$) plays the role that ancestors play in the graphical scheme, while J_i plays the role of induced ancestors. However, rather than being elicited from the graph, these elements are dependent on the particular value instantiation and can be uncovered during search. The variables *var-emc*($\vec{a}_i$) are a subset of the graph-based *anc*($\vec{a}_i$). The variables in *anc*($\vec{a}_i$) that are not included in *var-emc*($\vec{a}_i$) either participate only in nonaffecting constraints (do not exclude any value of x_{i+1}) relative to the current instantiation $\vec{a}_i$ or, even if the constraints are potentially affecting, they are superfluous, as they rule out values of x_{i+1} eliminated by earlier constraints. Consequently, using similar arguments as we employed in the graph-based case, it is possible to show the following:

PROPOSITION 6.3   Given a dead-end tuple $\vec{a}_i$, the latest variable in its jumpback set J_i is the earliest variable to which it is safe to jump.

Proof   *Sketch:* Let x_j be the latest variable in the jumpback set J_i of a dead-end $\vec{a}_i$. As in the graph-based case, jumping back to a variable later than x_j will not remove some of the no-goods that were active in causing this dead-end, and therefore the same dead-end will recur. To show that we cannot jump back any farther than x_j we must show that, because we generate the *var-emc* set by looking at earliest constraints first, it is not possible that there exists an alternative set of constraints for which $\vec{a}_i$ is a dead-end and for which the jumpback set yields an earlier culprit variable. Therefore, it is possible that changing the value of x_j will yield a solution, and that this solution might be missed if we jumped to an earlier variable. •

Algorithm CONFLICT-DIRECTED-BACKJUMPING is presented in Figure 6.6. It computes the jumpback sets for each variable and uses them to determine the variable to which it returns after a dead-end.

EXAMPLE 6.7   Consider the problem of Figure 5.4 using ordering $d_1 = (x_1, \ldots, x_7)$. Given the dead-end at x_7 and the assignment $\vec{a}_6 = (blue, green, red, red, blue, red)$, the *emc* set is $(\langle x_1, blue \rangle, \langle x_3, red \rangle)$, since it accounts for eliminating all the values of x_7. Therefore, algorithm CONFLICT-DIRECTED-BACKJUMPING jumps to x_3. Since x_3 is an internal dead-end whose own $var-emc$ set is $\{x_1\}$, the jumpback set of x_3 includes just x_1, and the algorithm jumps again, this time back to x_1. •

procedure CONFLICT-DIRECTED-BACKJUMPING
Input: A constraint network $\mathcal{R} = (X, D, C)$.
Output: Either a solution, or a decision that the network is inconsistent.

$i \leftarrow 1$	(initialize variable counter)
$D_i^i \leftarrow D_i$	(copy domain)
$J_i \leftarrow \emptyset$	(initialize conflict set)
while $1 \leq i \leq n$	
instantiate $x_i \leftarrow$ SELECT-VALUE-CBJ	
if x_i is null	(no value was returned)
$iprev \leftarrow i$	
$i \leftarrow$ index of last variable in J_i	(backjump)
$J_i \leftarrow J_i \cup J_{iprev} - \{x_i\}$	(merge conflict sets)
else	
$i \leftarrow i + 1$	(step forward)
$D_i^i \leftarrow D_i$	(reset mutable domain)
$J_i \leftarrow \emptyset$	(reset conflict set)
end while	
if $i = 0$	
return "inconsistent"	
else	
return instantiated values of $\{x_1, \ldots, x_n\}$	
end procedure	

subprocedure SELECT-VALUE-CBJ

    while D_i^i is not empty
        select an arbitrary element $a \in D_i^i$, and remove a from D_i^i
        $consistent \leftarrow true$
        $k \leftarrow 1$
        while $k < i$ and *consistent*
            if CONSISTENT$(\vec{a}_k, x_i = a)$
                $k \leftarrow k + 1$
            else
                $R_S \leftarrow$ the earliest constraint causing the conflict,
                add the variables in R_S's scope S excluding x_i, to J_i
                $consistent \leftarrow false$
        end while
        if *consistent*
            return a
    end while
    return null   (no consistent value)
end procedure

Figure 6.6 The CONFLICT-DIRECTED-BACKJUMPING algorithm.

6.2.4   *i*-Backjumping

The notion of a conflict set is based on a simple restriction: we identify conflicts of a single variable only. What if we lift this restriction so that we can look a little further ahead? For example, when backtracking instantiates variables in its forward phase, what happens if it instantiates two variables at the same time? This may lead to special types of hybrids between look-ahead and look-back.

We can define a set of parameterized backjumping algorithms, called *i-backjumping* algorithms, where *i* indexes the number of variables consulted in the forward phase. All algorithms jump back maximally at both leaf and internal dead-ends, as follows. Given an ordering of the variables, *i*-backjumping instantiates them one at a time, as does conflict-directed backjumping. However, when selecting a new value for the next variable, the algorithm makes sure the new value is both consistent with past instantiation, and consistently extendible by the next $i - 1$ variables (which will require revising the CONSISTENT procedure). Note that conflict-directed backjumping is *1-backjumping*. This computation will be performed at every node and can be exploited to generate conflict sets that conflict with *i* future variables, yielding *level-i conflict sets*. A tuple $\bar{a}_j$ is a level-*i* conflict set if it is not consistently extendible by the next *i* variables. Once a dead-end is identified by *i*-backjumping, its associated conflict set is a level-*i* conflict set. The algorithm can assemble the earliest level-*i* conflict set and jump to the latest variable in this set exactly as is done in 1-backjumping. The balance between computation overhead at each node and the savings on node pruning should, of course, be considered. (For elaboration, see Exercise 9.)

6.3   Complexity of Backjumping

We will now return to graph-based backjumping and demonstrate how graph information can yield graph-based complexity bounds relevant to all variants of backjumping.

Although the implementation of graph-based backjumping requires, in general, careful maintenance of each variable's induced ancestor set, some orderings facilitate a particularly simple rule for determining which variable to jump to. Given a graph, a depth-first search (DFS) ordering is one that is generated by a DFS traversal of the graph. This traversal ordering results also in a *DFS spanning tree* of the graph that includes all and only the arcs in the graph that were traversed in a forward manner. The depth of a DFS spanning tree is the number of levels in that tree created by the DFS traversal (see Even 1979). The arcs in a DFS spanning tree are directed toward the higher indexed node. For each node, its neighbor in the DFS tree preceding it in the ordering is called its *DFS parent*.

If we use graph-based backjumping on a DFS ordering of the constraint graph, finding the graph-based culprit requires following a very simple rule: if a dead-end (leaf or internal) occurs at variable x, go back to the DFS parent of x.

EXAMPLE 6.8

Consider, once again, the CSP in Figure 5.4. A DFS ordering $d_2 = (x_1, x_7, x_4, x_5, x_6, x_2, x_3)$ and its corresponding DFS spanning tree are given in Figure 6.4(c) and (d). If a dead-end occurs at node x_3, the algorithm retreats to its DFS parent, which is x_7. •

THEOREM 6.2

Given a *DFS* ordering of the constraint graph, if $f(x)$ denotes the *DFS* parent of x, then, upon a dead-end at x, $f(x)$ is x's graph-based earliest safe variable for both leaf and internal dead-ends.

Proof Given a DFS ordering and a corresponding DFS tree, we will show that if there is a dead-end at x (internal or leaf), $f(x)$ is the latest among the induced ancestors of x. Clearly, $f(x)$ always appears in the induced ancestor set of x since it is connected to x, and since it precedes x in the ordering. It is also the latest in the induced ancestors since all the relevant dead-ends that appear in x's session must be its descendents in the DFS subtree rooted at x. Let y be a relevant dead-end variable in the DFS subtree rooted at x. Because in a DFS tree of any graph the only nontree arcs are backarcs (connecting a node to one of its ancestors in the tree (Even 1979), y's ancestors that precede x must therefore lie on the path (in the DFS spanning tree) from the root to x. Therefore, they either coincide with $f(x)$ or appear before $f(x)$. •

We can now present the first of two graph-related bounds on the complexity of backjumping.

THEOREM 6.3

When graph-based backjumping is performed on a *DFS* ordering of the constraint graph, the number of nodes visited is bounded by $O((b^m k^{m+1}))$, where b bounds the branching degree of the *DFS* tree associated with that ordering, m is its depth, and k is the domain size. The time complexity (measured by the number of consistency checks) is $O(ek(bk)^m)$, where e is the number of constraints.

Proof Let x_i be a node in the DFS spanning tree whose DFS subtree has depth of $m - i$. We associate backjumping search along the DFS tree order with an AND-OR search space tree (rather than the usual search tree space) as follows. The AND-OR tree has two types of nodes: variable nodes are the OR nodes, and value nodes are the AND nodes. The variable and value nodes are alternating. The root of the AND-OR search tree is the root variable of the DFS tree. It has k value child nodes, each corresponding to a possible consistent value. From each of these value nodes emanate b variable nodes, one for each of the root's child variables in the DFS tree.

From each of these variable nodes, value child nodes emanate, each corresponding to a value consistent with the assignment on the path from the root, and so on. In general, any new value nodes that emanate from a variable node must be consistent with the assignment along the path to the root of the AND-OR search tree. You should convince yourself that backjumping traverses a portion of this AND-OR search tree and therefore its size bounds the number of values tested for consistency with a partial instantiation. Let T_i stand for the number of nodes in the AND-OR search subtree rooted at node x_i (at level $m - i$ of the DFS spanning tree). Since any assignment of a value to x_i generates at most b independently solvable subtrees of depth $i - 1$ or less, T_i obeys the following recurrence:

$$T_i = k \cdot b \cdot T_{i-1}$$
$$T_0 = k$$

Solving this recurrence yields $T_m = b^m k^{m+1}$. Thus, the worst-case number of nodes visited by graph-based backjumping is $O(b^m k^{m+1})$. Since creating each value node requires e consistency tests, we get $O(ek(bk)^m)$ consistency tests overall. Notice that when the DFS tree is balanced (when each internal node has exactly b child nodes), the bound can be improved to $T_m = O((n/b)k^{m+1})$, since $n = O(b^{m+1})$.   •

The above bound suggests a graph-based ordering heuristic: use a DFS ordering having a minimal depth. Unfortunately, finding a minimal depth DFS tree is NP-hard. Still, knowing what we should be minimizing may lead to useful heuristics.

It can be shown that DFS orderings of *induced* graphs also allow bounding backjumping's complexity as a function of the depth of a corresponding DFS tree. Let d be an ordering that is a DFS ordering of an induced graph (G^*, d_1), and let m_d^* be the DFS tree depth. It can be shown that graph-based backjumping, if applied along ordering d, has the same backjump rule we saw on a DFS ordering of the original graph.

PROPOSITION Let d be a DFS order of an induced graph of a constraint problem. Jumping
       6.4 back to parents in this DFS tree is safe for graph-based backjumping.   •

   THEOREM If d is a DFS ordering of (G^*, d_1) for some ordering d_1, having depth m_d^*,
       6.4 then the complexity of graph-based backjumping (measured by consistency checks) using ordering d is $O(ek(bk)^{m_d^*})$.   •

A proof, which uses somewhat different terminology and derivation, is given by Bayardo and Miranker (1995). The virtue of Theorem 6.4 is in allowing a larger set

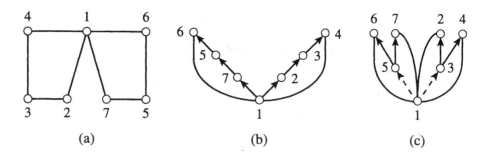

Figure 6.7 (a) A graph, (b) its DFS ordering, and (c) a DFS ordering of its induced graph.

of orderings to be considered, each yielding a bound on backjumping's performance as a function of its DFS tree depth. Since every DFS ordering of G is also a DFS ordering of its induced graph along d, (G^*, d) (the added induced arcs are back arcs of the DFS tree), DFS orderings of G are a subset of all DFS orderings of all of G's induced graphs that may lead to orderings having better bounds.

**EXAMPLE
6.9**
Consider the graph G displayed in Figure 6.7(a). Ordering $d_1 = 1, 2, 3, 4, 7, 5, 6$ is a DFS ordering having the smallest depth of 3. Consider now the induced graph along the same ordering, which has the two added arcs: $\{(1, 3), (1, 5)\}$. A DFS ordering of the induced graph can be provided by $d = 1, 3, 4, 2, 5, 6, 7$, which has a spanning tree depth of only 2. Consequently, graph-based backjumping is O(exp(4)) along d_1 and O(exp(3)) along d. Notice that while $f(x)$ is a safe backjump point, it may not be maximal; if, going forward from 1 to 3, we realize a dead-end at 3 (imagine the domain of x_3 is empty to begin with), we should jump back earlier than 1 and conclude that the problem is inconsistent.   •

6.4 **Learning Algorithms**

The earliest minimal conflict set of Definition 6.12 is a no-good explicated during search and used to guide backjumping. However, this same no-good may be rediscovered as the algorithm explores different paths in the search graph. By making this no-good explicit in the form of a new constraint, we can make sure that the algorithm will not rediscover it, since it will be available for consistency testing. Doing so may prune some subtrees in the remaining search space. This technique, called *constraint recording* or *learning*, is the foundation of the learning algorithms described in this section.

An opportunity to learn new constraints is presented whenever the backtracking algorithm encounters a dead-end, that is, when the current instantiation

$\vec{a}_i = (a_1, \ldots, a_i)$ is a conflict set of x_{i+1}. Had the problem included an explicit constraint prohibiting this conflict set, the dead-end would never have been reached. There is no point, however, in recording the conflict set $\vec{a}_i$ itself as a constraint at this stage because under the backtracking control strategy the current state will not recur.[1] However, if $\vec{a}_i$ contains one or more subsets that are in conflict with x_{i+1}, recording these smaller conflict sets as constraints may prove useful in the continued search; future states may contain these conflict sets, and they exclude larger conflict sets as well.

With the goal of speeding up search, the target of learning is to identify conflict sets that are as small as possible (i.e., minimal). As noted above, one obvious candidate is the earliest minimal conflict set, which is already identified for conflict-directed backjumping. Alternatively, if only graph information is used, the graph-based conflict set could be identified and recorded. Another (extreme) option is to learn and record *all* the minimal conflict sets associated with the current dead-end.

In learning algorithms, the savings yielded from a potentially pruned search (by finding out in advance that a given path cannot lead to a solution) must be balanced against the overhead of processing at each node generation a more extensive database of constraints.[2]

Learning algorithms may be characterized by the way they identify smaller conflict sets. Learning can be *deep* or *shallow*. Deep learning insists on recording only minimal conflict sets that require a deeper and costly analysis. Shallow learning allows recording nonminimal conflict sets as well. Learning algorithms may also be characterized by how they bound the arity of the constraints recorded. Constraints involving many variables are less frequently applicable, require additional memory to store, and are more expensive to consult than constraints having fewer variables. The algorithm may record just a single no-good or multiple no-goods per dead-end, and it may allow learning solely at leaf dead-ends, or at internal dead-ends as well.

We next present three primary types of learning: graph-based learning, deep learning, and jumpback learning. Each of these can be further restricted by bounding the scope size of the constraints recorded, referred to as *bounded learning*. These algorithms exemplify the main alternatives, although there are numerous possible variations.

6.4.1 Graph-Based Learning

Graph-based learning uses the same methods as graph-based backjumping to identify a no-good; information on conflicts is derived from the constraint graph alone.

---

1. Recording this constraint may be useful if the same initial set of constraints is expected to be queried in the future.

2. We make the assumption that the computer program represents constraints internally by storing the invalid combinations. Thus, increasing the number of stored no-goods increases the size of the data structure and slows down retrieval.

Given a leaf dead-end $\vec{a}_i = (a_1, \ldots, a_i)$, the values assigned to the ancestors of x_{i+1} are identified and included in the recorded conflict set. In internal dead-ends the induced ancestor set will be considered.

EXAMPLE 6.10

Consider the problem from Figure 5.4, when searching for *all solutions* in the ordering $d = x_6, x_3, x_4, x_2, x_7, x_1, x_5$. Figure 6.8(b) presents the search space explicated by naive backtracking and by backtracking, augmented with graph-based learning. Branches below the cut lines in Figure 6.8(b) are generated by the former but not by the latter. Leaf dead-ends are numbered (1) through (10) (only dead-ends that appear in the search with learning are numbered). At each dead-end, search with learning can record a new constraint. At dead-end (1), no consistent value exists for x_1. The ancestor set of x_1 is $\{x_2, x_3, x_4, x_7\}$, so graph-based learning records the no-good $(\langle x_2, green \rangle, \langle x_3, blue \rangle, \langle x_4, blue \rangle, \langle x_7, red \rangle)$. This no-good reappears later in the search, under the subtree rooted at $x_6 = teal$, and it can be used to prune the search at the dead-end numbered (9). The dead-ends labeled (2) and (4) occur because no consistent value is found for x_7, which has the ancestor set $\{x_3, x_4\}$. The no-goods $(\langle x_3, blue \rangle, \langle x_4, red \rangle)$ and $(\langle x_3, red \rangle, \langle x_4, blue \rangle)$ are therefore recorded by graph-based learning, in effect creating an "equality" between x_3 and x_4. (The dead-ends

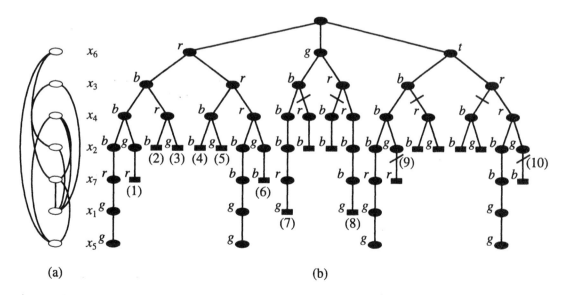

(a) (b)

Figure 6.8 The search space explicated by backtracking on the CSP from Figure 5.4, using the variable ordering $(x_6, x_3, x_4, x_2, x_7, x_1, x_5)$ and the value ordering (*blue, red, green, teal*): (a) the ordered constraint graph, and (b) the search space, where the cut lines indicate branches not explored when graph-based learning is used.

---

procedure GRAPH-BASED-BACKJUMP-LEARNING

    instantiate $x_i \leftarrow$ SELECT-VALUE

    if x_i is null   (no value was returned)

        record a constraint prohibiting $\vec{a}_{i-1}[l_i]$.

        iprev $\leftarrow i$

        (algorithm continues as in Figure 6.5)

Figure 6.9   GRAPH-BASED-BACKJUMP-LEARNING, modifying CBJ.

at (3) and (5) involve the same no-goods; if *graph-based* backjump-ing is used instead of backtracking, these dead-ends will be avoided, however.) This learned constraint prunes the remaining search four times. The following additional no-goods are also recorded by graph-based learning at the indicated dead-ends: (6) with dead-end variable x_1: $(\langle x_2, green \rangle, \langle x_3, red \rangle, \langle x_4, red \rangle, \langle x_7, blue \rangle)$; (7) with dead-end variable x_5: $(\langle x_4, blue \rangle, \langle x_6, green \rangle, \langle x_7, red \rangle)$; (8) with dead-end variable x_5: $(\langle x_4, red \rangle,$ $\langle x_6, green \rangle, \langle x_7, blue \rangle)$; (9) with dead-end variable x_7: $(\langle x_2, green \rangle, \langle x_3, blue \rangle,$ $\langle x_4, blue \rangle)$; and (10) with dead-end variable x_7: $(\langle x_2, green \rangle, \langle x_3, red \rangle, \langle x_4,$ $red \rangle)$. Note that dead-ends (9) and (10) occur at x_2 with learning, and at x_7 without learning.   •

To augment graph-based backjumping with graph-based learning, we need only add a line (in boldface) to GRAPH-BASED-BACKJUMPING after a dead-end is encountered, as shown in Figure 6.9.

Recording a new constraint may require adding a new relation to the list of constraints C. If a constraint with scope I_i already exists, it may only be necessary to remove a tuple from this constraint. The overhead of learning at each dead-end, with graph-based learning, is $O(n)$, since each variable is connected to at most $n - 1$ earlier variables.

6.4.2   Deep versus Shallow Learning

Identifying and recording only minimal conflict sets constitutes *deep learning*. Not insisting on minimal conflict sets is *shallow learning*. Discovering all minimal conflict sets means acquiring all the possible information out of a dead-end. For the problem and ordering of Example 6.10 at the first dead-end, deep learning will record the minimal conflict set of x_1 ($x_2 = green$, $x_3 = blue$, $x_7 = red$) (or perhaps ($x_2 = green$, $x_4 = blue$, $x_7 = red$), or both), instead of the nonminimal conflict sets including both x_3 and x_4 that are recorded by graph-based learning. Discovering *all* minimal conflict sets can be implemented by enumeration: first, recognize all conflict sets of one element; then, all those of two elements; and so on. Although deep learning is the most informative approach, its cost is prohibitive, especially if we want all minimal conflict sets, and in the worst case, exponential in the size of the initial conflict set. If r is the cardinality of the graph-based conflict set, we can envision a worst case where all the subsets of size $r/2$ are minimal conflict sets of the dead-end variable. The number of such minimal conflict sets may be $\binom{r}{r/2} \cong 2^r$, which amounts to exponential time and space complexity at each dead-end.

6.4.3 Jumpback Learning

To avoid the explosion in time and space of full deep learning, we may settle for identifying just one conflict set, minimal relative to prefix conflict sets. The obvious candidate is the jumpback set for leaf and internal dead-ends, as was explicated by conflict-directed backjumping. *Jumpback learning* uses the conflict set restricted to this jumpback set, as the conflict set to be learned. Because this conflict set is calculated by the underlying backjumping algorithm, the overhead in time complexity, at a dead-end, is only the time it takes to store the conflict set. As with graph-based learning, the modification required to augment CONFLICT-DIRECTED-BACKJUMPING with a learning algorithm is minor: specify that the conflict set is recorded as a no-good after each dead-end, as described in Figure 6.10.

EXAMPLE 6.11 For the problem and ordering of Example 6.10 at the first dead-end, jumpback learning will record the no-good $(x_2 = green, x_3 = blue, x_7 = red)$, since that tuple includes the variables in the jumpback set of x_1. •

In general, graph-based learning records the constraints with the largest scopes, and deep learning records the smallest ones. As noted for backjumping, the virtues

---

procedure CONFLICT-DIRECTED-BACKJUMP-LEARNING

    instantiate $x_i \leftarrow$ SELECTVALUE-CBJ

    if x_i is null   (no value was returned)

        record a constraint prohibiting $\vec{a}_{i-1}[J_i]$

        iprev $\leftarrow i$

        (algorithm continues as in Figure 6.6)

Figure 6.10 CONFLICT-DIRECTED-BACKJUMP-LEARNING, modifying CBJ.

of graph-based learning are mainly theoretical (see Section 6.4.6); using this algorithm in practice is not advocated since jumpback learning is always superior. Nor is the use of deep learning recommended, because its overhead cost is usually prohibitive.

6.4.4   Bounded and Relevance-Bounded Learning

Each learning algorithm can be compounded with a restriction on the size of the conflicts learned. When conflict sets of size greater than i are ignored, the result is i-order graph-based learning, i-order jumpback learning, or i-order deep learning. When restricting the arity of the recorded constraint to i, the *bounded learning* algorithm has an overhead complexity that is time and space exponentially bounded by i only.

An alternative to bounding the size of learned no-goods is to bound the learning process by discarding no-goods that appear, by some measure, to be no longer relevant.

DEFINITION 6.14   **(i-relevant)**

A no-good is i-relevant if it differs from the current partial assignment by at most i variable-value pairs.   •

DEFINITION 6.15   **(ith order relevance-bounded learning)**

An ith order relevance-bounded learning scheme maintains only those learned no-goods that are i-relevant and discards the rest.   •

6.4.5   Nonsystematic Randomized Backtrack Learning

Learning can be used to make incomplete search algorithms complete, that is, make them guaranteed to terminate with a solution, or with a proof that no solution exists. Consider a randomized backtracking-based algorithm (randomizing value or variable selection) that, after a fixed number of dead-ends, restarts with a different, randomly selected variable or value ordering, or one that allows unsafe backjumping points. Study of such algorithms has been motivated by observing the performance of incomplete stochastic local search algorithms that often outperform traditional backtracking-based algorithms (see Chapter 7).

Often randomization, restarts, or unsafe backjumping make the search algorithm incomplete. However, completeness can be reintroduced if all no-goods discovered are recorded and consulted. Such randomized learning-based algorithms are complete because, whenever they reach a dead-end, they discover and record a *new* conflict set. Since the number of conflict sets is finite, such algorithms are guaranteed to find a solution. This same argument allows bounding the complexity of learning-based algorithms, discussed in the next subsection.

6.4.6 **Complexity of Backtracking with Learning**

Graph-based learning yields a useful complexity bound on backtracking's performance, parameterized by the induced width w^*. Since it is the most conservative learning algorithm (when excluding arity restrictions), its complexity bound will be applicable to all variants of learning discussed here.

THEOREM 6.5 Let d be an ordering of a constraint graph, and let $w^*(d)$ be its induced width. Any backtracking algorithm using ordering d with graph-based learning has a space complexity of $O(n \cdot (k)^{w^*(d)})$ and a time complexity of $O(n^2 \cdot (2k)^{w^*(d)+1})$, where n is the number of variables and k bounds the domain sizes.

Proof Graph-based learning has a one-to-one correspondence between dead-ends and conflict sets. Backtracking with graph-based learning along d records conflict sets of size $w^*(d)$ or less, because the dead-end variable will not be connected to more than $w^*(d)$ earlier variables by both original constraints and recorded ones. Therefore the number of dead-ends is bounded by the number of possible no-goods of size $w^*(d)$ or less. Moreover, a dead-end at a particular variable x can occur at most $k^{w^*(d)}$ times, after which point constraints are learned excluding all possible assignments of its induced parents. So the total number of dead-ends for backtracking with learning is $O(n \cdot k^{w^*(d)})$, yielding space complexity of $O(n \cdot k^{w^*(d)})$. Since the total number of values considered between successive dead-ends is at most $O(kn)$, the total number of values considered during backtracking with learning is $O(kn \cdot n \cdot k^{w^*(d)}) = O(n^2 \cdot k^{w^*(d)+1})$. Since each value requires testing all constraints defined over the current variable, and at most $w^*(d)$ prior variables, at most $O(2^{w^*(d)})$ constraints are checked per value test, yielding a time complexity bound of $O(n^2(2k)^{w^*(d)+1})$.   ●

Recall that the time complexity of graph-based backjumping can be bounded exponentially by m_d^* where m_d^* is the depth of a DFS tree of an ordered induced graph, while the algorithm requires only linear space. Note that $m_d^* \geq w^*(d)$. However, it can be shown that for any graph, $m_d^* \leq \log n \cdot w^*(d)$. Therefore, to reduce the time bound of graph-based backjumping by a factor of $k^{\log n}$, we need to invest $O(k^{w^*(d)})$ in space, augmenting backjumping with learning. In Chapter 10 we show an alternative argument for this time-space trade-off.

6.5 **Look-Back Techniques for Satisfiability**

Incorporating backjumping and learning into a backtrack-based algorithm for satisfiability requires figuring out how to compute the jumpback conflict set for clausal propositional constraints and for bivalued domains.

For simplicity's sake assume a CNF-based backtracking algorithm like DPLL, but initially without any unit propagation. Here we do not distinguish between the variables in the jumpback set and the associated no-goods uncovered. Note that any no-good is a clause. Note also that a partial solution can be described by a set of literals. Thus, we define the jumpback set as a conflict set called a *J-clause*, which is determined as follows: whenever the algorithm encounters a leaf dead-end of variable x, there must be a clause that forces the literal x and another clause that forces $\neg x$ relative to the current partial solution.[3] We say that clause $(\alpha \vee x)$ forces x relative to a current partial solution σ if all the literals in α are reversed (negated) in σ. Let $(\alpha \vee x)$ and $(\beta \vee \neg x)$ be two such forcing clauses. By resolving these two clauses we generate a new no-good clause $J_x = (\alpha \vee \beta)$. Moreover, had we identified the two earliest clauses (see Definition 6.11) that forbid x and $\neg x$, their resolvent would have been the earliest conflict set of x.

In the case of internal dead-ends the J-clauses are updated as we saw for jump-back sets earlier. Let x be a leaf dead-end and let y be the most recent *literal* in σ that appears in the J-clause of x, J_x (let us assume without loss of generality that y appears positively in σ). Therefore, $J_x = (\theta \vee \neg y)$ (because x or $\neg x$ were forced). If $\neg y$ is consistent with the current prefix of σ truncated below y (namely, it is an alternative value), y inherits J_x's conflict set. That is, $J_y \leftarrow resolve(\theta \vee \neg y, J_x \vee y)$ (note that J_y may be empty here) and search continues forward. Otherwise, if $\neg y$ is not consistent with the prefix of σ below y, there must exist a J-clause of y $(\delta \vee y)$ that forces y. The algorithm then resolves $J_x = (\theta \vee \neg y)$ with $(\delta \vee y)$, yielding a new conflict set of y, $J_y = (\theta \vee \delta)$. The algorithm now jumps back to the recent variable in J_y, records J_y as a conflict, and so on. Algorithm SAT-CBJ-LEARN, given in Figure 6.11, maintains these earliest J_i conflict sets for each variable. Backjumping is implemented by jumping to the most recent variable in these J sets, while learning records these as clauses.

Notice that many details are hidden in the procedure CONSISTENT. Clearly the order by which clauses are tested can have a significant effect on what is learned. Our representation tests earlier clauses before later ones to allow a deep backjump. There are numerous variations of learning in the context of SAT formulas. At any dead-end different clauses can be learned, and the type of clauses learned is indeed the focus of several of the new improved learning schemes (e.g., Grasp). The scheme proposed here favors learning early clauses.

The analysis and intricacy in learning grows when unit propagation is allowed inside CONSISTENT. You can then distinguish between forced assignments (due to unit propagation) and choice-based assignments. An efficient implementation of learning in the presence of unit propagation can benefit from specialized efficient data structures (e.g., watch lists as proposed in Zhang 1997) that quickly recognize unit clauses. Indeed a sequence of learning algorithms for SAT with increased levels of implementation sophistication are being developed, often yielding remarkable

---

3. Note that we abuse notation when denoting by x both a variable and the literal over x denoting $x =$ true. The meaning should be clear from the context.

procedure SAT-CBJ-LEARN

Input: A CNF theory φ over a set of variables $X = \{x_1, \dots, x_n\}$, $\forall i$ $D_i = \{l_i, \neg l_i\}$.

Output: Either a solution, or a decision that the formula is unsatisfiable.

1. $J_i \leftarrow \emptyset$

2.   While $1 \le i \le n$

3.   instantiate $x_i \leftarrow$ SELECT-VALUE-SAT-CBJ-LEARN.

4.   If x_i is null (no value returned), then

5.   add J_i to φ (learning)

6. $iprev \leftarrow i$

7. $i \leftarrow$ index of last variable in J_i, l_i its σ value   (*backjump*)

8. $J_i \leftarrow resolve(J_i \vee l_i, J_{iprev})$ (merge conflict sets)

9.   else,

10.   Select the next variable: $x_i \in X$, $X \leftarrow X - \{x_i\}$, prefer variables
            appearing in unit clauses.

11. $D_i \leftarrow \{l_i, \neg l_i\}$ (go forward)

12. $J_i \leftarrow \emptyset$ (reset conflict set)

13.   Endwhile

14.   if $i = 0$ return "inconsistent"

15.   else, return the set of literals σ

end procedure

subprocedure SELECT-VALUE-SAT-CBJ-LEARN

1. While D_i is not empty

2. $l_i \leftarrow$ select $l_i \in D_i$, remove l_i from D_i.

3.   consistent $\leftarrow$ *true*

4.   If CONSISTENT($\sigma \cup l_i$) then return $\sigma \leftarrow \sigma \cup \{l_i\}$.

5.   else, determine the earliest clause $(\theta \vee \neg l_i)$ forcing $\neg l_i$.

6. $J_i \leftarrow J_i \vee \theta$ $(= resolve(J_i \vee l_i, \theta \vee \neg l_i)$

7. Endwhile

8. Return $x_i \leftarrow$ null (no consistent value)

end procedure subprocedure SELECT-VALUE-SAT-CBJ-LEARN

Figure 6.11 Algorithm SAT-CBJ-LEARN.

leaps in performance. In the algorithm we presented, the preference for unit variables in the variable selection (step 3) will have the effect of unit propagation as in DPLL.

6.6 Integration and Comparison of Algorithms

Complementary enhancements to backtracking can be integrated into a single procedure. The look-ahead strategies discussed in Chapter 5 can be combined with any of the backjumping variants. Additionally, a combined algorithm can employ learning and the dynamic variable and value ordering heuristics based on look-ahead information. Subsequently, once a collection of algorithms is available, the issue of comparison and evaluation needs to be addressed.

6.6.1 Integrating Backjumping and Look-Ahead

One possible combination of look-ahead with look-back is integrating conflict-directed backjumping with forward-checking-level look-ahead and dynamic variable ordering. We present such an integrated algorithm, FC-CBJ, in Figure 6.12.

The main procedure of FC-CBJ closely resembles CONFLICT-DIRECTED-BACKJUMPING (Figure 6.6). Recall that CBJ maintains a jumpback set J for each variable x. SELECTVALUE-CBJ adds earlier instantiated variables to J_i. Upon reaching a dead-end at x_i, the algorithm jumps back to the latest variable in J_i. When CBJ is combined with look-ahead, the J sets are used in the same way, but they are built in a different manner. While selecting a value for x_i, SELECT-VALUE-FC-CBJ puts x_i (and possibly other variables that precede x_i when nonbinary constraints are present) into the J sets of *future*, uninstantiated variables that have a value in conflict with the value assigned to x_i. On reaching a dead-end at a variable x_j that follows x_i, x_i will be in J_j if x_i, as instantiated, pruned some values of x_j.

FC-CBJ is derived from CONFLICT-DIRECTED-BACKJUMPING by making two modifications. The first is that the D' sets are initialized and reset after a dead-end, in the same manner as in GENERALIZED-LOOKAHEAD (Figure 5.7), since SELECT-VALUE-FC-CBJ is based on look-ahead and relies on the D' being accurate and current. The second modification is the call to SELECT-VARIABLE (Figure 5.11) in the initialization phase and during each forward step. These calls could be removed, and the algorithm would revert without other modification to a static variable ordering. But because look-ahead is being performed for the purposes of rejecting inconsistent values, there is little additional cost in performing SELECT-VARIABLE. In practice, this heuristic has been found most effective in reducing the size of the search space.

Apparently, there is some inverse relationship between look-ahead and look-back schemes; the more you look ahead, the less you need to look back. This can be shown at least for forward-checking and for the simplest form of backjumping.

procedure FC-CBJ

Input: A constraint network $\mathcal{R} = (X, D, C)$.

Output: Either a solution, or a decision that the network is inconsistent.

    $i \leftarrow 1$ (initialize variable counter)

    call SELECT-VARIABLE   (determine first variable)

    $D_i' \leftarrow D_i$ for $1 \le i \le n$ (copy all domains)

    $J_i \leftarrow \emptyset$ (initialize conflict set)

    while $1 \le i \le n$

        instantiate $x_i \leftarrow$ SELECT-VALUE-FC-CBJ

        if x_i is null   (no value was returned)

            iprev $\leftarrow i$

            $i \leftarrow$ latest index in J_i (backjump)

            $J_i \leftarrow J_i \cup J_{iprev} - \{x_i\}$

            reset each D_k', $k > i$, to its value before x_i was last instantiated

        else

            $i \leftarrow i + 1$ (step forward)

            call SELECT-VARIABLE   (determine next variable)

            $D_i' \leftarrow D_i$

            $J_i \leftarrow \emptyset$

    end while

    if $i = 0$, **return** "inconsistent"

    else, return instantiated values of $\{x_1, \ldots, x_n\}$

end procedure

subprocedure SELECT-VALUE-FC-CBJ

    while D_i' is not empty

        select an arbitrary element $a \in D_i'$, and remove a from D_i'

        empty-domain $\leftarrow$ *false*

        for all k, $i < k \le n$

            for all values b in D_k'

                if not CONSISTENT($\vec{a}_{i-1}$, $x_i = a$, $x_k = b$)

                    let R_S be the earliest constraint causing the conflict

                    add the variables in R_S's scope S, but not x_k, to J_k

                    remove b from D_k'

            endfor

            if D_k' is empty   ($x_i = a$ leads to a dead-end)

                empty-domain $\leftarrow$ *true*

        endfor

        if *empty-domain*   (don't select a)

            reset each D_k' and j_{k}, $i < k \le n$, to status before a was selected

        else, return a

    end while

    return null   (no consistent value)

end subprocedure

Figure 6.12 The main procedure of the FC-CBJ algorithm.

PROPOSITION   When using the same variable ordering, Gaschnig's backjumping always
     6.5   explores every node explored by forward-checking.

   Proof   See Exercise 13.   •

6.6.2   Comparison of Algorithms

Faced with a variety of backtracking-based algorithms and associated heuristics,
it is natural to ask which ones are superior in performance. Performance can be
assessed by a theoretical analysis of worst- or average-case behavior, or determined
empirically. Figure 6.13 shows the partial order relationships between several algorithms discussed in this chapter, based on their explored search space. Algorithm
A is superior to B (an arrow from B to A) if the search space of A is contained in
the search space of B.

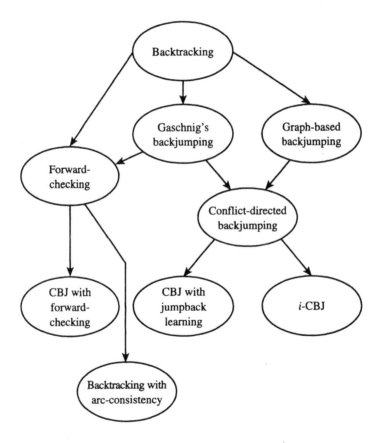

Figure 6.13   The relationships of selected backtracking-based algorithms. An arrow from A to B indicates that on the same problem and with the same variable and value orderings, the nodes
in A's search tree will contain the nodes in B's.

The study of algorithms for constraint satisfaction problems has often relied upon experimentation to compare the relative merits of different algorithms or heuristics. Worst-case analysis, the primary analytical performance evaluation method, has focused largely on characterizing tractable classes of problems. However, simple backtracking search, although exponential in the worst case, can have good average performance. The lack of effective analysis of backtracking search makes empirical evaluation mandatory.

Initially, empirical evaluations have been based on simple benchmark problems, such as the n-queens problem, and on small randomly generated problem instances. In the 1990s, the experimental side of the field blossomed, due to the increasing power of inexpensive computers and the identification of the "phase transition" phenomenon (described next), which has enabled hard random problems to be generated.

For an appropriate empirical study, researchers have to face the question of problem distributions and benchmarks. It is clear that multiple types of benchmarks and multiple ways of presenting the results are needed to be able to present a reliable picture. Benchmarks should include individual instances that come from various applications, parameterized random problems, and application-based parameterized problems. Several criteria are frequently measured: CPU time, size of generated search tree, or calls to a common subroutine, such as CONSISTENT. The general goal of such studies is to identify a small number of algorithms that are dominating—observed to be superior on some class of problems.

Individual Instances as Benchmarks

The merit of this approach is that it is close, if not identical, to the underlying goal of all research: to solve real problems. If the benchmark problems are interesting, then the results of such a comparison are likely to be interesting. The drawback of using benchmarks of this type is that it is often impossible to extrapolate the results. Algorithm A may beat algorithm B on one benchmark but lose on another.

Random Problems

A contrasting technique for evaluating or comparing algorithms is to run the algorithms on artificial, synthetic, parameterized, randomly generated data. Since a practically unlimited supply of such random problems is easily generated, it is possible to run an algorithm on a large number of instances, thereby minimizing sampling error. Moreover, because the problem generator is controlled by several parameters, the experimenter can observe the possibly changing efficacy of the algorithm as one or more of the parameters change.

Application-Based Random Problems

The idea is to identify a problem domain (e.g., job shop scheduling) that can be used to define parameterized problems having a specific structure, and to generate instances by randomly generating values for the problem's parameters. This approach combines the virtues of the two approaches above: it focuses on problems that are related to real applications, and it allows generating many instances for the purpose of statistical validity of the results.

The Phase Transition

The phase transition phenomenon was studied extensively in the context of satisfiability. The theory of NP-completeness is based on worst-case complexity. The fact that 3-SAT is NP-complete implies (assuming the $NP \neq P$) merely that any algorithm for 3-SAT will take an exponential time for some problem instances. To understand the behavior of algorithms in practice, average-case complexity is more appropriate. For this we need to supply a probability distribution on formulas for each input length. Initially, experiments were conducted using random clause length formulas. These were generated using a parameter p as follows. For each new clause of the m clauses, include each of the $2n$ literals in the new clause with probability p. It was shown, however, that DPLL solves these kinds of problems in polynomial average time (for a survey see Cook and Mitchell 1997). Subsequently it was found that the fixed-length formulas took exponential time on average and therefore were perceived as a more appropriate benchmark. Fixed-length formulas are generated by selecting a constant number m of clauses, uniformly at random from the set of all possible clauses of a given length k. The resulting distribution is called random k-SAT. When investigating the performance of DPLL on these problems, it was observed that when the number of clauses is small, most instances are satisfiable and very easily solved; when the number of clauses is very large, most instances can be determined unsatisfiable quickly as well. In between, as the number of clauses grows, difficulty in solution grows up to a peak and then goes down monotonically. If c is the ratio of clauses to variables $C = m/n$, it was shown that for 3-SAT the peak occurs around the ratio 4.2 (see Figure 6.14). Also between these ratios, the probability of satisfiability shifts smoothly from near 1 to near 0. It is intriguing that the peak in difficulty occurs near the ratio where about half of the formulas were satisfiable. The same pattern of hardness was found with some other algorithms and also for larger numbers of literals in a clause, k, but with the transition at higher ratios, and the peak difficulty for DPLL being much greater (Cook and Mitchell 1997).

The phase transition observation had a significant practical implication. It allowed researchers to test their algorithms on hard problem instances, sampled from the phase transition, thus deliberately testing the average performance of hard instances.

A similar phenomenon was observed for binary CSPs. To generate binary random CSPs over N variables of fixed length, a fixed number C of constraints are generated uniformly at random from the set of $N(N-1)/2$ constraints, and for each constraint, T pairs of values out of the possible K^2 values are selected uniformly at random as no-goods. Given a fixed number of variables N, values K, and tightness T, the value of C in the phase transition of any backtracking

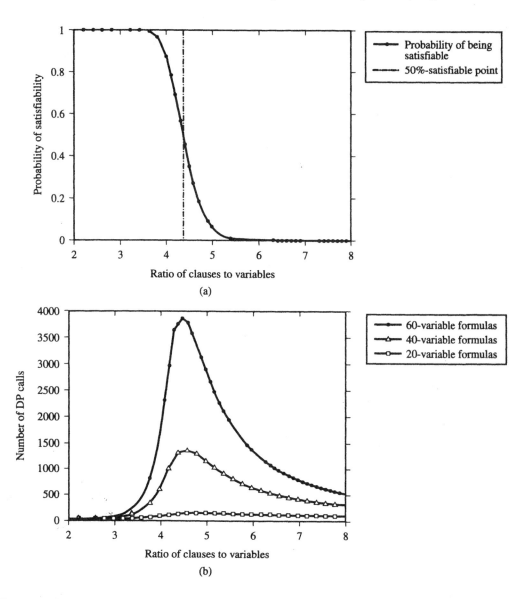

Figure 6.14 The phase transition for random 3-SAT. (a) The probability of a formula being satisfiable as a function of clauses to variables ratio. (b) DPLL performance.

search could be determined empirically while varying the number of constraints from small to large. Therefore, empirical studies first determine the value of C that corresponds to the phase transition and subsequently generate instances from this region. Experimentally derived formulas for number of constraints C' at the cross-over point, $C' = CN(N-1)/2$, is given in Table 6.1 (Frost 1997, page 51).

Table 6.1   Experimentally derived formulas for C' at the cross-over point, under Model B. $C' = CN(N-1)/2$ is the number of constraints in a CSP with parameters C and N.

D	T	Formula for C'
3	.111	$7.300N + 16.72$
3	.222	$3.041N + 13.72$
3	.333	$1.516N + 15.56$
3	.444	$0.725N + 16.78$
6	.111	$13.939N + 12.82$
6	.222	$6.361N + 6.56$
6	.333	$3.761N + 5.49$
6	.444	$2.408N + 5.41$
6	.556	$1.510N + 7.00$
9	.222	$8.284N + 3.86$
9	.333	$4.949N + 4.87$
9	.444	$3.208N + 4.32$

Some Empirical Evidence

Table 6.2 demonstrates results of some typical experiments comparing several backtracking algorithms. All algorithms here incorporate forward-checking-level look-ahead and a dynamic variable ordering scheme similar to that described in Figure 5.11. The names are abbreviated in the table: "FC" refers to backtracking with forward-checking and dynamic variable ordering; "FC + AC" refers to forward-checking with arc-consistency enforced after each instantiation; "FC-CBJ" refers to FC and conflict-directed backjumping; "FC-CBJ + LVO" adds a value ordering heuristic called LVO; "FC-CBJ + LRN" is CBJ plus fourth-order jumpback learning; "FC-CBJ + LRN + LVO" is CBJ with both LVO and learning. The columns labeled "Set 1" through "Set 3" report averages from 2000 randomly generated binary CSP instances. All instances had variables with three-element value domains, and the number of constraints was selected to generate approximately 50% solvable problems. The number of variables and the number of valid tuples per constraint was 200 and 8 for Set 1, 300 and 7 for Set 2, and 350 and 6 for Set 3. The rightmost two columns of the figure show results on two specific problems from the Second Dimacs Implementation Challenge (Johnson and Trick 1996): ssa7552-038 and ssa7552-158. For more details about the experiments, see Frost (1997).

These results show that interleaving an arc-consistency procedure with search was generally quite effective in these studies, as was combining learning and value ordering. An interesting observation can be made based on the nature of the constraints in each of the three sets of random problems. The problems with more restrictive, or "tighter," constraints had sparser constraint graphs. With the

Table 6.2 Empirical comparison of six selected CSP algorithms.

Algorithm	Set 1		Set 2		Set 3		ssa 038		ssa 158	
	Nodes (thousands)	CPU (seconds)	Nodes (thousands)	CPU (seconds)	Nodes (thousands)	CPU (seconds)	Nodes (thousands)	CPU (seconds)	Nodes (thousands)	CPU (seconds)
FC	207	68.5	—	—	—	—	46	14.5	52	20.0
FC+AC	40	55.4	1	0.6	1	0.4	4	3.5	18	8.2
FC-CBJ	189	69.2	222	119.3	182	140.8	40	12.2	26	10.7
FC-CBJ+LVO	167	73.8	132	86.8	119	111.8	32	11.0	8	4.5
FC-CBJ+LRN	186	63.4	32	15.6	1	0.5	23	5.5	19	8.6
FC-CBJ+LRN+LVO	160	74.0	26	14.0	1	3.8	16	3.8	13	7.1

looser constraints, the difference in performance among the algorithms was much less than on problems with tighter constraints. The arc-consistency enforcing and constraint-learning procedures were much more effective on the sparser graphs with tight constraints. These procedures are able to exploit the local structure in such problems. We also see that FC + AC prunes the search space most effectively.

The empirical results shown in Table 6.2 are only examples of typical experimental comparisons of algorithms. Unfortunately, it is not possible to conclude from this and similar studies how the algorithms will perform on all problems having different structural properties.

6.7 Summary

This chapter described the primary look-back methods, backjumping and learning, for improving backtracking. Both graph-based approaches for backjumping and learning, as well as constraint-based approaches, were presented and analyzed. We showed that backjumping's time complexity can be bounded exponentially as a function of the depth of a DFS tree traversing any of its induced graph, while its space complexity is linear. We also showed that the time and space complexity of learning during search can be bounded exponentially by the induced width. We also explicitly presented a look-back algorithm for satisfiability incorporated with DPLL. We discussed algorithms that combine look-ahead and look-back improvements, and compared the various algorithms using a partial order over their search spaces.

6.8 Bibliographical Notes

Truth maintenance systems were the earliest area to contribute to the look-back aspect of backtracking. Stallman and Sussman (1977) were the first to mention no-good recording, and their idea gave rise to look-back-type algorithms, called *dependency-directed backtracking*, that include both backjumping and no-good recording (McAllester 1990). Their work was followed by Gaschnig (1979), who introduced the backjumping algorithm and also coined the name. Researchers in the logic-programming community were also among the earliest to try and improve a backtracking algorithm used for interpreting logic programs. Their improvements, known under the umbrella term *intelligent backtracking*, have focused on the basic principal ideas for a limited amount of backjumping and constraint recording (Bruynooghe 1981; Rosiers and Bruynooghe 1986; Bruynooghe and Pereira 1984; Cox 1984).

Later, following the introduction of graph-based methods (Freuder 1982; Dechter and Pearl 1987b), Dechter (1990) described the graph-based variant of backjumping, which was followed by Prosser's conflict-directed backjumping (Prosser 1993). She also introduced learning no-goods into backtracking that includes graph-based learning (Dechter 1990). Dechter and Pearl (1987b) identified the induced-width bound on learning algorithms. Frueder and Quinn (1987) noted the dependence of backjumping's performance on the depth of the DFS tree of the constraint graph, and Bayardo and Miranker (1995) improved the complexity bound. They also observed that with (relevance-based) learning, the time complexity of graph-based backjumping can be reduced by a factor of $k^{\log n}$ at an exponential space cost in the induced width (Bayardo and Miranker 1995). Ginsberg (1993) introduced the dynamic backtracking algorithm, which employs a similar notion of keeping only relevant learned no-goods that are most likely to be consulted in the near-future search. Dynamic backtracking uses an interesting variable reordering strategy that allows exploiting good partial solutions constructed in earlier subtrees. The usefulness of the DFS ordering for distributed execution of backjumping was also shown (Dechter, Collin, and Katz 1999).

Subsequently, as it became clear that many of backtracking's improvements are orthogonal to one another (i.e., look-back methods and look-ahead methods), researchers have more systematically investigated various hybrid schemes in an attempt to exploit the virtues of each method. Dechter (1990) evaluated combinations of graph-based backjumping, graph-based learning, and the cycle-cutset scheme. An evaluation of hybrid schemes was carried out by Rosiers and Bruynooghe (1986) on coloring and crypto-arithmetic problems, who combined dynamic variable ordering and some limited look-back, and Prosser (1993), who combined known look-ahead and look-back methods and ranked each combination based on average performance, primarily on zebra problems. Dechter and Meiri (1994) have evaluated the effect of preprocessing by directional consistency algorithms on backtracking and backjumping.

Before 1993, most of the empirical testing was conducted on relatively small problems (up to 25 variables), and the prevalent conclusion was that only low-overhead methods are cost-effective. With improvements in hardware and recognition that empirical evaluation may be the best way to compare the various schemes, a substantial increase in empirical testing has been realized. Cheeseman, Kanefsky, and Taylor (1991) observed that randomly generated instances have a phase transition from easy to hard. Mitchell, Selman, and Levesque (1992) extended this observation to Boolean satisfiability. Subsequent extension to constraint networks are reported in Frost and Dechter (1994b) and in Prosser (1994). Using these observations, researchers began to focus on testing various hybrids of algorithms on larger and harder instances (Frost and Dechter 1994a, 1994b, 1995; Ginsberg 1993; Crawford and Auton 1993; Bayardo and Miranker 1996; Baker 1994). In addition, closer examination of various algorithms uncovered interesting relationships. For instance, as already noted, dynamic variable ordering performs the function of value selection as well as variable selection (Bacchus and van Run 1995), and when the order of variables is fixed, forward-checking eliminates the need for backjumping in leaf nodes, as is done in Gaschnig's backjumping (Kondrak and van Beek 1994).

The value of look-back improvements for solving propositional satisfiability was initially largely overlooked, when most algorithms focused on look-ahead improvements of DPLL (Crawford and Auton 1993; Zhang 1997). This was changed significantly with the work by Bayardo and Schrag (1997). They showed that their algorithm RELSAT, which incorporates both learning and backjumping, outperformed many of the best look-ahead-based SAT solvers based on hard benchmarks available at the time. Subsequently, several variants of learning were proposed for SAT solvers (e.g., Grasp in Marques-Silva and Sakalla 1999), all incorporating an efficient data structure called a *watch list* proposed in the DPLL solver SATO (Zhang 1997), followed by even more intricate engineering ideas in learning-based solvers such as Chaff (Zhao et al. 2001). We should note that these learning-based techniques work especially well on structured problems, while they normally are inferior to DPLL-based procedures on uniformly random instances. In particular, backjump-learning-based SAT solvers performed extremely well for planning instances and for symbolic model verification problems (Clark et al. 1999).

The idea of nonsystematic complete backtracking was introduced by Makoto Yokoo, who was the first to observe that the use of learning in the context of a distributed version of search maintains completeness (Yokoo 1995) and was tested for SAT by Richards and Richards (1998). This idea recently caught up in the community of SAT solver developers as well.

Constraint processing techniques have been incorporated into the *constraint logic programming* (CLP) languages. The inference engine of these languages uses a constraint solver as well as the traditional logic programming inference procedures. One of the most useful constraint techniques included in those languages is the use of various levels of arc-consistency in look-ahead search (Van Hentenryck 1989; Jaffar and Lassez 1994). It remains to be seen whether various styles of look-back methods can also be incorporated in a cost-effective manner.

6.9 **Exercises**

1. Let G be a constraint graph of a problem having five variables x_1, x_2, x_3, x_4, x_5 with arcs (x_1, x_2), (x_2, x_3), (x_3, x_4), (x_4, x_1), (x_4, x_5), (x_5, x_2), as in Figure 5.15 (page 147). For a problem having the constraint graph G and using ordering $d_1 = (x_1, x_2, x_3, x_4, x_5)$, answer, confirm, or reject the following:

   (a) Graph-based backjumping will always behave exactly as backtracking.

   (b) Gaschnig's backjumping will always behave like backtracking.

   (c) Conflict-directed backjumping and Gaschnig's backjumping are always identical on G.

   (d) Graph-based learning over G and ordering d_1 will never record constraints of size greater than two.

   (e) If a leaf dead-end occurs at x_5, what is the induced ancestor set $I_5(x_5)$? What are the induced ancestors $I_3(x_3, x_4)$? $I_3(x_3, x_4, x_5)$?

   (f) Propose a better ordering for graph-based backjumping. Justify your answer.

   (g) If a leaf dead-end occurs at x_5 and then there is another internal dead-end at x_4, what is the conflict set recorded by graph-based learning?

(h) How would your answer on all the previous questions be different if the constraint (x_2, x_3) is omitted?

2. Complete the proof of Proposition 6.1; that is, construct an example showing that backing up further from the culprit in leaf dead-ends skips solutions.

3. Prove the following claim: "For leaf dead-ends, jumping back to the parent in the ordered graph will not cause any solution to be missed."

4. Complete the proof of Theorem 6.1 by constructing a counterexample that proves that it is not safe to back up more than the graph-based culprit when using graph-based backjumping.

5. Let m_d be the depth of a DFS tree of an induced graph along some ordering d_1. Let d be the DFS ordering.

   (a) Prove that graph-based backjumping always jumps to the parent in the DFS tree or to an earlier variable.

   (b) Prove that backjumping along d is bounded exponentially by m_d.

6. Describe backjump- and graph-based learning algorithms for SAT that are incorporated in DPLL with unit propagation look-ahead.

7. Consider the crossword puzzle in Figure 1.1 (page 4), as described in Chapter 2, formulated using the dual-graph representation. Using the ordering $(x_1, x_2, x_5, x_6, x_4, x_3)$, show a trace, whose length is limited to a one-page description for parts (a), (b), and (c) and provide the required answer for parts (d) and (e).

   (a) Graph-based backjumping
   (b) Graph-based backjumping learning
   (c) Jumpback learning
   (d) Bound the complexity of graph-based backjumping on the crossword puzzle along the ordering above
   (e) Bound the complexity of graph-based backjumping learning using that ordering

8. Consider the graph in Figure 6.15. Provide a DFS ordering of the graph and bound the complexity of solving any problem having that graph.

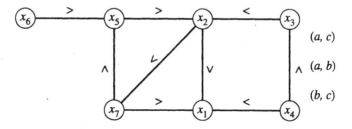

Figure 6.15 A constraint network, with domains $D = \{a, b, c\}$.

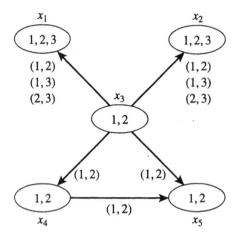

Figure 6.16 A small CSP. The constraints are $x_3 < x_1$, $x_3 < x_2$, $x_3 < x_5$, $x_3 < x_4$, $x_4 < x_5$. The allowed pairs are shown on each arc. The arrows only denote the direction of "$<$" relation.

9. Precisely define algorithm i-BACKJUMPING by defining its i-CONSISTENT procedure.

10. Suppose we try to solve the problem in Figure 6.16 along the ordering $d = (x_1, x_2, x_3, x_4, x_5)$.

    (a) Show the trace and no-goods recorded by graph-based learning.

    (b) Discuss the performance of deep learning on that problem.

    (c) Show how jumpback learning will behave upon a dead-end at x_5.

11. Prove that learning can provide a time complexity bound that is smaller by a factor of $n^{\log_2 k}$ of backjumping.

12. (a) Prove the correctness of FC-CBJ.

    (b) Analyze the overhead at each node of SAT-CBJ-LEARN.

13. Prove Proposition 6.5 (Kondrak and van Beek 1997): When using the same variable ordering, Gaschnig's backjumping always explores every node explored by forward-checking.

14. The Golomb ruler problem was described in Chapter 5 (Exercise 12). Discuss the relevance and effect of backjumping and learning for this problem.

15. Propose a learning and backjumping algorithm for the combinatorial auction problem presented in Chapter 5 (Exercise 13). Trace the performance of the algorithm on a small problem instance. To what extent do you think graph-based backjumping and conflict-directed backjumping are effective for this class of problems? Do the same for the rain problem (Chapter 5, Exercise 14).

chapter 7

Stochastic Greedy Local Search

A life spent making mistakes is not only more honorable,
but more useful than a life spent doing nothing.

George Bernard Shaw

As we have seen throughout this book, techniques for solving constraint problems fall into two main categories: search (also called *conditioning*) and inference. Search and inference can also be combined, trading off time and space, and improving overall performance (see Chapter 10). Nevertheless, even when combined, their worst-case time complexity is often prohibitive, requiring the use of approximations.

Greedy search is one of the most appealing approximation methods. One reason for this method's popularity is that it requires very little memory. A popular greedy approach for solving constraint problems is to start with an arbitrary *full* assignment to all variables, and then resolve inconsistencies by *local repairs*. For example, when solving the 8-queens problem, we can place 8 queens on the board, one on each row and each column, without paying attention to diagonal constraints. Then we try to resolve inconsistencies by moving a queen in its column to a row that removes as many conflicts as possible. These methods, although they may not guarantee success, have recently become popular because, when augmented with randomization and heuristics for escaping local minima, they work extremely well in some problem domains. They can often solve larger problems than those solvable by any complete algorithm.

For example, such *local search methods* can solve n-queens problems with a million queens in less than a minute. This is in contrast to backtracking search methods; even the most sophisticated ones can currently handle only a few hundred queens. Similarly, on hard random k-SAT problems, a local search algorithm can handle instances with several thousands of variables, while the current practical limit for complete methods (e.g., DPLL) is around 600 variables.

One of the earliest applications of this approach was aimed at finding good solutions to the traveling salesman problem (TSP) (Lin 1965; Lin and Kernighan 1973). TSP is an optimization problem where the goal is to find the shortest path for a salesperson needing to visit all cities (a tour) such that each city is visited only once. A greedy local search algorithm for TSP starts by picking a random sequence of cities, and then proceeds to improve it by making local changes, swapping the positions of two cities on the path. These changes are made until no swap leads to further improvement in the total tour. This procedure can be repeated a number of times, each time starting with a new random sequence, and then the best sequence is picked.

This chapter presents a class of such algorithms. Rather than systematically searching combinations of all instantiations, such algorithms use randomization augmented with a greedy component to search a subset of "preferred" instantiations. Since all variants improving on the basic greedy approach use a stochastic component, these algorithms are called *stochastic greedy local search* (or SLS for short, Section 7.1, 7.2). In Section 7.3 we present ideas for combining local search with exact inference.

7.1 Greedy Local Search

Local search algorithms differ from what we have seen in systematic search so far in two ways. First, such algorithms use greedy, hill-climbing traversal of the search space, and as greedy methods they are not guaranteed to find a solution. Second, they typically explore a search space whose states are complete, full (but not necessarily consistent) assignments to all the variables, rather than partially consistent assignments common in search.

7.1.1 The Algorithm

A local search algorithm starts from a randomly chosen complete instantiation and moves from one complete instantiation to the next. The search is guided by some cost function related to the task (e.g., the number of violated constraints, also called the *number of conflicts*) estimating the distance between the current assignment and a solution. In its most greedy variant, at each step the value of the variable that leads to the greatest reduction of the cost function is changed. Typically, moving from one state to the next involves only a *local change* to the value of a single variable, hence the name *local search*.[1] The algorithm stops either when the cost is zero (a *global minimum*), in which case the problem is solved, or when there is no way to improve the current assignment by changing just one variable (a *local minimum*). In the latter case the algorithm may be restarted from a different initial random assignment.

While this hill-climbing approach is appealing, its shortcomings are obvious: the algorithm may get stuck in a local minima. Figure 7.1 presents a basic stochastic

---

1. Clearly, this can be extended to changing two variables at a time, or more.

---

procedure SLS

Input: A constraint network $\mathcal{R} = (X, D, C)$, number of tries MAX_TRIES. A cost function defined on full assignments.

Output: A solution iff the problem is consistent, "false" otherwise.

  1. **for** i = 1 to MAX_TRIES

- **initialization: let** $\bar{a} = (a_1, \ldots, a_n)$ be a random initial assignment to all variables.

- **repeat**

    (a) **if** $\bar{a}$ is consistent, return $\bar{a}$ as a solution.

    (b) **else** let $Y = \{\langle x_i, a'_i \rangle\}$ be the set of variable-value pairs that when x_i is assigned a'_i, give a maximum improvement in the cost of the assignment; pick a pair $\langle x_i, a'_i \rangle \in Y$,

$$\bar{a} \leftarrow (a_1, \ldots, a_{i-1}, a'_i, a_{i+1}, \ldots, a_n) \text{ (just flip } a_i \text{ to } a'_i\text{)}.$$

- **until** the current assignment cannot be improved.

  2. **endfor**

  3. **return** false

Figure 7.1 Algorithm stochastic local search (SLS).

greedy local search (SLS) procedure. This procedure uses MAX_TRIES number of independent runs, each with a different random initial assignment.

SLS methods became especially popular for solving satisfiability (SAT), that is, finding a truth assignment to CNF formulas. Indeed, the notion of "flipping" a value emerged from the propositional case where changing the value of a variable is uniquely defined as "value flipping." A famous local search algorithm for SAT called GSAT (greedy satisfiability) is an SLS algorithm where the cost of an assignment is the number of unsatisfied clauses.

EXAMPLE 7.1   Consider the formula $\varphi = \{(\neg C)(\neg A \vee \neg B \vee C)(\neg A \vee D \vee E)(\neg B \vee \neg C)\}$. Assume that in the initial assignment all variables are assigned the value 1 (true). This assignment violates two clauses, the first and the last, so the cost is 2. Next we see that flipping A, E, or D will not remove any inconsistency. Flipping C to 0 will satisfy the two violated clauses but will violate the clause $(\neg A \vee \neg B \vee C)$, yielding a cost of 1. Flipping B to $\neg B$ will remove one inconsistency and has a cost of 1 as well. If we flip C to $\neg C$, subsequently flipping B to $\neg B$ yields a cost of 0—and a solution. •

Improvements to SLS can be made either in the selection of the initial assignment, and in the nature of the local changes considered, or by trying to escape from local minima. By using combinations of various heuristics we get a whole family of SLS algorithms. We next enumerate several specific heuristics for improving local search, aiming primarily at escaping from local minima. Subsequently, we introduce local search with random walk.

7.1.2 Heuristics for Improving Local Search

Several approaches for escaping local minima have proved useful.

Plateau Search

When a local optimum is reached, continuing search by nonimproving "sideways" moves can significantly improve the performance of SLS. This heuristic is called the *plateau search*.

Constraint Weighting

The *breakout method* or *constraint weighting* can also significantly improve the performance of local search. The guiding cost function is a weighted sum of the violated constraints, defined by $F(\bar{a}) = \sum_i w_i * C_i(\bar{a})$, where w_i is the current weight of constraint C_i, and $C_i(\bar{a}) = 1$ iff $\bar{a}$ violates constraint C_i, and equals 0 otherwise.

At each step, the algorithm first selects a variable-value pair such that when the value of the variable is changed to the designated value, it leads to the largest reduction in F. Then, at local minima, the weights are adjusted, increasing by 1 the weight of each constraint that is violated by the current assignment. This process ensures that the current assignment is no longer a local minimum relative to the new cost function.

Tabu Search

The idea of *tabu search* is to prevent the search from becoming stuck in local minima by preventing "backwards" moves. This is usually achieved by constructing a list of the last n variable-value assignments. When picking the next variable-value assignment, those on the list are forbidden, or tabu.

There are several additional nondeterministic steps that can be instrumental in improving the performance of local search algorithms. For example, *tie-breaking rules* between equally good flips (that is, between two or more values that would suggest the same greedy increase) may be conditioned by historic information. For example, in the event of a tie we select the variable that was flipped least recently. Other ideas are based on *value propagation*—for instance, using value propagation, such as unit propagation or arc-consistency over unsatisfied constraints, whenever reaching a local minimum, or using it to improve the initial assignment at each try.

Automating MAX-FLIPS

How do we decide how many runs of MAX_TRIES to try and how many steps to take during each try of MAX_FLIPS? Researchers proposed a range of ideas, either based on experiments with a given set of instances, or devising an automatic stopping rule. One rule used is to continue search so long as there is progress. Progress is determined as finding an assignment that satisfies more constraints than found so far in that particular run. For example, every time we find such an improved assignment, we may allow the algorithm additional time equal to the amount of time it has spent up until that point from the beginning of the try. Opinions on the significance of restarts vary; some even claim (based on empirical experiments) that restarts are completely irrelevant.

7.2 Random Walk Strategies

The random walk strategy, formulated primarily for SAT, combines a random walk search strategy with a greedy bias toward assignments that satisfy more constraints or clauses. The stochastic element can be perceived as another technique for escaping local minima. Instead of making a "greedy" move (i.e., a change that maximizes the improvement in the cost function) at each step, we do a random walk step. A pure random walk procedure for SAT starts with a random assignment. Assuming this assignment does not satisfy all clauses, we select an unsatisfied clause randomly and flip the value of one of its variables. This will cause the clause to be satisfied, but may cause others to become unsatisfied.

7.2.1 WalkSAT

One random walk variant of local search that proved highly successful empirically is WALKSAT. As its name suggests, it was introduced for solving satisfiability. While we will use the WALKSAT name, we present a variant of the algorithm for general constraints. The WALKSAT is based on a two-stage variable selection process. In the first stage of each step, a constraint violated by the current assignment is randomly selected. In the second stage, either the value of one of the variables appearing in the selected constraint is randomly changed (with probability p) or else (with probability $1 - p$) we greedily minimize the "break value"—the number of new constraints that become inconsistent due to a value change. For SAT, changing the value of any variable (flipping) is guaranteed to satisfy the clause. This is not the case for constraints, and therefore the break value should take into account the change to the selected constraint as well.

The number of random walk moves is controlled by the parameter p. In practice, you can often identify a good value for p given a class of problems. As another refinement, if there is a variable having a break value of zero, it is selected

---

procedure WALKSAT

Input: A network $\mathcal{R} = (X, D, C)$, number of flips MAX_FLIPS, MAX_TRIES, probability p.

Output: "True," and a solution, if the problem is consistent, "false," and an inconsistent best assignment, otherwise.

1. **for** i = 1 to MAX_TRIES **do**

2. **start** with a random initial assignment $\bar{a}$.

3. Compare best assignment with $\bar{a}$ and retain the best.

4. **for** i = 1 to MAX_FLIPS

   • **if** $\bar{a}$ is a solution, **return** true and $\bar{a}$.

   • **else,**

     i.   **pick** a violated constraint C, randomly

     ii. **choose** with probability p a variable-value pair $\langle x, a' \rangle$ for $x \in$ *scope* (C), or, with probability $1 - p$, choose a variable-value pair $\langle x, a' \rangle$ that minimizes the number of new constraints that break when the value of x is changed to a' (minus 1 if the current constraint is satisfied).

     iii. Change x's value to a'.

5. **endfor**

6. **return** false and the best current assignment.

Figure 7.2 Algorithm WALKSAT.

with probability 1. Figure 7.2 presents a simple version of WALKSAT. WALKSAT has been shown to be highly effective on a range of problem domains, such as hard random k-SAT problems, logistics planning formulas, graph coloring, and circuit synthesis formulas.

EXAMPLE 7.2   Following Example 7.1, with the initial assignment of value 1 to all the variables, we will first select an unsatisfied clause, such as $(\neg B \vee \neg C)$, and then select a variable. If we try to minimize the number of additional constraints that would be broken, we will select B and flip its value. Subsequently, the only unsatisfied clause is $\neg C$, which is selected and flipped.   •

Simulated Annealing

A famous stochastic local search method is *simulated annealing*. Simulated annealing uses a noise model inspired by statistical mechanics. At each step, the algorithm picks a variable and a value, and then computes δ, the change in the cost function when the value of the variable is changed to the value picked. If this change improves or has no impact on the cost function, we make the change. Otherwise, we make the change with probability $e^{-\delta/T}$, where T is a parameter called *temperature*. The temperature can be held constant, or slowly reduced from a high temperature to a near zero temperature according to some "cooling schedule." This algorithm converges to the exact solution if the temperature T is reduced gradually.

7.2.2 **Properties of Local Search**

The most notable property of local search is that it terminates at local minima. When randomness is introduced, the performance of local search can be illuminated using the theory of random walks. Consider a satisfiable 2-SAT formula having N variables and let $\bar{a}$ denote a satisfying assignment. The random walk procedure starts with a random assignment $\bar{a}'$. On the average this truth assignment will differ from $\bar{a}$ on $N/2$ propositional variables. Consider the unsatisfied clauses in the formula. Since the clause is unsatisfied, $\bar{a}'$ assigns negative values to both of its literals while $\bar{a}$ assigns "true" to at least one of these literals (since $\bar{a}$ satisfies every clause). Now, randomly select a variable in this clause and flip its value in $\bar{a}'$. Since there are only two literals, there is at least a 50% chance of selecting the variable corresponding to a literal set to true in $\bar{a}$. Therefore, with at least a 50% chance, the distance between the new assignment and $\bar{a}$ will be reduced by 1 and with less than a 50% chance we will increase the distance. Consider a general random walk that starts at a given location and takes L steps, either one step to the left or to the right with probability 0.5. It can be shown that after L^2 steps, such a walk will on the average travel a distance of L units from its starting point. Given that our random walk started at a distance of $N/2$ from the satisfying truth assignment $\bar{a}$, after an order of N^2 steps, the walk will hit a satisfying assignment, with probability going to 1.

The analysis for 2-SAT breaks down for k-SAT with $k \geq 3$ (see Exercise 2). In fact, it can be shown that a random walk strategy will take an exponential number of flips on 3-SAT formulas, in the worst case. Indeed, some local search methods such as WALKSAT can be shown to eventually hit a satisfying assignment with probability 1 if such an assignment exists. Others, such as GSAT, WalkSAT/TABU, Novelty, and R-Novelty (Hoos and Stutzle 1999), cannot.

A related property is that SLS algorithms are *anytime*—the longer they run, the better the solution they may produce (i.e., a solution that satisfies more and more constraints). Unlike complete algorithms, however, local search algorithms cannot prove inconsistency. When the problem does not have a solution, an SLS algorithm would run forever. In practice, a time limit is set, after which a failure is reported.

We can analyze the complexity of a local search step. In general, we can maintain information from one flip to the next and recompute only the changes caused by the previous flip. This computation is normally linear in the neighborhood size of each variable in the network.

7.2.3 **Examples of Empirical Evaluation**

Variant SLS algorithms are evaluated empirically, either on some given benchmarks or on randomly generated problems. In recent years, the practice has been
to generate hard random problems drawn from the phase transition as described in
Chapter 6.

Table 7.1 (Selman, Kautz, and Cohen 1994a) shows some typical empirical
evaluations comparing popular variants of local search (such as the basic GSAT
algorithm, simulated annealing, random walk, and random noise strategies) on a
test suite of randomly generated CNF problems. The *random walk strategy* (i.e.,
GSAT + walk) augments GSAT as follows: with a probability p, pick a variable occurring in an unsatisfied clause and flip its truth value. With probability
$1 - p$ do a regular greedy step. The *random noise strategy* is the same except the
variable can be picked from *any* clause. Both random walk and random noise
differ from WALKSAT in a subtle way. For each strategy the table gives the average time in seconds it took to find a satisfying assignment, the average number
of flips it required, and R, the average number of restarts needed before finding
a solution. At least 100 random restarts (MAX-TRIES setting in GSAT) were
applied on each problem instance (but in some cases the strategy was restarted
up to 1000 times). The parameters of each method were varied and optimized
empirically.

In Table 7.2 we show experiments comparing DPLL (called DP here) with WALK-
SAT and random walk (GSAT + walk) demonstrating the superiority of WALK-
SAT over its competitors. These experiments were conducted over test pattern
generation problems for VLSI circuits translated into SAT problems.

7.3 **Hybrids of Local Search and Inference**

We have seen that consistency-enforcing algorithms such as arc- and path-
consistency for general CSPs, and bounded resolutions for CNF formulas, may
help search either when applied in a preprocessing stage or when interleaved during search. It is natural to ask, therefore, if such inference-based methods similarly
affect stochastic local search methods.

7.3.1 **The Effect of Constraint Propagation on SLS**

Consider first a simple collaboration between local search and inference, where
SLS is applied only after applying a *consistency-enforcing* preprocessing algorithm.
Can we improve SLS by making the problem more explicit?

Indeed, it was shown that certain classes of structured problems, which are
very easy for systematic backtracking algorithms, are quite hard for local search,

Table 7.1 Comparing noise strategies on hard random 3CNF instances. "*" denotes terminated runs with no solutions.

Formula		GSAT									Simulated annealing		
		Basic			Walk			Noise					
Variables	Clauses	Time	Flips	R	Time	Flips	R	Time	Flips	R	Time	Flips	R
100	430	.4	7554	8.3	.2	2385	1.0	.6	9975	4.0	.6	4748	1.1
200	860	22	284,693	143	4	27,654	1.0	47	396,534	6.7	21	106,643	1.2
400	1700	122	2.6×10^6	67	7	59,744	1.1	95	892,048	6.3	75	552,433	1.1
600	2550	1471	30×10^6	500	35	241,651	1.0	929	7.8×10^6	20	427	2.7×10^6	3.3
800	3400	*	*	*	286	1.8×10^6	1.1	*	*	*	*	*	*
1000	4250	*	*	*	1095	5.8×10^6	1.2	*	*	*	*	*	*
2000	8480	*	*	*	3255	23×10^6	1.1	*	*	*	*	*	*

Table 7.2 Comparing complete DPLL method (DP) with local search strategies on circuit synthesis problems (time in seconds).

Formula			DP	GSAT+ walk	WSAT
ID	Variables	Clauses	Time	Time	Time
2bitadd_12	708	1702	*	0.081	0.013
2bitadd_11	649	1562	*	0.058	0.014
3bitadd_32	8704	32,316	*	94.1	1.0
3bitadd_31	8432	31,310	*	456.6	0.7
2bitcomp_12	300	730	23,096	0.009	0.002
2bitcomp_5	125	310	1.4	0.009	0.001

even when the best currently known heuristics, like constraint weighting and random walk, are used. In particular, 3-SAT problems, having tightly connected clusters of variables that, in turn, are loosely connected by another set of constraints, can be extremely hard for even the best implementations of SLS. However, these problems often become trivial for SLS once a restricted form of resolution is enforced. Moreover, the overhead associated with enforcing this kind of local consistency is still much less than the computation needed to solve the problem without it.

A possible explanation is that enforcing local consistency changes the state space of local search methods by eliminating many near solutions. Namely, assignments that satisfy *almost* all clauses, for which the value of the original cost function is therefore almost zero, become assignments whose cost is high due to consistency enforcing. On the other hand, for problems that have a uniform structure the effect of constraint propagation can be sharply different (Kask and Dechter 1995).

In the rest of this section we will address a more involved collaboration, interleaving local search and inference using the cycle-cutset decomposition.

7.3.2 Local Search on Cycle-Cutset

As discussed in Chapter 5, backtracking search can be improved if we instantiate first a cycle-cutset of the variables and solve the rest by arc-consistency. This idea is called the *cycle-cutset decomposition*. The effectiveness of cycle-cutset decomposition is founded on the fact that an *instantiated* variable cuts the flow of information on any path on which it lies and therefore changes the effective connectivity of the network. That is, the network is equivalent to one where the variable is deleted

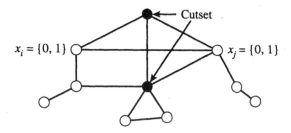

Figure 7.3 Constraint network with cycle-cutset.

and the influence of its assigned value is propagated to each of its neighboring variables. Consequently, when the group of instantiated variables cuts all cycles in the graph (e.g., a cycle-cutset), the remaining network can be viewed as cycle-free and can be solved by a tree inference algorithm like arc-consistency. The complexity of the cycle-cutset method when incorporated within backtracking search can be bounded exponentially in the size of the cutset of the graph because all instantiations to the cutset variables may need to be enumerated (see Proposition 5.2 and also Chapter 10). Figure 7.3 presents a constraint network with a cycle-cutset highlighted in black.

Hence, the cycle-cutset scheme alternates between two algorithms: a backtracking search algorithm on the cutset portion of the network and a tree algorithm on the remaining portion. Since an SLS algorithm approximates search, the next idea is to apply it to the search portion within the cycle-cutset scheme. For simplicity of presentation we assume networks of binary constraints.

Tree Inference for Networks with Cycles

To allow the collaboration between a tree algorithm and local search, we next define a tree algorithm for general networks with cycles. The target is that given an assignment to a cycle-cutset of the variables, any assignment it produces will minimize the number of violated constraints over all its tree subnetworks.

Assume that we have a constraint network $\mathcal{R} = (X, D, C)$ that is arc-consistent and has all of its variables X divided into two disjoint sets of variables, *cutset variables* Y and *tree variables* Z, such that the constraint subgraph induced by removing Y is a *forest*—it has no cycles. We can make each tree a rooted tree, for which the parent-child relationship is well-defined. (Each cutset variable is duplicated for each of its neighboring nodes and assigned its value.)

Let $T_{z_i}^{p_i}$ be the subproblem rooted at z_i (including z_i) where p_i is the parent of z_i. The cost $C_{z_i}(a_i, \bar{y})$ is the minimum number of violated constraints in $T_{z_i}^{p_i}$ when

procedure TREE

$(R_{z_i,z_j}(a_i, a_j)$ is the constraint between z_i and z_j and is either 0 if $(a_i, a_j) \in R_{z_i, z_j}$ or 1, otherwise.)

Input: An arc-consistent network $\mathcal{R} = (X, D, C)$. Variables X partitioned into cycle-cutset Y and tree variables Z, $X = Z \cup Y$. An assignment $Y = \bar{y}$.

Output: An assignment $Z = \bar{z}$ that minimizes the number of violated constraints of the entire network when $Y = \bar{y}$.

Initialization: For any value $\bar{y}[i]$ of any cutset variable y_i, the cost $C_{y_i}(\bar{y}[i], \bar{y})$ is 0.

1. Going from leaves to root on the tree compute costs:

   (a) **for** every variable, z_i and any value $a_i \in D_{z_i}$, compute

$$C_{z_i}(a_i, \bar{y}) = \sum_{\{z_j | z_j \text{ child of } z_i\}} \min_{a_j \in D_{z_j}} (C_{z_j}(a_j, \bar{y}) + R_{z_i, z_j}(a_i, a_j))$$

   (b) **endfor**

2. Compute, going from root to leaves, new assignments for every tree variable z_i:

   (a) **for** a tree variable z_i, let D_{z_i} be its consistent values with v_{p_i} the value assigned to its parent p_i, $(\langle p_i, v_{p_i} \rangle)$ compute

$$a_i \leftarrow \arg\min_{a_i \in D_{z_i}} (C_{z_i}(a_i, \bar{y}) + R_{z_i, p_i}(a_i, v_{p_i}))$$

   (b) **endfor**

3. **return** $(\langle z_1, a_1 \rangle, \ldots, \langle z_k, a_k \rangle)$.

Figure 7.4   procedure TREE.

$z_i = a_i$ and $Y = \bar{y}$. Let $C(\bar{z}, \bar{y})$ be the number of violated constraints in the entire network when $Y = \bar{y}$ and $Z = \bar{z}$, and C_{min} the minimum overall number of violated constraints. That is, $C_{min} = \min_{Y=y} \min_{Z=z} C(z, y)$.

Therefore, the TREE algorithm (see Figure 7.4) works by first computing the cost $C_{z_i}(a_i, \bar{y})$ for every tree variable z_i, assuming a fixed cycle-cutset assignment $Y = \bar{y}$, by propagating those cost values from leaves to root. At each node the cost is computed based on the cost of its child variables (see step 1). Once these values are computed, the algorithm computes an assignment to each tree variable z_i, going from root to leaves, using the cost values C_{z_i} computed earlier and the new value of the parent of z_i (see step 2). We can show the following:

THEOREM 7.1   The TREE algorithm in Figure 7.4 is guaranteed to find an assignment that minimizes the number of violated constraints over every constraint subnetwork, conditioned on the cycle-cutset values.   •

SLS with Cycle-Cutset

Since, the TREE algorithm minimizes the cost of tree subnetworks given a cycle-cutset assignment for every network, we can now replace the systematic backtracking search of assigning values to the cutset variables by an SLS search. The combined algorithm called SLS + CC will execute a number of tries, each of which starts from a new random initial assignment. Within one try, SLS + CC will alternate between SLS and the TREE algorithm. It first fixes the cycle-cutset values and runs the TREE algorithm on the problem. Once the TREE algorithm terminates, it will run SLS on the problem when fixing the values of the tree variables, and so on. One try of the combined algorithm SLS + CC is described in Figure 7.5.

Note that the only tree variables that have effect on SLS are those that are adjacent to the cycle-cutset variables. Therefore, a violated constraint involving a tree variable should be forced to be adjacent to a cutset variable, or else this information will not be visible to SLS applied to the cutset variables. It has been observed that if this condition is not enforced, the performance of SLS + CC will deteriorate by several orders of magnitude.

---

procedure: one try of SLS + CC

Input: A constraint network $\mathcal{R} = (X,D,C)$. X is divided into cycle-cutset variables Y and tree variables Z, $X = Y \cup Z$.

Output: An assignment $Z = \bar{z}$, $Y = \bar{y}$ that is a local minimum of the number of violated constraints $C(\bar{z}, y)$ and a global minimum over $C_z(z, \bar{y})$.

  1. Create a random initial assignment for all variables.

  2. Alternate between the following two steps until either the problem is solved, or the TREE algorithm does not change the values of the variables, or no progress is being made.

    (a) Run the TREE algorithm on the problem, where the values of cycle-cutset variables are fixed.

    (b) Run SLS on the problem, where the values of tree variables are fixed.

Figure 7.5   SLS with cycle-cutset inference (SLS + CC).

The cycle-cutset idea can be generalized (see Chapter [10]) as follows. We can apply search to an *arbitrary* subset of variables (conditioning variables), and then for each partial assignment apply inference to the rest of the problem. But, the subproblem conditioned on the cutset assignment may have induced width (w^*) larger than 1. When $w^* = 1$, we have the special, and by now familiar, cycle-cutset scheme. A stochastic local search algorithm can always replace the complete search algorithm within this hybrid framework.

Table 7.3 and Figure 7.6 show the flavor of some empirical results comparing pure SLS with SLS + CC on randomly generated problem instances. Table 7.3 organizes the results by increasing cycle-cutset size. The experimental results showed that when the cycle-cutset size is less than 30% of the variables, SLS + CC can solve up to 3–4 times more problems than SLS alone, given the same amount of CPU time. When the cycle-cutset size is about 30%, both algorithms

Table 7.3   SLS versus SLS + CC.

Binary CSP, 100 instances, 125 variables, 8 values, tightness 21/36				
Number of constraints	Average cutset size	Time bound (seconds)	SLS solved	SLS + CC solved
170	14%	36	81	100
180	16%	54	62	93
190	17%	66	30	72

Binary CSP, 100 instances, 125 variables, 8 values, tightness 18/36				
Number of constraints	Average cutset size	Time bound (seconds)	SLS solved	SLS + CC solved
245	26%	66	66	90
250	27%	77	42	79
255	28%	90	25	66

Binary CSP, 100 instances, 125 variables, 8 values, tightness 16/36				
Number of constraints	Average cutset size	Time bound (seconds)	SLS solved	SLS + CC solved
290	33%	41	84	76
300	34%	62	64	47
305	35%	86	41	34

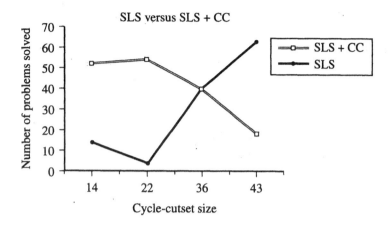

Figure 7.6 SLS versus SLS + CC with *N* = 100 and *K* = 8.

are roughly equal. When the cutset size grows further, SLS alone is better than SLS + CC.

Figure 7.6 plots two graphs (SLS and SLS + CC) using the data in the last row of each of the four blocks in Table 7.3. On the horizontal axis we have the cutset size, and on the vertical axis we have the number of problems solved. We can see that when the cutset size is 36%, the two graphs intersect. When the cutset size is less than 36%, SLS + CC is better, and when the cutset size is more than 36%, pure SLS is better. Clearly, these results are not conclusive, and research on such hybrids is ongoing.

7.4 **Summary**

This chapter introduced *stochastic local search*, a randomized greedy scheme that can be viewed as an approximation of systematic search. A local search algorithm starts from a randomly chosen complete instantiation of all the variables and moves from one complete instantiation to the next, using a random walk biased greedily by some cost function. At each step, a value is either selected randomly or a value of the variable that leads to the greatest reduction of the cost function is selected. The algorithm stops either when the cost is zero (a *global minimum*), in which case the problem is solved, or when there is no way to improve the current assignment by changing just one variable (a *local minimum*). In the latter case the algorithm may be restarted from a different initial random assignment. We have described the main approaches, greedy and random walk based, and showed how each can be augmented with a variety of heuristics that attempt to escape from local minima.

Subsequently, we have shown how local search can be incorporated within a hybrid of search and inference, such as the cycle-cutset scheme.

Unlike complete algorithms, local search algorithms cannot be used to prove the inconsistency of constraint problems. When the problem does not have a solution, a local search algorithm would run forever. In practice, a time limit is set after which a failure is reported.

7.5 **Bibliographical Notes**

Greedy local search algorithms were first developed for optimizations tasks in operations research, and in the context of neural networks (minimizing the energy function). One of the earlier applications was for finding good solutions to the traveling salesman problem (TSP) (Lin 1965; Lin and Kernighan 1973).

Recently, stochastic local search algorithms like min-conflicts were introduced by Philips et al. (1990) to CSP, showing that such methods can solve the million-queens problem, which cannot be solved by any complete search algorithm. Triggered by this success, local search methods were introduced for satisfiability by Selman, Levesque, and Mitchell (1992) and independently by Gu (1992), and were demonstrated to be successful for different classes of automated reasoning problems like graph coloring, scheduling, and planning.

The first local search method for SAT, called GSAT, was based on standard greedy hill-climbing search (Selman, Levesque, and Mitchell 1992; Gu 1992; Gent and Walsh 1993a). A major improvement of these algorithms was obtained by building the search around random walk strategy, which led to WalkSAT and related methods (Selman, Kautz, and Cohen 1994b). WalkSAT has been shown to be highly effective on a range of problem domains, such as hard random *k*-SAT problems, logistics planning formulas, graph coloring, and circuit synthesis formulas (Selman, Kautz, and Cohen 1994b; Kautz and Selman 1999).

A number of heuristics have been developed in recent years, all designed to overcome the problem of local minima. These heuristics greatly improve the performance of the basic scheme. The *plateau search* was proposed by Selman, Levesque, and Mitchell (1992); *simulated annealing* was introduced by Kirkpatrick and Johnson (Kirkpatrick, Gelatt, and Vecchi (1983) and Johnson et al. (1991)); and the *breakout method* or *constraint weighting* was proposed by Morris (1993) and in a different form by Selman and Kautz (1993). A related approach developed by Tsang (1999) for constraint satisfaction and optimization, called GENET, modifies the cost of no-goods whenever a dead-end in local search occurs. The *value propagation* heuristic was proposed for escaping local minima in Yugami, Ohta, and Hara (1994). Gent and Walsh (1993a) suggested using *historic information* instead of randomly breaking ties. The idea of *tabu search* was introduced by Glover (1986, 1989). The idea of automatically determining the length of every run is Hampson's (1993).

Recent extensive work by Hoos and Stutzle (1999, 2000) has empirically explored and compared various variants of local search and introduced the methodology of *run-time distributions* as a basis for comparison. In particular they observed exponential run-time distributions that seem to indicate that restart strategies are irrelevant. Yet, in a subsequent paper they qualified this observation (Hoos and Stutzle 2000).

Konolige (1994) was the first to demonstrate the inferiority of local search on structured problems, which triggered the work of combining inference with local search. The work on hybrids between local search and inference was first introduced by Pinkas and Dechter (1995) in the context of energy minimization in neural networks, and subsequently extended by Kask and Dechter (1996) to constraint satisfaction. Empirical evaluation of the effect of local consistency preprocessing on search is presented in Kask and Dechter (1995). Additional studies are available on various hybrids of local search with systematic search (Schaerf 1997; Zhang and Zhang 1996), local search with unit resolution (Hirsch and Kojevnikov 2001), and local search with learning (Richards and Richads 1998).

Random walk strategies capitalize on a property shown by Papadimitriou (1991) for 2-SAT, namely, that repeatedly picking an unsatisfied clause and flipping the truth assignment of one of the variables leads to an algorithm that finds solutions in $O(N^2)$ steps with a probability approaching 1, where N is the number of propositional variables. More recently, Schoening (1999) showed that a series of short unbiased random walks on a 3-SAT problem will find a satisfying assignment in $O(1.334^N)$ flips (assuming such an assignment exists).

A variety of worst-case bounds on the performance of variants of local search for SAT of the form $O(2^{\alpha N})$, where N is the number of variables and $0 < \alpha \le 1$, have been proposed (Gent and Walsh 1993b; Hirsch 2000).

7.6 **Exercises**

1. Consider stochastic local search algorithms (SLS) such as GSAT and WALKSAT. Apply algorithm SLS to the 5-queens problem when your initial assignment is that all the queens are on the diagonal. Give at most a one-page description of tracing the algorithm.

2. Explain why the argument for polynomial scaling of random walk on 2-SAT breaks down for 3-SAT. What is the effect of greedy bias used in WALKSAT on the random walk process?

3. Analyze the complexity of an SLS local search step.

4. Analyze the complexity of a WALKSAT step.

5. Prove Theorem 7.1.

6. (Due to Selman) Consider the GSAT procedure (greedy moves only) for finding satisfying assignments for Boolean formulas in clausal form, and the

following formula F consisting of the clauses

$$(x1 \lor \neg x2), (x1 \lor \neg x3), (x1 \lor \neg x4), \ldots, (x1 \lor \neg x100)$$

(a) What is the probability that a truth assignment selected uniformly at random from all possible truth assignments will satisfy F?

(b) Assuming that the initial random truth assignment selected by GSAT does not satisfy F, how many flips will GSAT take to reach a satisfying assignment?

(c) Give a pair of binary clauses, C1 and C2, such that when C1 and C2 are added to F, GSAT will almost certainly not be able to find a satisfying assignment for the resulting set of clauses, when starting from a random initial assignment. Briefly explain why GSAT would have trouble finding a satisfying assignment of F with the two added clauses.

7. Consider the WALKSAT procedure with $p = 0.5$. Consider an arbitrary satisfiable formula as input.

(a) Starting at a random assignment, will the procedure eventually reach a satisfying assignment? Explain your answer. (Assume that the procedure does *not* restart. That is, the procedure either continues flipping variables indefinitely or stops at a satisfying assignment.)

(b) In the walk step, assume that the procedure simultaneously flips all variables in the randomly selected unsatisfied clause. Will the procedure eventually reach a satisfying assignment (again, no restarts)? Explain your answer.

(c) In the walk step, assume that the procedure simultaneously flips one variable in each unsatisfied clause. Will the procedure eventually reach a satisfying assignment (no restarts)? Explain your answer.

part two

Advanced Methods

chapter 8

Advanced Consistency Methods

We cannot all hope to combine the pleasing qualities of
good looks, brains, and eloquence.

Homer, The Odyssey

Now that we have covered the spectrum of basic constraint processing techniques, discussing inference approaches, search approaches, and their approximations, we can delve more deeply into some of these methods and their hybrids. This chapter focuses on extending variable-based consistency-enforcing algorithms to relation-based algorithms. These definitions are then used to characterize the consistency level sufficient to guarantee global consistency for special classes of constraints having tight domains or that are row convex. This chapter also covers the specialized languages of propositional logic and linear constraints within this more generalized concept of bounded inference.

In Chapter 3 we bounded inference by the number of variables involved. It is more frequently practical, however, to restrict inference by the number of constraints participating in the inference rather than by the number of variables. In particular, when most of the constraints have arity greater than two, arc-consistency and path-consistency, as defined, rarely seem to be relevant.

EXAMPLE 8.1 Consider the constraint network $\mathcal{R}$ over five integer domain variables, where the constraints take the form of linear equations and the domains are integers bounded by closed intervals:

$$D_x \in [-2, 3]$$

$$D_y \in [-5, 7]$$

$$R_{xyz}: \quad x + y = z$$

$$R_{ztl}: \quad z + t = l$$

From the constraint R_{xyz} and the domain constraint D_x we can infer the new constraint $R_{zy} : z - y \in [-2, 3]$. From this new constraint and the domain D_y, we can also infer $D_z \in [-7, 10]$. Although these inferences seem quite basic, they do not fit within our previous definitions of arc- and path-consistency. Since only a single constraint and a single domain are involved in each of the above inferences, they do have a flavor of basic arc-consistency. However, by definition, z is already arc-consistent relative to both x and y, since there is no binary restriction on the pair $\{x, z\}$ or on the pair $\{y, z\}$. Consider now the two constraints, $x + y = z$ and $z + t = l$. From these two constraints we can infer the new constraint $x + y + t = l$. Since the two constraints involve five variables, this inference can be perceived as part of applying 5-consistency to the network. However, because this inference involves just two constraints, it seems to parallel path-consistency in a binary constraint network as well.   •

The above examples demonstrate that our vocabulary for discussing local consistency does not conveniently accommodate straightforward inferences between constraints of arity greater than two. It would be natural to view the first inference in Example 8.1 as enforcing arc-consistency of some sort, since only one constraint is involved (a hyperarc), and the second as enforcing path-consistency (or 2-consistency), since only two constraints are involved. The concept of *relational consistency* accommodates this intuition.

8.1 Relational Consistency

Let's start with relational arc-consistency. Which property of arc-consistency do we choose to keep when extending to higher-order constraints? Dealing with one constraint at a time? Recording only domain constraints? Both? We will eventually express both properties of arc-consistency, but we begin by focusing on the number of constraints involved.

8.1.1 Relational *m*-Consistency

A constraint is *relational arc-consistent* (in a network) if its projections over *any* subset of its scope are explicitly present in the network.

DEFINITION 8.1   **(relational arc-consistency)**

Let $\mathcal{R}$ be a constraint network over a set of variables $X = \{x_1, \ldots, x_n\}$, having domains $D_1, \ldots, D_n$, and let R_S be a relation (constraint) in $\mathcal{R}$ defined over a scope S. We say that R_S in $\mathcal{R}$ is *relational arc-consistent* relative to a variable $x \in S$ iff any consistent instantiation of the variables in $S - \{x\}$ has an extension to a value in D_x that satisfies R_S. That is, if

$$\rho(S - \{x\}) \subseteq \pi_{S-\{x\}}(R_S \bowtie D_x) \qquad (8.1)$$

(Recall that $\rho(A)$ is the set of all consistent instantiations of the subnetwork defined by A.) A relation R_S in $\mathcal{R}$ is relational arc-consistent if it is relational arc-consistent relative to every variable in S. A network is relational arc-consistent iff every relation contained within it is relational arc-consistent.   •

Naturally, if relational arc-consistency is not satisfied, it can be imposed by adding a constraint, as dictated by Equation (8.1). Namely, we can add the constraint $R_{S-\{x\}}$,

$$R_{S-\{x\}} \leftarrow \pi_{S-\{x\}}(R_S \bowtie D_x) \qquad (8.2)$$

If we want to ensure that only one constraint is defined over each scope, even in the case where arc-consistency already exists, then we can instead apply the rule that tightens the current constraint:

$$R_{S-\{x\}} \leftarrow R_{S-\{x\}} \cap \pi_{S-\{x\}}(R_S \bowtie D_x) \qquad (8.3)$$

Including such constraints ensures the condition in Equation (8.1), since determining the consistency of a partial solution on A will include testing the added constraint. The following two examples demonstrate the concept of relational arc-consistency.

EXAMPLE 8.2   Consider a network with one constraint $R_{xyz} = \{(a, a, a), (a, b, c), (b, b, c)\}$. This relation is not relational arc-consistent, but if we add the projection $R_{xy} = \{(a, a), (a, b), (b, b)\}$, then R_{xyz} will become relational arc-consistent relative to $\{z\}$. To make this network relational arc-consistent, we would have to add all the projections of R_{xyz} with respect to all subsets of its variables.   •

EXAMPLE 8.3   Consider again Example 8.1. We have already noticed that the network is arc-consistent relative to the *variable-based* definition. However, it is not relational arc-consistent because there is a consistent assignment to z and y that cannot be extended to a value in x's domain while satisfying the constraint $x + y = z$. If we add the constraints $R_{zy} : z - y \in [-2, 3]$, $R_{zx} : z - x \in [-5, 7]$, $D_z : z \in [-7, 10]$, and $R_{ft} : f - t \in [-7, 10]$, then the resulting network, $\mathcal{R}'$, augmented with the above four new constraints, is relational arc-consistent.   •

We next define *relational path-consistency*. The definition involves the simultaneous consistency of two constraints, without regard to their arity.

DEFINITION 8.2   **(relational path-consistency)**

Let $\mathcal{R}$ be a constraint network over a set of variables $X = \{x_1, \ldots, x_n\}$ having domains $D_1, \ldots, D_n$, and let R_S and R_T be two constraints in $\mathcal{R}$. We say that R_S and R_T are *relational path-consistent* relative to a variable $x \in S \cap T$ iff any consistent instantiation of the variables in $S \cup T - \{x\}$ has an extension to a value in the domain of x, D_x, that satisfies R_S and R_T simultaneously; that is, iff

$$\rho(A) \subseteq \pi_A(R_S \bowtie R_T \bowtie D_x) \tag{8.4}$$

where $A = (S \cup T) - \{x\}$. A pair of relations R_S and R_T is relational path-consistent iff it is relational path-consistent relative to every variable in $S \cap T$. A network is relational path-consistent iff every pair of its relations is relational path-consistent.   ●

Note that the definition of relational path-consistency subsumes relational arc-consistency if we allow nondistinct pairs of relations.

EXAMPLE 8.4   We saw that the network in Example 8.1 is not relational path-consistent since we can assign to x, y, l, and t values that are consistent relative to the relational arc-consistent network $\mathcal{R}'$ generated in Example 8.3. For example, the assignment $(\langle x, 2 \rangle, \langle y, -5 \rangle, \langle t, 3 \rangle, \langle l, 15 \rangle)$ is consistent, since only domain restrictions are applicable, but there is no value of z that simultaneously satisfies $x + y = z$ and $z + t = l$. To make the two constraints relational path-consistent relative to z we should deduce the constraint $x + y + t = l$ and add it to the network.   ●

Relational consistency can be extended to m relations in a similar way:

DEFINITION 8.3   **(relational m-consistency)**

Let $\mathcal{R}$ be a constraint network over a set of variables $X = \{x_1, \ldots, x_n\}$, and let $R_{S_1}, \ldots, R_{S_m}$ be m distinct relations in $\mathcal{R}$, where $S_i \subseteq X$. We say that $R_{S_1}, \ldots, R_{S_m}$ are *relational m-consistent* relative to $x \in \bigcap_{i=1}^{m} S_i$ iff any consistent instantiation of the variables in $A = \bigcup_{i=1}^{m} S_i - \{x\}$ has an extension to x that satisfies $R_{S_1}, \ldots, R_{S_m}$ simultaneously; that is, iff

$$\rho(A) \subseteq \pi_A(\bowtie_{i=1}^{m} R_{S_i} \bowtie D_x) \tag{8.5}$$

A set of relations $\{R_{S_1}, \ldots, R_{S_m}\}$ is *relational m-consistent* iff it is relational m-consistent relative to every variable in $\bigcap_{i=1}^{m} S_i$. A network is relational m-consistent iff every set of m relations is relational m-consistent. A network is strongly relational m-consistent if it is relational i-consistent for every $i \leq m$.   ●

Relational arc- and path-consistency correspond to relational 1- and relational 2-consistency, respectively.

EXAMPLE 8.5   Consider the constraint network over the set of variables $\{x_1, x_2, x_3, x_4, x_5\}$, where each variable has the domains $D_i = \{a, b, c\}$, $1 \le i \le 5$, and the relations are given by

$$R_{2,3,4,5} = \{(a, a, a, a), (b, a, a, a), (a, b, a, a), (a, a, b, a), (a, a, a, b)\}$$
$$R_{1,2,5} = \{(b, a, b), (c, b, c), (b, a, c)\}$$

The constraints are not relational arc-consistent. The instantiation ($x_2 = a$, $x_3 = b$, $x_4 = b$) is a consistent instantiation as it satisfies all the applicable constraints (trivially so—there are no constraints defined strictly over $\{x_2, x_3, x_4\}$ or over any of their subsets), but it does not have an extension to x_5 that satisfies $R_{2,3,4,5}$. Neither are the constraints relational path-consistent. The instantiation ($x_1 = c$, $x_2 = b$, $x_3 = a$, $x_4 = a$) is consistent (again, trivially so), but it does not have an extension to x_5 that satisfies $R_{2,3,4,5}$ and $R_{1,2,5}$ simultaneously. Now, if we add the unary constraints $R_2 = R_3 = R_4 = \{a\}$ and $R_1 = R_5 = \{b\}$, we get an equivalent network that is both relational arc- and relational path-consistent. Why? Because then all the variables' domains have a singleton value and the set of solutions over every subset of variables will contain a single tuple only, the one that can be extended to a full solution.   •

For binary constraints, relational m-consistency is identical (except for minor preprocessing) to variable-based i-consistency where $i = m + 1$; otherwise, the conditions are different. For example, given a set of m constraints $R_{S_1}, \ldots, R_{S_m}$, enforcing relational m-consistency relative to a variable x can also be accomplished by enforcing r-consistency if $r = |\cup S_i - 1|$. On the other hand, enforcing i-consistency may be accomplished by relational m-consistency where m ranges from 1 to 2^i, depending on the number of constraints in the network.

8.1.2   Space Bound versus Time Bound

Up to now, whether we used variable-based or relational-based consistency, if a subnetwork having i variables was used as the basis of inference, a constraint having scope $i - 1$ was always inferred and recorded. This dependency between the size of the consulted subnetwork and the arity of the generated constraint can be avoided. Indeed, we often want to bound the scope of inferred and recorded constraints even if inference is based on a large number of variables and constraints. We next discuss this option of separating the size of the network being consulted for inference from the scope of the resulting recorded constraint. In *relational* (i, m)-*consistency*, defined below, m is the cardinality of the set of relations consulted, and i corresponds to the the scope size of the recorded constraint.

RELATIONAL-CONSISTENCY($\mathcal{R}$, i, m) ($RC_{(i,m)}$)

Input: A network $\mathcal{R} = (X, D, C)$.

Output: A relational (i, m)-consistent network $\mathcal{R}'$, equivalent to $\mathcal{R}$.

1. **repeat**
2. $Q \leftarrow \mathcal{R}$
3.   **for** every m relations $R_{S_1}, \dots, R_{S_m} \in Q$
        and every subset A of size i, $A \subseteq \bigcup_{j=1}^{m} S_j$
4. $R_A \leftarrow R_A \cap \pi_A(\bowtie_{j=1}^{m} R_{S_j})$
5.   **if** R_A is the empty relation
6.   **then** exit and return the empty network
7.   **endif**
8.   **endfor**
9. **until** $Q = \mathcal{R}$

Figure 8.1   Relational (i, m)-consistency.

DEFINITION 8.4   **(relational (i, m)-consistency)**

A set of relations $\{R_{S_1}, \dots, R_{S_m}\}$ is *relationally (i, m)-consistent* iff for every subset of variables A of size i, $A \subseteq \cup_{j=1}^{m} S_j$, any consistent assignment to A can be extended to an assignment to $\bigcup_{j=1}^{m} S_j - A$ that satisfies $R_{S_1}, \dots, R_{S_m}$ and the respective domain constraints simultaneously. A network is relationally (i, m)-consistent iff every set of m relations is relationally (i, m)-consistent. A network is strong relational (i, m)-consistent iff it is relational (j, m)-consistent for every $j \leq i$.   •

Figure 8.1 presents algorithm RELATIONAL-CONSISTENCY, $RC_{(i,m)}$, a brute-force algorithm for enforcing strong relational (i, m)-consistency on a network $\mathcal{R}$ by tightening the relations among subsets of size i. It parallels brute-force algorithms such as AC-1 and PC-1. Algorithms for enforcing relational consistency that are not scope restricted will be referred to as RC_m, and they can be obtained from $RC_{(i,m)}$ by using size $i = |\cup_{i=1}^{m} S_i| - 1$ in step 3 of the algorithm. Notice that step 4 should also ensure that only values from the domains of the variables not in A are considered. That is, an exact operation is $R_A \leftarrow R_A \cap \pi_A((\bowtie_{i=1}^{m} R_{S_i}) \bowtie (\bowtie_{x \in \cup_{i=1}^{m} S_i - A} D_x))$, which we avoided for simplicity's sake. Step 4 is accurate if the network is relational arc-consistent already.

Note that R_A stands for the current unique constraint specified over the scope A. If no constraint exists, then R_A is the universal relation over A. We call the operation in step 4 *extended composition* since it generalizes the composition operation defined on binary relations.

DEFINITION 8.5   **(extended composition)**

The extended composition of relation $R_{S_1}, \ldots, R_{S_m}$ relative to a subset of variables $A \subseteq \bigcup_{i=1}^{m} S_i$, denoted $EC_A(R_{S_1}, \ldots, R_{S_m})$, is defined by

$$EC_A(R_{S_1}, \ldots, R_{S_m}) = \pi_A(\Join_{i=1}^{m} R_{S_i})$$

When the operator is applied to m relations, it is called *extended m-composition*. If the projection operation is restricted to subsets of size i, it is called *extended (i, m)-composition*.   •

Algorithm $RC_{(i,m)}$ computes the closure of $\mathcal{R}$ with respect to extended (i, m)-composition. It is computationally expensive for large i and m, although it can be improved in a manner parallel to the improvements of path-consistency algorithms.

The two most practical relational consistency algorithms are those that work with single constraints, only recording constraints on subsets of their variables. These are $RC_{(1,1)}$, which we called generalized arc-consistency, and the full relational arc-consistency algorithm RC_1. Generalized arc-consistency (also called *domain propagation*) derives domain restrictions from single constraints. It can be defined by the rule

$$D_x \leftarrow D_x \cap \pi_x(R_S \Join D_{s-\{x\}}) \tag{8.6}$$

where $x \in S$. Relational arc-consistency can be derived by a rule recording, for every constraint R_S, a constraint on $S - \{x\}$ for every $x \in S$. Namely:

$$R_{S-\{x\}} \leftarrow R_{S-\{x\}} \cap \pi_{S-\{x\}}(R_S \Join D_x) \tag{8.7}$$

Both rules consider all assignments that agree with a single constraint and variable domains. While the first rule records (projects over) the single variable, the second rule projects on all the variables in the constraint scope, excluding x. The first shrinks the domains of x, while the second makes the constraint on $S - \{x\}$ more explicit. Notice that for binary constraints, these two rules are identical. Specializing $RC_{(i,m)}$ for the two rules in Equations (8.6) and (8.7) yields an algorithm for enforcing generalized arc-consistency ($RC_{(1,1)}$) and relational arc-consistency (RC_1), respectively.

The complexity of an algorithm enforcing generalized arc-consistency is clearly polynomial. The complexity of relational arc-consistency is polynomial (in the input) as well, but unless all the constraints have bounded scopes, the algorithm may be exponential in the largest scope size.

8.2 **Directional Consistency Revisited**

The class DIC of variable-based directional consistency algorithms introduced in Chapter 4 can be extended to relational consistency in a natural way.

8.2.1 **Directional Relational Consistency**

We next adapt the definition of relational consistency to the directional case.

DEFINITION   (directional relational consistency)
8.6
Given a network $\mathcal{R}$ and an ordering $d = (x_1, \ldots, x_n)$, $\mathcal{R}$ is *m-directionally relationally consistent* iff for every subset of constraints $\{R_{S_1}, \ldots, R_{S_m}\}$ where the latest variable in any of the constraints' scopes is x_l, and for every A, $A \subseteq \{x_1, \ldots, x_{l-1}\}$, every consistent assignment to A can be extended to x_l while simultaneously satisfying all the relevant constraints in $\{R_{S_1}, \ldots, R_{S_m}\}$.   ●

Figure 8.2 presents algorithm DIRECTIONAL-RELATIONAL-CONSISTENCY, DRC$_m$. The algorithm, which uses the bucket data structure presented in Chapter 4, places in the bucket of x_j all the relations whose latest variable is x_j along a given ordering d. Buckets are subsequently processed in descending order of d from last to first, where in each bucket the extended m-composition operator (step 6 of DRC$_m$) is applied to every subset of m relations. In addition to extended composition, the algorithm may include two optional steps of *simplification* and *instantiation*. The simplification step ensures that each bucket contains relations defined on distinct subsets of variables that are not subsumed by each other. The instantiation step is invoked when a bucket contains a value assignment. In that case, instead of applying extended composition, each relation in the bucket is assigned the given value, and the resulting function is moved into its appropriate bucket. These two steps should also be included in any practical implementation of algorithm ADAPTIVE-CONSISTENCY, which was introduced in Chapter 4 (Figure 4.14).

EXAMPLE   We can use our familiar crossword puzzle (Figure 1.1 on page 4) to illus-
8.6   trate both DRC$_2$ and ADAPTIVE-CONSISTENCY, as the two algorithms coincide in this example. As we have seen in Chapter 2, one possible formulation of the problem is to have a variable for each square that can hold a character, $x_1, \ldots, x_{13}$; the domains of the variables are the alphabet letters and the constraints are the possible words. As we saw, for this example, the constraints are given by

$$R_{\{1,2,3,4,5\}} = \{(H, O, S, E, S), (L, A, S, E, R), (S, H, E, E, T), (S, N, A, I, L),$$
$$(S, T, E, E, R)\}$$
$$R_{\{3,6,9,12\}} = \{(A, L, S, O), (E, A, R, N), (H, I, K, E), (I, R, O, N), (S, A, M, E)\}$$
$$R_{\{5,7,11\}} = \{(E, A, T), (L, E, T), (R, U, N), (S, U, N), (T, E, N), (Y, E, S)\}$$

DIRECTIONAL-RELATIONAL-CONSISTENCY (DRC$_m$)

Input: A constraint network $\mathcal{R} = (X, D, C)$, an ordering $d = (x_1, \ldots, x_n)$.

Output: An m-directional consistent network, along d.

1. Partition the constraints (including domain constraints) into $bucket_1, \ldots, bucket_n$, where $bucket_i$ contains all constraints whose highest variable is x_i.

2. **for** $p \leftarrow n$ **downto** 1 **do**

3.   **simplification**: **for** every R_{S_i}, $R_{S_j} \in bucket_p$, such that $S_i \supseteq S_j$ **do**

   $R_{S_i} \leftarrow \pi_{S_i}(R_{S_i} \bowtie R_{S_j})$ and remove R_{S_j}

4.   **instantiation**: **if** $bucket_p$ contains the constraint $x_p = u$ **then**
      (assign $x_p = u$)

      for every $R_{S_i} \in bucket_p$ **do**

      $R_{S_i - \{x_p\}} \leftarrow \pi_{S_i - \{x_p\}}(\sigma_{x_p = u} R_{S_i})$

         if not empty, add the result to its appropriate bucket, else exit.

5.   **else** (the general case)

      $j \leftarrow \min\{\text{number of variables in } bucket_p, m\}$

6.   **for** every j relations $R_{S_1}, \ldots, R_{S_j}$ in $bucket_p$ **do**

      $A \leftarrow \cup\, S_i - \{x_p\}$, $R_A \leftarrow R_A \cap \pi_A(\bowtie_i R_{S_i})$

7.   **if** R_A is not empty **then** add R_A to its appropriate bucket

8.   **else** exit and return the empty network

9. **return** $\bigcup_{j=1}^n bucket_j$

Figure 8.2 Algorithm DRC$_m$.

$$R_{\{8,9,10,11\}} = \{(A, L, S, O), (E, A, R, N), (H, I, K, E), (I, R, O, N),$$
$$(S, A, M, E)\}$$
$$R_{\{10,13\}} = \{(B, E), (I, T), (N, O), (U, S)\}$$
$$R_{\{12,13\}} = \{(B, E), (I, T), (N, O), (U, S)\}$$

Let us perform several steps of DRC$_2$, where the ordering of the variables is $d = (x_{13}, x_{12}, \ldots, x_1)$. Thus, x_1 is the last variable in the ordering

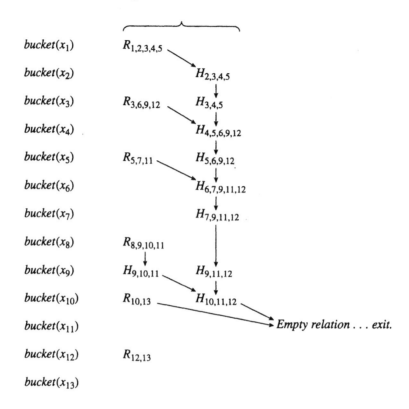

Figure 8.3   Example of applying DRC$_2$ to the crossword puzzle.

and x_{13} is the earliest. The derivation is described schematically in Figure 8.3, showing only the scopes of the recorded functions. As a shorthand, we will call the bucket for each x_i by the name *bucket$_i$*. We denote the original relations by Rs and the new relations (created during the processing of DRC$_2$) by Hs. Our first step is to distribute each original R relation into the bucket of the latest ordered variable in its scope. Next, we process each of the buckets, starting at the end of the ordering. The bucket for x_1 contains the single relation $R_{\{1,2,3,4,5\}}$. Processing *bucket$_1$* generates the relation

$$H_{2,3,4,5} = \pi_{2,3,4,5}(R_{1,2,3,4,5})$$
$$= \{(O, S, E, S), (A, S, E, R), (H, E, E, T), (N, A, I, L), (T, E, E, R)\}$$

and places it in the bucket of variable x_2, which is processed next. The bucket for x_2 contains only this single relation $H_{2,3,4,5}$. Processing *bucket$_2$* adds the relation

$$H_{3,4,5} = \pi_{3,4,5}(H_{2,3,4,5}) = \{(S, E, S), (S, E, R), (E, E, T), (A, I, L), (E, E, R)\}$$

to the bucket of variable x_3. This bucket is processed next, and we see that it contains the relations $R_{3,6,9,12}$ and $H_{3,4,5}$. Processing *bucket$_3$* adds the relation

$$H_{4,5,6,9,12} = \pi_{4,5,6,9,12}(H_{3,4,5} \bowtie R_{3,6,9,12})$$
$$= \{(E,S,A,M,E),(E,R,A,M,E),(E,T,A,R,N),(I,L,L,S,O),$$
$$(E,R,A,R,N)\}$$

to the previously empty bucket of variable x_4. Processing *bucket$_4$* adds the relation

$$H_{5,6,9,12} = \{(S,A,M,E),(R,A,M,E),(T,A,R,N),(L,L,S,O),$$
$$(R,A,R,N)\}$$

The bucket for x_5 now contains the relations $R_{5,7,11}$ and $H_{5,6,9,12}$. Processing *bucket$_5$* adds the relation

$$H_{6,7,9,11,12} = \{(A,U,M,N,E),(A,E,R,N,N),(L,E,S,T,O),$$
$$(A,U,R,N,N)\}$$

The bucket for x_6 contains only this newly generated relation $H_{6,7,9,11,12}$. Processing *bucket$_6$* adds the relation

$$H_{7,9,11,12} = \{(U,M,N,E),(E,R,N,N),(E,S,T,O),(U,R,N,N)\}$$

to the bucket for x_7. Processing *bucket$_7$* adds the relation

$$H_{9,11,12} = \{(M,N,E),(R,N,N),(S,T,O)\}$$

to the bucket of x_9. Next we process the bucket of x_8, containing only the original relation $R_{8,9,10,11}$, and when processed it adds the relation

$$H_{9,10,11} = \{(L,S,O),(A,R,N),(I,K,E),(R,O,N),(A,M,E)\}.$$

The bucket for x_9 now contains the relations $H_{9,10,11}$ and $H_{9,11,12}$. Processing *bucket$_9$* adds the relation

$$H_{10,11,12} = \{(O,N,N)\}$$

The bucket for x_{10} contains the relations $R_{10,13}$ and $H_{10,11,12}$. Processing *bucket$_{10}$* adds the empty relation. Since the empty relation was derived, the algorithm stops and reports that the network is inconsistent.   ●

8.2.2 Complexity

The complexity of DRC$_m$ is not likely to be polynomial, even for $m = 2$, since, as we will see, it solves NP-complete problems. Nevertheless, as observed for variable-based consistency enforcing, its worst-case complexity can be bounded using the induced width of the constraint graph. The primal and dual constraint graphs of the crossword puzzle of Figure 1.1 are given in Figure 2.5 (page 31).

We see that the induced width of the primal graph, along the processing ordering $d = x_{13}, \ldots, x_1$, is 5. As with variable-based directional consistency enforcing (see Chapter 4), directional relational consistency transforms its primal constraint graph into the induced ordered graph. Since the complexity of recording a new constraint is exponential in the scope of these constraints, and since the scope size of each new constraint is bounded by the induced width, we can bound the complexity of directional relational consistency using the induced width as well:

THEOREM   **(complexity of directional relational consistency)**
8.1
Given a network $\mathcal{R}$, the time complexity and size of the network generated by DRC_m along ordering d is $O(nm \cdot (2^m k^2)^{(w^*(d)+1)})$, where $w^*(d)$ is the induced width of the network's constraint graph along ordering d. Consequently, the time complexity of DRC_2 is $O(n(4k^2)^{(w^*(d)+1)})$.

Proof Since the number of variables mentioned in any bucket is at most $w^*(d)+1$, the number of relations in a bucket is bounded by $O(2^{w^*(d)+1})$, and the number of subsets of size m is $O(2^{(w^*(d)+1)m})$. Also, the number of tuples in each relation is bounded by $k^{w^*(d)+1}$ when k bounds the domain size. The complexity of an m-way join of relations of size $k^{w^*(d)+1}$ can be bounded by $O(m \cdot k^{2(w^*(d)+1)})$ since the size of the relation resulting from every pair-wise join is still bounded by $k^{w^*(d)+1}$, and thus m consecutive joins do not multiply but only add. Consequently, the overall complexity is $O((nm) \cdot 2^{(w^*(d)+1)m} \cdot k^{2(w^*(d)+1)})$, as stated.   •

The only case for which the complexity of DRC_m is guaranteed to be polynomial occurs when $m = 1$. You should convince yourself of the following:

LEMMA   The complexity of DRC_1 is $O(n \cdot e^2 \cdot t^2)$ where e is the number of input
8.1   relations and t bounds the number of tuples in each relation.   •

Interestingly, whenever we apply ADAPTIVE-CONSISTENCY to the crossword puzzle, at most two relations will ever reside in a single bucket, no matter what variable ordering is selected (see Figure 8.3). For the crossword puzzle, then, ADAPTIVE-CONSISTENCY coincides with DRC_2. We can show the following (see Exercise 5):

PROPOSITION   (1) Crossword puzzles can be made directional backtrack-free by
8.1 DRC_2, and (2) the complexity of DRC_2 applied to crossword puzzles is $O(n \cdot k^{2(w^*(d)+1)})$.   •

Interestingly, RC_2 and DRC_2 can generate backtrack-free representations for a variety of problems. Two such classes are Boolean formulas and linear algebraic inequalities over discrete integer domains. These are special cases of constraints having tight domains and row-convex constraints, respectively.

8.3 **Domain and Constraint Tightness**

We next discuss relevant properties that relate domain and constraint tightness to a level of local consistency that ensures global consistency.

8.3.1 **Domain Tightness**

Constraint networks having smaller domain size are easier to ensure global consistency and therefore to solve.

THEOREM 8.2   A strong relational 2-consistent constraint network over bivalued domains is globally consistent.

Proof   Let $\vec{a}_{i-1} = (a_1, \ldots, a_{i-1})$ be a consistent assignment to variables $x_1, \ldots, x_{i-1}$ in a strong relational 2-consistent constraint network over bivalued domains. We want to show that there is a value $\langle x_i, a_i \rangle$ that will be consistent with $\vec{a}_{i-1}$. Let's assume that such an extension does not exist and derive a contradiction. Since there are two possible values for x_i, let's call them 0 and 1. Let's denote by A_0 all the *relevant* constraints (those whose scope contains x_i and a subset of $x_1, \ldots, x_{i-1}$) that are violated by $(\vec{a}_{i-1}, x_i = 0)$ and by A_1 the corresponding set of relevant constraints violated by $(\vec{a}_{i-1}, x_i = 1)$. Clearly, A_0 and A_1 are not empty, or else we would have a consistent extension to x_i contrary to our assumption. Let's pick $R_1 \in A_0$ and $R_2 \in A_1$ (R_1 and R_2 may be equal). Therefore, R_1 and R_2 are at most two constraints that cannot consistently extend a common consistent partial assignment (the projection of $\vec{a}_{i-1}$ on the union of the scopes of R_1 and R_2 excluding x_i) to x_i, contradicting strong relational 2-consistency (if $R_1 = R_2$ we would be contradicting relational arc-consistency).   •

Theorem 8.2 implies that if we enforce strong relational 2-consistency, we will make any bivalued network globally consistent. The argument can easily be extended to *directional* relational consistency. That is, a bivalued network that is directional relational 2-consistent is also directionally globally consistent. In other words, algorithm DRC2 is complete for bivalued theories. Remember that we have already observed this property for binary constraints. However, while bivalued binary constraints are tractable, nonbinary bivalued networks are not, because variable-based path-consistency can be enforced in polynomial time while relational 2-consistency cannot be.

Can Theorem 8.2 be extended to larger domains? Indeed, if the domain size of a constraint network has at most k values, strong relational k-consistency ensures global consistency. Consequently DRC_k globally solves any k-domain constraint problem such as the graph k-coloring problem. We leave the proof of the general case to you.

THEOREM 8.3   **(domain tightness and local consistency)**

A strong relational k-consistent constraint network $\mathcal{R} = (X, D, C)$ over domains with at most k values is globally consistent.   •

COROLLARY 8.1 DRC_k makes any k-bounded constraint network with k-bounded domains directional backtrack-free.   •

8.3.2   Constraint Tightness

The notion of domain tightness can be extended from unary scope relations (domains) to arbitrary relations having any scope size, allowing a similar relationship with bounded local consistency.

DEFINITION 8.7   **(m-tight)**

A constraint relation R_S of arity r is called *m-tight* if, for any variable $x_i \in S$ and any instantiation $\bar{a}$ of the remaining $r - 1$ variables in $S - \{x_i\}$, either there are at most m extensions of $\bar{a}$ to x_i that satisfy R_S, or there are exactly $|D_i|$ such extensions.   •

Notice that given a constraint network with c constraints, each with arity of at most r and at most t tuples in the relation, determining the least m such that all c of the constraints are m-tight requires $O(c \cdot r \cdot t)$ time.

EXAMPLE 8.7   We illustrate the above definitions using the following network $\mathcal{R}$ with variables $\{x_1, x_2, x_3, x_4\}$, domains $D_i = \{a, b, c\}$, $1 \leq i \leq 4$, and constraints

$$R_{S_1} = \{(a, a, a), (a, a, c), (a, b, c), (a, c, b), (b, a, c),$$
$$(b, b, b), (b, c, a), (c, a, b), (c, b, a), (c, c, c)\}$$
$$R_{S_2} = \{(a, b), (b, a), (b, c), (c, a), (c, c)\}$$
$$R_{S_3} = \{(a, b), (a, c), (b, b), (c, a), (c, b)\}$$

where $S_1 = (x_1, x_2, x_3)$, $S_2 = (x_2, x_4)$, and $S_3 = (x_3, x_4)$.

It can be verified that all of the constraints are 2-tight. As a partial verification of the binary constraint R_{S_3}, consider the extensions to variable x_3 given instantiations of the variable x_4. For the instantiation $\langle x_4, a \rangle$ there is one extension to x_3; for $\langle x_4, b \rangle$ there are three extensions (but $|D_3| = 3$, so the definition of 2-tightness is still satisfied); and for $\langle x_4, c \rangle$ there is one extension. •

We next introduce the main relationship (for a proof see van Beek and Dechter 1997).

THEOREM 8.4   **(constraint tightness and local consistency)**

A strongly relationally $(m + 1)$-consistent constraint network that has m-tight constraints is globally consistent. •

Notice that Theorem 8.4 requires that a network has a level of strong consistency that is less than or equal to the level of strong consistency required by domain tightness in Theorem 8.3. The level of required consistency is equal in both theorems only when $m = k - 1$ and is less when $m < k - 1$. For example, the graph k-colorability problem provides examples of networks where domain tightness and constraint tightness give the same bound on the sufficient level of local consistency required because the constraints are $(k - 1)$-tight.

Notice also that once we enforce some level of relational consistency the tightness level of the network's constraints may increase or decrease. The parameter m will increase if a new constraint is being recorded on a subset of variables that were not explicitly constrained before, and the new constraint has a larger m-tightness value.

Another important special case are bivalued constraint networks. For example, the satisfiability of propositional CNFs (SAT) provides an example of networks with domains of size 2. Constraints having domains of size 2 are 1-tight by definition. Any additional constraints added to the network, as a result of enforcing strong relational 2-consistency, will also be 1-tight. This is another example where domain tightness and constraint tightness yield the same required consistency level.

8.4 **Inference for Boolean Theories**

In the previous section we saw that, for Boolean constraints, enforcing relational 2-consistency is sufficient for global consistency. It turns out that for CNF theories the extended 2-composition, which enforces relational 2-consistency, is equivalent to pair-wise resolution. Both these observations yield well-known algorithms for the task of propositional satisfiability.

8.4.1 **Consistency for Propositional CNF Theories**

To review notation, recall the definitions in Section 2.2.2 and take a look at the following additional definitions. We say a clause α is *entailed* by φ, $\varphi \models \alpha$, if and only if α is true in all models of φ. A clause α is a *prime implicate* of φ if and only if $\varphi \models \alpha$ and $\not\exists \beta \subset \alpha$ such that $\varphi \models \beta$. A Horn formula is a CNF formula whose clauses all have at most one positive literal. A clause is positive if it contains only positive literals, and it is negative if it contains only negative literals. A k-CNF formula is one whose clauses are all of length k or less.

EXAMPLE 8.8

Consider the following CNF formula:

$$\varphi = \{(F \vee X \vee Y \vee \neg Z) \wedge (F \vee Z) \wedge (X \vee Y \vee F)\}.$$

As noted, a formula φ can be viewed as a constraint network where each clause corresponds to a constraint defined by its models. It is easy to see that the clauses are relationally arc-consistent since the projection of each single clause on any subset of propositional symbols results in the universal relation allowing everything (no unary constraints are available). The first two clauses are also relationally path-consistent relative to F since any truth assignment to X, Y, Z can be extended by assigning "true" to F, thereby satisfying both clauses. Similarly, the two clauses are relationally path-consistent relative to Z since any consistent assignment to X, Y, F has to satisfy the third clause of φ and therefore by assigning $Z = true$ the first two clauses are satisfied. You are encouraged to check for yourself that the entire set of clauses is relationally path-consistent.   •

We next show that the notion of resolution is equivalent to extended 2-composition (see Definition 8.5).

EXAMPLE 8.9

Consider the two clauses $\alpha = (P \vee \neg Q \vee \neg O)$ and $\beta = (Q \vee \neg W)$. Now let the relation $R_{PQO} = \{000, 100, 010, 001, 110, 101, 111\}$ be the models of α and the relation $R_{QW} = \{00, 10, 11\}$ be the models of β. Resolving these two clauses over Q generates the resolvent clause $\gamma = res(\alpha, \beta) = (P \vee \neg O \vee \neg W)$. The models of γ are $\{(000, 100, 010, 001, 110, 101, 111\}$. It is easy to see that $EC_{POW}(R_{PQO}, R_{QW}) = \pi_{POW}(R_{PQO} \bowtie R_{Qw})$ yields the models of γ.   •

Indeed, we have the following:

LEMMA 8.2

The *resolution* operation over two clauses, $(\alpha \vee Q)$ and $(\beta \vee \neg Q)$, results in a clause $(\alpha \vee \beta)$ satisfying $models(\alpha \vee \beta) = EC_{Q'}(models(\alpha \vee Q), models(\beta \vee \neg Q))$, where Q' is the union of scopes of both clauses excluding Q.   •

Specializing algorithm RC$_2$ (Figure 8.1) to CNF theories, replacing extended 2-composition with resolution, yields an algorithm that applies pair-wise resolution to the theory until no new resolvents can be generated.

Since relational 2-consistent networks with bivalued domains are globally consistent (Theorem 8.2), the resolution algorithm, enforcing relational 2-consistency,

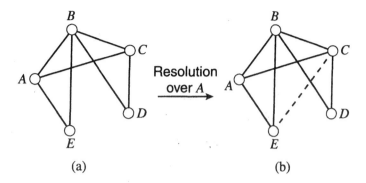

Figure 8.4 (a) The interaction graph of theory $\varphi_1 = \{(\neg C), (A \vee B \vee C), (\neg A \vee B \vee E),(\neg B \vee C \vee D)\}$, and (b) the effect of resolution over A on that graph.

generates a globally consistent, and therefore backtrack-free, representation. When the resolution algorithm terminates, and if we also eliminate redundant clauses by subsumption elimination (that is, if $\alpha \subseteq \beta$, we can delete β), we will get all the prime implicates of the CNF theory. We can therefore conclude that the set of all prime implicates of a theory is globally consistent.

As noted in Chapter 2, the structure of a propositional theory can be described by its *interaction graph*. The interaction graph $G(\varphi)$ of a propositional theory φ is an undirected graph that contains a node for each propositional variable and an edge for each pair of nodes that correspond to variables appearing in the same clause. For example, the interaction graph of theory $\varphi_1 = \{(\neg C), (A \vee B \vee C), (\neg A \vee B \vee E), (\neg B \vee C \vee D)\}$ is shown in Figure 8.4(a).

Notice that the interaction graph of a theory processed by resolution should be augmented with new edges reflecting the added resolvents. For example, as shown in Figure 8.4(b), resolution over variable A in φ_1 generates a new clause $(B \vee C \vee E)$, so the graph of the resulting theory has an edge between nodes E and C.

Next observe that since a domain constraint in a CNF theory appears as a unit literal, the relational arc-consistency rule in Equation (8.7) translates to unit resolution. Indeed, UNIT-PROPAGATION, the algorithm presented in Figure 3.16, applies relational arc-consistency for SAT. However, unlike general relational arc-consistency, unit propagation can be performed in linear time.

8.4.2 Directional Resolution

Specializing DRC$_2$ for CNFs, by replacing extended 2-composition with resolution and the instantiation step by unit resolution, results in algorithm DIRECTIONAL-RESOLUTION (DR), presented in Figure 8.5.

DIRECTIONAL-RESOLUTION (DR)

Input: A CNF theory φ, an ordering $d = Q_1,\ldots,Q_n$ of its variables.

Output: A decision of whether φ is satisfiable. If it is, a theory $E_d(\varphi)$, equivalent to φ, else an empty directional extension.

1. **Initialize:** generate an ordered partition of clauses into buckets $bucket_1,\ldots,bucket_n$, where $bucket_i$ contains all clauses whose highest variable is Q_i.

2. **for** i $\leftarrow$ n **downto** 1 process $bucket_i$:

3.   **if** there is a unit clause **then** (the instantiation step)
         apply unit resolution in $bucket_i$ and place the resolvents in their right buckets.

       if the empty clause was generated, theory is not satisfiable.

4.   **else** resolve each pair $\{(\alpha \vee Q_i),(\beta \vee \neg Q_i)\} \subseteq bucket_i$.

         if $\gamma = \alpha \vee \beta$ is empty, return $E_d(\varphi) = \{\}$, the theory is not satisfiable

         else determine the index of γ and add it to the appropriate bucket.

5. **return** $E_d(\varphi) \leftarrow \bigcup_i bucket_i$

Figure 8.5   Algorithm DIRECTIONAL-RESOLUTION.

We call its output theory, $E_d(\varphi)$, the *directional extension* of φ. Given an ordering $d = (Q_1, \ldots, Q_n)$, all the clauses containing Q_i that do not contain any symbol higher in the ordering are placed in the bucket of Q_i, denoted $bucket_i$. The algorithm processes the buckets in the reverse order of d. Processing of $bucket_i$ means resolving over Q_i all the possible pairs of clauses in the bucket and inserting the resolvents into appropriate lower buckets.

Note that if the bucket contains a unit clause (Q_i or $\neg Q_i$), only unit resolutions are performed. As implied by Theorem 8.2, DRC₂ is guaranteed to generate a backtrack-free representation along the order of processing. Indeed, once all the buckets are processed, and if the empty clause was not generated, a truth assignment (model) can be assembled in a backtrack-free manner by consulting $E_d(\varphi)$, using the order d.

EXAMPLE 8.10   Given the input theory $\varphi_1 = \{(\neg C), (A \vee B \vee C), (\neg A \vee B \vee E), (\neg B \vee C \vee D)\}$, and an ordering $d = (E, D, C, B, A)$, the theory is partitioned into buckets and processed by directional resolution in reverse order. Resolving over

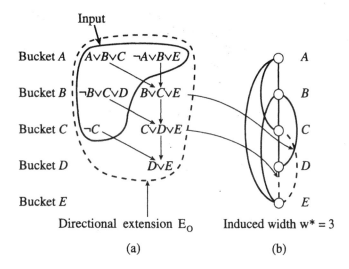

Figure 8.6 A schematic execution of directional resolution using ordering $d = (E, D, C, B, A)$.

variable A produces a new clause $(B \vee C \vee E)$, which is placed in *bucket*$_B$. Resolving over B then produces clause $(C \vee D \vee E)$, which is placed in *bucket*$_C$. Finally, resolving over C produces clause $(D \vee E)$, which is placed in *bucket*$_D$. Directional resolution now terminates, since no resolution can be performed in *bucket*$_D$ and *bucket*$_E$. The output is a nonempty directional extension $E_d(\varphi_1)$. Once the directional extension is available, model generation can begin. There are no clauses in the bucket of E, the first variable in the ordering, and therefore E can be assigned any value (e.g., $E = 0$). Given $E = 0$, the clause $(D \vee E)$ in *bucket*$_D$ implies $D = 1$, clause $\neg C$ in *bucket*$_C$ implies $C = 0$, and clause $(B \vee C \vee E)$ in *bucket*$_B$, together with the current assignments to C and E, implies $B = 1$. Finally, A can be assigned any value since both clauses in its bucket are satisfied by previous assignments. The initial partitioning into buckets along the ordering d as well as the buckets' contents generated by the algorithm following resolution over each bucket are depicted in Figure 8.6a.   •

Not surprisingly, the complexity of directional resolution is exponentially bounded (time and space) in the induced width of the theory's interaction graph along the order of processing. We can prove this based on the complexity of DRC2 (yielding $O(n16^{w*+1})$ when substituting $k = 2$ in Theorem 8.1). Notice that the graph of theory φ_1 along the ordering d depicted in Figure 8.6b has an induced width of 3. Simple direct arguments yield a somewhat tighter bound.

LEMMA 8.3   Given a theory φ and an ordering $d = (Q_1, \ldots, Q_n)$, if Q_i has at most k parents in the induced graph along d, then the bucket of Q_i in $E_d(\varphi)$ contains no more than 3^{k+1} clauses.

Proof Given a clause α in the bucket of Q_i, there are three possibilities for each parent P of Q_i: either P appears in α, $\neg P$ appears in α, or neither of them appears in α. Since Q_i also appears in α, either positively or negatively, the number of possible clauses in a bucket is no more than $2 \cdot 3^k < 3^{k+1}$. •

Since the number of parents of each variable is bounded by the induced width along the order of processing, we get the following:

THEOREM 8.5 **(complexity of DR)**

Given a theory φ and an ordering of its variables d, the time complexity of algorithm DR along d is $O(n \cdot 9^{w_d^*})$, and $E_d(\varphi)$ contains at most $n \cdot 3^{w_d^*+1}$ clauses, where w_d^* is the induced width of φ's interaction graph along d. •

8.4.3 Tractable Boolean Theories

This section revisits some tractable classes mentioned before.

2-SAT

Note that algorithm DIRECTIONAL-RESOLUTION is tractable for 2-CNF theories because 2-CNFs are closed under resolution (the resolvents are of size 2 or less) and because the overall number of clauses of size 2 is bounded by $O(n^2)$, yielding $O(n \cdot n^2) = O(n^3)$ complexity. In this case, unordered resolution is also tractable. We have already noted this tractable class in Chapter 3. Exploiting w^*, we can get the following:

THEOREM 8.6 Given a 2-CNF theory φ, its directional extension $E_d(\varphi)$ along any ordering d is of size $O(n \cdot w_d^{*2})$ and can be generated in $O(n \cdot w_d^{*2})$ time. •

DIRECTIONAL-RESOLUTION is not the best algorithm for solving 2-SAT problems, since we know that 2-SAT can be solved in linear time (Itai, Even, and Shamir 1976). Note, however, that DIRECTIONAL-RESOLUTION decides not only consistency but also compiles the theory into one that can produce each model in linear time in the output theory. In other words, in polynomial time we can have access to the exponential number of 2-CNF models. Generating them all takes exponential time, however.

Horn Theories

We also noted in Chapter 3 that Horn theories are tractable. These are CNF formulas where each clause has at most one positive literal. They can be written as a collection of implications, also called *Horn rules*, of the form

$$P \leftarrow Q_1 \wedge Q_2 \wedge \ldots \wedge Q_r$$

where all the Q_i's and P are positive atoms. P is called the head of the rule and $\{Q_1, \ldots, Q_r\}$ is its antecedent. Some of the rules may have empty heads.

Indeed, consistency of a Horn theory can be fully determined by unit propagation. Assume we apply unit propagation to a Horn theory. If the algorithm terminates without generating an empty clause, its outputs can be partitioned into a set of unit clauses and into a disjoint set of nonunit clauses that do not mention any of the unit clauses. Consequently, if we assign each unit clause its truth value and each of the rest of the propositions a negative truth value, the resulting assignment does not violate any clause, because each clause must contain a negative literal. That is, we have the following (see also Theorem 3.3):

THEOREM 8.7   The consistency of Horn theories can be determined by unit propagation. If the empty clause is not generated, the theory is satisfiable.   •

Since unit propagation is the same as relational arc-consistency, we have just shown that relational arc-consistency is complete for Horn satisfiability. In Chapter 11 we will show that Horn theories, as well as 2-CNF theories, can be extended to tractable classes over multivalued variables in general CSPs.

8.5 **Row-Convex Constraints**

This section identifies a property of constraints called *row convexity* and shows that in this case relational path-consistency is sufficient to guarantee global consistency. Row convexity extends some special binary constraint properties such as functional and monotone constraints. For the sake of simplicity, we first present definitions and analysis for the case of binary constraints.

DEFINITION 8.8   **(functional)**

A binary relation R_{ij} expressed as a $(0,1)$-matrix (see Chapter 1) is *functional* if and only if there is at most a single 1 in each row and in each column of R_{ij}.   •

DEFINITION 8.9   **(monotone)**

Given some ordering of the domain of values for all variables, a binary relation R_{ij} expressed as a $(0,1)$-matrix is *monotone* if the following conditions hold: if $(a, b) \in R_{ij}$ and $c \geq a$, then $(c, b) \in R_{ij}$, and if $(a, b) \in R_{ij}$ and $c \leq b$, then $(a, c) \in R_{ij}$.   •

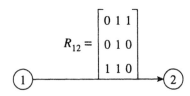

Figure 8.7 A row-convex constraint.

DEFINITION
8.10

DEFINITION   **(row convex)**
8.10

A binary relation R_{ij} represented as a $(0,1)$-matrix is *row convex* if in each row (column) all of the 1s are consecutive; that is, no two 1s within a single row are separated by a 0 in that same row (column).   ●

For example, consider the simple constraint network in Figure 8.7, with variables x_1 and x_2 and domains $D_1 = \{a, b, c\}$ and $D_2 = \{d, e, f\}$. The constraint R_{12} does not allow, for example, the pair (a, d) but does allow the pairs (a, e), (a, f). This constraint is row convex but not monotone.

The following well-known lemma on the intersection of $(0,1)$-row vectors that are row convex is instrumental for proving the properties of interest. The lemma is a discrete version of the well-known result that, for a set of mutually intersecting intervals, there is a point common to all.

LEMMA   Let F be a finite collection of $(0,1)$-row vectors that are row convex and of
8.4   equal length such that every pair of row vectors in F has a nonzero entry in common; that is, their intersection is not the vector with all 0s. Then all of the row vectors in F have a nonzero entry in common.   ●

THEOREM   Let $\mathcal{R}$ be a path-consistent binary constraint network. If there exists an
8.8   ordering of the domains $D_1, \ldots, D_n$ of $\mathcal{R}$ such that the relations of all constraints are row convex, the network is globally consistent and is therefore minimal.

Proof   The theorem is proved by showing that if the network is path-consistent and all of the $(0,1)$-matrices are row convex, then the network is k-consistent for all $k \leq n$. Suppose that variables $x_1, \ldots, x_{k-1}$ can be consistently instantiated. That is, let $a_1, \ldots, a_{k-1}$ be an instantiation satisfying all the relevant constraints. To show that the network is k-consistent, we must show that there exists at least one instantiation, a_k, of variable x_k that is not violated by any R_{ik}, $i = 1, \ldots, k - 1$. The $a_1, \ldots, a_{k-1}$ restrict the allowed instantiations of x_k. For each i, the nonzero entries in row a_i of the $(0, 1)$-matrix R_{ik} are the allowed instantiations of x_k. The key here is that all of these row vectors are row convex (i.e., the 1s are consecutive).

Hence, by Lemma 8.4, it is sufficient to show that any two row vectors have a nonzero entry in common to show that they all have a nonzero entry in common. But arc-consistency guarantees that each row vector contains at least one nonzero entry, and path-consistency guarantees that each pair of row vectors has a nonzero entry in common. Hence, all of the constraints have a nonzero entry in common, and there exists at least one consistent instantiation of x_k that satisfies all the constraints. Hence, we have shown that for any consistent instantiation of $k - 1$ variables, there exists an instantiation of any kth variable. The network therefore is k-consistent.

                                                           ●

EXAMPLE 8.11

We use the familiar scene-labeling example to illustrate the application of Theorem 8.8. Figure 2.7 (page 34) shows the constraint network when junctions are the variables. Figure 1.4 (page 7) shows the domains of the variables and the ordering imposed (from left to right). The constraints between variables are simple: if two variables share an edge, then the edge must be labeled the same at both ends. Not all of the constraints are row convex. However, in this case, once the path-consistency algorithm is applied, the relations become row convex. Therefore, in this example, no reordering of the domains is needed in order to satisfy row convexity. Note that the scene-labeling problem has been shown to be NP-complete in the general case (Kirousis and Papadimitriou 1985).

    As an immediate corollary of Theorem 8.8, if we know that the result of applying path-consistency will be that all of the relations become row convex, we can guarantee a priori that path-consistency will generate a globally consistent network. Thus, if the relations in our constraint network are row convex, and remain row convex under extended composition, the result applies.

                                                            ●

Let the domains of the variables be finite subsets of the integers, and let a binary constraint between two variables be a conjunction of linear equalities and inequalities of the form $ax_i - bx_j = c$, $ax_i - bx_j < c$, or $ax_i - bx_j \leq c$, where a, b, and c are integer constants. For example, the conjunction

$$(3x_i + 2x_j \leq 3) \wedge (-4x_i + 5x_j < 1)$$

is an allowed constraint between variables x_i and x_j. A network with constraints of this form can be formulated as a linear integer program where each constraint is on two variables and the domains of the variables are restricted to be finite subsets of the integers. However, it can be shown that each element in the closure under composition, intersection, and transposition of the resulting set of $(0,1)$-matrices is row convex, provided that when an element is removed from a domain by arc-consistency, the associated $(0,1)$-matrices are "condensed." This is best illustrated through an example. Let $D_i = D_j = \{-1, 0\}$ and $D_k = \{-1, 0, 1\}$. Let R_{ij} be the matrix constructed from the constraint $x_i + x_j < 0$ and R_{jk} be constructed from $-2x_j + x_k = 1$.

$$R_{ij} = \begin{bmatrix} 1 & 1 \\ 1 & 0 \end{bmatrix} \quad R_{jk} = \begin{bmatrix} 1 & 0 & 0 \\ 0 & 0 & 1 \end{bmatrix} \quad R_{ik} = \begin{bmatrix} 1 & 0 & 1 \\ 1 & 0 & 0 \end{bmatrix}$$

The matrix R_{ik}, the result of composing R_{ij} and R_{jk}, is not row convex. However, there is no solution with x_k assigned 0, so D_k becomes $\{-1, 1\}$ and row convexity can be restored by removing the middle column from matrices R_{ik} and R_{jk}. Hence, we can guarantee that the result of path-consistency will be row convex and therefore minimal, and that the network will be globally consistent for any binary linear equation over the integers.

8.5.1 Identifying Row-Convex Relations

As noted in the scene-labeling example, when constructing a constraint network and the (0,1)-matrices that represent the constraints, we must impose an ordering on the domains of the variables. Sometimes a natural ordering exists, as when the domain is a finite subset of the integers, but often the ordering imposed is arbitrary and with no inherent meaning. An unlucky ordering may hide the fact that the constraint network really is row convex or, more properly, can be made row convex. How can we distinguish this case from the case where no ordering of the domains will result in row convexity? The following theorem shows that we can efficiently test for row convexity.

THEOREM
8.9

(Booth and Lueker 1976)

An $m \times n$ (0,1)-matrix specified by its f nonzero entries can be tested for whether a permutation of the columns exists such that the matrix is row convex in $O(m + n + f)$ steps.   •

EXAMPLE
8.12

Maruyama (1990) shows that natural language parsing can be formulated as a problem on constraint networks. In this framework, intermediate parsing results are represented as a constraint network, and every solution to the network corresponds to an individual parse tree. We use an example network to illustrate the application of Theorems 8.8 and 8.9. Consider the following sentence:

Put	the block	on the floor	on the table	in the room.
V1	NP2	PP3	PP4	PP5

With 14 different parses the sentence is structurally ambiguous, as there are many ways to attach the prepositional phrases. Table 8.1 shows the original ordering of the domains, and Figure 8.8 and Table 8.2 show the variables in the constraint network and the constraints. For example, the constraint between variable PP3 and variable PP4 is given by the (0,1)-matrix at row PP3, column PP4, of Table 8.2 (the symbol I in the table denotes the

Table 8.1 Variables and domains for parsing example.

Variable	Domain	
	Original ordering	*New ordering*
V1	{Rnil}	{Rnil}
NP2	{O1}	{O1}
PP3	{L1, P2}	{L1, P2}
PP4	{L1, P2, P3}	{P2, P3, L1}
PP5	{L1, P2, P3, P4}	{P3, P4, L1, P2}

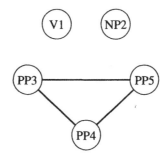

Figure 8.8 Graph of parsing constraint network.

identity matrix—the $(0,1)$-matrix consisting of 1s along the diagonal and 0s everywhere else). While the network is path-consistent, it can be seen that the constraints are not all row convex given the original domain ordering used. However, using the new domain ordering shown in Table 8.1, the constraints become row convex. •

Let's show how Theorem 8.9 can be used to determine whether an ordering of the domains of the variables exists such that all of the $(0,1)$-matrices R_{ij}, $1 \leq i, j \leq n$, are row convex. The procedure is simple: for each variable, x_j, we take the matrix defined by stacking up R_{1j} on top of R_{2j} on top of $\cdots$ R_{nj} and test whether the matrix can be made row convex. For example, with reference to Table 8.2, for variable PP4 we would test whether the columns of the matrix consisting of the 3 columns and 11 rows under the column heading PP4 can be permuted to satisfy the row convexity property. In this example such a permutation exists and corresponds to the new ordering of the domain of variable PP4 shown in Table 8.1.

8.5.2 **Nonbinary Row-Convex Constraints**

Informally, an r-ary relation is row convex if, in the multidimensional 0/1 matrix representing the constraint, each vector that is parallel to one of the axes has the consecutive 1s property.

Table 8.2 Tabular representation of constraint network.

	V1	NP2	PP3	PP4	PP5
V1	I	1	1 1	1 1 1	1 1 1 1
NP2	1	I	1 1	1 1 1	1 1 1 1
PP3	1	1	I	1 0 1	1 0 1 1
	1	1		1 1 1	1 1 1 1
PP4	1	1	1 1		1 0 0 1
	1	1	0 1	I	1 1 0 1
	1	1	1 1		1 1 1 1
PP5	1	1	1 1	1 1 1	
	1	1	0 1	0 1 1	I
	1	1	1 1	0 0 1	
	1	1	1 1	1 1 1	

DEFINITION 8.11 (row convex)

An r-ary relation R_S, where $S = \{x_1, \ldots, x_r\}$, is *row convex* if for any subset Z of $r - 2$ variables $Z \subseteq S$ and for every instantiation, $\vec{a}$, of Z, the binary relation $\pi_{(S-Z)}(\sigma_{\vec{a}}(R))$ is·row convex.   •

For binary constraint networks, we have identified an efficient procedure for determining whether a domain ordering exists such that the relations are all row convex. It is an open question whether such an efficient procedure exists for r-ary constraint networks. However, there are practical examples such as bivalued relations, implicational constraints (see Chapter 11), and many cases of linear inequalities that are all row convex.

As in the binary case, we now can see that general relational path-consistency ensures global consistency when the relations are row convex.

THEOREM 8.10 Let $\mathcal{R} = (X, D, C)$ be a network of constraints that is relationally path-consistent. If there exists an ordering of the domains $D_1, \ldots, D_n$ of $\mathcal{R}$ such that the relations are row convex, the network is globally consistent.

Proof See van Beek and Dechter (1995).   •

Therefore, we have the following:

THEOREM 8.11 For any network $\mathcal{R}$, whose closure under extended 2-composition is row convex, RC$_2$ will generate a globally consistent network of $\mathcal{R}$.   •

Consider a set of r-ary linear inequalities, where the domains of the variables are finite subsets of integers and the r-ary constraints over a subset of variables $x_1, \ldots, x_r$ are of the form $a_1 x_1 + \cdots + a_r x_r \leq c$, where the a_i's are rational constants. This is a general integer linear program. The r-ary inequalities define corresponding r-ary relations that are row convex. Since it is possible to show that r-ary linear inequalities that are closed under relational path-consistency are row convex, relative to any set of integer domains (using the natural ordering), we can conclude that,

PROPOSITION 8.2   A set of linear inequalities that is processed by RC$_2$ is globally consistent. •

Clearly, we then have the following:

THEOREM 8.12   For any network $\mathcal{R} = (X, D, C)$, whose directional closure relative to extended 2-composition is not empty and row convex, algorithm DRC$_2$ computes an equivalent network of $\mathcal{R}$ that is backtrack-free along the ordering d. •

In the next section we will see that DRC$_2$ specializes to a well-known algorithm for processing linear inequalities.

8.6 **Linear Inequalities**

In this section, we note the applicability of consistency enforcing to the special case of linear inequalities over infinite domains like the rational numbers, as well as over finite and infinite subsets of integers. In database theory, a k-ary relation r is a finite set of tuples, and a database is a finite set of relations. However, the relational calculus and relational algebra can be developed without the assumptions of finiteness for relations. We will use the term *unrestricted relation* for finite or infinite sets of points in a k-dimensional space.

8.6.1 **Linear Elimination**

Let us consider the case where a constraint between r or fewer variables is a linear inequality of the form

$$\sum_{i=1}^{r} a_i x_i \leq c$$

where a_i and c are rational constants.[1] For example, the conjunction $(3x_i + 2x_j \leq 3)$ $\land (-4x_i + 5x_j \leq 1)$ includes two constraints between variables x_i and x_j. We show that the standard operation of variable elimination for this class of expressions is equivalent to extended 2-composition. Let us denote by $sol(\alpha)$ the unrestricted relation of tuples from the domain satisfying a set of linear inequalities α. We define the elimination operation as follows.

DEFINITION 8.12   **(linear elimination)**

Let

$$\alpha = \sum_{i=1}^{(r-1)} a_i x_i + a_r x_r \leq c$$

and

$$\beta = \sum_{i=1}^{(r-1)} b_i x_i + b_r x_r \leq d$$

Then $elim_r(\alpha, \beta)$ is applicable only if a_r and b_r have opposite signs, in which case

$$elim_r(\alpha, \beta) \equiv \sum_{i=1}^{r-1} \left(-a_i \frac{b_r}{a_r} + b_i \right) x_i \leq -\frac{b_r}{a_r} c + d$$

If a_r and b_r have the same sign, the elimination implicitly generates the universal constraint.   ●

In principle, if the domains are finite, we can convert each linear inequality to a relational representation and then enforce relational path-consistency. Alternatively, we can apply linear elimination directly to the algebraic expressions.

The next lemma says that extended 2-composition is identical to linear elimination over the rationals, while it is not quite so over the integers.

LEMMA 8.5 $sol(elim_r(\alpha, \beta)) \supseteq EC_r(sol(\alpha), sol(\beta))$ when the domains are the integers. However, over the rationals $sol(elim_r(\alpha, \beta)) = EC_r(sol(\alpha), sol(\beta))$.

Proof Let

$$\alpha = \sum_{i=1}^{(r-1)} a_i x_i + a_r x_r \leq c$$

---

1. If we insist on a unique constraint for a given subset of variables in a scheme, we would have to define a constraint as a conjunction of linear inequalities, all defined on the same set of variables.

and

$$\beta = \sum_{i=1}^{(r-1)} b_i x_i + b_r x_r \le d$$

It is easy to see that if a_r and b_r have the same sign (both are positive or both are negative), then for any assignment to $x_1, \ldots, x_{i-1}$, there is always a value for x_r that extends $x_1, \ldots, x_{i-1}$ and satisfies both α and β. Therefore, the extended composition produces the universal relation. Assume now that a_r and b_r have opposite signs. Multiplying α by $-\frac{b_r}{a_r}$ and summing the resulting inequality with β yields the inequality

$$\sum_{i=1}^{r-1} \left(-a_i \frac{b_r}{a_r} + b_i \right) x_i \le -\frac{b_r}{a_r} c + d \tag{8.8}$$

We get

$$\sum_{i=1}^{r-1} -a_i \frac{b_r}{a_r} x_i + \frac{b_r}{a_r} c \le d - \sum_{i=1}^{r-1} b_i x_i \tag{8.9}$$

Now, there exists an intermediate value γ between the left and the right side of Equation (8.9). If $x_r = \frac{\gamma}{b_r}$, $b_r x_r$ will be greater than the left-hand side of (8.9), satisfying α, and it will also be smaller than the right-hand side of (8.9), satisfying β. In other words, any tuple satisfying Inequality (8.8) can be extended to a *rational value* of x_r in a way that satisfies both α and β. It is unclear, though, whether there exists an integer extension to x_r, which is the reason for partial containment for the integers. ●

Linear elimination, applied when one of the constraints is a domain constraint of the type $x \le a$, can yield both domain propagation and relational arc-consistency, and both rules are popular in processing systems of linear inequalities.

8.6.2 **Fourier Bucket Elimination**

Incorporating linear elimination into DRC$_2$, when the constraints are specified as linear inequalities, yields algorithm DIRECTIONAL-LINEAR-ELIMINATION (DLE), which is the well-known Fourier elimination algorithm.

As in the case of propositional theories, DRC$_2$ generates a directionally globally consistent problem. The algorithm decides the solvability of any set of linear inequalities over the rationals and generates a problem representation that is backtrack-free. The algorithm is summarized in Figure 8.9.

DIRECTIONAL-LINEAR-ELIMINATION (φ, d)

Input: A set of linear inequalities φ, an ordering $d = x_1, \ldots, x_n$.

Output: A decision of whether φ is satisfiable. If it is, a backtrack-free theory $E_d(\varphi)$.

1. **Initialize:** Partition inequalities into ordered buckets.

2. **for** $i \leftarrow n$ **downto** 1 **do**

3.   **if** x_i has one value in its domain **then**
              substitute the value into each inequality in the bucket and
              put the resulting inequality in the right bucket.

4.   **else,** for each pair $\{\alpha, \beta\} \subseteq bucket_i$, compute $\gamma = elim_i(\alpha, \beta)$
              if γ has no solutions, return $E_d(\varphi) = \{\}$, "inconsistency"
              else add γ to the appropriate lower bucket.

5. **return** $E_d(\varphi) \leftarrow \bigcup_i bucket_i$

Figure 8.9   Fourier elimination (DLE).

THEOREM 8.13   Given a set of linear inequalities φ, algorithm DLE (Fourier elimination) decides the consistency of φ over the rationals and the reals, and it generates an equivalent backtrack-free representation.   •

EXAMPLE 8.13   Consider the set of inequalities over the reals:

$$\varphi(x_1, x_2, x_3, x_4) = \{(1)\ 5x_4 + 3x_2 - x_1 \leq 5,\ (2)\ x_4 + x_1 \leq 2,\ (3)\ -x_4 \leq 0,$$
$$(4)\ x_3 \leq 5,\ (5)\ x_1 + x_2 - x_3 \leq -10,\ (6)\ x_1 + 2x_2 \leq 0\}$$

The initial partitioning into buckets is shown in Figure 8.10. Processing $bucket_4$, which involves applying elimination relative to x_4 over inequalities $\{(1),(3)\}$ and $\{(2),(3)\}$, respectively, results in $3x_2 - x_1 \leq 5$, placed into $bucket_2$, and $x_1 \leq 2$, placed into $bucket_1$. Next, processing the two inequalities $x_3 \leq 5$, and $x_1 + x_2 - x_3 \leq -10$ in $bucket_3$ eliminates x_3, yielding $x_1 + x_2 \leq -5$ placed into $bucket_2$. When processing $bucket_2$, containing $x_1 + 2x_2 \leq 0$, $3x_2 - x_1 \leq 5$, and $x_1 + x_2 \leq -5$, no new inequalities are added. The final set of buckets is displayed in Figure 8.11.   •

Once the algorithm is applied, we can generate a solution in a backtrack-free manner as usual. Select a value for x_1 from its domains that satisfies the unary inequalities in $bucket_1$. From there on, after selecting assignments for $x_1, \ldots, x_{i-1}$, select a value for x_i that satisfies all the inequalities in $bucket_i$. This is an easy task, since all the constraints are unary once the values of $x_1, \ldots, x_{i-1}$ are determined.

$$bucket_4 : \quad 5x_4 + 3x_2 - x_1 \leq 5, x_4 + x_1 \leq 2, -x_4 \leq 0$$
$$bucket_3 : \quad x_3 \leq 5, x_1 + x_2 - x_3 \leq -10$$
$$bucket_2 : \quad x_1 + 2x_2 \leq 0$$
$$bucket_1 :$$

Figure 8.10 Initial buckets.

$$bucket_4 : \quad 5x_4 + 3x_2 - x_1 \leq 5, x_4 + x_1 \leq 2, -x_4 \leq 0$$
$$bucket_3 : \quad x_3 \leq 5, x_1 + x_2 - x_3 \leq -10$$
$$bucket_2 : \quad x_1 + 2x_2 \leq 0 \parallel 3x_2 - x_1 \leq 5, x_1 + x_2 \leq -5$$
$$bucket_1 : \quad \parallel x_1 \leq 2$$

Figure 8.11 Final buckets.

The complexity of Fourier elimination is not, however, bounded exponentially by the induced width. The reason is that the number of linear inequalities that can be specified over a scope of size i cannot be bounded exponentially by i.

8.7 Summary

This chapter extended consistency definitions and algorithms from variable based to relation based, allowing us to express new types of bounded inference not captured by variable-based i-consistency. The concepts of relational arc-, path-, and i-consistency were defined, capturing inference operators for languages such as propositional theories and algebraic linear inequalities. Extension of relational consistency to directional relational consistency follows naturally and was described within the bucket elimination formulation. The chapter presented the notions of domain and constraint tightness and row convexity and also described relationships of bounded local consistency that can guarantee global consistency. Specializing DRC$_1$ and DRC$_2$ to CNF formulas and to linear inequalities yields well-known variable elimination algorithms such as the Davis-Putnam algorithm (which we call directional resolution) and Fourier elimination. We also explicitly addressed well-known tractable classes such as 2-SAT and Horn theories and have placed those within the general relational framework.

8.8 Bibliographical Notes

Relational consistency was defined by van Beek and Dechter in a sequence of four papers (van Beek and Dechter 1994, 1995, 1997; Dechter and van Beek 1997).

They proved that global consistency is guaranteed given bounded domains, tight constraints, or row convexity if accompanied with an appropriate level of bounded consistency. An explicit generalization of local consistency using the notion of the dual graph and its use for generalizing topological properties of constraint networks is given in Jégou (1993b). Relational consistency allowed expressing these relationships for nonbinary networks in a natural way. Mackworth (1977b) presented the definition of generalized arc-consistency, also called hyper-arc-consistency, which is equivalent to relational (1,1)-consistency.

The results on domain size and consistency were presented by Dechter (1992b). The class of row-convex binary constraint networks was introduced by van Beek (1992) and extended to the nonbinary case later (van Beek and Dechter 1995). Barette, Deville, and van Hentenryck (1999) showed that binary linear constraints that are closed under path-consistency are row convex, and therefore can be solved in polynomial time. The idea of row convexity has also been exploited in the context of continuous constraints (Haroud and Faltings, 1996). They show that for continuous domains, this result can be generalized to ternary and n-ary constraints using (3, 2)-consistency. The example network of natural language parsing is due to Maruyama (1990).

The observation that relational 2-consistency and adaptive consistency implies algorithm DIRECTIONAL-RESOLUTION for CNFs was presented in Dechter and Rish (1994) and Rish and Dechter (2000). It was observed that the resulting algorithm is the well-known Davis-Putnam algorithm (Davis and Putnam 1960). Indeed, this algorithm was immediately replaced with a backtracking-style algorithm due to its heavy space complexity (Davis, Logemann, and Loveland 1962; Rish and Dechter 2000).

8.9 **Exercises**

1. Consider the constraint network over the set of variables $\{x_1, x_2, x_3, x_4, x_5\}$, where each variable has domain $D_i = \{a, b, c\}$, $1 \leq i \leq 5$, and the relations are given by

$$R_{2,3,4,5} = \{(a,a,a,a), (b,a,a,a), (a,b,a,a), (a,a,b,a), (a,a,a,b)\}$$
$$R_{1,2,5} = \{(b,a,b), (c,b,c), (b,a,c)\}$$

Are the constraints relational arc- and path-consistent? If not, make the network relational arc- and path-consistent.

2. Prove Lemma 8.1: The complexity of DRC$_1$ is $O(n \cdot e^2 \cdot t^2)$, where e is the number of input relations and t bounds the number of tuples in each relation.

3. The definition of relational m-consistency is similar, but not identical, to that of variable-based m-consistency if applied to the dual view of the problem. (In this view, the constraints are perceived to be variables, their allowed tuples are their respective domains, and two such constraint variables are constrained by

binary constraints if they have variables in common.) Choose a network and demonstrate the relationship between relational m-consistency and variable-based consistency over the dual graph.

4. Prove Lemma 8.2 that resolution is equivalent to extended 2-composition.

5. Prove Proposition 8.1: (1) Crossword puzzles can be made directional backtrack-free by DRC$_2$, and (2) the complexity of DRC$_2$ applied to crossword puzzles is $O(n \cdot k^{2(w^*(d)+1)})$.

6. Prove that algorithm DLE can decide the consistency of a set of linear inequalities over the rationals and the reals.

7. Analyze the complexity of DLE over finite domains and over the rationals.

8. Prove that algorithm DLE is polynomial over the class of unary and binary inequalities of the form $x - y \leq a$, $x \leq b$. Prove also that the algorithm directionally globally solves such inequalities over the integers (if a and b are integers), the rationals, and the reals.

9. Consider linear inequalities over the integers:

   (a) Over integer domains algorithm DLE is no longer guaranteed to decide consistency since linear elimination is not identical to extended 2-composition. If the empty relation is generated by DLE, can you conclude that the problem is inconsistent? Explain your answer.

   (b) Would a backtrack algorithm be backtrack-free if applied following DLE? Would it have a smaller search space?

10. Consider the following CNF theory:

$$\varphi = \{(A, \neg B, D), (\neg D, F, C), (\neg C)\}$$

    (a) Define RC$_1$ and RC$_2$ for CNF theories using the resolution operator.
    (b) Apply RC$_1$ and RC$_2$ to φ.

11. Consider again the following CNF formula:

$$\varphi = \{(A, \neg B, D), (\neg D, F, C), (\neg C)\}$$

    Show the execution of algorithm DIRECTIONAL-RESOLUTION on this theory along ordering $d_1 = (A, B, C, D, F)$ and $d_2 = (F, D, C, B, A)$. Bound the complexity of the algorithm along each ordering.

12. Consider the following linear constraints over the *nonnegative* integers:

$$(1)\ l + x + y + z \leq 1, \quad (2)\ l - z \leq -1$$

    Show that the constraints are not relational arc- or path-consistent. Then show what constraints should be added to make them arc- and path-consistent. Is the resulting network row convex?

13. Prove that a theory that includes all its prime implicates is globally consistent.

chapter 9

Tree Decomposition Methods

> Everything should be made as simple as possible,
> but not one bit simpler.
>
> *Albert Einstein (attributed)*

As noted in Chapters 4 and 8, topological characterization of tractable classes is centered on the graph parameter called *induced width* or *tree width*. In this chapter, we provide related schemes that are based on the notion of tree decompositions. These methods are applicable across a wide variety of tasks, not exclusively to constraint processing, and have received different names in different research areas, such as join-tree clustering, clique-tree clustering and hypertree decompositions. We will refer to these schemes by the umbrella term *tree-clustering*. The complexity of these methods is governed by the induced width, the same parameter that controls the performance of directional (relational) consistency.

9.1 Acyclic Networks

In Chapter 4, we showed that trees of binary constraints can be processed efficiently. The primal graph of such binary constraint trees has induced width of 1. The notion of constraint trees can be extended beyond binary constraints to problems having scope higher than 2, using the notions of hypergraphs and hypertrees, leading to the creation of a class of *acyclic constraint networks*.

9.1.1 Solving Acyclic Problems

To review, a *hypergraph* is a structure $\mathcal{H} = (V, S)$ that consists of a set of vertices $V = \{v_1, \ldots, v_n\}$ and a set of subsets of these vertices $S = \{S_1, \ldots, S_l\}$, $S_i \subseteq V$, called *hyperedges*. The hyperedges differ from regular edges in that they each may "connect" more than two variables.

A hypergraph $\mathcal{H} = (V, S)$ can be mapped to a regular graph called a *dual graph* $\mathcal{H}^{dual}$ (for more details, see Chapter 2). The nodes of the dual graph are the hyperedges from the hypergraph, and a pair of such nodes are connected if they share vertices in V. The arc that connects two such nodes is labeled by the shared vertices. Formally, given $\mathcal{H} = (V, S)$, $\mathcal{H}^{dual} = (S, E)$ where $S = \{S_1, \ldots, S_r\}$ are edges in $\mathcal{H}$, and $(S_i, S_j) \in E$ iff $S_i \cap S_j \neq \emptyset$. A primal graph of a hypergraph $\mathcal{H} = (V, S)$ has V as its set of nodes, and any two nodes are connected by an arc if they appear in the same hyperedge. Note that if all the constraints of a network $\mathcal{R}$ are binary, then its hypergraph is identical to its primal graph.

Any constraint network $\mathcal{R} = (X, D, C)$, $C = \{R_{S_1}, \ldots, R_{S_r}\}$ can be associated with a hypergraph $\mathcal{H}_R = (X, H)$, where X is the set of nodes (variables), and H is the set of scopes of the constraints in C, namely, $H = \{S_1, \ldots, S_r\}$. Therefore, the dual graph of a constraint hypergraph associates a node with each constraint scope and an arc for each two nodes sharing variables. This association facilitates the transformation of a nonbinary constraint problem into a binary one, called the *dual problem* (see Chapter 2), as follows. The variables of the dual problem are the constraints, their domains are the legal tuples of the constraint, and there is a binary constraint between any two dual variables that share original variables, enforcing equality on the values assigned to the shared variables. Therefore, if a problem's dual graph happens to be a tree, it means that the dual constraint problem can be efficiently solved by the tree-solving algorithm.

It turns out, however, that sometimes, even when the dual graph does not look like a tree, it is in fact a tree, if some of its arcs (and their associated constraints) are *redundant* and can be removed, leaving behind a tree structure. A constraint is considered redundant if its removal from the constraint network does not change the set of all solutions. It is not normally easy to recognize redundant constraints. In the dual representation, however, some redundancies are easy to identify: since all the constraints in the dual network enforce equalities (over shared variables), a constraint and its corresponding arc can be deleted if the variables labeling the arc are shared by every arc along an *alternate* path between the two endpoints. This is because the alternate path (of constraints) already enforces that equality. Removing such constraints does not alter the problem.

EXAMPLE 9.1
Figure 9.1 depicts the hypergraph, the primal graph, and the dual graph representations of a constraint network with variables A, B, C, D, E, F and with constraints on the scopes $(ABC),(AEF)$, (CDE), and (ACE). The specific constraints are irrelevant to the current discussion; they can be arbitrary relations over domains of $\{0, 1\}$, such as $C = A \vee B$, $F = A \vee E$, and so on. We see that the arc between (AEF) and (ABC) in Figure 9.1(c) is redundant because variable A also appears along the alternative path $(ABC) - AC - (ACE) - AE - (AEF)$. A consistent

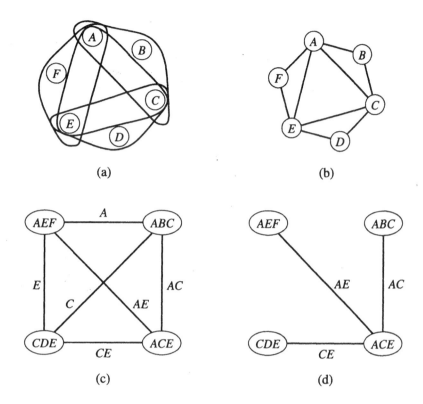

Figure 9.1 (a) Hypergraph, (b) primal graph, (c) dual graph, and (d) join-tree constraint graphs of a CSP.

assignment to *A* is thereby ensured by these constraints even if the constraint between *AEF* and *ABC* is removed. Likewise, the arcs labeled *E* and *C* are also redundant, and their removal yields the graph in Figure 9.1(d). •

We call the property that ensures such legitimate arc removal the *running intersection property* or *connectedness property*. The running intersection property can be defined over hypergraphs or over their dual graphs, and is used to characterize equivalent concepts such as *join-trees* (defined over dual graphs) or *hypertrees* (defined over hypergraphs). An *arc subgraph* of a graph contains the same set of nodes as the graph, and a subset of its arcs.

DEFINITION 9.1 **(connectedness, join-trees, hypertrees, and acyclic networks)**

Given a dual graph of a hypergraph, an arc subgraph of the dual graph satisfies the *connectedness* property iff for each two nodes that share a variable, there is at least one path of labeled arcs, each containing the shared variables. An arc subgraph of the dual graph that satisfies the connectedness property is called a *join-graph*. A join-graph that is a tree is called a *join-tree*. A *hypertree* is a hypergraph whose dual graph has a join-tree. A constraint network whose hypergrpah is a hypertree is called an *acyclic network*.

●

EXAMPLE 9.2   Considering again the graphs in Figure 9.1, we can see that the join-tree in Figure 9.1(d) satisfies the connectedness property. The hypergraph in Figure 9.1(a) has a join-tree and is therefore a hypertree.

●

An acyclic constraint network can be solved efficiently. Because the constraint problem has a join-tree, its dual problem is a tree of binary constraints and can therefore be solved by the tree-solving algorithm. Note that the domains of variables in the dual problem are bounded by the number of tuples in the input constraints. In Figure 9.2, we reformulate the tree algorithm for solving acyclic problems. The algorithm assumes that domain constraints are already *absorbed* into the relevant relations; that is, any tuple in a relation that has an illegal domain value of some variable is removed.

ACYCLIC-SOLVING

Input: An acyclic constraint network $\mathcal{R} = (X, D, C)$, $C = \{R_1,\ldots,R_r\}$.
S_i is the scope of R_i. A join-tree T of $\mathcal{R}$.

Output: Determine consistency, and generate a solution.

1. $d = (R_1,\ldots, R_r)$ is an ordering such that every relation appears before its descendent relations in the tree rooted at R_1.

2. **for** $j = r$ to 1, for edge (j,k), $k < j$, in the tree **do**

    $R_k \leftarrow \pi_{S_k} (R_k \bowtie R_j)$

    if the empty relation is created, exit, the problem has no solution.

   endfor

3. **return:** The problem is consistent. Generate a solution:

    Select a tuple in R_1 for $i = 2$ to r.
    After instantiating $R_1,\ldots,R_{i-1}$ select a tuple
    in R_i that is consistent with all previous assignments.

Figure 9.2 ACYCLIC-SOLVING algorithm.

**EXAMPLE
9.3**

Consider the tree dual problem in Figure 9.1(d) and assume that the constraints are given by $R_{ABC} = R_{AEF} = R_{CDE} = \{(0,0,1)(0,1,0)(1,0,0)\}$ and $R_{ACE} = \{(1,1,0)(0,1,1)(1,0,1)\}$. Assume the ordering $d = (R_{ACE}, R_{CDE}, R_{AEF}, R_{ABC})$. When processing R_{ABC}, its parent relation is R_{ACE}; we therefore generate $\pi_{ACE}(R_{ACE} \bowtie R_{ABC})$, yielding the revised relation $R_{ACE} = \{(0,1,1)(1,0,1)\}$. Next, processing R_{AEF} (likewise connected to R_{ACE}) we generate relation $R_{ACE} = \pi_{ACE}(R_{ACE} \bowtie R_{AEF}) = \{(0,1,1)\}$. Note that the revised relation R_{ACE} is now being processed. Subsequently, processing R_{CDE} we generate $R_{ACE} = \pi_{ACE}(R_{ACE} \bowtie R_{CDE}) = \{(0,1,1)\}$. A solution can then be generated by picking the only allowed tuple for R_{ACE}, $(A = 0, C = 1, E = 1)$, extending it with a value for D that satisfies R_{CDE}, which is only $D = 0$, and then similarly extending the assignment to $F = 0$ and $B = 0$, to satisfy R_{AEF} and R_{ABC}. ●

Algorithm ACYCLIC-SOLVING is correct, essentially applying directional arc-consistency from leaves to root (step 2) along the join-tree of the dual problem. Since the complexity of a tree-solving algorithm is $O(nk^2)$, where n is the number of variables and k bounds the domain size, the implied complexity here is $O(r \cdot l^2)$ if there are r constraints, each allowing at most l tuples. However, the complexity can be improved for this special case. The join operation can be performed in time linear in the maximum number of tuples of each relation, like so: project R_j on the variables shared by R_j and its parent constraint, R_k, an $O(l)$ operation, and then prune any tuple in R_k that has no match in that projection. If tuples are ordered lexicographically, which requires $O(l \cdot \log l)$ steps, the join operator has a complexity of $O(l)$, yielding an overall complexity of $O(r \cdot l \cdot \log l)$ steps. In summary, we have the following:

**THEOREM
9.1**

(correctness and complexity)

Algorithm ACYCLIC-SOLVING decides the consistency of an acyclic constraint network, and its complexity is $O(r \cdot l \cdot \log l)$ steps, where r is the number of constraints and l bounds the number of tuples in each constraint relation. ●

Another distributed version of algorithm ACYCLIC-SOLVING has every node sending the message in step 2 to each one of its neighbors in the join-tree. Once they all receive this message, each neighboring node can compute the *minimal relation* over its scope. We will revisit this issue in subsequent sections.

9.1.2 Recognizing Acyclic Networks

Several efficient procedures for identifying acyclic networks and for finding a representative join-tree were developed in the area of relational databases (Maier 1983).

DUAL-ACYCLICITY ($\mathcal{R}$)

Input: A hypergraph $\mathcal{H}_\mathcal{R} = (X, S)$ of a constraint network $\mathcal{R} = (X, D, C)$, $C = \{R_1, \ldots, R_t\}$ and S_i is the scope of R_i.

Output: A join-tree $T = (S, E)$ of $\mathcal{H}_\mathcal{R}$, if $\mathcal{R}$ is acyclic.

1. $T = (S, E)$ ← Generate a maximum spanning tree of the weighted dual constraint graph of $\mathcal{R}$.

2. **for** every two nodes, u and v in T, **do**

   if the unique path connecting them in T does not satisfy the connectedness property, exit ($\mathcal{R}$ is not acyclic).

   endfor

3. **return:** R is acyclic, and T is a join-tree of $\mathcal{H}_\mathcal{R}$.

Figure 9.3   Algorithm DUAL-ACYCLICITY.

Two alternative methods are discussed below, one based on processing the dual constraint graph and the other on consulting its primal graph.

Dual-Based Recognition

It turns out that if a hypergraph has a join-tree, then any maximum spanning tree of its dual graph is a join-tree when the arcs of the dual graph are weighted by the number of shared variables (Maier 1983). Therefore, testing whether a hypergraph has a join-tree can be done by generating a maximum spanning tree over its dual graph. Once a spanning tree is obtained, testing connectedness can be accomplished efficiently because there is only one path between every pair of nodes in the candidate join-tree. Algorithm DUAL-ACYCLICITY accomplishes this and is described in Figure 9.3.

THEOREM 9.2   **(correctness and complexity)**

Algorithm DUAL-ACYCLICITY decides if a constraint network $\mathcal{R}$ is acyclic. If it is, the algorithm returns a join-tree of $\mathcal{R}$'s dual graph. The algorithm's complexity is $O(e^3)$, where e is the number of constraints.

Proof The number of nodes in the dual graph equals the number of constraints, e. Since generating a maximum spanning tree of a graph can be done in $O(n^2)$, where n is the number of nodes in the graph, generating the spanning tree here is $O(e^2)$. A brute-force approach for testing the connectedness property takes $O(e^3)$ because there are $O(e^2)$ pairs of nodes and testing this property for the unique path between each pair is $O(e)$. For correctness see Maier (1983).

EXAMPLE
9.4

Had we applied a maximum spanning tree algorithm to the dual graph in Figure 9.1(c), the three arcs labeled by singleton variables would be removed, resulting in the join-tree in Figure 9.1(d), which, as already observed, satisfies connectedness.

Primal-Based Recognition

The second acyclicity recognition scheme is based on the fact that a primal graph of a hypertree must be chordal (Beeri et al. 1983). Therefore, an alternative approach to recognizing acyclicity is based on testing if the primal graph of the constraint network is chordal. If it is, its maximal cliques should be identified, which, as we saw in Chapter 4, is easy to do on chordal graphs. However, since different hypergraphs can map to the same primal graph, we need to further ensure another property called *conformality* that the maximal cliques of the chordal primal graph coincide with the scopes of the original constraints.

DEFINITION
9.2

(conformality)

A chordal primal graph is conformal relative to a constraint hypergraph iff there is a one-to-one mapping between maximal *cliques* and scopes of constraints.

It was shown that

THEOREM
9.3

(Maier 1983) A hypergraph has a join-tree iff its primal graph is chordal and conformal.

As discussed in Section 4.1.2, a graph is chordal if, in a *maximal cardinality ordering*, each node's parents are connected. If the primal graph is chordal, its maximal cliques can be identified in linear time, listing every node and its parents in the ordering. If the maximal cliques coincide with the scopes of the constraints, both conditions for acyclicity (chordality and conformality) are satisfied, and we know that the constraint network is acyclic. This leads to algorithm PRIMAL-ACYCLICITY described in Figure 9.4.

EXAMPLE
9.5

Consider again the constraint network of Example 9.1, whose primal graph is given again in Figure 9.5(a). A max-cardinality ordering is given in Figure 9.5(b). Since all the parents of each node are connected, the graph is chordal. The maximal cliques, enumerated from top to bottom, are *FAE*

PRIMAL-ACYCLICITY ($\mathcal{R}$)

Input: A network $\mathcal{R} = (X, D, C)$ and its primal graph G.

Output: A join-tree iff the problem is acyclic.

1. **Test chordality:** Using a max-cardinality ordering $d = (x_1, \ldots, x_n)$ of G,

   for $i = n$ to 1 **do**:

       if the parents of x_i are not connected, exit. The problem is not acyclic.

2. **Test conformality:** Let $C_1, \ldots, C_r$ be the cliques (a node and all its parents) indexed by their highest variable.

   if the maximal cliques correspond to scopes of constraints, $\mathcal{R}$ is acyclic.

   else, the network is not acyclic. exit.

3. *Create a join-tree:*

       Let $C_1, \ldots, C_r$ be the maximal cliques indexed by their highest variable.

       Going from r to 1, connect every clique to an earlier clique with which it shares a maximal number of variables.

5. **return** the tree of cliques.

Figure 9.4 Algorithm PRIMAL-ACYCLICITY.

(the clique of F), DEC (the clique of D), EAC (the clique of E), and ABC (the clique of A). The cliques of B and C are not maximal. Therefore, there are four maximal cliques, and these are identical to the constraints' scopes. The graph is recognized as acyclic. Next, clique FAE is connected to clique EAC, DEC is connected to EAC, which is connected to ABC. Now we have a join-tree representation equivalent to the original problem (see Figure 9.5(c)).   •

It is easy to see the following:

THEOREM 9.4   The complexity of algorithm PRIMAL-ACYCLICITY is $O(n^2)$.   •

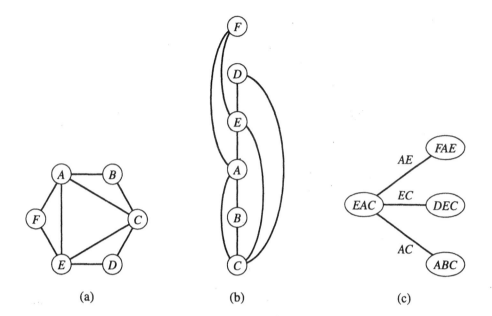

Figure 9.5 (a) A primal graph, (b) a max-cardinality ordering, and (c) its join-tree.

9.2 **Tree-Based Clustering**

Since acyclic constraint networks can be solved efficiently, we naturally aim at compiling an arbitrary constraint network into an acyclic one. This can be achieved by grouping subsets of constraints into clusters, or subproblems, whose scopes constitute a hypertree, thus transforming a constraint hypergraph into a constraint hypertree. Replacing each subproblem with its set of solutions yields an acyclic constraint problem. If the transformation process is tractable, including both graph transformation and finding all solutions to each subproblem, the resulting algorithm is polynomial. This compilation process is called *join-tree clustering*.

9.2.1 **Join-Tree Clustering**

The graphical input to the above clustering scheme is a constraint hypergraph $\mathcal{H} = (X, H)$, where H is the set of scopes of the constraint network, and the output is a hypertree $\mathcal{S} = (X, S)$ and a partition of the original hyperedges into the new hypertree edges.

DEFINITION
9.3

(hypertree embedding of a hypergraph)

A *hypertree embedding of a hypergraph* $\mathcal{H} = (X, H)$ is a hypertree $\mathcal{S} = (X, S)$ such that, for every $h \in H$, there is $h_1 \in S$ such that $h \subseteq h_1$.   •

Once a hypertree $\mathcal{S}$ is constructed, each of its edges defines a subproblem that contains a constraint if its scope is contained in the hyperedge. Each subproblem is then solved, and its set of solutions is a new constraint whose scope is the hyperedge. The resulting problem has one constraint per hyperedge of S and, by construction, is acyclic.

There are various specific methods that decompose a hypergraph into a hypertree. The aim is to generate hypertrees that have small-sized hyperedges because this implies small constraint subproblems. The most popular approach manipulates the constraint primal graph, and it emerges from the primal recognition process (Figure 9.4). Rather than stopping at step 1 of algorithm PRIMAL-ACYCLICITY (because some parents are not connected), chordality can be enforced by connecting all parents. If, during this process, conformality is violated (step 2), it can be subsequently enforced by generating a unique constraint for every maximal clique. The maximal cliques of the resulting chordal graph are the candidate scopes in the formed acyclic network. These cliques define the subproblems that must be independently solved. The procedure, called JOIN-TREE-CLUSTERING (JTC), is described in Figure 9.6.

While any variable ordering can be used in step 1 of the algorithm, the max-cardinality ordering may be good because when the graph is chordal, no edges will be added in step 2. The first three steps of the algorithm manipulate only the primal graph, embedding it in a chordal graph (whose maximal cliques make a hypertree), and then identifying its join-tree. Step 4 partitions the constraints into the cliques (the hypertree edges). Step 5 solves each clique's subproblem, and thus creates one new constraint for each clique. We conclude the following:

THEOREM
9.5

Algorithm JOIN-TREE-CLUSTERING transforms a constraint network into an equivalent acyclic network.   •

EXAMPLE
9.6

Consider the graph in Figure 9.7(a), and assume it is a primal graph of a binary constraint network. In this case, the primal and hypergraph are the same. Consider the ordering $d_1 = (F, E, D, C, B, A)$ in Figure 9.7(b). Performing tree-clustering connects parents recursively from the last variable to the first, creating the induced ordered graph by adding the new (broken) edges of Figure 9.7(b). The maximal cliques of this induced graph are $Q_1 = \{A, B, C, E\}$, $Q_2 = \{B, C, D, E\}$, and $Q_3 = \{D, E, F\}$. Alternatively, if ordering d_2 in Figure 9.7(c) is used, the induced graph generated has only one added edge. The cliques in this case are $Q_1 = \{D, F\}$, $Q_2 = \{A, B, E\}$, $Q_3 = \{B, C, D\}$, and $Q_4 = \{A, B, C\}$. The corresponding join-trees of both orderings are depicted in Figure 9.8 (broken arcs are not part of the

JOIN-TREE-CLUSTERING (JTC)

Input: A constraint problem $\mathcal{R} = (X, D, C)$ and its primal graph $G = (X, E)$.

Output: An equivalent acyclic constraint problem and its join-tree:

$T = (X, D, C')$.

1. Select a variable ordering, $d = (x_1, \ldots, x_n)$.

2. **Triangulation** (create the induced graph along d and call it G^*):

   for $j = n$ to 1 by -1 **do**

   $E \leftarrow E \cup \{(i, k) \mid (i, j) \in E, (k, j) \in E\}$

3. **Create a join-tree of the induced graph G^*:**

   a. Identify all maximal cliques in the chordal graph (each variable and its parents is a clique).

   Let $C_1, \ldots, C_r$ be all such cliques, created going from last variable to first in the ordering.

   b. Create a tree structure T over the cliques:

   Connect each C_i to a C_j ($j < i$) with whom it shares the largest subset of variables.

4. Place each input constraint in one clique containing its scope, and let P_i be the constraint subproblem associated with C_i.

5. Solve each P_i and let R_i' be its set of solutions.

6. Return $C' = \{R_1', \ldots, R_t'\}$, the new set of constraints and their join-tree, T.

Figure 9.6 Algorithm JOIN-TREE-CLUSTERING.

join-trees). Next, focusing on the join-tree in Figure 9.8(b), we partition the constraints into the tree-nodes. We place the following subproblems into the nodes: $P_1 = \{R_{FD}\}$ is placed in node (FD), $P_2 = \{R_{BD}, R_{CD}\}$ is placed in node (BCD), $P_3 = \{R_{AB}, R_{AC}\}$ is placed in node (ABC), and $P_4 = \{R_{AB}, R_{BE}, R_{AE}\}$ is placed in (ABE). Next, applying step 4 of the algorithm, we solve the subproblems P_1, P_2, P_3, P_4, and replace each with R_1, R_2, R_3, R_4, where R_i is the solution relation of P_i, yielding a desired acyclic network. •

In general, the maximal clique size of an induced ordered graph equals its induced width + 1. The running time of join-tree clustering is dominated by computing the set of solutions of each subproblem.

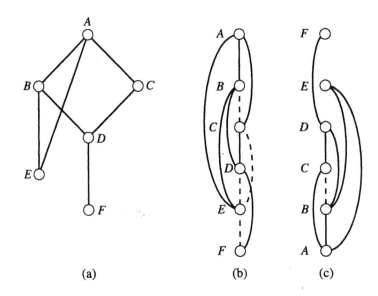

Figure 9.7   (a) A graph; (b) and (c) two of its induced graphs.

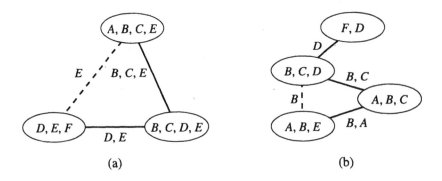

Figure 9.8   Join-graphs of the induced graphs (a) from Figure 9.7(b) and (b) from Figure 9.7(c). (All arcs included.) The corresponding join-trees are the same figures with the broken arcs removed. Note that sometimes, but not always, we use commas between characters in a cluster.

THEOREM   **(complexity of JTC)**

9.6

Given a constraint network having n variables and r constraints, the time and space complexity of join-tree clustering is $O(r \cdot k^{w^*(d)+1})$, where k is the maximum domain size and $w^*(d)$ is the induced width of the ordered graph.

Proof   Finding a tree decomposition of a hypergraph (step 1) is performed over the constraint primal graph requiring $O(n^2)$ steps. The most expensive is step 5, which computes all the solutions of each subproblem. Since the size of each subproblem corresponds to a clique in the induced (triangulated) ordered graph, it is bounded by the induced width $+ 1$. Solving a problem P_i with at most $w^*(d) + 1$ variables and r_i constraints costs $O(r_i \cdot k^{w^*(d)+1})$. Summing over all subproblems $\sum_i r_i k^{w^*(d)+1}$ yields the desired bound.   ●

9.2.2   Unifying Tree Decomposition Schemes

Next we describe JTC within a more general and formal setting that unifies algorithms appearing in a variety of reasoning areas. Our exposition divides tree-clustering algorithms into two parts. The first portion defines the notion of hypergraph embeddings precisely as tree decomposition without committing to any specific algorithm that creates such a decomposition. The second is an algorithm that processes a given tree decomposition (essentially combining the solution process of subproblems with the acyclic problem solving). The algorithm is described in a distributed fashion, as a message passing between adjacent nodes in the tree decomposition.

DEFINITION 9.4   **(tree decomposition)**

Let $\mathcal{R} = (X, D, C)$ be a CSP problem. A *tree decomposition* for $\mathcal{R}$ is a triple $\langle T, \chi, \psi \rangle$, where $T = (V, E)$ is a tree, and χ and ψ are labeling functions that associate each vertex $v \in V$ with two sets, $\chi(v) \subseteq X$ and $\psi(v) \subseteq C$, that satisfy the following conditions:

1. For each constraint $R_i \in C$, there is *at least* one vertex $v \in V$ such that $R_i \in \psi(v)$, and $scope(R_i) \subseteq \chi(v)$.

2. For each variable $x \in X$, the set $\{v \in V | x \in \chi(v)\}$ induces a connected subtree of T. (This is the connectedness property.)   ●

DEFINITION 9.5   **(tree width, hyperwidth, separator)**

The tree width of a tree decomposition $\langle T, \chi, \psi \rangle$ is $tw = max_{v \in V} |\chi(v)|$, and its hyperwidth is $hw = max_{v \in V} |\psi(v)|$. Given two adjacent vertices u and v of a tree decomposition, the separator of u and v is defined as $sep(u, v) = \chi(u) \cap \chi(v)$.   ●

EXAMPLE 9.7   Consider the binary constraint problem whose primal graph appears in Figure 9.7(a). The join-trees in Figure 9.8(a) and (b) are redescribed in Figure 9.9, using the two labeling functions described above. The labeling X is the set inside each node.   ●

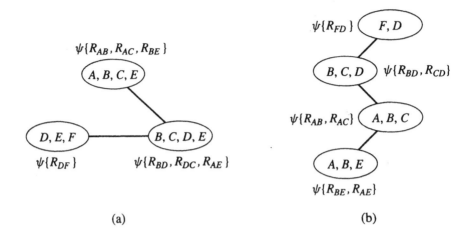

Figure 9.9 Two tree decompositions.

Graphically, a tree decomposition defines a hypertree embedding of a hypergraph. The smallest tree width and hyperwidth among all such embeddings are called the tree width and the hyperwidth of the constraint hypergraph, respectively.

Once a tree decomposition is available, algorithm CLUSTER-TREE-ELIMINATION (CTE) in Figure 9.10 processes the decomposition. The algorithm is applicable to a wide variety of tasks where the join and project operators are given a general interpretation.

The algorithm is presented as a message-passing algorithm, where each vertex of the tree sends a constraint to each of its neighbors. If the tree contains m edges, then a total of $2m$ messages will be sent. Node u takes all the constraints in $\psi(u)$ and all the constraint messages received by u from all adjacent nodes, joins them, and projects the combined function onto the separator of u and v. The projected constraint is then sent to v (remember that v is adjacent to u in the tree). For clarity of exposition we do not mention the special case of processing (instantiated) constraints that share no variables with the eliminated variables. Those will just be passed along separately in the message. The output of the CTE algorithm is the input tree decomposition where each node is augmented with the constraints sent from neighboring nodes, called *clusters*. For each node, the augmented set of constraints is a *minimal subproblem* relative to the input constraint problem $\mathcal{R}$. Intuitively, a subproblem of a constraint network is minimal if you can correctly answer any query on it without having to refer back to information in the whole network. More precisely, a subproblem over a subset of variables Y is minimal relative to the whole network if its set of solutions is identical to the projection of the network's solutions on Y.

CLUSTER-TREE-ELIMINATION (CTE)

Input: A tree decomposition $\langle T, \chi, \psi \rangle$ for a problem $\mathcal{R} = \langle X, D, C \rangle$.

Output: An augmented tree whose nodes are clusters containing the input constraints as well as messages received from neighbors. A minimal problem for each node v.

Compute messages:

for every edge (u, v) in the tree, **do**

- Let $m_{(u, v)}$ denote the message sent by vertex u to vertex v.

   Let $cluster(u) = \psi(u) \cup \{m_{(i, u)} | (i, u) \in T, i \neq v\}$

   After node u has received messages from all adjacent vertices, except maybe from v, compute and send to v:

$$m_{(u,v)} = \pi_{sep(u,v)}(\bowtie_{R_i \in cluster(u)} R_i)$$

endfor

Return: A tree decomposition augmented with constraint messages. For every node $u \in T$, return the minimal subproblem $cluster(u) = \psi(u) \cup \{m_{(i,u)} | (i, u) \in T\}$

Figure 9.10 Algorithm CLUSTER-TREE-ELIMINATION (CTE).

DEFINITION 9.6

(minimal subproblem)

Given a constraint problem $\mathcal{R} = (X, D, C)$ and a subset of variables $Y \subseteq X$, and let D_Y and C_Y be the respective domains and constraints a subproblem over Y, $\mathcal{R}_Y = (Y, D_Y, C_Y)$, is minimal relative to $\mathcal{R}$ if $sol(R_Y) = \pi_Y sol(\mathcal{R})$ where $sol(\mathcal{R})$ is the set of all solutions of network $\mathcal{R}$. ●

Convergence of CTE is guaranteed, but it may take as long as the diameter of the tree in the worst case when messages are not ordered. If processing is performed from leaves to root and back, convergence is guaranteed after two passes, where only one constraint message is sent on each edge in each direction.

EXAMPLE 9.8

Figure 9.11 shows the messages propagated for the join-tree in Figure 9.9(b). Since cluster 1 contains only one relation, the message from cluster 1 to 2 is the projection of R_{FD} over the separator between cluster 1 and 2, which is variable D. The message $m_{(2,3)}$ from cluster 2 to cluster 3

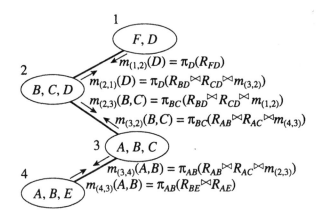

Figure 9.11   Example of messages sent by CTE.

joins the relations in cluster 2 with the message $m_{(1,2)}$, and projects over the separator between cluster 2 and 3, which is $\{B, C\}$, and so on.   •

Since CTE can be shown to be equivalent to generating and solving an acyclic constraint problem by a tree-solving algorithm, we can conclude the following:

THEOREM   **(correctness and completeness)**
9.7
Given a tree decomposition of a constraint problem $\mathcal{R}$, algorithm CTE is sound and complete for generating minimal subproblems over $\chi(v)$ for every node v in the tree.   •

Complexity of CTE

Algorithm CTE can be subtly varied to influence its time and space complexities. As described in Figure 9.10, the algorithm's time complexity can be far larger than its space complexity. At first glance, it seems that the space complexity is also expo-nential in w^*. Indeed, if we first record the joined relation in the equation in Figure 9.10 and subsequently project on the separator, we will have space complexity exponential in w^*. However, we can interleave the join and project operations, and thereby make the space complexity identical to the size of the sent constraint message. In the equation in Figure 9.10, we compute the message m, which is a function defined over the separator, *sep*, because all the variables in the *eliminator*, $elim(u) = \chi(u) - sep$, are eliminated by projection. This can be implemented by enumeration (or search) as follows: for each assignment v to $\chi(u)$, we can test if v is consistent with each constraint in $cluster(u)$, and if it is, we will project the tuple v over *sep*, creating v_{sep}, and add it to the relation $m(sep)$.

THEOREM 9.8

(time-space complexity by tree width)

Let N be the number of nodes in a tree decomposition T, w^* be its tree width, *sep* be its maximum separator size, r be the number of constraints, and *deg* be the maximum degree in T. The time complexity of CTE is $O((r + N) \cdot deg \cdot k^{w^*})$ and the space complexity is $O(N \cdot k^{sep})$.

Proof Let deg_u be the degree of u. The time complexity of processing a node u is $deg_u \cdot (|\psi(u)| + deg_u - 1) \cdot k^{|\chi(u)|}$ because the number of constraints that are processed by u for each neighbor is $|\psi(u)| + deg_u - 1$. By bounding deg_u by *deg* and $|\chi(u)|$ by w^*, and summing over all nodes, we can bound the entire time complexity by $O(deg \cdot (r+N) \cdot k^{w^*})$. Assuming the enumeration algorithm described above, the time is k^{w^*} while the space is k^{sep}. For each edge, CTE will record two constraints. Since the number of edges is bounded by N, and the size of each recorded constraint is bounded by k^{sep}, the space complexity is bounded by $O(N \cdot k^{sep})$. If $r \geq n$, this yields time complexity of $O(deg \cdot r \cdot k^{w^*})$. •

It is possible to have an implementation of the algorithm whose time complexity will not depend on *deg*, but this improvement will be more expensive in memory (Shenoy 1996; Kask 2001).

The performance of CTE can also be bounded exponentially in the hyperwidth, but this may also require paying more in terms of space complexity. Assume that every constraint has at most t tuples. Clearly, a join operation requires at most t^2 time and space. Since we have at most hw relations in a cluster, we can first join them and record the resulting relation, using $O(t^{hw})$ time and space. Joining the resulting relation and the message from each neighbor (whose size is also $O(t^{hw})$) may take at most $O(t^{2hw})$ per neighbor, yielding $deg \cdot t^{2hw}$ per outgoing message. Since this only tightens the relation generated at node u, and since the message sent to each neighbor is a projection on a separator of this tightened relation, it yields $2deg \cdot t^{2hw}$ per node and overall $O(2N \cdot t^{2hw})$ time complexity and $O(N \cdot t^{hw})$ space complexity. It is important to note that t can be exponential in the tree width (or induced width) of the problem. However, when the input relations are tight and explicitly expressed, the hyperwidth can provide a tighter bound on complexity than that provided by the tree width, and can characterize a wider class of tractability. In summary we have the following:

THEOREM 9.9

(Time-space complexity by hyperwidth)

Let N be the number of nodes in a tree decomposition T, hw be its hyperwidth, r be the number of constraints, and *deg* be the maximum degree in T; t bounds the relation size. The time complexity of CTE is $O(N \cdot t^{2hw})$ and the space complexity is $O(N \cdot t^{hw})$. •

Join-Tree Clustering as Tree Decomposition

Algorithm JTC is committed to a specific algorithm for creating the tree decomposition (steps 1–3 of JTC in Figure 9.6). As mentioned, solving the subproblems in the tree and then applying the tree-solving algorithm is equivalent to CTE when applied to the same tree decomposition. JTC is a compilation algorithm. Because it generates the full set of solutions for each node, its space complexity is exponential in the tree width w^*, while, as we saw, CTE's space complexity is exponential in the separator's size only. On the other hand, while the time complexity of CTE is $O(r \cdot deg \cdot k^{w^*})$ if $N \leq r$, the time complexity of JTC is just $O(r \cdot k^{w^*})$. This is because CTE recomputes the relation associated with a node for each neighboring node in order to save space. Clearly, this distinction matters only if there is a substantial difference between the tree width and the maximum separator size of a given tree decomposition.

The following example demonstrates that there are tree decompositions that will not be created by the first three steps of JTC in Figure 9.6. That is, there are tree decompositions that cannot be derived by triangulation.

EXAMPLE 9.9   Consider a problem, with constraints defined on all pairs of variables, whose graph is complete. Clearly, the only possible tree decomposition created by triangulation will have one node containing all the variables and all the constraints. An alternative tree decomposition has a node C_1 whose variables are $\{1, \ldots, n\}$ and whose constraints are defined over the pairs of variables:

$$\{(1, 2)(3, 4), \ldots, (i, i + 1)(i + 2, i + 3) \ldots\}.$$

Then there is a node, $C_{i,j}$, for each other constraint that is not included in C_1, and the tree connects C_1 with each other node. Figure 9.12 demonstrates these two cases for a network having four nodes $\{1, 2, 3, 4\}$ and binary constraints $\{R_{12}, R_{13}, R_{14}, R_{23}, R_{24}, R_{34}\}$.   ●

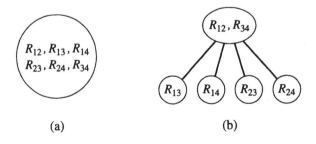

(a)   (b)

Figure 9.12   Two tree decompositions of a complete binary constraint network: (a) can be created by JTC and (b) cannot be obtained by JTC.

9.3 ADAPTIVE-CONSISTENCY as Tree Decomposition

We next show that the bucket elimination algorithm, ADAPTIVE-CONSISTENCY (ADC), discussed in Chapter 4, (Figure 4.15) can be viewed as a message-passing algorithm along a bucket-tree, which is a special case of tree decomposition. Let us first redefine the notion of buckets.

Let $\mathcal{R} = (X, D, C)$ be a problem and d an ordering of its variables, $d = (x_1, \ldots, x_n)$. Let $B_{x_1}, \ldots, B_{x_n}$ be a set of buckets, one for each variable. Each bucket B_{x_i} contains those constraints in C whose latest variable in d is x_i. A *bucket-tree* of $\mathcal{R}$ given an ordering d has buckets as its nodes, and bucket B_x is connected to bucket B_y if the constraint generated by ADAPTIVE-CONSISTENCY in bucket B_x is placed in B_y. The variables of B_{x_i} are those appearing in the scopes of any of its original constraints, as well as those received from other buckets. Therefore, in a bucket-tree, every node B_x has one parent node B_y and possibly several child nodes $B_{z_1}, \ldots, B_{z_t}$. The structure of the bucket-tree can also be extracted from the induced ordered graph of $\mathcal{R}$ along d using the following definition:

DEFINITION 9.7
(bucket-tree, graph-based)

Let (G^*, d) be the induced ordered graph along d of a problem $\mathcal{R}$ whose primal graph is G. Each variable x and all of its earlier neighbors in the induced graph reside in bucket B_x. The nodes of the bucket-tree are the n buckets. Each node B_x points to B_y (B_y is the parent of B_x) if y is the latest earlier neighbor of x in (G^*, d). If B_y is the parent of B_x in the bucket-tree, then the separator of x and y is the set of variables appearing in $B_x \cap B_y$. •

EXAMPLE 9.10

Consider a constraint network defined over the graph in Figure 9.13. Figure 9.14(a) shows the initial buckets along the ordering $d = (A, B, C, D, F, G)$, and the ρ constraints that will be created and passed by ADAPTIVE-CONSISTENCY from top to bottom. Figure 9.14(b) displays the same computation as a message passing along its bucket-tree. •

THEOREM 9.10

A bucket-tree of a constraint network $\mathcal{R}$ is a tree decomposition of $\mathcal{R}$.

Proof We need to provide two mappings, χ and ψ, and show that tree decomposition properties hold for a bucket-tree:

1. $\chi(B_x)$ contains x and its earlier neighbors in the induced graph (G^*, d) along ordering d.

2. $\psi(B_x)$ contains all constraints whose highest-ordered argument is x.

By construction, the first tree decomposition property holds.

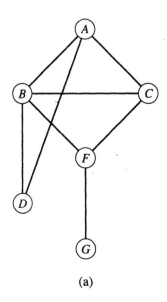

(a)

Figure 9.13 A constraint network example.

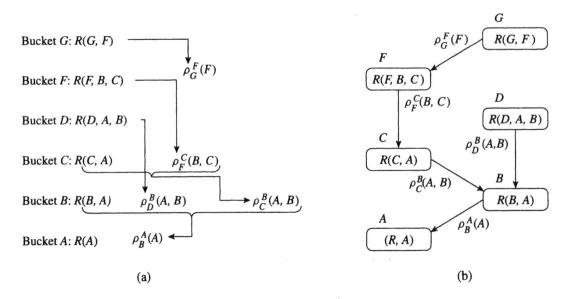

(a)   (b)

Figure 9.14 Execution of *ADC* along the bucket-tree.

To prove connectedness, let's assume that there are two buckets B_i and B_j both containing a variable z, and let B_k be the bucket of z (where z is removed). Clearly, $k < i, k < j$.

By construction, there must be a path from B_i to B_k containing z (z is removed only at B_k) as well as a path containing z from B_j to B_k (those two paths may be shared). This clearly yields a path from B_i to B_j containing z.   ●

Since the bucket-tree is a tree decomposition, it can be processed by CTE. It adds a bottom-up message passing to ADAPTIVE-CONSISTENCY yielding ADAPTIVE-TREE-CONSISTENCY (ATC) presented in Figure 9.15. In the top-down phase, each bucket receives constraint messages ρ from its children and sends a ρ constraint

---

ADAPTIVE-TREE-CONSISTENCY (ATC)

Input: A problem $\mathcal{R} = (X, D, C)$, ordering d.

Output: Augmented buckets containing the original constraints and all the ρ constraints received from neighbors in the bucket-tree.

0. Preprocessing:

Place each constraint in the latest bucket, along d, that mentions a variable in its scope. Connect bucket B_x to B_y, $y < x$ in d, if variable y is the latest earlier neighbor of x in the induced graph G_d.

1. Top-down phase (ADC):

For $i = n$ to 1, process bucket B_{x_i}:

Let $\rho_1, \ldots, \rho_j$ be all the constraints in B_{x_i} at the time B_{x_i} is processed, including original constraints of $\mathcal{R}$. The constraint $\rho_{x_i}^y$ sent from x_i to its parent y is computed by

$$\rho_{x_i}^y(sep(x_i y)) = \pi_{sep(x_i y)} \bowtie_{i=1}^j \rho_i$$

2. Bottom-up phase:

For $i = 1$ to n, process bucket B_{x_i}:

Let $\rho_1, \ldots, \rho_j$ be all the constraints in B_{x_i} at the time B_{x_i} is processed, including the original constraints of $\mathcal{R}$. The constraint $\rho_{x_i}^{z_j}$ sent to each child bucket z_j is computed by

$$\rho_{x_i}^{z_j}(sep(x_i, z_j)) = \pi_{sep(x_i, z_j)}(\bowtie_{i=1}^j \rho_i)$$

Figure 9.15 Algorithm ADAPTIVE-TREE-CONSISTENCY (ATC).

message to its parent. This portion is equivalent to ADC. In the bottom-up phase, each bucket receives a ρ constraint from its parent and sends ρ constraints to each child.

EXAMPLE
9.11
Figure 9.16 shows a complete execution of ATC along the linear order of buckets and along the bucket-tree. The ρ constraints are displayed as messages placed on the outgoing arcs.   ●

Since a bucket-tree is a tree decomposition, and since it can be shown that CTE applied to a bucket-tree is equivalent to ATC, then ATC both generates a backtrack-free representation along certain orderings and augments this representation with

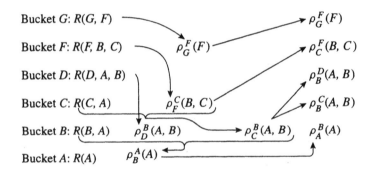

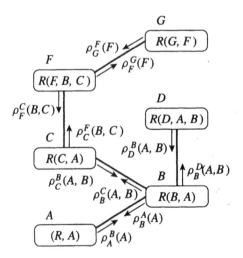

Figure 9.16 Propagation of ρ messages along the bucket-tree.

the generation of minimal subproblems. Furthermore, we can state the following:

THEOREM 9.11   **(complexity of ATC)**

Let w^* be the induced width of G along ordering d. The time complexity of ATC is $O(r \cdot deg \cdot k^{w^*})$, where deg is the maximum degree in the bucket-tree and k bounds the domain size. The space complexity of ATC is $O(n \cdot k^{w^*})$.

Proof   Since the number of buckets is n, from the analysis of CTE we can derive that the time complexity of ATC is $O((r + n) \cdot deg \cdot k^{w^*})$. Assuming that $r > n$, we get the desired bound for time complexity. Since the size of each message is k^{sep}, and since for bucket-trees the separator size is just w^*, we get space complexity of $O(n \cdot k^{w^*})$. It is possible to modify ATC so that its time complexity will be bounded by just $O(r \cdot k^{w^*+1})$, without increasing space complexity.

9.4 Summary

The chapter presents the class of acyclic constraint networks that provides a generalization of tree problems to nonbinary constraints and shows that such networks can be solved by a form of relational arc-consistency. We present join-tree clustering (JTC), a technique that transforms any constraint network into an acyclic one. The transformation involves a graph-based step that embeds the constraint hypergraph in a hypertree, also called a *join-tree*, which induces a collection of subproblems. The transformation's second step solves the subproblems, concluding the creation of an acyclic problem.

We present, subsequently, a unifying representation of tree-clustering that can accommodate many tree-based algorithms appearing in many areas of computation (probabilistic reasoning, combinatorial optimization) for defining a tree decomposition and an associated cluster tree elimination algorithm. The relationship with bucket elimination algorithms is explicated. It is shown that variable elimination algorithms can be viewed as message-passing algorithms along specific tree decompositions.

All algorithms are shown to be time exponential in the tree width and hyperwidth and space exponential in the separator of the tree decomposition or the tree width as well.

9.5 Bibliographical Notes

Join-tree clustering was introduced for constraint processing by Dechter and Pearl (1989) and for probabilistic networks by Lauritzen and Spiegelhalter (1988). Both methods are based on the characterization by relational database researchers that acyclic databases have an underlying tree structure, called *join-tree*, that allows polynomial query processing using join-project operations and easy identification procedures (Beeri et al. 1983; Maier 1983; Tarjan and Yannakakis 1984). In both constraint networks and belief networks, it was observed that the complexity of compiling any knowledge base into an acyclic one is exponential in the cluster size, which is characterized by the induced width or tree width. At the same time, variable elimination algorithms developed by Bertele and Brioschi (1972), Seidel (1981), and Dechter and Pearl (1987b) (e.g., adaptive consistency and bucket elimination) were also observed to be governed by the same complexity graph parameter. The similarity between the two approaches from the constraint perspective was analyzed by Dechter and Pearl (1989). Independently of this investigation, the tree width parameter was undergoing intensive investigation in the theoretic graph community. It characterizes the best embedding of a graph (or a hypergraph) in a hypertree. Various connections between hypertrees, chordal graphs, and k-trees were made by Arnborg and his colleagues (Arnborg 1985; Corneil, Arnborg and Proskourowski 1987). They showed that finding the smallest tree width of a graph is NP-complete, but deciding if the graph has a tree width below a certain constant k is polynomial in k. A more recent analysis is given by Bodlaender (1997).

Another decomposition into (so-called) hinges was presented by Jeavons, Gyssens, and Cohen (1994). A *hinge decomposition* is a special case of hypertree decomposition, and a best hinge decomposition can be obtained in polynomial time. Another decomposition into a tree of biconnected components that can also be optimally achieved in polytime is described in Chapter 10. It can be shown that any hinge decomposition is closely related to biconnected component tree decomposition of the dual graph whose redundant arcs are removed.

In recent years, research has focused on a variety of greedy and other approximation algorithms for tree width and induced width (Becker and Geiger 1996; Shoiket and Geiger 1997). More recently a new parameter called *hyperwidth* was introduced by Gottlob, Leone, and Scarcello (1999) and shown to provide another characterization of tractability. They provide a framework for systematically comparing structural CSP decomposition methods relative to their power for identifying large tractable cases of constraints.

9.6 Exercises

1. Prove the complexity of algorithm PRIMAL-ACYCLICITY (Theorem 9.4).

2. Consider the crossword puzzle described in Chapter 2.

   (a) Use join-tree clustering to transform the problem into an acyclic constraint network. What is the complexity of this transformation? Explicitly present the constraint problem generated.

   (b) Apply CTE (show the messages schematically).

(c) Compare the above two approaches (JTC, CTE) for solving the problem in terms of time and space complexity.

3. Consider the graph problem in Figure 9.7(a) and assume that all the constraints are binary "not-equal" constraints and all the domains of the variables have the values $\{1, 2\}$, except the domain of B is $\{1, 2, 3\}$.

(a) Generate a tree decomposition.

(b) Apply CTE to this problem fully (show the messages exactly).

4. Consider a grid problem with nine variables and binary constraints. Describe a join-tree decomposition created by JTC.

5. (Gottlob, Leone, and Scarcello 1999) Consider the hypergraph over $X = \{x_1, x_2, \ldots, x_{11}\}$, with the hyperedges $H = \{(x_1, x_{10}, x_{11}), (x_1, x_2, x_3), (x_1, x_4), (x_3, x_6), (x_4, x_5, x_6), (x_4, x_7), (x_5, x_8), (x_6, x_9), (x_2, x_3, x_{10}, x_{11})\}$.

(a) Generate a biconnected decomposition of the primal graph of the hypergraph.

(b) Find a cycle-cutset of the primal graph.

(c) Find a biconnected component of the dual graph whose redundant edges are removed.

(d) Find a hypertree decomposition.

(e) What are the tree width, hyperwidth, and separators of your decomposition?

(f) What is the time and space complexity of CTE on the decomposition?

(g) Show schematically how ADAPTIVE-TREE-CONSISTENCY will work on this problem. What would be the time and space complexity?

6. Show that algorithm ATC can be modified so that its time complexity is bounded by $O(r \cdot k^{w^*+1})$, where r is the number of constraints, k bounds the domain size, and w^* is the induced width of the ordering (Shenoy 1996).

chapter 10

Hybrids of Search and Inference: Time-Space Trade-Offs

The more constraints one imposes
the more one frees oneself.

Igor Stravinski

Throughout this book two primary constraint processing schemes emerge—those based on *conditioning* or *search*, and those based on *inference* or *derivation*. Search in constraint satisfaction takes the form of depth-first backtracking, while inference is performed by variable elimination and tree-clustering algorithms, or by bounded local consistency enforcing. Compared to human problem-solving techniques, conditioning is analogous to guessing (a value of a variable), or reasoning by assumption. The problem is divided into subproblems, conditioned on the instantiation of a subset of variables, each of which should be solved. On the other hand, inference corresponds to reinterpreting or redefining the problem at hand. Inference-based algorithms derive and record new information, generating equivalent problem representations that facilitate an easier solution.

Search and inference algorithms have their relative advantages and disadvantages. Inference-based algorithms are efficient when the problem is sparse (when the induced width of the problem is low), but otherwise require substantial time and memory. Search algorithms require exponential time in the worst case, but need very little memory. Search often exhibits a much better average performance than their worst-case bounds. Given their complementary properties, the key to designing efficient algorithms is to combine inference-based and conditioning-based algorithms, and try to tailor the balance of inference and search to the problem instance. This combined approach may better utilize the benefit of each scheme and allow improved performance guarantees, reduced space complexity, and increased overall average performance.

Because of its better average performance and minimal space requirements, search is more popular than variable elimination for finding a single solution to

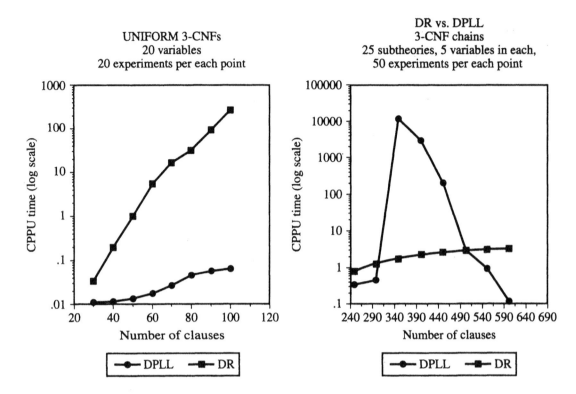

Figure 10.1   Average time performance of DPLL versus DR (a) on uniform 3-CNFs, w^* = 10 to 18, and (b) on chain 3-CNFs, w^* = 4 to 7.

constraint problems. For problems with low width, however, variable elimination techniques exploit the problems' structure and can be more efficient than back-tracking, as empirically demonstrated in Figure 10.1. The figure summarizes experiments over randomly generated satisfiability instances of two types, comparing DPLL backtracking for SAT with DIRECTIONAL-RESOLUTION (DR), and the bucket elimination algorithm for CNFs presented in Chapter 8.

The figure shows that, as expected, on uniform random 3-CNFs having large w^*, the complexity of the variable elimination algorithm, DR, grew exponentially with the problem density, while the performance of backtracking was much better. Even small problems having 20 variables already demonstrate the exponential behavior of DR as a function of the number of clauses (Figure 10.1(a)). On larger problems DR often ran out of memory. However, the behavior of the algorithms on chain problems, characterized as having a small induced width, was completely different. Here, variable elimination was far more efficient than backtracking search.

Table 10.1 Comparison between backtracking and variable elimination.

	Backtracking	*Variable elimination*
Worst-case time	$O(\exp(n))$	$O(n \times \exp(w^*))$ $w^* \leq n$
Average time	Better than worst case	Same as worst case
Space	$O(n)$	$O(n \times \exp(w^*))$ $w^* \leq n$
Task	One solution	Knowledge compilation

An important property of variable elimination algorithms is that they are knowledge compilation algorithms. Instead of finding one solution, they compile a problem into another representation from which all solutions can be found in linear time. These complementary characteristics of backtracking and variable elimination are summarized in Table 10.1.

There are several ways of combining search with inference, some of which we have already hinted at in previous chapters. One way is to use a restricted version of inference procedures as a preprocessing to search, thus yielding a restricted search space. Another approach is to alternate between both methods: apply search to a subset of the variables, and then perform inference on the rest. One instantiation of this second approach was explored in look-ahead backtracking algorithms. There, at every state of the search, namely, at each partial variable assignment, an approximate *bounded* inference algorithm (e.g., arc-consistency) is applied.

This chapter presents two orthogonal architectures for hybrids. The first reduces the general problem, via conditioning, to specific subproblems that are easy to solve by variable elimination. The second starts with bounding the separators' sizes of tree decompositions (see Chapter 9) and then applies conditioning search inside each cluster of the tree decomposition clusterings that have bounded separator sizes.

10.1 Specialized Cutset Schemes

We will start with the special case of the first hybrid scheme, called the *cycle-cutset decomposition*, and will follow with a recursive cutset search approach.

10.1.1 The Cycle-Cutset Scheme

The hybrid algorithm presented in this section is based on identifying a *cycle-cutset*, a set of nodes that, once removed, would render the constraint graph cycle-free. This method, called the *cycle-cutset decomposition*, was briefly discussed in Chapter 5 (see Section 5.3.3).

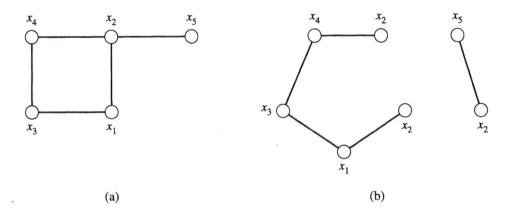

(a)   (b)

Figure 10.2 An instantiated variable cuts its own cycles: (a) a loopy constraint graph; (b) the graph associated with conditioning on x_2.

The method exploits the fact that variable instantiation changes the effective connectivity of the constraint graph. Consider a constraint problem whose graph is given in Figure 10.2(a). For this problem, instantiating x_2 to some value, say, a, renders the choices of values to x_1 and x_5 independent, as if the pathway $x_1 - x_2 - x_5$ were blocked at x_2. Similarly, this instantiation blocks dependency in the pathway $x_1 - x_2 - x_4$, leaving only one path between any two variables. In other words, given that x_2 was assigned a specific value, the "effective" constraint graph for the rest of the variables is shown in Figure 10.2(b). Here, the instantiated variable x_2 and its incident arcs are first deleted from the graph, and x_2 subsequently is duplicated for each of its neighbors. The constraint problem having the graph shown in Figure 10.2(a) when $x_2 = a$ is identical to the constraint problem having the graph in Figure 10.2(b) with the same assignment $x_2 = a$.

In general, when the group of instantiated variables constitutes a cycle-cutset, the resulting network is cycle-free (as shown in Figure 10.2(b)) and can be solved by the inference-based tree-solving algorithm. Note that in most practical cases it would take more than a single variable to cut all the cycles in the graph. Thus, a general way of solving a problem whose constraint graph contains cycles is to identify a subset of variables that cut all cycles in the graph, find a consistent instantiation of the variables in the cycle-cutset, and then solve the remaining problem by the tree algorithm. If a solution to this restricted problem (conditioned on the cycle-cutset values) is found, then a solution to the entire problem is at hand. If not, another instantiation of the cycle-cutset variables should be considered until a solution is found. If the task is to solve a constraint problem whose constraint graph is presented in Figure 10.2(a) (assume x_2 has two values $\{a, b\}$ in its domain), first $x_2 = a$ must be assumed, and the remaining tree problem relative to this instantiation is solved. If no solution is found, it is assumed that $x_2 = b$ and another attempt is made.

The number of times the tree-solving algorithm needs to be invoked is bounded by the number of partial solutions to the cycle-cutset variables. A small cycle-cutset is, therefore, desirable. However, since finding a minimal-size cycle-cutset can be shown to be computationally hard, it will be more practical to settle for a compromise and incorporate this scheme within backtracking search. Because backtracking works by progressively instantiating sets of variables, we only need to keep track of the connectivity status of the constraint graph. As soon as the set of instantiated variables constitutes a cycle-cutset, the search algorithm is switched to the tree-solving algorithm on the restricted problem, that is, either finding a consistent extension for the remaining variables (thus finding a solution to the entire problem) or concluding that no such extension exists (in which case backtracking takes place and another instantiation for the cutset variables is tried).

Some simple heuristic ordering of the variables that aims at finding a small cycle-cutset could be very beneficial here. One is to order the variables in decreasing order of their degree in the constraint graph. Several greedy and approximation algorithms for this problem can be found in the literature.

EXAMPLE 10.1   Assume that backtracking instantiates the variables of the CSP represented in Figure 10.3(a) in the order C, B, A, E, D, F, as in Figure 10.3(b). Backtracking will instantiate variables C, B, and A, and then, realizing that these variables cut all cycles, will invoke a tree-solving routine on the rest

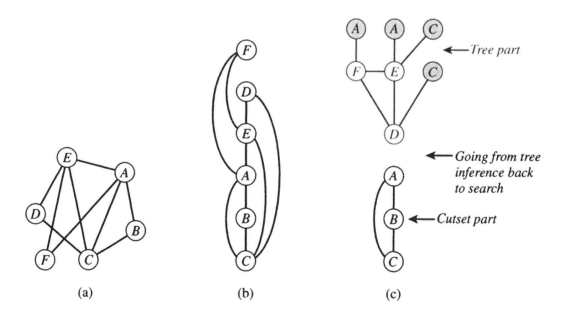

(a)   (b)   (c)

Figure 10.3 (a) A constraint graph and (b) its ordered graph. (c) The constraint graph of the cutset variable and the conditioned variable, where the assigned variables are darkened.

of the problem; the tree problem in Figure 10.3(c), with variables C, B, and A assigned, should then be attempted. If no solution is found, control returns to backtracking, which will go back to variable A.   •

Observe that the applicability of this idea is independent of the particular type of backtracking algorithm used over the cycle-cutset variables (e.g., naive backtracking, backjumping, backtrack with learning, etc.). Also note that when the original problem has a tree constraint graph, the cycle-cutset scheme coincides with a tree algorithm, and when the constraint graph is complete, the algorithm reverts to regular backtracking.

In the worst case, all possible assignments to the cutset variables need to be tested. If c is the cycle-cutset size, k^c is the number of tree-structured subproblems that need to be solved, each requiring $O((n - c)k^2)$ steps for the tree algorithm, yielding the following theorem:

THEOREM   Algorithm CYCLE-CUTSET-DECOMPOSITION has time complexity of $O(n \cdot k^{c+2})$
10.1   where n is the number of variables, c is the cycle-cutset size, and k is the
               domain size. The space complexity of the algorithm is linear.   •

10.1.2 Structure-Based Recursive Search

We will next provide a simple argument and an algorithm that performs search only, but consults a tree decomposition in a way that reduces its complexity. The argument is easiest to digest using a binary constraint network that is a tree. Given a tree network, we can identify a node x_1 that, when removed, generates two subtrees of size $n/2$ (approximately). Let T_n be the time to solve such a binary tree starting at x_1. When x_1 is instantiated, we need to solve two subproblems of size $n/2$. Thus, since x_1 has at most k values, T_n obeys the recurrence relation

$$T_n = k \cdot 2T_{n/2}$$

with

$$T_1 = k$$

It is easy to see that

$$T_n = n \cdot k^{\log n + 1} \tag{10.1}$$

We can apply the same argument to any tree decomposition of an arbitrary network, viewing each solution to a cluster as an instantiation of a metavariable (having the dual constraint view of the tree-decomposed problem). In this view the domain sizes are bounded by k^{w^*}, where w^* is the tree width of the decomposition and therefore bounds the cluster size. Substituting in Equation (10.1) k^{w^*} for k yields $T_n = n \cdot k^{w^* \cdot (\log n + 1)}$. However, since generating each tuple in a cluster by search can take $O(k^{w^*})$ time (but linear space), we get a total time complexity of $O(n \cdot k^{w^* \cdot (\log n + 2)})$. We call an algorithm that applies this search idea recursively to each subtree *recursive search*. We can summarize as follows:

THEOREM 10.2
A constraint problem with n variables and k values having a tree decomposition of tree width w^* can be solved by recursive search in linear space and in $O(n \cdot k^{2w^* \cdot (\log n + 1)})$ time.   ●

It can be shown that for some instances the cycle-cutset method is superior to recursive search, while for others, recursive search is superior (see Exercise 5).

The idea of recursively dividing a tree decomposition into two balanced subtrees can be terminated with subproblems that may be solved efficiently by other methods, instead of going all the way with (recursive) search.

For example, when a subproblem has a small induced width it can be solved by inference, yielding a possible hybrid between inference and search. Alternatively, we can solve a subproblem with a cycle-cutset scheme. You will be asked to consider such algorithms in Exercise 6. Such hybrids can be viewed as a special case of a "conditioning first" hybrid described next.

10.2 Hybrids: Conditioning First

The cycle-cutset scheme can be generalized. Rather than insisting on conditioning a subset (cutset) that cuts all cycles and yields width-1 subproblems, we can allow cutsets that create subproblems whose bounded width is higher than 1. This suggests a framework of hybrid algorithms parameterized by a bound b on the induced width of subproblems solved by inference.

10.2.1 The Idea

The idea is to instantiate a set of cutset variables, yielding a constraint graph with an induced width bounded by b. We call such a conditioning set a *b-cutset*.

DEFINITION 10.1
(b-cutset)

Given a graph G, a subset of nodes is called a b-cutset iff when the subset is removed the resulting graph has an induced width less than or equal to b. A minimal b-cutset of a graph has a smallest size among all b-cutsets of the graph. A cycle-cutset is a 1-cutset of a graph.   ●

It is clear that finding a minimal b-cutset is a hard task, although we can easily identify a b-cutset relative to a given variable ordering. Given an ordering $d = x_1, \ldots, x_n$ of G, a b-cutset relative to d is obtained by processing the nodes from last to first. When node x is processed, if its induced width is greater than b, it is added to the b-cutset and removed from the graph. Otherwise, its earlier neighbors are connected. By definition, the induced width relative to a cutset is called the *adjusted induced width*. The adjusted induced width relative to a b-cutset is b.

DEFINITION 10.2   **(adjusted ordered graph, adjusted induced width)**

Given a graph $G = (X, E)$, an ordering d, and a subset of nodes $V \subseteq X$, the adjusted ordered graph relative to V and d is (G', d) where $G' = (X - V, E')$ where $E' \subseteq E$ are edges among $X - V$. The adjusted induced width with respect to V is the induced width of the adjusted ordered graph. •

Since conditioning on a value assignment translates to node deletion in the constraint graph, conditioning on a b-cutset creates subproblems that can be solved by variable elimination in time and space exponential in b. This yields algorithm ELIM-COND(b), described in Figure 10.4. It runs backtracking search on the cutset variables and bucket elimination (e.g., adaptive consistency) on the remaining variables. The constraint problem $\mathcal{R} = (X, D, C)$ conditioned on an assignment $Y = \bar{y}$ and denoted by $\mathcal{R}_{\bar{y}}$ is defined as $\mathcal{R}$ augmented with the unary constraints dictated by the assignment $\bar{y}$. Remember that when adaptive consistency processes a network $\mathcal{R}$ having a set of assignments $\bar{y}$, it may process the variables of assigned buckets first, each by the instantiation step (see Figure 8.2).

Algorithm ELIM-COND(b) allows bounding the amount of memory required while still maintaining desirable performance guarantees. In other words, the constant b can be used to control the balance between search and variable elimination, and thus affect the trade-off between time and space.

ELIM-COND(b)

Input: A constraint network $\mathcal{R} = (X, D, C)$, $Y \subseteq X$, which is a b-cutset. d is an ordering that starts with Y such that the adjusted induced width, relative to Y along d, is bounded by b, $Z = X - Y$.

Output: A consistent assignment, if there is one.

1. **while** $\bar{y} \leftarrow$ next partial solution of Y found by backtracking, **do**

    (a) $\bar{z} \leftarrow$ ADC ($\mathcal{R}_{Y = \bar{y}}$).

    (b) **if** $\bar{z}$ is not *false*, return solution = $(\bar{y}, \bar{z})$.

2. **endwhile**

3. **return:** the problem has no solutions.

Figure 10.4 Algorithm ELIM-COND(b).

THEOREM 10.3 Given $\mathcal{R} = (X, D, C)$, if ELIM-COND(b) is applied along ordering d when Y is a b-cutset of size c_b, then the space complexity of ELIM-COND(b) is bounded by $O(n \cdot exp(b))$, and its time complexity is bounded by $O(n \cdot 2^b exp(c_b+b))$.

Proof Given a b-cutset assignment, the time and space complexity of the inference portion (by variable elimination) is bounded by $O(n \cdot (2k)^b)$. Since in the worst case, backtracking involves enumerating all possible instantiations of the b-cutset in $O(k^{c_b})$ time and linear space, the total time complexity is $O(n \cdot (2k)^b \cdot k^{c_b}) = O(n \cdot 2^b k^{(b+c_b)})$.   ●

Theorem 10.3 calls for a new optimization task on graphs:

Finding a b-cutset

Given a graph $G = (V, E)$ and a constant b, find a minimal b-cutset. That is, find a smallest subset of nodes U, such that the adjusted induced width relative to V is G' less than or equal to b.

Note that for a given constant b, verifying that a given subset of nodes is a b-cutset can be accomplished in polynomial time (in the number of nodes). Verification can be accomplished by deleting the b-cutset from the graph and verifying that the remaining graph has an induced width bounded by b that is $O(exp(b))$. Moreover, given an ordering, you can test if a conditioning set is a b-cutset relative to the ordering by inspecting the induced width of the adjusted ordered graph. Therefore, ELIM-COND(b) can be applied using backtracking to all the variables in a given ordering until the problem conditioned on the partial assignment has an induced width b or less *along the ordering*. Search and variable elimination can also be interleaved dynamically, as we demonstrate in the following section.

In summary, the parameter b can be used to control the trade-off between search and inference. If $b \geq w_d^*$, where d is the ordering used by ELIM-COND(b), the algorithm coincides with adaptive consistency. As b decreases, the algorithm requires less space and more time. There is no guaranteed worst-case time improvement of ELIM-COND(b) over pure adaptive consistency. For example, it can be shown that the size of the smallest cycle-cutset (1-cutset), c_1, and the smallest induced width, w^*, obey the inequality $c_1 \geq w^* - 1$. Therefore, $1 + c_1 \geq w^*$, where the left side of this inequality is the exponent that determines the time complexity of ELIM-COND($b = 1$), while w^* governs the complexity of adaptive consistency. In general,

$$1 + c_1 \geq 2 + c_2 \geq \ldots b + c_b \ldots \geq w^* + c_{w^*} = w^*$$

But, since by definition $c_{w^*} = 0$, we get a hybrid scheme whose time complexity decreases as its space increases until it reaches the induced width.

10.2.2   Hybrid Algorithm for Propositional Theories

In this section we present a variant of ELIM-COND(b) for processing propositional CNFs. As we know, the most celebrated backtracking search algorithm for propositional CNF theories is the backtracking DPLL algorithm that applies look-ahead using unit propagation at each node. The bucket elimination algorithm for CNFs is DIRECTIONAL-RESOLUTION (DR), described in Chapter 8, which uses resolution as its variable elimination operator.

Remember that the structure of a propositional theory can be described by an *interaction graph*. The interaction graph of a propositional theory φ, denoted $G(\varphi)$, is an undirected graph that contains a node for each propositional variable and an edge for each pair of nodes that correspond to variables appearing in the same clause. For example, the interaction graph of theory $\varphi_1 = \{(\neg C), (A \vee B \vee C), (\neg A \vee B \vee E), (\neg B \vee C \vee D)\}$ was shown in Figure 8.4(a) (page 227). The interaction graph of a theory processed by resolution should be augmented with new edges reflecting the added clauses. For example, resolution over variable A in φ_1 generates a new clause $(B \vee C \vee E)$, so the graph of the resulting theory has an edge between nodes E and C, as shown in Figure 8.4(b).

The theory φ conditioned on the assignment $Y = \bar{y}$ is called a *conditional theory* of φ relative to $\bar{y}$ and is denoted by $\varphi_{\bar{y}}$. Since the effect of conditioning on a subset of propositions Y is their deletion from the constraint graph, the *conditional graph* of $\varphi_{\bar{y}}$, denoted $G(\varphi_{\bar{y}})$, is obtained by deleting the nodes in Y (and all their incident edges) from $G(\varphi)$. The *conditional induced width* of a theory $\varphi_{\bar{y}}$, denoted $w_{\bar{y}}^*$, is the induced width of the graph $G(\varphi_{\bar{y}})$. It is similar to the adjusted induced width, but it also depends on the particular assignment.

EXAMPLE 10.2   Figure 10.5 shows the interaction graph of theory $\varphi = \{(\neg C \vee E), (A \vee B \vee C \vee D), (\neg A \vee B \vee E \vee D), (\neg B \vee C \vee D)\}$ along the ordering $d = (E, D, C, B, A)$, having induced width 4. Conditioning on A yields two conditional theories: $\varphi_{A=0} = \{(\neg C \vee E), (B \vee C \vee D), (\neg B \vee C \vee D)\}$, and $\varphi_{A=1} = \{(\neg C \vee E), (B \vee E \vee D), (\neg B \vee C \vee D)\}$. The ordered graphs of $\varphi_{A=0}$ and $\varphi_{A=1}$ are also shown in Figure 10.5. Clearly, $w_d^*(B) = 2$ for theory $\varphi_{A=0}$, and $w_d^*(B) = 3$ for theory $\varphi_{A=1}$. Besides deleting A and its incident edges from the interaction graph, we can also delete some other edges because some clauses subsuming the assignment can be deleted as well. For example, $A = 0$ can remove the edge between B and E because the clause $(\neg A \vee B \vee E \vee D)$ becomes satisfied and is removed.   •

Algorithm DP-DR(b) combines DPLL and DR, and is a special version of ELIM-COND(b) that incorporates dynamic variable ordering. The algorithm, presented in Figure 10.6, takes as an input a propositional theory φ and a parameter b. If no inconsistency is discovered by unit propagation, DP-DR(b) proceeds to its primary activity: choosing between resolution and conditioning. So long as there exists a variable Q connected to at most b other variables in the conditional interaction

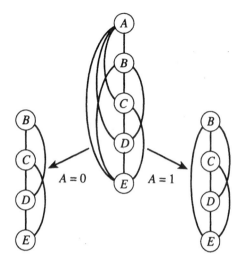

Figure 10.5 The effect of conditioning on A on the interaction graph of theory $\varphi = \{(\neg C \vee E), (A \vee B \vee C \vee D), (\neg A \vee B \vee E \vee D), (\neg B \vee C \vee D)\}$.

DP-DR(φ, b)

Input: A CNF theory φ over variables X; a bound b.

Output: A decision of whether φ is satisfiable. If it is, an assignment $\bar{y}$ to a cutset variable Y, and the conditional directional extension $E_d(\varphi_y)$.

1. **if** unit_propagate(φ) = *false*, return(*false*);
2. **else** $X \leftarrow X - \{$variables in unit clauses$\}$
3. **if** no more variables to process, return *true*;
4. **else while** $\exists Q \in X$ such that *degree* $(Q) \leq b$ in the current conditioned graph
5.   resolve over Q
6.   **if** no empty clause is generated,
7.   add all resolvents to the theory
8.   **else** return *false*
9. $X \leftarrow X - \{Q\}$
10. **endWhile**
11. Select a variable $Q \in X$; $X \leftarrow X - \{Q\}$.
12. $Y \leftarrow Y \cup \{Q\}$;
13. **return**(DP-DR($\varphi \wedge \neg Q, b$) $\vee$
            DP-DR($\varphi \wedge Q, b$)).

Figure 10.6 Algorithm DP-DR(b).

graph, DP-DR(b) resolves upon Q (steps 4–9). Otherwise, it selects an unassigned variable (step 11), adds it to the b-cutset (step 12), and continues recursively with the conditional theory $\varphi \wedge \neg Q$ or $\varphi \wedge Q$. Clearly, by limiting resolution to variables that are connected to at most b neighbors we limit the size of the resolvents, yielding a bounded inference. If the algorithm does not find any consistent partial assignment, it deems the theory inconsistent. Otherwise, it returns an assignment $\bar{y}$ to the cutset Y and the conditional directional extension $E_d(\varphi_{\bar{y}})$, where d is the variable ordering dynamically constructed by the algorithm.

EXAMPLE 10.3

Figure 10.7 demonstrates algorithm DP-DR(2) for the theory $\varphi = \{(\neg C \vee E),$ $(A \vee B \vee C \vee D), (\neg A \vee B \vee E \vee D), (\neg B \vee C \vee D)\}$. Every variable is initially connected to at least three other variables in $G(\varphi)$. Consequently, no resolution can be done, and a conditioning variable is selected. Assume that A is selected. Assignment $A = 0$ adds the unit clause $\neg A$, which causes unit resolution in $bucket_A$ and produces a new clause $(B \vee C \vee D)$ from $(A \vee B \vee C \vee D)$. The assignment $A = 1$ produces clause $(B \vee E \vee D)$. In Figure 10.7, the original clauses are shown on the left as a partitioning into buckets. The new clauses are shown on the right, within the

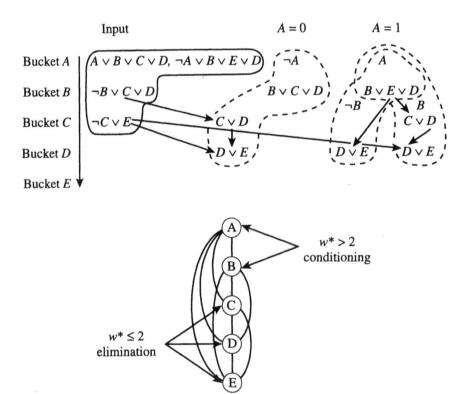

Figure 10.7   A trace of DP-DR(2) on the theory $\varphi = \{(\neg C \vee E), (A \vee B \vee C \vee D), (\neg A \vee B \vee E \vee D), (\neg B \vee C \vee D)\}$.

corresponding search-tree branches. The branch for $A = 0$ (i.e., $\neg A$) yields a conditional theory $\{(\neg B \vee C \vee D), (B \vee C \vee D), (\neg C \vee E)\}$. Since the degrees of all the variables in the corresponding (conditional) interaction graph are now 2 or less (see Figure 10.5), we can proceed with DIRECTIONAL-RESOLUTION. We select B, perform resolution in its bucket, and record the resolvent $(C \vee D)$ in $bucket_C$. The resolution in $bucket_C$ creates clause $(D \vee E)$. At this point, the algorithm terminates, returning the assignment $A = 0$, and the conditional directional extension $\varphi \wedge (B \vee C \vee D) \wedge (C \vee D) \wedge (D \vee E)$. Following the alternative branch of $A = 1$ results in the conditional theory $\{(B \vee E \vee D), (\neg B \vee C \vee D), (\neg C \vee E)\}$. Since each variable is connected to three other variables (see Figure 10.5), no resolution is possible. Conditioning on B yields the conditional theory $\{(E \vee D), (\neg C \vee E)\}$ when $B = 0$, and the conditional theory $\{(C \vee D), (\neg C \vee E)\}$ when $B = 1$. In both cases, the algorithm terminates, returning $A = 1$, the assignment to B, and the corresponding conditional directional extension.

As a specialized version of ELIM-COND(b), algorithm DP-DR(b) is guaranteed to generate clauses restricted to length b or less, by resolution. We can conclude directly, and also based on Theorem 10.3, the following:

THEOREM 10.4   **(complexity of DP-DR(b))**

The time complexity of algorithm DP-DR(b) is $O(n \cdot exp(b + c_b))$, where c_b is the largest cutset to be conditioned upon. The space complexity is $O(n \cdot exp(b))$. •

Empirical Evaluation of DP-DR(b)

We conclude our discussion of conditioning-first hybrids by presenting some typical empirical results from experiments with different structured CNFs. The experiments focus on random uniform 3-CNFs having 100 variables and 400 clauses, as well as on $(2, 5)$-trees with 40 cliques and 15 clauses per clique, and with $(4, 8)$-trees with 50 cliques and 20 clauses per clique. In general, (k, m)-trees are trees of cliques each having $m + k$ nodes and separators of size k. The randomly generated 3-CNFs were designed to have an interaction graph that corresponds to (k, m)-trees.

As expected, the performance of DP-DR(b) depends on the induced width of the theories. Figure 10.8 summarizes the results for DP-DR(0), DP-DR(5), and DP-DR(13) on the three classes of problems. The intermediate bound, $b = 5$, seems to be overall more cost-effective than both extremes, $b = 0$ and $b = 13$. We even observe a time gain with intermediate values of b for the class of (4,8)-trees.

10.3 Hybrids: Inference First

We next present an orthogonal approach for combining conditioning and inference, based on tree decomposition. In Chapter 9, we saw that the main drawback of the

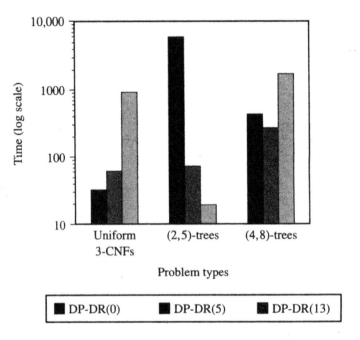

Figure 10.8   Performance of DP-DR(b) for $b = 0, 5, 13$ on different types of problems.

CLUSTER-TREE-ELIMINATION (CTE) algorithm (Figure 9.10) is its memory needs: the space complexity of CTE is exponential in the largest separator size, which may be prohibitive.

Algorithm CTE already contains a hidden combination of variable elimination and search: while it computes functions on the separators using variable elimination and is space exponential in the separator's size, the clusters themselves can be processed by search in time exponential in the cluster size. Thus, you can trade even more space for time by allowing larger cliques but smaller separators. This can be achieved by combining adjacent nodes in a tree decomposition that are linked by "fat separators," and keeping apart only those nodes that are linked by bounded size separators. We elaborate on this general approach in the following pages.

10.3.1   The SUPER-CLUSTER-TREE-ELIMINATION Algorithm

Assume a problem whose tree decomposition has tree width r and separator size s. Assume further that our space restrictions do not allow the necessary $O(\exp(s))$ memory required by CTE on such a tree. One way to overcome this problem is to collapse these nodes in the tree that are connected by large separators to include the variables and constraints from both nodes. The resulting tree decomposition has larger subproblems but smaller separators. This idea suggests a sequence of tree decompositions parameterized by the sizes of their separators.

Let T be a tree decomposition of hypergraph $\mathcal{H}$. Let $s_0, s_1, \ldots, s_n$ be the sizes of the separators in T, listed in strictly descending order. With each separator size s_i we associate a secondary tree decomposition T_i, generated by combining adjacent nodes whose separator sizes are strictly greater than s_i. We denote by r_i the largest set of variables in any cluster of T_i. Note that as s_i decreases, r_i increases. Clearly, the next theorem follows from Theorem 9.8:

THEOREM 10.5   Given a tree decomposition T of a constraint problem, where n bounds the number of constraints and the number of nodes in the tree, separator sizes $s_0, s_1, \ldots, s_t$ and secondary tree decompositions having a corresponding maximal number of nodes in any cluster, $r_0, r_1, \ldots, r_t$, the complexity of CTE when applied to each secondary tree decompositions T_i is $O(n \cdot deg \cdot exp(r_i))$ time and $O(n \cdot exp(s_i))$ space (i ranges over all the secondary tree decompositions) and *deg* bounds the degree in T.   ●

Note again that each clique is processed by search. That is, each solution created by backtracking is projected on the separator and the projected solutions are accumulated. Any backtracking scheme can be used. We will call the resulting algorithm SUPER-CLUSTER-TREE-ELIMINATION(b), or SCTE(b). It takes a primary tree decomposition and generates a tree decomposition whose separator's size is bounded by b, which is subsequently processed by CTE. In the following example we assume a naive backtracking search processing each clique.

EXAMPLE 10.4   Consider the constraint problem having the constraint graph in Figure 10.9. The graph can be decomposed into the join-tree in Figure 10.10(a). If we allow only separators of size 2, we get the join tree T_1 in Figure 10.10(b). This structure suggests that applying CTE takes time exponential in the largest cluster, 5, while requiring space exponential in 2. If space considerations allow only singleton separators, we can use the secondary tree T_2 in Figure 10.10(c). We conclude that the problem can be solved either in $O(k^4)$ time (k being the maximum domain size) and $O(k^3)$ space using T_0, or in $O(k^5)$ time and $O(k^2)$ space using T_1, or in $O(k^7)$ time and $O(k)$ space using T_2. (We focus on cluster processing only.)   ●

Super-Buckets

Since bucket elimination algorithms can be extended to bucket-trees as we saw in Section 9.3, and since a bucket-tree is a tree decomposition, by merging adjacent buckets we generate a *super-bucket-tree* (SBT) in a similar way to how we generated super-clusters. Consequently, in the top-down phase of bucket elimination (or ATC) several variables are eliminated at once. Algorithm SUPER-BUCKET-ELIMINATION(b) is not presented explicitly, but in Figure 10.11(a) we illustrate the

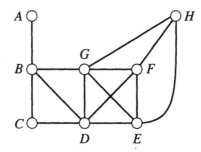

Figure 10.9 A primal constraint graph.

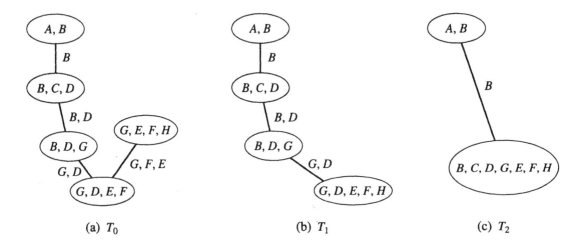

Figure 10.10 A tree decomposition with separators equal to (a) 3, (b) 2, and (c) 1.

bucket-tree of the graph in Figure 9.13 along the order $d = (A, B, C, D, F)$. In (b) and (c) we see two super-bucket-trees that collapse a few buckets into one. (See also Exercise 7.)

10.3.2   Decomposition into Nonseparable Components

A special tree decomposition occurs when all the separators are singleton variables. This type of tree decomposition is attractive because it requires only linear space. While we generally cannot find the best tree decompositions having a bounded separators' size in polynomial time, this is a feasible task when the separators are singletons. To this end, we use the graph notion of *nonseparable components* (Even 1979).

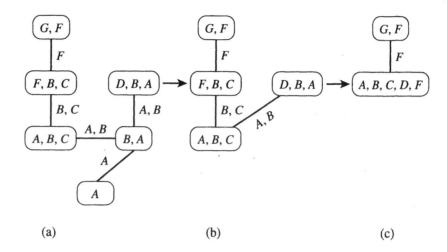

(a)   (b)   (c)

Figure 10.11 From (a) a bucket-tree to (b) join-tree to (c) a super-bucket-tree.

DEFINITION   (nonseparable components)
10.3

A connected graph $G = (V, E)$ is said to have a *separation node* v if there exist nodes a and b such that all paths connecting a and b pass through v. A graph that has a separation node is called *separable*, and one that has none is called *nonseparable*. A subgraph with no separation nodes is called a *nonseparable component* or a *biconnected component*.   •

An $O(|E|)$ algorithm exists for finding all the nonseparable components and the separation nodes. It is based on a depth-first search traversal of the graph. An important property of nonseparable components is that they are interconnected in a tree-structured manner. That is, for every graph G there is a tree SG, whose nodes are the nonseparable components $C_1, C_2, \ldots, C_r$ of G. The separating nodes of these trees are $V_1, V_2, \ldots, V_t$, and any two component nodes are connected through a separating node vertex in SG. Clearly, the tree of nonseparable components suggests a tree decomposition where each node corresponds to a component, the variables of the nodes are those appearing in each component, and the constraints can be freely placed into a component that contains their scopes. Applying CTE to such a tree requires only linear space, but is time exponential in the components' sizes.

EXAMPLE   Assume that the graph in Figure 10.12(a) represents a constraint network
10.5   having unary, binary, and ternary constraints as follows:

$$\mathcal{R} = \{R_{AD}, R_{AB}, R_{DC}, R_{BC}, R_{GF}, D_G, D_F, R_{EHI}, R_{CFE}\}$$

The nonseparable components and their tree structure are given in Figure 10.12(b) and (c). The ordering of components $d = (C_1, C_2, C_3, C_4)$ dictates

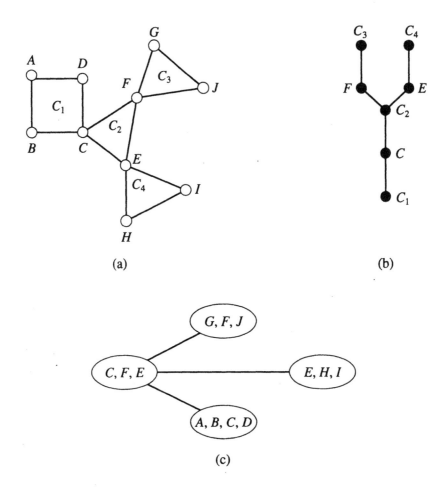

(a)   (b)

(c)

Figure 10.12 A graph and its decomposition into nonseparable components.

super-clusters associated with variables $\{G, J, F\}$, $\{E, H, I\}$, $\{C, F, E\}$, and $\{A, B, C, D\}$. The initial partition into super-clusters and a schematic execution of CTE are displayed in Figure 10.13. We show the execution as a message passing along a super-cluster-tree. The message ρ_A^B computed by cluster A and sent to cluster B is placed inside the receiving bucket.   •

THEOREM   **(nonseparable components)**
10.6
If $\mathcal{R} = (X, D, C)$, and $|X| = n$ is a constraint network whose constraint graph has nonseparable components of at most size r, then the SUPER-CLUSTER-ELIMINATION algorithm, whose clusters are the nonseparable components, is time $O(n \cdot \exp(r))$ but requires only linear in space.   •

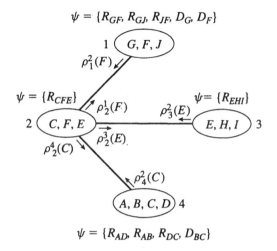

Figure 10.13 A schematic execution of ATC when the super-buckets are the nonseparable components. R denotes original constraints and ρ denotes new domain constraints.

10.3.3 Hybrids of Hybrids

We can now combine the two hybrid approaches—conditioning and inference—in a straightforward manner. Once we have decided on a space parameter b_1, we can first find a tree decomposition with separators bounded by b_1 as suggested by the super-clustering approach. The decomposition suggests a collection of subproblems that can be solved by search. Instead of pure search, we can reduce the time complexity further by applying, independently, ELIM-COND(b_2) to each subproblem. Clearly, we must have $b_2 \leq b_1$ to maintain the space requirement, but the time complexity in each clique can be significantly reduced as a result.

We call the combined algorithm HYBRID(b_1, b_2). First, a tree decomposition having separators bounded by b_1 is created, followed by application of the CTE algorithm, but each clique is processed by ELIM-COND(b_2). If $c_{b_2}^*$ is the size of the maximum b_2-cutset in each clique of the b_1-tree decomposition, the resulting algorithm is space exponential in b_1 but time exponential in $c_{b_2}^*$.

Two special cases are worth mentioning. The first is when we apply the cycle-cutset scheme (HYBRID($b_1, 1$)) in each cluster. In the next subsection we will demonstrate this method on structured networks that are associated with real circuits (for circuit diagnosis tasks) and show that the reduction in complexity bounds for complex circuits is tremendous.

The second special case is when $b_1 = b_2$. For $b = 1$, HYBRID(1,1) corresponds to applying the nonseparable components as a tree decomposition and utilizing the cycle-cutset in each component. The space complexity of this algorithm is linear, but its time complexity can be much better than the cycle-cutset scheme or the nonseparable component approach alone.

10.4 **A Case Study of Combinatorial Circuits**

A variety of diagnosis and testing tasks over combinatorial circuits can be modeled as constraint processing or constraint optimization tasks. Such circuits can shed light on the structural parameters associated with a real benchmark of significant importance. The analysis uses benchmark combinatorial circuits, widely used in the fault diagnosis and testing community (Brglez and Fujiwara 1996) (see Table 10.2). None of the circuits are trees. An example is shown in the schematic diagram of circuit c432 in Figure 10.14.

Each circuit is associated with a primal graph, where a node corresponds to each variable in the circuit. For every gate in the circuit, the graph has edges connecting all the variables of the gate's inputs and output. Table 10.3 gives the number of nodes and edges of the primal graph for each circuit.

Join-tree decompositions of each circuit graph were generated using the triangulation approach (see Figure 9.6). Several ordering heuristics were considered including maximum-cardinality, minimum-width, and induced-width (see Chapter 4 for definitions). The reported results use the min-induced-width ordering, as it was by far the best, yielding the smallest cluster sizes and separators.

Table 10.2 ISCAS '85 benchmark circuit characteristics.

Circuit name	Circuit function	Total gates	Input lines	Output lines
c17		6	5	2
c432	Priority decoder	160 (18 EXOR)	36	7
c499	ECAT	202 (104 EXOR)	41	32
c880	ALU and control	383	60	26
c1355	ECAT	546	41	32
c1908	ECAT	880	33	25
c2670	ALU and control	1193	233	140
c3540	ALU and control	1669	50	22
c5315	ALU and selector	2307	178	123
c6288	16-bit multiplier	2406	32	32
c7552	ALU and control	3512	207	108

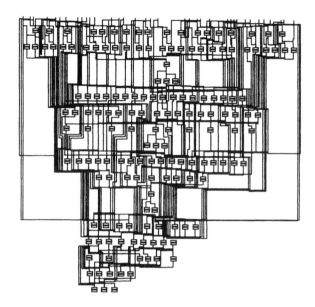

Figure 10.14 Schematic of circuit c432: 36 inputs, 7 outputs, and 160 components.

Table 10.3 Number of nodes and edges for the primal graphs of the circuits.

Circuit	c17	c432	c499	c880	c1355	c1908	c2670	c3540	c5315	c6288	c7552
Number of nodes	11	196	243	443	587	913	1426	1719	2485	2448	3719
Number of edges	18	660	692	1140	1660	2507	3226	4787	7320	7184	9572

10.4.1 Parameters of Primary Join-Trees

For each primary join-tree generated, three parameters are computed: (1) the size of clusters, (2) the size of cycle-cutsets in each of the subgraphs defined by the clusters, and (3) the size of the separator sets. The nodes of the join-tree are labeled by the cluster sizes. We present the results on two circuits, c432 and c3540, having 196 and 1719 variables, in Figures 10.15 and 10.16, respectively.

For example, Figure 10.15 shows that the cluster sizes range from 2 to 28. The root node has 28 nodes, and the descendant nodes have strictly smaller sizes. The depth of the tree is 11, and all nodes whose distance from the root is greater than 6 have sizes strictly less than 10. The leaves have sizes ranging from 2 to 6. The corresponding numbers for the primary join-tree of the larger circuit c3540 are shown in Figure 10.16.

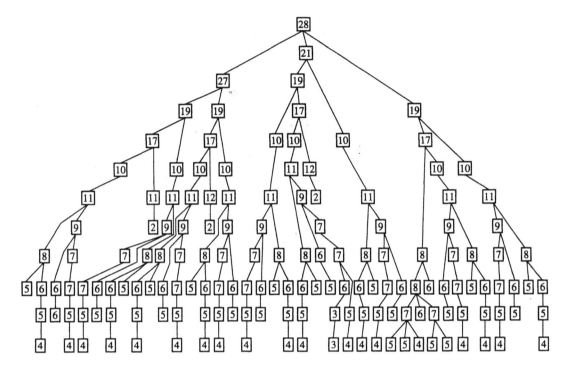

Figure 10.15   Primary join-tree (157 cliques) for circuit c432 (196 variables); the maximum separator size is 23.

As we can see, some clusters and separators require memory space exponential in 23 for circuit c432 and exponential in 89 for circuit c3540. This is clearly not feasible. We will next evaluate the potential of HYBRID($b, 1$).

10.4.2   Parameters Controlling Hybrids

Let s_0 and c_0 be the maximum separator and cutset size, respectively, of the primary join-tree T_0 obtained by some tree decomposition. Let $s_0, s_1, \ldots, s_n$ be the size of the separators in T_0 listed from largest to smallest. As discussed earlier, with each separator size, s_i, we associate a tree decomposition T_i generated by combining adjacent clusters whose separators' sizes are strictly larger than s_i. We denote by c_i the largest cycle-cutset size computed in any cluster of T_i.

Figure 10.17 displays the structure of secondary join-trees for c432. The primary join-tree for the circuit is shown in Figure 10.15. The secondary trees are indexed by the separator sizes of the primary tree, which range from 1 to 23 (see Figure 10.17). As the separator size decreases, the maximum cluster size increases, and both the size and the depth of the tree decreases. Like the primary join-tree,

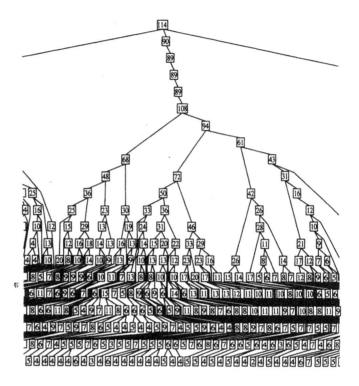

Figure 10.16 Part of primary join-tree (1419 cliques) for circuit c3540 (1719 variables) showing the descendants of the root node down to the leaves; the maximum separator size is 89.

each secondary join-tree also has a skewed distribution of the cluster sizes. Note that the cluster size for the root node is significantly larger than for all other nodes and increases as the separator decreases.

Figure 10.18 gives six graphs presenting the emerging bounds for time versus space for each circuit. Each point in the graphs corresponds to a specific secondary join-tree decomposition T_i and has space complexity measured by the separator size, s_i, and time complexity measured by the cycle-cutset size in each cluster.

Each graph in Figure 10.18 can be used to select the parameter b that best controls the balance between time and space for the respective circuits. We see that reducing space has the gradual effect of increasing the time required by a corresponding HYBRID$(*, 1)$ algorithm. For example, circuit c432 shows the separator size (space), which is initially 23 (for the primary join-tree), gradually reduced down to 1 in a series of secondary trees. The figure demonstrates that reducing the separator size (to meet the space restrictions) increases the worst-case time complexity of the HYBRID algorithm. The time increases because of the large clusters contained in the secondary join-tree, and the corresponding increase in the size of their cutsets. Note that the graphs in Figure 10.18 all display a "knee" phenomenon

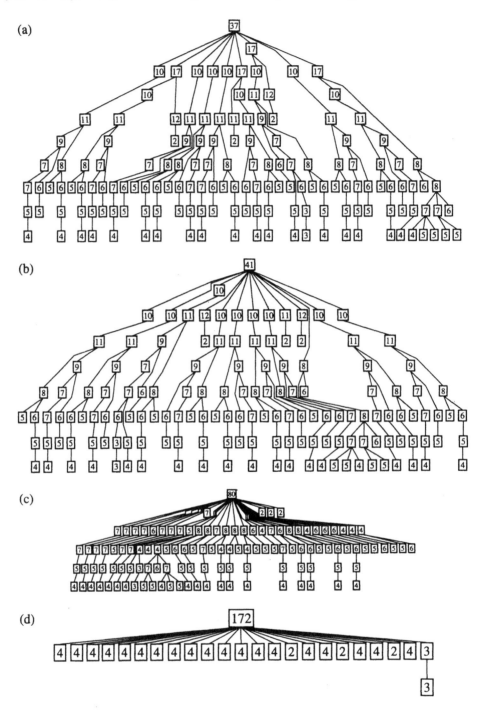

Figure 10.17 Secondary trees for c432 with separator sizes (a) 16, (b) 11, (c) 7, and (d) 3.

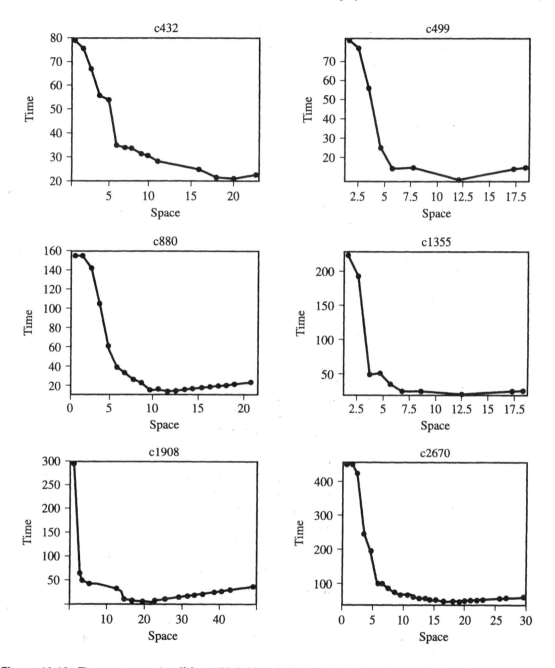

Figure 10.18 Time-space trade-off for c432 (196 variables), c499 (243 variables), c880 (443 variables), c1355 (587 variables), c1908 (913 variables), and c2670 (1426 variables). Time is measured by the maximum of the separator size and the cutset size, and space by the maximum separator size.

in the time-space trade-off, where time increases only slightly for a wide range of space reduction, beyond which further reduction in space causes a significant rise in the time bound.

10.5 Summary

Problem-solving methods can be viewed as hybrids of two main techniques: inference and search. Tree clustering and variable elimination are examples of inference algorithms, while backtracking is an example of a search method. Variable elimination algorithms are time and space exponential in the size of the induced width, while search algorithms are time exponential in the number of variables but require only linear memory. This chapter presented a structure-based hybrid scheme that uses inference and search as its two extremes and, using a single design parameter, permits the user to control and tailor the storage-time trade-off in accordance with the problem domain and the available resources.

The structural parameters of interest are (1) the size of clusters in a tree decomposition (i.e., the induced width), (2) the size of cycle-cutsets in each of the subgraphs defined by the clusters, and (3) the size of the separator sets.

The hybrid is allowed by observing different effects of conditioning and elimination on the constraint graph. Assigning to x_i a value (conditioning on x_i) corresponds to deleting it from the constraint graph, while variable eliminating x_i requires connecting all its neighbors (in the current graph) and then eliminating the corresponding node from the graph. Indeed, in bucket elimination, when x_i is assigned a value, no new constraints are created, while processing the bucket of x_i by elimination adds new components to the buckets of x_i's parents. We demonstrated such a framework for both constraint satisfaction and propositional satisfiability.

Two architectures for hybrids were proposed. The conditioning-first idea is to find a small subset of conditioning-cutset variables Y, such that conditioning (that is, assigning them values) results in a subproblem having low w^* graph. Algorithm ELIM-COND(b) searches the space of partial assignments over the b-cutset variables and solves the rest of the problem by variable elimination. The special case of conditioning on a cycle-cutset is called the cycle-cutset decomposition. We demonstrated a specialization of this hybrid principle for satisfiability, incorporating dynamic variable ordering and dynamic order of elimination and conditioning.

The inference-first approach is to limit space by using tree decompositions whose separators are bounded by b. In particular, the tree of nonseparable components is a special case whose separators' size equals 1, yielding a linear space algorithm.

Finally, a hybrid of the two hybrids allows even better time complexity for every fixed space restriction.

This chapter also demonstrated the applicability of the scheme to real-life domains through the case study of structural parameters of benchmark circuits widely used in the fault diagnosis and testing community (Brglez and Fujiwara 1996). We also presented a recursive search scheme that exploits a tree decomposition, yielding an involved variable ordering scheme with structure-based complexity bounds.

10.6 Bibliographical Notes

Hybrid algorithms of inference and search were first introduced using the cycle-cutset decomposition (Dechter and Pearl 1987a; Dechter 1990) for constraints and were also termed *loop-cutset* in the area of probabilistic inference (Pearl 1988). Extensions of this approach to the general case were presented in propositional CNFs (Rish and Dechter 2000), and for optimization tasks (Larrosa 2000), as well as by Darwiche (1999). The inference-first idea for trading space for time was introduced in Dechter and El Fattah (2001). Additional ideas of extending the combination of conditioning and tree-clustering beyond the cycle-cutset scheme appear in the work of Jégou (1990) for constraint networks and in the work of Anderson, Shachter, and Solovitz (1999) and Cooper, Suermondt, and Heckerman (1991) for probabilistic networks. In Cooper, Suermondt, and Heckerman (1991) the idea is applied to the probabilistic inference for a pathfinder system, when the conditioning set is restricted to the set of diseases.

These hybrids suggest a secondary optimization task of finding the minimal b-cutset in graphs. The special case of cycle-cutset, also known as *minimal feedback set*, was shown to be NP-complete. Approximation algorithms were investigated by Bar-Yehuda, Becker, and Geiger (1999). It would be interesting to extend such algorithms for the more general case of finding the minimal b-cutset of a graph. The idea of recursive tree search was introduced recently by Darwiche (1999) in the context of probabilistic reasoning (under the name *recursive conditioning*).

10.7 Exercises

1. Develop approximation algorithms for finding a minimal b-cutset for a given constant b.

2. Prove that deciding the consistency of a constraint network whose constraint graph has nonseparable components of size at most r can be solved in time exponential in r while in linear space.

3. Consider the crossword puzzle in Figure 4.22 (page 114).

   (a) Suppose you want to solve the crossword puzzle using the cycle-cutset scheme. Discuss the approach. Can you bound the complexity of the cycle-cutset scheme for problems having this constraint graph? Compare with previous approaches.

(b) Bound the complexity of solving problems having the crossword constraint graph using the nonseparable-components method.

(c) What are the best time-space guarantees you can get for this instance of the crossword puzzle? What are the best time-space guarantees you can provide for a crossword puzzle of size $n \times n$?

(d) In your opinion, which of the methods you have learned in the constraint class is best suited for crossword puzzles?

4. Given a graph $G = (X, E)$, and $|X| = n$, given constants b and r, can we decide if there is a b-cutset of size r or less in polynomial time in n?

5. Based on worst-case complexity analysis, show an example of a problem class where the cycle-cutset scheme is superior to recursive conditioning, and vice versa. Show a class where recursive conditioning is better than the cycle-cutset scheme.

6. Propose a "conditioning-first" hybrid of search and inference that is based on recursive search and provide an analysis of its performance.

7. The SUPER-CLUSTER-TREE-ELIMINATION algorithm, when applied to a super-bucket-tree, is called SBTE (super-bucket-tree elimination). Show how SBTE works over the super-bucket-trees in Figure 10.11. Use the constraints specified in Figure 9.14.

chapter 11

Tractable Constraint Languages

David Cohen, Royal Holloway, University of London
Peter Jeavons, Oxford University Computing Laboratory

> The simplicities of natural laws arise through the
> complexities of the language we use for their expression.
>
> *Eugene Wigner*

Practical constraint solvers allow you to define constraint networks and (with luck) solve them. They often define a set of basic constraints that you can apply to variables. These basic constraints may well be called the *language* of the constraint solver.

Naturally you want to be able to offer some performance guarantees when you generate a constraint network model of a real-world problem using your constraint language. However, if the language allows arbitrary restrictions to general subsets of the variables, then the set of instances to which your solver can be applied forms an NP-hard problem.

There are some restricted constraint languages for which polynomial time solution algorithms are known. It is worthwhile to be able to identify and to understand such tractable languages.

Unfortunately, restricting the language of CSPs will restrict the problems that can be modeled in the language. We would thus like to be able to offer with our language a description of all those relations that can be expressed. We (usually) want the list of expressible relations to be as large as possible.

In short, we want a performance guarantee, for which we have to restrict our language. We also want an expressiveness guarantee, for which we need an extensive basic set of relations in our language. This contention between expressiveness and complexity is a key problem of the theory of designing constraint languages.

In this chapter we present a theory both of the expressiveness and the complexity of constraint languages. We will be able to characterize both for constraint languages over finite domains.

We will also briefly consider other practical (nonstructural) restrictions to the general CSP problem that make it tractable.

11.1 The CSP Search Problem

In this chapter we have a single domain for all the variables in our problems. This really is a notational convenience as the actual domain of a variable is restricted by the constraint relations. It is possible to think of our unified domain as the union of all of the actual problem domains.

We will augment the usual definitions in this book with specific notations as follows:

DEFINITION   **(CSP instance)**
11.1
A constraint satisfaction problem instance P is a triple, $\langle X, D, C \rangle$, where

- X is a finite set of variables.
- D is any set (called the "domain" of P).
- C is a finite set of constraints $\{C_1, C_2, \ldots, C_q\}$. Each constraint C_i is a pair $\langle S_i, R_i \rangle$, where S_i is a tuple of variables of length m_i (the "constraint scope"), and R_i is an m_i-ary relation over D (the "constraint relation").•

As usual, for each constraint, $\langle S_i, R_i \rangle$, the tuples of R_i indicate the allowed combinations of simultaneous value assignments for the variables in S_i.

Because we are interested in complexity results, we also require the following:

DEFINITION   **(general CSP)**
11.2
The general CSP (search) problem is the following: Given a CSP P, as defined above, we are interested in finding a solution to P, or determining that there is no solution.   •

11.1.1 Restricting the General CSP

We can limit a general CSP in two essentially different ways. We can ask that the hypergraph formed by the constraint scopes (network scheme) has some property, or we might restrict the allowable constraint relations.

We will say that a subclass obtained by restricting the network scheme is a *structural* subclass. If, on the other hand, we restrict the form of the relations allowed when modeling a CSP, we say that we have restricted the CSP *language*. The set of allowed relations is then called the *constraint language*. We will call a class of CSPs obtained in this way a *relational* subclass.

Previous chapters have largely focused on structural properties of constraint networks, together with some hybrid properties of both structure and language. In this chapter we will mostly concentrate on the theory of constraint languages.

11.2 Constraint Languages

Before continuing, we need to formalize some of the definitions of the concepts introduced in the previous section.

DEFINITION 11.3

(constraint language)

A *constraint language* Γ is any set of relations over some (given) domain. We denote by $D(\Gamma)$ the domain of the constraint language Γ. •

For any constraint language Γ, we define the relational subclass, $\mathbf{C}_\Gamma$, of the general CSP restricted to the language Γ in the following way: A CSP instance $P = \langle X, D, C \rangle$ is in $\mathbf{C}_\Gamma$ if, for every constraint $\langle S, R \rangle \in C$, we have $R \in \Gamma$.

DEFINITION 11.4

(tractable)

We will say that a finite constraint language Γ is tractable if $\mathbf{C}_\Gamma$ has a polynomial algorithm that will solve all instances. For brevity we will call an individual relation R tractable if $\{R\}$ is tractable. We will say that an infinite constraint language is tractable if every finite subset of the language is tractable. •

EXAMPLE 11.1

Scheduling

In this example, we are going to construct a constraint language capable of describing a simple job shop. (The example is intended to demonstrate the concept of a constraint language rather than the best way to model a scheduling problem.)

We have a set of machines $\{M_1, \ldots, M_k\}$ and a set of jobs $\{J_1, \ldots, J_s\}$ to perform. We model the problem by defining two variables J_i^t and J_i^p for each job J_i, $i = 1, \ldots, s$. The value of the variable J_i^t indicates the time that job J_i starts, while the value of variable J_i^p indicates the machine that is used to complete job J_i. In the nature of such scheduling problems there are three kinds of constraints:

Machine Constraints

For each job there is a set of machines that is capable of doing the job. This is a unary constraint on each of the J_i^p variables.

Precedence Constraints

Some jobs must be completed before others can be started. This requires binary constraints on some pairs of job times. If job J_i must complete before job J_k can start, and job J_i requires t_i time to complete, then we have the constraint that $J_i^t + t_i < J_k^t$.

Rationality Constraints

Lastly we need to specify that a machine can only do one thing at a time. In other words two jobs can either occur on the same machine, or overlap in time, but not both. This is a 4-ary constraint involving the times and places of every pair of jobs. For job J_i and job J_k it is the constraint

$$\left(J_i^t + t_i < J_k^t\right) \vee \left(J_k^t + t_k < J_i^t\right) \vee \left(J_i^p \neq J_k^p\right).$$

The important observation is that we do not require to use all possible relations to be able to model our (simple) scheduling problems. We only require relations of three different "types." Perhaps it might be possible to optimize our algorithm to process these three types of constraint relations. It may be that certain types of local consistency are appropriate for these cases, or certain classes of backtracking.

Unfortunately, this language can be shown to be NP-hard. Luckily though, the machine and precedence constraints, without the rationality constraints, form a tractable language (they are *max-closed* constraints—see Example 11.4). This suggests a possible solution strategy: we can find solutions easily to the machine/precedence constraints and then try to extend them to solutions of the whole problem.   ●

EXAMPLE 11.2   The widely used constraint language CHIP incorporates a number of constraint-solving techniques for arithmetic and other constraints. In particular it provides an algorithm for a restricted class of constraints over natural numbers, referred to as *basic constraints*. These basic constraints are of two kinds, referred to as "domain constraints" and "arithmetic constraints". The domain constraints are unary constraints that restrict the value of a variable to some specified finite subset of the natural numbers. The arithmetic constraints are unary and binary constraints that have one of the following forms:

$$ax \neq b$$

$$ax = by + c$$

$$ax \leq by + c$$

$$ax \geq by + c$$

where variables are represented by the letters x and y, and constants by the letters a, b, and c. All constants are nonnegative integers, and a is a nonzero integer.

As we will see, this language is actually tractable (see Example 11.5). We can even extend this language by adding, for instance, the following constraint types:

$$a_1 x_1 + a_2 x_2 + \ldots + a_r x_r \geq by + c$$

$$a x_1 x_2 \ldots x_r \geq by + c$$

$$(a_1 x_1 \geq b_1) \vee (a_2 x_2 \geq b_2) \vee \ldots \vee (a_r x_r \geq b_r) \vee (ay \leq b)$$

and the resulting (larger, more expressive) language is still tractable. Amazingly, after ensuring arc-consistency for a problem in this language, we can find a solution in linear time, if one exists!   •

11.2.1 Tractable Constraint Languages

A naive discussion of constraint languages concentrates on just two parameters: the size of the domain and the arity of the constraint relations. Recall from Chapter 3 that if we restrict both the domain size and the arity of the relations to 2, then we get the tractable 2-SAT language (see Example 11.10 on page 307). However, if we allow even domain size 3, then we can already express the graph 3-colorability problem, which is NP-hard. If we keep the domain size to 2, but allow relations of arity 3, then we have the NP-hard language of 3-SAT.

On the other hand, we have seen in the previous section that much more expressive languages, such as the basic constraints in CHIP, can still be tractable. Clearly, it is the specific language composition, not just its domain size or simple arity, that makes a language tractable. The space of constraint languages is illustrated in Figure 11.1. The example languages later in this section are included to show the wide variety of known tractable constraint languages.

All the constraint languages in this section appear to be tractable for very different reasons. These languages do not, of themselves, indicate how we can direct our search for new tractable languages. In Section 11.4 we will partly solve this problem. We will give a straightforward necessary condition for a constraint language over a finite domain to be tractable. We will also give a number of sufficient conditions for a constraint language over a finite domain to be tractable. In particular, this theoretical work will provide a unified framework for all of the tractable languages of this section.

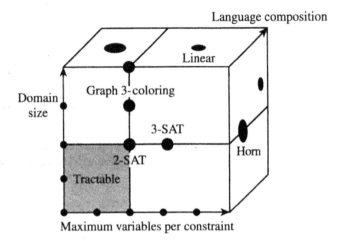

Figure 11.1   There is more to tractability than domain size and relation arity.

Examples of Tractable Languages

We now list a few examples of tractable languages. These are by no means all of the known tractable languages, but they are chosen to indicate the wide variety of reasons for tractability. One of the advantages of the CSP approach is that we unify problems from apparently diverse areas.

The first example is very straightforward. It describes a language that is clearly tractable, and where the proof of tractability is given as a solution algorithm. In Section 11.4, we will explain the tractability of all the languages mentioned in this section using a unifying algebraic theory.

EXAMPLE
11.3

Constant

Let D be any domain containing the value 0, and let Γ_0 be the class of all relations that allow the all 0s tuple, together with the empty relation. Clearly, we can solve a problem over this language by setting all variables to value 0. If this is a solution, then output the solution; otherwise report that there is no solution (because at least one constraint relation is empty).   •

EXAMPLE
11.4

Max-closed

Consider a domain D that is linearly ordered, and a binary function max defined on D in the obvious way:

$$max(a, b) \stackrel{\text{def}}{=} \begin{cases} a & \text{if } a > b \\ b & \text{otherwise} \end{cases}$$

We now extend *max* to *n*-tuples:

$$max(\langle a_1, \ldots, a_n \rangle, \langle b_1, \ldots, b_n \rangle) \stackrel{\text{def}}{=} \langle max(a_1, b_1), \ldots, max(a_n, b_n) \rangle$$

We call a relation R over D *max-closed*, if, whenever $\langle a_1, \ldots, a_n \rangle$ and $\langle b_1, \ldots, b_n \rangle$ are tuples in R, so is $max(\langle a_1, \ldots, a_n \rangle, \langle b_1, \ldots, b_n \rangle)$.

Finally, our language is the set of max-closed relations over D.

It turns out that if the constraint relations are max-closed, then the problem can be solved by establishing generalized arc-consistency. If any domain in the arc-consistent problem is empty, then there is no solution. Otherwise setting the value of each variable to its maximum remaining domain value is a solution.   •

EXAMPLE 11.5

The basic constraints of the CHIP language of Example 11.2 are in fact max-closed. So any set of equations of the form given in that example can be solved by establishing arc-consistency.

Consider a problem instance with domain $\{1, 2, 3, 4, 5\}$, variables $\{v, w, x, y, z\}$, and constraints

$$w \neq 3$$

$$z \neq 5$$

$$3v \leq z$$

$$y \geq z + 2$$

$$3x + y + z \geq 5w + 1$$

$$wz \geq 2y$$

After establishing arc-consistency, the domains are as follows:

$$D(v) = \{1\}, D(w) = \{4\}, D(x) = \{3, 4, 5\}, D(y) = \{5\}, \text{ and } D(z) = \{3\}$$

Since none of the domains is empty, we get the solution $v = 1$, $w = 4$, $x = 5$, $y = 5$, $z = 3$.   •

EXAMPLE 11.6

0/1/all or implicational

Let D be any finite domain. For any two subsets $A, B \subseteq D$:

- $A \times B$ is called *complete*.
- For any bijection $\pi : A \mapsto B$, $\{\langle a, \pi(a) \rangle : a \in A\}$ is called a *permutation*.
- For any values $x \in A, y \in B$, $(x \times B) \cup (A \times y)$ is called a *two-fan*.

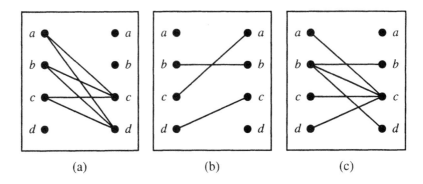

Figure 11.2 Three types of 0/1/all or implicational relations: (a) complete, (b) permutation, and (c) two-fan.

A *0/1/all* or *implicational* relation over D is, by definition, either complete, a permutation, or a two-fan. These three types of constraints are illustrated in Figure 11.2.[1]

Any CSP instance over this language can be solved by first establishing path-consistency. After this the instance can be solved without backtracking in quadratic time, using, for example, forward-checking.   •

It is often convenient to describe a relation as the set of solutions of some equation. The following definition formalizes this.

DEFINITION
11.5

Let D be a domain and P be a proposition or equation, and let $l = \langle x_1, \ldots, x_k \rangle$ be some ordering for the free variables of P. Define the relation $R(P, l)$ by

$$R(P, l) \stackrel{\text{def}}{=} \{ \langle d_1, \ldots, d_k \rangle \in D^k \mid x_1 := d_1, \ldots, x_k := d_k \text{ is a solution of } P \}$$

We then say that P and l define the k-ary relation $R(P, l)$.   •

EXAMPLE
11.7

Over the domain of integers modulo 2, the equation $x + y + z = 1$, together with the ordering $\langle x, y, z \rangle$, defines the ternary relation

$$\{ \langle 0, 0, 1 \rangle, \langle 0, 1, 0 \rangle, \langle 1, 0, 0 \rangle, \langle 1, 1, 1 \rangle \}$$

---

1. Relations are shown diagrammatically by drawing a single point for each domain value for each position of the relation, and then connecting two points if the corresponding combination of values is allowed, as in Chapter 2.

Over the Boolean domain, $\{0, 1\}$, where 0 corresponds to the Boolean value *false* and 1 corresponds to the Boolean value *true*, the proposition $x \Rightarrow (y \vee z)$, together with the ordering $\langle z, y, x \rangle$, defines the relation

$$\{\langle 0,0,0 \rangle, \langle 0,1,0 \rangle, \langle 0,1,1 \rangle, \langle 1,0,0 \rangle, \langle 1,0,1 \rangle, \langle 1,1,0 \rangle, \langle 1,1,1 \rangle\}$$

which is also defined by the clause $\neg z \vee x \vee y$ with order $\langle x, y, z \rangle$. •

We can now consider the language of general linear constraints. The CSP instances over this language correspond exactly to sets of simultaneous linear equations.

EXAMPLE 11.8

Linear constraints

Let D be any field (for instance, the real numbers, or the integers modulo p for some prime p). A *linear relation* is any relation defined by a linear equation over D, that is, a relation defined by an equation of the form $a_1 x_1 + \ldots + a_k x_k = r$, where $a_1, \ldots, a_k, r \in D$. Gaussian elimination is a polynomial algorithm for the language consisting of all linear relations. •

The tractability of the next problem class is well-known in logic programming and is the basis for the usefulness of the programming language Prolog.

EXAMPLE 11.9

Horn-SAT

Let D be the Boolean domain $\{0, 1\}$. A *Horn relation* is a relation over D defined by a Horn clause, which is a clause with at most one nonnegated literal. In other words, a Horn relation is a relation defined by a formula of the form $p_0 \vee \neg p_1 \vee \neg p_2 \vee \ldots \vee \neg p_k$. We saw in Chapter 3 that unit resolution will solve any set of Horn clauses in polynomial time. •

EXAMPLE 11.10

2-SAT

Let D be the Boolean domain $\{0, 1\}$. A *2-SAT relation* is a relation over D defined by a clause containing at most two literals, that is, a relation defined by a formula of the form $q_1 \vee q_2$ or just q_1. We saw in Chapters 3 and 8 that resolution, which is guaranteed to solve SAT problems, is polynomial for this class. •

The class of row-convex constraints was first described by van Beek and Dechter (1995). These constraints can be used to describe a hybrid (neither relational nor structural) tractable subclass of the general CSP problem (see Chapter 8 and Section 11.5 in this chapter). Unfortunately they do not form a tractable language since further conditions are necessary in order to ensure the tractability of problems involving row-convex constraints. On the other hand, the following more restricted constraint language is tractable.

EXAMPLE   **Connected Row Convex**
11.11
Let D be any totally ordered domain. We associate with each binary relation R on D^2 a square matrix M_R, with $M_R[d, e] = 1 \Leftrightarrow (d, e) \in R$. The order of the rows and columns of M_R is determined by the ordering on D.

A 0/1 matrix is row convex if, in each of its rows, the 1s are consecutive.

A 0/1 matrix is *connected row convex* if, after removing empty rows, it is row convex and connected (i.e., the positions of the 1s in two consecutive rows intersect or are consecutive).

A binary relation R is connected row convex if both M_R and M_R^T are connected row convex.

Any CSP instance over the language consisting of connected row-convex relations can be solved by first establishing path-consistency. A solution can then be found in a simple backtrack-free manner. The algorithm is the same as that used to solve implicational constraint problems. The reason that the same algorithm works for both examples will be made clear in Section 11.4, which will unify these two classes.   ●

11.3 Expressiveness of Constraint Languages

In the introduction to this chapter we described the key problems of constraint languages to be those of expressiveness and complexity. In this section we will give a complete description of the set of relations that can be expressed in any given constraint language over a finite domain.

In fact we will describe a family of *gadgets* for expressing relations. Each gadget will itself be a constraint satisfaction problem over the language of concern. We will show how these gadgets can be used to construct any expressible relation.

The same gadgets will also be used in Section 11.4 to determine the complexity of a constraint langauge.

11.3.1 Gadgets for Expressing Relations

First, we formally define what it means to express a relation in a constraint language.

DEFINITION   We say that a constraint language Γ is able to express a relation R if there
11.6   exists a constraint satisfaction problem $P = \langle X, D, C \rangle \in C_\Gamma$ and a list of variables L from X such that the projection of the solutions of P onto the list L is the relation R. We call P a *gadget* for expressing R in C_Γ, and we call L the *construction site* for R.

Formally, Γ *expresses* R if R is a relation over $D(\Gamma)$, and

$$\exists P = \langle X, D, C \rangle \in \mathbf{C}_\Gamma, \quad \text{and} \quad \exists x_1, \ldots, x_k \in X,$$
$$\text{such that } \pi_{\langle x_1, \ldots, x_k \rangle}(\text{Sol}(P)) = R \qquad \bullet$$

This definition means that we can express the relation R in the language Γ if and only if R is the projection of the set of solutions to some problem instance in $\mathbf{C}_\Gamma$.

For notational simplicity in our models, and for ease of construction of solving algorithms, it is desirable to keep the number of relations in a constraint language as small as possible. Any relation that is expressible in a language does not have to be included explicitly because we can exclude it without affecting the set of problems that can be modeled in the language. This concept is best understood using an example.

EXAMPLE 11.12   Consider the constraint satisfaction problem of Figure 11.3, over the domain $\{R, G, B\}$. The question is, as a gadget it expresses some relation on the construction site $\langle P, Q \rangle$. What is this relation?

First consider the case when the variable P is assigned value R. It follows that neither V nor W may have value R, and since they must have different values from each other, exactly one must take value B, and one value G. It follows immediately that Q must now take value R. By the symmetry of the problem we see that this gadget actually expresses the binary equality relation.

So, over a domain with three elements, any language containing the binary "not-equals" relation, $\neq$, is able to express the binary equality relation.

Any constraint language that includes the binary not-equals relation, $\neq$, can therefore make use of a gadget for the binary equality relation instead of including the relation itself. $\qquad \bullet$

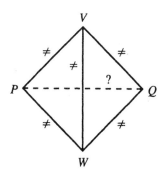

Figure 11.3 An example gadget. What is expressed at the construction site $\langle P, Q \rangle$?

The previous example demonstrates that it is a hard enough problem to determine exactly what is expressed by a given gadget. It is clearly harder to construct a gadget for a given relation, or even to work out if such a gadget exists.

11.3.2   A Universal Gadget for Finite Domains

In this section we will give a characterization of expressible relations for languages over finite domains. In fact we give a class of gadgets that are adequate to express any expressible relation in any given finite domain language.

The construction is complicated, but it is worth persevering because of its remarkable properties. It is called both the *indicator problem*, since its solutions indicate the complexity of a constraint langauge, and the *universal gadget*, since it can be used to construct arbitrary expressible relations.

DEFINITION 11.7   We define the *k*th-order *indicator problem* $I_k(\Gamma)$, for $k \geq 1$, over a language Γ as the following problem instance in $\mathbf{C}_\Gamma$:

- The variables of $I_k(\Gamma)$ correspond to all the *k*-tuples of the domain of Γ. We call the *k*-tuple associated with variable v the *name* of v, and denote the ith component of the name $v[i]$.

- The *name relation* of a list of variables $\langle v_1, \ldots, v_n \rangle$ in $I_k(\Gamma)$ is the *n*-ary relation $\{\langle v_1[i], \ldots, v_n[i] \rangle, i = 1, \ldots, k\}$, defined by the components of their names.

- An *n*-ary relation R *matches* a list of variables $\langle v_1, \ldots, v_n \rangle$ in $I_k(\Gamma)$ if and only if the name relation of $\langle v_1, \ldots, v_n \rangle$ is a subset of R.

- For each *n*-ary relation $R \in \Gamma$, and each *n*-tuple of variables S, $I_k(\Gamma)$ has the constraint $\langle S, R \rangle$ if and only if R matches S.   •

Now we can state the result that solves the expressibility problem for finite domains.

THEOREM 11.1   Let Γ be a constraint language over a finite domain D, and let R be any relation over D.

Let k be the number of rows in R, and let L_R be any list of variables in $I_k(\Gamma)$ whose name relation is R. Either

- $I_k(\Gamma)$ is a gadget for expressing R, with construction site L_R, or
- R is not expressible in Γ.   •

To demonstrate the use of this result we will now solve two expressibility problems.

EXAMPLE 11.13   Can $\Rightarrow$ (logical implication) be expressed in the Boolean language $\{\neg, \oplus\}$ (logical not, exclusive or)?

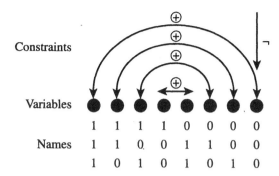

Figure 11.4 The third-order indicator problem for the Boolean language comprising unary not (¬) and exclusive or (⊕). This indicator problem has five constraints. Double-headed arrows indicate the scope of constraints with relation ⊕, and the single-headed arrow indicates the scope of the constraint with relation ¬.

Since the "implies" relation, ⇒, has three rows (there are three satisfying assignments in its truth table), we will use the indicator problem of order 3 as a gadget. This indicator problem is shown in Figure 11.4. According to the definition of this indicator problem, we should have a constraint with relation ⊕ on exactly those pairs of variables that the relation ⊕ matches, and similarly we should have a unary constraint with relation ¬ on exactly those variables whose name relation only contains ⟨0⟩s. In the figure, the double-headed arrows indicate the scope of the constraints whose relations are ⊕, and the single-headed arrow indicates the scope of the constraint whose relation is ¬. It is straightforward to check the name relations of these scopes to see that the associated constraint relations match them.

Consider the two variables v and w whose names are ⟨1, 0, 0⟩ and ⟨1, 0, 1⟩, respectively (these are the fourth and third variables from the left in Figure 11.4). The three tuples of the name relation of ⟨v, w⟩ are ⟨0, 0⟩, ⟨0, 1⟩, and ⟨1, 1⟩, so the name relation of ⟨v, w⟩ is the "implies" relation, ⇒.

Theorem 11.1 states that either this gadget constructs the relation ⇒ on the construction site ⟨v, w⟩, or else ⇒ cannot be expressed in this language. Now all we need to do is to solve the constraint satisfaction problem shown in Figure 11.4 and consider the values of solutions on ⟨v, w⟩.

The solutions are shown in Table 11.1, in which the construction site is in boldface. It can be seen that all four possible assignments to the two variables in the construction site can be extended to solutions of the whole constraint satisfaction problem.

Table 11.1 Solutions to the third-order indicator problem for the language $\{\neg, \oplus\}$. A construction site for $\Rightarrow$ is in boldface. The first four solutions show that the relation $\Rightarrow$ is not expressible in this language.

Variable names							
1	1	**1**	**1**	0	0	0	0
1	1	**0**	**0**	1	1	0	0
1	0	**1**	**0**	1	0	1	0
Solution							
1	0	**1**	**1**	0	0	1	0
1	0	**1**	**0**	1	0	1	0
1	0	**0**	**1**	0	1	1	0
1	0	**0**	**0**	1	1	1	0
1	1	**1**	**1**	0	0	0	0
1	1	**1**	**0**	1	0	0	0
1	1	**0**	**1**	0	1	0	0
1	1	**0**	**0**	1	1	0	0

It follows that this gadget actually expresses the complete relation, $D \times D$, at this site. So we can deduce from Theorem 11.1 that the relation $\Rightarrow$ is *not* expressible in the language $\{\neg, \oplus\}$.   •

EXAMPLE 11.14   Over a domain of size 3, can the binary equality relation be expressed in the language just containing the binary not-equals relation?

The equality relation has three satisfying tuples, so we need to construct the indicator problem of order 3. This problem, shown in part in Figure 11.5, has 27 variables and 108 constraints.

It is easy to check that the projection of all solutions onto any valid construction site gives the binary equality relation. Hence, the binary equality relation can be expressed in this language.

In fact, we have already seen a gadget for expressing the equality relation using this language in Example 11.12. That example used just four variables and five constraints. This shows that we may not get the smallest possible gadget from Theorem 11.1.   •

It is surprising that a single gadget can be used to derive all expressible relations (of a given size) for a constraint language. However, it is not the whole answer,

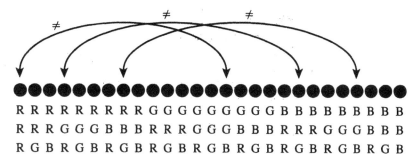

27 variables with their names

Figure 11.5 Using the third-order indicator problem to express binary equality from binary not-equals.

as the size of the indicator problem is exponential in the number of rows of the expressed relation. That is, for a relation with k rows over a domain of size d, we construct a gadget with d^k variables. This is even the case when the relation to be expressed is already contained in the constraint language! (In this case we could simply use the relation as its own gadget.)

It is an open research question to identify when it is possible to find smaller (i.e., not exponential) gadgets for constructing the expressible relations for a given language.

11.4 **Complexity of Constraint Languages**

Having obtained a characterization of the expressiveness of any constraint language over a finite domain, we now move on to the problem of determining the complexity of the relational subclass of constraint networks defined over such a language.

The gadget that we used to express any relation that can be expressed in a language over a finite domain was the indicator problem. Luckily, the set of solutions to the same indicator problems can also be used to determine the complexity of the language.

11.4.1 **Why Develop a Theory of Tractability?**

Before introducing the theory it is useful briefly to discuss the concept.

Algorithm Selector

For any constraint language, what we actually want is an algorithm for solving problems in the language. Actually we want the most efficient such algorithm. In any practical sense, then, a general theory of tractability of constraint languages is useful only if it suggests an algorithm for tractable languages. A theory that merely identifies all tractable languages will be of theoretical interest but of little practical value. We present a theory of the tractability of languages over finite domains that does indeed suggest an algorithm for each of them. It explains and unifies all of the finite domain examples in Section 11.2.1.

Maximal Languages

If any language is tractable, then certainly any subset of the language is tractable: we simply use the same algorithm to solve the subset in polynomial time. For this reason we are interested only in maximal tractable languages. A maximal tractable language is tractable, but if we add even a single new relation, then we get an intractable language. It is basic languages for expressing these maximal tractable languages that are the very best that can be offered as the basis for a constraint solver with a performance guarantee.

Determining whether a tractable language is maximal is in general very hard. If we only have a proof of tractability because we have a polynomial algorithm, then we can ask, "What other relations can I add to my language and still have this algorithm work?" If there are no such relations, then we may be tempted to assume that our language is indeed a maximal tractable language. But, we may have not chosen the right algorithm! Perhaps there is a better algorithm that solves a superset of this constraint language.

It is the unifying nature of the theory, the proofs of maximality that it offers, and the fact that it provides an algorithm selector that make the algebraic theory presented in Sections 11.4.3, 11.4.5, and 11.4.6 so significant.

11.4.2 Tractable Constraint Languages over a Domain with Two Elements

If Γ is a set of relations over a domain with two elements, then we may assume that the domain is the set $\{0, 1\}$ and that 0 corresponds to the Boolean value *false* and that 1 corresponds to the Boolean value *true*. The problem C_Γ is then sometimes called the *generalized satisfiability problem* over the set of Boolean relations Γ.

The tractability of the languages over a two-element domain is completely understood, and there is a dichotomy theorem for this domain.

THEOREM 11.2 Let Γ be a set of relations over the two-element domain $\{0, 1\}$. The problem C_Γ is NP-complete unless *every* relation in Γ either

1. allows the tuple $\langle 0, 0, \ldots, 0 \rangle$;

2. allows the tuple $\langle 1, 1, \ldots, 1 \rangle$;

3. is definable by a formula in conjunctive normal form in which each conjunct has at most one negated variable;

4. is definable by a formula in conjunctive normal form in which each conjunct has at most one unnegated variable;

5. is definable by a formula in conjunctive normal form in which each conjunct contains at most two literals;

6. is the set of solutions to some system of linear equations over GF(2).[2]   •

This dichotomy theorem is astounding. It defines six constraint languages and states that any set of relations that is not contained in one of these six is NP-hard.

Five of the six classes identified in Theorem 11.2 seem natural to logicians. The sixth class, consisting of solutions to linear equations, does not seem so natural in this context. A common framework for these six classes is provided by the unifying algebraic theory that we will present in Sections 11.4.5 and 11.4.6.

The original proof of Theorem 11.2 by Schaefer (1978) involved a case analysis that showed that any class of propositions not contained in one of these six languages can be used to express hard propositions and so is not tractable. This long proof has been greatly simplified in the algebraic approach.

It is not hard to show that the six classes mentioned in the theorem are all tractable; the hard part is to show that there are no other tractable constraint languages over a two-valued domain.

The tractability of classes 1 and 2 is clear (see Example 11.3). Three of the other four classes are well-known to be tractable for the following reasons:

- Class 4 is the satisfiability problem Horn-SAT (see Example 11.9);

- Class 5 is the satisfiability problem 2-SAT (see Example 11.10);

- Class 6 is solvable using, for instance, Gaussian elimination (see Example 11.8).

Class 3 is solvable using similar methods to those used for solving Horn-SAT problems. We may, perhaps, call it anti-Horn-SAT!

---

2. GF(2) is the unique field with two elements and can be thought of as arithmetic modulo 2; that is, $1 + 1 = 0$. It is well-defined to write and solve linear equations in modulo 2 arithmetic.

Of course, having a dichotomy result for the two-valued domain just motivates the search for such a result over larger finite, or perhaps infinite, domains. The holy grail of research into the complexity of constraint languages is a dichotomy theorem of this type for all constraint languages.

11.4.3   Tractability and Reduced Languages

When considering individual constraint networks, we have seen in previous chapters that it can be effective to enforce some level of consistency before searching for a solution. There is an analogous procedure for constraint languages. If a language has certain properties, then we may be able to reduce its domain and so simplify problems over the language. We will replace every relation over the original domain with a new relation over the reduced domain.

We are able to work in the reduced language, and so simplify the problems we are dealing with, so long as any problem instance has a solution in the reduced domain if and only if it has a solution in the original domain.

The possibility of such a reduction is determined by the existence of certain kinds of functions. These so-called squashing functions map sets of domain elements to a single representative from the set.

DEFINITION
11.8

Let Γ be a constraint language, and let $D = D(\Gamma)$ be the domain of Γ. Suppose that $D = \bigcup_{i=1}^{n} D_i$ where the D_i are mutually disjoint, and that $r_i \in D_i, i = 1, \ldots, n$. Furthermore, at least one of the sets D_i must contain at least two elements. Define $\mu : D \to D$, which takes each $x \in D_i$ to the value r_i.

Given a relation R, we say that μ is a squashing function for R if, for any $(x_1, \ldots, x_k)$ in R, we have that $(\mu(x_1), \ldots, \mu(x_k))$ is also in R.

We say that μ is a squashing function for Γ if it is a squashing function for every R in Γ.

When μ is a squashing function for Γ we define the squashed domain to be $\mu(D) = \{r_1, \ldots, r_n\}$, we define the squashed relation for any $R \in \Gamma$ to be

$$\mu(R) = \{(\mu(x_1), \ldots, \mu(x_k)) | (x_1, \ldots, x_k) \in R\}$$

and the squashed language $\mu(\Gamma)$ over $\mu(D)$ is the set of squashed relations.

●

We can use the first-order indicator problem for Γ to find any possible squashing functions, as explained below. Discovery of the squashing functions and application of the reductions has been shown to be achievable in time dependent only on the domain size.

If a nontrivial squashing function exists, we call a language *reducible*. After applying any possible reductions, we end up with a reduced constraint language. Since at least one of the sets D_i has two elements, the reduced domain is smaller than the original domain.

Not only is the tractability theory simpler for reduced languages, but we never want to work too hard when solving constraint problems so we are only interested in reduced languages. In the next sections we will only consider the tractability of reduced constraint languages.

11.4.4 Maximal Tractable Languages

The next result shows that adding all expressible relations to a constraint language does not alter its tractability.

THEOREM 11.3 Let Γ be a tractable language over a finite domain, and let Δ be the set of relations expressible over Γ. Then $\Gamma \cup \Delta$ is also a tractable language.   •

This theorem implies that a *maximal* tractable constraint language will be exactly the set of expressible relations over some base tractable language. It has been shown that each of these sets is exactly the set of *invariant relations of an algebraic clone*. Such sets are known as *relational clones* and are beyond the scope of this introductory chapter. We simply note that the study of maximal tractable constraint languages is really the study of relational clones.

Relational clones have been much studied in universal algebra, and quite a lot is known about their structure. Some of these known algebraic results can be adapted to obtain proofs of the results about tractable constraint languages given in the next two subsections.

11.4.5 A Necessary Condition for Tractability over a Finite Domain

In this section we will determine a necessary condition for a reduced language over a finite domain to be tractable. This condition will depend on a classification of the possible types of solutions to the indicator problems. Results of this type arise from the algebraic study of relational clones and are most easily expressed using the notion of k-ary operations.

DEFINITION 11.9 A k-ary *operation* from D^k to D is any mapping that assigns a member of D to each k-tuple of elements from D.   •

There are many simple examples of k-ary operations.

**EXAMPLE
11.15**

Let D be the set of real numbers. Define the 3-ary operation *mid*, which chooses the middle (in size) of its three arguments. So, for instance, $mid(3, 4, 17) = mid(17, 3, 4) = 4$.   •

Every k-tuple of domain values is the name of exactly one variable in the kth-order indicator problem so each solution to the kth-order indicator problem is in fact a k-ary operation.

**DEFINITION
11.10**

Let s be any solution to the kth-order indicator problem for Γ over domain D. We define the associated k-ary operation $\hat{s}$ as follows: The value of $\hat{s}(x)$ is the value assigned to the variable with name x in the solution s.   •

Many results about the complexity of a constraint language have been reduced to statements about the operations associated with the solutions to indicator problems. Naturally we need to define some particular types of operations.

**DEFINITION
11.11**

Let φ be a k-ary operation from D^k to D.

- If φ is such that, for all $d \in D$, $\varphi(d, d, \ldots, d) = d$, then φ is said to be *idempotent*.

- If there exists an index $i \in \{1, 2, \ldots, k\}$ such that for all $\langle d_1, d_2, \ldots, d_n \rangle \in D^k$, we have $\varphi(d_1, d_2, \ldots, d_n) = f(d_i)$, where f is a nonconstant operation on D, then φ is called *essentially unary*. If f is the identity operation, then φ is a *projection*.

- If $k \geq 3$ and there exists an index $i \in \{1, 2, \ldots, k\}$ such that for all $d_1, d_2, \ldots, d_k \in D$ with $|\{d_1, d_2, \ldots, d_k\}| < k$ we have $\varphi(d_1, d_2, \ldots, d_k) = d_i$, but φ is not a projection, then φ is called a *semi-projection*.

- If $k = 3$ and for all $d, d' \in D$, we have $\varphi(d, d, d') = \varphi(d, d', d) = \varphi(d', d, d) = d$, then φ is called a *majority operation*.

- If $k = 3$ and for all $d_1, d_2, d_3 \in D$ we have $\varphi(d_1, d_2, d_3) = d_1 - d_2 + d_3$, where $+$ and $-$ are binary operations on D such that $\langle D, +, - \rangle$ is an Abelian group, then φ is called an *affine operation*.   •

We can now present a necessary condition for reduced languages over finite domains to be tractable.

**THEOREM
11.4**

Assuming that P is not equal to NP, any tractable constraint language over a finite domain must have a solution to an indicator problem associated with either a constant operation, or a majority operation, or an idempotent binary operation, or an affine operation, or a semi-projection.   •

This result simplifies a great deal for a domain with two elements since over such a domain there are no semi-projections. In this case all of the necessary operations have arity at most 3, and we can determine tractability by examining solutions to the third-order indicator problem, as described in the following example.

EXAMPLE 11.16

The complexity of any language over a domain of size 2 can be determined by considering only the solutions to its third-order indicator problem. In fact the language is intractable unless the third-order indicator problem has one of exactly six specific solutions. Furthermore, each of these six solutions indicates which algorithm will solve the problems in the constraint language. These six solutions correspond to the six maximal tractable classes discovered by Schaefer (Theorem 11.2) and are shown in Table 11.2. In each case we specify to which of Schaefer's six tractable classes the language belongs.

The third-order indicator problem for the tractable language $\{\oplus, \neg\}$ is given in Figure 11.4, and for the intractable language $\{(p \vee q \vee r) \wedge (\neg p \vee \neg q \vee \neg r)\}$, in Figure 11.6.

The solutions to these problems are given in Table 11.3. It is easy to check that none of the six possible solutions that give tractability occur for the intractable language. The solution that guarantees tractability for the tractable langauge is in boldface and is actually a majority operation. •

In the general case, Theorem 11.4 gives us a necessary condition for tractability based on the existence of certain associated operations with arity at most $|D|$.

Table 11.2 The solutions to the third-order indicator problem for a Boolean language tell us what algorithm to use, or tell us that the langauge is NP-hard. The six "tractable" solutions are named here.

Variable names									
1	1	1	1	0	0	0	0		
1	1	0	0	1	1	0	0		
1	0	1	0	1	0	1	0		

Solution								Schaefer's class	Name
0	0	0	0	0	0	0	0	1	Constant 0
1	1	1	1	1	1	1	1	2	Constant 1
1	1	1	1	1	1	0	0	3	Anti-Horn
1	1	0	0	0	0	0	0	4	Horn-SAT
1	1	1	0	1	0	0	0	5	2-SAT
1	0	0	1	0	1	1	0	6	Linear

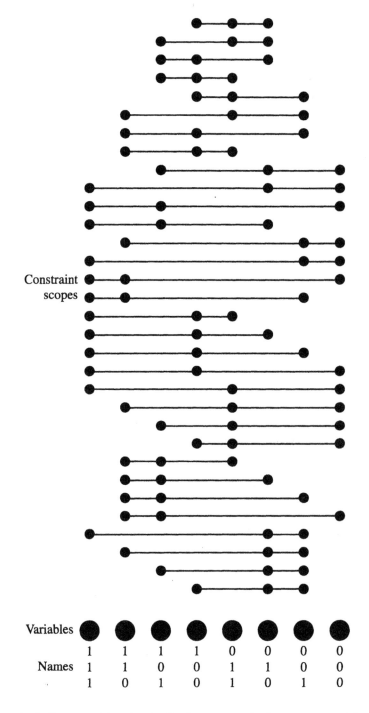

Figure 11.6 The third-order indicator problem for the Boolean constraint language containing only the (symmetric) ternary relation defined by $(p \vee q \vee r) \wedge (\neg p \vee \neg q \vee \neg r)$. This indicator problem should also have eight binary not equals constraints, arising from ternary scopes with repeated variables. They have been omitted (for clarity), see Exercise 10.

Table 11.3 The solutions to the third-order indicator problems for two Boolean languages. Checking against Table 11.2 shows that the language $\{\oplus, \neg\}$ is tractable (class 5), and that the language $\{(p \vee q \vee r) \wedge (\neg p \vee \neg q \vee \neg r)\}$ is not.

Variable names							
1	1	1	1	0	0	0	0
1	1	0	0	1	1	0	0
1	0	1	0	1	0	1	0
Solutions of I_3 ($\{\oplus, \neg\}$)							
1	0	0	0	1	1	1	0
1	0	0	1	0	1	1	0
1	0	1	0	1	0	1	0
1	0	1	1	0	0	1	0
1	1	0	0	1	1	0	0
1	1	0	1	0	1	0	0
1	**1**	**1**	**0**	**1**	**0**	**0**	**0**
1	1	1	1	0	0	0	0
Solutions of I_3 ($((p \vee q \vee r) \wedge (\neg p \vee \neg q \vee \neg r))$)							
0	0	0	0	1	1	1	1
1	1	1	1	0	0	0	0
1	0	1	0	1	0	1	0
0	1	0	1	0	1	0	1
0	0	1	1	0	0	1	1
1	1	0	0	1	1	0	0

This implies that we can employ the versatile indicator problem to give a straightforward test for intractability.

COROLLARY 11.1 For any set of relations Γ over a finite domain D, with $|D| \geq 3$, if all solutions to $I_{|D|}(\Gamma)$ are essentially unary, then $\mathbf{C}_\Gamma$ is NP-complete. •

11.4.6 Sufficient Conditions for Tractability

Many tractable languages over finite domains are known, and some examples were given at the start of this chapter in Section 11.2.1.

In this section we will describe some of the known tractable languages in terms of the solutions to their indicator problems. Each example we give will be a class of maximal tractable languages that extends one or more of the examples given in Section 11.2.1. In all of these cases tractability happens to be guaranteed simply by the existence of a single solution of a particular kind to an indicator problem.

It is convenient to define the following:

DEFINITION 11.12   Given any k-ary operation $\varphi : D^k \to D$, we say that a relation R *allows* φ if φ is a solution to the kth-order indicator problem for $\{R\}$.

We define $Inv(\varphi) \overset{\text{def}}{=} \{R \mid R \text{ allows } \varphi\}$.   ●

In all of the following cases of tractable languages, D is any finite domain.

Constant Operations

- Let κ be any constant operation (with one argument) on D.
- Let $\Gamma = Inv(\kappa)$

Γ is a maximal tractable language. If any problem instance in $\mathbf{C}_\Gamma$ has a constraint with an empty relation, then it has no solution. Otherwise, setting all variables to the value $\kappa(x)$ gives a solution.

Example 11.3, the constant language, falls into this class since its first-order indicator problem has solution $\kappa(x) = 0$.

Semilattice Operations

- Let $\otimes$ be any binary operation that satisfies
  - $\forall x, y, z \in D, (x \otimes y) \otimes z = x \otimes (y \otimes z)$ (Associativity)
  - $\forall x, y \in D, x \otimes y = y \otimes x$ (Commutativity)
  - $\forall x \in D, x \otimes x = x$ (Idempotency)
- Let $\Gamma = Inv(\otimes)$

Γ is a maximal tractable language. The following procedure solves any problem instance $P \in \mathbf{C}_\Gamma$:

1. Establish generalized arc-consistency.
2. If any domain is empty, then P has no solutions.
3. Otherwise, return the solution that assigns to variable v with domain $\{d_1, \ldots, d_k\}$, the value $d_1 \otimes \cdots \otimes d_k$.

Example 11.4, the max-closed language, falls into this class since *max* is an associative, commutative, idempotent operation that is a solution to its second-order indicator problem.

Example 11.9, the Horn-SAT language, falls into this class of tractable languages since

$$\wedge(a,b) \stackrel{\text{def}}{=} \begin{cases} \textit{false} & \text{if} \quad \textit{false} \in \{a,b\} \\ \textit{true} & \text{otherwise} \end{cases}$$

is an associative, commutative, idempotent operation that is a solution to its second-order indicator problem.

Near-Unanimity Operations

- Let v be any k-ary operation that, if all but at most one of its arguments have the same value, returns that value.
- Let $\Gamma = Inv(v)$.

Γ is a tractable language. If $k = 3$, then Γ is a maximal tractable language. A possible algorithm for C_Γ is simply to make any instance $P \in C_\Gamma$ strong k-consistent, as it can be shown that this will always give a new instance P' that is globally consistent.

Example 11.6, the 0/1/all or implicational language, falls into this class of tractable languages since

$$v_0(a,b,c) \stackrel{\text{def}}{=} \begin{cases} b & \text{if} \quad b=c \\ a & \text{otherwise} \end{cases}$$

is a ternary near-unanimity (majority) operation[3] that is a solution to its third-order indicator problem.

Example 11.10, the 2-SAT language, falls into this class of tractable languages since v_0 is a solution to its third-order indicator problem.

Example 11.11, the CRC language, falls into this class since the majority operation, $mid(a,b,c)$, which returns the middle of its three arguments with respect to the order on the domain, is a solution to its third-order indicator problem.

Affine Operations

- Let $+$ be any binary operation that makes D into a finite Abelian group, and let $\nabla(d_1, d_2, d_3) \stackrel{\text{def}}{=} d_1 - d_2 + d_3$.
- Let $\Gamma = Inv(\nabla)$.

Γ is a maximal tractable language.

---

3. This operation is known in universal algebra as the "dual discriminator."

Example 11.8, the linear constraints language (when the domain is finite), falls into this class since ∇ is a solution to its third-order indicator problem.

The different examples of tractable languages presented in Section 11.2.1 appeared to have no unifying principle, but we have now shown that they have a common structural feature involving solutions to an associated indicator problem.

We now have a much better understanding of the questions of expressiveness and complexity: it is the solutions to the indicator problems of a constraint language that hold the answers to both questions.

11.4.7   **Necessary and Sufficient Conditions for Tractability**

We would ideally like to find some condition on a language over a finite domain that is both necessary and sufficient for tractability.

At present we have a straightforward test for intractability, Corollary 11.1. We also have many examples of tractable languages. However, many languages fail the test for intractability, and yet we have no demonstration that they are tractable.

The problem of identifying tractable languages is completely solved for domain size 2. Schaefer's result, Theorem 11.2, is a true dichotomy, and in this case we see that every tractable language can be identified by the existence of a single solution to one of its indicator problems.

Over larger domains many known tractable languages are tractable because their set of associated operations contains one of a particular kind. It is the existence of this associated operation that guarantees tractability. We can find this operation associated with the language, and it tells us what solution technique to use to solve all instances of that relational subclass.

However, it may be that for larger domains there are further kinds of associated operations ensuring tractability, which are currently unknown. Also, in some cases it may be that a collection of several associated operations is needed to ensure tractability. It is therefore still an open research problem to obtain a complete classification of complexity for languages over arbitrary finite domains.

11.5   **Hybrid Tractability**

To determine whether a constraint problem lies in a structural class, we have only to consider the underlying hypergraph. To determine whether it lies in a relational class, we have only to consider the language of the problem instance. However, there are some important classes of tractable constraint satisfaction problems that are neither structural nor relational.

As yet there is no unifying principle for the hybrid cases. This of course makes them more intriguing. Would a unifying description of hybrid results link together the structural and relational classes?

In this section we give just three well-known examples and leave it to the interested reader to solve the research problem of how they are related to the examples in the previous sections. These three classes have already been discussed in earlier chapters. They are described here to contrast them with the tractable constraint languages described earlier.

The first example is an apparently structural subclass. It gives a condition for tractability based on the graph width of the underlying graph of a binary constraint satisfaction problem. However, we shall show here that it is not purely structural.

EXAMPLE 11.17

Let G be a graph with vertices V and edges E. Given an ordering $<$ on V, we define the predecessors of x with respect to $<$ as

$$\{y \in V \mid y < x \wedge \{y, x\} \in E\}$$

Recall that the width of the ordering is the maximum size of a predecessor set for the vertices of the graph. The width of the graph is the minimum of all the widths of the possible orderings of its vertices.

If the underlying graph of a binary constraint problem has width k and the problem is strong $(k + 1)$-consistent, then it is globally consistent. This result is not purely structural because the process of establishing strong $(k + 1)$-consistency may increase the width of the constraint problem instance. Hence we cannot decide whether a given instance is in this tractable class solely by considering the underlying hypergraph.   •

Our second example class is, on the face of it, entirely relational. It appears that we are limiting ourselves to a particular relational language and showing the tractability of all problems over that language. However, a close examination reveals that this is in fact a hybrid case as it requires some structural component in order to guarantee tractability.

EXAMPLE 11.18

Consider two ordered sets D_v and D_w and $R \subseteq D_v \times D_w$. We can express R as a $\{0, 1\}$-matrix M_R. We simply set $M_R[i, j] = 1$ if and only if $\langle v_i, w_j \rangle \in R$, where v_i is the ith element of D_v, and w_j is the jth element of D_w.

A $\{0, 1\}$-matrix is *row convex* if and only if, in each row of the matrix, all the 1s are consecutive; that is, no two 1s in the same row are separated by a 0 in that row. This definition of row convexity extends in the natural way to binary constraints (given an ordering of the domain at each variable).

For any path-consistent binary CSP, if there exist orderings of all domains that make all of the constraint relations row convex, then the CSP is globally consistent.

Unfortunately, it is possible to have a row-convex constraint problem that, when made path-consistent, does not remain row convex. So, we cannot state that the *language* of row-convex relations is tractable. In fact this constraint language has been shown to be NP-hard.   •

Our third and last example is a tractable class that depends only on counting.

EXAMPLE   Given any constraint problem C with domain size d and maximum con-
11.19   straint arity r, then if C is strong $d(r + 1)$-consistent, it is globally consistent.

This result is clearly hybrid, since the tractability depends on the domain size, the constraint arity, and a certain level of consistency.   •

11.6 Summary

This chapter has introduced the notion of a relational subclass of the general constraint satisfaction problem defined over a constraint language. When this language is over a finite domain, we have shown that the expressibility problem is solved, and we have presented a unifying framework for solving the complexity problem.

In both cases we still have important open questions. We do not yet have *efficient* gadgets for expressing constraints, nor do we know when such gadgets exist. We also do not yet have a general classification result for the complexity of languages over finite domains with more than two elements.

The case of infinite domains is harder. We have no real theory for unifying the results over infinite domains. At present there are just a few sporadic examples of tractable languages, but no effective general techniques to determine either complexity or expressiveness.

Although we now have a wide class of tractable languages from which to build solving algorithms, this is not yet a truly practical field. We really need to make more progress on the problem of identifying tractable problem instances, or subinstances, and determining which algorithms can be used to solve them efficiently. This will allow us to incorporate results on tractability into general constraint solvers.

11.7 Bibliographical Notes

Many constraint languages have been studied, and some have been shown to be tractable. This has led to the publication of a wide variety of research papers describing one or other technique for solving problems over particular constraint languages (Jeavons, Cohen, and Gyssens 1995, 1997; Jeavons and Cohen 1995; Jeavons 1998; Jeavons, Cohen, and Pearson 1999; Bjäreland and Jonsson 1999; Bulatov, Krokhin, and Jeavons 2001; Dalmau 2000; Dalmau and Pearson 1999; Feder and Vardi 1998; Bulatov and Jeavons 2000).

Historically, it was the hybrid tractable languages discussed in Section 11.5 that were the first to be identified. The hybrid class of bounded width constraint problems (Example 11.17) was first described by Freuder (1985).

The hybrid result giving tractability based on domain size and maximum arity of constraints (Example 11.19) was proved by Dechter (1992b).

The hybrid class of row-convex constraints (Example 11.18) was first described by van Beek (1992a) and van Beek and Dechter (1995). Their results on row-convex constraints extended earlier results on monotone and functional constraints (van Hentenryck, Deville, and Teng 1992).

The tractable language consisting of connected row-convex constraints (Example 11.11) was first described by Deville, Barette, and van Hentenryck (1997, 1999), where the algorithm given in this chapter is described.

The tractable language consisting of 0/1/all or implicational constraints was discovered independently (Cooper, Cohen, and Jeavons 1994; Kirousis 1993). A generalization of this constraint language was first described by Jeavons, Cohen, and Cooper (1998), where a simple criterion is given to identify all languages for which some specified level of consistency is a decision procedure.

The CHIP language of Example 11.2 is well-known, and there are many sources for further reading (Beldiceanu and Contejean 1994; Dincbas et al. 1988b; Aggoun and Beldiceanu 1993; Aggoun et al. 1987; Simonis 1995). The tractability of the max-closed language of Example 11.4 was first proven by Jeavons and Cooper (1995). In this paper they also describe the tractable extension to the basic constraints of the CHIP language of Example 11.2. This result has been used, for instance, to design an efficient algorithm for certain scheduling problems (Purvis and Jeavons 1999).

The extension of linear equations to the more general class of maximal tractable languages containing arbitrary affine relations was first proved by Feder and Vardi (1998). It is a generalization of the result of Example 11.8 for linear equations. In general, affine relations are defined by cosets of subgroups of direct products of Abelian groups, rather than just subspaces of vector spaces.

A good introduction to computational complexity can be found in Papadimitriou (1994), and an overview of tractable and intractable problem classes can be found in Garey and Johnson (1979).

A description of Gaussian elimination as required to solve linear equations can be found in any introductory text on linear algebra (see, for example, Herstein 1975).

A description of a polynomial algorithm for 2-SAT can be found in most introductory texts on satisfiability or complexity (see, for example, Papadimitriou 1994).

Schaefer (1978) gives the first proof of Theorem 11.2, and hence a complete characterization of the tractable relational subclasses of the Boolean CSP (which he calls the generalized satisfiability problem).

Generalized arc-consistency, as required for Example 11.4, has been described by several authors (van Hentenryck, Deville, and Teng 1992; Mohr and Masini 1988; Mackworth 1977b; Bessière and Régin 1997).

The notion of projecting solutions of constraint problems to derive new relations was first described as *constructing derived relations* by Cohen, Gyssens, and Jeavons (1996), where a proof of the expressibility result for finite domains (Theorem 11.1) may be found.

Jeavons, Cohen, and Gyssens (1996) give a full explanation of the indicator problem. They also show the importance of squashing functions and describe the algebraic test for tractability. The existence of a squashing function for Γ indicates that constraints with relations chosen from Γ allow a form of global "substitutability," very similar to a notion defined by Freuder (1991).

Jeavons (1998) develops the algebraic theory of maximal tractable constraint languages. A detailed study of this theory requires some knowledge of universal algebra and relational clones (Rosenberg 1986; Szendrei 1986).

Recently, Bulatov, Krokhin, and Jeavons (2000, 2001) have extended the algebraic theory of tractability and obtained certain limited dichotomy results over larger domains.

In this chapter we have characterized complexity of constraint languages over a finite domain in terms of solutions to indicator problems. An alternative approach is to demonstrate techniques for obtaining new tractable classes from existing examples. This work is beyond the scope of a short introductory chapter. Two such examples are the work on disjoint domains (Cohen, Jeavons, and Gault 2000) and the work on disjunctive constraints (Cohen et al. 2000; Broxvall, Jonsson, and Renz 2000).

Over an infinite domain there has been success in classifying all of the tractable subclasses of Allen's interval algebra for temporal constraints (Drankengren and Jonsson 1998; Krokhin, Jeavons, and Jonsson 2001). For other examples of work on the complexity of temporal constraints over infinite domains, see Koubarakis (1997), Nebel and Bürckert (1995), and van Beek (1991).

11.8 **Exercises**

1. Show that the precedence constraints of Example 11.1 are max-closed with the natural order on the time domain.

2. In this question you will determine the answer to some expressibility questions.

    (a) List the eight variables for any third-order indicator problem for the Boolean domain.

    (b) Write down the Boolean relations defined by

        i. $\vee$ (OR),

        ii. $\Rightarrow$ (IMPLIES),

        iii. $R_3 = (p \wedge q \wedge r) \vee (\neg p \wedge q \wedge \neg r) \vee (\neg p \wedge \neg q \wedge \neg r)$

(with any fixed variable ordering) and determine which lists of variables of the third-order Boolean indicator problem these relations match.

(c) Describe and solve the third-order indicator problem for the language $\Gamma = \{\vee, \Rightarrow, R_3\}$.

(d) By finding suitable constructor sites and projecting your solutions onto these sites, determine whether or not Γ is able to express

   i. $\vee$ (OR)

   ii. $(\neg p \wedge q \wedge \neg r) \vee (\neg p \wedge \neg q \wedge r) \vee (p \wedge \neg q \wedge \neg r)$

3. What are "maximal tractable constraint languages" and why are they important?

4. Determine the relations expressed by the following gadgets:

  (a) Domain $D = \{0, 1, 2, 3, 4, 5\}$ with the natural order; variables $\{v, w, z\}$; constraints $\{\langle(v, w), "<"\rangle, \langle(w, z), "<"\rangle\}$; construction site (v, z).

  (b) Domain $D = \{R, B, G, Y\}$; variables $\{a, b, c, d\}$; constraints $\{\langle(a, b), "\neq"\rangle, \langle(b, c), "\neq"\rangle, \langle(c, d), "\neq"\rangle, \langle(a, c), "\neq"\rangle, \langle(b, d), "\neq"\rangle\}$; construction site (a, d).

  (c) Domain is the integers modulo 5; variables $\{x, y, z, v, w\}$; constraints $\{x + 2y + 3z \equiv 4,\ 2x + z + 3w \equiv 1,\ z \equiv 3,\ v + 4y \equiv 2,\ x + y + z + v + w \equiv 0\}$; construction site $\{x, z, w\}$.

5. This question is about squashing functions.

  (a) Show that $\mu : \{a, b, c, d, e\} \rightarrow \{a, b, c, d, e\}$ defined by

$$\mu(x) = \begin{cases} b & \text{if } x \in \{a, b, e\} \\ c & \text{otherwise} \end{cases}$$

is a squashing function for the language $\Gamma = \{R_1, R_2, R_3, R_4\}$ depicted in Figure 11.7.

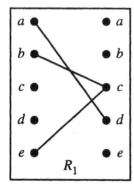 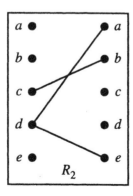 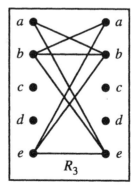 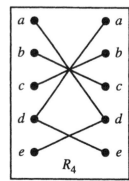

Figure 11.7 The four relations of the constraint language for Exercise 5.

(b) Use the squashing function of part (a) to reduce the language Γ.

(c) Consider the constraint satisfaction problem $P = \langle X, D, C \rangle$, where

$$X = \{x_1, x_2, x_3, x_4\}$$
$$D = \{a, b, c, d, e\}$$
$$C = \{c_1, c_2, c_3, c_4, c_5\}$$
$$c_1 = \langle (x_1, x_2), R_1 \rangle$$
$$c_2 = \langle (x_2, x_3), R_2 \rangle$$
$$c_3 = \langle (x_3, x_4), R_4 \rangle$$
$$c_4 = \langle (x_1, x_4), R_4 \rangle$$
$$c_5 = \langle (x_1, x_3), R_3 \rangle$$

i. Apply μ to squash each of the relations in P.

ii. Squash P to P' and solve this reduced problem.

iii. Demonstrate that the solution you obtained to P' is indeed a solution to P.

(d) Show how any solution to a constraint satisfaction problem over a language with a squashing function can be converted (squashed) into a solution for a squashed problem.

(e) Show that a reduced language is tractable whenever the original language is tractable.

6. Show that the following are equivalent for a constraint language:

- There is a solution to the first-order indicator problem that does not use every domain value.

- There exists a squashing function for the language.

7. Here you will prove that a language is intractable using solutions to its indicator problems.

(a) Solve the Boolean third-order indicator problem for the ternary Boolean "not all equal" relation defined by $(p \vee q \vee r) \wedge (\neg p \vee \neg q \vee \neg r)$. Use Table 11.2 to show that this relation is not tractable.

(b) Use Corollary 11.1 and the solutions to the appropriate indicator problem to show that the standard graph 3-colorability problem is NP-hard.

8. (a) Show that every projection is a solution to every indicator problem.

(b) Show that if an indicator problem of order k has only projections as solutions, then the language expresses all possible relations with k rows.

(c) Show that any language for which the indicator problems have only projections as solutions is intractable.

(d) Show that the Boolean language consisting of the ternary relation "not all equal," (from Exercise 7(a)), and the unary relation defined by the single literal p, is intractable.

9. (a) Write down the constraint network for Example 11.5 and make it generalized arc-consistent.

(b) Show that choosing the largest domain element for each variable in this arc-consistent problem gives a solution.

(c) Do the same for the network of equations over the domain $\{0, 1, 2, 3, 4, 5, 6\}$, with variables $\{v, w, x, y, z\}$, and constraints

$$z \neq 4$$
$$3v \leq w$$
$$2z \leq 4$$
$$2x + 3z + w \geq 2y$$
$$yz \geq 3x$$
$$y \geq v + 4$$

10. (a) Verify the construction of the third-order indicator problem depicted in Figure 11.6 for the constraint language just consisting of the ternary Boolean relation defined by $(p \vee q \vee r) \wedge (\neg p \vee \neg q \vee \neg r)$. You should also identify eight scopes with repeated variables giving rise to binary constraints.

(b) Solve this indicator problem to verify the list of solutions given in Table 11.3.

chapter 12

Temporal Constraint Networks

It usually takes more than three weeks to prepare a good impromptu speech.

Mark Twain

Philosophers, psychologists, and linguists have struggled for many years with the difficulties inherent in representing time. Representing and reasoning about time also play an important role in artificial intelligence. Almost any area within AI—commonsense reasoning, natural language cognition, plan recognition, scheduling, planning, and qualitative reasoning, to name but a few—involves some sort of reasoning about time.

A temporal reasoning system should consist of a temporal knowledge base, a routine to check its consistency, a query-answering mechanism, and an inference mechanism capable of discovering new information. The primitive entities in the knowledge base are *propositions*, such as "I was driving a car" or "the book was lying on the table," with which we mentally associate temporal intervals; each interval represents the time period during which the corresponding proposition holds. For example, the first proposition may be embedded in the sentence "I was driving a car last night," and the second in "The book was on the table when I left the room." The temporal information might be relative (e.g., "P occurred before Q") or metric (e.g., "P had started at least three hours before Q was terminated"). To express less specific information, disjunctive sentences may also be needed (e.g., "You can come in before or after lunch hour"). We should also allow references to absolute time (e.g., 4:00 P.M.) and to the duration of propositions (e.g., "P lasted at least two hours"). Given temporal information of this kind, we wish to derive answers to queries such as "Is it possible that a proposition P holds at time t_1?," "What are the possible times at which a proposition P holds?," and "What are the possible temporal relationships between two propositions P and Q?"

This chapter applies the constraint processing framework and techniques to such temporal reasoning issues. How can temporal reasoning be viewed as a CSP?

First, we need to identify the entities in our temporal domain. We shall consider two types of temporal objects: points and intervals. Intervals correspond to time periods during which events occur or propositions hold, and points represent beginning and ending points of some events, as well as neutral points of time. These objects will be the variables in our CSP. Temporal statements will be treated as constraints on the location of these objects along the time line. There are two types of constraints: qualitative and quantitative. *Qualitative* constraints specify the relative position of paired objects, and *quantitative* constraints place absolute bounds, or restrict the temporal distance between points.

Another important and related class of constraints is spatial constraints, which also received a lot of attention in recent years. The basic treatment in this chapter can be perceived as an introduction to the spatial case as well (Koubarakis 1997). In the remainder of this chapter, we will introduce the algebra framework of qualitative temporal networks and then focus on quantitative temporal constraint satisfaction problems (TCSPs).

12.1 **Qualitative Networks**

Interval algebra (Allen 1983) and point algebra (Vilain and Kautz 1986) can be regarded as qualitative constraint-based approaches to temporal reasoning, as their representation languages allow only qualitative statements. In interval algebra, the temporal objects are intervals, and constraints are specified by the relative location of paired intervals. For example, we can specify that intervals I and J intersect, that they are disjoint, or that I occurred before J. In point algebra, on the other hand, the temporal objects are points, and constraints are specified by the relative location of paired points. For example, we can say that P occurred at the same time as Q or that P and Q did not occur at the same time, where P and Q are time points.

12.1.1 **The Interval Algebra**

The interval algebra (IA) formulates temporal knowledge in terms of qualitative statements regarding the relative locations of paired intervals. Consider a pair of intervals I and J. There are seven basic (atomic) relations that can hold between intervals: *before, meets, overlaps, starts, during, finishes,* and *equal,* as depicted in Table 12.1. Each one of these relations is associated with an inverse relation; for example, the inverse of the relation *before* is the relation *after,* because I *before* J is equivalent to J *after* I. Because the inverse of "equal" is "equal" overall, there are 13 total relations that can exist between a pair of intervals: $\{b, m, o, s, d, f, bi, mi, oi, si, di, fi, =\}$ (see Table 12.1).

A subset of basic relations corresponds to an ambiguous, disjunctive relationship between intervals. If the relative location of intervals I and J is specified by

Table 12.1 The basic relations between a pair of intervals and their inverses.

Relation	Symbol	Inverse	Example
X before Y	b	bi	
X equal Y	=	=	
X meets Y	m	mi	
X overlaps Y	o	oi	
X during Y	d	di	
X starts Y	s	si	
X finishes Y	f	fi	

a relation set $\{r_1, \ldots, r_k\}$ (written as $I \{r_1, \ldots, r_k\} J$), then the following disjunction holds:

$$(I \; r_1 \; J) \vee \cdots \vee (I \; r_k \; J)$$

For example, the relationship $I \{s, si, d, di, f, fi, o, oi, =\} J$ expresses the fact that intervals I and J are not disjoint. It excludes the basic relations *before*, *after*, *meets*, and *met by* between I and J (see Table 12.1), thus forbidding basic relations whereby I and J are disjoint. To represent a given body of knowledge in the IA formalism, we simply translate the temporal statements into IA relationships between event intervals.

EXAMPLE 12.1

Consider the following information:

> *John was not in the room when I touched the switch to turn on the light, but John was in the room later when the light went out.*

Let *Switch* be the time of touching the switch, *Light* be the time the light was on, and *Room* be the time that John was in the room. The above information is translated into a set of IA relations between *Switch*, *Light*, and *Room*:

1. *Switch* overlaps or meets *Light*:   *Switch* $\{o, m\}$ *Light*.

2. *Switch* is before, meets, is met by, or after *Room*: *Switch* $\{b, m, mi, a\}$ *Room*.

3. *Light* overlaps, starts, or is during *Room*:   *Light* $\{o, s, d\}$ *Room*.   ●

Having represented the given knowledge within the IA framework, we are now interested in solving several reasoning tasks:

1. Determine whether the given information is *consistent*, that is, whether it is possible to arrange the intervals along the time line according to the given information.

2. If the information is consistent, find one, some, or all arrangements of the intervals along the time line, each corresponding to a possible *scenario*.

DEFINITION **(Interval algebra constraint network)**
12.1

The IA network can be expressed as a constraint network, involving a set of variables $\{x_1, \ldots, x_n\}$, where each variable represents a temporal interval. The domain of each variable is the set of ordered pairs of real numbers (i.e., $D_i = \{(a, b)|a, b \in \Re, a < b\}$), representing the beginning and ending points of the corresponding interval. Binary constraints between pairs of interval variables are given as IA relations—the constraint C_{ij} between x_i and x_j is defined as $C_{ij} \subseteq \{b, m, o, s, d, f, bi, mi, oi, si, di, fi, =\}$. A solution is an assignment of a pair of numbers to each variable such that no constraint is violated. Testing contraint violation requires translating the relationship between a pair of intervals $(a_1, b_1), (a_2, b_2)$ into a disjunction of qualitative relations. A solution can also be associated with a consistent labeling, assigning an atomic relation to each constraint that is consistent with a solution.   •

Note that a unique property of this representation is that constraints are not given as explicit relations over domains of variables, but as enumerated atomic relationships between the interval variables.

Once expressed as a constraint network, an IA network can be associated with a *constraint graph*, where nodes represent variables and an edge between nodes i and j represents a *direct constraint* C_{ij} between variables x_i and x_j. Each edge is labeled by the corresponding IA relation set. As usual, the lack of an edge between nodes i and j stands for a *universal constraint* permitting all relationships. The constraint graph representing Example 12.1 is depicted in Figure 12.1(a). One solution to the network of Figure 12.1(a) is $\{Switch = (1, 2), Light = (2, 3), Room = (2, 4)\}$, which represents the scenario shown in Figure 12.1(b). This solution corresponds to the feasible relations: (*Switch m Light*), (*Light s Room*), and (*Switch m Room*).

A constraint C' can be *tighter* than constraint C'', denoted by $C' \subseteq C''$, yielding a partial order between IA networks. A network N'' is tighter than network N' if the partial order $\subseteq$ is satisfied for all the corresponding constraints. Remember that two networks are *equivalent* if they possess the same solution set and that the minimal network is the *unique* equivalent network M, which is minimal with respect to $\subseteq$. The minimal network provides a more explicit representation of the

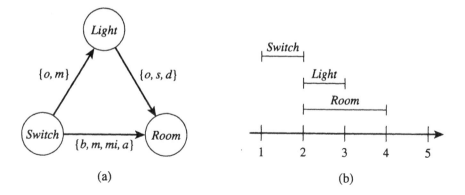

Figure 12.1 The constraint graph of Example 12.1.

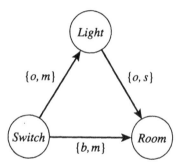

Figure 12.2 The minimal network of Example 12.1.

given knowledge and is therefore useful in answering many types of queries. The minimal network of Example 12.1 is shown in Figure 12.2.

As another example, consider the following description of events.

EXAMPLE
12.2
Fred was reading the paper while eating his breakfast. He put the paper down and drank the last of his coffee. After breakfast he went for a walk. ●

The first sentence tells us that the interval of time over which Fred read the paper intersects with the interval of time over which Fred ate breakfast. We represent this as "Paper {= $d, di, o, oi, s, si, f, fi$} Breakfast." The second sentence fixes the relationship between some of the endpoints of the intervals over which Fred read his paper and over which Fred drank his coffee, but it remains indefinite about others. We represent this as "Paper {d, o, s} Coffee." We also assume that drinking coffee is

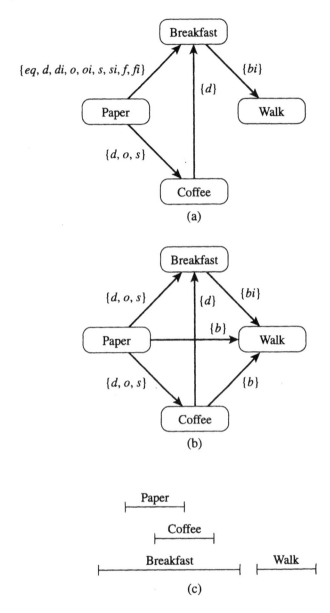

Figure 12.3 Representing qualitative relations between intervals: (a) an example network, (b) a minimal network, and (c) a consistent scenario.

a part of breakfast and so occurs during breakfast. We represent this as "Coffee {d} Breakfast." Finally, the information in the third sentence is represented as "Walk {bi} Breakfast." The resulting network is shown in Figure 12.3(a), where we have drawn the arc from "Breakfast" to "Walk" and have labeled it with the "bi" (after) relation.

The minimal network expressing all feasible relations between all pairs of intervals is shown in Figure 12.3(b). One possible consistent scenario is shown in Figure 12.3(c). With IA networks, it is the qualitative arrangement of the intervals that interests us, not the particular consistent instantiation that led to the arrangement. There are either zero or an infinite number of different consistent instantiations of the variables in an IA network, but there are only a finite number of different consistent arrangements of the intervals. One possible consistent instantiation that would lead to the arrangement shown in Figure 12.3(c) is Paper ← (1, 3), Breakfast ← (0, 5), Walk ← (6, 7), and Coffee ← (2, 4), where we are equating the names of the vertices with the variables they represent.

The reasoning tasks for IA networks are deciding consistency, finding one or more solutions, and since these networks have binary constraints only, computing the full minimal network. As expected, all these tasks are generally intractable, and it is therefore unlikely that polynomial-time algorithms exist. Therefore, we will try to improve exponential search algorithms such as backtracking, or resort to local inference procedures, as discussed next.

12.1.2 Path-Consistency in Interval Algebra

Next we focus on path-consistency for IA networks, defined using two binary operations on constraints: intersection and composition.

The *intersection* of two IA relations R' and R'', denoted by $R' \oplus R''$, is the set-theoretic intersection $R' \cap R''$. The *composition* of two IA relations, R' between intervals I and K and R'' between intervals K and J, is a new relation between intervals I and J, induced by R' and R'' as follows. The composition of two basic relations r' and r'' is defined by a *transitivity table*, a portion of which is shown in Table 12.2. For example, the basic relations I *meets* K and K is *during* J induce a new (composite) relation on I and J: I *overlaps*, is *during*, or *starts* J, depending on the location of J's starting point. It follows that the entry for $m \otimes d$ in the transitivity table is the set $\{o, d, s\}$. The composition of two *composite* relations R' and R'', denoted by $R' \otimes R''$, is the composition of the constituent basic relations:

$$R' \otimes R'' = \{r' \otimes r'' | r' \in R', r'' \in R''\}$$

Table 12.2 Composition in the interval algebra.

	b	s	d	o	m
b	b	b	$b\,o\,m\,d\,s$	b	b
s	b	s	d	$b\,o\,m$	b
d	b	d	d	$b\,o\,m\,d\,s$	b
o	b	o	$o\,d\,s$	$b\,o\,m$	b
m	b	m	$o\,d\,s$	b	b

```
QPC-1

Input: An IA network T.

Output: A path-consistent IA network.

1. repeat
2.     S ← T
3.     for k := 1 to n do
4.         for i, j := 1 to n do begin
5.             C_ij ← C_ij ⊕ C_ik ⊗ C_kj
9. until S = T
```

Figure 12.4 Algorithm QUALITATIVE-PATH-CONSISTENCY (QPC-1).

DEFINITION   **(path-consistency of IA)**
12.2
An IA network is *path-consistent* if for every three variables x_i, x_j, x_k, $C_{ij} \subseteq C_{ik} \otimes C_{kj}$.   •

Like any constraint network, an IA network can be converted into an equivalent path-consistent form by repeatedly applying the relaxation operation

$$C_{ij} \leftarrow C_{ij} \oplus (C_{ik} \otimes C_{kj}) \tag{12.1}$$

which corresponds to executing the PC-1 algorithm, given in Figure 12.4, until either a fixed point is reached or some constraint becomes empty, indicating inconsistency. Using this method, path-consistency can be achieved in $O(n^3)$ time (see Exercise 1).

EXAMPLE   Consider the network of Figure 12.1(a). Enforcing path-consistency by
12.3   repeatedly applying Equation (12.1) yields the network in Figure 12.2 as follows. (We will abbreviate *Switch* as S, *Room* as R, and *Light* as L.)

1. Apply $C_{SR} \leftarrow C_{SR} \oplus (C_{SL} \otimes C_{LR})$. Composing the constraints C_{SL} and C_{LR} induces a new constraint between S and R: $C'_{SR} = \{o, m\} \otimes \{o, s, d\} = \{b, o, m, d, s\}$. Then, intersecting C'_{SR} with the original constraint $C_{SR} = \{b, m, mi, bi\}$ yields a new constraint between S and R: $C_{SR} \leftarrow \{b, m\}$.

2. Apply $C_{LR} \leftarrow C_{LR} \oplus (C_{LS} \otimes C_{SR})$. This results in a new constraint between L and R: $C_{LR} \leftarrow \{o, s\}$.

3. Further applications of Equation (12.1) will not change the network; thus, we have reached a fixed point.   •

In some cases, path-consistency algorithms are *exact*— they are guaranteed to generate the minimal network (as we saw in Example 12.1) and therefore decide consistency. In the next section, we present some classes of IA networks for which 3- (path) or 4-consistency is guaranteed indeed to compute the minimal network. However, IA networks are generally NP-complete. Indeed, to solve the general IA network and to generate a solution, we will need to use backtracking search. Even when the minimal network is available, it is not guaranteed to be globally consistent to allow backtrack-free search. We can consider backtrack search when the variables are the intervals, the domains are the given temporal labelings, and the constraints are based on the composition table of the interval algebra. A backtracking scheme can use path-consistency as its look-ahead engine at each node of the search space.

12.1.3 The Point Algebra

Because of the computational limitations of IA an alternative model, *point algebra* (PA), which is less expressive, is often considered. In this model information is expressed by means of constraints on points. There are three possible basic relations that can hold between a pair of points P and Q: $P < Q$, $P = Q$, and $P > Q$. The elements of the PA are, therefore, all 2^3 subsets of the basic relations $\{<, =, >\}$. As we will show, reasoning tasks over this class of networks are polynomial.

DEFINITION
12.3

(point algebra networks)

A *point algebra network* (*PA network*) involves a set of variables $\{x_1, \ldots, x_n\}$, where each variable represents a time point. The domain of each variable is the set of real numbers $\Re$, standing for the set of time points the variable may assume. The constraints are given as PA elements, having their algebraic meaning over the reals.   ●

EXAMPLE
12.4

As an example of representing temporal information in the PA framework, consider the description of events shown in Figure 12.5(a). The sentence shown fixes the relationship between some of the endpoints of the intervals of time over which Fred read his paper and over which Fred drank his coffee, but it remains indefinite about others. We represent this by the network shown in Figure 12.5(a), where Paper$^-$ and Paper$^+$ represent the starting and ending points of the interval. The network is already the minimal network and also shows the feasible relations between all pairs of points. One possible consistent scenario is shown in Figure 12.5(b).   ●

As with IA networks, it is the qualitative arrangement of the points that interests us, not the particular consistent instantiation that led to the arrangement.

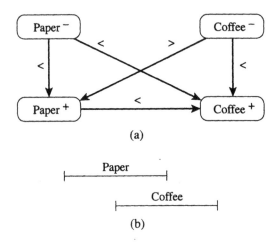

(a)

(b)

Figure 12.5 Representing qualitative relations between points: (a) Example: _Fred put the paper down and drank the last of his coffee._ (b) A consistent scenario.

One possible consistent instantiation that would lead to the arrangement shown in Figure 12.5(b) is Paper$^-$ ← 0, Paper$^+$ ← 2, Coffee$^-$ ← 1, and Coffee$^+$ ← 3. Consider another example:

EXAMPLE 12.5   Suppose we are given the following relationship between intervals I and J:

$$I \{s, d, f, =\} J \qquad (12.2)$$

That is, I _starts_, is _during_, _finishes_, or is _equal_ to J. Let x and y be the starting and ending points, respectively, of interval I (i.e., $I = [x, y]$), and z and t be the starting and ending points, respectively, of interval J (i.e., $J = [z, t]$). The relationship in Equation (12.2) can be expressed by the following PA constraints:

$$x < y, \ z < t, \ x < t, \ x \geq z, \ y \leq t, \ y > z \qquad (12.3)$$

Note that $\leq$ and $\geq$ are shorthand notation for the PA elements $\{<, =\}$ and $\{>, =\}$, respectively. The constraint graph of this example is given in Figure 12.6.   •

Any PA network can be expressed as an IA network. There are, however, problems that can be expressed by binary relations between intervals but not by binary relations between points.

EXAMPLE 12.6   Consider the IA relation

$$I \{b, a\} J \qquad (12.4)$$

In this case, I is _before_ or _after_ J, where intervals I and J are given by $I = [x, y]$ and $J = [z, t]$. This relationship cannot be encoded by binary PA

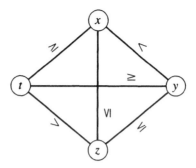

Figure 12.6 The constraint graph of a PA of Example 12.5.

Table 12.3 Composition in the point algebra.

	<	=	>
<	<	<	?
=	<	=	>
>	?	>	>

relations on points; it requires the 4-ary constraint $(y < z) \vee (t < x)$. Since the PA is limited to binary constraints, the IA network of Equation (12.4) cannot be represented as a PA network. ●

Algorithms

Path-consistency for the point algebra will also be defined using its particular composition operation, which is defined by the transitivity table of Table 12.3, where "?" expresses the universal relation.

While the IA network in Example 12.4 was fully expressed by a PA network, this is not always possible, as we will see later. The limited expressiveness of PA is compensated by its tractability. It turns out that most reasoning tasks for problems expressed in the PA can be solved in polynomial time, using path-consistency or 4-consistency. Specifically, a given PA network is consistent if and only if after executing path-consistency the resulting network is nonempty (Ladkin and Maddux 1989). Thus, deciding the consistency of a PA network is $O(n^3)$. A faster $O(n^2)$ algorithm for deciding consistency and for finding a consistent scenario is also available. However, path-consistency can also be used in computing the minimal network. Consider a subset of PA networks, called *convex PA (CPA) networks*. In these networks, the constraints are taken from the set $\{<, \le, =, \ge, >\}$. That is, the $\ne$ relation is excluded. It can be shown that path-consistency is exact for CPA networks (see Exercise 4). Thus, computing the minimal network of a CPA network is $O(n^3)$. Path-consistency is not exact, however, in the full PA (where the $\ne$ relation is allowed). In order to compute the minimal network for a PA network, we need to enforce 4-consistency, which requires $O(n^4)$ time. In summary we can briefly state these results:

THEOREM
12.1

(PA path-consistency)

1. Path-consistency decides the consistency of a PA network in $O(n^3)$ steps (Ladkin and Maddux 1989).

2. Consistency and solution generation of PA networks can also be accomplished in $O(n^2)$ (van Beek 1989).

3. The minimal network of a PA consistent network can be obtained using 4-consistency in $O(n^4)$ steps (van Beek 1992b).

4. The minimal network of CPA networks can be obtained by path-consistency in $O(n^3)$ (van Beek and Cohen 1990).   •

The PA can be used to identify classes of easy cases of IA networks. As we have seen before, some IA relations can be expressed as a conjunction of binary PA relations. Let IA_{PA} be the set of all these relations. Similarly, let IA_{CPA} be the set of all IA relations that can be expressed by a conjunction of binary CPA relations. An IA network whose constraints are IA_{PA} or IA_{CPA} relations will be called an IA_{PA} network or an IA_{CPA} network, respectively. To solve such a network, we simply translate it into an equivalent point network (in $O(n^2)$ time), solve the resulting PA network, and then, if necessary, translate the resulting network back into interval representation (again in time $O(n^2)$). Clearly, these restricted IA networks are easy to solve.

12.2 Quantitative Temporal Networks

One of the requirements of a temporal reasoning system is its ability to deal with metric information. For instance, we may need to express information on duration of events ("Fred reading the paper") or timing of events ("The time Fred was out for a walk"). Quantitative temporal networks provide a convenient formalism to deal with such information because they consider time points as the variables. A time point may be a beginning or an ending point of some event, as well as a neutral point of time. We will use a form of temporal distance for constraints. Consider the following temporal scenario.

EXAMPLE
12.7

John travels to work either by car (30–40 minutes) or by bus (at least 60 minutes). Fred travels to work either by car (20–30 minutes) or in a carpool (40–50 minutes). Today John left home between 7:10 and 7:20 A.M., and Fred arrived at work between 8:00 and 8:10 A.M. We also know that John arrived at work 10–20 minutes after Fred left home.   •

We wish to answer queries such as "Is the information in the story consistent?," "Is it possible that John took the bus and Fred used the carpool?," and "What are the possible times at which Fred left home?"

Let P_1 be the proposition "John was traveling to work" and P_2 the proposition "Fred was traveling to work." P_1 and P_2 are associated with intervals $[x_1, x_2]$ and $[x_3, x_4]$, respectively, where x_1 represents the time John left home and x_4 represents the time Fred arrived at work. Several quantitative constraints are given in the story. Because it takes John either 30–40 minutes or more than 60 minutes to travel to work, the temporal distance between x_1 and x_2 is constrained by

$$30 \leq x_2 - x_1 \leq 40 \text{ or } x_2 - x_1 \geq 60$$

Similar constraints apply to $x_4 - x_3$, namely,

$$20 \leq x_4 - x_3 \leq 30 \text{ or } 40 \leq x_4 - x_3 \leq 50$$

Assigning $x_0 = 7{:}00$ A.M., the fact that John left home between 7:10 and 7:20 A.M. imposes the following additional constraint:

$$10 \leq x_1 - x_0 \leq 20$$

The constraint on $x_4 - x_0$ assumes a similar form:

$$60 \leq x_4 - x_0 \leq 70$$

Finally, John's arrival time relative to Fred's departure time can be described by the constraint

$$10 \leq x_3 - x_2 \leq 20$$

DEFINITION
12.4

(TCSP)

A temporal constraint satisfaction problem (TCSP) involves a set of variables $\{x_1, \ldots, x_n\}$ having continuous domains; each variable represents a time point. Each constraint is represented by a set of intervals[1] $\{I_1, \ldots, I_k\} = \{[a_1, b_1], \ldots, [a_k, b_k]\}$.

A unary constraint T_i restricts the domain of variable x_i to the given set of intervals; that is, it represents the disjunction

$$(a_1 \leq x_i \leq b_1) \vee \cdots \vee (a_k \leq x_i \leq b_k)$$

---

1. For simplicity, we assume closed intervals; however, the same treatment applies to open and semi-open intervals.

A binary constraint T_{ij} constrains the permissible values for the distance $x_j - x_i$; it represents the disjunction

$$(a_1 \leq x_j - x_i \leq b_1) \vee \cdots \vee (a_k \leq x_j - x_i \leq b_k)$$

We assume that constraints are given in a *canonical form* in which all intervals are pair-wise disjoint. ●

A *network of binary temporal constraints* (a *binary* TCSP) consists of a set of variables $\{x_1, \ldots, x_n\}$ and a set of unary and binary constraints. Such a network can be represented by a *directed constraint graph*, where nodes represent variables and an edge $i \rightarrow j$ indicates that a constraint T_{ij} is specified between x_i and x_j; it is labeled by the interval set. Each input constraint T_{ij} implies an equivalent constraint T_{ji}. However, only one of these is usually shown in the constraint graph. A special time point, x_0, is introduced to represent the "beginning of the world." All times are relative to x_0; thus, we may treat each unary constraint T_i as a binary constraint T_{oi} (having the same interval representation). For simplicity we assume $x_0 = 0$. The constraint graph of Example 12.7 is given in Figure 12.7.

As usual, a tuple $x = (a_1, \ldots, a_n)$ is called a *solution* if the assignment $(x_1 = a_1, \ldots, x_n = a_n)$ does not violate any constraint.

Since a TCSP is binary it can assume the usual definition of minimality and binary decomposability, or global consistency, defined in Chapter 2 and explicated next.

DEFINITION   **(minimal and binary decomposable networks)**
12.5
Given a TCSP, a value v is a *feasible value* for variable x_i if there exists a solution in which $x_i = v$. The set of all feasible values of a variable is called the *minimal domain*. A minimal constraint T_{ij} between x_i and x_j is the set of all feasible values for $x_i - x_j$. A network is minimal iff its domains and constraints are minimal. A network is binary *decomposable* if every

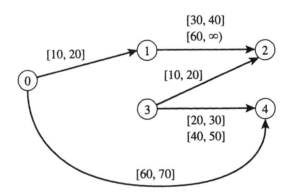

Figure 12.7 A constraint graph representing Example 12.7.

consistent assignment of values to a set of variables S can be extended to a solution.   •

Inference and constraint propagation over TCSPs are defined using the three binary operations on constraints: union, intersection, and composition, respecting their usual set-theoretic definitions.

DEFINITION
12.6

Let $T = \{I_1, \ldots, I_l\}$ and $S = \{J_1, \ldots, J_m\}$ be two constraints. Each is a set of intervals of a temporal variable or a temporal binary constraint.

1. The union of T and S, denoted by $T \cup S$, only admits values that are allowed by either T or S, that is, $T \cup S = \{I_1, \ldots, I_l, J_1, \ldots, J_m\}$.

2. The intersection of T and S, denoted by $T \oplus S$, admits only values that are allowed by both T and S, that is, $T \oplus S = \{K_1, \ldots, K_n\}$ where $K_k = I_i \cap J_j$ for some i and j. Note that $n \leq l + m$.

3. The composition of T and S, denoted by $T \otimes S$, admits only values r for which there exist $t \in T$ and $s \in S$, such that $t + s = r$, that is, $T \otimes S = \{K_1, \ldots, K_n\}$, where $K_k = [a + c, b + d]$ for some $I_i = [a, b]$, and $J_j = [c, d]$. Note that $n \leq l \times m$.   •

A pictorial illustration of the intersection and composition operations is given in Figure 12.8. Note that for some of these operations the resulting interval representation is not in canonical form. For instance, the composition operation results in four intervals, while, due to overlap, only three of them appear in the canonical form.

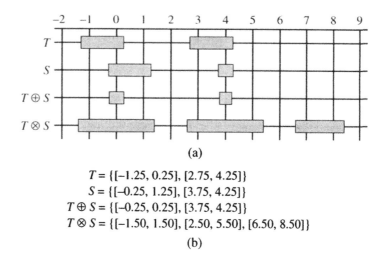

(a)

$$T = \{[-1.25, 0.25], [2.75, 4.25]\}$$
$$S = \{[-0.25, 1.25], [3.75, 4.25]\}$$
$$T \oplus S = \{[-0.25, 0.25], [3.75, 4.25]\}$$
$$T \otimes S = \{[-1.50, 1.50], [2.50, 5.50], [6.50, 8.50]\}$$

(b)

Figure 12.8 Operations on constraints: (a) intersection and (b) composition.

Given a constraint network, the first interesting problem is to determine its consistency. If the network is consistent, we may wish to find some specific solutions representing possible scenarios, or to answer queries concerning the set of all solutions. In particular, we can ask:

1. What are the possible times at which x_i could occur? (What is the minimal domain of x_i?)

2. What are all the possible relationships between x_i and x_j? (What is the minimal constraint between x_i and x_j?)

All these queries are NP-hard. The following section introduces a special class of temporal problems that can be processed in polynomial time.

12.2.1   The Simple Temporal Problem

A TCSP in which all constraints specify a single interval is called a *simple temporal problem* (STP). In such a network, each edge $i \to j$ is labeled by a single interval $[a_{ij}, b_{ij}]$ that represents the constraint

$$a_{ij} \leq x_j - x_i \leq b_{ij}$$

Alternatively, the constraint can be expressed as a pair of inequalities:

$$x_j - x_i \leq b_{ij}, \quad \text{and} \quad x_i - x_j \leq -a_{ij}$$

The problem of solving a system of linear inequalities is well-known in the operations research literature. It can be solved by the (exponential) simplex method (Dantzig 1962) or by Khachiyan's algorithm (Khachiyan 1979), which is rather complicated in practice. Fortunately, the special class of linear inequalities characterizing the STP admits a simpler solution. As we will see next, the inequalities can be given a convenient graph representation, to which a shortest-path algorithm can be applied.

An STP can be associated with a directed edge-weighted graph $G_d = (V, E_d)$, called a *distance graph* (to be distinguished from the constraint graph G). It has the same node set as G, and each edge $i \to j \in E_d$ is labeled by a weight a_{ij} representing the linear inequality $x_j - x_i \leq a_{ij}$. In Example 12.7, if we assume that John used a car and Fred used a carpool, we get an STP having

$$T_{12} = \{[30, 40]\} \text{ and } T_{34} = \{[40, 50]\}$$

and the distance graph depicted in Figure 12.9.

Each path from i to j in G_d, $i_0 = i, i_1, \ldots, i_k = j$, induces the following constraint on the distance $x_j - x_i$:

$$x_j - x_i \leq \sum_{j=1}^{k} a_{i_{j-1}, i_j} \tag{12.5}$$

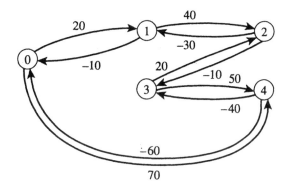

Figure 12.9 A distance graph representing a portion of Example 12.7.

If there is more than one path from i to j, then it can be easily verified that the intersection of all the induced path constraints yields

$$x_j - x_i \leq d_{ij} \qquad (12.6)$$

where d_{ij} is the length of the shortest path from i to j. Based on this observation, the following can be shown:

**THEOREM
12.2** (Shostak 1981; Leiserson and Saxe 1983) An STP T is consistent if and only if its distance graph G_d has no negative cycles.   •

The theorem holds because if there is a negative cycle C consisting of nodes $i_1, \ldots, i_k = i_1$, then summing the inequalities along C yields $X_{i_1} - X_{i_1} < 0$, which cannot be satisfied. If an STP is consistent, namely, if there is no negative cycle in G_d, then the shortest-path distances between each pair of nodes is well-defined. For any pair of connected nodes i and j, the shortest paths satisfy $d_{0j} \leq d_{0i} + a_{ij}$; thus,

$$d_{0j} - d_{0i} \leq a_{ij}$$

Hence, the tuple $(x_1 = d_{01}, \ldots, x_n = d_{0n})$ is a solution of the given STP. It is similarly easy to show that the tuple of negative reverse shortest distances is also a solution. We can conclude the following corollary:

**COROLLARY
12.1** Let G_d be the distance graph of a consistent STP. Two consistent scenarios are given by

$$S_1 = (d_{01}, \ldots, d_{0n})$$
$$S_2 = (-d_{10}, \ldots, -d_{n0})$$

which assign to each variable its latest and earliest possible times, respectively.   •

It follows that a given STP can be effectively specified by a complete directed graph, called a *d-graph*, where each edge $i \rightarrow j$ is labeled by the shortest-path length d_{ij} in G_d. The d-graph corresponds to a more explicit representation of the STP (see Equation (12.5) and Equation (12.6)). Furthermore, the following can be shown:

THEOREM **(decomposability)**
12.3
Any consistent STP is backtrack-free (decomposable) relative to the constraints in its d-graph.   •

As usual, the importance of decomposability lies in allowing a backtrack-free algorithm for assembling a solution to a given STP. We simply assign to each variable any value that satisfies the d-graph constraints relative to previous assignments (starting with $x_0 = 0$). A second beneficial by-product of decomposability is that the domains and the constraints characterized by the d-graph are minimal.

COROLLARY Let G_d be the distance graph of a consistent STP, T. The equivalent STP M,
12.2 defined by $\forall i, j, M_{ij} = \{[-d_{ji}, d_{ij}]\}$, is the minimal network representation of T, and the set of feasible values for variable X_i is $[d_{i0}, d_{0i}]$. For a proof, see Exercise 6.   •

EXAMPLE Consider the distance graph of Figure 12.9. Since there are no negative
12.8 cycles, the corresponding STP is consistent. The shortest-path distances, d_{ij}, are shown in Table 12.4. The minimal domains are $10 \leq x_1 \leq 20, 40 \leq x_2 \leq 50, 20 \leq x_3 \leq 30$, and $60 \leq x_4 \leq 70$. In particular, one special solution is the tuple $(d_{01}, \ldots, d_{04})$, namely, the assignment $\{x_1 = 20, x_2 = 50, x_3 = 30, x_4 = 70\}$, which selects for each variable its latest possible time. According to this solution, John left home at 7:10 A.M. and arrived at work at 7:50 A.M., while Fred left home at 7:30 A.M. and arrived at work at 8:10 A.M. The minimal network is given in Table 12.5. An alternate scenario, in which John used a bus and Fred used a carpool (i.e., $T_{12} = \{[60, \infty]\}$ and $T_{34} = \{[40, 50]\}$), results in a negative cycle and is therefore inconsistent.   •

Table 12.4 Lengths of shortest paths (d_{ij}) in the distance graph of Figure 12.9.

	0	1	2	3	4
0	0	20	50	30	70
1	−10	0	40	20	60
2	−40	−30	0	−10	30
3	−20	−10	20	0	50
4	−60	−50	−20	−40	0

Table 12.5 The minimal network corresponding to Figure 12.9.

	0	1	2	3	4
0	[0]	[10, 20]	[40, 50]	[20, 30]	[60, 70]
1	[−20, −10]	[0]	[30, 40]	[10, 20]	[50, 60]
2	[−50, −40]	[−40, −30]	[0]	[−20, −10]	[20, 30]
3	[−30, −20]	[−20, −10]	[10, 20]	[0]	[40, 50]
4	[−70, −60]	[−60, −50]	[−20, −30]	[−50, −40]	[0]

The d-graph of an STP can be constructed by applying Floyd-Warshall's ALL-PAIRS-SHORTEST-PATHS algorithm to the distance graph (Figure 12.10). The algorithm runs in time $O(n^3)$ and detects negative cycles simply by examining the sign of the diagonal elements d_{ii}. It constitutes, therefore, a polynomial time algorithm for determining the consistency of an STP and for computing both the minimal domains and the minimal network. Once the d-graph is available, assembling a solution requires only $O(n^2)$ time, because each successive assignment only needs to be checked against previous assignments and is guaranteed to remain unaltered. Thus, finding a solution can be achieved in $O(n^3)$ time.

THEOREM 12.4   The consistency and the minimal network of an STP can be determined in $O(n^3)$ where n is the number of variables.   ●

12.2.2 Solving the General TCSP

Having solved the STP, we now return to the general problem in which edges may be labeled by several intervals. A straightforward way of solving the general TCSP is to decompose it into several STPs, solve each one of them, and then combine

---

ALL-PAIRS-SHORTEST-PATHS

Input: A distance graph $G = (V, E)$ with weights a_{ij} for $(i, j) \in E$.

Output: A d-graph.

1. **for** $i := 1$ **to** n **do** $d_{ii} \leftarrow 0$
2. **for** $i, j := 1$ **to** n **do** $d_{ij} \leftarrow a_{ij}$
3. **for** $k := 1$ **to** n **do**
4.   **for** $i, j := 1$ **to** n **do**
5. $d_{ij} \leftarrow \min \{d_{ij}, d_{ik} + d_{kj}\}$

Figure 12.10 Floyd-Warshall's algorithm.

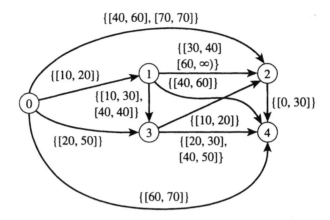

Figure 12.11 The minimal network of Example 12.7.

the results. Given a TCSP T, we define a *labeling* of T as a selection of one interval from each constraint. Each labeling defines an STP graph whose edges are labeled by the selected intervals. We can solve any of the TCSP's tasks by considering all its STPs. Specifically, the original network is consistent if and only if there is a labeling whose associated STP is consistent. Any solution of T is also a solution of one of its STPs and vice versa. Also, the minimal network of T can be computed from the minimal networks associated with its individual STPs, as stated in Theorem 12.5. The minimal network of Example 12.7 is shown in Figure 12.11. In this case, only three of the four possible labelings contribute to the minimal network.

THEOREM 12.5   The minimal network M of a given TCSP T satisfies $M = \bigcup_l M_l$, where M_l is the minimal network of the STP defined by labeling l, and the union is over all the possible labelings.

The complexity of solving a general TCSP by generating all the labelings and solving them independently is $O(n^3 k^e)$, where k is the maximum number of intervals labeling an edge and e is the number of edges. This brute-force enumeration process can be pruned significantly by running a backtracking search on a meta-CSP in which the variables are the TCSP's edges and the domains are the possible intervals. The backtracking algorithm assigns intervals to edges so long as no negative cycle of the current STP may be encountered. If such a partial assignment cannot be extended, it backtracks.

Formally, let T be a given TCSP, and let $G = (V, E)$ be its associated constraint graph. Let CSP(T) be a discrete CSP with variables $x_1, \ldots, x_m$, where $m = |E|$ and variable x_i corresponds to edge $e_i \in E$. The domain of x_i consists of the intervals $I_1, \ldots, I_k$ that label e_i in G. The constraints are not given explicitly (as a list of allowed or disallowed combinations), but implicitly: any assignment $(x_{i_1} = l_{i_1}, \ldots, x_{i_s} = l_{i_s})$ is consistent if and only if the corresponding STP is consistent.

In the following sections we present alternative approaches for processing the general TCSP. In particular, we discuss path-consistency algorithms that can be used as either an approximation or a preprocessing step before applying backtracking.

12.2.3 Path-Consistency in Quantitative Networks

In this section we study the applicability of path-consistency and its weaker version, directional path-consistency, to the TCSP framework. The Floyd-Warshall's algorithm, used for solving the STP, is such a *local consistency enforcing* algorithm. It imposes path-consistency on an STP. The general path-consistency is defined using the operations $\oplus$ and $\otimes$.

DEFINITION 12.7   A temporal constraint T_{ij} is path-consistent iff $T_{ij} \subseteq \oplus_{\forall k} (T_{ik} \otimes T_{kj})$, and a temporal network is path-consistent iff all its constraints are path-consistent.   •

The general temporal mirror of PC-1, called NPC-1 (numerical PC), is given in Figure 12.12. Since the domains of the variables are continuous, the issue of termination is no longer obvious. Nevertheless, it is simple to show that NPC-1 terminates for *integral* TCSPs, in which the extreme points of all intervals are integers. This is so because each intersection operation at step 5 must tighten a constraint by an integral amount. For nonintegral TCSPs, the same argument holds if the extreme points are rational numbers.

```
NPC-1
Input: A TCSP, T.
Output: S: the path-consistent network of T.
1. repeat
2.      S ← T
3.      for k := 1 to n do
4.          for i, j := 1 to n do begin
5.              T_ij ← T_ij ⊕ T_ik ⊗ T_kj
6.              if T_ij = ∅ then
7.                  exit (the network is inconsistent)
8.          end
9. until S = T
```

Figure 12.12 NPC-1—a path-consistency algorithm.

```
NPC-2

Input: A TCSP, T.

Output: The path-consistent network of T.

1. Q ← {(i, k, j) | i < j, k ≠ i, j}

2. while Q ≠ ∅ do begin

3.      select and delete a path (i, k, j) from Q

4.      if Tij ≠ Tik ⊗ Tkj then

5.           Tij ← Tij ⊕ Tik ⊗ Tkj

6.                if Tij = ∅ then exit (inconsistency)

7.           Q ← Q ∪ {(i, j, k) | 1 ≤ k ≤ n, i ≠ k ≠ j}

8. end
```

Figure 12.13   NPC-2—a more efficient path-consistency algorithm.

A more efficient path-consistency algorithm, the temporal equivalent of PC-2, called NPC-2, is shown in Figure 12.13. As shown in Chapter 3, path-consistency can be achieved for discrete CSPs in time polynomial in n (the number of variables) and k (the maximum domain size). For temporal networks, NPC-2 achieves path-consistency in $O(n^3 R^3)$, where R is the range of the network (expressed in terms of the coarsest possible time units) as follows:

DEFINITION   **(range)**
12.8
Let T be an integral TCSP. The range of a constraint $T_{ij} = \{[a_1, b_1], \ldots, [a_n, b_n]\}$ is $b_n - a_1$. The range of T is the maximum range over all constraints.   •

THEOREM   Temporal path-consistency of a TCSP can be achieved by NPC-2 in $O(n^3 R)$
12.6   composition steps (step 5 of NPC-2) and $O(n^3 R^3)$ arithmetic operations, where R is the range of the TCSP expressed in the coarsest possible time units.

Proof   Let T be a given TCSP. Without loss of generality, we may assume T is integral (otherwise, we can simulate the algorithm on the equivalent integral network). The worst-case running time of NPC-2 occurs when every constraint interval is decreased by only one time unit each time it is tightened by composition and intersection. In this case, if R is the maximum constraint range, each constraint might be updated $O(R)$ times. Also in the worst case, when a constraint is modified, $O(n)$ paths are added to Q. Thus, if we use the number of composition steps as the complexity measure,

```
DPC

Input: A TCSP, T, and a variable ordering d = (x_1, ... , x_n).

Output: A directional path-consistent network along d.

1. for r := n downto 1 by -1 do
2.      for all i, j < k such that (i,k), (j, k) ∈ E do begin
3.          T_ij ← T_ij ⊕ T_ik ⊗ T_kj
4.          E ← E ∪ (i, j)
5.          if T_ij = ∅ then
6.              exit (the network is inconsistent)
7. end
```

Figure 12.14 DPC—an algorithm enforcing directional path-consistency.

then the total complexity of NPC-2 is $O(n^3 R)$, since there are $O(n^2)$ constraints. Each composition step involves $O(k^2)$ arithmetic operations, since R can bound the number of intervals of a single constraint.

Note that R must be at least as large as k (the number of intervals per constraint). However, if the edges are labeled by a few intervals, $O(k^e)$ may reflect a lower complexity than $O(R^3)$. ●

EXAMPLE 12.9 Consider a constraint $x_i - x_j \in [-1000, -990] \cup [-800, 800] \cup [990, 1000]$. The range R of this constraint is $[-1000, 1000]$. For such a range R, the previous theorem implies that NPC-2 might need to update the constraints thousands of times. ●

As we by now know, although path-consistency algorithms are not guaranteed to compute the minimal network, they often provide a practical alternative and a complementary approach to the full decomposition scheme. In addition, some problems may benefit from the weaker version of path-consistency, *directional path-consistency*, which can be enforced more efficiently, and which is presented in Figure 12.14.

Fragmentation and Its Remedies

Enforcing path-consistency on TCSPs is problematic when the range R is large. An upper bound on the number of intervals in $T \otimes S$ is $|T| \cdot |S|$, where $|T|$ and $|S|$ are the number of intervals in T and S, respectively. As a result, the total number of intervals in the path-consistent network might be exponential relative to the number of intervals per constraint in the input network (yet bounded by R for integer domains).

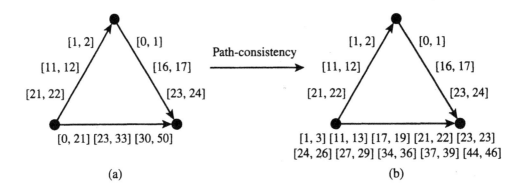

Figure 12.15 The fragmentation problem.

EXAMPLE 12.10

Consider the network presented in Figure 12.15a, having three variables, three constraints, and three intervals per constraint. After enforcing path-consistency, two constraints remain unchanged while the third is broken into 10 subintervals. As this behavior is repeated over numerous triangles in the network, the number of intervals may become exponential. The result is in Figure 12.15b. •

The fragmentation problem can be avoided by enforcing looser consistency than path-consistency, one which imposes fewer intervals that subsume all the intervals in the path-induced constraint. One such algorithm, called UPPER-LOWER-TIGHTENING (ULT), applies the STP algorithm to the network, even though the network is not simple. The idea is to use the extreme points of all intervals associated with a single constraint as one big interval, yielding an STP, and then to apply path-consistency (i.e., a shortest-path procedure) on that STP. Finally, the resulting network is intersected with the input network. This process can only decrease the number of intervals per constraint. Algorithm ULT is given in Figure 12.16.

EXAMPLE 12.11

An example run of ULT is given in Figure 12.17. The first iteration removes two intervals, while the second iteration removes one. •

THEOREM 12.7

Algorithm ULT terminates in $O(n^3 ek + e^2 k^2)$ steps, where n is the number of variables, e is the number of edges, and k is the number of intervals in each constraint. •

Note that in contrast to path-consistency, ULT is guaranteed to converge in $O(ek)$ iterations, even if the interval boundaries are not rational. Algorithm ULT and its advanced versions have been shown to be effective alternatives to path-consistency for quantitative networks, especially when incorporated inside a backtracking procedure.

```
ULT
Input: A TCSP T.
Output: A tighter TCSP equivalent to T.
1. N ← T.
2. repeat
3.    Compute N' ← STP(N). (STP(N) is generated by upper-lower bounds of
      range on disjunctive intervals.)
4.    N" ← compute the minimal network of N' using shortest-path algorithm.
5.    N = N''' ← N" ⊕ N.
6. until no change or inconsistent.
7. end
```

Figure 12.16   Algorithm UPPER-LOWER-TIGHTENING (ULT).

12.2.4 **Network-Based Algorithms**

As with general constraint satisfaction problems, temporal constraint networks may potentially exploit the topology of their constraint graphs. However, since temporal networks allow only binary constraints, they can only exploit structures having induced width of 1 or 2, or tree decompositions whose separator size is 1 or 2. The former corresponds to the case of nonseparable components. Applying a general tree decomposition algorithm, however, is not natural since it requires enforcing constraints of larger scopes, which are not in the language of binary temporal networks. Moreover, the idea of cycle-cutset cannot be employed beneficially in quantitative temporal problems because the backtracking used in the solution of TCSPs instantiates arcs, rather than variables, and such instantiations do not decompose the original network in the same way.

12.3 **Translations between Representations**

In this section, we relate the temporal TCSP model to two qualitative models of temporal reasoning: IA and PA. To facilitate such encoding, we allow the interval representation of constraints to include open and semi-open intervals, with the obvious effect on the definitions of the union and intersection operations.

Any constraint network in PA is a special case of a TCSP lacking metric information. Translating a PA network into a TCSP is straightforward. Constraints of the form $x_j < x_i$ and $x_j \leq x_i$ are expressed by the interval representations $T_{ij} = \{(-\infty, 0)\}$ and $T_{ij} = \{(-\infty, 0]\}$, respectively. The constraint $x_i = x_j$ translates into $T_{ij} = \{[0]\}$.

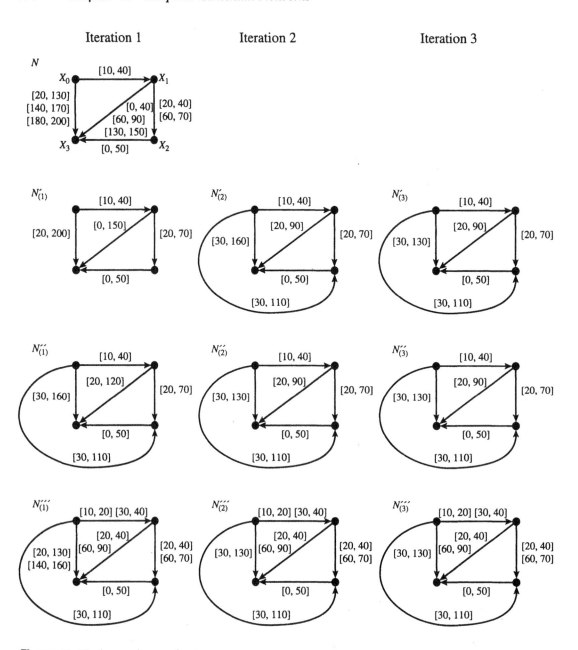

Figure 12.17 A sample run of ULT.

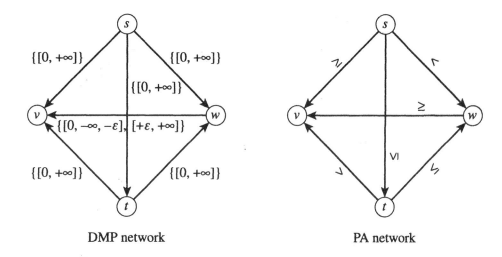

Figure 12.18 A PA network and its encoding as a TCSP.

The only relation that needs to be represented by a disjunction is $x_i \neq x_j$, translated into $T_{ij} = \{(-\infty, 0), (0, \infty)\}$. For example, in Figure 12.18, we see a PA network and its exact translation into a numerical TCSP network. Both networks are path-consistent but not minimal.

Thus, the full PA, including the $\neq$ relation, translates into TCSPs with disjunctions, for which the general methods can be applied and the special structure of the constraints exploited. In contrast, IA networks cannot always be translated into binary TCSPs because such a translation may require nonbinary constraints.

12.4 **Summary**

This chapter presented a basic constraint network approach for handling constraints conveying temporal information as developed in the artificial intelligence literature in the past two decades. The two main approaches of qualitative networks (point and interval) as well as quantitative networks were introduced, and the basic algorithms and concepts for their processing were presented and analyzed. Specifically, Allen's interval algebra (Allen 1983) and Vilain and Kautz's point algebra (Vilain and Kautz 1986) were given a formal constraint treatment. The quantitative network model expresses only binary constraints between variables that denote points from the domains of the reals. The constraints are disjunctions of intervals bounding the distances between pairs of variables. The tractable case of a simple temporal network was discussed. The general reasoning in both quantitative and qualitative networks is hard. But special cases of the point algebra as well as the simple temporal quantitative network are polynomial. Path-consistency for all these networks is defined, and a general backtracking scheme can be used to compute a solution in each of the networks incorporating path-consistency as a look-ahead scheme. We showed how the simple network can be used for approximating the solution of the general quantitative TCSP using an algorithm called ULT. Finally, a mapping of qualitative constraints to quantitative ones was given.

12.5 **Bibliographical Notes**

The work on temporal reasoning within the framework of constraint satisfaction problems was initiated with the influential interval algebra of Allen (1983), and was followed by Vilain and Kautz's (1986) point algebra. They also proved that IA is NP-complete. Other advances for qualitative networks appear in van Beek (1989,1990). These works provide the basis for temporal qualitative constraint networks. Koubarakis (1995) showed that minimal interval networks are not necessarily backtrack-free. The work on quantitative temporal reasoning was introduced by Dechter, Meiri, and Pearl (1990), which firmly laces temporal reasoning within the framework of constraint processing terminology and algorithms. These works were preceded and influenced by earlier papers involving computation of linear inequalities by Malik and Binford (1983), by Valdes-Perez (1986,1987), by Shostak (1981) and Leiserson and Saxe (1983), by Dean and McDermott's time map (Dean and McDermott 1987; Dean 1989), as well as by the work by Davis (1987) and Ladkin, Maddux, and Reinfeld (Ladkin 1988,1989; Ladkin and Maddux 1989; Ladkin and Reinfeld 1992). For more details, see the survey by Schwalb and Villa (1998).

Example 12.1 is due to to Allen (1983) and Example 12.2 is due to Kautz, Vilain, and van Beek (1989). The proof that path-consistency for interval algebra is $O(n^3)$ is due to Allen (1983), and Example 12.6 is from Vilain and Kautz (1986).

Since temporal constraint satisfaction has become a subarea of constraint processing, there has been an influx of research interest. The work presented in this chapter is based primarily on work in the late 1980s and early 1990s describing the interval algebra, the point algebra, and the quantitative numerical network. Some advancement into approximation methods investigated by Schwalb and Dechter (1997) was also included. All subsequent work, which is quite substantial, is outside the scope of this chapter, however. We will briefly mention some of these developments.

One recent direction has been to combine interval-based and point-based formalisms. Since in many cases we need to express information about both time points and intervals, hybrid systems were obviously required. Early on, Vilain (1982) presented a hybrid system that consisted of both points and intervals. Allen and Hayes (1985) have also noted that a theory that can accommodate both types of objects is needed. Indeed, following the characterization of qualitative and quantitative networks, a few proposals for combining the two frameworks were considered, most notably Meiri's approach (Meiri 1991, 1996) and Kautz and Ladkin's approach (Kautz and Ladkin 1991). Meiri defined a class of networks, called *interval-point algebra* (IPA) networks, where the constraints are relations between points and intervals. Kautz and Ladkin proposed keeping the two networks, quantitative and qualitative, distinct and suggested algorithms that migrate information between the two.

The majority of the current research focuses on the task of identifying tractable classes of temporal networks. This research was started by the influential work of Golumbic and Shamir (1993), who looked at all the subsets of interval algebra and identified some hard and easy subclasses. This work was followed by Nebel and Bürckert (1995), who characterized a maximal tractable subclass of the interval algebra. This research was followed by numerous papers, including Koubarakis (1992, 1995, 1996), the work of Drankergren and Jonsson (1996, 1997), and the work of Gerevini and Schubert (1995). See also Schwalb and Villa (1998). Finally, approximation algorithms such as ULT have been developed, including the work of Schwalb (1998) and Schwalb and Dechter (1997).

12.6 **Exercises**

1. Prove that path-consistency for the interval algebra can be achieved in $O(n^3)$.

2. Define IA as a CSP where the variables are relationships between pairs of intervals, their values are the possible relations, and constraints are defined via the composition tables.

3. Consider the IA network in Figure 12.3.

   (a) Generate the path-consistent network of this example.

   (b) Is the path-consistency network minimal?

   (c) Present one possible scenario.

4. Prove that path-consistency for convex point algebra networks yields the minimal network.

5. Consider the point algebra network in Figure 12.6. Find a path-consistent network. Is it minimal?

6. Prove the following:

   Let G_d be the distance graph of a consistent STP, T. The equivalent STP M, defined by $\forall i, j, M_{ij} = \{[-d_{ji}, d_{ij}]\}$, is the minimal network representation of T, and the set of feasible values for variable X_i is $[d_{i0}, d_{0i}]$ (see also, Dechter, Meiri, and Pearl 1990).

   Hint: Show that the domains cannot be tightened; that is, every value in the given domains can be extended to a full solution.

7. Prove the following:

   Any consistent STP is backtrack-free relative to the constraints in its d-graph.

8. Prove the following:

   Given a consistent STP T, the equivalent STP M, defined by $\forall i, j, M_{ij} = \{[-d_{ji}, d_{ij}]\}$, is the minimal network representation of T.

chapter 13

Constraint Optimization

Doing a thing well is often a waste of time.

Robert Byrne

Real-life problems frequently involve both *hard* and *soft* constraints. For example, in time-tabling problems, while a resource constraint such as "a teacher can teach only one class at a time" must be satisfied, a teacher's request to have her "schedule concentrated in just two days" is only a preference, not essential.

When we formalize problems that have both hard and soft constraints, we get a constraint network augmented with a *global cost function* (also called *criterion function* or *objective function*) over all the variables. *Constraint optimization problems* (COPs) find a complete assignment of values to all the variables, satisfying the hard constraints and optimizing the global cost function.

Numerous industrial problems can be modeled as constraint optimization tasks. In particular, scheduling and design tasks involve both hard and soft constraints. Consider the example of maintenance scheduling for power-generating units. A typical power plant consists of one or two dozen power-generating units that can be individually scheduled for preventive maintenance. Both the required time for each unit's maintenance and a reasonably accurate estimate of the plant's power demands are known in advance. The general purpose of determining a maintenance schedule is to determine the duration and sequence of outages of individual power units over a given time period, while minimizing operating and maintenance costs over the planning period in question, subject to various constraints. The schedule is influenced by many factors, including the length of the maintenance period for each unit, restrictions on when maintenance can be performed, the anticipated power demand for the entire plant, and the varying cost of maintenance and fuel at different times of the planning period.

An example from electronic commerce is the combinatorial auction problem. In combinatorial auctions bidders are allowed to place one bid for multiple items. This presents the auctioneer with the problem of determining the optimal selection of bids to maximize revenue. More formally, given a set of items $S = \{a_1, \ldots, a_n\}$ and a set of bids $B = \{b_1, \ldots, b_m\}$, each bid is $b_i = (S_i, r_i)$, where $S_i \subseteq S$ is a set of items and r_i is the cost to be paid for bid b_i. The task is to find a subset of bids $B' \subseteq B$ such that any two bids in B' do not share an item and to maximize $C(B') = \sum_{b_i \in B'} r_i$.

Another rich source of optimization problems is found in the area of planning in artificial intelligence. In the deterministic framework, the task is to find a short sequence of actions (a plan) that achieves a set of goals from a given initial state. Planning problems can be formulated as constraint satisfaction tasks assuming a fixed-length plan. Planning can be alternatively phrased as a constraint optimization tasks, when the global cost function to be optimized is the number of actions (or more generally, the cost) of the plan.

Ultimately, every constraint satisfaction task can be viewed as a constraint optimization problem. When all the constraints cannot be satisfied, you may want to find a solution that maximizes the number of satisfied constraints. This problem is known as the *Max-CSP* problem, and the SAT version is called *Max-SAT*. Constraints can also be assigned importance weights, in which case the task is to *minimize* the weighted sum of violated constraints.

The area of combinatorial optimization was researched extensively in the operation research (OR) community in the past few decades. More recently a new approach for formulating, modeling, learning, and solving soft constraints emerged inside the constraint processing community. In this chapter we adapt the traditional OR approach, which captures the nature of soft constraints as cost components within a global cost function. We will remark on current trends toward the end of the chapter.

In this chapter we will describe the primary approaches for solving discrete constraint optimization tasks and show that they extend constraint satisfaction methods. Specifically, constraint optimization methods can be divided into search-based schemes and inference-based schemes. The most common search algorithm for constraint optimization is *branch-and-bound*, while the most celebrated inference algorithm is *dynamic programming*. We will see the extent to which enhancement schemes for pure constraint satisfaction, such as look-ahead methods for backtracking, constraint propagation, and combined search and inference, can be applied to constraint optimization.

13.1 Constraint Optimization and Cost Networks

A constraint optimization problem is a constraint network augmented with a cost function. Let $X = \{x_1, \ldots, x_n\}$, let $F_1, \ldots, F_l$ be real-valued functional components defined over scopes $Q_1, \ldots, Q_l, Q_j \subseteq X$, let $\bar{a} = (a_1, \ldots, a_n)$, where a_i is in the domain of x_i, and let $\bar{a}_i$ be an assignment to the first i variables. The *global cost function F* is defined by

$$F(\bar{a}) = \sum_{j=1}^{l} F_j(\bar{a})$$

where $F_j(\bar{a})$ means F_j applied to assignments in $\bar{a}$ restricted to the scope of F_j. That is, $F_j(\bar{a}) = F_j(\bar{a}[Q_j])$.

We can view a constraint optimization problem as defined over an extended constraint network called a *cost network*. A cost network is a 4-tuple $\mathcal{C} = (X, D, C_h, C_s)$, where (X, D, C_h) is a constraint network and $C_s = \{F_{Q_1}, \ldots, F_{Q_l}\}$ is an additional set of cost components defined over scopes $Q_1, \ldots, Q_l$, $Q_i = \{x_{i_1}, \ldots, x_{i_l}\}$, $F_{Q_i} : \bowtie_{j=1}^{l} D_{i_j} \rightarrow Reals^+$ (the nonnegative real numbers). Functions in C_s will also be called *soft constraints*. The optimization task is to find $\bar{a}^o = (a_1, \ldots, a_n)$, satisfying all constraints, such that, $F(\bar{a}^o) = \max_{\bar{a}} F(\bar{a})$ or $F(\bar{a}^o) = \min_{\bar{a}} F(\bar{a})$. The cost graph of a cost network has a node for each variable. Arcs connect nodes, denoting variables that appear in the same *hard* or *soft* constraint.

Note that in this and the subsequent chapters we often denote variables by $A, B, C, \ldots$, and their respective domain values by $a, b, c, \ldots$. That is, when letters from the beginning of the alphabet are used, upper case denotes variables and lower case denotes a representative value. However, letters from the end of the alphabet (e.g., x, y, z) will always denote variables.

EXAMPLE 13.1   Consider the cost function $C(a, b, c, d, f, g) = F_0(a) + F_1(a, b) + F_2(a, c) + F_3(b, c, f) + F_4(a, b, d) + F_5(f, g)$, where each F_i is a real-valued function over the domains of the variables A, B, C, D, F, G. The cost network is presented in Figure 13.1.   ●

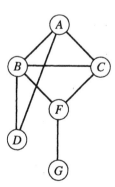

Figure 13.1 The cost graph of the cost function $C(a, b, c, d, f, g) = F_0(a) + F_1(a, b) + F_2(a, c) + F_3(b, c, f) + F_4(a, b, d) + F_5(f, g)$.

EXAMPLE
13.2
Consider the combinatorial auction problem. A simple approach for modeling this problem as a COP is to associate each bid b_i with a variable having two values $\{0, 1\}$, where $b_i = 1$ means that the bid is selected by the auctioneer. Otherwise, it is assigned $b_i = 0$. For every two bids that share an item there is a binary constraint prohibiting the assignment of 1 to both bid variables. Therefore, the variables are $b_1, \ldots, b_r$ having domains $\{0, 1\}$, and the constraints are the following: $\forall i, j$, if b_i and b_j share an item, there is a constraint R_{ij} such that $(b_i = 1, b_j = 1) \notin R_{ij}$. The cost functions are the following: for every b_i $F(b_i) = r_i$ if $b_i = 1$ and otherwise 0. The global cost function is $C = \sum_i F_i(b_i)$. The task is to find a consistent assignment to $b_1, \ldots, b_5$ having $\max_{b_1, \ldots, b_5} \sum_i F_i(b_i)$.

Consider a problem instance given by the following bids: $b_1 = \{1, 2, 3, 4\}$, $b_2 = \{2, 3, 6\}$, $b_3 = \{1, 5, 4\}$, $b_4 = \{2, 8\}$, $b_5 = \{5, 6\}$, and the costs $r_1 = 8$, $r_2 = 6, r_3 = 5, r_4 = 2, r_5 = 2$. In this case the variables are b_1, b_2, b_3, b_4, b_5, their domains are $\{0, 1\}$, and the constraints are $R_{12}, R_{13}, R_{14}, R_{24}, R_{25}, R_{35}$. The cost network for this problem formulation is identical to its constraint network, since all the cost components are unary. You can verify for yourself that an optimal solution is given by $b_1 = 0, b_2 = 1, b_3 = 1$, $b_4 = 0, b_5 = 0$. That is, selecting bids b_2 and b_3 is an optimal choice with total cost of 11. •

13.1.1 Solving COP as a Series of CSPs

We can always find a solution to a COP by solving a series of CSPs $\mathcal{R}^i$: each R^i is the constraint portion of the problem augmented with a constraint $\sum_{j=1}^{l} F_j \geq C^i$, where $C^1 \geq C^2 \geq \cdots \geq C^j$. Initially, a solution is found with a very low cost-bound C^j. The cost-bound is then gradually increased, with a new solution found each time. Eventually, the cost-bound is so high that no solution exists, and the most recently found solution is optimal, within the limit of the amount by which the cost-bound was increased. We can envision a more sophisticated control algorithm based on a binary search approach.

This reduction of constraint optimization to constraint satisfaction clearly permits applying *all* constraint processing techniques to optimization. However, solving multiple CSP problems can be avoided using a more direct approach along the paradigms of search, inference, and their hybrids.

13.2 Branch-and-Bound Search

Let us start with the simplest and most naive way to search for an optimal solution by extending backtracking search. Rather than halt with the first solution, backtracking traverses the search space seeking all solutions. Whenever a solution is found, its cost is evaluated and compared with the best solution found so far, and the current best is retained. This naive approach allows exploiting any backtracking search technique guided by the hard constraints. It is possible, however, to exploit the cost function for further pruning of search. For example, given a partial solution in a minimization task, if the sum of cost functions over its instantiated variables is already higher than the best solution found so far, the partial solution can be aborted. This idea can be generalized to a variety of bounding functions that can help in pruning search.

The above idea is the foundation of a popular optimization algorithm called *depth-first branch-and-bound* (BnB). Branch-and-bound maintains the cost of the best solution found so far. This cost is a lower bound, L, for the optimal cost in a maximization task. In addition, for each partial solution, $\vec{a}_i$, the algorithm also computes an upper bound using a *bounding evaluation function* $f(\vec{a}_i)$, which overestimates the best-cost solution that can extend $\vec{a}_i$. Therefore, when $f(\vec{a}_i) \leq L$, the partial solution $\vec{a}_i$ cannot be extended to a higher-cost solution than the current best one, and the algorithm backtracks, pruning the subtree below $\vec{a}_i$. BnB returns to $\vec{a}_{i-1}$ and attempts to find a new assignment to x_i. The BnB algorithm can also use the bounding function f as a heuristic guide for choosing the next best value for x_i. The algorithm terminates when the first variable has no values left, in which case the algorithm has found an optimal solution.

When hard constraints are included, the search space can be traversed by any of the search methods introduced throughout this book. Search can then be augmented at each node with a test comparing the upper bounding evaluation function f with the current global lower bound for potential pruning.

When the optimization task is *minimization*, the same branch-and-bound algorithm can be used, replacing upper bounds with lower bounds and maximization with minimization. In this case, the current best solution provides a global upper bound on the best solution (U), and the evaluation function at each node should underestimate the best-cost extension. When the bounding value associated with the current partial assignment is higher than the current value of the best solution ($f(\vec{a}_i) \geq U$), pruning can occur.

A generic branch-and-bound algorithm that extends naive backtracking for a maximization tusk is given in Figure 13.2. To focus the exposition on the new aspects associated with cost components, we will assume, unless otherwise noted, that the constraint optimization task has soft cost components only. We will also assume a maximization task throughout the remainder of this chapter. The minimization case is completely analogous.

13.2.1   A "First-Choice" Bounding Function

The primary way to enhance BNB is to improve the accuracy of its (upper) bounding evaluation function. Branch-and-bound algorithms were developed and enhanced substantially for a class of problems, known as *integer programs*, that were developed

procedure BRANCH-AND-BOUND (BNB)

Input: A cost network $\mathcal{C} = (X, D, C_h, C_s)$, L current lower bound. An upper-bound function f defined for every partial solution.

Output: Either an optimal (maximal) solution, or notification that the network is inconsistent.

$i \leftarrow 1$	(initialize variable counter)
$D_i' \leftarrow D_i$	(copy domain)

While $1 \leq i \leq n$

instantiate $x_i \leftarrow$ SELECTVALUE

If x_i is null	(no value was returned)
$i \leftarrow i - 1$	(backtrack)

Else

$i \leftarrow i + 1$	(step forward)
$D_i' \leftarrow D_i$	

Endwhile

If $i = 0$

    Return "inconsistent"

Else

Compute $C = C(x_1, \ldots, x_n)$, $L \leftarrow \max\{C, L\}$

$i \leftarrow n - 1$

end procedure

subprocedure SELECTVALUE

If $i = 0$ **return** L as the solution value and the most recent assignment
    as solution.

While D_i' is not empty

    select an element $a \in D_i'$ having max $f(\vec{a}_{i-1}, a)$

    and remove a from D_i'

If $\langle x_i, a \rangle$ is consistent with $\vec{a}_{i-1}$ and $f > L$, then

Return a	(else prune a)

Endwhile

Return null	(no consistent value)

end procedure

Figure 13.2 The BRANCH-AND-BOUND algorithm.

in the operations research community. Integer programming problems are constraint optimization tasks whose hard constraints and global cost function are linear, and whose variables are defined over the integers. The evaluation function is normally computed by solving a *linear programming problem* at each node over continuous variables that can be accomplished relatively efficiently.

The work in the constraint community extends such ideas to general constraints and general cost functions. In Section 13.4 we will describe a systematic scheme for generating bounding functions in a look-ahead manner based on bounded inference, extending constraint propagation methods. We conclude this section with the *first-choice* (*fc*) bounding functions. Consider a partial assignment $\vec{a}_i$. We define

$$f_{fc}(\vec{a}_i) = \sum_{F_j \in C} \max_{a_{i+1}, \ldots, a_n} F_j(\vec{a}_i, a_{i+1}, \ldots, a_n) \qquad (13.1)$$

where C is the set of all (soft) constraints. Note that computing this upper bound function f_{fc} is a form of look-ahead similar to forward-checking. Since each constraint is considered independently, $f_{fc}(\vec{a}_i)$ provides an upper bound on the maximal full cost assignment of extending $\vec{a}_i$. (For a minimization task we can just replace max with min; the resulting function yields a lower bound on the minimal cost solution extending $\vec{a}_i$.)

EXAMPLE 13.3 Consider the auction problem described in Example 13.2. Searching for a solution in the order $d = b_1, b_2, b_3, b_4, b_5$ yields the search space in Figure 13.3, traversed from left to right. The search space is highly constrained in this case. The evaluation bounding function at each node should *overestimate* its best extension for a solution. The first-choice bounding function for the root node (the empty assignment) is 23. The first solution encountered (selecting $\langle b_1, 1 \rangle$ and $\langle b_5, 1 \rangle$) has a cost of 10, which becomes the current global *lower bound*. The next solution encountered has the cost of 11 (when $\langle b_2, 1 \rangle$ and $\langle b_3, 1 \rangle$), while the rest of the variables are assigned 0. Subsequently, the partial assignment $(\langle b_1, 0 \rangle, \langle b_2, 0 \rangle)$ is explored. Since $f_{fc}(\langle b_1, 0 \rangle, \langle b_2, 0 \rangle) = 9$, this upper bound is lower than 11, and therefore search can be pruned. •

13.2.2 The Russian Doll Search

The Russian doll search algorithm is an elegant idea that can boost many bounding evaluation functions. The idea is to run n successive branch-and-bound searches, each involving a single additional variable (and the relevant added constraints). The first subproblem includes just the nth variable, and the ith subproblem includes the last i variables (from the $n - i + 1$ variable to the nth variable).

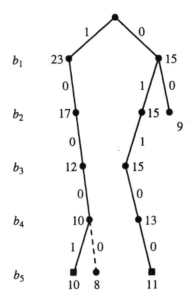

Figure 13.3 Branch-and-bound search space for the auction problem.

Each subproblem is solved by BnB, whose upper and lower bound evaluation functions use information recorded in earlier runs as follows. The $(n - i + 1)$th subproblem involves variables $x_i, x_{i+1}, \ldots, x_n$. Given a partial assignment to this subproblem, $(a_i, a_{i+1}, \ldots, a_{i+j})$ whose variables $A = \{x_{i+j+1}, \ldots, x_n\}$ are not assigned, the evaluation function is improved by adding to the first-cut function the optimal cost derived for the $n-i-j$ subproblem. That is, if $C_{i \ldots c+j}$ are all the cost components whose scopes are included in $\{x_i, \ldots, x_{i+j}\}$ and if a_i^o denotes the optimal cost for the ith subproblem, then $f(a_i, \ldots, a_{i+j}) = \sum_{F \in C_{i \ldots i+j}} F(a_i, \ldots, a_{i+j}) + a_{n-i-j-1}^o$.

In addition, previous optimal solutions are used to heuristically guide value selection and to improve the initial upper bound of each search. It turns out that the pruning power derived by this approach is often cost-effective, despite the increased overhead of having n searches.

13.3 **Bucket Elimination for Optimization**

We will now describe the inference algorithm for solving constraint optimization. The algorithm is a dynamic programming algorithm, analogous to adaptive consistency for constraint processing.

13.3.1   **Deriving** ELIM-OPT

We will develop the algorithm using the example in Figure 13.1. Consider the variables in the order $d_1 = A, C, B, F, D, G$. By definition, we need to compute

$$M = \max_{a,c,b,f,d,g} F_0(a) + F_1(a, b) + F_2(a, c) + F_3(b, c, f) + F_4(a, b, d) + F_5(f, g)$$

We can now apply some simple symbolic manipulation, migrating each cost component to the left of the maximization over variables that it does not reference. We get

$$M = \max_a \max_c F_0(a) + F_2(a, c) + \max_b F_1(a, b) + \max_f F_3(b, c, f)$$

$$+ \max_d F_4(a, b, d) + \max_g F_5(f, g) \tag{13.2}$$

Carrying the computation from right to left (from G to A), we first compute the rightmost maximization, which generates a function over F, $h^G(f)$ defined by $h^G(f) = \max_g F_5(f, g)$ and place it as far to the left as possible, yielding

$$M = \max_a \max_c F_0(a) + F_2(a, c) + \max_b F_1(a, b) + \max_f F_3(b, c, f) + h^G(f)$$

$$+ \max_d F_4(a, b, d) \tag{13.3}$$

Maximizing next over D (generating a function denoted $h^D(a, b)$, defined by $h^D(a, b) = \max_d F_4(a, b, d)$), we get

$$M = \max_a \max_c F_0(a) + F_2(a, c) + \max_b F_1(a, b) + h^D(a, b)$$

$$+ \max_f F_3(b, c, f) + h^G(f) \tag{13.4}$$

Next, maximizing over F (generating $h^F(b, c) = \max_f F_3(b, c, f) + h^G(f)$, we get

$$M = \max_a \max_c F_0(a) + F_2(a, c) + \max_b F_1(a, b) + h^D(a, b) + h^F(b, c) \tag{13.5}$$

Maximizing over B (generating $h^B(a, c)$), we get

$$M = \max_a \max_c F_0(a) + F_2(a, c) + h^B(a, c) \tag{13.6}$$

Finally, maximizing over C (generating $h^C(a)$), we get

$$M = \max_a F_0(a) + h^C(a) \tag{13.7}$$

The bucket elimination algorithm mimics the above algebraic manipulation by the familiar organizational data structure of *buckets*, each bucket holding a set of functions, as follows. First, the cost functions are partitioned into buckets relative to

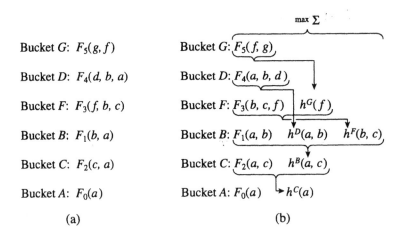

Figure 13.4 Bucket elimination along ordering $d_1 = A, C, B, F, D, G$. (a) The initial buckets. (b) The augmented buckets.

the order used, $d_1 = A, C, B, F, D, G$. In bucket G we place all functions mentioning G. From the remaining cost components F_j, we place all those mentioning D in bucket D, and so on. In general, in x_i's bucket (denoted $bucket_{x_i}$ or $bucket_i$) we place all the functions that mention x_i without mentioning any variable having a higher index. The resulting initial partitioning for our example is given in Figure 13.4(a), and it corresponds to deriving the expression in Equation (13.2). Now we process the buckets from last to first (in the figures, top to bottom), implementing the right-to-left computation of Equation (13.2). Processing a bucket amounts to summing its functions and eliminating the bucket's variable by maximization. *Bucket*$_G$ is processed first. The function $h^G(f) = \max_g F_5(f, g)$ is computed and placed in *bucket*$_F$ (this corresponds to deriving Equation (13.3) from Equation (13.2)).

Bucket$_D$ is processed next. We maximize out D, getting $h^D(b, a) = \max_d F_4(a, b, d)$, which is placed in *bucket*$_B$ (which corresponds to deriving Equation (13.4) from Equation (13.3)). The next variable is F. *Bucket*$_F$ contains two functions $F_3(b, c, f)$ and $h^G(f)$. Following Equation (13.5), we generate the function $h^F(b, c) = \max_f (F_3(b, c, f) + h^G(f))$, which is placed in *bucket*$_B$. In processing the next *bucket*$_B$, the function $h^B(a, c) = \max_b (F_1(a, b) + h^D(b, a) + h^F(b, c))$ is computed and placed in *bucket*$_C$ (deriving Equation (13.6) from Equation (13.5)), and so on. Figure 13.4(b) summarizes the flow of computation.

Subsequently, an optimizing tuple can be computed by selecting a value a that maximizes the function $h^C(a) + F_0(a)$ in its bucket, then selecting a value c that maximizes the function in bucket C given the value a, $(h^B(a, c) + F_2(a, c))$, and so on. Throughout this process we record at most two-dimensional functions. The complexity of the algorithm using ordering d_1 is (roughly) time and space quadratic in the domain sizes.

What will occur if we use a different variable ordering? For example, let's apply the algorithm using $d_2 = A, F, D, C, B, G$. Applying algebraic manipulation from right to left along d_2 yields the initial expression

$$M = \max_{a,f,d,c,b,g} F_0(a) + F_1(a,b) + F_2(a,c) + F_3(b,c,f) + F_4(a,b,d) + F_5(f,g)$$

$$= \max_a \max_f F_0(a) + \max_d \max_c F_2(a,c) + \max_b F_1(a,b) + F_3(b,c,f)$$

$$+ F_4(a,b,d) + \max_g F_5(f,g)$$

The following computation occurs in the respective buckets:

Bucket G: $h^G(f) = \max_g F_5(f,g)$

Bucket B: $h^B(a,c,d,f) = \max_b(F_4(a,b,d) + F_1(a,b) + F_3(b,c,f))$

Bucket C: $h^C(a,d,f) = \max_c(h^B(a,c,d,f) + F_2(a,c))$

Bucket D: $h^D(a,f) = \max_d h^C(a,d,f)$

Bucket F: $h^F(a) = \max_f(h^D(a,f) + h^G(f))$

Bucket A: $h^A = \max_a(F_0(a) + h^F(a))$

$M = h^G$

The flow of computation along ordering d_2 will be depicted in Figure 13.11(a), which we will discuss later. Note that in this case functions on four variables were created.

The same derivation can be generalized, yielding algorithm ELIM-OPT, described in Figure 13.5. It is a variable elimination process similar to adaptive consistency, where the join operation is replaced by summation and the projection by maximization. If the task at hand is minimization, the only change required is to replace the maximization operator by a minimization operator.

From the above derivation we can conclude that the ELIM-OPT algorithm is guaranteed to find the value of the optimal solutions in its backward phase (step 2). Going forward (step 3) it generates an optimal solution by consulting all the bucket's functions, guiding it to choose a maximizing value for each variable.

THEOREM
13.1   Given a cost network, step 2 of ELIM-OPT generates an augmented cost network representation from which the optimal solution can be generated in linear time by a greedy procedure (step 3). (For proof see Exercise 5.)   ●

Incorporating Hard Constraints

When a problem involves both hard and soft constraints, ELIM-OPT can be adjusted to the hard constraints. The revised algorithm ELIM-OPT-CONS in Figure 13.6 allows

---

ELIM-OPT

Input: A cost network $\mathcal{C} = (X,D,C)$, $C = \{F_1,\ldots,F_l\}$; ordering d.

Output: The maximal cost assignment to $\sum_j F_j$.

1. **Initialize:** Partition the cost components into ordered buckets.

2. **Process buckets** from $p \leftarrow n$ downto 1

For costs $h_1, h_2, \ldots, h_j$ defined over scopes $Q_1, \ldots, Q_j$ in $bucket_p$, do:

- **If** (observed variable) $x_p = a_p$, assign $x_p = a_p$ to each h_j and put in appropriate buckets.

- **Else** (sum and maximize)
  $A \leftarrow \cup_i Q_i - \{x_p\}$
  $h^p = \max_{x_p} \sum_{i=1}^{j} h_i$
  Place h^p in the latest lower bucket mentioning a variable in A.

3. **Forward:** From $i = 1$ to n, given $\vec{a}_{i-1}$, assign x_i a value a_i that maximizes the sum values of functions in its bucket.

4. **Return** the optimal cost computed in the bucket of x_1 and the optimal assignment.

Figure 13.5 Dynamic programming as ELIM-OPT.

constraint operations that are processed by join-project as well as by the cost function operation. Note that it is always possible to treat constraints as cost functions and apply ELIM-OPT. This, however, may result in an inferior algorithm. Hard constraints have stronger properties that can be exploited only if expressed explicitly.

Generating a hard constraint in a bucket (step 2 of the "else" part in ELIM-OPT-CONS) is *optional*. It can be dropped without affecting the algorithm's correctness since the constraints are taken into account in the maximization operator. It is worthwhile maintaining this operator because it permits the use of local consistency enforcing, which may have the computational benefits observed for directional *i*-consistency (see Chapters 4 and 8).

13.3.2 Complexity

We see that although ELIM-OPT can be applied using any ordering, its complexity varies considerably depending on the ordering used. Using ordering d_1 we recorded functions on pairs of variables only, while using d_2 we had to record functions on four variables (see *Bucket$_C$* in Figure 13.11(a)). The arity of the functions recorded

---

ELIM-OPT-CONS

Input: A cost network $\mathcal{C} = (X, D, C_h, C_s)$, $C_h = \{R_{S_1}, \ldots, R_{S_m}\}$; $C_s = \{F_{Q_1}, \ldots, F_{Q_l}\}$; ordering d.

Output: A consistent solution that maximizes $\sum_{F_i \in C_s} F_i$.

1. **Initialize:** Partition the C_s and C_h into buckets using the usual rule.

2. **Process buckets** from $p \leftarrow n$ downto 1,

For costs $h_1, h_2, \ldots, h_j$ defined over scopes $Q_1, \ldots, Q_j$, for hard constraint relations $R_1, R_2, \ldots, R_t$ defined over scopes $S_1, \ldots, S_t$ in $bucket_p$, do:

- **If** (observed variable) $x_p = a_p$, assign $x_p = a_p$ to each h_i and each R_i and put in appropriate buckets. Terminate if value is inconsistent.

- **Else** (sum and maximize, join and project)

    1. Let $U_p = \cup_i S_i - \{x_p\}$, $V_p = \cup_i Q_i - \{x_p\}$, $W_p = U_p \cup V_p$.

    2. $R^p = \pi_{U_p} (\bowtie_{i=1}^t R_i)$ (generate the hard constraint).

    3. For every tuple t over W_p do (generate the cost function):
       $h^p(t) = \max_{\{a_p | (t, a_p) \text{ satisfies } \{R_1, \ldots, R_l\}\}} \sum_{i=1}^j h_i(t, a_p)$.
       Place h^p in the latest lower bucket mentioning a variable in W_p. Place R^p in the bucket of the latest variable in U_p.

3. **Forward:** Assign maximizing values in ordering d, consulting functions in each bucket.

4. **Return** the optimal cost computed in the bucket of x_1 and the optimal assignment.

Figure 13.6 Algorithm ELIM-OPT-CONS.

in a bucket equals the number of variables appearing in that bucket, excluding the bucket's variable. Since computing and recording a function of arity r is time and space exponential in r, the complexity of the algorithm is exponential in the size (number of variables) of the largest bucket.

Fortunately, as was observed in earlier chapters for ADAPTIVE-CONSISTENCY and DIRECTIONAL-RESOLUTION, the bucket sizes for a given ordering are easily predicted.

Since a function is recorded during processing on all the variables appearing in the bucket of a variable (which is the set of its earlier neighbors in the ordered graph), these nodes should be connected. If we perform this graph operation recursively from last node to first (for each node connecting its earliest neighbors), we get the *induced graph*, which we saw already in Chapter 4. The induced width, denoted $w^*(d)$, equals the maximal width in the induced graph and is identical

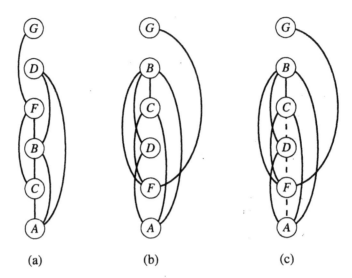

Figure 13.7 Two orderings of the cost graph of our example problem: (a) ordering $d_1 = A, C, B, F, D, G$, (b) $d_2 = A, F, D, C, B, G$. (c) The induced ordered graph along d_2.

to the size of the largest bucket. For more discussion and a formal definition, see Section 4.1.

EXAMPLE 13.4 The induced graph of the cost graph in Figure 13.1, relative to ordering $d_1 = A, C, B, F, D, G$, is depicted in Figure 13.7(a). In this case, the ordered graph and its induced ordered graph are identical, since all the earlier neighbors of each node are already connected. The maximum induced width is 2. Indeed, in this case, the maximum arity of functions recorded by the variable elimination algorithms is 2. For $d_2 = A, F, D, C, B, G$ the induced graph is depicted in Figure 13.7(c). The width of C is initially 2, while its induced width is 3. The maximum induced width over all variables for d_2 is 4, and so is the scope of the recorded function.   •

In summary, we have the following:

THEOREM 13.2 Given an ordering d, the complexity of ELIM-OPT (and ELIM-OPT-CONS) over a cost network having r hard and soft constraints is $O(r \cdot K^{w^*(d)+1})$ time and space when $w^*(d)$ is the induced width $w^*(d)$ of the network's ordered cost graph (See Theorem 4.9).   •

EXAMPLE 13.5 Consider again the auction problem in Example 13.2. The problem involves only binary constraints between bid variables. We denote the constraint between variable b_i and b_j by R_{ij}. Let's pick the ordering

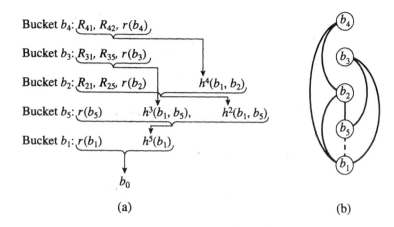

Bucket b_4: R_{41}, R_{42}, $r(b_4)$,

Bucket b_3: R_{31}, R_{35}, $r(b_3)$,

Bucket b_2: R_{21}, R_{25}, $r(b_2)$ $h^4(b_1, b_2)$,

Bucket b_5: $r(b_5)$ $h^3(b_1, b_5)$, $h^2(b_1, b_5)$,

Bucket b_1: $r(b_1)$ $h^5(b_1)$,

b_0

(a)

(b)

Figure 13.8 (a) Schematic execution of ELIM-OPT on the auction problem. (b) A corresponding induced-ordered graph.

$d = b_1, b_5, b_2, b_3, b_4$ whose induced width is 2. The execution of the bucket elimination algorithm along d is depicted schematically in Figure 13.8(a), while the induced graph is given in Figure 13.8(b). As before, we denote the generated functions by h and use a superscript to denote the bucket where they were created. In this example the constraints generated by the join-project operation in each bucket (by ELIM-OPT-CONS) are universal constraints and are therefore not accounted for. We start by processing bucket b_4. In this bucket we compute $h^4(b_1, b_2) = \max_{\{(b_4 | (b_1, b_2, b_4)) \in R_{41} \bowtie R_{42}\}} r(b_4)$, yielding

$$h^4(b_1, b_2) = \begin{cases} 0 & \text{if } b_1 = 1, \text{ or } b_2 = 1 \\ 2 & \text{if } b_1 = 0, b_2 = 0 \end{cases}$$

Processing bucket b_3 we compute $h^3(b_1, b_5) = \max_{\{(b_3 | (b_1, b_3, b_5)) \in R_{31} \bowtie R_{35}\}} r(b_3)$, yielding

$$h^3(b_1, b_5) = \begin{cases} 0 & \text{if } b_1 = 1, \text{ or } b_5 = 1 \\ 5 & \text{if } b_1 = 0, b_5 = 0 \end{cases}$$

Processing bucket b_2, which now includes a new function, gives us $h^2(b_1, b_5) = \max_{\{(b_2 | (b_1, b_2, b_5)) \in R_{21} \bowtie R_{25}\}} (r(b_2) + h^4(b_1, b_2))$, yielding

$$h^2(b_1, b_5) = \begin{cases} 0 & \text{if } b_1 = 1, b_5 = 1 \\ 0 & \text{if } b_1 = 1, b_5 = 0 \\ 2 & \text{if } b_1 = 0, b_5 = 1 \\ 6 & \text{if } b_1 = 0, b_5 = 0 \end{cases}$$

Next we process bucket b_5, computing $h^5(b_1) = \max_{b_5}(r(b_5) + h^2(b_1, b_5) + h^3(b_1, b_5))$, and yielding

$$h^5(b_1) = \begin{cases} 2 & \text{if } b_1 = 1 \\ 11 & \text{if } b_1 = 0 \end{cases}$$

Finally, in the bucket of b_1 we compute $h^1 = \max_{b_1}(r(b_1) + h^5(b_1))$, yielding $h^1 = \max\{11, 10\} = 11$.

The maximal value is therefore 11. To compute the maximizing tuple we select in bucket b_1 the value $b_1 = 0$, which maximizes $r(b_1) + h^5(b_1)$. Given $b_1 = 0$, the value of b_5 that maximizes the functions in bucket b_5 is 0. Subsequently, the assignment $b_2 = 1$ is selected, maximizing $r(b_2) + h^4(b_1 = 0, b_2)$. Then $b_3 = 1$ is selected, maximizing $r(b_3)$, and finally the only choice is $b_4 = 0$.   ●

13.3.3 **Counting the Number of Solutions**

Counting the number of solutions to a CSP is an important task that is known to be very hard (#P-complete) and has received substantial attention. Nevertheless, the problem can be elegantly solved by a variable elimination algorithm. It is particularly easy to introduce the algorithm here since it resembles ELIM-OPT so closely. Given a constraint network, and assuming its input relations are described via cost functions with costs of 1 for a consistent tuple and 0 for an inconsistent tuple, we replace maximization in ELIM-OPT by summation and summation by product. We get ELIM-COUNT, the bucket elimination algorithm for counting. Thus, when the bucket of a variable is processed, the algorithm multiplies all the functions in the bucket and sums over the bucket's variable. This yields a new function that associates with each tuple (over the bucket's scope excluding the bucket's variable) the number of consistent extensions to the eliminated variables. Figure 13.9 presents the ELIM-COUNT algorithm. The complexity of ELIM-COUNT obeys the general time and space complexity of bucket elimination algorithms. The correctness of the algorithm can be proved (see Exercise 5).

THEOREM   The time and space complexity of algorithm ELIM-COUNT is $O(e \cdot$
13.3 $exp(w^*(d)))$ where e is the number of constraints and $w^*(d)$ is the induced width of the network's ordered constraint graph along d.   ●

Clearly, the counting problem can also be solved by search, traversing the search space using any of the backtracking search algorithms we encountered. Any of the hybrid algorithms of search and inference can then be applied.

ELIM-COUNT

Input: A constraint network $\mathcal{R} = (X, D, C)$, ordering d.

Output: Augmented output buckets including the intermediate count functions and the total number of solutions.

1. **Initialize:** Partition C (0-1 cost functions) into ordered buckets $bucket_1, \ldots, bucket_n$. We denote a function in a bucket N_i, and its scope S_i.

2. **Backward:** For $p \leftarrow n$ downto 1, do
   Generate the function N^p: $N^p = \sum_{X_p} \prod_{N_i \in bucket_p} N_i$.
   Add N^p to the bucket of the latest variable in $\bigcup_{i=1}^{j} S_i - \{X_p\}$.

3. **Return** the number of solutions, N^1 and the set of output buckets with the original and computed functions.

Figure 13.9 Algorithm ELIM-COUNT.

13.4 **Mini-bucket Elimination**

As observed for constraint processing, bucket elimination algorithms have a serious drawback. They require exponential space unless the problem is sparse enough to yield a small induced width. Constraint processing responds to this problem by replacing full inference with bounded constraint propagation algorithms that enforce local consistency (Chapters 3, 4, and 8). We have seen how such sound but incomplete inference methods (arc-, path-, and i-consistency) can be used prior to or during search, making the problem more explicit, and how they can facilitate look-ahead improvements to backtracking.

Can such bounded inference propagation be extended to optimization? Given a set of constraints $\mathcal{R} = \{R_1, \ldots, R_l\}$, extended composition is the primary *global* inference operation. It eliminates a variable x, recording its impact on the rest of the variables by

$$\pi_{A-\{x\}} \bowtie_{j=1}^{l} R_j \tag{13.8}$$

where A is the scope of all participating constraints. Instead, this operator can be approximated by applying extended composition only to subsets of these constraints, thus reducing computation. In relational arc-consistency, for example, we compute for every R_i, $\pi_{A-\{x\}} R_i$, thus replacing Equation (13.8) with

$$\bowtie_{j=1}^{l} \pi_{A-\{x\}} R_j \tag{13.9}$$

In *i*-consistency, we consider B^i, which is the set of *all* subsets of the constraints $\mathcal{R}$ having at most *i* variables altogether, and replace Equation (13.8) by

$$\bowtie_{B \in B^i} \pi_{A-\{x\}} \bowtie_{R \in B} R \tag{13.10}$$

We can do the same, it seems, for optimization. Replacing pure relational constraints with cost components, the join operator by summation, and the projection by maximization in Equation (13.8) yields the inference operation computed in each bucket of ELIM-OPT:

$$\max_x \sum_{j=1}^{l} F_j \tag{13.11}$$

Similarly, we can replace Equation (13.10) by

$$\sum_{B \in B^i} \max_x \sum_{F_j \in B} F_j$$

There is an inherent difference, however, between constraints and cost components: cost functions do not allow full chaotic constraint propagation. They do allow, however, an organized form of propagation such as directional constraint propagation, called *mini-bucket propagation*.

The idea here is to approximate the function recorded by the algorithm in each bucket with a collection of smaller-arity functions. Let $h_1, \ldots, h_t$ be the functions in the bucket of x_p, and let $S_1, \ldots, S_t$ be their scopes. When ELIM-OPT processes the bucket of x_p, the function $h^p = \max_{x_p} \sum_{i=1}^{t} h_i$ is computed. A simple approximation idea is to compute an upper bound on h^p by "migrating" the maximization inside the summation. Since, in general, for any two nonnegative functions $Z(x)$ and $Y(x)$, $\max_x(Z(x) + Y(x)) \leq \max_x Z(x) + \max_x Y(x)$, this approximation will compute an upper bound. Therefore, we can compute a new function $g^p = \sum_{i=1}^{t} \max_{x_p} h_i$, which is an upper bound on h^p. Procedurally, this approach means that maximization is applied separately to each cost function, requiring less computation.

The idea can be generalized to any partitioning of a set of functions $h_1, \ldots, h_t$ into subsets called *mini-buckets*. Let $Q = \{Q_1, \ldots, Q_m\}$ be a partitioning into minibuckets of the functions $h_1, \ldots, h_t$ in x_p's bucket, where the mini-bucket Q_l contains the functions $h_{l_1}, \ldots, h_{l_r}$. The exact algorithm, ELIM-OPT, computes $h^p = \max_{x_p} \sum_{i=1}^{t} h_i$, which can be rewritten as $h^p = \max_{x_p} \sum_{l=1}^{m} \sum_{l_i} h_{l_i}$. By migrating maximization into each mini-bucket we compute $g^p = \sum_{l=1}^{m} \max_{x_p} \sum_{l_i} h_{l_i}$. The new functions, derived by $\max_{x_p} \sum_{l_i} h_{l_i}$ are placed separately into the buckets of the highest variable in their scope, and the algorithm proceeds with the next variable. Functions without arguments (i.e., constants) are placed in the lowest bucket. The maximized summand generated in the first bucket is thus an upper bound on the maximum cost solution. Subsequently, a lower bound can also be computed (in the same way as it is done by ELIM-OPT) as the cost of an assignment found in the forward step of the algorithm.

The quality of the bounds (lower and upper) depends on the degree of the partitioning into mini-buckets. Given a bounding parameter i, the algorithm creates an i-partitioning, where each mini-bucket includes no more than i variables. This is similar to directional i-consistency algorithms. The difference is that in the constraint case, mini-buckets were allowed to share constraints, while for optimization, a bounding approximation (upper or lower) is desired. To avoid redundancy a function should only appear in a single mini-bucket. Algorithm MBE-OPT(i), described in Figure 13.10, is parameterized by this i-bound. The algorithm outputs not only an upper bound on the cost of the optimal solution and an assignment, but also the collection of augmented buckets. By comparing the bound computed by MBE-OPT(i) in its Backward step to the cost of the assignment output by MBE-OPT(i) in its Forward step, we can always have an interval bound on the error for the given instance.

Clearly, there are many legitimate ways to partition a bucket into mini-buckets whose scopes are bounded by i, leading to different accuracies in the resulting upper bounds. Therefore, good heuristics for partitionings should be explored.

MBE-OPT(i)

Input: A cost network $\mathcal{C} = (X, D, C)$; an ordering d; parameter i.

Output: (a) An upper bound on the optimal cost solution, (b) an approximate solution, (c) a lower bound, and (d) the ordered augmented buckets.

1. **Initialize:** Partition the functions in C into $bucket_1, \dots, bucket_n$, where $bucket_i$ contains all functions whose highest variable is x_i. Let $S_1, \dots, S_m$ be the scopes of functions (new or old) in the processed bucket.

2. **Backward** For $p \leftarrow n$ downto 1, do

   - **If** variable x_p is instantiated ($x_p = a_p$), assign $x_p = a_p$ to each h_i and put each resulting function into its appropriate bucket.

   - **Else,** for $h_1, h_2, \dots, h_m$ in $bucket_p$, generate an (i)-partitioning, $Q' = \{Q_1, \dots, Q_t\}$.

   For each $Q_l \in Q'$ containing $h_{l_1}, \dots, h_{l_t}$ generate function h^l, $h^l = \max_{x_p} \sum_{i=1}^{t} h_{l_i}$.
   Add h^l to the bucket of the largest-index variable in U_l, $U_l = \bigcup_{i=1}^{m} scope(h_{l_i}) - \{x_p\}$.

3. **Forward** For $p = 1$ to n do, given $a_1, \dots, a_{p-1}$ choose a value a_p of x_p that maximizes the sum of all the functions in x_p's bucket.

4. **Return** the ordered set of augmented buckets, an assignment $\bar{a} = (a_1, \dots, a_n)$, an interval bound (the value computed in $bucket_1$ and the cost $F(\bar{a})$).

Figure 13.10 Mini-bucket elimination algorithm.

The algorithm's complexity is time and space $O(\exp(i))$ where $i \leq n$. When the bound i is large enough (i.e., when $i \geq w^*$), the mini-bucket algorithm coincides with ELIM-OPT. We conclude the following:

THEOREM 13.4

Algorithm MBE-OPT(i) generates an interval bound on the cost of the optimal solution, and its time and space complexity is $O(r \cdot \exp(i))$ and $O(r \cdot \exp(i-1))$, respectively, where r is the total number of cost functions. (For a proof, do Exercise 6.)   •

EXAMPLE 13.6

Figure 13.11 illustrates how algorithms ELIM-OPT and MBE-OPT(i) for $i = 3$ process the network in Figure 13.1 along the ordering $d = (A, F, D, C, B, G)$. Algorithm ELIM-OPT generates the functions $h^B(a, c, d, f)$, $h^C(a, d, f)$, $h^D(a, e)$, and $h^E(a)$. In the bucket of A, the algorithm then computes the cost $\max_a[h^E(a) + F_0(a)]$. Subsequently, an optimal tuple $(A = a', B = b', C = c', D = d', E = e')$ is computed for each variable along d_1 by selecting a value that optimizes the sum of functions in the corresponding buckets, conditioned on the previously assigned values. That is, $a' = \arg\max_a[h^E(a) + F_0(a)]$, $f' = \arg\max_f h^G(f) + h^D(a', f)$, $d' = \arg\max_{d \in D} h^C(a', d, f')$, and so on.

Algorithm MBE-OPT(3) splits bucket B into two mini-buckets, each containing no more than three variables, and generates $h^B(c, f)$ and $h^B(a, d)$. An upper bound on the maximizing cost is computed in bucket A by $\max_a[h^F(a) + h^D(a) + F_0(a)]$. Subsequently, a suboptimal tuple is

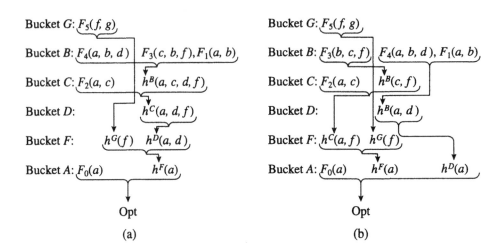

Figure 13.11   Execution of (a) ELIM-OPT and (b) MBE-OPT(i).

$$\text{Bucket } b_4 : \quad [R_{41}], [R_{42}, r(b_4)]$$

$$\text{Bucket } b_3 : \quad [R_{31}], [R_{35}, r(b_3)]$$

$$\text{Bucket } b_2 : \quad [R_{21}], [R_{25}, r(b_2) \ || \ h^4(b_2)]$$

$$\text{Bucket } b_5 : \quad [r(b_5) \ || \ h^3(b_5), h^2(b_5)]$$

$$\text{Bucket } b_1 : \quad r(b_1) \ || \ h^5$$

$$\text{Yielding: opt: } \ h^1 = M'$$

Figure 13.12 Schematic execution of MBE-OPT(2) on the auction problem.

computed by MBE-OPT(i) similarly to the way it is computed by ELIM-OPT, by assigning a value to each variable that maximizes the sum of functions in the corresponding bucket, given the assignments to the previous variables. The cost of this assignment is a lower bound on the optimal cost. ●

If the problem also has hard constraints the mini-bucket approach can approximate ELIM-OPT-CONS. This means that each mini-bucket may contain both hard and soft constraints and be processed by the bucket operators of ELIM-OPT-CONS.

EXAMPLE 13.7

Let us apply algorithm MBE-OPT(2) to the auction problem along the ordering $d = b_1, b_5, b_2, b_3, b_4$. Figure 13.12 shows the resulting mini-buckets; square brackets denote the choice for partitioning.

We start with processing bucket b_4. A possible partitioning places the constraint R_{41} in one mini-bucket and the rest in the other. We compute a constraint $R^4(b_1) = \pi_{b_1} R_{41}$, which is the universal constraint so it need not be recorded. In the second mini-bucket, we also compute $h^4(b_2) = \max_{\{(b_4|(b_4,b_2))\in R_{42}\}} r(b_4)$, yielding

$$h^4(b_2) = \begin{cases} 0 & \text{if } b_2 = 1 \\ 2 & \text{if } b_2 = 0 \end{cases}$$

Processing the first mini-bucket of b_3, which includes only hard constraints, will also not affect the domain of b_1. Processing the second mini-bucket of b_3 by $h^3(b_5) = \max_{\{(b_3|(b_3,b_5))\in R_{35}\}} r(b_3)$ yields

$$h^3(b_5) = \begin{cases} 0 & \text{if } b_5 = 1 \\ 5 & \text{if } b_5 = 0 \end{cases}$$

Processing the second mini-bucket of b_2 (the first mini-bucket includes a constraint whose projection is a universal constraint) by $h^2(b_5) = \max_{\{(b_2|(b_2,b_5))\in R_{25}\}} (r(b_2) + h^4(b_2))$ gives us

$$h^2(b_5) = \begin{cases} 2 & \text{if } b_5 = 1 \\ 6 & \text{if } b_5 = 0 \end{cases}$$

Processing bucket b_5 (with full buckets now), the algorithm computes $h^5 = \max_{b_5}(r(b_5) + h^2(b_5) + h^3(b_5))$, yielding

$$h^5 = 11$$

Finally, in the bucket of b_1 the algorithm computes $h^1 = \max_{b_1}(r(b_1)+h^5)$, yielding

$$h^1 = \max\{0 + 11, 8 + 11\} = 19$$

The maximal upper-bound cost is therefore 19. To compute a maximizing tuple, we select in bucket b_1 the value $b_1 = 1$, which maximizes $r(b_1)+h^5$. Given $b_1 = 1$, we choose $b_5 = 0$, which maximizes the functions in bucket b_5. Then, in bucket b_2, we can choose only $b_2 = 0$, due to the constraint R_{12}. Likewise, the only subsequent choices are $b_3 = 0$ and $b_4 = 0$. Therefore, the cost of the generated solution is 8, yielding the interval [8, 19] bounding the maximal solution.   ●

13.5 Search with Mini-bucket Heuristics

By comparing the bound computed by MBE-OPT(i) with the cost of the solution it returned, we see that the error of the solution can be bounded. If the error is large, we can rerun MBE-OPT(i) with increased i-bound. However, if the approximation still yields a large error, the mini-bucket approach can be augmented with search. The primary approach in hard constraint processing is to strengthen backtracking search using bounded consistency propagation in a look-ahead manner. In branch-and-bound this parallels to improving the accuracy of the (upper-bounding) evaluation function.

13.5.1 Generating a Bounding Function for Search

A search algorithm that exploits an evaluation function at each node is often called a *heuristic search algorithm*. The heuristic function estimates the cost of the optimal completion of every partial assignment to a full assignment. Thus, depth-first branch-and-bound can be viewed as a heuristic search algorithm that searches the space of partial assignments in a depth-first manner. It discards any partial assignment whose bounding evaluation function is not better (not larger) than the value of the current global best solution.

There are numerous ways to generate bounding evaluation functions. Naturally, more computation power may yield more accurate functions, and the right trade-off between the computational overhead at each node and the pruning power yielded during search may be hard to predict. One evaluation function already mentioned is the first-cut function defined in Equation (13.1). We next present a scheme for generating heuristic functions of varying strength using the MBE-OPT(i) algorithm.

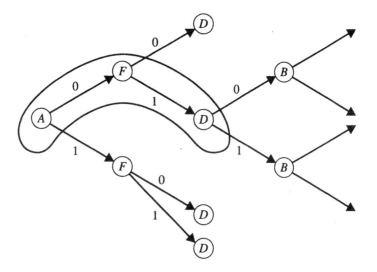

Figure 13.13 Search space for $f^*(a', f', d')$.

Consider again the cost network in Figure 13.1, and consider the output buckets resulting from the mini-bucket algorithm along ordering $d_1 = (A, F, D, C, B, G)$, as displayed in Figure 13.11b. Assume, without losing generality, that variables A, F, and D have been instantiated during search (see Figure 13.13). If an oracle proclaiming the exact best-cost solution extending this partial assignment was available, it could guide BnB to the optimal solution in a greedy, backtrack-free manner. Computing such an exact value is too costly, however. Instead we will develop an easy-to-compute bound. Let us denote by f^* the function returning the true best-cost completion of any partial solution. For example, $f^*(a', f', d')$ is the cost of the best completion of the partial assignment $(A = a', F = f', D = d')$. By definition,

$$f^*(a', f', d') = \max_{c, b, g} F(a', b, c, d', f', g)$$

$$= \max_{b, c, g}(F_0(a') + F_2(a', c) + F_3(b, c, f') + F_1(a', b)$$

$$+ F_4(a', b, d') + F_5(f', g))$$

$$= F_0(a') + \max_{c, b} F_2(a', c) + F_3(b, c, f') + F_1(a', b)$$

$$+ F_4(a', b, d) + \max_g F_5(f', g) \tag{13.12}$$

The last expression can be rewritten as

$$f^*(a', f', d') = g(a', f', d') + h^*(a', f', d') \tag{13.13}$$

where g is the cost portion defined only over variables that are already instantiated and h^* expresses the rest of the optimization task. That is, $g(a', f', d') = F_0(a')$ and $h^*(a', f', d') = \max_{c,b}(F_2(a', c) + F_3(b, c, f') + F_1(a', b) + F_4(a', b, d')) + \max_g F_5(f', g)$. We can derive

$$
\begin{aligned}
h^*(a', f', d') &= \max_c F_2(a', c) + \max_b F_3(b, c, f') + F_1(a', b) + F_4(a', b, d') \\
&\quad + \max_g F_5(f', g) \\
&= h^G(f') + \max_c F_2(a', c) + \max_b F_3(b, c, f') + F_1(a', b) \\
&\quad + F_4(a', b, d') \\
&= h^G(f') + \max_c F_2(a', c) + h^B(a', c, d', f') \\
&= h^G(f') + h^C(a', f', d')
\end{aligned}
$$

where

$$
h^G(f') = \max_g F_5(f', g)
$$

and

$$
h^B(a', c, d', f') = \max_b F_3(b, c, f') + F_1(a', b) + F_4(a', b, d')
$$

and

$$
h^C(a', f', d') = \max_c F_2(a', c) + h^B(a', c, d', f') \tag{13.14}
$$

Notice now that the functions $h^B(a, c, d, f)$ and $h^C(a, d, f)$ are exactly the functions produced by the bucket elimination algorithm ELIM-OPT (Figure 13.11(a)). Specifically, the function $h^B(a, c, d, f)$ is generated in *bucket$_B$*. In practice, however, this function may be too hard to compute as it requires processing a function on five variables and recording a function on four variables. It can be replaced by an approximation by migrating the maximization operation into the summation operation. That is, instead of computing $h^B(a', c, d', f')$ as defined above, we compute $\max_b F_3(f', b, c) + \max_b(F_1(a', b) + F_4(a', b, d')) = h^B(c, f') + h^B(a', d')$, and therefore, $h^B(a', d', c, f') \le h^B(c, f') + h^B(a', d')$. Notice that $h^B(c, f')$ and $h^B(a', d')$ are computed by MBE-OPT(i) (Figure 13.11(b)). The computation can continue in that fashion for the rest of the expression.

We will now present a general derivation showing how the functions recorded by the mini-bucket algorithm can, in general, be used as a bounding heuristic evaluation function in branch-and-bound. Given a cost network and a variable ordering $d = x_1, \ldots, x_n$, the mini-bucket algorithm outputs an ordered set of augmented buckets $bucket_1, \ldots, bucket_n$, containing both the input functions and the newly generated functions. We denote by *buckets*$(1..p)$ the union of all functions in the bucket of x_1 through the bucket of x_p.

Let $\vec{a}_p = (a_1, \ldots, a_p)$ be an assignment to the first p variables of COP $\mathcal{C} = (X, D, C)$ where $C = \{F_1, \ldots, F_l\}$. The maximal cost extension of $\vec{a}_p$, denoted $f^*(\vec{a}_p)$ is defined by

$$f^*(\vec{a}_p) = max_{a_{p+1}, \ldots, a_n} \sum_k F_k(\vec{a}_p, a_{p+1}, \ldots, a_n)$$

The above sum defining f^* can be divided into two smaller summands expressed by the functions in the ordered augmented buckets. In the first summand, called g, all the arguments are instantiated (their scope is contained in $x_1, \ldots, x_p$), and therefore the maximization operation is applied only to the second summand, denoted h^*. F_i denotes an original function, and h_i denotes original or new functions generated by MBE-OPT.

$$g(\vec{a}_p) = \left(\sum_{F_i \in buckets(1..p)} F_i \right)(\vec{a}_p)$$

and

$$h^*(\vec{a}_p) = max_{(a_{p+1}, \ldots, a_n)} \left(\sum_{F_i \in buckets(p+1\ldots n)} F_i \right)(\vec{a}_p, a_{p+1}, \ldots, a_n) \qquad (13.15)$$

and

$$f^*(\vec{a}_p) = g(\vec{a}_p) + h^*(\vec{a}_p)$$

During search, the g function can be evaluated over the partial assignment $\vec{a}_p$, while h^* can be estimated instead by a bounding function h, composed from the functions recorded by the mini-bucket algorithm, as defined next:

DEFINITION 13.1

[mini-bucket heuristic]

Given an ordered set of augmented buckets generated by the mini-bucket algorithm, the bounding function $h(\bar{a}^p)$ is the sum of all the new h_j^k functions that are generated in buckets $p + 1$ through n and reside in buckets 1 through p. That is, $h(\bar{a}^p) = \sum_{i=1}^{p} \sum_{h_j^k \in bucket_i} h_j^k$, where $k > p$. •

EXAMPLE 13.8

In Figure 13.11(b), the buckets of variables A, F, and D contain a total of four functions generated by the mini-bucket algorithm: $h^B(a, d)$, $h^C(a, f)$, $h^F(a)$, and $h^D(a)$. However, when computing the heuristic functions $h(a, d, f)$, only $h^B(a, d)$ and $h^C(a, f)$ are used, yielding $h(a, d, f) = h^B(a, d) + h^C(a, f)$, because $h^F(a)$ and $h^D(a)$ were already computed in buckets D and F from $h^C(a, f)$ and $h^B(a, d)$, respectively. •

The following properties can be proved:

THEOREM
13.5

For every partial assignment $\vec{a}_p = (a_1, \ldots, a_p)$ of the first p variables, the evaluation function $f(\vec{a}_p) = g(\vec{a}_p) + h(\vec{a}_p)$ as defined above never underestimates the cost of the best extension of $\vec{a}_p$. Also f is monotonic, that is, $f(\vec{a}_{p+1}) \leq f(\vec{a}_p)$.   •

Notice that monotonicity means better accuracy at deeper nodes in the search tree. In the extreme case, when each bucket p contains exactly one mini-bucket, the heuristic function h equals h^*, and the heuristic function f computes the optimal cost extension.

13.5.2   Algorithm BBMB(i)

The tightness of the bound generated by the mini-bucket approximation depends on its i-bound. Larger values of i generally yield better bounds, but require more computation. Since the mini-bucket algorithm is parameterized by i, when using the heuristics we get an entire class of branch-and-bound search algorithms that are parameterized by i and that allow a controllable trade-off between preprocessing and search, or between bounding function strength and its overhead. We call the resulting algorithm BBMB(i) (branch-and-bound with mini-bucket heuristics).

When algorithm BBMB(i) processes variable x_p in its depth-first search, all the variables preceding x_p are instantiated, so it can compute $f(\vec{a}_{p-1}, x_p = a_p) = g(\vec{a}_{p-1}, a_p) + h(\vec{a}_{p-1}, a_p)$ for each extension $x_p = a_p$ and prune all values a_p whose heuristic estimate $f(\vec{a}_{p-1}, a_p)$ is not better (that is, not greater for maximization problems; not smaller for minimization problems) than the current global bound.

EXAMPLE
13.9

We next demonstrate branch-and-bound search on the auction problem with two bounding functions. The first bounding function is first-cut f_{fc}, and the second is computed by MBE-OPT(2), denoted f_{mb}. Figure 13.14 shows the search space with the two bounding functions searching along ordering b_1, b_5, b_2, b_3, b_4. We start with f_{fc}.

Starting with b_1 we get $f_{fc}(b_1) = r(b_1) + 15$. Thus, $f_{fc}(b_1 = 0) = 15$ and $f_{fc}(b_1 = 1) = 8 + 15 = 23$. Therefore $b_1 = 1$ is selected first. Next, the algorithm decides a value for b_5. We get $f_{fc}(b_1 = 1, b_5 = 0) = 8 + 0 + 13 = 21$, while $f_{fc}(b_1 = 1, b_5 = 1) = 8 + 2 + 13 = 23$; consequently $b_5 = 1$ is selected. For the rest of the variables the constraints dictate $b_2 = 0, b_3 = 0, b_4 = 0$, yielding a solution with cost of 10 and a current lower bound of $L = 10$. The f_{fc} values are denoted next to each node. We backtrack to the closest choice node and choose the only alternative $b_5 = 0$, whose value is 21. Then, $b_2 = 0$ is the only choice due to the constraint with $b_1 = 1$.

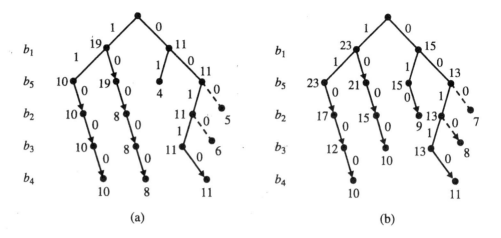

Figure 13.14 The search space using branch-and-bound with (a) the mini-bucket function f_{mb} and (b) lower bounding function f_{fc}.

Since $f_{fc}(b_1 = 1, b_5 = 0, b_2 = 0) = 8 + 7 = 15$, pruning will not occur. The only choice for b_3 is 0, with the value $8 + 2 = 10$. Since the upper bound for this node equals the lower bound, we prune. BnB backtracks to the next choice point of $b_1 = 0$, whose bound value is $(0 + 15 = 15)$, and so on. The next variable is b_5. Since $f_{fc}(b_1 = 0, b_5 = 1) = 15$, and $f_{fc}(b_1 = 0, b_5 = 0) = 0 + 13 = 13$, $b_5 = 1$ is selected. Then, the only value possible for b_2 is 0 with $f_{fc}(b_1 = 0, b_5 = 1, b_2 = 0) = 9$. Since this upper bound is lower than the global lower bound, 10, pruning occurs and the algorithm backtracks to $b_5 = 0$. The next variable is b_2. We get $f_{fc}(b_1 = 0, b_5 = 0, b_2 = 1) = 13$, while $f_{fc}(b_1 = 0, b_5 = 0, b_2 = 0) = 7$. We select $b_2 = 1$. Subsequently, for b_3 we have the choice of $f_{fc}(b_1 = 0, b_5 = 0, b_2 = 1, b_3 = 1) = 13$, or $f_{fc}(b_1 = 0, b_5 = 0, b_2 = 1, b_3 = 0) = 8$. We select $b_3 = 1$ and are left with $b_4 = 0$, with cost of $f(b_1 = 0, b_5 = 0, b_2 = 1, b_3 = 1, b_4 = 0) = 11$. We update the global lower bound to $L = 11$. Backtracking to the next choice point, the algorithm tries $b_3 = 0$ but its function evaluates to 8, causing another backtracking to $b_2 = 0$ with bounding value 7, causing backtracking to the root.

Let us now apply BnB with f_{mb}, which is the bounding function extracted from MBE-OPT(2). Based on the functions in the augmented bucket of b_1 produced by MBE-OPT(2), $f_{mb}(b_1 = 0) = r(b_1) + h^5 = 8 + 11 = 19$, while $f_{mb}(b_1 = 1) = 0 + 11 = 11$. Consequently, $b_1 = 1$ is chosen. We next evaluate $f_{mb}(b_1 = 1, b_5) = 8 + h^3(b_5) + h^2(b_5)$, yielding $f_{mb}(b_5 = 0) = 19$ and $f_{mb}(b_5 = 1) = 10$. Consequently, $b_5 = 0$ is chosen. The path is now deterministic, allowing the only choices: $b_2 = b_3 = b_4 = 0$. We end up with a solution having a cost of 8, which becomes the first global lower bound $L = 8$. BnB backtracks. The path is deterministic, dictating the choices $(b_2 = b_3 = b_4 = 0)$ whose bounding cost equals 10, yielding a solution with cost 10 $(b_1 = 1, b_5 = 1, b_2 = 0, b_3 = 0, b_4 = 0)$. The global lower bound L is updated to 10. The algorithm backtracks to the next choice point, which is $(b_1 = 0)$, whose bounding cost is 11. Next, for b_5, $f_{mb}(b_1 = 0, b_5) = 0 + r(b_5) + h^2(b_5) + h^3(b_5)$, yielding $f_{mb}(b_5 = 1) = 4$, which can be immediately pruned (less than 10), and $f_{mb}(b_5 = 1) = 11$. We select $b_5 = 0$. Subsequently, choosing a value for b_2, we get $f_{mb}(b_1 = 0, b_5 = 0, b_2) = r(b_2) + h^4(b_2) + h^3(b_5)$ (note that $h^2(b_5)$ is not included since it is created in bucket b_2). This yields $f_{mb}(b_2 = 1) = 11$, while $f_{mb}(b_2 = 0) = 5$, which is pruned. The next choice for b_3 is determined using the bounding function $f_{mb}(b_1 = 0, b_5 = 0, b_2 = 1, b_3) = 6 + r(b_3) + h^4(b_2 = 1)$, yielding for $b_3 = 1$ the bound 11, while for $b_3 = 0$ the bound 6, which will be pruned. $b_3 = 1$ is selected. Subsequently, only $b_4 = 0$ is feasible, and we get the best-cost solution of value 11. The global lower bound L is updated to 11, and BnB will lead to only pruned choices.

We see in this example that the performance of BnB using these two bounding functions yields similar performance (same number of nodes visited during search) but clearly the upper-bound function generated by f_{mb} is far more accurate than f_{fc}.   •

13.6 **Empirical Demonstration**

To get the flavor of how these algorithms perform, we present some empirical results with BBMB(i) on randomly generated problems conducted for Max-CSPs.[1] We present the results of BBMB(i) and compare them with a best-first search algorithm that uses the same mini-bucket heuristic, called BFMB(i). The best-first algorithm searches the state space in a "breadth-first manner" guided by an evaluation function, at each step expanding the node with the largest evaluation function. The first solution it finds is guaranteed to be an optimal one (Nillson 1980). We show typical experiments over sets of random binary CSPs. Each problem in this class is characterized by four parameters: $\langle N, K, C, T \rangle$, where N is the number of variables, K is the domain size, C is the number of constraints, and T is the tightness of each constraint, defined as the number of tuples not allowed. Each problem is generated by randomly picking C constraints out of $\binom{N}{2}$ total possible constraints, and picking T no-goods out of K^2 maximum possible for each constraint. We also present results from running two state-of-the-art algorithms for solving Max-CSPs: PFC-MPRDAC as defined in Meseguer, Larrosa, and Schiex (1999) and a stochastic local search (SLS) algorithm for CSPs (Kask and Dechter 1995). PFC-MPRDAC is a

---

1. These experiments were done on a 450 MHz Pentium II with 386 MB of RAM running Windows NT 4.0.

specialized branch-and-bound search algorithm developed for solving Max-CSPs. It uses a forward-checking step based on a partitioning of unassigned variables into disjoint subsets of variables. This partitioning is used for computing a heuristic evaluation function that is used for determining variable and value ordering, as well as pruning. At present, it is one of the best-known complete algorithms for Max-CSP.

We measure the accuracy ratio $opt = F_{Max-CSP}/F_{alg}$ between the true value of the optimal solution ($F_{Max-CSP}$) and the value of the solution found by the test algorithm (F_{alg}), whenever $F_{Max-CSP}$ is available. We report the distribution of the accuracy measure opt over the range 0.95. Problems in this range were solved optimally. Table 13.1 reports the results of experiments with three classes of overconstrained binary CSPs with domain sizes $K = 5$ and $K = 3$. It contains three blocks, each corresponding to a set of CSPs with a fixed number of variables and constraints and two levels of constraint tightness.

Each entry in the table gives a percentage of the problems that were solved exactly (falling in the 0.95 range) within our time bound, and the average CPU time for these problems.

As expected, as i increases, mini-bucket elimination solves more problems, while using more time. Focusing on BBMB, we see that it solved all problems when the i-bound is 5 or 6. Its total running time as a function of i forms a U-shaped curve. At first ($i = 2$) it is high (180), then as the i-bound increases the total time decreases, but then as the i-bound increases further the total time starts to increase again. For each set of problems, we have highlighted in bold the results corresponding to the optimal value of i.

This demonstrates a trade-off between the amount of preprocessing performed by MBE and the amount of subsequent search using the heuristic upper bound function generated by MBE. The optimal balance between preprocessing and search corresponds to the value of i-bound at the bottom of the U-shaped curve. We also report the results of PFC-MRDAC. When the constraint graph is dense, PFC-MRDAC is up to 2–3 times faster than the best-performing BBMB. When the constraint graph is sparse, the best BBMB is up to two orders of magnitude faster than PFC-MRDAC.

In Figure 13.15 we provide an alternative view of the performance of BBMB(i) and BFMB(i). Let $F_{BBMB(i)}(t)$ and $F_{BFMB(i)}(t)$ be the fraction of the problems solved completely by BBMB(i) and BFMB(i), respectively, by time t. Each graph in Figure 13.15 plots $F_{BBMB(i)}(t)$ and $F_{BFMB(i)}(t)$ for several values of i. These figures display the trade-off between preprocessing and search in a clear manner. When $F_{BBMB(i)}(t)$ (and $F_{BBMB(j)}(t)$) intersect for different values of i, they display a trade-off as a function of time. For example, if we have less than 70 seconds (see $N = 15$, $K = 10$, $C = 50$, $T = 85$), BBMB(4) is better than BBMB(6). However, when sufficient time is allowed, BBMB(6) is superior.

In Figure 13.16 we show results comparing the anytime performance of BBMB, which returns a (suboptimal) solution any time during search, with that of stochastic local search (SLS), which is inherently incomplete but has been shown to work well on CSPs in practice. The implementation of SLS used the basic greedy scheme combined with the constraint reweighting. When the constraint graph is

Table 13.1 Search completion times for problems with five values and 100 samples.

T	MBE BBMB BFMB i=2 %/time	MBE BBMB BFMB i=3 %/time	MBE BBMB BFMB i=4 %/time	MBE BBMB BFMB i=5 %/time	MBE BBMB BFMB i=6 %/time	MBE BBMB BFMB i=7 %/time	MBE BBMB BFMB i=8 %/time	PFC-MRDAC %/time
	*N = 15, K = 5, C = 105. Time bound 180 sec. Avg w* = 14. Dense network.*							
18	0/- 10/180 0/-	0/- 32/180 0/-	0/- 64/148 0/-	12/0.56 96/81.4 13/111	13/2.27 100/33.4 59/64.5	31/11.7 **100/21.9** 88/47.4	34/49.7 100/52.5 100/58.1	100/9.61
19	0/- 16/180 0/-	0/- 40/180 0/-	0/- 77/155 2/188	0/- 100/76.8 3/182	5/2.78 100/29.7 42/54.0	12/14.6 **100/22.8** 88/39.2	40/60.3 100/60.9 100/61.9	100/7.69
	*N = 20, K = 5, C = 100. Time bound 180 sec. Avg w* = 12. Medium density.*							
18	0/- 5/180 0/-	0/- 15/180 0/-	7/0.17 38/170 1/183	10/0.71 71/132 2/60.0	11/3.12 86/82.3 9/76.9	23/14.4 **95/57.4** 33/81.5	29/68.7 96/90.6 59/98.9	100/18.7
19	0/- 4/180 0/-	0/- 24/180 0/-	0/- 56/160 0/-	4/0.70 64/121 12/89.5	4/3.21 84/97.5 12/76.5	4/14.9 **96/85.4** 32/77.3	4/70.7 92/90.0 52/96.8	100/17.4
	*N = 40, K = 5, C = 55. Time bound 180 sec. Avg w* = 5.1. Sparse network.*							
18	0/- 44/87.7 3/4.56	12/0.02 100/4.41 92/14.9	36/0.07 **100/0.21** 100/0.45	54/0.19 100/0.23 **100/0.27**	88/0.53 100/0.56 100/0.57	100/1.03 100/1.04 100/1.04	100/1.14 100/1.15 100/1.16	100/4.94
19	0/- 38/104 1/25.4	7/0.03 99/8.35 83/14.4	25/0.07 100/0.34 100/1.28	55/0.20 **100/0.25** **100/0.30**	79/0.56 100/0.61 100/0.63	96/1.29 100/1.35 100/1.36	100/1.89 100/1.90 100/1.90	100/8.04

dense (Figure 13.16(a)), SLS is substantially faster than BBMB. However, when the constraint graph is sparse (Figure 13.16(b)), BBMB(4) and BBMB(6) are faster than SLS.

13.7 Summary

This chapter extends constraint processing techniques covered throughout the book to constraint optimization. In constraint optimization the task is to find a consistent

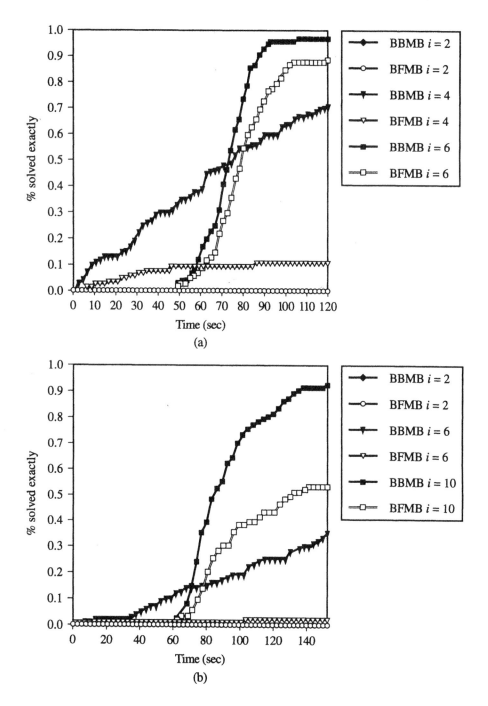

Figure 13.15 Max-CSP: Distribution of search completion. (a) $N = 15$, $K = 10$, $C = 50$, $T = 85$ and (b) $N = 20$, $K = 5$, $C = 100$, $T = 18$.

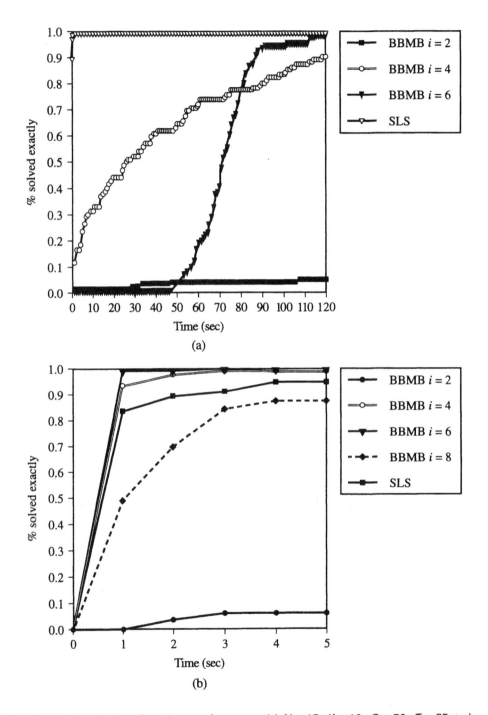

Figure 13.16 Max-CSP: Distribution of anytime performance. (a) $N = 15$, $K = 10$, $C = 50$, $T = 85$ and
(b) $N = 40$, $K = 5$, $C = 55$, $T = 19$.

solution that optimizes some cost function. The chapter described the branch-and-bound search algorithms and the inference-based variable elimination approach. All the hybrid schemes of search and inference described for constraints can be applied to optimization. In particular, the chapter also presented a sound but incomplete inference, inspired by constraint propagation, called mini-bucket elimination. The principal idea of mini-bucket elimination is to bound inference by partitioning the functions into subsets that are processed independently, and consequently restrict the number of arguments in the inferred functions. Finally, we show how the mini-bucket algorithm can be exploited for creating a bounding heuristic evaluation function that can be consulted for value selection and for pruning at any state in the search.

It is possible to use additional hybrid ideas along the principles described in Chapter 10. For example, given a bound on the size of inferred functions, a hybrid algorithm can alternate between variable elimination (recording a function) or branching, based on the potential size of recorded functions, yielding methods similar to algorithm DCDR(i) described in Chapter 10. For more information see Larrosa (2000).

13.8 **Bibliographical Notes**

Algorithms for discrete combinatorial optimization tasks were developed in the past five decades by the operations research community under the umbrella term *integer programming*. While it is known how to solve optimization problems when the constraints and cost functions are linear over continuous domains, the task is hard when the domains are discrete. Branch-and-bound search for integer programming uses a lower bounding function derived by relaxing the integrality constraints and solving a continuous linear programming problem (Fulkerson, Dantzig, and Johnson (1954). This idea of branch-and-bound can be traced back to the work of Fulkerson, Dantzig, and Johnson (1954, 1959) on integer programming and the traveling salesman problem (Rinnoy Kan et al. 1985). An early survey appears in Lawler and Wood (1956).

In the late 1970s and early 1980s, formal descriptions of the branch-and-bound methods were given by Ibaraki (1976, 1978) and Kohler and Stieglitz (1974) in the more general setting of state-space search, and a relationship with dynamic programming for sequential decision making was discussed (Ibaraki 1978; Kumar and Kanal 1983). In artificial intelligence, branch-and-bound algorithms were investigated under the umbrella term *heuristic search*. It was recognized that best-first search and depth-first branch-and-bound were special cases of branch-and-bound (Nillson 1980; Pearl 1984).

Dynamic programming was developed by Bellman (1957) as an alternative to branch-and-bound search. He introduced the idea in the context of sequential decision making. The perception of nonserial dynamic programming as a variable elimination algorithm is described in detail in Bertele and Briochi (1972).

They observed the dependence of nonserial dynamic programming, or variable elimination, on an order-based graph parameter that they called "dimension" and that we call induced width. They also presented several greedy algorithms for bounding a graph dimension.

Constraint processing in the past two decades has shifted toward constraint optimization. The work of extending backtracking algorithms for optimization was initiated by Freuder (1992). More recent research has focused on extending constraint propagation ideas to optimization, especially for bounding the evaluation functions. A variety of lower bound functions were developed that can be related to constraint propagation (Meseguer, Larrosa, and Schiex 1999; Kask and Dechter 2001; Schiex 2000). The first-cut lower bound function is an example of extending forward-checking. The mini-bucket scheme presented in this chapter was introduced by Dechter (1997) and Dechter and Rish (1997, 2003), and its use for lower bounding function generation was introduced by Kask and Dechter (2001). The Russian doll idea is due to Lematre, Verfaillie and Schiex (1996).

A significant effort addressing a variety of soft constraint types and algorithms was introduced recently. There are several frameworks for soft constraints, such as the *semi-ring-based formalism* (Bistarelli, Montanari, and Rossi 1997), where each tuple in each constraint has an associated element taken from a partially ordered set (a semi-ring), and the *valued constraint formalism*, where each constraint is associated with an element from a totally ordered set. These formalisms are general enough to model classical constraints, weighted constraints, fuzzy constraints, and overconstrained problems. Current research effort is focused on extending propagation and search techniques into this more general framework.

13.9 **Exercises**

1. The Golomb ruler was described in Exercise 12 in Chapter 5. Here we repeat and extend some of the previous questions. It can be described as follows: Place a set of n markers $X_1 > \cdots > X_n$ on the integer line (assigning a positive integer to each marker), such that the distances between any two markers are all different, and such that the length of the ruler, that is, the assignment to X_n, is the smallest possible.

   (a) Provide two ways of formulating the Golomb ruler as a constraint optimization problem. Demonstrate your formulation on a problem of small size (five variables).

   (b) Discuss the solution of the Golomb ruler problem by branch-and-bound algorithms and by bucket elimination algorithms.

2. The combinatorial auction problem was described in this chapter and earlier as Exercise 13 in Chapter 5. Answer Exercise 1 for this problem.

3. The rain problem (defined first as Exercise 14 in Chapter 5) is defined as follows: Given a communication network modeled as a graph $G = (N, E)$, where the set of nodes are processing nodes and the links are bidirectional communication links, each link e is associated with *bandwidth capacity* $c(e)$. A *demand* is a communication need between a pair of nodes $d_u = (x_u, y_u, \beta_u)$, where x_u is the source, y_u is the destination, and β_u is the required bandwidth. Given a set of demands $\{d_1, \ldots, d_m\}$, the task is to assign a route (a simple path) from source to destination for each demand such that the total capacity used over each link is below the available bandwidth.

   Answer Exercise 1 for the rain problem.

4. Consider a graph-coloring problem that has four variables (A, B, C, D), where the domains of A and C are $\{1, 2, 3\}$ and the domains of B and D are $\{1, 2\}$. The constraints are not-equal constraints between adjacent variables. Apply the ELIM-COUNT algorithm to this problem. Compare its performance with a simple search algorithm for counting.

5. Prove that algorithms ELIM-OPT and ELIM-COUNT are sound and complete.

6. Prove Theorem 13.4.

14

Probabilistic Networks

It's choice—not chance—that determines your destiny.

Jean Nidetch

So far we have dealt with hard, deterministic constraints or with preferences expressed via a cost function in a constraint optimization framework. Yet, many real-life problems involve substantial uncertainty that cannot be captured by categorical constraints. The main source of uncertainty is lack of knowledge about the problem domain. This lack of knowledge may be due to user's ignorance or due to an inherent inability to acquire the necessary knowledge. For example, in medical diagnosis, the uncertainty in precisely predicting the symptoms of a disease arises from the inability to model every factor associated with the disease.

The main framework for expressing and reasoning with uncertain information is *probabilistic networks*, also called *belief networks* or *Bayesian networks*. This framework aims at modeling primarily natural phenomena and natural processes. Constraints, on the other hand, model human processes of intervention that aim at changing the natural course of events. Like constraint networks, the probabilistic framework is built upon a graphical representation whose semantics guide representation and inference, and is accompanied by computational principles similar to those encountered throughout this book. An important aspect of Bayesian networks is that they are declarative. They are direct representations of the world, not of reasoning processes. Still, inference and conditioning search, the two guiding computational paradigms we observed for constraints, are applicable here as well. We therefore expand briefly into this area, providing a glimpse into the computational issues of probabilistic frameworks. For a recent overview see Pearl and Russel (2001), and for a full treatment of belief networks please refer to Pearl (1988) and Koller and Friedman (2003). This chapter assumes familiarity with the basic concepts of probability theory.

Belief networks provide a formalism for reasoning about partial beliefs under conditions of uncertainty. Like any complete probabilistic model of a domain, they must represent a joint probability distribution: the probability of every possible value assignment to all the variables. Belief networks are defined by

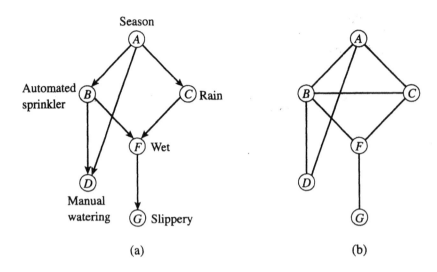

Figure 14.1   (a) Belief network $P(g, f, d, c, b, a) = P(g|f)P(f|c, b)P(d|b, a)P(b|a)P(c|a)P(a)$. (b) Its moral graph.

a directed acyclic graph over nodes representing random variables of interest (e.g., the temperature of a device, the gender of a patient, a feature of an object, the occurrence of an event). The arcs represent direct causal influences between the linked variables. The strength of these influences are quantified by conditional probabilities for each node, given its parents in the network. For example, the network in Figure 14.1(a) can express causal relationships between "season" (A), "the configuration of an automatic sprinkler system" (B), "the amount of rain expected" (C), "the wetness of the pavement" (F), "whether or not the pavement is slippery" (G), and "the amount of manual watering necessary" (D).[1] The absence of a direct link between A and G, for example, captures our understanding that there is no direct dependency (or cause) between "season" and "slipperiness," which is not mediated by F, the wetness of the pavement. A belief network relies on the notion of a directed graph. For convenience, we repeat some of the definitions from Chapter 1.

DEFINITION 14.1   **(graph concepts)**

A *directed graph* is a pair, $G = \{V, E\}$, where $V = \{x_1, \ldots, x_n\}$ is a set of elements and $E = \{(x_i, x_j)|x_i, x_j \in V, i \neq j\}$ is the set of edges. If $(x_i, x_j) \in E$, we say that x_i points to x_j. For each variable x_i, the set of parent nodes of x_i, denoted $pa(x_i)$, comprises the variables pointing to x_i in G, while the set of child nodes of x_i, denoted $ch(x_i)$, comprises the variables that

---

1. Note that Figure 14.1(b) is identical to Figure 13.1.

x_i points to. When no possibility of confusion exists, we abbreviate $pa(x_i)$ by pa_i and $ch(x_i)$ by ch_i. The family of x_i, F_i, includes x_i and its parent variables. A directed graph is *acyclic* if it has no directed cycles. The moral graph of a directed graph G is an undirected graph obtained by connecting the parents of each node in G and removing the directionality.   •

DEFINITION 14.2

(belief network)

Let $X = \{x_1, \ldots, x_n\}$ be a set of random variables over domains, $D_1, \ldots, D_n$, respectively. A *belief network* is a pair $\langle G, P \rangle$ where $G = (X, E)$ is a directed acyclic graph over the variables, and $P = \{P_i\}$, where P_i denotes conditional probability tables $P_i = \{P(x_i|pa_i)\}$ (called CPTs). The belief network represents a probability distribution over X having the product form

$$P(a_1, \ldots, a_n) = \Pi_{i=1}^{n} P(a_i | \bar{a}_{pa_i})$$

where an assignment $(x_1 = a_1, \ldots, x_n = a_n)$ is abbreviated to $\bar{a} = (a_1, \ldots, a_n)$ and where $\bar{a}_S$ denotes the restriction of a tuple $\bar{a}$ over a subset of variables S (this is an alternative notation to $\bar{a}[s]$). An evidence set E is an instantiated subset of variables. We call $x_i \cup pa_i$ the *scope* of P_i.   •

EXAMPLE 14.1

The belief network in Figure 14.1 is defined by six CPTs each associated with a node and its parents. For example, the CPT of G describes the probability that the pavement is wet $(F = 1)$ for each status combination of the sprinkler and raining. A possible CPT is given by

B	C	F	$P(G = 1|B,C)$
0	0	1	0.1
1	0	1	0.9
0	1	1	0.9
1	1	1	1.0

The conditional probability for $F = 0$ is implied because the probabilities need to sum up to 1. The belief network represents the joint probability distribution

$$\forall a, b, c, d, f, g, \quad P(g, f, d, c, b, a)$$
$$= P(g|f)P(f|c, b)P(d|b, a)P(b|a)P(c|a)P(a)$$

In this case, $pa(F) = \{B, C\}$. The moral graph is given in Figure 14.1(b). •

The primary queries posed over probabilistic networks are the following:

1. *Belief assessment.* Given a set of observations (or evidence), the task is to compute the posterior probability of each value of each variable, given the evidence.

2. *Finding the most probable explanation (mpe)*. Given some observed variables, the task is to find a maximum probability assignment to all unobserved variables given the observation.

3. *Finding the maximum a posteriori hypothesis (map)*. Finding an assignment to a *subset* of the unobserved hypothesis variables that maximizes their conditional probability.

These queries are applicable to tasks such as situation assessment, diagnosis, probabilistic decoding, as well as planning and decision making. They are all known to be computationally hard. Nevertheless, they can be assisted by the underlying graph in the same manner as constraint processing are. In particular, all queries permit a polynomial propagation inference algorithm for singly connected networks.

Extending this propagation algorithm to multiply connected networks involves familiar ideas such as the cycle-cutset approach (also known as *loop-cutset conditioning*), join-tree clustering, and variable elimination. As we have seen, these methods work well for sparse networks with small cycle-cutsets or small clusters. In the rest of this chapter we will describe variants of these algorithms that are based on variable elimination and search, and comment on the relevance of other ideas that we have seen to this probabilistic framework.

14.1 Bucket Elimination for Belief Assessment

Belief updating, the primary inference task over belief networks, is the process of maintaining the posterior probability distribution of single variables once new evidence arrives. For instance, in our example, if we observe that the pavement is slippery, we want to assess the likelihood that the sprinkler was on. The primary algorithms used for belief updating are inference based and known as join-tree clustering (Lauritzen and Spiegelhalter 1988). The variable elimination algorithm presented next is a close variant of these methods.

14.1.1 Deriving ELIM-BEL

The derivation of ELIM-BEL, the bucket elimination algorithm, for belief updating, is very similar to the one we saw for ELIM-OPT in Chapter 13. For your convenience we will repeat some of this derivation here. The only difference is that the summation operator in ELIM-OPT is replaced with a product operator and maximization is replaced by summation.

Let $x = a$ be an atomic proposition. The problem is to assess and update the belief in $x = a$, given evidence $E = e$. That is, we wish to compute

$P(x = a|e) = \alpha \cdot P(x = a, e)$, where α is a normalization constant that ensures that all probabilities sum to 1,

$$\alpha = \frac{1}{\sum_{a \in D_x} P(x = a, e)}$$

We will develop the algorithm using the example in Figure 14.1. Assume we have evidence that $g = 1$. Consider the variables in the order $d_1 = A, C, B, F, D, G$. We need to compute

$$P(a, g = 1) = \sum_{c, b, f, d, g=1} P(g|f)P(f|b, c)P(d|a, b)P(c|a)P(b|a)P(a)$$

As we have shown for ELIM-OPT, we can apply some simple symbolic manipulation (migrating conditional probability tables to the left of the summation variables) to get

$$= P(a) \sum_c P(c|a) \sum_b P(b|a) \sum_f P(f|b, c) \sum_d P(d|b, a) \sum_{g=1} P(g|f) \qquad (14.1)$$

Carrying the computation from right to left, we first generate a function over G, $\lambda_G(f)^2$, defined by $\lambda_G(f) = \sum_{g=1} P(g|f)$, and place it as far to the left as possible, yielding

$$= P(a) \sum_c P(c|a) \sum_b P(b|a) \sum_f P(f|b, c)\lambda_G(f) \sum_d P(d|b, a) \qquad (14.2)$$

Summing next over D (generating a function denoted $\lambda_D(a, b)$, defined by $\lambda_D(a, b) = \sum_d P(d|a, b)$), we get

$$= P(a) \sum_c P(c|a) \sum_b P(b|a)\lambda_D(a, b) \sum_f P(f|b, c)\lambda_G(f) \qquad (14.3)$$

Next, summing over F (generating $\lambda_F(b, c) = \sum_f P(f|b, c)\lambda_G(f)$), we get

$$= P(a) \sum_c P(c|a) \sum_b P(b|a)\lambda_D(a, b)\lambda_F(b, c) \qquad (14.4)$$

Summing over B (generating $\lambda_B(a, c)$), we get

$$= P(a) \sum_c P(c|a)\lambda_B(a, c) \qquad (14.5)$$

---

2. Note that we used superscript in Chapter 13 for created functions (e.g., $\lambda^G(x)$) while here we use subscript (e.g., $\lambda_G(x)$).

Finally, summing over C (generating $\lambda_C(a)$), we get

$$P(a)\lambda_C(a) \tag{14.6}$$

The answer to the query $P(a|g=1)$ can be computed by normalizing the last product:

$$P(a|g=1) = \frac{P(a) \cdot \lambda_C(a)}{\sum_{a \in D_x} P(a) \cdot \lambda_C(a)}$$

The resulting bucket elimination algorithm that mimics this computation is identical to ELIM-OPT when the cost functional components are replaced with probability tables and when the corresponding operators are replaced. Given ordering $d = x_1, \dots, x_n$, where the queried variable appears first, the CPTs are partitioned using the usual rule. Then buckets are processed from last to first. To process each bucket, all the bucket's functions, denoted $\lambda_1, \dots, \lambda_j$ and defined over scopes $S_1, \dots, S_j$ are multiplied. The bucket's variable is then eliminated by summation. The computed function is $\lambda_p : U_p \to R$, $\lambda_p = \sum_{x_p} \prod_{i=1}^{j} \lambda_i$, where $U_p = \cup_i S_i - x_p$. This function is placed in the bucket of its largest-index variable in U_p. Once all the buckets are processed, the answer is available in the first bucket. The algorithm is presented in Figure 14.2.

ELIM-BEL

Input: A belief network $\langle G, P \rangle$, $P = \{P_1, \dots, P_n\}$; an ordering of the variables, $d = x_1, \dots, x_n$; evidence e.

Output: The belief $P(x_1|e)$.

1. **Initialize:** Generate an ordered partition of the conditional probability matrices, $bucket_1, \dots, bucket_n$, where $bucket_i$ contains all matrices and relevant evidence whose highest variable is X_i. Put each observed variable in its bucket. Let $S_1, \dots, S_j$ be the subset of variables in the processed bucket on which matrices (new or old) are defined.

2. **Backward:** For $p \leftarrow n$ downto 1, do

   for all the matrices $\lambda_1, \lambda_2, \dots, \lambda_j$ in $bucket_p$, do

   - **If** (observed variable) $x_p = a_p$ appears in $bucket_p$, assign $x_p = a_p$ to each λ_i and then put each resulting function in appropriate bucket.

   - **else**, $U_p \leftarrow \cup_{i=1}^{j} S_i - \{x_p\}$. Generate $\lambda_p = \sum_{x_p} \prod_{i=1}^{j} \lambda_i$ and add λ_p to the largest-index variable in U_p.

3. **Return:** $Bel(x_1) = \alpha \prod_i \lambda_i(x_1)$ (where the λ_i are in $bucket_1$, α is a normalizing constant).

Figure 14.2 Algorithm ELIM-BEL.

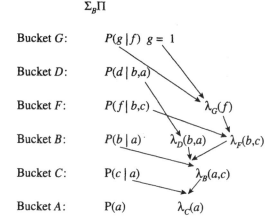

Figure 14.3 Bucket elimination along ordering $d_1 = A, C, B, F, D, G$.

In our example, the initialization step corresponds to deriving the expression in Equation (14.1). $Bucket_G$ is processed first. To eliminate G we sum over all values of G. Since in this case we have an observed value $g = 1$, the summation is over a singleton value. The function $\lambda_G(f) = \sum_{g=1} P(g|f)$ is computed and placed in $bucket_F$ (this corresponds to deriving Equation (14.2) from Equation (14.1). $Bucket_D$ is processed next. We sum out D, getting $\lambda_D(b, a) = \sum_d P(d|b, a)$, which is placed in $bucket_B$ (which corresponds to deriving Equation (14.3) from Equation (14.2)), and so on as shown in Figure 14.3. Throughout this process we have recorded at the most two-dimensional functions; the complexity of the algorithm using ordering d_1 is (roughly) time and space quadratic in the domain sizes.

As we have seen, a different variable ordering can be used by the algorithm, but this yields different computational complexity. For example, if we apply the algorithm using $d_2 = A, F, D, C, B, G$, we get the process summarized in Figure 14.4(a). In summary, we have the following:

THEOREM 14.1   Algorithm ELIM-BEL computes the posterior belief $P(x_1|e)$ for any given ordering of the variables initiated by x_1.   •

14.2 **An Elimination Algorithm for mpe**

In this section we focus on finding the most probable explanation. This task appears in applications such as diagnosis and design as well as in probabilistic decoding. For example, given data on clinical findings, it may suggest the most likely disease a patient is suffering from. In message decoding, the task is to identify the most likely input message that was transmitted over a noisy channel, given the observed output.

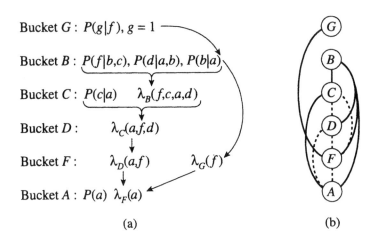

Bucket G : $P(g|f)$, $g = 1$

Bucket B : $\underbrace{P(f|b,c), P(d|a,b), P(b|a)}$

Bucket C : $\underbrace{P(c|a) \quad \lambda_B(f,c,a,d)}$

Bucket D : $\lambda_C(a,f,d)$

Bucket F : $\lambda_D(a,f)$ $\lambda_G(f)$

Bucket A : $P(a)$ $\lambda_F(a)$

(a)   (b)

Figure 14.4 (a) The bucket's output when processing along $d_2 = A, F, D, C, B, G$. (b) The corresponding induced graph.

The relevant task here is finding the most likely assignment over a *subset* of hypothesis variables. While mpe focuses on all variables, it is close enough and is often used in applications.

The problem is to find x^0 such that $P(x^0) = \max_x P(x, e) = \max_x \prod_i P(x_i, e|x_{pa_i})$, where $x = (x_1, \ldots, x_n)$ and e is a set of observations, on subsets of the variables. Computing the mpe for a given ordering $x_1, \ldots, x_n$, can be accomplished as previously shown by performing the maximization operation along the ordering from right to left, while migrating to the left all components that do not mention the maximizing variable. You can immediately see that this task is identical to the constraint optimization task in Chapter 13 without hard constraints, where summation is replaced by a product. Indeed, the bucket elimination algorithm for mpe, called ELIM-MPE, is identical to ELIM-OPT up to the mentioned changes and is described explicitly in Figure 14.5.

EXAMPLE 14.2   Consider again the belief network in Figure 14.1. Given the ordering $d = A, C, B, F, D, G$ and the evidence $G = g'$, process variables from last to first after partitioning the conditional probability matrices and evidence into buckets, such that $bucket_G = \{P(g|f), G = g'\}$, $bucket_D = \{P(d|b, a)\}$, $bucket_F = \{P(f|b, c)\}$, $bucket_B = \{P(b|a)\}$, $bucket_C = \{P(c|a)\}$, and $bucket_A = \{P(a)\}$. To process G, assign it evidence $G = g'$, get $h_G(f) = P(g'|f)$, and place the result in $bucket_F$. Process $bucket_D$ by computing $h_D(b, a) = \max_d P(d|b, a)$ and put the result in $bucket_B$. Bucket F, next to be processed, now contains two matrices: $P(f|b, c)$ and $h_G(f)$. Compute $h_F(b, c) = \max_f p(f|b, c) \cdot h_G(f)$, and place the resulting function in $bucket_B$. To eliminate B, we record the function $h_B(a, c) = \max_b P(b|a) \cdot h_D(b, a) \cdot h_F(b, c)$ and place it in $bucket_C$. To eliminate C, we compute

---

ELIM-MPE

Input: A belief network $\langle G,P \rangle$, $P = \{P_1,\ldots,P_n\}$; an ordering of the variables, d; observations e.

Output: The most probable assignment.

1. **Initialize:** as in ELIM-BEL

2. **Backward:** For $p \leftarrow n$ downto 1, do

for all the functions $h_1, h_2, \ldots, h_j$ in $bucket_p$, do

- **If** (observed variable) $bucket_p$ contains $x_p = a_p$, assign $x_p = a_p$ to each h_i and put each in appropriate bucket.

- **else**, $U_p \leftarrow \bigcup_{i=1}^{j} S_i - \{x_p\}$. Generate functions $h_p = \max_{x_p} \prod_{i=1}^{j} h_i$. Add h_p to bucket of largest-index variable bucket in U_p.

3. **Return:** The mpe value is obtained by the constant computed in $bucket_1$.

An mpe tuple is obtained by assigning values in the ordering d consulting recorded functions in each bucket as follows.

Given the assignment $a = (a_1,\ldots,a_{i-1})$ choose

$a_i = argmax_{x_i} \prod_{\{h_j \in bucket_i | a = (a_1,\ldots,a_{i-1})\}} h_j$

Figure 14.5 Algorithm ELIM-MPE.

$h_C(a) = \max_c P(c|a) \cdot h_B(a, c)$ and place it in $bucket_A$. Finally, we determine the mpe value given in $bucket_A$, $M = \max_a P(a) \cdot h_C(a)$. Next we generate the mpe tuple by going forward through the buckets. First, select the value a^0 satisfying $a^0 = argmax_a P(a) h_C(a)$. Then, determine the value of C, $c^0 = argmax_c P(c|a^0) h_B(a^0, c)$. Next $b^0 = argmax_b P(b|a^0) h_D(b, a^0) h_F(b, c^0)$ is selected, and so on. The schematics computation is summarized by Figure 14.3, where λ plays the role of h.   •

14.3 **Complexity**

As for all bucket elimination algorithms (e.g., ADAPTIVE-CONSISTENCY, DIRECTIONAL-RESOLUTION, ELIM-OPT, and ELIM-COUNT), the complexity of algorithm ELIM-BEL and ELIM-MPE is dominated by the time and space needed to process a bucket. Recording a function on all the bucket's variables is time and space exponential in the number of variables mentioned in the bucket. The induced width bounds the scope of the functions recorded.

In our wet pavement example, the moral graph is identical to Figure 13.1 (page 365), and therefore Figure 13.7(a) and (b) depicts the ordered moral graph using two orderings $d_1 = A, C, B, F, D, G$ and $d_2 = A, F, D, C, B, G$ and their corresponding effect on the induced width. Thus, as usual, given an ordering d, the complexity of ELIM-BEL and ELIM-MPE is (time and space) exponential in the induced width $w^*(d)$ of the network's ordered moral graph.

We know that variable instantiations are handled in a special way during the processing of buckets. This is particularly significant for belief updating, since evidence may change the belief in a variable. The mechanics of exploiting observations is as described earlier for optimization.

Continuing with our example, using elimination order d_1, suppose we wish to compute the belief in A, having observed $B = b'$. This observation is relevant only when processing $bucket_B$. When the algorithm arrives at that bucket, the bucket contains the three functions, $P(b|a)$, $\lambda_D(b, a)$, and $\lambda_F(b, c)$, as well as the observation $B = b'$ (see Figure 14.3). The processing rule dictates computing $\lambda_B(a, c) = P(b'|a)\lambda_D(b', a)\lambda_F(b', c)$, that is, generating and recording a two-dimensional function. It would be more effective, however, to separately apply the assignment b' to each function in the bucket, and then put the individual resulting functions into lower buckets. In other words, we can generate $P(b'|a)$ and $\lambda_D(b', a)$, both of which will be placed in bucket A, and $\lambda_F(b', c)$, which will be placed in bucket C. By doing so, we avoid increasing the dimensionality of the recorded functions. Processing buckets containing observations in this manner automatically exploits the cutset conditioning effect.

To capture this refinement we remember the notion of an *adjusted induced width*:

DEFINITION 14.3   Given a graph G, a set of observed nodes E, and an ordering of all the nodes d, the *adjusted induced width* of G relative to E along d, $w^*(d, E)$, is the induced width along d when all the nodes corresponding to observed nodes are removed.   •

In summary, we have the following theorem:

THEOREM 14.2   Given a belief network having n variables, algorithms ELIM-BEL and ELIM-MPE, when using ordering d and evidence variables E, are time and space exponential in the adjusted induced width $w^*(d, E)$ of the network's ordered moral graph.   •

14.4 Hybrids of Elimination and Conditioning

As noted for deterministic reasoning, a serious drawback of elimination and clustering algorithms is that they require considerable memory for recording the intermediate functions. Conditioning search, on the other hand, requires only linear space. In Chapter 10 we showed that by combining search and inference we may be able to reduce the amount of memory needed while still maintaining reasonable performance guarantees. Indeed, all the ideas described in Chapter 10 are immediately applicable for probabilistic reasoning.

14.4.1 Search for Probabilistic Reasoning

Full search for belief updating requires traversing the tree of partial value assignments and accumulating the appropriate sums of probabilities. For mpe, search can take the form of branch-and-bound, as discussed in Chapter 13. For example, observing that $G = 0$ and $D = 1$, we can compute $P(a, G=0, D=1)$ for the Bayesian network of Figure 14.1, given by

$$P(a, G = 0, D = 1) = \sum_{a,c,b,f,d=1,g=0} P(g|f)P(f|b,c)P(d|a,b)P(c|a)P(b|a)P(a)$$

$$= \sum_a P(a) \sum_c P(c|a) \sum_b P(b|a) \sum_f P(f|b,c).P(d = 1|a,b)P(g = 0|f) \quad (14.7)$$

by traversing the tree in Figure 14.6, going along the ordering from first variable to last variable in a depth-first manner.

14.4.2 Cycle-Cutset and Other Hybrids

Let Y be a subset of conditioned variables, $Y \subseteq X$, and $V = X - Y$. We denote by v an assignment to V, by $\bar{y}$ an assignment to Y, and by $f(X)|_{\bar{v}}$ the function f,

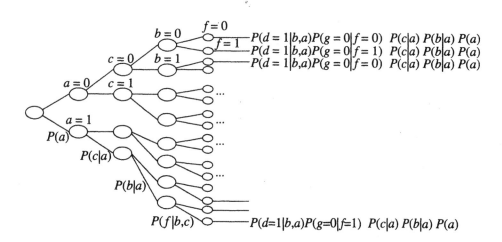

Figure 14.6 Probability tree.

ELIM-COND-BEL

Input: A belief network $\langle G, P \rangle$, $G = (X, E)$, $P = \{P_1, \ldots, P_n\}$; an ordering of the variables, d; a subset Y of conditioned variables; observations e.

Output: The join probability of $P(x_1, e)$.

Initialize: $p = 0$.

1. For every assignment $Y = \bar{y}$, do

   - $p_1 \leftarrow$ The output of ELIM-BEL with $\bar{y} \cup e$ as observations.

   - $p \leftarrow p + p_1$

2. **Return** p.

Figure 14.7 Algorithm ELIM-COND-BEL.

where the arguments in $X \cap V$ are assigned the values in $V = \bar{v}$. Clearly,

$$P(e) = \sum_{\bar{x}} P(\bar{x}, e) = \sum_{\bar{y}} \sum_{\bar{v}} P(\bar{y}, \bar{v}, e) = \sum_{\bar{y}} \sum_{\bar{v}} \prod_i P(x_i | \bar{x}_{pa_i})|_{(\bar{y}, \bar{v}, e)}$$

Therefore, we can use variable elimination to compute $\sum_{\bar{v}} P(\bar{v}, \bar{y}, e) = \sum_{\bar{v}} \prod_i P(x_i | \bar{x}_{pa_i})|_{(\bar{y}, e)}$ for every partial tuple $\bar{y}$, while treating the conditioned variables in Y and E as observed variables. The basic computation will be enumerated for all value combinations of Y. This straightforward approach was presented in Chapter 10 (Figure 10.4). Adapting the algorithm for belief updating yields algorithm ELIM-COND-BEL in Figure 14.7.

Alternatively, we can use a dynamic selection of variables for either variable elimination or search, similar to the way algorithm DP-DR (b) does in Chapter 10, as in Figure 14.8. The algorithm is described recursively.

As we have seen before, given a particular value assignment $\bar{y}$, the time and space complexity of computing the sum probability over $X - Y$ is bounded exponentially by the adjusted induced width $w^*(d, E \cup Y)$ of the ordered moral graph along d, adjusted for both observed and conditioned nodes.

THEOREM 14.3   Given a set of conditioning variables, Y, the space complexity of algorithm ELIM-COND-BEL is $O(n \cdot exp(w^*(d, Y \cup E)))$, while its time complexity is $O(n \cdot exp(w^*(d, E \cup Y) + |Y|))$.   •

When the variables in $E \cup Y$ constitute a cycle-cutset of the moral graph, the graph can be ordered so that its adjusted induced width $= 1$ and ELIM-COND-BEL reduces to the cycle-cutset algorithm.

```
ELIM-COND-BEL-DY (b)
```
Input: A belief network $\langle G,P \rangle$, $G = \langle X, E \rangle$, $P = \{P_1 .. P_n\}$, observation e, a bound b.
  $X \leftarrow X - \{X_1\}$

Output: The join probability $P(X_1, e)$
  Assign all observed values into functions
while: $\exists x \in X$ such that degree $(x) \leq b$ in the current conditional moral graph of
  G, and x is not observed.
  $\lambda_x \leftarrow \sum \Pi \lambda_j$, $X \leftarrow X - \{x\}$
      x λ_j in bucket(x)
  $P \leftarrow P - \{\lambda_j\} \cup \{\lambda_x\}$
Endwhile: Select a variable $y \in X, X \leftarrow X - \{y\}$
Return: ELIM-COND-BEL $(b, P, y = 0)$ +
        ELIM-COND-BEL $(b, P, y = 1)$

Figure 14.8 Algorithm ELIM-COND-BEL (b).

14.5 **Summary**

This chapter introduced probabilistic networks, which arise from the need to represent uncertainty about the world domain. The probabilistic framework can be perceived as an extension of constraint networks for capturing uncertain or fuzzy constraints. Since the computational aspects of processing probabilistic networks and constraint networks are similar, the chapter briefly re-derived these relevant techniques. We focused on bucket elimination algorithms for belief updating and for finding the most probable explanation, and showed that they fit the same pattern of performance as their counterparts in constraint processing. We briefly described conditioning search and hybrids of search and conditioning capturing, in particular, the cycle-cutset method.

Despite the similarities, there are substantial inherent differences in semantics and even computation between constraints, cost functions, and probabilistic functions. Computationally, constraints are a special case that permits constraint propagation in a chaotic manner. These primary building blocks of constraint processing do not translate immediately to either costs or probability functions.

In Chapter 13 we observed a specific, organized extension of bounded inference using a scheme called mini-bucket elimination. This same idea can be applied to probabilistic networks. For more information see Dechter and Rish (2003).

14.6 **Bibliographical Notes**

As described in a recent survey (Pearl and Russel 2001), probabilistic models based on directed acyclic graphs (DAGs) have a long tradition, which began with geneticist Sewall Wright (1921). Variants have appeared in many fields; within cognitive science and artificial intelligence, such models are known as Bayesian networks. Their initial development in the late 1970s was motivated by the need to model top-down (semantic) and bottom-up (perceptual) combinations of evidence in reading.

In artificial intelligence the area flourished with the introduction of Pearl's book in 1988 (Pearl 1988). This book outlines the main properties of these networks as well as the basic principal inference algorithms. The most popular algorithms for probabilistic reasoning are join-tree clustering algorithms, which are similar to the variable elimination algorithms presented in this chapter. The idea of cycle-cutset algorithms is also given in Pearl (1988). Variable elimination algorithms trace back to the peeling algorithm for genetic trees (Cannings, Thompson, and Skolnick 1978), Zhang and Poole's algorithm (Zhang and Poole 1996), as well as the SPI algorithm by D'Ambrosio, Shactor, and Del Favero (1990). In 1996, Dechter introduced bucket elimination algorithms as a unifying framework for both probabilistic and deterministic reasoning (Dechter 1996, 1999a).

chapter 15

Constraint Logic Programming

Francesca Rossi, University of Padova, Italy

The limits of my language are the limits of my mind.
All I know is what I have words for.

Ludwig Wittgenstein

In previous chapters we have seen how to solve a given constraint satisfaction problem by means of algorithms that usually employ some form of consistency enforcing combined with some variant of backtracking search. Specific features, like the shape of the constraint graph or the nature of the constraints, can be used to make the search for a solution more efficient, and also to identify tractable classes of constraint problems.

This style of constraint processing provides many techniques and tools to efficiently solve constraint problems. However, it also makes several assumptions that are sometimes not present in practice. For example, it is assumed that all constraints are available at the beginning of the search process, and that constraints are represented extensionally as sets of allowed tuples. In contrast, in some real-life scenarios, you may want to construct incrementally the constraint problem to be solved, and to represent constraints via formulas of a certain language rather than sets of tuples.

Embedding constraints into high-level programming languages can help in both these directions. In fact, it usually allows for a more flexible and practical constraint processing environment, where constraints can also be represented as formulas and can be incrementally accumulated following a certain program structure. The presence of constraints in a programming language is also useful to make the programming language more expressive because constraints add a declarative mechanism to model properties and efficient techniques to prove them.

Constraints can be, and have been, embedded in many programming environments, but some are more suitable than others to deal with constraints.

For example, the fact that constraints can be seen as relations or predicates, that their conjunction can be seen as a logical AND, and that backtracking search is the base methodology to solve them, makes them very compatible with logic programming, which is based on predicates, logical conjunctions, and depth-first search. This is why in this chapter we will focus on the addition of constraints within the logic programming paradigm.

After giving the main notions of the syntax and operational semantics of logic programming (LP), we will show how to model and solve CSPs within LP. Then we will describe how constraints are embedded in LP, generating the constraint logic programming (CLP) framework, and we will show how the CLP features allow for a more natural and efficient modeling of CSPs. Finally, we will discuss several concepts and techniques that are directly related to the use of constraints in constraint programming languages, but that can also be useful in more general environments.

15.1 **Logic Programming**

The logic programming paradigm is based on a very unique declarative programming idea, where programs are not made of statements (like in imperative programming) nor of functions (as in functional programming), but of logical implications between collections of predicates (Lloyd 1993).

15.1.1 **Syntax**

A logic program is seen as a logical theory and has the form of a set of rules (called *clauses*) that relate the truth value of a literal (the *head* of the clause) to that of a collection of other literals (the *body* of the clause).

DEFINITION 15.1
A clause has the form H :- B, where $B = B_1, \ldots, B_m$ and both the B_i's and H are positive literals. Each literal involves an n-ary predicate, say, p, and has the form $p(t_1, \ldots, t_n)$ where the t_i's are terms. A term can be

- a variable x,

- a constant a, or

- the application of an n-ary function to n terms: $f(t_1, \ldots, t_n)$.   ●

The body of a clause is interpreted as a logical conjunction of literals. The meaning of the :- symbol is an implication from the body B to the head H: if B is true, then H must be true as well. Since B is a conjunction of literals, saying that B is true means that all the literals in B must be true.

Since both the body and the head of a clause may contain variables, it is important to include in the above logical interpretation of a clause also such variables, and to understand whether they are existentially or universally quantified. Given a clause H :- B, where S_H is the set of variables appearing in H and S_B is the set of the other variables appearing in the clause (that is, those appearing in B but not in H), this clause can be interpreted as the following logical formula: for all values for the variables in S_H, there exist values for the variables in S_B such that B implies H.

EXAMPLE 15.1

For example, the logical interpretation of the clause

```
p(X,Y) :- q(X), r(X,Y,Z).
```

is that, for all values of x and y, there exist values of z such that, if $q(x)$ and $r(x,y,z)$ are both true, then also $p(x,y)$ is true. Notice that in LP variable names always start with an uppercase letter, while predicate and function names always start with a lowercase letter. Therefore we will follow this convention whenever we write LP clauses. However, when we mention some variable name in the text in some mathematical formula, we will use the usual lowercase convention as in the rest of the book.   •

For those more accustomed with imperative programming environments, another way to see a clause is that the head of the clause is the definition of a procedure (the predicate) with its arguments (the terms), and the body is its code, which is just a collection of calls to other procedures. The variables in the head of the clause can be thought of as the parameters of the procedure, while the variables not in the head but in the body can be seen as local variables.

EXAMPLE 15.2

Then, the operational interpretation of the above clause is as follows: to execute procedure p over arguments x and y, we must execute procedure q over argument x and procedure r over arguments x, y, z. Variables x and y are formal parameters of procedure p, while z is a local variable.   •

Clauses with no body, usually written as H., are called *facts*. Their meaning, according to what was said above, is that the literal H is true for any value of its variables. In other words, if $H = p(t_1, \ldots, t_n)$, it means that, for all values of the variables in terms t_i's, predicate p with arguments $t_1, \ldots, t_n$ is true. Logically, a fact is just an axiom. Operationally, a fact means that any call to procedure p with parameters matching $t_1, \ldots, t_n$ ends with success without the need to call any other procedure.

DEFINITION 15.2

A logic program is just a collection of clauses.   •

EXAMPLE 15.3

For example, the following program has three clauses:

```
reach(X,X).
reach(X,Y) :- flight(X,Y).
reach(X,Y) :- flight(X,Z), reach(Z,Y).
```

and describes the reachability between two cities (x and y) via a sequence of one or more direct flights. Notice that here we have a recursive definition of predicate reach, and its three clauses have different roles: the first two describe the base case, and say that from x we can reach y either if x and y are the same city, or if there is a direct flight between x and y, while the third clause describes the recursive case, and says that from x we can reach y if there is a direct flight between x and z, and if from z we can reach y.   •

15.1.2 Operational Semantics

Executing a logic program means asking for the truth value of a certain statement, called the *goal*, written as :- G. G can be any collection of positive literals, say, $A_1, \ldots, A_n$. Asking for the truth value of G means asking whether there are suitable values for the variables in G such that all the A_i's are true, given the clauses of the logic program. Therefore the variables appearing in a goal are existentially quantified.

EXAMPLE 15.4   For example, giving the goal :- p(X,Y). means asking whether there are values for the variables x and y such that $p(X, Y)$ is true in the given logic program.   •

The answer to a goal is found by using the clauses of the program, and recursively *unifying* the current goal with the head of a clause.

DEFINITION 15.3   Unification of two literals A_1 and A_2 consists of finding an assignment of terms to the variables of A_1 and A_2 that makes the literals equal. An assignment of terms to variables is called a *substitution*. Given a substitution σ and a literal A, the application of σ to the variables of A returns a new literal written as $A\sigma$.   •

Usually, among all the unifiers, you want the most general one (because it subsumes all the others), which is the substitution that instantiates the variables as little as possible and still makes the two literals equal.

EXAMPLE 15.5   For example, the substitution $\sigma = \{x = b, y = a, v = f(z)\}$ unifies $A_1 = p(x, a, f(z))$ with $A_2 = p(b, y, v)$, since $A_1\sigma = A_2\sigma$. Moreover, it is their most general unifier (mgu). Also $\{x = b, y = a, v = f(c), z = c\}$ unifies these two literals, but it is not the most general unifier because variable v is instantiated, while there is no need to do so to make A_1 and A_2 equal.   •

Given a goal $G = A_1, \ldots, A_n$, the aim is to prove that it is possible to find values for its variables that make it true in the given logic program. Or, in other words, we need to prove that G is a theorem of the logical theory that contains the axioms (i.e., the facts) and the logical implications (i.e., the clauses) of the given logic program. Operationally, this is done by repeatedly transforming the goal via a sequence of *resolution steps*, until either we end up with the empty goal (in this case the proof is successful), or we cannot continue and we don't have the empty goal (and in this case we have a failure), or we continue forever (and in this case we have an infinite computation).

Each resolution step involves the unification between a literal A that is part of a goal, say, $G = A, R$, and the head H of a clause, say, $H : -B$. If A and H unify, with most general unifier σ, then the whole goal G can be replaced by the new goal $(B, R)\sigma$. That is, we replace A with the body of the clause, and we apply σ to the whole new goal. This can be described more formally by the following rewriting rule, which shows how to pass from a goal G to a goal G'. The statements above the line are the preconditions to the application of the rule, and below the line we have the new goal:

$$\frac{G = A, R \quad H : -B \quad \sigma = mgu(A, H)}{G' = (B, R)\sigma}$$

If, using one or more occurrences of such a rule, we get to the empty goal, the answer of the program to the given goal is the accumulated substitution (that is, the composition of all the mgu's used in the resolution steps), projected over the variables of the goal.

DEFINITION 15.4

A sequence of resolution steps is called a *derivation*. If a derivation ends with success it is called a *refutation*. Given a goal, the set of all derivations starting from it can be represented as a tree (its *derivation tree*), where the goal is the root, each internal node is an intermediate goal, the leaves are empty goals or failure nodes, and the parent-child relationship coincides with a resolution step. •

EXAMPLE 15.6

For example, given the program

```
reach(X,X).
reach(X,Y) :- flight(X,Y).
reach(X,Y) :- flight(X,Z), reach(Z,Y).
flight(losangeles, sanfrancisco).
flight(sanfrancisco, newyork).
flight(newyork, portland).
```

the goal :- reach(losangeles, sanfrancisco) can be transformed by using the second clause with mgu $\{x = losangeles, y = sanfrancisco\}$. This generates the new goal :- flight(losangeles, sanfrancisco). Then this goal can be transformed by using the first fact for predicate flight producing

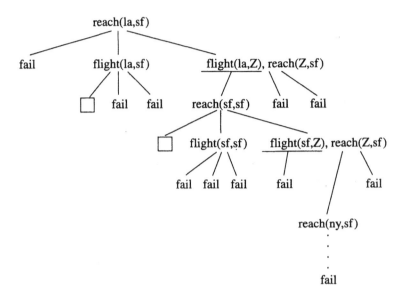

Figure 15.1 The derivation tree for goal :- reach(losangeles, sanfrancisco).

the empty goal. Thus the computation has succeeded. The derivation tree for this goal, in Figure 15.1, shows this successful computation and also parts of other computations. At each node of the tree, which contains a current goal, if there is more than one literal, the literal used for resolution is underlined. Moreover, the links of the tree starting from each node are as many as the clauses whose head has the same predicate symbol as the underlined literal, and they are ordered from left to right following the way clauses and facts are written (from the first one to the last one). Empty goals are denoted by boxes, as is common in the theory of logic programming, and failing unifications are denoted by "fail" leaves. Part of the tree, which produces just failing derivations, is not shown to avoid a large picture. Notice that this derivation tree does not contain any infinite derivation.

A success can be obtained also by starting for the goal :- reach(losangeles, newyork), while failure is obtained for the goal :- reach(losangeles, portland). In fact, there is no way to apply some resolution steps to this last goal and end up with the empty goal. Notice that the goals considered so far do not contain any variables; thus the result of the computation is either success or failure, with no mention of any substitution. If instead we have the goal :- flight(X,Y), then there are six possibilities for success, with substitutions {$x = losangeles$, $y = sanfrancisco$}, {$x = sanfrancisco$, $y = newyork$}, {$x = sanfrancisco$, $y = portland$},

$\{x = losangeles,\ y = newyork\}$, $\{x = losangeles,\ y = portland\}$, and $\{x = newyork,\ y = portland\}$. •

15.1.3 Logic Programming versus Prolog

It is easy to see that, at every step in the resolution process, there are in general several literals in the current goal that could be replaced using a resolution step to produce a new goal. Moreover, for each such literal, there are in general several clauses whose head unifies with the chosen subgoal. While a theoretical treatment of logic programming can avoid making these choices, because the order in which such items are chosen does not influence the set of resulting refutations, real logic programming languages, such as Prolog (Sterling and Shapiro 1994), have to take such decisions to avoid nondeterminism. For example, Prolog always chooses the leftmost literal within a goal and the first (that is, the uppermost) clause in the program (among those with the same head predicate as in the chosen subgoal). Moreover, Prolog performs a depth-first traversal (or, better, construction) of the derivation tree. When a failure is reached, chronological backtracking is performed until either we reach a success node (that is, a leaf with empty goal), or we continue forever in an infinite branch.

It is important to notice that these choices make the overall search engine unsafe because there could be a goal that has a solution, but Prolog could be unable to find it.

EXAMPLE 15.7 This is what happens, for example, in the following program when we consider the goal :- stupid(X,Y).:

```
stupid(X,Y) :- stupid(X,Y).
stupid(X,Y) :- stop(X,Y).
stop(X,Y).
```

In fact, the Prolog execution strategy always chooses the first of the two clauses for predicate stupid, which leads to an infinite chain of identical

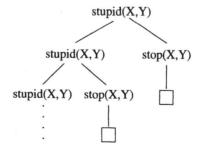

Figure 15.2 The derivation tree for goal :- stupid(X,Y).

calls to goal stupid(X,Y). The second clause would be used only if the goal and the head of the first clause do not unify, which is never the case in this example. Nevertheless, the derivation tree for such a goal, which can be seen in Figure 15.2, contains this choice and thus also refutations.   •

There is also another source of unsafeness in Prolog, which is related to the fact that, for efficiency reasons, unification is usually performed without the so-called *occur check*, which checks if some term equations are recursive. Recursive term equations make the unification algorithm run forever; thus avoiding the occur check could generate an infinite behavior in some cases.

15.1.4   Data Structures in LP: Records and Lists

The main data structures that can be used in logic programming are records and lists. Records with n fields are just defined using n-ary functions, whose arguments define the fields. This makes record definition and usage very natural.

For example, if you need a record defining a point over the Cartesian plane, with two fields corresponding to the two coordinates, it is enough to use a 2-ary function point. Notice that this is not a built-in function; thus the name of the function can be chosen arbitrarily by the programmer. The following program defines predicates coordinatex and coordinatey, which compute the x or y coordinate of a point.

```
coordinatex(point(X,Y),X).
coordinatey(point(X,Y),Y).
```

Lists are instead available in LP via a built-in syntax such that

- [ ] is the empty list.
- [H | T] is the list with H as its first element (i.e., the *head* of the list) and T as the rest of the list (i.e., the *tail* of the list).
- [X1,X2,...,Xn] is the list containing the n elements $x_1, ..., x_n$.

For example, the following program defines a predicate append that appends two lists.

```
append([ ], Y, Y).
append([F|R], Y, [F|Z]) :- append(R,Y,Z).
```

More precisely, predicate append has three arguments: the two lists to be appended, and the list that results from the append operation. Notice in this program the use of recursion to scan the first list and to construct, as a third argument, the concatenation of the two lists corresponding to the first and the second arguments of the predicate. The first clause applies when the first list is empty, and in this case returns the second list as the result. The second clause applies when the first list is not empty. In this case, let us assume it is made of a first element, say, f, and the rest of the list, say, r, and let us call y the second list. Then the resulting list will have f as its first element, and the remainder of the list, call it z, will be the result of appending r and y.

15.2 **Logic Programming as a Constraint Programming Language**

We have seen that the logic programming execution engine performs a depth-first traversal of the derivation tree of the goal. This is obviously very similar to the backtracking search used to find a solution of a finite domain constraint satisfaction problem. Also, sets of facts with the same predicate describe several ways to make the predicate true; thus it is a relation, or a finite domain constraint. Therefore it is easy to see that logic programming is a natural programming framework where finite domain constraint satisfaction problems can be modeled, and then solved by the execution engine. In fact, a finite domain CSP is just a set of relations, or constraints, each of which can be modeled by a set of facts where the predicate name corresponds to the constraint name. Then, the task of satisfying all constraints can be described by a clause whose body contains all the constraint predicates (since literals in the body are combined via logical AND). The head of such a clause must then contain all variables of the constraints. Giving a goal that matches this head means asking for one solution of the CSP.

EXAMPLE 15.8
For example, consider the CSP with three variables (x, y, and z), all with domain $D = \{a, b, c\}$, and two constraints: $c_1(x, y) = \{(a, a), (a, b), (b, b)\}$ and $c_2(y, z) = \{(b, a)\}$. Then a corresponding logic program could be the following one:

```
csp(X,Y,Z) :- c1(X,Y),c2(Y,Z).
c1(a,a).
c1(a,b).
c1(b,b).
c2(b,a).
```

Giving the goal :- csp(X,Y,Z) means asking whether there are values for x, y, and z such that both $c1(x, y)$ and $c2(y, z)$ can be true. The derivation tree for this goal is shown in Figure 15.3; there is no infinite derivation, and all successful derivations correspond to solutions of the original CSP. Notice that this tree is similar to the search tree for this problem as described in Chapter 5.

Notice that we can also give the goal :- csp(a,b,b), which means that we want to check if $x = a, y = b, z = b$ is a solution. The derivation tree for this goal, shown in Figure 15.4, has just failing derivations, meaning that the instantiation of the goal is not a solution.

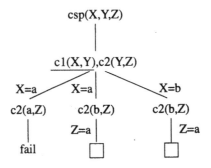

Figure 15.3 The derivation tree for goal :- csp(X,Y,Z).

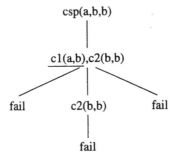

Figure 15.4 The derivation tree for goal :- csp(a,b,b).

Or we can also give the goal :- csp(a,b,Z), which means that we want to check whether there are solutions in which $x = a$ and $y = b$. The derivation tree for this goal, shown in Figure 15.5, contains a successful derivation, which means that there are indeed solutions in which $x = a$ and $y = b$. Notice that the logic programming engine not only says that there are solutions, but also returns one (that is, a value for Z, in this case $Z = a$) or all of them. •

It is thus clear that any finite domain CSP can be described by a logic program having one clause and several ground facts. The execution engine is then able both to find one or all solutions of the CSP and to find complete solutions if given a partial one. However, logic programs can express much more complex relationships, allowing also for recursion and function symbols. In addition, the use of functions and variables in the description of a problem also can allow for a more compact representation of the constraints.

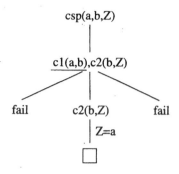

Figure 15.5 The derivation tree for goal :- csp(a, b, Z).

EXAMPLE
15.9   For example, if we want to express a binary constraint that requires two variables to be equal, we don't need to write as many facts as the number of domain elements, but just one fact where the same variable is used in both arguments of the predicate, like in c(X,X). Another example is a binary constraint that requires that two variables are different: in this case, we don't need to write as many facts as the number of pairs of distinct domain elements, but just two clauses, as follows:

```
c(X,X) :- !, fail.
c(X,Y).
```

The first clause is used when the two variables involved in constraint *c* have the same value, and its body always fails (fail is a built-in predicate with no arguments that always fails). The second clause is instead used when the two variables have different values, and it always succeeds, since there is no body. The exclamation mark in the first clause, called a *cut*, makes sure that the second clause is not tried upon failure in the body of the first one, which otherwise would be done by the LP engine.   •

In this section we have seen that, while modeling and solving CSPs using ordinary LP programs is easy, LP poses restrictions on the solution algorithm and thus may result in a slow solution process. In fact, LP's execution engine corresponds to depth-first search with chronological backtracking—not the most efficient way to solve CSPs. Also, no notion of constraint propagation can be inserted into the solution algorithm. We will see in the next section that constraint logic programming languages extend LP by providing many tools to improve the solution efficiency using CN techniques, and they extend CSPs by allowing for constraints defined not only as sets of tuples but also via formulas over a specific language of constraints (like arithmetic equations and disequations over the reals, or term equations, or linear disequations over finite domains).

15.3 **Syntax and Semantics of Constraint Logic Programming**

Syntactically, constraints are added to logic programming by just considering a specific constraint type (for example, linear equations over the reals) and then allowing constraints of this type in the body of the clauses. Besides the usual resolution engine of logic programming, you have a (complete or incomplete) constraint solving system, which is able to check the consistency of constraints of the considered type. This simple change provides many improvements over logic programming:

- First, the concept of unification is generalized to constraint solving: the relationship between a goal and a clause (to be used in a resolution step) can be described not just via term equations but via more general statements, that is, constraints. This allows for a more general and flexible way to control the flow of the computation.

- Second, expressing constraints by some language (for example, linear equations and disequations) is more compact.

- Finally, the presence of an underlying constraint solver, usually based on incomplete constraint propagation of some sort, allows for the combination of backtracking search and constraint propagation, thus generating more efficient complete solvers.

We will now look in more detail at each of these points, which characterize the class of constraint logic programming (CLP) languages (Jaffar and Maher 1994; Marriott and Stuckey 1998).

We first need to define which constraints we are interested in and provide a suitable constraint system for them. The constraint system must be able to both test the consistency of any set of constraints that could arise in the CLP language and perform variable elimination (to project a solution onto the variables of the goal). These two tasks are the only ones that are needed when using constraints within LP. Notice that such tasks are performed by the unification algorithm, which therefore can be seen as a constraint solver over sets of term equations. For example, if we want to work with linear arithmetic equations over the rationals, we may use the Gauss-Jordan elimination algorithm, which is a complete constraint solver for such constraints. Or, if we want to work with arithmetic constraints over a finite domain, we may use arc-consistency as an incomplete solver to test for consistency.

In general, we need a *constraint language* that specifies which kind of constraints we may use, and a corresponding consistency test of any set of constraints expressible in this language, as well as a suitable variable elimination procedure. Notice that we do not require to be able to find one or all solutions of a given set of constraints.

15.3.1 **Syntax**

Once we have chosen a constraint language, a CLP clause is just like an LP clause, except that its body may also contain constraints of the considered language.

EXAMPLE 15.10

For example, if we can use linear disequations over the reals, a CLP clause could be

```
p(X,Y) :- X < Y+1, q(X), r(X,Y,Z).
```

This clause states that p(X,Y) is true if q(X) and r(X,Y,Z) are true, and if the value of x is smaller than that of $y + 1$.   ●

If we work with finite domains, we can always replace a constraint such as $x < y + 1$ with a literal of the form $c(X, Y, Z)$ in the body of the above clause, and as many ground facts as the number of pairs of values for x and y that satisfy the relation $x < y + 1$. However, this representation would obviously be less compact. In addition, it would not allow the use of constraint propagation as described ahead.

To use a clause in a resolution step in LP, we just have to check the existence of an mgu between the selected subgoal and the head. Here, we also have to check the consistency of the current set of constraints with the constraints in the body of the clause. Thus two solvers are involved: unification and the specific constraint solver for the constraints in use.

More precisely, instead of dealing with just term equations of the form $x = t$, which can be seen as a specific kind of constraint over x and the variables in t, we can use any kind of constraints, such as $x + y \leq 6$ or $x < y + 1$. Therefore, besides unification of terms, you have to use a suitable algorithm to perform constraint solving over the desired class of constraints.

15.3.2 **Operational Semantics**

While in LP a computation state consists of a goal and a substitution, in CLP we have a goal and a set of constraints, called the *constraint store*. Then, resolution steps work as follows:

DEFINITION 15.5

Given a state of the form $\langle G, S \rangle$, where G is the current goal and S is the current constraint store, assume $G = A, R$ (and that we want to rewrite A). Then:

- If A is a constraint, A is added to S; thus the new state is $\langle R, prop(S \wedge A) \rangle$, where prop(C) is the result of applying some constraint propagation algorithm (like arc-consistency) to the constraint store C.

- If instead A is a literal, and there is a clause $H : -B$ with the same head predicate as A, then we add the constraint $A = H$ to the constraint store, we replace A with B, and the new goal is then $\langle (B, R), S \wedge \{A = H\} \rangle$.   ●

Notice that $A = H$ may involve both term equations and constraints of the considered constraint language.

DEFINITION
15.6

A CLP computation is successful if there is a way to get from the initial state $\langle G, \text{true} \rangle$ to the goal $\langle G', S \rangle$, where G' is the empty goal and S is satisfiable.   •

Therefore, while in LP we just accumulate substitutions during a computation, in CLP we also accumulate constraints.

Derivation trees are defined in the same way as in LP, except that each node in the tree now represents both the current goal and the current constraint store. Also, in working CLP systems, the usual Prolog traversal mode is retained: depth-first, with subgoals selected from left to right, and clauses from the first to the last one.

Early detection of failing computations is achieved by checking the consistency of the current constraint store. At each node, having a constraint store containing the constraints accumulated so far (both term equations and other kinds of constraints), the underlying constraint system is automatically invoked (via function *prop* above) to check consistency, and the computation along this path continues only if the check is successful (although the check itself could be incomplete). Otherwise, backtracking is performed. Notice that this consistency check can use some form of constraint propagation, thus applying the principle of combining depth-first backtracking search with constraint propagation, as usual in complete constraint solvers for CSPs.

EXAMPLE
15.11

A typical example of a CLP program is the one describing the factorial function:

```
fac(0,1).
fac(N, N * F) :- N ≥ 1, fac(N-1,F).
```

For this program, goal fac(2,X) succeeds with answer $x = 2$, after two backtrackings. Its derivation tree (Figure 15.6) shows that a depth-first traversal of such a tree would first encounter two failing computations and then the only successful one. More precisely, the CLP run-time system first tries to rewrite the goal by using the first clause, that is, the fact fac(0,1), failing to do so. Then it tries to use the head of the second clause, that is, fac(N,N*F), obtaining the new goal fac(1,F) and the constraint Y=2*F. Thus the new state is $\langle fac(1, F), Y = 2 * F \rangle$. Notice that, in this second rewriting step, unification would not be enough, because the second argument of the goal (that is, y), is not unifiable with the second argument of the head of the clause (that is, $n*f$). Thus we need to add the constraint $Y = N * F$ in the current store.[1]

---

1. In our case we added a simplified version of this constraint because we also have the constraint $N = 2$ due to the unification of the first arguments.

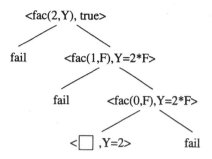

Figure 15.6 The derivation tree for goal :- fac(2,X).

Now the CLP system tries again to rewrite the current goal by using the fact, failing, and then by using the head of the clause, obtaining the new state $\langle fac(0, F), Y = 2 * F \rangle$. At this point, rewriting the current goal with the fact is possible and produces the new state $\langle \square, Y = 2 \rangle$, which is a successful state. If we ask the CLP system for further answers to the initial goal, it will continue the expansion of the derivation tree in a depth-first way until a new successful state is found, or all states have been considered. In this example, the CLP system will try a different rewriting for the last goal $(\langle fac(0, F), Y = 2 * F \rangle)$, failing to use the head of the clause. Since there are no other nodes in the tree awaiting further expansion, the system will return that there is no other answer to the initial goal.   ●

EXAMPLE 15.12

Another typical CLP program is one describing a mortgage, where p is the amount borrowed, i is the interest rate, t is the number of time periods, r is the repayment made after each time period, and b is the final balance:

```
mortgage(P,T,I,R,B) :- T=0, B=P.
mortgage(P,T,I,R,B) :- T≥1, mortgage(P+P*I-R,T-1,I,R,B).
```

The first clause states that when the number of time periods is 0 $(t = 0)$, the final balance (b) coincides with the amount borrowed $(b = p)$. The second clause instead states that, if the number of time periods is 1 or more $(t \geq 1)$, we recursively call procedure mortgage over the same i, r, and b, but a new borrowed amount, $p + p * i - r$, taking into account the interest and the amount paid at the previous time period, and the number of time periods, $t - 1$.

If we want to know what happens if we borrow $1000 for 10 years at an interest rate of 10% and repay $150 a year, we have to use the goal

```
:- mortgage(1000,10,10/100,150,B).
```

which returns the answer $b = 203.129$. If instead we use the goal

```
:- mortgage(P,10,10/100,150,0).
```

that is, we ask how much to borrow to reach a zero balance with the conditions given above, then the answer generated is $p = 0.3855 * b + 6.1446 * r$. Notice that in CLP we may have constraints as answers, not just variable substitutions. Thus the relationship among the variables of the goal can be expressed in a more general way than just term equations.   ●

CLP is not a single programming language, but a programming *paradigm*, which is parametric with respect to the class of constraints used in the language. Working with a particular CLP language means choosing a specific class of constraints (for example, finite domains, linear, or arithmetic) and a suitable constraint system for that class. Notice that unification is not *replaced*, rather it is assisted by the constraint solver, since every CLP language also applies LP-style unification over its variables.

Denoting a CLP language over a constraint class X as CLP(X), we can say that logic programming is just CLP(Tree), where Tree identifies the class of term equalities (a term is just a tree), with their unification algorithm to solve classes of them. The language CLP(R) (Jaffar et al. 1992), instead, works with both terms and arithmetic constraints over the reals. The mortgage program, for instance, is an example of a program in CLP(R).

A popular class of constraints, which is directly related to the subject of this book, is the class of constraints with variables ranging over finite domains. Constraint logic programming using finite domain constraints is a useful language scheme, referred to as CLP(FD). The next section will be devoted to the description of this particular class of CLP languages, which are most suited to model and solve the CSP classes described in previous chapters of this book.

15.4 CLP over Finite Domain Constraints

Finite domain constraints, as used within CLP languages, are usually intended to be arithmetic constraints over finite domain variables. Also, although in principle the finite domains for the variables can contain any element, in practice each element is mapped onto an integer, and thus a finite domain of any variable is always represented as a set (actually a list) of integers. Thus CLP(FD) needs a constraint system that is able to perform consistency checks and projection over these kinds of constraints. Usually, the consistency check is based on constraint propagation similar to, but weaker than, arc-consistency (called *bounds-consistency*, see Section 15.5).

One of the peculiarities of CLP(FD) languages, as opposed to generic CLP languages, is that they have a specific mechanism to define the initial finite domains of the variables. The usual way is to represent a domain as an interval over the integers.

EXAMPLE 15.13

For example, a typical CLP(FD) syntax to say that the domain of variable x contains all integers between 1 and 10 is X in [1..10] or X:[1,10] or fd_domain(X,1,10). In the remainder of this chapter, we will not use the syntax of any specific CLP(FD) language, but we will use the simplest syntax at hand to understand the concept to be explained.   •

Another common feature of all CLP(FD) languages is that it provides a built-in predicate called labeling that works over a list of variables, and finds values for them such that all constraints in the current store are satisfied. As noted before, CLP languages do not necessarily return a value for each variable in the goal, but in general return the set of accumulated constraints. Since usually in CSPs you need to find the solutions and are not interested in the relationship among the variables of the goal, the labeling predicate provides a mechanism to have such solutions. More precisely, this predicate triggers backtracking search over a set of variables.

EXAMPLE 15.14

For example, the following clause defines a problem with three finite domain variables (x, y, and z), each with domain containing the integers from 1 to 10, and sets a constraint over them ($x + y = 9 - z$). After this, it triggers backtracking search via predicate labeling:

p(X,Y,Z) :- [X,Y,Z]: [1,10], X + Y = 9 - Z, labeling([X,Y,Z]).

The result of executing the goal :- p(X,Y,Z). is any instantiation of the three variables over their domains that satisfies the constraint $x + y = 9 - x$.

Notice that without the labeling predicate, this same goal would return just the new domains obtained after applying constraint propagation. For example, running this goal in the CLP(FD) language GNU Prolog (Codognet and Diaz 1996), which uses bounds-consistency (to be described later), would return the answer [X,Y,Z]:[1,7],[2] meaning that the domains have been reduced from [1..10] to [1..7] via constraint propagation. Notice that, in this example, after constraint propagation, all the variable domains are the same interval, but in general they may be different intervals, even starting from the same initial domain.   •

The clause in the example above presents the typical shape of a CLP(FD) program: first the variable domains are specified, then the constraints over such variables are defined, and finally the backtracking search is invoked via a labeling predicate. A CLP(FD) program can consist of many clauses, but the overall

---

2. Although not exactly in this syntax.

structure of the program always reflects this order, which refers to a methodology called *constraint-and-generate*—first variables are constrained and only later (when the domains are smaller) backtracking search is invoked. This is done with the aim of avoiding useless work as much as possible. If we first give values to the variables (via labeling) and then check the constraints, in most cases the proposed instantiation will be rejected because it is inconsistent. Notice that it is the task of the programmer to make sure that the *constraint-and-generate* principle is followed by his/her program.

Many constraints and literals can be present in the body of a CLP clause. While the order in which they are written does not influence the answers given by the program to a goal, such an order is very important in determining the efficiency with which such answers are found. In fact, different orders may yield very different times in producing an answer to a goal. Not only that: some orders may also result in infinite derivations, while others may find the solution in finite time.

EXAMPLE 15.15

Consider, for example, the CLP program

```
sum(0,0).
sum(N, N+S) :- sum(N-1,S), N ≥ 1.
```

which is supposed to compute the sum of the first N integer numbers. If we give the goal sum(1,0), the computation never ends. In fact, because of the left-to-right processing of a goal, each step uses the second clause, adding a sum literal and a new constraint to the store, and then expanding the sum literal again. The constraints are never checked for consistency because they are never reached by the left-to-right processing scheme. Reordering the elements of the body of the second clause as

```
sum(0,0).
sum(N, N+S) :- N ≥ 1, sum(N-1,S).
```

we correctly get a failure after a finite time as the answer to goal sum(1,0). •

As a rule, it is always better to move constraints before the literals in the body of the clauses, so that failures are discovered earlier. More generally, when there are several literals in a clause, it is better to write first (that is, more to the left) those literals that have a smaller number of answers, since this reduces the size of the search tree.

EXAMPLE 15.16

Typical finite domain constraint problems are those that arise in crypto-arithmetic: the task is to assign different integer digits to different variables (expressed as letters) such that some equations among the variables are satisfied. A typical example is SEND + MORE = MONEY, which can be described by the following CLP(FD) program:

```
smm(S,E,N,D,M,O,R,Y) :-
      [S,E,N,D,M,O,R,Y] : [0,9],
      constrain([S,E,N,D,M,O,R,Y]),
      labeling([S,E,N,D,M,O,R,Y]).
constrain([S,E,N,D,M,O,R,Y]) :-
      S ≠ 0, M ≠ 0,
      alldifferent([S,E,N,D,M,O,R,Y]),
      1000*S + 100*E + 10*N + D + 1000*M + 100*O + 10*R + E =
      10000*M + 1000*O + 100*N + 10*E + Y.
```

In this program, the first clause defines the problem in terms of variable domains, constraint predicate, and backtracking search, while the second clause defines the constraints. The domains are defined by saying, through a specific syntax, that all the variables must range between 0 and 9. The constraints say that all variables must be different (via predicate alldifferent, defined by other clauses not written here), and that the desired equation must be satisfied.

Given the goal :- smm(S,E,N,D,M,O,R,Y)., the CLP system rewrites this goal by using the first clause; the new goal is thus

```
constrain([S,E,N,D,M,O,R,Y]), labeling([S,E,N,D,M,O,R,Y]),
```

while the constraint store, initially empty, becomes the domain constraint (that is, all variables in [0, 9]). Then, the current goal is expanded by rewriting the first predicate using the second clause. This leads to the new goal labeling ([S,E,N,D,M,O,R,Y]), and to the constraint store that contains all accumulated constraints, that is, $[S, E, N, D, M, O, R, Y] :: [0, 9]$, $S \neq 0, M \neq 0$, *alldifferent*$([S, E, N, D, M, O, R, Y])$, $1000*S+100*E+10*N+D+1000*M+100*O+10*R+E = 10000*M+1000*O+100*N+10*E+Y$. At this point, the labeling predicate starts a classical depth-first traversal of the search tree by instantiating each of the variables to a value in its current domain and by backtracking every time the next variable cannot be instantiated consistently with the constraints and previous assignments. A constraint propagation algorithm can be used at each step of the search procedure to speed it up. For this example, the only solution that is found is $S = 9, E = 5, N = 6, D = 7, M = 1, O = 0, R = 8, Y = 2$. •

As mentioned earlier, the labeling predicate usually has a default definition; thus it does not need to be redefined explicitly via some clauses. However, if we decided to define it ourselves, it could be done via the following clauses:

```
labeling([ ]).
labeling([V|Vs]) :- indomain(V), labeling(Vs).
indomain(V) :- dom(V,D), member(V,D).
```

In words, predicate labeling iterates through each variable v of the list of variables to be labeled, to give it a value in its domain. This is done via predicate indomain, which finds the current domain of the variable (via dom(V,D)) and makes sure that the value given to v is one of the elements of the domain (via member(V,D), which is a built-in predicate). Since both the variables and the domain elements are stored in lists, which are then scanned sequentially from the first to the last element, this built-in definition always selects the next variable in the list (thus using a static variable selection strategy) and the next value in the domain (thus values are chosen from the smallest one to the larger one).

However, other more sophisticated backtracking-based search procedures, with specific heuristics for variable and value selection, can be modeled by writing personalized clauses for a new labeling predicate. For example, it is possible to select as the next variable the one with the smallest domain, via the following clauses:

```
labeling([ ]).
labeling(L) :- smallestdom(L,V,L1), indomain(V), labeling(L1).
indomain(V) :- dom(V,D), member(V,D).
```

where predicate smallestdom(L,V,L1), whose clauses are not written here (see Marriott and Stuckey 1998 for details), finds in the list of variables l the variable v that has the smallest current domain, and returns in l_1 the list of all remaining variables.

Predicate alldifferent, as used in the last example, in its most naive version can be defined by a clause that sets as many inequality constraints as the pair of distinct variables. This means that we have many binary inequality constraints. A possible definition could be the following one:

```
alldifferent([ ]).
alldifferent([H|L]) :- diff(H,L), alldifferent(L).
diff(X,[ ]).
diff(X,[H|L]) :- X ≠ H, diff(X,L).
```

However, we will see later that usually there is a built-in definition of the alldifferent predicate that uses just one n-ary constraint (where n is the number of variables that have to be different) and uses a specialized constraint propagation algorithm for such a constraint to achieve more pruning. This is done via the notion of *global constraints*, which will be explained in more detail in Section 15.5.3.

EXAMPLE 15.17   Another typical CLP(FD) program is the one describing the n-queens problem:

```
goal(N, Queens) :-
    length(Queens,N), Queens :: [1,N],
    queens(Queens), labeling(Queens).
```

```
queens([ ] ).
queens([X|Y]) :- safe(X,Y,1), queens(Y).
safe(_,[ ], _).
safe(X,[F|T],Nb) :- noattack(X,F,Nb), Newnb = Nb + 1,
safe(X,T,Newnb).
noattack(X,Y,Nb) :- Y + Nb ≠ X, X + Nb ≠ Y, X ≠ Y.
```

Predicate goal is the main predicate and defines the whole problem: first predicate length, whose definition we did not write here, forces list Queens to be a list of n distinct variables. Then, the domain of each variable in such a list is set to the interval $[1, n]$, constraints are posed over such variables by predicate queens, and backtracking search is invoked by predicate labeling (which, in its built-in definition, performs naive chronological backtracking). Predicate queens scans the entire list of queens and sets the usual binary constraints over any pair of queens, via predicate safe. In fact, predicate safe sets the appropriate inequality constraints between queens on the same row or on the same diagonal. More precisely, predicate safe sets the necessary constraints between queen X and all queens in list [F|T]. Variable NB is the distance (in terms of columns) between queen X and queen F, and it is used by predicate noattack to set the right disequations between variables X and Y.

A coding of this program in LP can be done in a similar way as for the previous example, and showing the same problems with respect to the CLP formulation. Moreover, in this case we also have an additional restriction, since the LP formulation needs a fixed value for n, because otherwise the predicate describing the domain (which contains the integers from 1 to n) cannot be properly defined. •

There are many CLP(FD) languages or environments that have been developed, either in academic or commercial environments. Among them, some of the most successful are ECLiPSe (IC-PARC 1999), GNU Prolog (Diaz 2000), SICStus Prolog (Carlsson and Widen 1999), and CHIP (Dincbas et al. 1988a).

15.5 **Issues and Notions Coming from CLP Use**

As noted above, CLP languages provide the features of a high-level declarative programming paradigm like logic programming on top of one or more constraint solvers. This is useful for many reasons: flexibility, efficiency, generality, and compactness. However, the coexistence of constraint solvers and logic programming notions also raises some issues that are not present when considering constraint solvers alone. In this section we will describe some of these issues, and the new notions and techniques that are related to them.

15.5.1 Variables, Constraints, Domains

Flexible Number of Variables

The presence of lists—and, in general, of functions—in LP and CLP allows for a flexible scenario, where, for example, it is possible to have a nonspecified number of variables for some constraints. Consider, for example, the variables and constraints that are needed to specify a set of houses, each with its own features, like the number of rooms, the size in terms of square meters, the price, and the size of each room, plus some constraints among such features.

The natural way to represent this situation is to have one variable for each of the first three features, and as many variables as the number of rooms, to express the square meters of the rooms. However, this modeling works well for one house, but not in a situation where there are many houses, with varying numbers of rooms. In order to have a uniform structure variable/constraints for all houses, we need to specify the maximum number of rooms in a house, and use dummy values for houses having a smaller number of rooms.

This solution modeling is obviously undesirable, especially if new houses having larger numbers of rooms are added later. It is easy to see that CLP (and LP) allows for more flexible representations, via the use of lists. In this example it is enough to consider a list for each house, containing as many elements as the number of rooms.

EXAMPLE 15.18

For example, a CLP(FD) clause that could describe such a situation is the following one:

```
house(N,S,P,L): -
    N :: [1,20], S :: [50,600], P :: [100,1000], L :: [5,20],
    constrain(N,S,P,L), labeling([N,S,P,L]).
```

In this clause, variables N, S, P represent the first three features (that is, number of rooms, square meters, and price), while variable L is a list that contains as many elements as the number of rooms (thus we will have the constraint $N = \text{length}(L)$). Variable domains are set as appropriate, and predicate `constrain` sets (in a part of the program not written here) the appropriate constraints over all the features of a house. •

Compact Representation of Constraints

In CSPs, constraints are assumed to be represented extensively, by listing all tuples that are allowed by the constraint. This representation is possible, but not encouraged in a CLP language, since it would generate very big clauses. Therefore, the use of constraint languages, like arithmetic constraints, allows for a compact description. Thus usually CLP languages use either arithmetic constraints, or term equations, or other compact ways to represent constraints within clauses.

Ordered Domains

Another restriction that is often placed on CLP(FD) languages is that variable domains are ordered, while in general, in finite domain constraints, domains are any set of elements. The order allows the assimilation of domains to intervals over the integers. This allows for coding a domain by just two values (the upper and the lower bounds of the interval), while a set of values needs an explicit representation of all the elements of the set.

15.5.2   Bounds-Consistency

Bounds-consistency is a form of constraint propagation (or *local consistency* technique) that emerged within CLP(FD) languages. This is why, although we introduced it in Chapter 3, we define it again here and discuss its significance in greater depth.

Bounds-consistency is related to the fact that variable domains are represented as intervals of the integers, which in turn are represented by two elements: their minimum and their maximum. However, constraint propagation techniques like arc-consistency could destroy this representation by removing elements internal to the interval. Consider, for example, the variable domain X :: [1,10] and the constraint X $\neq$ 5: arc/node-consistency would remove the value 5 from the domain of X, thus producing two intervals instead of one for the new domain.

To avoid this phenomenon, CLP(FD) usually uses an approximation of arc-consistency, called *bounds-consistency*, which removes an element from a domain only if the resulting domain is still an interval. More precisely:

DEFINITION 15.7   A constraint is *bounds-consistent* if, for each of its variables, say, X, there is an assignment for the other variables that is compatible with min(X) and another assignment that is compatible with max(X).   •

Notice that this definition is much weaker than (n-dimensional) arc-consistency, which instead requires the condition above not just for min(X) and max(X), but for all values of X.

EXAMPLE 15.19   For example, the constraint $X = 3Y + 5Z$, with domains $D(X) = [2, 7]$, $D(Y) = [0, 2]$, and $D(Z) = [-1, 2]$, is not bounds-consistent. To obtain bounds-consistency, we must update the domains to $D(X) = [2, 7]$, $D(Y) = [0, 2]$, and $D(Z) = [0, 1]$.   •

To achieve bounds-consistency efficiently, you need to define appropriate *propagation rules* for each constraint, to compute new domains that are bounds-consistent. For example, the propagation rules for the constraint $X = Y + Z$

are the following ones:

$$X \geq \min(Y) + \min(Z) \qquad X \leq \max(Y) + \max(Z)$$
$$Y \geq \min(X) - \max(Z) \qquad Y \leq \max(X) - \min(Z)$$
$$Z \geq \min(X) - \max(Y) \qquad Z \leq \max(X) - \min(Y)$$

It is easy to see that, using such rules, the domains of the three variables X, Y, and Z are *shrunk*, while maintaining an interval representation, in such a way that the constraint $X = Y + Z$ is bounds-consistent.

When there are several constraints, bounds-consistency is achieved in the same way as arc-consistency: each constraint is considered in turn (following any fair strategy), until no domain is modified.

This technique is used in most CLP languages, since it is both efficient (in time and space) and sufficiently powerful.

15.5.3   Global Constraints

We already discussed briefly the concept of global constraints in Chapter 3. However, since this notion was developed within constraint programming, we reintroduce it here and present it in more detail.

Global constraints sometimes appear with different names, for example, *specialized* or *special* constraints, to avoid confusion with the notion of globality that relates to the entirety of a CSP, but the name *global constraints* is the one usually used in the CLP literature, where they have been introduced, so we stick to it in this book as well. They are usually nonbinary constraints that appear often and for which specialized constraint propagation methods are developed. Usually, such methods are stronger than applying arc-consistency yet still efficient.

A typical example is the alldifferent constraint that we saw in the cryptoarithmetic example, which enforces that a set of variables have different values. Although such a constraint can be defined by as many binary inequality constraints as the number of pairs of variables, such a representation allows for poor pruning by arc-consistency. For example, if variables x, y, and z have the same domain $\{1,2\}$, the constraint alldifferent([X,Y,Z]) has no solution, but arc-consistency over the corresponding set of binary inequalities cannot detect this.

Since such a constraint appears so often, it is worthwhile to strengthen the propagation method. In fact, there are other techniques that could be more powerful than arc-consistency, if we consider all the variables involved and not two at a time. For example, consider an algorithm that removes the value of any assigned variable (that is, a variable with a singleton domain) from the domains of the other variables and, after that, checks that the resulting number of nonfixed variables, say, nv, does not exceed the total number of values for them, say, r. If it does exceed it, it returns false, meaning that it has detected an inconsistency. For example, for the same situation considered above, this consistency algorithm would not remove any value (since no variable is fixed) and then it would compute $nv = 3$ and $r = 2$. Since $nv > r$, it would return false, therefore detecting the inconsistency that arc-consistency could not detect.

Clearly, while this algorithm is more powerful than arc-consistency, it is still not complete. For example, given variables X, Y, Z, and T with domains $D(X) = D(Y) = D(Z) = \{1, 2\}$, and $D(T) = \{2, 3, 4, 5\}$, and the constraint alldifferent([X,Y,Z,T]), the constraint has no solution, but the algorithm does not return false.

An even more powerful consistency algorithm for the alldifferent constraint can be devised by observing that this constraint basically requires a maximal bipartite matching between variables and values, such that each variable must be matched to a different value.

In general, the current store in a CLP computation contains both binary and nonbinary constraints, and also specialized global constraints such as alldifferent. At each step, when constraint propagation is performed, bounds-consistency is applied to all binary and nonbinary constraints, and a specialized propagation algorithm is applied to each global constraint (a different one for each kind of global constraint). Notice that not all nonbinary constraints are given a specialized constraint propagation algorithm, just those that occur more frequently in applications.

Another example of a global constraint is the so-called cumulative constraint, which is mainly used in scheduling and resource assignment problems. The constraint

```
cumulative([S1,...,Sm], [D1,...,Dm], [R1,...,Rm],L)
```

describes a situation in which there are m tasks with start times $s_1, \ldots, s_m$ and durations $d_1, \ldots, d_m$ and that require $r_1, \ldots, r_m$ units of a single resource. At most l units of the resource are available simultaneously.

For example, if we need to say that three persons want to perform two tasks, one of which requires two people and lasts 30 minutes, and another one that requires two people and lasts 40 minutes, we can say it via the following cumulative constraint:

```
cumulative([S1,S2], [30,40], [2,2],3)
```

Solving this constraint means finding the start times for the two tasks that satisfy the required conditions. A specialized propagation algorithm for the cumulative constraint aims at reducing the domains of s_1 and s_2. Otherwise, a brute-force algorithm would define many binary constraints and apply arc-consistency or bounds-consistency over them.

15.6 **Summary**

This chapter was intended to provide enough knowledge about constraint logic programming to enable readers with constraint-solving expertise to code and solve their problems using a CLP language. The exposition started from logic programming, which can already be seen as a programming language to work with finite domain constraints, and then showed how CLP languages are superior, in terms of compactness and efficiency, as a modeling and solving tool for finite domain constraints. We also outlined the main concepts that have been introduced in the constraint-solving arena by the CLP community, such as global constraints and bounds-consistency.

15.7 **Bibliographical Notes**

The concept of logic programming was first developed in the 1970s. The first constraint logic programming language was Prolog II (Colmerauer 1982), which was designed by Colmerauer in the early 1980s. Prolog II could treat term equations like Prolog, but in addition could also handle term disequations. After this, Jaffar and Lassez observed that both term equations and disequations were just a special form of constraints, and developed the concept of a constraint logic programming scheme in 1987 (Jaffar and Lassez 1987).

From then on, several instances of the CLP scheme were developed: Prolog III (Colmerauer 1990), with constraints over terms, strings, Booleans, and real linear arithmetic; CLP(R) (Jaffar et al. 1992), with constraints over terms and real arithmetics; and CHIP (Dincbas et al. 1988a), with constraints over terms, finite domains, and finite ranges of integers.

Constraint logic programming over finite domains was first implemented in the late 1980s by Pascal Van Hentenryck (1989) within the language CHIP. The notions of constraint propagation that were embedded in CHIP were very preliminary. Since then, more up-to-date constraint propagation algorithms have been developed and added to more recent CLP(FD) languages, like GNU Prolog (Diaz 2000) and ECLiPSe (IC-PARC 1999).

A very good book from which to learn about many aspects of CLP, from techniques to propagation algorithms, to applications, to modeling and efficiency issues, is the one by Marriott and Stuckey (1998). Anybody who is interested in modeling and solving CSPs in any CLP language should refer to that book.

Although CLP(FD) languages are very expressive and allow a declarative style of programming that goes hand in hand with the intrinsic declarative nature of constraints, many application domains already have their preferred languages, which mainly belong to the imperative paradigm, where computation evolves through a sequence of state changes. This paradigm is fundamentally different from the CLP framework, where, as we have seen, a computation consists instead of a sequence of goal rewritings that monotonically add constraints to the variable values. Although several companies have understood the added value of a declarative style of programming and have used a CLP-like programming language for some of their applications, there are also many companies that prefer to stick to the imperative programming paradigm, mainly for ease of introducing constraint-based technology in their structure and tools. For this reason, several constraint solvers and constraint-based tools have been embedded in an imperative programming environment, usually in the form of libraries that can be imported and used in several other programs. The typical programming languages that are used to develop such solvers are C++ and Java. ILOG (1995) is one of the most successful companies that produce such constraint-based libraries and tools. In particular, ILOG produces a constraint solver that uses many of the techniques described in this book, as well as a constraint-based configurator and a scheduler.

15.8 **Exercises**

1. Consider the following pairs of literals (where a, b, c are constants, x, y, z, v, w are variables, p and q are predicate symbols, and f is a function symbol):

   - $p(a, b, c)$ and $p(x, b, y)$
   - $p(a, x, z)$ and $p(b, y, z)$
   - $p(x, f(y), a)$ and $p(z, v, w)$
   - $p(x, y, z)$ and $q(a, b, z)$

   Which pairs unify and which don't? If they unify, find their most general unifier.

2. Given the logic program

   ```
   p(X,Y) :- q(X,Y,Z).
   p(X,Y) :- r(X,a).
   q(X,Y,a) :- r(a,Y).
   r(a,a).
   r(b,a).
   ```

   build the derivation tree for the goals p(X,Y) and p(b,Y). Consider also the Prolog way of building the derivation tree, and determine which solution (if any) Prolog would find first.

3. Take any CSP from the previous chapters and write the logic program that would model it and find its solutions.

4. Given the CLP(FD) program

   ```
   p(0.0).
   p(X,Y) :- p(X-1,Z), Y=Z+X-1.
   ```

   build the derivation tree for p(2,Y).

5. Consider the following conjunction of constraints:

$$X \neq 4 \wedge X \neq Y \wedge X \leq Y + 2$$

with {3, 4, 5} as the domain of variable X, and {0, 1, 2, 3, 4, 5} as the domain of variable Y. Apply both node/arc-consistency and bounds-consistency over these constraints, and compare the results.

Bibliography

Aggoun, A., and N. Beldiceanu. 1993. Extending CHIP in order to solve complex scheduling and placement problems. *Mathl. Comput. Modelling*, 17(7): 57–73.

Aggoun, A., M. Dincbas, A. Herold, H. Simonis, and P. Van Hentenryck. 1987. The CHIP System. Technical Report TR-LP-24, ECRC, Munich, Germany.

Allen, J. 1983. Maintaining knowledge about temporal intervals. *Communications of the ACM*, 26:832–843.

Allenand, J. F., and P. J. Hayes. 1985. A common-sense theory of time. In *International Joint Conference on Artificial Intelligence (IJCAI-85)*, 528–531.

Anderson, S. K., R. D. Shachter, and P. Solovitz. 1994. Global conditioning for probabilistic inference in belief networks. In *Uncertainty in Artificial Intelligence (UAI'94)*, 514–522.

Appel, K. I., and W. Haken. 1976. Every planar map is four colorable. *Bull. Amer. Math. Soc.*, 82:711–712.

Arnborg, S. A. 1985. Efficient algorithms for combinatorial problems on graphs with bounded decomposability—a survey. *BIT*, 25:2–23.

Arnborg, S., and A. Proskourowski. 1989. Linear time algorithms for NP-hard problems restricted to partial *k*-trees. *Discrete and Applied Mathematics*, 23: 11–24.

Bacchus, F. 2002. Enhancing Davis Putnam with extended binary clause reasoning. In *18th National Conference on Artificial Intelligence (AAAI-02)*, 613–619.

Bacchus, F., and P. van Run. 1995. Dynamic variable ordering in CSPS. In *Principles and Practice of Constraints Programming (CP'95)*, Cassis, France. Available as *Lecture Notes on CS*, 976:258–277, 1995.

Baker, A. B. 1994. The hazards of fancy backtracking. In *Proceedings of National Conference of Artificial Intelligence (AAAI'94)*.

Baker, A. B. 1995. Intelligent backtracking on constraint satisfaction problems: experimental and theoretical results. Technical report, Ph.D. thesis, University of Oregon.

Barette, O., Y. Deville, and P. Van Hentenryck. 1999. Constraint satisfaction over connected row-convex constraints. *Artificial Intelligence*, 109:243–271.

Bar-Yehuda, R., A. Becker, and D. Geiger. 1999. Random algorithms for the loop-cutset problem. In *Uncertainty in AI (UAI'99)*, 81–89.

Bayardo, R., Jr., and D. P. Miranker. 1995. On the space-time trade-off in solving constraint satisfaction problems. In *14th International Joint Conference on Artificial Intelligence(1995)*, 558–562.

Bayardo, R., and D. Miranker. 1996. A complexity analysis of space-bound learning algorithms for the constraint satisfaction problem. In *AAAI'96: Proceedings of the 13th National Conference on Artificial Intelligence*, 298–304.

Bayardo, R. J., Jr., and R. C. Schrag. 1997. Using CSP look-back techniques to solve real world SAT instances. In *14th National Conference on Artificial Intelligence (AAAI97)*, 203–208.

Becker, A., and D. Geiger. 1996. A sufficiently fast algorithm for finding close to optimal junction trees. In *Uncertainty in AI (UAI'96)*, 81–89.

Beeri, C., R. Fagin, D. Maier, and M. Yannakakis. 1983. On the desirability of acyclic database schemes. *Journal of the ACM*, 30(3):479–513.

Beldiceanu, N., and E. Contejean. 1994. Introducing global constraints in CHIP. *Math and Computational Modelling*, 20(12):97–123.

Bellman, R. E. 1957. *Dynamic Programming*. Princeton University Press.

Bertele, U., and F. Brioschi. 1972. *Nonserial Dynamic Programming*. Academic Press.

Bessière, C., and M. Cordier. 1993. Arc-consistency and arc-consistency again. In *National Conference of Artificial Intelligence (AAAI-93)*, 108–113.

Bessière, C., and J.-C. Régin. 1997. Arc consistency for general constraint networks: Preliminary results. In *Proceedings of IJCAI'97*, 398–404, Nagoya, Japan.

Bessière, C., and J.-C. Régin. 2001. Refining the basic constraint propagation algorithm. In *International Joint Conference on Artificial Intelligence (IJCAI-01)*, 309–315.

Bistarelli, S., U. Montanari, and F. Rossi. 1997. Semiring-based constraint satisfaction and optimization. *Journal of the Association of Computing Machinery*, 44(2):165–201.

Bitner, J. R., and E. M. Reingold. 1975. Backtracking programming techniques. *Communications of the ACM*, 18(11):651–656.

Bjäreland, M., and P. Jonsson. 1999. Exploiting bipartiteness to identify yet another tractable subclass of CSP. In J. Jaffar, editor, *Principles and Practice of Constraint Programming—CP'99*, volume 1713 of *Lecture Notes in Computer Science*, 118–128, Springer-Verlag.

Bodlaender, H. L. 1997. Treewidth: Algorithmic techniques and results. In *MFCS-97*, 19–36.

Booth, K. S., and G. S. Lueker. 1976. Testing for the consecutive ones property, interval graphs, and graph planarity using pq-tree algorithms. *Computational System Science*, 13:335–379.

Brglez and Fujiwara. 1996. A neutral netlist of 10 combinatorial benchmark circuits and a target translator in Fortran. In *Proceedings of the IEEE International Symposium on Circuits and Systems*.

Broxvall, M., P. Jonsson, and J. Renz. 2000. Refinements and independence: A simple method for identifying tractable disjunctive constraints. In R. Dechter, editor, *Principles and Practice of Constraint Programming*, 114–127, Springer-Verlag.

Brunaldi, R. A. 1977. Introductory combinatorics.

Bruynooghe, M. 1981. Solving combinatorial search problems by intelligent backtracking. *Information Processing Letters*, 12:36–39.

Bruynooghe, M., and L. M. Pereira. 1984. Déduction revision by intelligent backtracking. In J. A. Campbell, editor, *Implementation of Prolog*, 194–215, Ellis, Horwood, Chichester.

Bulatov, A. A., and P. G. Jeavons. 2000. Tractable constraints closed under a binary operation. Technical Report PRG-TR-12-00, Oxford University Computing Laboratory.

Bulatov, A. A., A. A. Krokhin, and P. G. Jeavons. 2000. Constraint satisfaction problems and finite algebras. In *Proceedings of the 27th International Colloquium on Automata, Languages and Programming—ICALP'00*, volume 1853 of *Lecture Notes in Computer Science*, 272–282, Springer-Verlag.

Bulatov, A. A., A. A. Krokhin, and P. G. Jeavons. 2001. The complexity of maximal constraint languages. In *Proceedings of STOC'01*.

Cannings, C., E. A. Thompson, and H. H. Skolnick. 1978. Probability functions on complex pedigrees. *Advances in Applied Probability*, 10:26–61.

Carlsson, M., and J. Widen. 1999. SICStus Prolog User's Manual. On-line version at *www.sics.se/sicstus/*. Technical report, Swedish Institute of Computer Science (SICS).

Caseau, Y., and F. Laburthe. 1996. Commutative scheduling with task intervals. In *Joint International Conference and Symposium on Logic Progamming*. MIT Press.

Cheesman, P., B. Kanefsky, and W. Taylor. 1991. Where the *really* hard problems are. In *International Joint Conference on Artificial Intelligence (IJCAI-91)*, 331–337.

Clark, E., M. Fujita, A. Biere, A. Cimatti, and Y. Zhu. 1999. Symbolic model checking using SAT procedures instead of BDDS. In *Proceedings of the 36th Design Automation Conference*, 317–320.

Codognet, P., and D. Diaz. 1996. Compiling constraints in CLP(FD). *Journal of Logic Programming*, 27(3).

Cohen, D. A., M. Gyssens, and P. G. Jeavons. 1996. Derivation of constraints and database relations. In *Proceedings of the Second International Conference on Constraint Programming—CP'96 (Boston, August 1996)*, volume 1118 of *Lecture Notes in Computer Science*, 134–148, Springer-Verlag.

Cohen, D. A., P. G. Jeavons, and R. L. Gault. 2000. New tractable classes from old. In *Principles and Practice of Constraint Programming—CP 2000*, volume 1894 of *Lecture Notes in Computer Science*, R. Dechter, editor, 160–171, Springer-Verlag.

Cohen, D. A., P. G. Jeavons, P. Jonsson, and M. Koubarakis. 2000. Building tractable disjunctive constraints. *Journal of the ACM*, 47:826–853.

Colmerauer, A. 1982. Prolog II reference manual and theoretical model. Technical report, Groupe Intelligence Artificielle, Universite' Aix-Marseille.

Colmerauer, A. 1990. An introduction to Prolog-III. *Communications of the ACM*.

Cook, S. A., and D. G. Mitchell. 1997. Finding hard instances of the satisfiability problem: A survey. *DIMACS Series in Discrete Mathematics and Theoretical Computer Science*. American Mathematical Society.

Cooper, G. F., H. J. Suermondt, and D. E. Heckerman. 1991. A combination of cutset conditioning with clique-tree propagation in the path-finder system. In *Uncertainty in Artificial Intelligence (UAI'91)*, 245–253.

Cooper, M. C. 1990. An optimal k-consistency algorithm. *Artificial Intelligence*, 41(1):89–95.

Cooper, M. C., D. A. Cohen, and P. G. Jeavons. 1994. Characterising tractable constraints. *Artificial Intelligence*, 65:347–361.

Cormen, T. H., C. E. Leiserson, and R. L. Rivest. 1990. *Introduction to Algorithms*. MIT Press.

Corneil, D. G., S. A. Arnborg, and A. Proskourowski. 1987. Complexity of finding embeddings in a k-tree. *SIAM Journal of Discrete Mathematics*, 8:277–284.

Cox, P. T. 1984. Finding backtrack points for intelligent backtracking. In J. A. Campbell, editor, *Implementation of Prolog*, 216–233, Ellis, Horwood, Chichester.

Crawford, J., and L. Auton. 1993. Experimental results on the crossover point in satisfiability problems. In *AAAI'93: Proceedings of the 11th National Conference on Artificial Intelligence*, 21–27.

Dalmau, V. 2000. A new tractable class of constraint satisfaction problems. In *Sixth International Symposium on Mathematics and Artificial Intelligence*.

Dalmau, V., and J. Pearson. 1999. Closure functions and width 1 problems. In J. Jaffar, editor, *Principles and Practice of Constraint Programming—CP'99*, volume 1713 of *Lecture Notes in Computer Science*, 159–173, Springer-Verlag.

D'Ambrosio, B., R. D. Shachter, and B. A. Del Favero. 1990. Symbolic probabilistic inference in belief networks. In *National Conference on Artificial Intelligence (AAAI'90)*, 126–131.

Dantzig, G. B. 1962. *Linear Programming and Extensions*. Princeton University Press.

Darwiche, A. 1999. Recursive conditioning. In *Proceedings of the 11th Conference on Uncertainty in Artificial Intelligence (UAI99)*.

Davis, E. 1987. Constraint propagation with interval labels. *Artificial Intelligence*, 32:281–331.

Davis, M., G. Logemann, and D. Loveland. 1962. A machine program for theorem proving. *Communications of the ACM*, 5:394–397.

Davis, M., and H. Putnam. 1960. A computing procedure for quantification theory. *Journal of the Association of Computing Machinery*, 7(3).

Dean, T. L. 1989. Using temporal hierarchies to efficiently maintain large temporal databases. *Journal of the ACM*, 36:687–714.

Dean, T. L., and D. V. McDermott. 1987. Temporal database management. *Artificial Intelligence*, 32:1–55.

Debruyne, R. 1998. Removing more values than max-restricted path consistency for the same cost. Technical Report TR98041, LIRMM, Ph.D. thesis, Universit de Montpellier.

Dechter, R. 1990. Enhancement schemes for constraint processing: Backjumping, learning and cutset decomposition. *Artificial Intelligence*, 41:273–312.

Dechter, R. 1992a. Constraint networks. In S. C. Shapiro, editor, *Encyclopedia of Artificial Intelligence*, 2nd edition, 276–285. John Wiley & Sons.

Dechter, R. 1992b. From local to global consistency. *Artificial Intelligence*, 55(1): 87–107.

Dechter, R. 1996. Bucket elimination: A unifying framework for probabilistic inference algorithms. In *Uncertainty in Artificial Intelligence (UAI'96)*, 211–219.

Dechter, R. 1997. Mini-buckets: A general scheme of generating approximations in automated reasoning. In *IJCAI-97: Proceedings of the 15th International Joint Conference on Artificial Intelligence*, 1297–1302.

Dechter, R. 1999a. Bucket elimination: A unifying framework for reasoning. *Artificial Intelligence*, 113:41–85.

Dechter, R. 1999b. Constraint satisfaction. In *The MIT Encyclopedia of Cognitive Sciences (MITECS)*, 195–197.

Dechter, R., Z. Collin, and S. Katz. 1999. Self-stabilizing distributed constraint satisfaction. In *Chicago Journal of Theoretical Computer Science (CJTCS)*.

Dechter, R., and Y. El Fattah. 2001. Topological parameters for time-space tradeoff. *Artificial Intelligence*, 125:93–188.

Dechter, R., and I. Meiri. 1994. Experimental evaluation of preprocessing algorithms for constraint satisfaction problems. *Artificial Intelligence*, 68:211–241.

Dechter, R., and J. Pearl. 1987a. The cycle-cutset method for improving search performance in AI applications. In *Proceedings of the Third IEEE Conference on AI Applications*, 224–230, Orlando, Florida.

Dechter, R., and J. Pearl. 1987b. Network-based heuristics for constraint satisfaction problems. *Artificial Intelligence*, 34:1–38.

Dechter, R., and J. Pearl. 1989. Tree clustering for constraint networks. *Artificial Intelligence*, 33(3):353–366.

Dechter, R., and I. Rish. 1994. Directional resolution: The Davis-Putnam procedure, revisited. In *Principles of Knowledge Representation and Reasoning (KR-94)*, 134–145.

Dechter, R., and I. Rish. 1997. A scheme for approximating probabilistic inference. In *Uncertainty in Artificial Intelligence* (VAI-97), 132–141.

Dechter, R., and I. Rish. 2003. Mini-buckets; a general scheme for approximating inference. *Journal of HCM* (at press).

Dechter, R., and P. van Beek. 1997. Local and global relational consistency. *Theoretical Computer Science*, 283–308.

Deville, Y., O. Barette, and P. Van Hentenryck. 1997. Constraint satisfaction over connected row convex constraints. In *Proceeedings of IJCAI'97*, 405–411.

Deville, Y., O. Barette, and P. Van Hentenryck. 1999. Constraint satisfaction over connected row convex constraints. *Artificial Intelligence*, 109:243–271.

Deville, Y., and P. Van Hentenryck. 1991. An efficient arc consistency algorithm for a class of CSP problems. In *IJCAI-91*, 325–330, Sydney, Australia.

Deville, Y., P. Van Hentenryck, and C. Teng. 1992. A generic arc-consistency algorithm and its specialization. *Artificial Intelligence*, 57:291–321.

Diaz, D. 2000. The GNU Prolog web site, *http://pauillac.inria.fr/diaz/gnu-prolog/*.

Dincbas, M., P. Van Hentenryck, H. Simonis, A. Aggoun, T. Graf, and F. Berthier. 1988a. The constraint logic programming language CHIP. In *Proceedings of the International Conference on Fifth Generation Computer Systems*, Tokyo, Japan.

Dincbas, M., P. Van Hentenryck, H. Simonis, A. Aggoun, and T. Graf. 1988b. Applications of CHIP to industrial and engineering problems. In *First International Conference on Industrial and Engineering Applications of Artificial Intelligence and Expert Systems*, Tullahoma, Tennessee.

Drankengren, T., and P. Jonsson. 1996. Maximal tractable subclasses of Allen's interval algebra: Preliminary report. In *National Conference on Artificial Intelligence (AAAI'96)*, 389–394.

Drankengren, T., and P. Jonsson. 1997. Towards a complete classification of tractability in Allen's algebra. In *International Joint Conference on Artificial Intelligence (IJCAI-97)*, 389–394.

Drankengren, T., and P. Jonsson. 1998. A complete classification of tractability in Allen's algebra relative to subsets of basic relations. *Artificial Intelligence*, 106:205–219.

Even, S. 1979. *Graph Algorithms*. Computer Science Press.

Feder, T., and M. Y. Vardi. 1998. The computational structure of monotone monadic SNP and constraint satisfaction: A study through datalog and group theory. *SIAM Journal of Computing*, 28(1):57–104.

Freuder, E. C. 1978. Synthesizing constraint expressions. *Communications of the ACM*, 21(11):958–965.

Freuder, E. C. 1982. A sufficient condition for backtrack-free search. *Journal of the ACM*, 29(1):24–32.

Freuder, E. C. 1985. A sufficient condition for backtrack-bounded search. *Journal of the ACM*, 32:755–761.

Freuder, E. C. 1991. Eliminating interchangeable values in constraint satisfaction problems. In *Proceedings of AAAI-91*, 227–233.

Freuder, E. C. 1992. Partial constraint satisfaction. *Artificial Intelligence*, 50:510–530.

Freuder, E. C., and M. J. Quinn. 1987. The use of lineal spanning trees to represent constraint satisfaction problems. Technical Report 87-41, University of New Hampshire, Durham.

Frost, D. H. 1997. Algorithms and heuristics for constraint satisfaction problems. Technical report, Ph.D. thesis, Information and Computer Science, University of California, Irvine.

Frost, D., and R. Dechter. 1994a. Dead-end driven learning. In *AAAI'94: Proceedings of the 12th National Conference on Artificial Intelligence*, 294–300.

Frost, D., and R. Dechter. 1994b. In search of best search: An empirical evaluation. In *AAAI'94: Proceedings of the 12th National Conference on Artificial Intelligence*, 301–306.

Frost, D., and R. Dechter. 1995. Look-ahead value ordering for constraint satisfaction problems. In *Proceedings of the International Joint Conference on Artificial Intelligence (IJCAI-95)*, 572–578.

Frost, D., and R. Dechter. 1996. Looking at full look-ahead. In *Proceedings of the Second International Conference on Constraint Programming (CP-96)*, 539–540.

Fulkerson, D. R., G. B. Dantzig, and S. M. Johnson. 1959. On a linear programming, combinatorial approach to the traveling salesman problem. *Operations Research*, 7:58–66.

Fulkerson, D. R., G. B. Dantzig, and S. M. Johnson. 1954. Solution of a large scale traveling salesman problem. *Operations Research*, 2:393–410.

Garey, M., and D. S. Johnson. 1979. *Computers and Intractability: A Guide to the Theory of NP-Completeness*. Freeman.

Gaschnig, J. 1978. Experimental case studies of backtrack vs. waltz-type vs. new algorithms for satisfying assignment problems. In *Proceedings of the Second Canadian Conference on Artificial Intelligence*, 268–277, Toronto, Ontario.

Gaschnig, J. 1979. Performance measurement and analysis of search algorithms. Technical Report CMU-CS-79-124, Carnegie Mellon University.

Gent, I., and T. Walsh. 1993a. An empirical analysis of search in GSAT. *Artificial Intelligence Research (JAIR)*, 1993.

Gent, I., and T. Walsh. 1993b. Towards understanding of hill-climbing procedures in SAT. In *11th National Conference on Artificial Intelligence (AAAI93)*, 28–33.

Gerevini, A., and L. Schubert. 1995. Efficient algorithms for qualitative reasoning about time. *Artificial Intelligence*, 74(3):207–248.

Ginsberg, M. L. 1993. Dynamic backtracking. *Journal of Artificial Intelligence Research*, 1:25–46.

Glover, F. 1986. Future paths for integer programming and links to artificial intelligence. *Computers and Operational Research*, 13:533–549.

Glover, F. 1989. Tabu search—part I. *ORSA Journal of Computing*, 1:190–206.

Golomb, S., and L. Baumert. 1965. Backtrack programming. *Journal of the ACM*, 12:516–524.

Golumbic, M. C., and R. Shamir. 1993. Complexity and algorithms for reasoning about time: A graph-theoretic approach. *Journal of the ACM*, 40:1108–1133.

Gomes, C., and B. Selman. 2001. Algorithm portfolios. *Artificial Intelligence*, 126: 43–62.

Gomes, C., B. Selman, N. Crato, and H. Kautz. 2000. Heavy-tailed phenomena in satisfiability and constraint satisfaction. In *Journal of Automated Reasoning*, 24:67–100.

Gomes, C., B. Selman, and H. Kautz. 1998. Boosting combinatorial search through randomization. In *Proceedings of the National Conference on Artificial Intelligence (AAAI98)*.

Gottlob, G., N. Leone, and F. Scarcello. 1999. A comparison of structural CSP decomposition methods. In *Proceedings of the 16th International Joint Conference on Artificial Intelligence (IJCAI)*, 394–399, Morgan Kaufmann.

Gu, J. 1992. Efficient local search for very large-scale satisfiability problems. *Sigart Bulletin*, 3:8–12.

Hampson, S. 1993. Changing max-flips automatically. Personal communication.

Haralick, M., and G. L. Elliot. 1980. Increasing tree-search efficiency for constraint satisfaction problems. *Artificial Intelligence*, 14:263–313.

Haroud, D., and B. Faltings. 1996. Consistency techniques for continuous constraints. *Constraints, International Journal*, 85–118.

Herstein, I. N. 1975. *Topics in Algebra*, 2nd edition. Wiley.

Hirsch, E. H. 2000. SAT local search algorithms: Worst-case study. *Journal of Automated Reasoning*, 24(1/2):127–143.

Hirsch, E. H., and A. Kojevnikov. 2001. Solving Boolean satisfiability using local search guided by unit clause elimination. In *Seventh International Conference on Principles and Practice of Constraint Programming (CP01)*.

Hoos, H. H., and T. Stutzle. 1999. Towards a characterization of the behaviour of stochastic local search algorithms for SAT. *Artificial Intelligence*, 112:213–232.

Hoos, H. H., and T. Stutzle. 2000. Local search algorithms for SAT: An empirical evaluation. *Journal of Automated Reasoning*, 24(1/2):1–62.

Huffman, D. A., 1971. Impossible objects as nonsense sentences. In Meltzer, B. and Michie, D. (Eds.), *Machine Intelligence 6*, 295–324, Edinburgh, Scottland: Edinburgh University Press.

Ibaraki, T. 1976. Theoretical comparisons of search strategies in branch-and-bound algorithms. *Computer and Information Sciences*, 5:315–344.

Ibaraki, T. 1978. Branch-and-bound procedure and state-space representation of combinatorial optimization problems. *Information and Control*, 36:1–27.

IC-PARC. 1999. The ECLiPSe 4.2 Constraint Logic Programming System. *www.icparc.ic.ac.uk/eclipse/*.

ILOG, editor. 1995. *ILOG SOLVER: Object Oriented Constraint Programming*.

Itai, A., S. Even, and A. Shamir. 1976. On the complexity of timetable and multicommodity flow. *SIAM Journal on Computing*, 5:691–703.

Jaffar, J., and J. Lassez. 1987. Constraint logic programming. In *Proceedings of Programming Languages*. ACM.

Jaffar, J., and J. Lassez. 1994. Constraint logic programming: A survey. *Journal of Logic Programming*, 19(20):503–581.

Jaffar, J., and M. J. Maher. 1994. Constraint logic programming: A survey. *Journal of Logic Programming*, 19 and 20.

Jaffar, J., S. Michaylov, P. Stucky, and R. Yap. 1992. The CLP(R) language and system. *ACM Transactions on Programming Languages and Systems*, 14(3).

Jeavons, P. G. 1998. On the algebraic structure of combinatorial problems. *Theoretical Computer Science*, 200:185–204.

Jeavons, P. G., and D. A. Cohen. 1995. An algebraic characterization of tractable constraints. In *Computing and Combinatorics. First International Conference COCOON'95 (Xi'an, China, August 1995)*, volume 959 of *Lecture Notes in Computer Science*, 633–642, Springer-Verlag.

Jeavons, P. G., D. A. Cohen, and M. Cooper. 1998. Constraints, consistency and closure. *Artificial Intelligence*, 101:251–265.

Jeavons, P. G., D. A. Cohen, and M. Gyssens. 1995. A unifying framework for tractable constraints. In *Proceedings of the First International Conference on*

Constraint Programming—CP'95 (Cassis, France, September 1995), volume 976 of *Lecture Notes in Computer Science*, 276–291, Springer-Verlag.

Jeavons, P. G., D. A. Cohen, and M. Gyssens. 1996. A test for tractability. In *Proceedings of the Second International Conference on Constraint Programming—CP'96 (Boston, August 1996)*, volume 1118 of *Lecture Notes in Computer Science*, 267–281, Springer-Verlag.

Jeavons, P. G., D. A. Cohen, and M. Gyssens. 1997. Closure properties of constraints. *Journal of the ACM*, 44:527–548.

Jeavons, P. G., D. A. Cohen, and J. K. Pearson. 1999. Constraints and universal algebra. *Annals of Mathematics and Artificial Intelligence*, 24:51–67.

Jeavons, P. G., and M. C. Cooper. 1995. Tractable constraints on ordered domains. *Artificial Intelligence*, 79(2):327–339.

Jeavons, P., M. Gyssens, and D. Cohen. 1994. Decomposing constraint satisfaction problems using database techniques. *Artificial Intelligence*, 66:57–89.

Jégou, P. 1990. Cyclic clustering: A compromise between tree-clustering and the cycle-cutset method for improving search efficiency. In *European Conference on AI (ECAI-90)*, 369–371, Sweden.

Jégou, P. 1993a. Decomposition of domains based on the micro-structure of finite constraint satisfaction problems. In *Proceedings of the 11th National Conference on Artificial Intelligence*, 731–736, Washington, DC.

Jégou, P. 1993b. On the consistency of general constraint satisfaction problems. In *National Conference on AI (AAAI93)*, 114–119.

Johnson, D. S., C. R. Aragon, L. A. McGeoch, and C. Schevon. 1991. Optimization by simulated annealing: An experimental evaluation; part II, graph coloring and number partitioning. *Operations Research*, 39:378–406.

Johnson, D. S., and M. A. Trick, editors. 1996. *Cliques, Coloring and Satisfiability*. Volume 26 of *DIMACS Series in Discrete Mathematics and Theoretical Computer Science*. American Mathematical Society.

Kask, K. 2001. Approximation algorithms for graphical models. Technical report, Ph.D. thesis, Information and Computer Science, University of California, Irvine.

Kask, K., and R. Dechter. 1995. GSAT and local consistency. In *International Joint Conference on Artificial Intelligence (IJCAI'95)*, 616–622, Montreal, Canada.

Kask, K., and R. Dechter. 1996. A graph-based method for improving GSAT. In *National Conference on Artificial Intelligence (AAAI'96)*, 350–355, Portland, Oregon.

Kask, K., and R. Dechter. 2001. A general scheme for automatic search heuristics from specification dependencies. *Artificial Intelligence*, 91–131.

Kautz, H., and P. B. Ladkin. 1991. Integrating metric and qualitative temporal reasoning. In *National Conference of Artificial Intelligence (AAAI-91)*, 241–246.

Kautz, H., and B. Selman. 1999. Unifying SAT-based and graph-based in planning. *International Joint Conference on Artficial Intelligence (IJCAI99)*, 318–325.

Kautz, H., M. Vilain, and P. van Beek. 1989. Constraint propagation algorithms for temporal reasoning: A revised report. In D. Weld and J. de Kleer, *Readings in Qualitative Reasoning about Physical Systems*, Morgan Kaufmann, 373–381.

Khachiyan, L. G. 1979. A polynomial algorithm in linear programming. *Soviet Mathematics Doklady*, 191–194.

Kirkpatrick, S., C. D. Gelatt, and M. P. Vecchi. 1983. Optimization by simulated annealing. *Science*, 220:671–680.

Kirousis, L. 1993. Fast parallel constraint satisfaction. *Artificial Intelligence*, 64: 147–160.

Kirousis, L. M., and C. H. Papadimitriou. 1985. The complexity of recognizing polyhedral scenes. In *Proceedings of the 26th Symposium on Foundations of Computer Science*, 175–185, Portland, Oregon.

Kjaerulff, U. 1990. Triangulation of graph-based algorithms giving small total state space. Technical Report 90-09, Department of Mathematics and Computer Science, University of Aalborg, Denmark.

Kjaerulff, U. 1992. Optimal decomposition of probabilistic networks by simulated annealing. *Statistics and Computing*, 2:7–17.

Kohler, W. H., and K. Stieglitz. 1974. Characterization and theoretical comparison of branch-and-bound algorithms for permutation problems. *Journal of the ACM*, 21:140–156.

Koller, D., and N. Friedman. 2003. Bayesian networks and beyond: reasoning and learning with probabilistic models. MIT press (at press).

Kondrak, G., and P. van Beek. 1994. A theoretical evaluation of selected back-tracking algorithms. In *Proceedings of International Joint Conference of Artificial Intelligence (IJCAI-94)*.

Kondrak, G., and P. van Beek. 1997. A theoretical valuation of selected algorithms. *Artificial Intelligence*, 89:365–387.

Konolige, K. 1994. Easy to be hard: Difficult problems for greedy algorithms. In *Principles of Knowledge Representation and Reasoning (KR-94)*, 374–378.

Koubarakis, M., 1992. Dense time and temporal constraints with inequalities. In *Proceedings of the 3rd International Conference on Principles of Knowledge-Bases and Reasoning (KR-92)*, 24–35.

Koubarakis, M., 1995. From local to global consistency in temporal constraint networks. In *Proceedings of the First International Conference on Principles and Practice of Constraint Programming (CP'95)*, 53–69.

Koubarakis, M. 1996. Tractable disjunctions of linear constraints. In *Principles and Practice of Constraint Programming (CP'96)*, 297–307.

Koubarakis, M. 1997. From local to global consistency in temporal constraint networks. *Theoretical Computer Science*, 173(1):89–112.

Koubarakis, M. 2000. Querying temporal and spatial constraint networks in PTIME. *Artificial Intelligence*, 223–263.

Krokhin, A., P. Jeavons, and P. Jonsson. 2001. A complete classification of complexity in Allen's algebra in the presence of a non-trivial basic relation. In *Proceedings IJCAI'01*.

Kumar, V. 1992. Search with branch-and-bound. In S. C. Shapiro, editor, *Encyclopedia of Artificial Intelligence*, 1468–1472. Wiley-Interscience.

Kumar, V., and L. N. Kanal. 1983. A general branch-and-bound formulation for understanding and synthesizing and/or tree search procedures. *Artificial Intelligence*, 21:179–198.

Ladkin, P. B. 1988. Time representation: A taxonomy of interval relations. In *National Conference of Artificial Intelligence (AAAI-86)*, 360–366.

Ladkin, P. B. 1989. Metric constraint satisfaction with intervals. Technical report, TR-89-038, International Computer Science Institute, Berkeley, California.

Ladkin, P. B., and R. D. Maddux. 1989. On binary constraint networks. Technical report, Kerstel Institute, Palo Alto, California.

Ladkin, P., and A. Reinfeld. 1992. Effective solution of qualitative interval constraint problems. *Artificial Intelligence*, 57:105–124.

Larrosa, J. 2000. Boosting search with variable-elimination. In *Principles and Practice of Constraint Programming (CP2000)*, 291–305.

Lauriere, J. L. 1978. A language and a program for stating and solving combinatorial problems. *Artificial Intelligence*, 10(1).

Lauritzen, S. L., and D. J. Spiegelhalter. 1988. Local computation with probabilities on graphical structures and their application to expert systems. *Journal of the Royal Statistical Society, Series B*, 50(2):157–224.

Lawler, E. L., and D. E. Wood. 1956. Branch and bound methods: A survey. *Operations Research*, 14:699–719.

Leiserson, C. E., T. H. Cormen, and R. L. Rivest. 1990. *Introduction to Algorithms*. MIT Press.

Leiserson, C. E., and J. B. Saxe. 1983. A mixed-integer linear programming problem which is efficiently solvable. In *21st Annual Allerton Conference on Communication, Control and Computing*, 204–213.

Lematre, M., G. Verfaillie, and T. Schiex. 1996. Russian doll search for solving constraint optimization problems. In *Proceedings of the National Conference on Artificial Intelligence (AAAI-96)*.

Lin, S., 1965. Computer solutions of the traveling salesman problem. *BSTJ*, 44:2245–2269.

Lin, S., and W. Kernighan. 1973. An effective heuristic for the traveling salesman problem. *Operations Research*, 21:498–516.

Lloyd, J. W. 1993. *Foundations of Logic Programming*. Springer-Verlag.

Mackworth, A. K. 1977a. Consistency in networks of relations. *Artificial Intelligence*, 8(1):99–118.

Mackworth, A. K. 1977b. On reading sketch maps. In *Fifth International Joint Conference on Artificial Intelligence*, 598–606.

Mackworth, A. K. 1992. Constraint satisfaction. In S. C. Shapiro, editor, *Encyclopedia of Artificial Intelligence*, 285–293, John Wiley & Sons.

Mackworth, A. K., and E. C. Freuder. 1985. The complexity of some polynomial network consistency algorithms for constraint satisfaction problems. *Artificial Intelligence*, 25.

Maier, D. 1983. *The Theory of Relational Databases*. Computer Science Press.

Malik, J., and T. O. Binford. 1983. Reasoning in time and space. In *International Joint Conference on Artificial Intelligence (IJCAI83)*, 343–345.

Marques-Silva, J. P., and K. A. Sakalla. 1999. Grasp-a search algorithm for propositional satisfiability. *IEEE Transactions on Computers*, 506–521.

Marriott, K., and P. J. Stuckey. 1998. *Programming with Constraints: An Introduction*. MIT Press.

Maruyama, H. 1990. Structural disambiguation with constraint propagation. In *Proceedings of the 28th Conference of the Association for Computational Linguistics*, 31–38, Pittsburgh, Pennsylvania.

McAllester, D. A. 1980. An outlook on truth-maintenance. Technical Report AI Memo 551, MIT, Boston, Massachusetts.

McAllester, D. A. 1990. Truth maintenance. In *AAAI'90: Proceedings of the Eighth National Conference on Artificial Intelligence*, 1109–1116.

McGregor, J. J. 1979. Relational consistency algorithms and their application in finding subgraph and graph isomorphisms. *Information Science*, 19:229–250.

Mehlhorn, K., and S. Thiel. 2000. Faster algorithms for bounds-consistency of the sortedness and the alldifferent constraint. *Principles and Practice of Constraint Programming (CP2000)*, 306–319.

Meiri, I. 1991. Combining qualitative and quantitative constraint satisfaction problems. In *Proceedings of the Ninth National Conference on Artificial Intelligence (AAAI'91)*, 1–8, Anaheim, California.

Meiri, I. 1996. Combining qualitative and quantitative constraints in temporal reasoning. *Artificial Intelligence*, 87:343–385.

Meiri, I., R. Dechter, and J. Pearl. 1990. Temporal constraint networks. *Artificial Intelligence*, 49:61–95.

Meseguer, P., J. Larrosa, and T. Schiex. 1999. Maintaining reversible dac for max-CSP. *Artificial Intelligence*, 149–163.

Mitchell, D., B. Sellman, and H. Levesque. 1992. Hard and easy distributions of SAT problems. In *Proceedings of the 10th National Conference on Artificial Intelligence*, 459–465.

Mohr, R., and T. C. Henderson. 1986. Arc and path consistency revisited. *Artificial Intelligence*, 28:225–233.

Mohr, R., and G. Masini. 1988. Good old discrete relaxation. In *Proceedings of ECAI-88*, 651–656, Munich, Germany.

Montanari, U. 1974. Networks of constraints: Fundamental properties and applications to picture processing. *Information Science*, 7(66):95–132.

Morris, P. 1993. The breakout method for escaping from local minima. In *Proceedings of the 11th National Conference on Artificial Intelligence (AAAI'93)*, 40–45.

Nadel, B. A. 1989. Constraint satisfaction algorithms. *Computational Intelligence*, 5:188–299.

Nadel, B. A. 1990. Some applications of the constraint satisfaction problem. In *AAAI-90: Workshop on Constraint Directed Reasoning Working Notes*, Boston.

Nebel, B., and H. Bürckert. 1995. Reasoning about temporal relations: A maximal tractable subclass of Allen's interval algebra. *Journal of the ACM*, 42(1):43–66.

Nillson, N. J. 1980. *Principles of Artificial Intelligence*. Tioga.

Nudel, B. 1983. Consistent-labeling problems and their algorithms: Expected complexities and theory-based heuristics. *Artificial Intelligence*, 21:135–178.

Papadimitriou, C. H. 1991. On selecting a satisfying truth assignment. In *Proceedings of the Conference on the Foundations of Computer Science*.

Papadimitriou, C. H. 1994. *Computational Complexity*. Addison-Wesley.

Pearl, J. 1984. *Heuristics: Intelligent Search Strategies*. Addison-Wesley.

Pearl, J. 1988. *Probabilistic Reasoning in Intelligent Systems*. Morgan Kaufmann.

Pearl, J., and S. Russel. 2001. *Bayesian Networks*. MIT Press.

Philips, A. B., S. Minton, M. D. Johnston, and P. Laired. 1990. Solving large scale constraint satisfaction and scheduling problems using heuristic repair methods. In *National Conference on Artificial Intelligence (AAAI'90)*, 17–24, Anaheim, California.

Pinkas, G., and R. Dechter. 1995. Improving connectionist energy minimization. *Journal of Artificial Intelligence Research (JAIR)*, 223–248.

Prestwich, S. 2000. A hybrid search architecture applied to hard random 3-SAT and low autocorrelation binary sequences. *Principles and Practice of Constraint Programming (CP2000)*, 337–352.

Prosser, P. 1993. Hybrid algorithms for constraint satisfaction problems. *Computational Intelligence*, 9(3):268–299.

Prosser, P. 1994. Binary constraint satisfaction problems. Some are harder than others. In *Proceedings of the 11th European Conference on Artificial Intelligence ECAI'94*, 95–99.

Prosser, P., I. P. Gent, E. MacIntyre, and T. Walsh. 1996. The constrainedness of search. In *13th National Conference on Artificial Intelligence*.

Prosser, P., B. M. Smith, I. P. Gent, E. MacIntyre, and T. Walsh. 1995. An empirical study of dynamic variable ordering heuristics for the constraint satisfaction problem. In *Principles and Practice of Constraint Programming (CP95)*, 179–193.

Puget, J. 1998. A fast algorithm for the bound consistency of Alldiff constraints. In *National Conference on Artificial Intelligence, AAAI98*, 359–366.

Purdom, P. W. 1983. Search rearrangement backtracking and polynomial average time. *Artificial Intelligence*, 21:117–133.

Purvis, L., and P. Jeavons. 1999. Constraint tractability theory and its application to the product development process for a constraint-based scheduler. In *Proceedings of the First International Conference on the Practical Application of Constraint Technologies and Logic Programming—PACLP'99*, 63–79, Practical Applications Company.

Regin, J.-C. 1994. A filtering algorithm for constraints of difference in CSPS. *Proceedings of National Conference of Artificial Intelligence (AAAI94)*, 362–367.

Regin, J.-C. 1996. Generalized arc-consistency for global cardinality constraints. In *National Conference on Artificial Intelligece (AAAI-96)*, 209–215.

Richards, T. T., and B. Richards. 1998. Non-systematic search and learning: An empirical study. In *Principles and Practice of Constraint Programming—CP98*, 370–384.

Rinnoy Kan, A. H. G., E. L. Lawler, J. K. Lenstra, and D. B. Shmoys. 1985. *The Traveling Salesman Problem*. John Wiley and Sons.

Rish, I., and R. Dechter. 2000. Resolution vs. search; two strategies for SAT. *Journal of Automated Reasoning*, 24(1/2):225–275.

Rosenberg, I. G. 1986. Minimal clones I: The five types. In *Lectures in Universal Algebra (Proc. Conf. Szeged 1983)*, volume 43 of *Colloq. Math. Soc. Janos Bolyai*, 405–427, North-Holland.

Rosiers, W., and M. Bruynooghe. 1986. Empirical study of some constraint satisfaction algorithms. In *Artificial Intelligence II, Methodology Systems Applications (AIMSA86)*, 173–180.

Sabin, D., and E. C. Freuder. 1994. Contradicting conventional wisdom in constraint satisfaction. In *ECAI-94*, 125–129, Amsterdam.

Schaefer, T. J. 1978. The complexity of satisfiability problems. In *Proceedings of the 10th ACM Symposium on Theory of Computing (STOC)*, 216–226.

Schaerf, A. 1997. Combining local search and look-ahead for scheduling and constraint satisfaction problems. In *National Conference on Artificial Intelligence (AAAI97)*, 1254–1259.

Schiex, T. 1999. Radio Link Frequency Assignment. *Constraints*, 4:79–89.

Schiex, T. 2000. Arc consistency for soft constraints. *Principles and Practice of Constraint Programming (CP2000)*, 411–424.

Schoening, U. 1999. A probabilistic algorithm for k-SAT and constraint satisfaction problems. In *Foundations of Computer Science 99*.

Schwalb, E. 1998. Temporal reasoning with constraints. Technical report, Ph.D. thesis, Information and Computer Science, University of California, Irvine.

Schwalb, E., and R. Dechter. 1997. Processing disjunctions in temporal constraint networks. *Artificial Intelligence*, 93(1–2):29–61.

Schwalb, E., and L. Villa. 1998. Temporal constraints: A survey. *Constraints*, 1–20.

Seidel, R. 1981. A new method for solving constraint satisfaction problems. In *International Joint Conference on Artificial Intelligence (IJCAI-81)*, 338–342.

Selman, B., and H. Kautz. 1993. An empirical study of greedy local search for satisfiability testing. In *Proceedings of the 11th National Conference on Artificial Intelligence*, 46–51.

Selman, B., H. Kautz, and B. Cohen. 1994a. Local search strategies for satisfiability testing. In *Dimacs Series in Discrete Mathematics and Theoretical Computer Science*.

Selman, B., H. Kautz, and B. Cohen. 1994b. Noise strategies for local search. In *Proceedings of the 11th National Conference on Artificial Intelligence*, 337–343.

Selman, B., H. Levesque, and D. Mitchell. 1992. A new method for solving hard satisfiability problems. In *Proceedings of the 10th National Conference on Artificial Intelligence*, 440–446.

Shenoy, P. P. 1996. Binary join trees. In *Proceedings of Conference on Uncertainty in Artificial Intelligence (UAI96)*, 492–499.

Shoiket, K., and D. Geiger. 1997. A practical algorithm for finding optimal triangulations. In *14th National Conference on Artificial Intelligence (AAAI'97)*, 185–190.

Shostak, R. 1981. Deciding linear inequalities by computing loop residues. *Journal of the ACM*, 28:769–779.

Simonis, H. 1995. The CHIP system and its applications. *Lecture Notes in Computer Science*, 976:643–646.

Sinclair, A., M. Luby, and D. Zuckerman. 1993. Optimal speedup of Las Vegas algorithms. *Information Processing Letters*, 47:173–180.

Smith, B., and S. A. Grant. 1998. Trying harder to fail first. In *European Conference on Artificial Intelligence (ECAI-92)*, 249–253.

Stallman, M., and G. J. Sussman. 1977. Forward reasoning and dependency-directed backtracking in a system for computer-aided circuit analysis. *Artificial Intelligence*, 9:135–196.

Sterling, L., and E. Shapiro. 1994. *The Art of Prolog*. MIT Press.

Stone, S., and J. M. Stone. 1986. Efficient search techniques—an empirical study of the *n*-queens problem. Technical Report RC #54343, IBM T. J. Watson.

Szendrei, A. 1986. *Clones in Universal Algebra*, volume 99 of *Seminaires de Mathematiques Superieures*. University of Montreal.

Tarjan, R. E., and M. Yannakakis. 1984. Simple linear-time algorithms to test chordality of graphs, test acyclicity of hypergraphs and selectively reduce acyclic hypergraphs. *SIAM Journal of Computation*, 13(3):566–579.

Tsang, E. 1993. *Foundation of Constraint Satisfaction*. Academic Press.

Tsang, E, Wang, C. J., Davenport, A., Voudouris, C., and T. L. Lav. 1999. A family of stochastic methods for constraint satisfaction and optimization. In the *First International Conference on the Practical Applications of Constraint Technologies and Logic Programming (PACLP)*, 359–383.

Ullman , J. D. 1991. Personal communication.

Ullman, J. D. 1998. *Principles of Database and Knowledge-Base Systems, Vol. 1*. Computer Science Press.

Valdes-Perez, R. E. 1986. Spatio-temporal reasoning and linear inequalities. Technical Report AIM-875, Artificial Intelligence Lab, MIT, Cambridge, Massachusetts.

Valdes-Perez, R. E. 1987. The satisfiability of temporal constraint networks. In *National Conference of Artificial Intelligence (AAAI-87)*, 256–260.

van Beek, P. 1989. Approximation algorithms for temporal reasoning. In *International Joint Conference on Artificial Intelligence (IJCAI89)*, 1291–1296.

van Beek, P. 1990. Exact and approximate reasoning about qualitative temporal relations. Ph.D. thesis, University of Waterloo. Available as Department of Computing Science Technical Report TR-90-29, University of Alberta.

van Beek, P. 1991. Temporal query processing with indefinite information. *Artificial Intelligence in Medicine*, 3:325–339.

van Beek, P. 1992a. On the minimality and decomposability of row-convex constraint networks. In *Proceedings AAAI-92 (San Jose, CA)*, 447–452.

van Beek, P. 1992b. Reasoning about qualitative temporal information. *Artificial Intelligence*, 58:297–326.

van Beek, P., and R. Cohen. 1990. Exact and approximate reasoning about temporal relations. *Computational Intelligence*, 6:132–144.

van Beek, P., and R. Dechter. 1994. Constraint tightness versus global consistency. In *Proceedings of Knowledge Representation (KR-94)*, 572–582, Bonn, Germany.

van Beek, P., and R. Dechter. 1995. On the minimality and global consistency of row-convex constraint networks. *Journal of the ACM*, 42(3):543–561.

van Beek, P., and R. Dechter. 1997. Constraint tightness and looseness versus local and global consistency. *Journal of the ACM*, 44(4):549–566.

Van Hentenryck, P. 1989. *Constraint Satisfaction in Logic Programming*. MIT Press.

Van Hentenryck, P., Y. Deville, and C.-M. Teng. 1992. A generic arc-consistency algorithm and its specializations. *Artificial Intelligence*, 57:291–321.

van Hoeve, W. J. 2001. The alldifferent constraint: A survey. *Constraints, an International Journal*, 15(10):1–26.

Vilain, M. 1982. A system of reasoning about time. In *National Conference of Artificial Intelligence (AAAI'82)*, 197–201.

Vilain, M., and H. Kautz. 1986. Constraint propagation algorithms for temporal reasoning. In *National Conference on Artificial Intelligence (AAAI'86)*, 377–382.

Wallace, R. J. 1993. Why ac-3 is almost always better than ac-4. In *International Joint Conference on Artificial Intelligence (IJCAI-93)*, 239–245.

Wallace, R., A. Morozov, S. L. Epstein, E. C. Freuder, and B. Samuels. 2002. The adaptive constraint engine. *Principles and Practice of Constraint Programming (CP2002)*, 525–540.

Waltz, D. 1975. Understanding line drawings of scenes with shadows. In *The Psychology of Computer Vision*.

Wright, S. 1921. Correlation and causation. *Journal of Agricultural Research*, 20:557–585.

Yokoo, M. 1995. Asynchronous weak commitment search for solving distributed constraint satisfaction problems. In *First International Conference on Constraint Programming*, France.

Yugami, N., Y. Ohta, and H. Hara. 1994. Improving repair-based constraint satisfaction methods by value propagation. In *Proceedings of the National Conference of Artificial Intelligence (AAAI-94)*.

Zhang, H. 1997. Sato: An efficient propositional prover. In *Proceedings of the International Conference on Automation Deduction (CADE)*, 272–275.

Zhang, J., and H. Zhang. 1996. Combining local search and backtracking techniques for constraint satisfaction. In *National Conference of Artificial Intelligence (AAAI96)*, 369–374.

Zhang, N. L., and D. Poole. 1996. Exploiting causal independence in Bayesian network inference. *Journal of Artificial Intelligence Research (JAIR)*.

Zhang, Y., and R. H. C. Yap. 2001. Making ac-3 an optimal algorithm. In *International Joint Conference on Artificial Intelligence (IJCAI-01)*, 316–321.

Zhao, Y., L. Zhang, M. Moskewicz, C. Madigan, and S. Malik. 2001. Chaff: Engineering an efficient SAT solver. *Proceedings of Design and Automation Conference*.

Index

Printed and bound by CPI Group (UK) Ltd, Croydon, CR0 4YY

03/10/2024

01040339-0006